THE BUMPY ROAD
— of mother and daughter
THE ROUGH ROAD
— of mother and daughter

Qiu Niao

ISBN 978-1-956696-70-7 (paperback)
ISBN 978-1-956696-71-4 (hardcover)
ISBN 978-1-956696-72-1 (digital)

Copyright © 2021 by Qiu Niao

All rights reserved. No part of this publication may be reproduced, distributed, or transmitted in any form or by any means, including photocopying, recording, or other electronic or mechanical methods without the prior written permission of the publisher. For permission requests, solicit the publisher via the address below.

Rushmore Press LLC
1 800 460 9188
www.rushmorepress.com

Printed in the United States of America

This book is dedicated to thousands upon ————
of great, strong and selfless mums!

I'm wish every woman in the world ————
live happy life and have wonderful marriage!

I hope that my mother's ————
soul rest in peace in heaven!

PREFACE

We always hear people say, "Novel and film are fictitious." However, it is not true. What is in this autobiographical novel, it is entirely based on the author's personal experience and described.

Among so many young people in this contemporary world, hardly understand how several "grand political movements", be in China have exerted Chinese people's life in a profound and direct way.

When I was just one month old and left my birthplace Jiangsu in a small boat, the rough journey seemed to have forecasted a life in turmoil. And that even my life was on the brink three number of times of life death line…

In those years when life is so hard as to make one shed a bitter tear, my mother made it with her perseverance and diligence. She just struggled in a desperate plight. Finally, she was beaten down with diseases and passed away with a belief that "death is better than surviving" and endless physical pain.

During those changeable and unpredictable times, I also like a lonely bird with injuries covering my whole body struggling to fly in the sky of autumn, longed to find light and warmth, to see a good defeat the evil, and I hope the happiness that would fill the whole world.

This book through a vivid description of the destiny of two generations, the book demonstrates a profound life philosophy if a woman wants to acquire real happiness, she must possess the following three elements,

Qiu Niao

<u>First,</u> the superior social system is an indispensable prerequisite

<u>Second,</u> your own tenacious efforts are the basic guarantee of seeking happiness.

<u>Third,</u> a trustworthy and reliable good man who can share joys and sorrows with you.

    I hope that the novel will exert an educational influence on our society to bring about a better life.

Qiu Niao (Autumn Bird)
The Hague, Netherlands Aug 31, 2021

CONTENTS

Preface vii

Chapter 1. The world is change unpredictable 1
1.1 "Jade Girl" of the remote and backward place 1
1.2 The war, make the family ruptured 6
1.3 Reorganized family 15

Chapter 2. Age of rapid change 23
2.1 The survivor of a great disaster 23
2.2 A Selfless mother 31
2.3 Take the lead walk on the way of collectivism 41
2.4 Innocence 46
2.5 A young girl in her high school days 57
2.6 Under the route of Liu and Deng 69
2.7 Trumped-up charge 80
2.8 Unexpected disaster 90

Chapter 3. The golden age was ruined 110
3.1 The days' time of fix the earth 110
3.2 The cow herding girl 125
3.3 A Trip to Changsha and Wuhan during in the
       Cultural Revolution 134
3.4 Beijing, the elegant demeanor of blood dye 150
3.5 A trip to fathers' hometown 174
3.6 Hazy first love 187
3.7 The tumultuous years 201
3.8 Among the quiet mountains 210
3.9 Mother and daughter's anxiety 222

Chapter 4. Lose one's bearings 236
4.1 Between the people. 236
4.2 Heavy cross. 250
4.3 Touchstone of love 265
4.4 Be born at the wrong time 277
4.5 Returning to the city and my resist 291
4.6 The future, be enveloped in smoke 308
4.7 Love, cannot set foot into two boats 325
4.8 True love falls into Xiang Jiang 341

Chapter 5. Injured lonely bird 379
5.1 The counterrevolutionary of implicate all of one's
    close relatives. 379
5.2 The god bird fly to heaven 391
5.3 Hapless fate. 422
5.4 Resignation and engagement in medicine 439
5.5 Another married man 452

Chapter 6. Wander about the ends of the earth. 464
6.1 She lingered at the cape. 464
6.2 Shenzhen SAR Entrepreneurship 481
6.3 Happiness depends on oneself to create. 489
6.4 The test of life. 511
6.5 People have unpredictable vicissitudes in the life. 531
6.6 Fly far and high. 551

Random Thoughts 569
Appendix. 571
1. See notes below: 571
2. Reference: 583
3. The Kuomintang and The Republic of China -. 586

CHAPTER 1

The world is change unpredictable

1.1 "Jade Girl" of the remote and backward place

Shao Guizhen was born to a poor farmer's family in Jiangsu, 1923. When she was born, her grandfather who had been live under the same roof had passed away. Grandmother died when Shao Guizhen was barely aware of things and followed by her father's death, when she turned just seven. Shao Guizhen survived along with her mother, two elder brothers of roughly thirteen and fourteen, and one elder sister not yet ten. It was a time when the countryside was poor, and farming relied heavily on primitive methods. The losses of able-bodied adults in Shao Guizhen's family made their lives very difficult.

Soon after father died, an opportunity came along when the local temple started recruiting Golden Boy and Jade Maiden – servants who functioned as intermediaries to Buddhist deities. Shao Guizhen's mother sent her in to see if she might qualify.

When the host of temple saw Shao Guizhen, she took an immediate liking of her, "The girl's skin is as smooch and delicate as a porcelain doll." With that, Shao Guizhen soon became the Jade Maiden of the temple.

In the year when Shao Guizhen was turning sixteen, a Buddhist nun who was very fond of her told her, "The temple is preparing for your entrance into Buddhist nun hood. The formal ceremony will be in a few days." "But that means will I remain at the temple for the rest of my life?" Shao Guizhen asked. "That's right. On the day of the ceremony, they will shave off every strand of your hair, and burn nine incense marks on your scalp, three on each row." "Surely that must hurt?" "Yes, but it shall hurt only this once. From then on, you will never have to worry about any worldly affairs. Your days will be spent chanting the sacred sutras while knocking on the wooden fish with eyes closed, shutting off the world."

That night, troubled thoughts of what the future would hold for her kept Shao Guizhen wide awake. She remembered how much it had hurt when incense sticks and candles accidentally burned her skin and shivered at the thought of having nine incense marks burned onto her scalp; then she thought of what it would be like spending an eternity at the temple. Finally, she decided, she was going to run away the following night.

The next night, all was quiet at the temple. The moon was bright and clear and somewhat eased Shao Guizhen's fear of the dark. She had been pondering her escape route. When she was certain that the other Buddhist nuns were sound asleep, she sat up from the bed quietly. Shao Guizhen had wrapped up her belongings in a cotton bundle during the day and took it out from underneath the bed. She ran to the back gate in silence, careful to conceal herself in the shadows. At the back gate, she pulled out the large wooden bolt and softly pushed the gate open.

Once outside, Shao Guizhen scurried towards home along the bank of a stream that stretched on for miles. The riverbank was rank with dew-saturated grass. Shao Guizhen was in such a hurry that she made a misstep and slipped into the river. She struggled in a panic to stay above water and threw about her limbs searching for the bank. At last, her feet felt a pothole in the bank, and she tried bringing herself up. But as soon as she stepped onto the pothole, the soft mud underneath gave, and she once again sank back down. Shao Guizhen had already swallowed some water. She was frightened by the idea of drowning and an instinct to stay alive forced her to keep on fighting for life with every last bit of strength. In her violent struggle, Shao Guizhen thought she saw the image of her deceased grandmother bending down by the bank and extending out an arm trying to grab her. She tried to reach for her grandmother's hand, but instead found that she had gotten ahold of some long weed growing by the bank. She pulled on the weed and at last brought herself out of the water and carefully climbed onto the bank from a gentle slope. Shao Guizhen's cotton package had fallen in the river, but she was in no shape or mood to retrieve the package. Despite her soaking wet clothes, she was huddled the body and ran towards home tremblingly.

A loud and urgent knock came at the door in the middle of the night and woke up Shao Guizhen's mother and her elder brothers and sister. They were shocked to find Shao Guizhen at the doorway. After hearing Shao Guizhen's brief recount of what had happened, her mother ached for her daughter's ordeal and held her in her arms. Then, she found some dry clothes for her to change into and told her to rest a bit on her bed.

Lying in bed, Shao Guizhen began to weep. Her feet had been bound in the past though they were later released. Nonetheless, the night's ordeal had been too much for her feet. "The skin on my feet is chafed and they really hurt. I don't bind my feet, can I?" Shao Guizhen pleaded with her mother. "If foot binding is too much pain for you, then let's forget about it. You can the wrap foot cloth untie" Her mother said.

Shao Guizhen's mother hurriedly packed some of her daughter's clothes and sent her to her uncle's home before daybreak in the Buddhist nuns came looking for her.

As expected, the abbess came looking for Shao Guizhen. "I did not send my daughter to your temple to become a Buddhist nun," Shao Guizhen's mother said. "I can't let her remain in your temple forever and not get married." Therefore, the matter was left unsettled.

Shao Guizhen's uncle and aunt had been married for many years, but they had no child of their own. Seeing which, Shao Guizhen's mother decided to let them adopt Shao Guizhen as their daughter. The couple was fond of the idea and treated Shao Guizhen as their own daughter. Since then, Shao Guizhen settled down at their home and spent two peaceful years. Uncle's home was at the edge of the town. He had opened a small meat shop in front of his home. Aunt did some needlework on the side to make ends meet. If uncle's meat shop had bones and meat scraps left over at the end of the day, uncle often brought those back and made soup and dishes with the scraps for aunt. Pork bones were worth practically nothing at the time and very few customers cared for them. Though uncle was not a wealthy man, he never let Shao Guizhen starve. Uncle even sent her to a private tutor house so that she could receive some basic education. One day, uncle gave Shao Guizhen some household items that they didn't need and asked her to sell them to the pawnshop so that she could pay the tuition for her new school year.

This is a sunny morning in summer. Birds warbled from the branches overhead, producing a melodious harmony. The fields smelled fresh and sweet from last night's rain. There was a gentle breeze and the stream rippled onwards with golden gleam. In the distance, the sun could be seen half concealed behind the mountains, its rays radiating into the blue sky and tinted the clouds with golden rims. Shao Guizhen walked light-footedly along a well-trodden path by the river. Her pitch-black hair was smooth like silk and swayed gently in the soft breeze from the canal; her rosy cheeks brimmed with the dazzling feminine beauty of youth. When she almost arrived at the pawnshop, she saw some cargo ships unloading salt and other goods.

The world is change unpredictable

After Shao Guizhen entered the pawnshop, she saw the shop owner talking to a gentleman of about fifty.

Dressed in a new suit, he looked smart and brimming with health. When the gentleman saw Shao Guizhen, he paused the conversation and cast a long and hard stare at her from head to toe. This made Shao Guizhen rather uncomfortable. She hurriedly sold the items to the shop owner, picked up the copper coins from the counter and rushed back home.

A few days later, when Shao Guizhen just finished washing the dishes, uncle walked inside from the meat shop and said excitedly, "My poor daughter will soon have a change of luck. You will be married off to a wealthy household." Shao Guizhen had no idea what this was about and appeared at a loss. "Remember the pawnshop you went to a few days ago? "Uncle explained hurriedly. "The owner of the pawnshop knows me. Sometimes he comes to my shop to buy pork bones for his dogs. He wondered who you were in the past and asked me about you. When you visited the pawnshop a few days ago, Master Jiang happened to be at the shop. He is the wealthiest and most powerful man in the area, and a regimental commander of the Nationalist Party, and he even has his own salt business. He has a son two years older than you. His son is studying at the Military Academy of the Nationalist Party. Master Jiang found you most suitable to be his daughter-in-law. He has asked the pawnshop owner as the matchmaker. He hopes you can marry his son. As soon as you agree, the ceremony can be held right away. Once you become Master Jiang's daughter-in-law, you will enjoy a noble and wealthy life for the rest of your life." "But I have never met his son before," Shao Guizhen said. "I don't even know what kind of man he is. How could I risk marrying a total stranger?" "Silly girl, this is the kind of marriage every girl dream of! Think about it, Master Jiang is an important man in the Nationalist Party and owes large business. The pawnshop owner even told me that his son is rather handsome. You will never run into such a wonderful marriage in a million years!

You can't remain unmarried for the rest of your life, so why not take this opportunity?" Uncle's words persuaded Shao Guizhen. She shyly agreed to the marriage.

A few days later, Master Jiang sent over ample presents for the engagement. Uncle gave half the presents to Shao Guizhen's mother, who was overjoyed and said, "from now on, my days in poverty have come to an end!" One month later, the Jiang mansion was decorated anew with lanterns and colorful banners in preparation for the wedding. Gongs, drums and fireworks accompanied the wedding procession. In such a merry and cheerful atmosphere, Shao Guizhen was wedded to the most powerful family in the area.

1.2 The war, make the family ruptured

Shao Guizhen's husband, Jiang Jianming, a good-looking. The young man fair complexion and be refined in manner, studied at the Military Academy of the Nationalist Party.

He returned home every weekend and always rushed to see Shao Guizhen the first thing after extending one's regards to his parents. The newlyweds held each other in affection and enjoyed their intimacies. While Jiang Jianming was away in school, Shao Guizhen spent most of her days in idleness. To pass the time, she often visited the training ground in the courtyard with her maid where Nationalist soldiers trained with American-made military equipment. Her father-in-law supervised and observed the training. He was often clad in mustard-colored woolen military coat with floral emblems on his shoulders in the shape of plum blossom. Occasionally, he would cast a glance at her and nod with a smile. Shao Guizhen's in-laws held her very dear, considering that she was the only daughter-in-law to their only son. Every morning, even in winter, if water did not freeze, the soldiers that trained in the courtyard washed their faces and brushed teeth with icy cold tap water. The soldiers had been accustomed to the routine and none appeared to flinch at the coldness. Shao Guizhen

The world is change unpredictable

had been watching them and followed suit. At first, the frosty water hurt her fingers, but very soon she learned to enjoy the refreshing feel.

Shortly after the marriage, Shao Guizhen began to feel out of sorts, she nauseated at the sight of greasy food, and she had been without her menses for two, three months. When Shao Guizhen told this to her mother-in-law, she was overjoyed and excited and said, "Looks like you are pregnant. We must have a doctor look at you." Shao Guizhen's mother-in-law soon found a renowned doctor for her. The doctor felt her pulse and said, "I must congratulate you, Lady Shao, you are pregnant!" Father-in-law and mother-in-law were extremely happy to hear this good news, not only added some precious jewelry to her, and add to her another maid. Shao Guizhen gave birth to a baby girl on a very cold winter day. The Jiang household named the girl "Xiao-dong", meaning "baby girl born in winter". Though a girl, Xiao-dong was the first grandchild to the Jiang household and the apple of their eye.

Six months after Xiao-dong was born, Jiang Jianming began to spend less and less time at home. When he returned from school, he often went out and loitered about to pass the night; sometimes, he would not return until well past midnight. Shao Guizhen began to think this was becoming an issue. Her husband hardly spent any time with her and Xiao-dong and had been lagging on his schoolwork.

One night, Jiang Jianming was not home as usual. Shao Guizhen had one of the maids look after Xiao-dong and went with another maid fetching for him. They headed towards the entertainment quarter in the military camp where Shao Guizhen knew she would find him.

When she arrived at the entryway, she heard somebody calling out to her husband, "Jiang Jianming, your wife is here looking for you!" When Shao Guizhen walked into the entertainment venue in the barracks, but Jiang Jianming was out of sight. Shao Guizhen wondered where he could have hidden himself in such a short time.

Shao Guizhen looked everywhere before she finally caught sight of a few mahjong tables. On one of the tables, a game appeared to be suspended in the middle with mahjong tiles and copper coins tossed about. Three players sat around the table; the fourth seat was empty. As Shao Guizhen was walking towards the table to ask about her husband, she caught sight of a pair of feet half concealed underneath the table. She looked more closely and realized she recognized the feet, the shoes and socks. Shao Guizhen to laughed to oneself at her husband's silly act. She pulled the empty chair away so that Jiang Jianming had nowhere to hide but crawl out on his feet. This caused a roar of laughter from the other soldiers. "Jiang Jianming, isn't you a bit young to be such a henpeck?" Someone said half-jokingly. "I'm just playing hide-and-seek with her." Jiang Jianming stood up and spoke. But this only brought out another round of laughter from the other soldiers. "So, you have been addicted to gambling. No wonder you are not doing your homework anymore when you come home from school. Wait till your dad and mom hear about this!" Shao Guizhen said with displeasure.

Jiang Jianming dreaded the thought of his parents learning about his gambling habits. "Honey, could you please look the other way this time? I promise I will never gamble again." Jiang Jianming put on his jacket and hurriedly followed Shao Guizhen home. Since then, Jiang Jianming rarely touched mahjong. When he did, he always made sure to return home early. Jiang Jiaming's grades improved. Shao Guizhen's in-laws were very pleased to see her positive influence over their son. For several years, Shao Guizhen enjoyed a close-knit and joyful relationship with her husband and in-laws until life took an unexpected turn in the year Jiang Jianming was to graduate and Xiao-dong ready for school.

After the victory of the Anti-Japanese War, the Chinese Civil War, also known as the War of Liberation, launched in full scale in July of 1946. The People's Liberation Army led by the Communist

Shao Guizhen looked everywhere before she finally caught sight of a few mahjong tables. On one of the tables, a game appeared to be suspended in the middle with mahjong tiles and copper coins tossed about. Three players sat around the table; the fourth seat was empty. As Shao Guizhen was walking towards the table to ask about her husband, she caught sight of a pair of feet half concealed underneath the table. She looked more closely and realized she recognized the feet, the shoes and socks. Shao Guizhen to laughed to oneself at her husband's silly act. She pulled the empty chair away so that Jiang Jianming had nowhere to hide but crawl out on his feet. This caused a roar of laughter from the other soldiers. "Jiang Jianming, isn't you a bit young to be such a henpeck?" Someone said half-jokingly. "I'm just playing hide-and-seek with her." Jiang Jianming stood up and spoke. But this only brought out another round of laughter from the other soldiers. "So, you have been addicted to gambling. No wonder you are not doing your homework anymore when you come home from school. Wait till your dad and mom hear about this!" Shao Guizhen said with displeasure.

Jiang Jianming dreaded the thought of his parents learning about his gambling habits. "Honey, could you please look the other way this time? I promise I will never gamble again." Jiang Jianming put on his jacket and hurriedly followed Shao Guizhen home. Since then, Jiang Jianming rarely touched mahjong. When he did, he always made sure to return home early. Jiang Jiaming's grades improved. Shao Guizhen's in-laws were very pleased to see her positive influence over their son. For several years, Shao Guizhen enjoyed a close-knit and joyful relationship with her husband and in-laws until life took an unexpected turn in the year Jiang Jianming was to graduate and Xiao-dong ready for school.

After the victory of the Anti-Japanese War, the Chinese Civil War, also known as the War of Liberation, launched in full scale in July of 1946. The People's Liberation Army led by the Communist had been watching them and followed suit. At first, the frosty water hurt her fingers, but very soon she learned to enjoy the refreshing feel.

Shortly after the marriage, Shao Guizhen began to feel out of sorts, she nauseated at the sight of greasy food, and she had been without her menses for two, three months. When Shao Guizhen told this to her mother-in-law, she was overjoyed and excited and said, "Looks like you are pregnant. We must have a doctor look at you." Shao Guizhen's mother-in-law soon found a renowned doctor for her. The doctor felt her pulse and said, "I must congratulate you, Lady Shao, you are pregnant!" Father-in-law and mother-in-law were extremely happy to hear this good news, not only added some precious jewelry to her, and add to her another maid. Shao Guizhen gave birth to a baby girl on a very cold winter day. The Jiang household named the girl "Xiao-dong", meaning "baby girl born in winter". Though a girl, Xiao-dong was the first grandchild to the Jiang household and the apple of their eye.

Six months after Xiao-dong was born, Jiang Jianming began to spend less and less time at home. When he returned from school, he often went out and loitered about to pass the night; sometimes, he would not return until well past midnight. Shao Guizhen began to think this was becoming an issue. Her husband hardly spent any time with her and Xiao-dong and had been lagging on his schoolwork.

One night, Jiang Jianming was not home as usual. Shao Guizhen had one of the maids look after Xiao-dong and went with another maid fetching for him. They headed towards the entertainment quarter in the military camp where Shao Guizhen knew she would find him.

When she arrived at the entryway, she heard somebody calling out to her husband, "Jiang Jianming, your wife is here looking for you!" When Shao Guizhen walked into the entertainment venue in the barracks, but Jiang Jianming was out of sight. Shao Guizhen wondered where he could have hidden himself in such a short time.

Party and the National Army led by the Kuomintang and the battle for power is getting fiercer and fiercer.

On the one hand of successive Soviet assistance to the Chinese Communist Party. But on the other one hand, in 1948 when U.S. aid was slow in coming, the situation of the Kuomintang troops is already very sinister.

Within the Nationalist Party, news that the situation was becoming grim had begun to spread. Shao Guizhen's father-in-law, Master Jiang, was a keen man and held a key military position in the Nationalist Party. He was aware of corruption within the Party and its grim outlook in the war against the Communists. He gradually shrank his salt business until finally closing it down altogether, so that he could make a speedy escape out of the Chinese mainland as soon as the Nationalist Party was defeated. The situation was getting worse day by day. In the second year of the war, the corrupt and incompetent Nationalist troops suffered a casualty of 1.52 million as it was defeated by the Chinese People's Liberation Army said to rely on merely "millet and rifles". The Communist Party quickly expanded its Liberation Zone while the Nationalist regime tottered. <See Appendix 3. A>

In the final days of the spring Festival of 1948, Shao Guizhen sensed something was wrong, seeing how for several days in a row her father-in-law had been packing up valuable belongings and the soldiers had been busily. Troubled with anxiety and fear, Shao Guizhen dreamt one night that she was all alone and an enormous cat with bulging eyes was chasing her. She tried running away yet found her feet glued to the ground. Shao Guizhen stirred from her sleep screaming and panting. Jiang Jianming leaned over as he was roused from sleep and asked, "Did you have a bad dream?" After hearing Shao Guizhen's recount, Jiang Jianming said, "You must be too tired and tense from all the packing and whatnot. Why don't you take Xiao-dong with you and pay a visit to your uncle tomorrow?"

The following day turned out to be a fine day. Early in the morning, Shao Guizhen left for uncle's home with Xiao-dong and a maid. Yet she arrived at uncle's home only to learn that uncle might have traveled to nearby villages to buy pigs. Shao Guizhen asked around in the neighborhood without any luck of finding out exactly which village her uncle had left for. Shao Guizhen thought she had n 't seen her mother for a long time and might as well pay a visit. She hurriedly bought some of her mother's favorite food and clothes from shops in the town and rented a boat. The boatman rowed the boat down the river all the way towards her mother's village.

Arriving at the village a little before noon, Shao Guizhen paid the boatman and paced hurriedly home. Her mother was more than glad to see her and Xiao-dong. Shao Guizhen's two brothers had been out working; her older sister had been married off a short time ago. Shao Guizhen sipped some tea, rested briefly and helped her mother with house cleaning chores. They had a simple lunch and resumed cleaning afterwards. By the time they were sipping afternoon tea, the sun had begun to set. Shao Guizhen had to rush home for dinner with her husband and in-laws. The villagers helped her found another boat and she parted in a hurry with her mother.

When the boat docked in town, Shao Guizhen stepped ashore with Xiao-dong and her maid and headed toward her uncle's home, which was at the other end of the town from her own, hoping that she would be able to talk with him briefly. While walking down the street, Shao Guizhen noticed the shops had closed for business earlier than usual; the town appeared to be in a state of disarray. Shao Guizhen feels that the atmosphere is different from usual.

At that moment, she caught sight of a man darting up and down the street making inquiries. She knew the man to be her husband's best friend Li Anping. When Li Anping spotted Shao Guizhen, he swung his arms at her agitatedly and shouted, "Aiyar, Lady Shao, where in the world have you been?" It turned out that Li Anping had been looking desperately for Shao Guizhen. Li Anping ran towards Shao

The world is change unpredictable

Guizhen and said hurriedly, "Jiang Jianming came to see me around noon today. He had been looking desperately for you! He thought he'd find you at your uncle's place, but you weren't there. He told me his father received a top-secret order from the Combat Division of the Defense Ministry for him to take his infantry division up north; they will join other legion and prepare for a final showdown with the Communists. He told me 'If we manage to win the war, I will come back for her and Xiao-dong. If not, well, if I manage to survive, I will be on the run. I mustn't linger any longer --orders are orders. I suppose this means I will have to part with my family.' I'm sorry you couldn't leave with Jianming, but I don't think it's necessarily a bad thing. He sounded uncertain about winning the war. You wouldn't be safe with him."

The devastating news instantly crushed Shao Guizhen. She sank back on the ground and broke down into a wild sob, "Good heavens! What am I supposed to do? I must follow my husband even if he is going to the war. A married woman follows his husband despite of what fate holds for him."

Tears flowed freely down her cheeks. Shao Guizhen's maid stared in shock at her lady who was beyond consolation. Xiao-dong nestle up to her mother, looking up at her with fear and confusion in her eyes. Shao Guizhen clutched Xiao-dong tightly and wailed, "My family is ruined just like that. What are we supposed to do?" Li Anping watched helplessly, failing to find any words of condolence.

He caught sight of a boy of eight or nine that suddenly appeared at the other end of the street. He recognized it was his son and called for him to come over. "Don't be running around at a time like this, it's not safe!" Li Anping scolded and turned to Shao Guizhen. "You must not cry on like that, it won't do you any good. Why don't you come over to my place for supper?"

Shao Guizhen suddenly remembered she and Jianming placed some valuable jewelry in a hidden compartment at the bottom of a large wardrobe in their bedroom. "I must go back home at once and pack some necessary things, supper will have to wait. Would you be

11

so kind to take the maid and Xiao-dong with you home? I will be back as soon as I'm finished packing." Shao Guizhen said.

"Good heavens!" Li Anping said in disbelief, "Your home is a targeted military camp! You must be out of your mind going there at this time. When the Liberation Army drops a bomb there is anybody's guess! Look for yourself, anybody with a bit of fortune has already fled after the Nationalist troops; even the shops have closed early. Look here, Communist troops are swift and unpredictable. The Nationalists don't even have a plan how to confront them. If the Communists decide to attack your husband military camp, you'd be become involved right into them." "I know all of that. But I need to go and pack some clothes at least; it just wouldn't do otherwise. I will be fast." "If you insist on going, all right then. We will be waiting for you right at my home. But you mustn't linger there longer than you have to!"

When Shao Guizhen returned to the Jiang household, she found the front gate had not been latched. She entered the gate and saw the abandoned living quarter and the empty courtyard in a state of disarray. Dusk approached. There was no bird tweeting and not a dog and cat around. The silence gave Shao Guizhen an eerie chill. Heart fluttering with fear, she quickly headed towards the bulky yet exquisitely carved wardrobe in her bedroom. She knelt, prostrated her upper body and reached underneath the wardrobe until her left cheek almost touched the ground. Finally, she felt a lacquered jewelry box sitting undisturbed in a hidden compartment. Shao Guizhen was relieved and pulled the box out. It was a fine jewelry box carved with flowers and birds. She opened the box and saw all her jewelry safely in place. Furthermore, husband had placed a handful of silver pieces and a few gold bricks the size of mahjong tile wrapped in a piece of red silk. She found a short note with cursive writing along with the valuables and began reading,

"The money I left for you will be used of raising Xiao Dong to adulthood, you must not use the money for anything else! Originally, we thought that with the victory of the war against Japan, our family would be able to live a happier and more secure life. To our surprise, the Communists party, with the assistance of the Soviet Union, treated the KMT as the enemy, launched an even fiercer battle against the Kuomintang. At this juncture, the U.S. stopped aiding us. This home is a nest for the Kuomintang, you are absolute mustn't live here anymore. Take Xiao-dong with you and find a place to hide. I'm a soldier so I must obey orders. I must leave you and Xiao-dong for the moment. If we can defeat military of the Communist, I will go and find you and we will all go to Nanjing. Jianming." <See App. 3. A.>

Shao Guizhen put the note away in her pocket and thrown open the wardrobe doors. Jiang Jianming had taken most of his clothes but left hers and Xiaodong's untouched. She hurriedly took out some of their garments, threw them on the bed and wrapped them with the bed sheet. Then she slung the bundle of clothes and valuables over her shoulder and scurried back as fast as she could before it was totally dark.

She was completely out of breath when she saw Xiao-dong standing at the front door of Li Anping's home, anxiously waiting for her. Li Anping's wife ushered her to the supper table hospitably, "You really had us worried. Why don't you have something to eat first and take it easy."

While eating, Shao Guizhen asked Li's wife, "Aren't you going to leave this town? Other merchants had already begun to leave." To which Li's wife said, "I couldn't bear to leave this home. Li and I worked hard for years to get where we are today. I'm not going nowhere." "Did you not hear what the Nationalists said? When the Communists get here, they will take away your properties and give them to the people. Aren't you afraid of that?" Li Anping teased. "Ai, that's nonsense. Our shop sells nothing but everyday goods like salt, soy sauce, vinegar and cooking oil. We barely make our ends meet. What is there for them to take away?

No matter who holds the power, peoples have to use oil, salt, soy sauce and vinegar to eat, we do this way our own small business. Common folks like us ask for nothing, but we just want to live a peaceful life."

At this point, Shao Guizhen said, "Jianming left some money for me and Xiao-dong. I will be extremely grateful if Mr. Li could help me find an affordable lodging nearby for us to settle down."

Li's wife said hospitably, "We have an extra room we use for storage. You and Xiao-dong can stay with us for now if you'd like to." Shao Guizhen said, "My father-in-law's troops march day and night. I have not the least idea where to go looking for them. There is no telling how long I will have to wait for them in this town. I mustn't trouble you with extended stay. Besides, you need that room to store goods." Li's wife said, "In that, you don't need to worry about finding lodging yourself. Li will make the necessary arrangements. He knows all the inn owners in town." Li Anping hurriedly finished his supper and left to find a rent affordable inn for Shao Guizhen and Xiao-dong.

One hour later, he returned and said cheerfully, "I managed to find a great deal. Business is slow for inns, so the inn owner I found agreed to let you live there with a very affordable monthly rent, not much more expensive than living in a regular household and paying a fee. Besides, the room is furnished and has all the necessary household items. So, you don't need to spend money buying them." Shao Guizhen was relieved to hear the good news. That night, she insisted on giving some money to Li and his wife and moved with Xiao-dong and the maid to the inn Li Anping had found for her in the center of the town. The next day, Shao Guizhen paid the maid a full month's wage and traveling expense and let her go.

Shao Guizhen had wanted to run to Nanjing to find her husband. However, she took a daughter who was six-or-seven-year-old, the road will be very difficult. Helpless, she can only stay in the hotel every day with Xiaodong. As for whether her husband died in

No matter who holds the power, peoples have to use oil, salt, soy sauce and vinegar to eat, we do this way our own small business. Common folks like us ask for nothing, but we just want to live a peaceful life."

At this point, Shao Guizhen said, "Jianming left some money for me and Xiao-dong. I will be extremely grateful if Mr. Li could help me find an affordable lodging nearby for us to settle down."

Li's wife said hospitably, "We have an extra room we use for storage. You and Xiao-dong can stay with us for now if you'd like to." Shao Guizhen said, "My father-in-law's troops march day and night. I have not the least idea where to go looking for them. There is no telling how long I will have to wait for them in this town. I mustn't trouble you with extended stay. Besides, you need that room to store goods." Li's wife said, "In that, you don't need to worry about finding lodging yourself. Li will make the necessary arrangements. He knows all the inn owners in town." Li Anping hurriedly finished his supper and left to find a rent affordable inn for Shao Guizhen and Xiao-dong.

One hour later, he returned and said cheerfully, "I managed to find a great deal. Business is slow for inns, so the inn owner I found agreed to let you live there with a very affordable monthly rent, not much more expensive than living in a regular household and paying a fee. Besides, the room is furnished and has all the necessary household items. So, you don't need to spend money buying them." Shao Guizhen was relieved to hear the good news. That night, she insisted on giving some money to Li and his wife and moved with Xiao-dong and the maid to the inn Li Anping had found for her in the center of the town. The next day, Shao Guizhen paid the maid a full month's wage and traveling expense and let her go.

Shao Guizhen had wanted to run to Nanjing to find her husband. However, she took a daughter who was six-or-seven-year-old, the road will be very difficult. Helpless, she can only stay in the hotel every day with Xiaodong. As for whether her husband died in we thought that with the victory of the war against Japan, our family would be able to live a happier and more secure life. To our surprise, the Communists party, with the assistance of the Soviet Union, treated the KMT as the enemy, launched an even fiercer battle against the Kuomintang. At this juncture, the U.S. stopped aiding us. This home is a nest for the Kuomintang, you are absolute mustn't live here anymore. Take Xiao-dong with you and find a place to hide. I'm a soldier so I must obey orders. I must leave you and Xiao-dong for the moment. If we can defeat military of the Communist, I will go and find you and we will all go to Nanjing. Jianming." <See App. 3. A.>

Shao Guizhen put the note away in her pocket and thrown open the wardrobe doors. Jiang Jianming had taken most of his clothes but left hers and Xiaodong's untouched. She hurriedly took out some of their garments, threw them on the bed and wrapped them with the bed sheet. Then she slung the bundle of clothes and valuables over her shoulder and scurried back as fast as she could before it was totally dark.

She was completely out of breath when she saw Xiao-dong standing at the front door of Li Anping's home, anxiously waiting for her. Li Anping's wife ushered her to the supper table hospitably, "You really had us worried. Why don't you have something to eat first and take it easy."

While eating, Shao Guizhen asked Li's wife, "Aren't you going to leave this town? Other merchants had already begun to leave." To which Li's wife said, "I couldn't bear to leave this home. Li and I worked hard for years to get where we are today. I'm not going nowhere." "Did you not hear what the Nationalists said? When the Communists get here, they will take away your properties and give them to the people. Aren't you afraid of that?" Li Anping teased. "Ai, that's nonsense. Our shop sells nothing but everyday goods like salt, soy sauce, vinegar and cooking oil. We barely make our ends meet. What is there for them to take away?

the war or fled to Taiwan, In the chaotic situation of the civil war between the Kuomintang and the Communist Party, she could not inquire at all. <See App. 3. B>

1.3 Reorganized family

There was a rumor that the infantry division led by Jiang Jiaming's father went north. The Nationalist Army of the Kuomintang is preparing for a final battle with the People's Liberation Army of the Communist Party.

At first, Shao Guizhen attempted to go to Nanjing with Xiaodong and look for Jiang's family member. But the hotel owner said, "Are you risking your life? Everyone wants to get away from the war, except soldiers, who have no other option. It is said that the fifth army corps of Kuomintang have been heavily defeated in the North. How can you take a six-or-seven-year-old daughter who is and rush to the battlefield, not knowing your husband is still alive? Besides, how can you get to know where Kuomintang soldiers live from ordinary people?" Hearing that, Shao had to give up her plan. Disappointedly, she stayed in the hotel with Xiaodong as usual.

The spring festival had passed of 1948 year, and the spring was coming. Then Kuomintang troops were badly beaten by the People's Liberation Army and the battle has failed one after another. In the days of armistice between battles, people still ran their businesses. Sometimes hotel guests were large in number, sometimes small. One day the hotel owner came to Shao Guizhen and said, "Some guests offered to pay for washing clothes. What do you think of the job?" At that time Shao was pondering, "Sit idle and you will eat away your fortune. I cannot maintain this life with Xiaodong in the hotel, doing nothing but sleep and eat." So as soon as she heard the offer, she accepted it without hesitation. In less than a month since she began the washing, her hands, with tender skin, was peeling. Later, the dirty water mixed with soap foam and washing soda, made her hands inflamed and rotten. They hurt so severely that she could not sleep all night. Having no choice, she continued her toil, one tub and another.

Late spring in this year, two guests booked in at the hotel and proposed to Shao Guizhen at different times. The first one was a local tradesman on silk business, about thirty years old, 170 centimeters tall, polite in behavior and handsome in looking. He always gave Shao Guizhen tips after she ironed his clothes. He said to Shao, "As a single parent with a little kid, you must suffer a lot. Accept that." Once when he earned some good money from business, he eagerly told Shao Guizhen about it. Then he asked in an earnest way, "Will you marry me?" Shao asked, "Aren't you married?" He replied, "My wife died in a difficult labor and left me a kid, who is taken care of by my mother." Shao grew very embarrassed and answered, "Let me think about it carefully…" She told herself, "He seems to be a nice man with good temper and personality…Still having no news about Jianming, what shall I do?"

Shortly after that, a guest named Qiu Zhongyuan, over thirty years old, about 180 centimeters tall with luminous eyes, checked in, who came across. He looks like a fashionable movie star in his well-cut wool suit and elegant tie. He noticed Shao Guizhen as soon as he entered the hotel, thinking, "This woman looks clean, well-cultured and feminine and seems to be a good lady. Why does she actually condescended to wash clothes in the hotel?" Two or three days later, he found some clothes, went to Shao and said, "Will you wash some extra clothes today?" Shao answered, "I will at any time." Then Qiu asked, "Would you like to have dinner with me in the dining hall this evening?" Shao replied, "But I had to wash your clothes first." Qiu said, "You can do it tomorrow." Shao said, "OK, but I have to bring my daughter Xiaodong." Qiu said, "Sure."

At dinner, they naturally exchanged their life experiences. Qiu was the first to introduce himself, "My name is Qiu Zhongyuan.

I'm a traditional Chinese medicine practitioner. I came from Caiyuangou Village, Zhengzhou, Henan Province. I was captured by guerrilla forces who wanted me to follow the troops go to northeast and serve as military doctor. Having my mother, my wife and three young daughters at home, I was reluctant to go. One day they troop was marching on a road besides a large corn field, I took the precious opportunity. I crouched, pretending to fasten my shoelaces and lagged. Being unnoticed, I sneaked into the corn field and ran away when they troop went by. I'm not daring to go home; I've been living of wandering life witch practicing medicine. I led a vagrant of practices medicine life until I arrived here. It's a good thing to acquaintance witch you in Jiangsu. The hotel owner told me your husband suddenly left followed his father's troop and your family fell apart. I guess he might have either lost his life in the battlefield or escaped. It's said the Eighth Route Army is fierce. That's why I dare not to serve as a doctor in Kuomintang troops. Now I plan to run a clinic, but I need an assistant for operation. Will you help me?" Shao Guizhen said, "But I have no medical knowledge." Qiu said, "It's never too late to learn." Shao said, "How can I manage that with only two years of education?" Qiu said, "Medicine is a technique. It doesn't necessarily need academic background. My education background is no better than yours. I consider you very smart and I'm sure you can manage it." Shao thought, "It's not bad to learn a technique which will set me free from the hard work of washing clothes." Additionally, Qiu's appearance left her a favorable impression. She thought for a while and gladly accepted the offer.

That silk businessman, noticing the closer relationship between Shao and Qiu, felt jealous and refrained from chatting with Shao. Soon after that, he left the hotel without informing Shao in advance.

One day at dinner, Qiu Zhongyuan, to Shao's surprise, accidentally talked about his family. He said, "My wife, who came from the North, hasn't given birth for seven or eight years since she bore three girls. I don't have a boy, isn't the family without offspring?

I brought her a lot of tonics and all my endeavors failed. Will you marry me?" Shao asked, "You've got a wife already. Why are you asking for another wife?" Qiu said, "It's an arranged marriage. She is three years older than I. In the North, many women are older than their husband because parents say older women are more capable of doing housework and taking care of their husbands. Furthermore, I'm afraid the lineage of my family will be broken off." At that time, affection had arisen between them. Shao thought his requirement was reasonable and accepted it silently. In old China, allowing the men to find several wives.

So, they slept together in the same room at that night. Qiu did everything to please her and their romantic intercourse continued until midnight. Next day when the sun had not risen, Shao was taken by Xiaodong's shouting outside and had to bring her to her own room and slept with her for a while. When she got up, the sun was very high in the sky. She washed her face in a hurry and ran to the clinic to help Qiu Zhongyuan to treat patients without even taking her breakfast.

The next day, Qiu said to Shao, "I think you don't need to rent that room anymore. Now you sleep with me and Xiaodong can sleep in the clinic. Why shall we pay for an extra room?" Shao agreed. She canceled the renting and lived with Qiu in his room. They also put a little bed in a corner of the clinic and separated it from other parts with a cloth curtain. So Xiaodong got a tolerable place for sleep. Though small in body Xiaodong was very clever. Shao Guizhen had been considering sending her to school shortly before she found her pregnant. The delightful couple decided to pay a few days' visit to Qiu's hometown. Meanwhile, they hoped Xiaodong would stay there with Qiu's mother, wife and children and go to school.

The late autumn of 1948, it was after the "Zheng Zhou Battle". Despite the continual defeats, Chiang Kai-shek would not give up his power. At the end of October, he drafted the "Xu Bang launch a mass campaign" plan in Nanjing (Mainland called "Battle of Huaihai").

The world is change unpredictable

The Kuomintang army of the Republic of China is in Xuzhou stand ready for the Communist People's Liberation Army put up a stubborn resistance. Although China's Anti-Japanese War has achieved victory in the August 15, 1945, but in order to compete for political power, "Kuomintang-Communist civil war" still results in China was thick with gunpowder fumes ... Qiu's hometown, located in a small valley besides the Yellow River, it isn't many trees and river view. In the time of turmoil, hire is seemed tranquil without. Maybe it was not an ideal place for soldiers to live or fight. Bathed in warm sunshine every day, the village looked safe in the golden autumn. To Shao's surprised, Qiu Zhongyuan has a large and strong house, it is made of stones and thick, wood piles. The house standing upright on a plain not far from the ravine, adding a view like oil painting to the barren.

Because Shao Guizhen, being pregnant, felt sick after taking train and horse-drawn carriage. Qiu made bed for her to take a rest as soon as they entered the house. Then he sat with his mother chatting. Qiu's mother lived with his wife Wan and his three daughters whose ages followed a sequence of two years' interval. The youngest daughter Weifen was at about the same age with Xiaodong but much taller. Maybe due to this reason, they liked each other at the first sight. Soon they carried vine-made baskets and went out hand in hand to pick sweet potatoes in the field.

Wan's first and second daughters were playing around when Qiu, his mother and his wife Wan were chatting. Qiu said to his mother, "Mum, she is the new daughter-in-law I found for you. Wan hasn't given birth for eight years after she bore three daughters. We tried our best but failed. I fear that without a son, the lineage of our family will be broken off. I have no choice but to find another wife in Jiangsu. You will not disagree, will you?" Qiu's mother said, "Of course I will since you like her and can afford to feed one's family." Hearing that, Mrs. Wan felt unhappy but could not say noon the side. Because in old China men were allowed by the government to have two or three or even more wives. Furthermore, boys were regarded as the ones who carry on the family lineage, especially in the North. Qiu Zhongyuan introduced the basic information of Shao Guizhen. After a few minutes, Qiu said to his mother, "Mum, I want to visit some old friends who grew up with me." Qiu's mother said, "Fine. I will stay home and chat with Guizhen." Weizhen and Weifen, Qiu's first two daughters, said at the same time, "Daddy, we want to go with you." Qiu said with one leg outside by the door, "That is all right." He stepped over the threshold immediately to call on his friends, with his two girls followed gleefully.

Only Qiu Zhong yuan's mother, Wan and Shao Guizhen were left at home. Shao rested for a while and Qiu's mother began chat with her. Mrs. née Wan went to cook.

Shao asked first, "Mum, I heard from Zhongyuan that he has four sisters and brothers, whose ages follow a sequence of nearly two years' interval. When his father passed away, he and his younger brother were less than ten years old. His two elder sisters were young as well. How did you manage to feed four children?" Qiu's mother said, "Wow! When Zhong yuan's father passed away, he left me five children. The oldest one was born by his first wife, who died of acute peritonitis when her daughter was three or four years old. The girl was fifteen or sixteen when Zhong yuan's father died. She lived with me since then until she got married when she was eighteen or nineteen. The 2nd oldest daughter also got married at the age of less than twenty. After the death of Zhong yuan's father, I had to sell lands to carry out the duty of affording five sons and daughters."

Shao asked, "Sell lands? Do you have so many lands to sell?" Qiu's mother said, "I used to have, but few of them were left now. But I didn't worry. Zhongyuan had learned medical skill from his uncle in Xi'an. His brother Zhonglin, ten years younger, also became a doctor. And Zhonglin married the daughter of a Kuomintang official in Hankou. It's heard that he lived very well. Now I don't have to worry about anything." Shao felt quite curious and asked, "Ten years younger than Zhongyuan? Then he is of the same age regarded as the ones who carry on the family lineage, especially in the North. Qiu Zhongyuan introduced the basic information of Shao Guizhen. After a few minutes, Qiu said to his mother, "Mum, I want to visit some old friends who grew up with me." Qiu's mother said, "Fine. I will stay home and chat with Guizhen." Weizhen and Weifen, Qiu's first two daughters, said at the same time, "Daddy, we want to go with you." Qiu said with one leg outside by the door, "That is all right." He stepped over the threshold immediately to call on his friends, with his two girls followed gleefully.

Only Qiu Zhong yuan's mother, Wan and Shao Guizhen were left at home. Shao rested for a while and Qiu's mother began chat with her. Mrs. née Wan went to cook.

Shao asked first, "Mum, I heard from Zhongyuan that he has four sisters and brothers, whose ages follow a sequence of nearly two years' interval. When his father passed away, he and his younger brother were less than ten years old. His two elder sisters were young as well. How did you manage to feed four children?" Qiu's mother said, "Wow! When Zhong yuan's father passed away, he left me five children. The oldest one was born by his first wife, who died of acute peritonitis when her daughter was three or four years old. The girl was fifteen or sixteen when Zhong yuan's father died. She lived with me since then until she got married when she was eighteen or nineteen. The 2nd oldest daughter also got married at the age of less than twenty. After the death of Zhong yuan's father, I had to sell lands to carry out the duty of affording five sons and daughters."

Shao asked, "Sell lands? Do you have so many lands to sell?" Qiu's mother said, "I used to have, but few of them were left now. But I didn't worry. Zhongyuan had learned medical skill from his uncle in Xi'an. His brother Zhonglin, ten years younger, also became a doctor. And Zhonglin married the daughter of a Kuomintang official in Hankou. It's heard that he lived very well. Now I don't have to worry about anything." Shao felt quite curious and asked, "Ten years younger than Zhongyuan? Then he is of the same age

The world is change unpredictable

The Kuomintang army of the Republic of China is in Xuzhou stand ready for the Communist People's Liberation Army put up a stubborn resistance. Although China's Anti-Japanese War has achieved victory in the August 15, 1945, but in order to compete for political power, "Kuomintang-Communist civil war" still results in China was thick with gunpowder fumes ... Qiu's hometown, located in a small valley besides the Yellow River, it isn't many trees and river view. In the time of turmoil, hire is seemed tranquil without. Maybe it was not an ideal place for soldiers to live or fight. Bathed in warm sunshine every day, the village looked safe in the golden autumn. To Shao's surprised, Qiu Zhongyuan has a large and strong house, it is made of stones and thick, wood piles. The house standing upright on a plain not far from the ravine, adding a view like oil painting to the barren.

Because Shao Guizhen, being pregnant, felt sick after taking train and horse-drawn carriage. Qiu made bed for her to take a rest as soon as they entered the house. Then he sat with his mother chatting. Qiu's mother lived with his wife Wan and his three daughters whose ages followed a sequence of two years' interval. The youngest daughter Weifen was at about the same age with Xiaodong but much taller. Maybe due to this reason, they liked each other at the first sight. Soon they carried vine-made baskets and went out hand in hand to pick sweet potatoes in the field.

Wan's first and second daughters were playing around when Qiu, his mother and his wife Wan were chatting. Qiu said to his mother, "Mum, she is the new daughter-in-law I found for you. Wan hasn't given birth for eight years after she bore three daughters. We tried our best but failed. I fear that without a son, the lineage of our family will be broken off. I have no choice but to find another wife in Jiangsu. You will not disagree, will you?" Qiu's mother said, "Of course I will since you like her and can afford to feed one's family." Hearing that, Mrs. Wan felt unhappy but could not say noon the side. Because in old China men were allowed by the government to have two or three or even more wives. Furthermore, boys were

The world is change unpredictable

with me. I heard the Communist troops are undefeatable and about to take hold of the entire country. Is Zhonglin's father-in-law still at ease? Isn't he terrified?" Qiu's mother said, "The old man is said to be a little nervous, but not terrified. He said he had never done anything wrong to the public and committed no crime, so he didn't want to escape."

Shao kept silent for a while after hearing that. She thought, "Things might be different in the combating battlefield." Then she asked another question, "Why did your family have so many lands in the past?" Qiu's mother said, "I heard from Zhong Yuan's father that Zhong Yuan's grandpa used to serve as a clerk in the county government since he was young. He was very famous for his good articles even in remote areas, and many people came to ask him to write official complaint for filing a lawsuit. For this reason, he could earn a lot of extra money besides his salary. He didn't visit prostitute, drug and gambling, rather, he bought land once he had some money and thus owned many lands. Zhong Yuan's father was also a decent man. What he cared about are lands and children. I didn't sell land until I became a widow. Now most of the lands are sold. Only two or three of them are left for us to grow vegetables for our own use."

After taking the rest, Shao felt much better. She got up and helped Wan to cook. Qiu Zhongyuan arrived home no sooner than the meal was ready, so did his daughters. The whole family enjoyed the dishes. At the table, Qiu Zhongyuan said, "Mum, please come with us to Jiangsu when we leave. I'm busier and busier and Guizhen is pregnant. You can cook for us or provide other help." Hearing that, Qiu's mother had a wide smile on her face, "Sure! I am eager to see the outside world with you. It's dulled to stay in Caiyuangou." Qiu Zhongyuan said, "Mum, we want to leave Xiaodong here to accompany Wan's daughters. Moreover, she should go to school instead of living with us. We rented the hotel room in Jiangsu only to run our business." Qiu's mother said, "Sure! But she must change her surname, or people here will not know whose daughter she is." Shao Guizhen smiled and accepted the suggestion at once, "Of course.

It's quite easy. Just change Jiang Xiaodong into Qiu Xiaodong." They reached the agreement and Xiaodong inherited his stepfather's surname ever since.

    The couple decided to go back to Jiangsu after less than ten days' stay in hometown because some of his patients had not fully recovered although they did refuse to accept new patients when they left. Qiu Zhongyuan decided to return to the hotel in Jiangsu with his mother and wife on the ninth day. On that day, Qiu's mother carry some local products like red dates and dried persimmons and together lived in the hotel followed her son and daughter-in-law.

    A few months later, Shao Guizhen gave birth to their first girl with Qiu Zhongyuan in the rented room. Qiu Zhongyuan adored the baby despite her gender because she resembled his appearance very much and the little girl is a real delight by everyone who saw her. He later named her Qiu Weiying. Sometimes Qiu Zhongyuan said with pride to his patients, "Look, the eyes of my daughter were so brilliant. She must be smart and have a promising future." According to the old belief, parents will benefit from their children if the son resembles his mother or daughter resembles her father.

    Due to Qiu's outstanding medical skills and the couple's responsible attitude, more and more patients came to them. Now with Qiu's mother and the new-born daughter, the two rooms they rented became too small for them to live and treat patients. The rooms were narrow, stuffy and especially uncomfortable in the scorching summer. So, the couple decides to move out and trying to find another place to live and practice medicine.

CHAPTER 2

Age of rapid change

2.1 The survivor of a great disaster

One day after Weiying was one-month old, Zhang Yumou, apprentice to Qiu Zhong Yuan's younger brother--Qiu Zhonglin went to the hotel at the request after taking part in the funeral procession of his father.

He also brought a letter of Qiu Zhonglin, which said, "...I have bought a relatively large house in Hankou where Guang Feng's parents live with us. You cannot do with renting and living in the hotel. I have a plan to send our mother to here and you can come along. And I suggest you opening a clinic in Changsha, which may be a good way out, one reason being that it will facilitate us visiting each other since I live in Hubei. And this time Zhang Yumou can pick you all up here." This letter just met the intention of Qiu Zhongyuan and his wife.

Their mother agreed with great pleasure after being told the news, for the two rented rooms, one for treating patients and the other for accommodating the whole family were not enough with more and more patients. Qiu's mother had always thought that such a living environment was crowded with stale air, much worse than my previous Caiyuangou. Therefore, with the mother's support, the couple stopped receiving new patients to be operated on and treated old patients immediately. They asked the patients who had almost recovered to go back home and take some medicine that they could cope with by themselves and those who could not leave temporarily to stay for more days. After a few days when all old patients would get recovered, the whole family could leave Jiangsu.

One evening Zang Yumou saw Qiu Zhongyuan checking the account. Suddenly he said to Qiu secretly, "Could you borrow some money for me to start up a business?" Qiu asked, "How do you develop such an idea?" Zhang answered, "We have spent all of our money on my father's funeral, and my 50-odd-year-old mother is in bad health so that my younger brother can hardly afford the family just by farming. That's why I want to borrow some money from you to open a small shop for him." Qiu agreed, "Good idea. You are quite filially devoted for your mother. How much do you need?" Zhang smiled, "I do not need much. Just 200 teals." Qiu said, "That's not a small amount of money." Then Zhang immediately answered, "I will pay you back as soon as my brother earns money form the shop or I myself make some by being a doctor." Qiu agreed, "OK, I'll help you out. But I do not have that much at hand. I'll give it to you together with the ship ticket fees tomorrow morning." Hearing this, Zhang became so glad.

When Zhang Yumou took money from Qiu and went to buy ship tickets after breakfast the next morning, Qiu exhorted him, "Buy the ticket of tomorrow afternoon. Though there's only one ship for Shanghai per week here, few people went to big cities including Nanjing, so we are likely to get tickets." Holding the money in hand, Zhang replied without looking back, "I knew that when I was at the dock." The couple then began to wrap up with the last few patients and check accounts with them.

Zhang came back before lunch and took out the tickets and remaining money from his pocket. Confused at the different colors of one ticket that Zhang held aside from the others, Qiu asked, "Why is your own ticket different from ours?" Zhang answered with a cold smile, "This one is in a better position on the ship. It's the last one but costs a bit more. You better be frugal, for you can get to Hankou anyway, or you must wait until next week." With this, he pressed the three tickets into Qiu's hand while Qiu staring at his face with a hooknose, got too angry to say a word. However, he did not want to wait for another week; moreover, the family had made preparation for leaving. With no alternative, Qiu borrowed Zhang 200 yuan as he promised. Then Zhang left when Qiu fell into his own thought. Not asking more, Qiu continued to be engaged in the treatment of remaining patients.

After breakfast the next morning, the family began to wrap up medical facilities and daily commodities in their bedroom as well as their baggage. Grandma was also busy with it. In the afternoon, they settled their bills with the hotel and bid farewell to the boss and servants. They left the hotel of Jiangsu province where they had lived for more than one year.

They set out in a hurry. With a bag made of satin embroidered with flowers on her right arm, Shao Guizhen held little Weiying who was still asleep with her head against her mother's. Grandma Qiu, with a small-sized cloth wrapper, walked alongside the river in the town by her small feet. And Qiu Zhongyuan carried a rattan full of medical articles in one hand and a heavy canvas bag on another shoulder. Zhang Yumou, then, carrying light baggage and his own bamboo pretentiously, frigged about along a narrow path. It had not rained for a long time and there was no breeze over the riverside. With the earth basked in the afternoon sun, it was hot and suffocating. A stray dog beside the street was gasping with its tongue stretched out. Despite clouds above, there was no sign for rain. Zhang saw an empty boat rowed slowly in the river first, and Qiu shouted together with him. The boatman rowed the boat towards them and stopped by the riverside. Zhang and the Qiu family hurried onto the boat and felt relieved. Then the boatman strived to row to the dock where the ship was anchored.

Passers were boarding when they got off the boat and onto the dock. Zhang did not care about the Qiu family at all; instead, he hurried to the ticket examiner and passed the inspection quickly. However, the ticket inspector check tickets suddenly became confused at the tickets handed to him by Qiu Zhongyuan, saying, "The three tickets are not for the passenger ship but for the small freighter on that tugboat down there. But how can you spend the whole night on a freighter, which will be more dangerous when the weather changes." Qiu pointed to Zhang, who had then already entered the cabin, "It was him who has bought all the tickets. We had no idea at all. So, could we board the ship and pay the rest of the ticket then?" The ticket inspector replied, "Tickets for both the sleeping cabin and the seats have been sold today. Nevertheless, you may refund your tickets." Qiu was surprised, "It would cause great trouble, for we used to live here by renting rooms in a hotel…" "Then there is no alternative." "You mean we have to take the freighter down there?" "Eh…that's up to you," the examiner answered in a helpless tone. With vixen whistling, the ship was to leave the dock immediately. Time was so pressing that the family could not turn back and hurry along the slope to board the freighter, full of caused reluctance.

Seeing the goods on board, Qiu Zhongyuan was so angry that he cursed, "Shit! How can we sleep here, let alone sit down?" Then he touched the parcels of various sizes and realized that they were filled with cotton. A long wooden board, which could be used as a seat was fixed in the middle part of the tugboat. Two biggest parcels were put on each side of the board. Qiu asked his mother and Guizhen to sit on the wooden board and backed on the parcels he had pushed aside. And he himself, finally sitting on the deck behind the parcels, faced the boundless river and thought crossly, "Damn it! Why didn't he tell us the truth about our tickets?"

When they got board in the afternoon, it was clear with breeze blowing over the river and waves patting against the bank. But when felt relieved. Then the boatman strived to row to the dock where the ship was anchored.

Passers were boarding when they got off the boat and onto the dock. Zhang did not care about the Qiu family at all; instead, he hurried to the ticket examiner and passed the inspection quickly. However, the ticket inspector check tickets suddenly became confused at the tickets handed to him by Qiu Zhongyuan, saying, "The three tickets are not for the passenger ship but for the small freighter on that tugboat down there. But how can you spend the whole night on a freighter, which will be more dangerous when the weather changes." Qiu pointed to Zhang, who had then already entered the cabin, "It was him who has bought all the tickets. We had no idea at all. So, could we board the ship and pay the rest of the ticket then?" The ticket inspector replied, "Tickets for both the sleeping cabin and the seats have been sold today. Nevertheless, you may refund your tickets." Qiu was surprised, "It would cause great trouble, for we used to live here by renting rooms in a hotel…" "Then there is no alternative." "You mean we have to take the freighter down there?" "Eh…that's up to you," the examiner answered in a helpless tone. With vixen whistling, the ship was to leave the dock immediately. Time was so pressing that the family could not turn back and hurry along the slope to board the freighter, full of caused reluctance.

Seeing the goods on board, Qiu Zhongyuan was so angry that he cursed, "Shit! How can we sleep here, let alone sit down?" Then he touched the parcels of various sizes and realized that they were filled with cotton. A long wooden board, which could be used as a seat was fixed in the middle part of the tugboat. Two biggest parcels were put on each side of the board. Qiu asked his mother and Guizhen to sit on the wooden board and backed on the parcels he had pushed aside. And he himself, finally sitting on the deck behind the parcels, faced the boundless river and thought crossly, "Damn it! Why didn't he tell us the truth about our tickets?"

When they got board in the afternoon, it was clear with breeze blowing over the river and waves patting against the bank. But when of one ticket that Zhang held aside from the others, Qiu asked, "Why is your own ticket different from ours?" Zhang answered with a cold smile, "This one is in a better position on the ship. It's the last one but costs a bit more. You better be frugal, for you can get to Hankou anyway, or you must wait until next week." With this, he pressed the three tickets into Qiu's hand while Qiu staring at his face with a hooknose, got too angry to say a word. However, he did not want to wait for another week; moreover, the family had made preparation for leaving. With no alternative, Qiu borrowed Zhang 200 yuan as he promised. Then Zhang left when Qiu fell into his own thought. Not asking more, Qiu continued to be engaged in the treatment of remaining patients.

After breakfast the next morning, the family began to wrap up medical facilities and daily commodities in their bedroom as well as their baggage. Grandma was also busy with it. In the afternoon, they settled their bills with the hotel and bid farewell to the boss and servants. They left the hotel of Jiangsu province where they had lived for more than one year.

They set out in a hurry. With a bag made of satin embroidered with flowers on her right arm, Shao Guizhen held little Weiying who was still asleep with her head against her mother's. Grandma Qiu, with a small-sized cloth wrapper, walked alongside the river in the town by her small feet. And Qiu Zhongyuan carried a rattan full of medical articles in one hand and a heavy canvas bag on another shoulder. Zhang Yumou, then, carrying light baggage and his own bamboo pretentiously, frigged about along a narrow path. It had not rained for a long time and there was no breeze over the riverside. With the earth basked in the afternoon sun, it was hot and suffocating. A stray dog beside the street was gasping with its tongue stretched out. Despite clouds above, there was no sign for rain. Zhang saw an empty boat rowed slowly in the river first, and Qiu shouted together with him. The boatman rowed the boat towards them and stopped by the riverside. Zhang and the Qiu family hurried onto the boat and it grew dark, the only stars that gave off dim light hid into clouds quietly. It was so dark that they could not see their fingers or the remote horizontal line, even clouds up in the sky and mountains beside the river. Unless he saw vague someone walking here and there on the deck with a kerosene lamp and heard the wave sounds, he might feel that the small boat carried his whole family progressing through the horrible world.

At midnight when people on the passenger ship were asleep, Qiu Zhongyuan bended over a small parcel of cotton and fell asleep with tiredness. Backed on the two parcels closely, Grandma Qiu and Shao Guizhen slept in a trance. Out of a sudden, it began to rain with wind, cooling all of them though it was summertime. Shao Guizhen dragged out a small cotton quilt from their baggage quickly to wrap little Weiying up. The howling wind and torrential rain caused waves in the river, striking the poor tugboat violently as if it was to be overturned. The whole family became nervous. Under such circumstances, Qiu Zhongyuan, although everyone in the passenger ship was asleep, shouted, "Help! Help! The tugboat is being turned over..." Such a wretched and horrible scream passed onto the ship immediately and Passengers on board got to know what happened and thus got up and ran to the end of the ship. Standing on the deck with a shelter, they all stared at the poor tugboat, some shouted, "Oh! How terrible t is! The whole family is being drowned. Hurry up ..." At this time, a sailor pushed his way through the crowd, crept on the end of the stern and stretched his head out of the ship, hoping to drag the cable linking the small boat. Some warm-hearted men hurried to drag his legs or feet in that he might fall into the water. Suddenly there came such a furious storm that the cable was snapped, and the boat was thrown away. Passengers in the ship screamed and shouted, only to witness the tugboat being flung further and further by the ruthless water.

Qiu Zhongyuan was so scared that he held onto that big bundle of cotton, and Shao Guizhen held little Weiying more and more tightly, thinking that if they must leave the world, they must be together. Grandma Qiu was in despair, only longing for God's blessing. Kneeing on the board panicked, she kept on murmuring and kowtowing, "Dear God, thank God. Please make sure that we arrive safely and once we do, I'll light candles three days and nights to express my appreciation…" However, the God might not hear her prayer immediately and have not yet begun to show compassion. The wind was still roaring and the storm still raging, striking hardly the poor little boat, which was gradually filled with water. And dozens of the bundles of cotton covered with water-proof canvas were soaked soon. The boat, with more weight, began to sink. The whole family felt entirely desperate, except little Weiying who was sleeping and crying alternatively in her mother's arms, without the knowledge that the God was playing a death game with the four of them. While Grandma was unceasingly kowtowing, Qiu Zhongyuan was rapidly throwing the bundles into the river and at the same time scooping up the water in the boat with a big porcelain cup. Finally, only the two biggest bundles of cotton were left, though Shao helped him to move them after handing Weiying to Grandma for a moment. Qiu gave up out of breath, "Just let it be." Then he lay on the board, tired. The tiny boat went up and down through the river like this without an identified direction…

The storm gradually ceased as the morning twilight which was fish belly white appeared on the oriental horizon when dawn came. Suddenly, had a row of waves with a mountainous force towards the was boat directly impacted, the boat drifted with the waves to the harbor of the Huangpu River.

The family were so exhausted that they fell asleep on board without being to move a bit but to accept their destiny. The boat stopped swinging and sinking as the storm halted and began to drift towards the riverbank together with the waves. On hearing vixen of the passenger ship coming from the center of the river, which was lit by the sunglow, the whole family felt that they could survive anyhow. The ship came nearer with louder siren. Passers on the ship stretched out their heads from doors and windows to look for them. And the ship drove to their side quite soon. People on board were quiet and surprised and pleasant, "It is a miracle that you could survive." "We thought we could never see you again. This is just unbelievable."

At this exact moment, Zhang Yumou wormed his way into the crowd at the stern and cast his eyes to the whole family. Facing the passenger ship, Qiu Zhongyuan seated himself on the boat, totally worn out. Seeing the pointed skull of Zhang, Qiu showed great indignation and grudge against him. Not knowing what to say, he pointed with his finger to Zhang, who hid away with a guilty conscience. A sailor hooked the boat nearer with a bamboo pole and then put a ladder made of rope. Another sailor brought some food and drinks and jumped onto the boat with the help of the ladder. Then he rowed the survived boat to the gulf of Shanghai. While rowing, he talked with the couple, telling them that a train in Shanghai station could from where that they could go on to Wuhan. On hearing this, the family were very pleased and feel refreshed. They finally survived after going through so many hardships.

Qiu Zhongyuan bought four train tickets as soon as they went ashore at the dock of Shanghai. And he bought something to eat and drink while waiting for the train. The couple had nothing to say with Zhang Yumou, who felt boring and turned to Grandma Qiu for a talk. However, Granny, who was also very angry, did not pay attention to him. Zhang moved aside, pretending to be drowsy.

The train was coming at dusk. Zhang followed the Qiu family to get on the train. Seated, Shao felt some pain in her arms and thus handed Weiying to Qiu who played with their little girl. Perhaps due to the heavy storm on the river, Weiying began to have diarrhea soon, staining Qiu's fashionable suit. In the times when the civil war just ended, water supply on the train had not been recovered and there was not a drop from the tap. Qiu had no alternative but to wipe with paper. When the train stopped midway, he rushed down and washed out the filth with the water he found. Then he returned to the train immediately. After several stops, the family arrived at their destination---Wuhan at last.

Qiu called two rickshaws, one for the couple and little Weiying and the other for Granny and Zhang Yumou. The rickshaws took them to Qiu Zhonglin's house at Derunli of Hankou district very soon.

As soon as he got to his brother's home and put down the luggage, Qiu Zhongyuan described the risky trip to Qiu Zhonglin. Hearing the whole story, Qiu Zhonglin scolded Zhang Yumou loudly, "What were you thinking about? My mother and my brother's family might have died in the river due to the ship tickets you had bought. Get out of here. I'll not have you as my apprentice anymore." Zhang looking nervous somewhat and quibbled, "I had no idea that those tickets were for the small tugboat. I thought they were for the seats on the bottom. I have not learned enough and where will you send me?" Qiu Zhongyuan denounced, "You have lost your conscience and my whole family were at risk of dying. So, where you go has nothing to do with us." Qiu Zhonglin added, "Go back to your hometown!" And Qiu Zhongyuan walked towards Zhang, "Take out the money I have lent you." Zhang became nervous suddenly and murmured, "I have no money to go back home…" Qiu replied, "I'll give you enough for your ticket and food, so be quick." Zhang had to take out the 200 silver dollars from the pocket of his underwear. Giving him enough money for buying tickets and food, Qiu required him never to come back again.

After Zhang left with reluctance, Qiu Zhonglin said to his brother, "Even I dare not lend him so much. How could you do so without even knowing about him?" Qiu Zhongyuan answered, "I thought it would be all right because he was your apprentice…" Qiu Zhonglin replied, "My brother, you must first know the nature of a person who borrows a relatively large amount of money from you, or…" Qiu Zhongyuan replied, "Exactly, or we would not have survived, let alone the money."

The couple rested for several days at Qiu Zhonglin's home in Hankou. After discussion with Qiu Zhonglin and his wife, they decided to arrange for Granny to stay and by the way accompany Guang Feng's parents and bring little Weiying to leave for Hankou to start their own career. The next day, they went on the train to Changsha.

2.2 A Selfless mother

Changsha is a city with a long history and rich culture. Located at the east bank down Xiang River, it is the metropolis of Hunan Province, with Jingguang Railway passing through. Throughout history, Hunan has trained the births of many cultural intellects as well as brilliant military leaders and great politicians, especially in the turbulent days when the hero of the Communist Party, Mao Zedong stood out.

There were many Mao's distinguished townsmen who fought by him regardless of the threat of death, and at last established new China. Among them was Vice President Liu Shaoqi, who died from the persecution in Cultural Revolution, Defense Minister Peng Dehuai, Vice Supreme Military Command and Director of Physical Culture and Sports Commission He Long, Hu Yaobang, who used to be the Secretary of Chinese Communist League Central but later died, and so on. Even nowadays, in addition to Peng Liyuan, there are several famous singers in China, most are Hunan. Tian Han, the great songwriter of the national anthem, is also from Hunan people <See App, 2. C)> perhaps, Hunan has a distinct four seasons climate; and it has mountains, water, rivers are unique geographical location, maybe can bring some talent to some people.

Qiu Zhongyuan did not expect at first that his move after taking his younger brother, Qiu Zhonglin's advice, was one that tied the fate of his whole family to everything that took place in the city.

Upon arrival at Changsha, the couple bought a house which was long and narrow, located at Pozi Street, downtown. The estimated 100 square meters house had only outer walls; the rooms inside were divided by wooden boards. It was opposite the famous traditional restaurant of Changsha, The Fire Palace. There were two large rooms in the house, one facing the street, on behind all the other rooms. The one facing the street was adapted to a waiting room, where they made a high counter with wooden bars. A small window connected the railings and the counter, for residence permit and payment. Right of the counter was a small door to the passageway, with another door to its left, facing the passageway. Inside the door was a long room which was divided into two in the middle. The outer half was for dressing change and the inner for operations. There was a wooden attic above the two halves to store the absorbent cottons, gauzes and other medicines and instrument. Continuing the passageway to enter the next door would bring one to the kitchen. Another door opened in the left corner of the kitchen, inside of which the passageway turned its direction to the left. A door to a small room faced the right of the passage. The passageway leaded to a small courtyard, under the roof of which, next to the back room, was a toilet. The large room at the end of the linear house was the bedroom of couple.

The linear house was built before liberation, when Changsha City got burnt in the Anti-Japan War. It was said that the Kuomintang did not want to leave the well-preserved city of Changsha to the Communist Party, so that an ill-decided order was given that Changsha be burnt down. As the fire got its way, the whole city was swallowed by the flame, scaring a large crowd of people to Orange Isle at the west bank of Xiang River. After the fire, the then high-ranking officials of Kuomintang in Hunan were dismissed and prosecuted. However, the beautiful, famous cultural city was deprived of almost all its nice buildings. As a result, the streets had to welcome the new houses build with wooden boards in rush. (This, however, made removals very convenient, which contributes to the reconstruction of Changsha in the modern times when economy develops fast.)

Upon arrival at Changsha, the couple bought a house which was long and narrow, located at Pozi Street, downtown. The estimated 100 square meters house had only outer walls; the rooms inside were divided by wooden boards. It was opposite the famous traditional restaurant of Changsha, The Fire Palace. There were two large rooms in the house, one facing the street, on behind all the other rooms. The one facing the street was adapted to a waiting room, where they made a high counter with wooden bars. A small window connected the railings and the counter, for residence permit and payment. Right of the counter was a small door to the passageway, with another door to its left, facing the passageway. Inside the door was a long room which was divided into two in the middle. The outer half was for dressing change and the inner for operations. There was a wooden attic above the two halves to store the absorbent cottons, gauzes and other medicines and instrument. Continuing the passageway to enter the next door would bring one to the kitchen. Another door opened in the left corner of the kitchen, inside of which the passageway turned its direction to the left. A door to a small room faced the right of the passage. The passageway leaded to a small courtyard, under the roof of which, next to the back room, was a toilet. The large room at the end of the linear house was the bedroom of couple.

The linear house was built before liberation, when Changsha City got burnt in the Anti-Japan War. It was said that the Kuomintang did not want to leave the well-preserved city of Changsha to the Communist Party, so that an ill-decided order was given that Changsha be burnt down. As the fire got its way, the whole city was swallowed by the flame, scaring a large crowd of people to Orange Isle at the west bank of Xiang River. After the fire, the then high-ranking officials of Kuomintang in Hunan were dismissed and prosecuted. However, the beautiful, famous cultural city was deprived of almost all its nice buildings. As a result, the streets had to welcome the new houses build with wooden boards in rush. (This, however, made removals very convenient, which contributes to the reconstruction of Changsha in the modern times when economy develops fast.)

The couple rested for several days at Qiu Zhonglin's home in Hankou. After discussion with Qiu Zhonglin and his wife, they decided to arrange for Granny to stay and by the way accompany Guang Feng's parents and bring little Weiying to leave for Hankou to start their own career. The next day, they went on the train to Changsha.

2.2 A Selfless mother

Changsha is a city with a long history and rich culture. Located at the east bank down Xiang River, it is the metropolis of Hunan Province, with Jingguang Railway passing through. Throughout history, Hunan has trained the births of many cultural intellects as well as brilliant military leaders and great politicians, especially in the turbulent days when the hero of the Communist Party, Mao Zedong stood out.

There were many Mao's distinguished townsmen who fought by him regardless of the threat of death, and at last established new China. Among them was Vice President Liu Shaoqi, who died from the persecution in Cultural Revolution, Defense Minister Peng Dehuai, Vice Supreme Military Command and Director of Physical Culture and Sports Commission He Long, Hu Yaobang, who used to be the Secretary of Chinese Communist League Central but later died, and so on. Even nowadays, in addition to Peng Liyuan, there are several famous singers in China, most are Hunan. Tian Han, the great songwriter of the national anthem, is also from Hunan people <See App, 2. C)> perhaps, Hunan has a distinct four seasons climate; and it has mountains, water, rivers are unique geographical location, maybe can bring some talent to some people.

Qiu Zhongyuan did not expect at first that his move after taking his younger brother, Qiu Zhonglin's advice, was one that tied the fate of his whole family to everything that took place in the city.

Age of rapid change

Changsha was already peacefully liberated under the military munity launched by senior generals of Kuomintang, Cheng Qian and Chen Mingyi on August 4th, 1949, before the establishment of People's Republic of China on October 1st. however, the headquarters of Kuomintang was not willing to hand over Changsha to Communist Party after their loss of their metropolis, Nanjing, in April. As a dying kick, they sent planes to drop bombs at Changsha for a few times, once happened to be at the time when the Qius arrived. In the bombardment, the family hid in the shelter under the ancient circumvallation of Tianxin Pavilion. There, you can also the clouds in the sky.

Mrs. Qiu held Qiu Weiying tightly in her arms, lowering her head to protect the tiny body of her baby from the splinters. In fact, those minor attacks barely had any effect; Chairman Mao, the first leader of PRC, stood on the Tiananmen Rostrum on October 1st as scheduled, and announced to the world, "The People's Republic of China will forever since stand on her own feet!"

After the war, the Qiu family hurriedly renovated the old house they bought. Later, Qiu Zhongyuan and his wife employed a mid-aged man, Zheng Huaxian, as their accountant. One day, Qiu Zhongyuan said to Zheng, "The new China advocates monogamy. My marriage was arranged by my parents before liberation when we were in the north, and it was no procedure. As the war came to an end, the Qiu's embellished their house in simple style. Later needed at that time, so I don't have any credentials. Now that I have lived with Guizhen for one year and a half already, I think it's time for us to go to the governmental office to register. So, would you be the chief witness at our wedding?" Zheng replied delightfully, "Why wouldn't I? What a blissful job it is! I am more than happy to take it!" So, Qiu Zhongyuan and Shao Guizhen registered, and invited some neighbors they got along well with to the Fire Palace, where they had a simple wedding with Zheng being their chief witness.

33

It was the first winter of new China, 1949. Eight years of Anti-Japan War and four years of Civil War had consumed much of the country's wealth. The notes issued by Kuomintang government turned waste papers, and the prices went up. When the Qius had everything ready and was about to receive their first patient, they suddenly realized that they were lacking anesthetics. Anesthetic is the primary medicine in proctologic operations; without it they could do nothing in their clinic. For anesthetics were quite expensive at that time, they couldn't manage to start their business, they didn't even have one large bill, and there left only a few eggs, some vegetables and a jar of American milk powder which Weiying occasionally got to drink. Depressed by the fact, Qiu Zhongyuan stood in a trance at his consulting room. Shao Guizhen, holing Weiying in her arms, saw the scene. She said to him in comfort, "The black satin cotton-padded cheongsam I am wearing has a woolen lining and is very warm. I figure the Jiang 's family spent a lot to have the tailor made it when I was to marry their son. Let's put it on sale. We might get a good price if somebody wants it, and we can use the money for quite some time." With these words, Shao Guizhen put little Weiying, who was sleeping tight, into the cradle.

Then, she took Qiu Zhong Yuan's hand and went to the T-junction of the street and the main road. She put off her cheongsam by Huangxing road without any hesitation and turned the woolen side out and started peddling. Some passersby came close curiously, looked and commented, "Wow, I have never seen a cheongsam with such decent fabric from inside out!" Shao Guizhen herself did not feel easy to sell the garment at low price, but she had no other way to get money. However, people only came to look and consult, but no one could afford to buy it. Shao shivered in cold, her face turning blue. Tears welled up in Qiu Zhong Yuan's eyes. He said in incitation, "I will never forget your selling your woolen cheongsam in such freezing winter days for the family." At this moment, a well-dressed couple came up to examine the cheongsam from inside out.

After asking the reason why they wanted to sell it, the couple offered a satisfying price and left with the garment.

The Qius took the money home, exhilarated. Afterwards, Qiu went to the pharmacy company to purchase the anesthetics, and Shao went to the nearby butcher's and bought a fish and some green vegetables. The next morning, they glued the paper ads by the roadside windows, and hang up a wooden board on the door, telling their business hours. Right in the afternoon there were people coming for the doctor. Before long, they made some money and Shao Guizhen bought an ordinary cotton-padded jacket made of black satin.

Shao Guizhen's mother died in the countryside of their hometown Jiangsu in the winter of 1951. In grief, Shao took Weiying back, while Qiu left to attend to the clinic. Shao often sent money to her mother after she was married, but her mother used them to help her friends and relatives in need while leading a frugal life herself. She was quite thin when she died. Looking at the body of her mother, Shao regretted not having been more considerate for her. Now that her mother had died, she would have no more chance to perform her duty of filialness. The thought brought her to endless tears…

After a while, she suddenly realized that one-year-old Weiying was not in bed. She asked her second sister who was just walking out of the kitchen unsettled, "Have you seen Weiying?" Her sister replied, "My son Weikang might have taken her out." Hearing the words, Shao wiped her tears and dashed out. As she got several steps away from the house, she saw that Weiying was put into a hand-made sleigh, while Zong Weikang was about to sit inside himself and sleigh down along the slope. Shao was frightened at the scene. She shouted while running to them, and almost fell to the ground. Seeing her coming, Zong Weikang stood still. Shao ran to them, snatched little Weiying from the sleigh, and complained, "Good heavens! You are only a child yourself; how can you take her out to sleigh! How old are you?" Zong Weikang replied that he was sixteen. Shao thought to herself, "He isn't as young as he seems. It is likely that my sister is too poor to nourish him." So, shao went back and said to her sorrowful-looking sister, "Sister, I think Weikang is too thin for the labors in the countryside. I think I can take him with me and teach him medicine. When you get old, he may have become a doctor and you can depend on him." Her sister was cheered up by her words, and said smilingly, "You cannot be righter. Not to mention whether I can depend on him when I am old, I think it will even be a huge problem for him to get married, he has always been a weak boy with poor health. If you take him to Changsha and educate him to be a doctor, he won't be troubled by economic problems and won't end up being a bachelor." So, after the funeral, Shao took sixteen - year-old Zong Weikang to Changsha.

Qiu Zhongyuan was a bit unhappy seeing Zong Weikang. He said, "I remember the year when we went to my hometown. I didn't tell you then that my sister asked me to teach his son medicine and I didn't agree. What's more, we already have an assistant now. Wouldn't it be of more trouble if you have him with us?" Shao said, "We are having more and more patients now. When he finishes his apprenticeship, he can help us with the patients." Qiu contemplated for a while in silence, and then he said, "Li (the first wife of Qiu Zhongyuan) wrote to me saying 'I want to take mom and our daughters to Changsha.' What do you say about it?" Shao answered, "What do I say? We are family. We have enough rooms. Just let them come if they want to!" Before long, the first wife of Qiu took her three daughters, Qiu Xiaodong, who had always been living with Grandma Qiu in their hometown, and Qiu's mother to Changsha, and settled down in Pozi Street. Later they had more patients in the clinic, and the house got crowded. Grandma could not stand that many people, so she took Li, Li's two daughters and Xiaodong back to their hometown. Only Wan's eldest daughter left in Changsha for middle school, for it was not so convenient to go to school in her hometown. She did not move until her mother took her other two sisters to Beijing and sent her to Beijing for school too. Xiaodong came back to Changsha when it came the time for middle school, and had been living with mother ever since then, even after she got married.

Zheng Huaxian, the accountant of Qiu's clinic, was a man in his forties. He had an interesting talent, that is, he could keep his face unmoved and only slant his mouth to make his ears moving back and forth. He often played the trick for little Weiying when he was free. He would move his left ear when Weiying trotted to his left and move the right ear when Weiying ran to his right. This would bring the innocent little girl to chuckles, adding much fun to her childhood.

When Weiying was about three, Shao gave birth to a boy, which made Qiu Zhongyuan jump and clap in joy. He would tell whomever he met, "This is my fifth kid. Finally, I have a boy when I'm forty!" They named the boy Qiu Juecong and hired a nanny to live at their house to cater to the baby. When Juecong was almost one year old and taken on a bus, he waved his arms and legs in happiness. So Qiu Zhongyuan gave some extra money to the nanny to have her take Juecong on a bus around the city every day.

Shao was pregnant again when Juecong was one. This time she suffered more than ever, not only having no appetite but also feeling dizzy at times. Their business, however, was flourishing each day, so she insisted on seeing the patients with her husband. Later her stomach became especially large, and examination told them that she was having twins. Nevertheless, she went on with her work with big belly. Qiu Zhongyuan thought, "It will be perfect if these are two boys, or at least one. Then I don't want it anymore."

One afternoon, Shao was tired and went to rest in bed. Aches took over her the moment she lay down, and she was at the verge of breaking down. Qiu was nervous in sixes and sevens, for it was too late to send her to a hospital. So, he hurried to send for a female doctor to help deliver the babies. After long toil and labor, two girls were born. Seeing two girls only, but not a boy, Qiu was almost disappointed to tears. He immediately set aside and paid no attention to them. The girl that came out first started crying, while the later one was quiet. Shao sensed something wrong and tried to sit up and check on her regardless of the pain. The doctor picked up the quiet girl by her feet, hit her hard on her bums, which at last brought the baby to crying. Shao Guizhen let out a sigh of relief and lay back relaxed. But when the doctor left and she had just had a few minutes of break, Qiu said to her directly, "Let's send the two girls to someone else!" Shao immediately opposed, "Why? We are more than able to raise them!" Qiu said angrily, "I already have seven girls. Why would I want more?" Shao said, "No matter if it is a boy or a girl, it is our own flesh and bones. I won't give them to others as long as we can afford to put food in their mouths." Hearing his wife's speech, Qiu insisted no more.

Half a year later, Qiu became insufficient with breast milk, and they too busy with their clinic. So, with introduction of their patients, they sent the twins to a kind and reliable couple. The husband worked at a hardware and electric material shop, and the wife stayed at home with a schoolboy, while undertaking some embroidery job by a sewing machine. To accomplish this, she fixed some satin or left-over cloth painted with patterns on bamboo circles and embroidered different patterns on them with thread evolving around the sewing machine. The called the twins Damao and Xiaomao, as named by the Qius. They treated the girls as if they were the biological parents, taking every detail into perfect consideration. Shao Guizhen could only visit the twins when it came the time to pay the monthly alimony or occasionally at Sundays. Sometimes she would bring some food and clothes along. Damao and Xiaomao grew up, being comfortable in their new home, and never felt nostalgic. They appeared indifferent every time Shao and little Weiying went to visit them. They lived there until they were seven and should go to school. Even after they doctor to help deliver the babies. After long toil and labor, two girls were born. Seeing two girls only, but not a boy, Qiu was almost disappointed to tears. He immediately set aside and paid no attention to them. The girl that came out first started crying, while the later one was quiet. Shao sensed something wrong and tried to sit up and check on her regardless of the pain. The doctor picked up the quiet girl by her feet, hit her hard on her bums, which at last brought the baby to crying. Shao Guizhen let out a sigh of relief and lay back relaxed. But when the doctor left and she had just had a few minutes of break, Qiu said to her directly, "Let's send the two girls to someone else!" Shao immediately opposed, "Why? We are more than able to raise them!" Qiu said angrily, "I already have seven girls. Why would I want more?" Shao said, "No matter if it is a boy or a girl, it is our own flesh and bones. I won't give them to others as long as we can afford to put food in their mouths." Hearing his wife's speech, Qiu insisted no more.

Half a year later, Qiu became insufficient with breast milk, and they too busy with their clinic. So, with introduction of their patients, they sent the twins to a kind and reliable couple. The husband worked at a hardware and electric material shop, and the wife stayed at home with a schoolboy, while undertaking some embroidery job by a sewing machine. To accomplish this, she fixed some satin or left-over cloth painted with patterns on bamboo circles and embroidered different patterns on them with thread evolving around the sewing machine. The called the twins Damao and Xiaomao, as named by the Qius. They treated the girls as if they were the biological parents, taking every detail into perfect consideration. Shao Guizhen could only visit the twins when it came the time to pay the monthly alimony or occasionally at Sundays. Sometimes she would bring some food and clothes along. Damao and Xiaomao grew up, being comfortable in their new home, and never felt nostalgic. They appeared indifferent every time Shao and little Weiying went to visit them. They lived there until they were seven and should go to school. Even after they sisters to Beijing and sent her to Beijing for school too. Xiaodong came back to Changsha when it came the time for middle school, and had been living with mother ever since then, even after she got married.

Zheng Huaxian, the accountant of Qiu's clinic, was a man in his forties. He had an interesting talent, that is, he could keep his face unmoved and only slant his mouth to make his ears moving back and forth. He often played the trick for little Weiying when he was free. He would move his left ear when Weiying trotted to his left and move the right ear when Weiying ran to his right. This would bring the innocent little girl to chuckles, adding much fun to her childhood.

When Weiying was about three, Shao gave birth to a boy, which made Qiu Zhongyuan jump and clap in joy. He would tell whomever he met, "This is my fifth kid. Finally, I have a boy when I'm forty!" They named the boy Qiu Juecong and hired a nanny to live at their house to cater to the baby. When Juecong was almost one year old and taken on a bus, he waved his arms and legs in happiness. So Qiu Zhongyuan gave some extra money to the nanny to have her take Juecong on a bus around the city every day.

Shao was pregnant again when Juecong was one. This time she suffered more than ever, not only having no appetite but also feeling dizzy at times. Their business, however, was flourishing each day, so she insisted on seeing the patients with her husband. Later her stomach became especially large, and examination told them that she was having twins. Nevertheless, she went on with her work with big belly. Qiu Zhongyuan thought, "It will be perfect if these are two boys, or at least one. Then I don't want it anymore."

One afternoon, Shao was tired and went to rest in bed. Aches took over her the moment she lay down, and she was at the verge of breaking down. Qiu was nervous in sixes and sevens, for it was too late to send her to a hospital. So, he hurried to send for a female left, they would go back to visit their foster parents every now and then and lived with them occasionally. There was an especially strong emotional tie between the twins and their foster parents, and when the foster parents died, they cried harder than they would cry for their real parents.

Shao was also too busy to take care of Weiying and Juecong. So, When Weiying was four and Juecong was one, Shao sent them to a very good kindergarten at that time, where there were nursery class and junior, middle and senior class for children of different ages. Every Saturday afternoon, Shao would pick the children home after work, and send them back in Monday mornings. When Juecong was two, though being little, he could sense it when mom was leaving. So, every time when Shao was about to leave the kindergarten, Juecong would hold mom by her thigh or her clothes, crying and shouting to keep her from going away. Mrs. Qiu's eyes would water at such moment, but to cater to the clinic and her patients, she had to manage to comfort her son and go away. At this moment, Weiying would be very sensible to come and take his hand and follow the teacher to take him to his dormitory. Weiying herself liked the kindergarten very much, for there she could learn singing, dancing, and sometimes some easy book knowledge and painting. The teachers also liked her a lot and would assign her as the leading actress in the festival galas or parent days. Once she was assigned with the character of Sister Lamb in the play Grandma Wolf. Instead of following the script, she opened the door and pushed Grandma Wolf to the ground and tried to remove her mask. The teacher asked her, "Why don't you do it like we've practiced before?" She answered, "She will eat people when she turns a wolf! If I get the wolf face away, she will not be a wolf and will not eat my sister." This brought the parents and teachers to laughter. The happy and well-educated childhood has left her an obscure but beautiful memory. This was the beginning road start of her life.

The second year after the twins were born, Shao had another boy whom they named Juele. At first the nanny raised him at their house, but later she couldn't manage to take care of her own group of children, so Shao decided to send Juele to the nanny's place. At that time, Shao had already mastered the expertise of medicine due to her consistent hard work. As more and more patients came to their clinic, The Qius had no time to cater to so many children. Qiu thought that he already had five children with Guizhen and taking the three daughters of him and his ex-wife and the daughter of Guizhen and her ex-husband into account, they already had nine children. Too many children would become a burden to their energies, so they could not have any more. Also, having given birth to six children and being busy with the work, Guizhen's health may be at risk. So, he decided to have the spermatic ligation.

At that time, the Soviet Union was the friendliest country with China, so their policy that encourages more births was followed suit. When the news spread in the neighborhood that Qiu was to take the operation, people came to discourage him, "Just keep on having children as long as you can, so as to make your contribution to our country!" The Qius replied, "If we have fewer children, we will have more time and energy for our patients. Isn't this contributing to our country?" Before long, Qiu Zhongyuan had an expert to perform the operation. At that time, few people took such surgeries, for China was learning almost everything from Soviet, sometimes even copy without consideration. The more children a couple have, the more honored they are. Women who gave birth to an especially large number of children would be given the title of "Heroic Mother". China, a country with an already large population at the beginning, was brought to a rapid growth in population.

In 1959, Ma Yinchu, a professor at Beijing University expressed his criticism for such a policy and was severely persecuted at that time. It was 20 years later when the Cultural Revolution came to an end that he was redressed.

2.3 Take the lead walk on the way of collectivism

As the private clinic of the Doctor Qiu's became more famous, more severe patients came for help. Qiu Zhongyuan felt it necessary to purchase some more medicine and new equipment in Guangzhou.

One day in the spring of 1955, Qiu bought a train ticket and set out for Guangzhou alone, leaving his wife home to cater to the clinic and children. That day he finished his supper early, so he took off his coat to have a nap in bed. He didn't expect that he would fall into sound sleep after a few minutes in bed, and Mrs. Qiu did not bother for she thought that he would get up in time. As she finished all the work at hand and was about to go to sleep, she was surprised to see her husband still sleeping. So, she shook him awake and asked, "When does your train leave? Why are you still sleeping?" When he got sober, he looked at the golden Omega watch on his hand, then jumped immediately off his bed, grabbed his luggage and ran out of the door.

Upon arrival at the train station, he saw the waiting room was already empty. Worried, he ran to the platform at once. A staff member there stopped him and asked, "Excuse me, which train do does you take? Why are you in such a hurry?" Qiu showed him the ticket in hand. He pointed to a train leaving the station and said, "See, it has just left. You shouldn't have been so late!" Qiu looked at the disappearing train, feeling rather gloomed. In low spirits, he took his luggage back home.

As he arrived at the gate, an idea of testing his wife's loyalty dawned on him. He was thinking of going to the north to visit his mother in hometown, or to Beijing to see his three other daughters and their mother when time allowed. Will the charming wife of his stay loyal to him when he is away? With such thought, he opened the gate with his keys, quietly put down his luggage, and crept towards their bedroom all the way to the bedside. He intentionally avoided waking his wife up; instead, he gasped by her ears and moved his lips towards her face. Mrs. Qiu, who had just fallen asleep, soon woke in shock. All she knew was that her husband has left home. Before she could figure things out, she gathered all her strengths to smack at the shadow by her bed, which, caused the shout of her husband, "Ouch! It hurts so much…" Not until then did she realized that her husband has missed the train and came back. Of course, she did not feel sorry for him. But rather annoyed and amused. She thought that the smack served him right, nobody is to blame for the trouble; you brought it on yourself.

A few days later, Qiu Zhongyuan left for Guangzhou again. Upon arrival, he was delighted by the beautiful spring sceneries, which were quite different from the gloomy, rainy weather in Changsha the night before. He got on a rickshaw to the hotel. On the way, extravagant buildings constantly came into his horizon; trendy cars ran past occasionally; flowers were sold on stalls almost everywhere on the street or held by hawking flower girls. Attracted to everything in the modern city, Qiu just couldn't help looking and contemplating…

After paying for the rickshaw and checking in the hotel, he tidied himself up a bit and put on a delaine western-style suit. He entered a restaurant in the street and had his lunch. Instead of heading straight to pharmacies, he took a walk around the large southern city, where his 180-centemeter height, shiny eyes, high spirits and charming manners caught the attention of many passersby. For the whole afternoon, Qiu just strolled and toured, and bought some gifts for his family. The afternoon slid by with barely any notice. As darkness of the night dimed the evening glow, he realized it was time to go back to the hotel for supper and sleep. After meal and bath, he lay in bed quietly, kept awake by thoughts. Several years of hard work has enriched the family with a good sum of money, allowing him to buy a large house in Guangzhou and move his clinic and family there.

After breakfast the next morning, Qiu Zhongyuan set about collecting information of real estate. He went to see two houses in the morning, but neither met his expectations. After lunch, he saw

Age of rapid change

some ads for house renting and selling in the newspaper, so after having his cup of tea, he set out for the address of the houses on sale.

There was the house spotted in a quiet place downtown, in an unfrequented, clean alley. The surroundings looked secluded, with a flowery yard behind the iron railings. The yard was surrounded by two-meter-high walls and faced the street. Entering the iron double-door and walking down a path inside, one could see a two-and-a-half-story building of round corners. Qiu sounded the round iron knocker on the door and stepped in the house. After a look around, he decided that it was a very good house. He started thinking that the house could be adapted to a larger clinic than that in the Pozi Street and would still have enough room left for the six kids and the nanny. So, he asked the owner, "If I am to buy the house, when can I own it?" The owner said, "I've gone through all the procedures needed to immigrate to America where my relative lives. If you pay me all the money, I can give it to you in three to five days." Qiu said, "Good. But my family live in Changsha. I came to Guangzhou only to buy some medicine and equipment, so I don't have enough money with me, and I haven't talked with my wife yet." The owner said, "Alright, but I can only wait for 10 days at most. And you have to pay the handsel first." Qiu asked, "How much do you need?" The man answered, "Five hundred." Qiu said, "No way. I wasn't expecting buying a house before, so I don't have that much right now. And I need to shop and pay for the hotel. Two hundred or three is the best I can offer." The owner said, "Give me three hundred then. It's a deal!" Qiu did as he said.

Three days later, Qiu went back to Changsha. To his surprise, his cheerful suggestion was steadily opposed by his wife, who said, "Guangzhou is too close to Hong Kong. The Communist Party has driven the Kuomintang away from mainland China. There will be a day when they take Hong Kong back from the foreigners. If they fail, Guangzhou could be enrolled in a war." Qiu said, "We can go to Hong Kong in times of war, even to America. I heard it is a free, rich and modernized country. What's more, I've already paid the earnest."

Shao answered immediately, "I heard they are having trouble getting drinking water in Hong Kong; each family has to line up to carry water outside. Busy as we are, how can we manage to do that? Our life here is already settled; I don't feel like moving again. Think of it, if we buy the house at Guangzhou, it might be blown off in times of war! What shall we do about our kids? I've had enough of wars, and I will never go to Guangzhou!" The speech made sense to Qiu. At last, he had to give up his plan.

In early 1956, China saw the climax of socialist transformation, with Beijing taking the lead in achieving industry-wide public-private partnerships. Subsequently, the country's major cities, as well as more than 50 medium-sized cities, achieved industry-wide public-private partnerships one after another. While in the countryside socialist cooperative transformation was advocated. The Qiu 's, who had already had a career, was inevitably enrolled in the new policies of transformation toward owned economy. To respond to the call for public-private partnership of the Party and government, Qiu Zhongyuan decided to donate all of his savings, plus some of the money he borrowed from his brother Qiu Zhonlin.

And along with other famous orthopedics and pediatrics experts in Changsha, to buy a two-story house covering 2000 square meters at the most bustling street, Mid-Huangxin Road. Thus, Changsha South district United Hospital (which is now Changsha Traditional Chinese Medicine Research Institute) was established, with Qiu Zhongyuan being the leader. The Qius also donated all their equipment and medicines to collectivism.

At first, people all voted for Qiu Zhongyuan to be the dean, but he refused, arguing, "I am specified in technical work in Proctology, and I know nothing about management. I have neither experience nor interest in administrative work. If you want a dean, ask someone else!" However, the other doctors who invested did not want the position either. As a result, Wang Huijun, a female party member

Shao answered immediately, "I heard they are having trouble getting drinking water in Hong Kong; each family has to line up to carry water outside. Busy as we are, how can we manage to do that? Our life here is already settled; I don't feel like moving again. Think of it, if we buy the house at Guangzhou, it might be blown off in times of war! What shall we do about our kids? I've had enough of wars, and I will never go to Guangzhou!" The speech made sense to Qiu. At last, he had to give up his plan.

In early 1956, China saw the climax of socialist transformation, with Beijing taking the lead in achieving industry-wide public-private partnerships. Subsequently, the country's major cities, as well as more than 50 medium-sized cities, achieved industry-wide public-private partnerships one after another. While in the countryside socialist cooperative transformation was advocated. The Qiu 's, who had already had a career, was inevitably enrolled in the new policies of transformation toward owned economy. To respond to the call for public-private partnership of the Party and government, Qiu Zhongyuan decided to donate all of his savings, plus some of the money he borrowed from his brother Qiu Zhonlin.

And along with other famous orthopedics and pediatrics experts in Changsha, to buy a two-story house covering 2000 square meters at the most bustling street, Mid-Huangxin Road. Thus, Changsha South district United Hospital (which is now Changsha Traditional Chinese Medicine Research Institute) was established, with Qiu Zhongyuan being the leader. The Qius also donated all their equipment and medicines to collectivism.

At first, people all voted for Qiu Zhongyuan to be the dean, but he refused, arguing, "I am specified in technical work in Proctology, and I know nothing about management. I have neither experience nor interest in administrative work. If you want a dean, ask someone else!" However, the other doctors who invested did not want the position either. As a result, Wang Huijun, a female party member

Age of rapid change

some ads for house renting and selling in the newspaper, so after having his cup of tea, he set out for the address of the houses on sale.

There was the house spotted in a quiet place downtown, in an unfrequented, clean alley. The surroundings looked secluded, with a flowery yard behind the iron railings. The yard was surrounded by two-meter-high walls and faced the street. Entering the iron double-door and walking down a path inside, one could see a two-and-a-half-story building of round corners. Qiu sounded the round iron knocker on the door and stepped in the house. After a look around, he decided that it was a very good house. He started thinking that the house could be adapted to a larger clinic than that in the Pozi Street and would still have enough room left for the six kids and the nanny. So, he asked the owner, "If I am to buy the house, when can I own it?" The owner said, "I've gone through all the procedures needed to immigrate to America where my relative lives. If you pay me all the money, I can give it to you in three to five days." Qiu said, "Good. But my family live in Changsha. I came to Guangzhou only to buy some medicine and equipment, so I don't have enough money with me, and I haven't talked with my wife yet." The owner said, "Alright, but I can only wait for 10 days at most. And you have to pay the handsel first." Qiu asked, "How much do you need?" The man answered, "Five hundred." Qiu said, "No way. I wasn't expecting buying a house before, so I don't have that much right now. And I need to shop and pay for the hotel. Two hundred or three is the best I can offer." The owner said, "Give me three hundred then. It's a deal!" Qiu did as he said.

Three days later, Qiu went back to Changsha. To his surprise, his cheerful suggestion was steadily opposed by his wife, who said, "Guangzhou is too close to Hong Kong. The Communist Party has driven the Kuomintang away from mainland China. There will be a day when they take Hong Kong back from the foreigners. If they fail, Guangzhou could be enrolled in a war." Qiu said, "We can go to Hong Kong in times of war, even to America. I heard it is a free, rich and modernized country. What's more, I've already paid the earnest."

among the janitors employed by Qiu, was chosen as the dean. She was overwhelmed by joy and agreed at once.

Next, a meeting was held to decide the monthly salary of the staff. Considering his contribution to Changsha South district United Hospital and rich experience in medicine, Qiu Zhongyuan was offered a salary of 224 yuan per month, the highest in the hospital at that time, which equaled the salary of a vice Governor. It was also said to be the same as the sum Jiang Qing, the wife of Chairman Mao got. For he was outstanding in all aspects, no one objected the decision. However, he was not benefited as a big shareholder, which he himself did not object either.

Because he was only responding positively to the call of the then government about taking the road to collectivization. Same time, at that time, the social climate was different, and he was not calculating power and money at all. (However, two years later, when the Southern Region Hospital had developed into such a famous and frequented hospital that a branch hospital was needed, Qiu's salary was lessened to 184 yuan per month by the then dean, Wang Huijun, with which he still had no opinion, for it was still more than what most others got.)

However, Shao Guizhen was offered only sixty-something per month. But she was a selfless, thrift woman, who thought she could do with both wealth and poverty. Even though she was earning much less than when she was in a private clinic, she was quite content with her peaceful and carefree new life. As to Zong Weikang, he worked at Northern Changsha Hospital (which is now Changsha Senile Hospital) For he has very different characters and he couldn't get along with uncle. The business and salary standard of Changsha Southern United Hospital was approved by the authorities. Shao Guizhen also joined in the hospital, where her husband performed as the attending physician.

Since then, they stopped the business in their private clinic, which left much room to their house at Pozi Street. Xiaodong had completed her studies in primary school with satisfying scores several months before and was hoping to go to middle school in the Changsha. When the Qius finished their visit to their hometown during Spring Festival, they took Xiaodong back. Xiaodong was smart in nature. She spent some time studying at home, and then got admitted to a key school, No. 2 Middle School, in September. Weiying also started her study at Pozi Street Primary School the same month that year.

2.4 Innocence

At the summer 1956, 7-year-old Qiu Weiying left Xinmin Kindergarten for grade one at Changsha Pozi Street Primary School. The kindergarten she used to be at was the most expensive and one of the bests in Changsha. The teachers there gave specified instructions to children of different ages, to prepare the young kids with the right principles of life.

Qiu Weiying got along quite well with all male and female classmates in her class. Despite that she had her own characteristics and personalities, bullying was never her thing. She was especially friendly with a girl named Zhang Tairan in her class. The two girls were even closer than sisters. Zhang Tairan had almost the same figure as Qiu Weiying, but different from her brown hair, Zhang's shiny black hair was tied into two circles above her ear, looking exactly like a little juggler performing flower biting. Zhang lived right opposite their school, so she only needed to cross the street to go home. She usually took Qiu Weiying back to her house after school. The first time little Weiying entered the gate guarded by a doorkeeper; she widened her eyes in surprise and said, "What a big place! Your father must be a high-ranking official…" Zhang did not deny, "He used to be a cadre in the Long March, and a general in war." Then, she pointed to some soldiers exercising on the parallel bars and said, "They are here to protect my father." At first, Weiying was confused. She asked, "What is 'Long March'?" Zhang said, "It's climbing the snow-covered mountains and crossing the grassland for

Age of rapid change

revolution. A lot of people died then." Her answer confused Weiying even more, who continued to ask, "Why do they do it then, if so, many should die?" Zhang scratched her head and replied, "I… have no idea either. I shall go to ask Daddy. He told me all about it. He was an official during the Long March, but not as big as he is now." <See App 1. A>

Zhang's father was in his fifties, and though being tall and skinny, he looked rather healthy. On his kind, handsome face, there was a pair of dark, slanting eyebrows and intelligent eyes.

Her mother was forty-something, plump, and had light-toned, flawless skin. There was always a nice smile on her sincere face. She seemed as glad as seeing her own daughter every time she saw Qiu Weiying, and she had always treated her like family.

Zhang's brother was one or two years younger than his sister Qiu. His face and figure were exactly like his father's, but he has got the skin of from his mother. Every time Qiu visited their house, he would smile with barely any words, but his dark, smart eyes would always reveal that he was bright and adorable in nature.

One day after school, Zhang ran to Qiu and invited her to her place for supper so that they could play together. Qiu agreed and went along. Zhang's parents were especially pleased to see her, and served her with big bowls of various food, including fish, meat, vegetables and soup. It was by the table that Qiu was informed that day was Zhang's birthday. After supper, Zhang asked her, "Would you sleep here tonight?" Qiu said, "I haven't told my parents yet, I'm afraid that they will be worried and scold me when I get home tomorrow." Hearing the talk, Zhang's mother said, "If so, Tairan and I can go to your home with you and tell your mother." Qiu said happily, "Great!" They were living in the same street, so it did not take long for them to arrive at The Qius. Mrs. Qiu had seen Zhang Tairan several times before and was informed that Mr. Zhang was a former cadre in the Long March, and that Zhang Tairan was Weiying's best friend in class, whom she herself liked a lot. So, she gladly approved their request.

After they got back to Zhang's house, Qiu Weiying entered the large room of Mr. and Mrs. Zhang with Tairan and her mother, and saw Mr. Zhang sitting in a single sofa, absorbed in a newspaper. There was his teacup on the table besides, steaming with jasmine tea in it. Seeing them coming, he raised his head and smiled. Weiying walked quietly to him, looked up at him and asked, "Uncle Zhang, your soldiers have guns, you must also have a gun. Can I look at it?" Uncle Zhang smiled mildly and said, "What an interesting girl! Alright, alright, I'll show it to you." Then he picked up a black pistol from the drawer of his bed stand, a gun that was not new but quite clean. Qiu tried to reach out for it, but Mr. Zhang raised it up and said, "This is no toy for you. Wait a minute." After unloading the gun, he gave it to Qiu. She took it over with both her hands and tried to do an aiming pose, but it was too heavy for her to hold. She said, "It's too heavy!" Mr. Zhang took it back, showed the shooting move to her and said, "It is heavy for little children like you, not for me." Then, he put the pistol back to his drawer.

Leaving the room, the two girls ran to the back yard to play. It was empty and quiet there. Under the cement bridge behind the yard, there were two iron railing doors on the wall, through the gaps of which they could see the darkness inside, but it was hard to tell how deep it was or what was inside. Weiying asked curiously, "What's inside the door? Why do you lock it with big locks?" Zhang said, "Daddy said 'children cannot enter', maybe there are monsters inside." Hearing the words, Weiying couldn't help feeling afraid. She said, "Oh, I'm so scared. Let's go to the front yard!" So, the two little girls ran to the stairs, chasing each other towards the front yard.

The sun set. The girls were tired and went to sleep in Zhang Tairan's room. Even though there were other small beds in the room, the two girls still slept in the same bed which was not very big. As Weiying gradually fell asleep, she sensed Zhang's mother coming to their bed. She looked at them amiably for a while, and then put down the curtain. The next morning, they had breakfast together, and then the two little girls held each other's hand and went to school intimately side by side.

In the spring of 1957, when Qiu Weiying was in the second term of her first year in primary school, her parents bought a more than 200-square-meter house in an alley of Laozhaobi. It would take her more than half an hour if she were to walk to school, and it was not safe for a little girl like her to commute alone that far. As a result, she had to transfer to another school. Before they moved, Qiu Weiying told Zhang Tairan that she was leaving, which brought Zhang to tears. She urged, "Promise to visit me at my house every Sunday!" Qiu agreed.

But her mother was too busy to spruce the new place up to take her to Zhang's the first Monday after they moved and was occupied too the next Sunday. So Qiu took a bus to Zhang's house without informing her mother. However, she hesitated by the gate and did not dare to enter, for she was worried that she would be blamed for not coming on the previous Sunday. Consequently, she went home melancholy. The longer the time was, the more afraid she was to visit Zhang Tairan. So, the pure and sacred friendship between them came to an end.

Ten years later, on a farm for intellectual youth in Chen County, Qiu Weiying accidentally heard a female classmate who had been in the same class mention her deep friendship with Zhang Tairan and said, "…before Zhang Tairan's father was dispatched to Beijing, she cried at school, saying, '…I will never see Qiu Weiying again.' All our classmates felt sorry for her." Hearing these words, Qiu Weiying was astonished and sorrowful as she had never been before. She did not spend a long time with Zhang, but the innocent and profound friendship stayed in her memory as the most glorious page of her life. One could safely say that the friendship between children is no way less than family tie and romantic love, for it sprouts deep down one's heart, unaffected by the complicated social codes.

The house in the alley of Lao Zhaobi that the Qius bought in the spring of 1957 covered 207 square meters. It was located at a quiet place downtown. Stepping out the door, making a turn to the entrance of the alley, was the Laozhaobi. Most of the houses on the street were built with wooden boards, except for their house and Guangming Ophthalmology Hospital, which were built with red bricks. Entering the alley, walking a couple of steps towards the left and then keeping heading straight for about ten meters, one can get to the end of the alley where their house was. A couple and their daughter lived at the turning. The man was old, and his wife, though of almost the same age, had rosy cheeks and a nice face, indicating that she used to be a beauty. Their daughter, Wei Meiling, was around eighteen, and had a sweet and lovely face. Later she worked as an actress in the August 1st Film Studio in Beijing. Opposite their house, there was a two-story house behind a small door, merged among the other houses around. There lived a street director and her husband, a forty-year-old engineer and his wife and daughter, and a couple downstairs that people seldom saw. Outside the door, there was a leafy old pagoda tree. Deeper into the alley right to the Qius lived an old lady, Wu. Her husband used to be a doctor of traditional Chinese medicine but had already passed away. She lived with her daughter, her son-in-law, and her granddaughter. She had a thirteen-year-old grandson nicknamed "Bean Bean", who often came to visit her and often likes to joke around.

The house that the Qiu's bought had a stone path made of sixty-something white rectangle granites behind the entrance by the stairs. It was about six meters wide, four meters long. The roof was flat, painted by white lime powder, forming a vertical angle against the walls. The stone path leads to a large yard, where a line cut in between, dividing it into two patches. Right of the line was a hard-beaten earth land, to the right corner of which was a six-square-meter garden surrounded by brick walls of two feet height. They shared the wall right to the garden with Xiangzhong Printing House next door. Up in the middle of the wall were some windows. Left of the line was

The house in the alley of Lao Zhaobi that the Qius bought in the spring of 1957 covered 207 square meters. It was located at a quiet place downtown. Stepping out the door, making a turn to the entrance of the alley, was the Laozhaobi. Most of the houses on the street were built with wooden boards, except for their house and Guangming Ophthalmology Hospital, which were built with red bricks. Entering the alley, walking a couple of steps towards the left and then keeping heading straight for about ten meters, one can get to the end of the alley where their house was. A couple and their daughter lived at the turning. The man was old, and his wife, though of almost the same age, had rosy cheeks and a nice face, indicating that she used to be a beauty. Their daughter, Wei Meiling, was around eighteen, and had a sweet and lovely face. Later she worked as an actress in the August 1st Film Studio in Beijing. Opposite their house, there was a two-story house behind a small door, merged among the other houses around. There lived a street director and her husband, a forty-year-old engineer and his wife and daughter, and a couple downstairs that people seldom saw. Outside the door, there was a leafy old pagoda tree. Deeper into the alley right to the Qius lived an old lady, Wu. Her husband used to be a doctor of traditional Chinese medicine but had already passed away. She lived with her daughter, her son-in-law, and her granddaughter. She had a thirteen-year-old grandson nicknamed "Bean Bean", who often came to visit her and often likes to joke around.

The house that the Qiu's bought had a stone path made of sixty-something white rectangle granites behind the entrance by the stairs. It was about six meters wide, four meters long. The roof was flat, painted by white lime powder, forming a vertical angle against the walls. The stone path leads to a large yard, where a line cut in between, dividing it into two patches. Right of the line was a hard-beaten earth land, to the right corner of which was a six-square-meter garden surrounded by brick walls of two feet height. They shared the wall right to the garden with Xiangzhong Printing House next door. Up in the middle of the wall were some windows. Left of the line was and then the two little girls held each other's hand and went to school intimately side by side.

In the spring of 1957, when Qiu Weiying was in the second term of her first year in primary school, her parents bought a more than 200-square-meter house in an alley of Laozhaobi. It would take her more than half an hour if she were to walk to school, and it was not safe for a little girl like her to commute alone that far. As a result, she had to transfer to another school. Before they moved, Qiu Weiying told Zhang Tairan that she was leaving, which brought Zhang to tears. She urged, "Promise to visit me at my house every Sunday!" Qiu agreed.

But her mother was too busy to spruce the new place up to take her to Zhang's the first Monday after they moved and was occupied too the next Sunday. So Qiu took a bus to Zhang's house without informing her mother. However, she hesitated by the gate and did not dare to enter, for she was worried that she would be blamed for not coming on the previous Sunday. Consequently, she went home melancholy. The longer the time was, the more afraid she was to visit Zhang Tairan. So, the pure and sacred friendship between them came to an end.

Ten years later, on a farm for intellectual youth in Chen County, Qiu Weiying accidentally heard a female classmate who had been in the same class mention her deep friendship with Zhang Tairan and said, "…before Zhang Tairan's father was dispatched to Beijing, she cried at school, saying, '…I will never see Qiu Weiying again.' All our classmates felt sorry for her." Hearing these words, Qiu Weiying was astonished and sorrowful as she had never been before. She did not spend a long time with Zhang, but the innocent and profound friendship stayed in her memory as the most glorious page of her life. One could safely say that the friendship between children is no way less than family tie and romantic love, for it sprouts deep down one's heart, unaffected by the complicated social codes.

paved with smaller granite. It was next to the corridor and the stair attached to it.

Inside the 207-square-meter house, there were four large bedrooms and one small one, each has two or three doors; in the middle of the house, there was a living room of the same size as the large bedrooms, having a door on each of the walls. The front door faced the stair, the other three led to the bedrooms; besides the rooms, there was a small yard, a toilet and a storehouse, and there was a 10-square-meter terrace made of wood above the kitchen. Behind the bedrooms, there was a back yard. There was a window of Wu's on the wall next to their house facing their backyard. The ground level of their house was taller by half than that of the Wu's. The inside of the house was paved by red wooden floor. It was empty down the floor, about one meter apart from the ground. The first door in the left corner led to Juele's bedroom. In the room, there was another door in the right corner of it, leading to Mr. and Mrs. Qiu's bedroom. Another door opposite to it in the corner led to the back yard facing Wu's window; the second door in the right corner of the living room led to Weiying's bedroom, where was also another door in the same position, facing the small yard. There was a rectangle bathtub in the yard. In front of the door to her bedroom, there was another door in on the right corner, leading to Xiaodong's bedroom, which had a window on the wall between hers and Weiying's bedroom that faced the yard, and a door in the left corner to the back yard; the third door in the center of the right wall of the living room led to the room of the twins. There was also a door to the small yard and another to the corridor, facing the kitchen; the kitchen was one meter higher than the front garden, and was to the right of it. It was a large and long kitchen, in which the stairs to the terrace led to the center of the wall. Down the stairs by the wall was a groove for the coals. The toilet and storehouse were behind the kitchen, to the right of the house. The toilet, the store house and the terrace shared the same wall with the "Another Village" restaurant next door; the fourth door in the living room, the front door, faced the corridor and the stair in the front yard. Outside the living room in the right was the entrance to Juecong and Juele's bedroom. The corridor next to the front yard stretched past the doors to the boys' bedrooms, the doors of the living room and of the twins' and the kitchens, and at last led to the toilet behind. Down the four-step stair outside the living room was the front yard. When they needed to go out, they should walk down the stair, cross the front yard and turn right to the gate.

One could tell that the owner of the house was not an ordinary person, for its two halves of gate were about seven centimeters thick and three meters high, forming a square when they were closed. There was a gold brass bell on each half, with a diameter of 20 centimeters. When somebody walked up the three-step stair to the gate and rang the brass doorbells, the sound would spread around the small hutong on the red-brick wall above the gate, was the characters "Hong Wu", made of protruding bricks. It was said to be the name of the son of the previous owners, who became insane in love. His parents built the house for him. They used to be national capitalists dealing cotton yam in Shanghai before liberation, and later left for somewhere with their son after selling the house to the Qiu's. Qiu Zhongyuan was grateful that Shao Guizhen followed him all along after their marriage and did all her best for the well-being of their family. She had drawn all her -dough from the bank and chipped in for the purchase of their new house. So, Qiu Zhongyuan decided to put her name only on the house proprietary certificate to show his gratitude.

After their move, Qiu transferred from Pozi Street Primary School to Fuzheng Street Primary school near Lao Zhaobi and continued her studies in her second term of first grade. She joined her new class not long after school started and finished six years of studies there. In her last three years, her class adviser was Ms. Zhang, a serious but nice lady in her forties who taught Chinese. As soon as she took over the class, she paid special attention and care to Qiu Weiying, which made Weiying felt going to school very pleasing.

The desk mate of Weiying was Li Diguang, a gentle, polite boy who followed all the rules in school. Young as he was, he was rather masculine, with strong bone structure of the face and a pair of dark slanting eyebrows. There was always a slight smile on his face. He did quite well in his studies and served as the medium detachment captain of the Young Pioneers in their class, while Qiu Weiying served as the Squad Leader. However, Qiu, who was probably rather conservative in nature, never talked or smiled to the well-behaved boy. What's more, she would use a white chalk to draw a line on the desk, dividing the desk into two equal parts, warning him not to cross the boundary. Li Diguang did not argue; he only smiled. They sat in the back of the classroom, for the two kids were relatively taller than their classmates, so Qiu continued the practice for several days without being noticed by others. One day before their Chinese class, Teacher Zhang saw her emphasizing the line, and asked curiously, "Qiu Weiying, what are you doing?" She answered, "We each own one half of the desk. He should not cross the boundary." Before Teacher Zhang could respond, she added, "My mom says, 'it is improper for men and women to touch each other while passing objects'." Teacher Zhang was amused and surprised, "How conservative you are for your age! How can this be 'improper'? Ask your mother again when you go back."

That day, Weiying went home and told the incident to her mother, who smiled and said, "Silly girl, you're only sharing a desk with your classmate. What does it have to do with that saying?" Weiying asked, "What does it mean then?" Mrs. Qiu said, "It has nothing to do with children. It's about grown-ups being improperly close with the opposite sex. I'll tell you what it means, when you grow up."

The next day in school Qiu wiped the line clean with a rag she brought along. Later one day at noon, Li Diguang accidentally hurt his finger while sharpening a pencil. Qiu saw his finger bleeding slightly, but she did not know what to do. Li Diguang put the finger in his mouth to stop the bleeding and went home.

Qiu told it that to her mother when having lunch at home. Mrs. Qiu immediately put down her bowl and chopsticks and gave her some absorbent cotton, gauzes, antiphlogistic powder and a small bottle of mercurochrome, and told her to give it to Li when she returned to school. Qiu hurried to finish her meal and went back to school at once. Before long, Li Diguang arrived too. The minute he sat down, Qiu put all the articles on the table, and then seriously started to deal with the wound as if she were a little doctor. She sterilized his finger with mercurochrome, dressed the wound with antiphlogistic powder and then wrapped it up. Li Diguang sat straight, smiling while she was catering to his finger. At that time, the tallest boy in class who sat in the last row in the corner was laughing at her, but she did not care at all.

Not long after Qiu Weiying's 10th birthday, was the 10th anniversary of PRC. According to a popular saying of the mainland, people born in 1949 were called "Liberation Brands". One day, Teacher Zhang told Qiu to choose some classmates who could sing and dance for two performances for the school celebration of the 10th National Day. Qiu considered it as a task of honor, and accepted with pleasure, for she had been fond of singing and dancing since kindergarten. She remembered the Xinjiang girls she saw in movies and on stage, whose dance was interesting and attractive. So, she picked some lively, adorable girls in her class and designed a Xinjiang-styled dance, Our Motherland is Like a Garden, and a singing performance. The main feature of Xinjiang dance is that the dancer moves the neck left and right in an easy manner and matches the move with elegant hand gestures and body movements, coordinating into a kind of nice, bubbly dance. At first, some girls had trouble moving their necks, and thus danced stiffly, moving their shoulders before their necks. Qiu came up with an idea and told them to stand at the corner of walls at home, so as to fix their body, and then practice moving their necks. This worked, and a few days later everybody could move the neck easily. On the big day, the girls all asked their parents to braid their hair into tiny braids and put on their best vest and skirts before coming to school. At that time, the cloth on sale was limited; one had to buy it with tickets. Thus, they had difficulty making the large, loose sleeves. Having thought of it earlier, Qiu asked her mother for some large pieces of clean medical gauzes, cut them into certain shapes, bent them into sleeves and used some pins to fix them to the vests. Teacher Zhang helped her in the task and praised the brilliant idea. Their dance was quite popular among the audience, and they later represented the school in a district competition and ended up winning a good prize. Since then, Qiu became more interested in singing and dancing. Sometimes at home, when she was in the mood, she could sing for two hours in a row.

There was a girl in her class named Zhou Wenzao, who was very close with her. Zhou lived in the dormitory of Xinhua Bookstore near the school. One day after school, Qiu and a girl named Zhou Xiong, who liked painting, went to Wenzao's home. Wenzao took some miniatures of color wall hangings out of the drawer, which were as small as pages of a book, for them to appreciate and choose.

Qiu delightfully picked dozens of miniatures she liked, among which were the Goldfish Dance, Peacock Dance, The Goddess' Marriage, The Butterfly Lovers and The Flood in Gold Mountain. Afterwards she took the miniatures to Xinhua Bookstore and bought a few pictures she liked to hang up in her room. Later, she put a beautiful green fish tank she found in the store house on her scarlet desk and put some nice-looking goldfish in the tank decorated with artistic plants. She decorated her room into a pretty, comfortable place, adding much fun to her life. She felt cozy in her own room, so she liked to stay in the room and read books in holidays. While reading, she found that she could recognize some new words among the learned ones. Sometimes she liked to tidy up the drawers or the entire room. At that time, her father had a salary much higher than others (184 yuan per month was 10 times more than a green hand apprentice), and her mother also had a salary as a doctor. They hired a nanny to do the house works, allowing her and her brothers and sisters to lead a delicate life. As she got elder, she would occasionally take the twins to Xinhua Cinema or the shopping mall nearby. Sometimes on Sundays, the family would go to the park or climb Mount Yuelu.

One afternoon in the summer vacation of 1960, the Qius were napping in their own rooms. Qiu Weiying put her story book aside, got off her bed and headed for the toilet in the alley by the kitchen. As she walked pass the kitchen door and took a few steps into the alley, she heard some abnormal noise. She raised her head and looked at the urinal behind the unlocked door – Good Heavens! A big boa of about 10 centimeters wide was glaring at her with merciless glow in its eyes, head raised, and mouth opened. It seemed to be starting to stretch its soft, spiraled body. Frightened, Weiying turned immediately and ran away. She ran at her best speed, hopped into her parents' room and hit the wooden pillar of their bed, as if she could not feel any pain. Her father was waked at once. He asked, "What's wrong? Why, the panic?" Her mom also woke up. Qiu Weiying pointed to the direction of the toilet and stammered, "Snake, snake! In the toilet…" Hearing this, her father got up at once, slipped into his leather slippers and grabbed a painted wooden stick, and then hurried to the toilet. Mrs. Qiu also got up and ran after him with Weiying. Weiying stopped near the men's urinal, she stood behind her parents with lingering fears looked to the urinal, but she did not see the snake, of course the snake has slipped away.

She gathered her courage and said, "I saw it here!" Then she observed the toilet and the dark store house behind her parents. Mr. Qiu said, "No snake found!" Mrs. Qiu said, "Hush, listen, there's some noise." Mr. Qiu held the stick tight and turned on the light in the house. Still, the snake was not found. Mrs. Qiu said, "Forget it. The house is too big, and it's empty down the floor. We can't possibly pry the floor to search for it. It is probably our 'house snake' that came from underground." Mr. Qiu said, "It'll be nice if we catch a nanny to do the house works, allowing her and her brothers and sisters to lead a delicate life. As she got elder, she would occasionally take the twins to Xinhua Cinema or the shopping mall nearby. Sometimes on Sundays, the family would go to the park or climb Mount Yuelu.

One afternoon in the summer vacation of 1960, the Qius were napping in their own rooms. Qiu Weiying put her story book aside, got off her bed and headed for the toilet in the alley by the kitchen. As she walked pass the kitchen door and took a few steps into the alley, she heard some abnormal noise. She raised her head and looked at the urinal behind the unlocked door – Good Heavens! A big boa of about 10 centimeters wide was glaring at her with merciless glow in its eyes, head raised, and mouth opened. It seemed to be starting to stretch its soft, spiraled body. Frightened, Weiying turned immediately and ran away. She ran at her best speed, hopped into her parents' room and hit the wooden pillar of their bed, as if she could not feel any pain. Her father was waked at once. He asked, "What's wrong? Why, the panic?" Her mom also woke up. Qiu Weiying pointed to the direction of the toilet and stammered, "Snake, snake! In the toilet…" Hearing this, her father got up at once, slipped into his leather slippers and grabbed a painted wooden stick, and then hurried to the toilet. Mrs. Qiu also got up and ran after him with Weiying. Weiying stopped near the men's urinal, she stood behind her parents with lingering fears looked to the urinal, but she did not see the snake, of course the snake has slipped away.

She gathered her courage and said, "I saw it here!" Then she observed the toilet and the dark store house behind her parents. Mr. Qiu said, "No snake found!" Mrs. Qiu said, "Hush, listen, there's some noise." Mr. Qiu held the stick tight and turned on the light in the house. Still, the snake was not found. Mrs. Qiu said, "Forget it. The house is too big, and it's empty down the floor. We can't possibly pry the floor to search for it. It is probably our 'house snake' that came from underground." Mr. Qiu said, "It'll be nice if we catch

Age of rapid change

girls all asked their parents to braid their hair into tiny braids and put on their best vest and skirts before coming to school. At that time, the cloth on sale was limited; one had to buy it with tickets. Thus, they had difficulty making the large, loose sleeves. Having thought of it earlier, Qiu asked her mother for some large pieces of clean medical gauzes, cut them into certain shapes, bent them into sleeves and used some pins to fix them to the vests. Teacher Zhang helped her in the task and praised the brilliant idea. Their dance was quite popular among the audience, and they later represented the school in a district competition and ended up winning a good prize. Since then, Qiu became more interested in singing and dancing. Sometimes at home, when she was in the mood, she could sing for two hours in a row.

There was a girl in her class named Zhou Wenzao, who was very close with her. Zhou lived in the dormitory of Xinhua Bookstore near the school. One day after school, Qiu and a girl named Zhou Xiong, who liked painting, went to Wenzao's home. Wenzao took some miniatures of color wall hangings out of the drawer, which were as small as pages of a book, for them to appreciate and choose.

Qiu delightfully picked dozens of miniatures she liked, among which were the Goldfish Dance, Peacock Dance, The Goddess' Marriage, The Butterfly Lovers and The Flood in Gold Mountain. Afterwards she took the miniatures to Xinhua Bookstore and bought a few pictures she liked to hang up in her room. Later, she put a beautiful green fish tank she found in the store house on her scarlet desk and put some nice-looking goldfish in the tank decorated with artistic plants. She decorated her room into a pretty, comfortable place, adding much fun to her life. She felt cozy in her own room, so she liked to stay in the room and read books in holidays. While reading, she found that she could recognize some new words among the learned ones. Sometimes she liked to tidy up the drawers or the entire room. At that time, her father had a salary much higher than others (184 yuan per month was 10 times more than a green hand apprentice), and her mother also had a salary as a doctor. They hired it." It was the hard times when meat was offered in monthly rations. Weiying knew that father would take Juecong occasionally to the restaurant and each order an expensive bowl of snake soup. Walking out of the alley, she asked her mother, "Does it eat people?" Mrs. Qiu answered, "House snakes don't eat people generally. They mainly feed on small animals like rats and frogs. But look out for the vipers! Even though they don't eat people, one people can poison die from a bite, people can because the poisoning death." Qiu felt quite scared at these words and asked immediately, "What does a viper look like?" Her mother said, "A viper usually has a triangle head, and can spurt poisonous liquid. If one gets bitten by it, the poison will infiltrate his blood and kill him." Weiying listened carefully and kept the description in mind. Being a young girl knowing almost nothing about life, she could only depend on the instructions from teachers and parents.

2.5 A young girl in her high school days

Qiu Weiying completed her elementary school education in the summer of 1962. At that time, each student was required to choose three targeted schools within the city, the first target should be a key school, the second a common and the third a private one. Because Weiying remained conservative and not used to talking with boys, she chose "No. 4 Middle School" a key girls' school---as her first target, "No. 14 Middle School" ---a common girls' school---as her second, and a private one admitting both boys and girls as her third target as there was no private schools exclusively for girls. As a result, she is in the key school of the first target (Less than 10% of the class slots), was "in the city fourth middle school" admitted.

The former of which had been "Changsha Zhounan Girls' School". Established before the liberation, it had high teaching quality and a long history. For example, it had cultivated several famous women social activists in early China including Cai Chang.

The big school was in Beizheng Street near the downtown, with a relatively complete set of facilities, teaching buildings, auditoriums, dormitories, gardens and lawns, as well as indoor and outdoor sports venues. The then principal was a tall and thin man at the age of about 50 years old with a pair of glasses.

And though China remained friendly ties with the Soviet Union and the Chinese usually called its "elder big brother". The Soviet Union had torn its cooperation agreements with China because of political disputes in July of 1961, but this rupture was not publicly manifested at the time. Therefore, Weiying was assigned to one of three Russian classes after being enrolled in the early autumn of 1962 while there were another three English classes.

There were over 40 students in her class and all the students were divided into six rows. They were seated according to height and Weiying sat in the fifth row. Since the students were all girls, she felt happy and easy in such an environment. Whenever a class period was over, some girls liked surrounding her and talking beside the green bushes. They were often made laugh by her humorous words. Once a girl named Shao Runzhi smiled to her, "Why don't you laugh, Qiu Weiying? I laugh so much that I feel a stomachache." She said, "I just feel that talking like this is easy and pleasant, but I don't think these jokes are interesting." Their teachers would also take part in their talks occasionally. The head-teacher of her class in one term taught politics and she liked the most Cao Li who had two retroussé braids. After class, Cao Li liked talking with Weiying, Mo Shuchun, Wu Xiaoping and Yang Runzhi so the head-teacher often joined in their chat.

On the way back to the classroom during one break, she said to Weiying, "I find you have a very strong ability of expression. The school can guarantee your admission to a teacher's university after graduation. You will then become a teacher after graduation and cultivate more talents for our country." At this, Weiying remained silent because she had several ideal professions in mind, singer, actress, surgeon and writer on. She had never intended to be a teacher.

Would she have the interest in preparing classes, giving lessons and correcting homework?

While walking outside the school, Weiying looked straight ahead. If a strange man glared see at her, she would think him "disgusting". However, she can be a "naughty girl" herself. Although she abided by the rules and regulations of the school, she also liked to imitate male teachers' expressions, tones and posies, making her classmates bursting into laughter.

The mathematics teachers of her class were a man with the surname of Liu from Yueyang. He liked using this province Yueyang dialect while teaching, so many students often made fun of him after class.

Once in self-learning class, Weiying and several others could not make out a math's question, so she proposed to ask Mr. Liu. They walked to Liu's office and arriving at the door, Weiying called, "Mr. Liu." He, who was correcting homework, lifted his head to look at them and smile, "Oh, a long team has come." When having class, the next day, Weiying came after him into the classroom, who said, "Qiu Weiying, you are late for one minute." She replied in his dialect immediately, "Not only me. Look, 'a long team has come!'". Then several students came inside following her, making him a little embarrassed the whole class laugh.

Meanwhile, Weiying loved to give nicknames for some teachers and her classmates would adopt them immediately if they read smoothly. The Russian teacher at Weiying's class was a forty-year-old man at the height of more than 170 centimeters and with tidy hair. He had perfume sprayed on his body every day and walked as if dancing. As he had the surname of Zheng, Weiying gave him the nickname of "Zheng Niuniu" (It is walking like the "Yangge dance" of Chinese twist). Whenever the bell rang for Russian class, a student on duty standing by the door would call "stand up", and the teacher would begin class after saying "sit down".

One day the student on duty stood by the door, but Mr. Zheng did not come after the bell rang. So, she stretched her neck to look outside and suddenly stood straight, laughing to her classmates, "'Zheng Niuniu' is coming…" However, Zheng heard that and asked in a rage, "Who asked you to give me such a nickname?" The student answered, "Not me…" Zheng was unhappy, "Then who?" Thinking that one should bear what one did, Weiying stood up and said, "It's me." Zheng looked at her with an expression of reproach, "Qiu Weiying, come to my office after class."

Weiying came there after class. Entering the door, she sat by the other side of the table of Mr. Zheng, who lifted his head, "Qiu Weiying, do you know that I came here to be a translator. When experts of the Soviet Union had left, many translators changed their professions. Although I became a teacher, some of my habits have not been changed. You can make suggestions to me in public if you do not like some aspects of me, but you can't give nicknames to teachers. Actually, we all like you and I can take you to learn ballroom dancing at weekends." Weiying dare not say anything at this. She had seen some men and women dancing together at the open dance area of Youth Palace near her home. Nevertheless, though people at that time did not do anything "out of line", but Weiying who had been very reserved since childhood thought it shameful and she did not have that courage to hug with a man to learn ballroom dance. So, she walked out as soon as Zheng finished criticizing her. But since then, she dares not call him "Zheng Niuniu" anymore.

However, it was hard for her to change the habit of giving nicknames for teachers with special features. And they also became popular among students of other classes. The physical education teacher was an unmarried man at the age of more than 30. Perhaps because he was single and didn't know how to take care of himself, his clothes always looked dirty, and his face and hairs always took on a brightly oily appearance. Therefore, Weiying gave him a nickname of "Youtiao (Chinese fried food) bachelor". Later this nickname became popular in the school.

Age of rapid change

The head-teacher of Weiying's class was a man teaching philology. One of his ears was left half perhaps because he was pressed when being born or because he encountered a doctor without outstanding skills. Weiying called him "one and a half" (a figure in math), which became quite popular in the class.

Once in physics class, Weiying wanted to speak with a classmate in the last row. But when she turned around, she found their head-teacher siting by the back wall and listening to the class. Because his two ears were not symmetrical, his glasses were slant hung on his ear, unparalleled. And Weiying felt funny also at his expression. Therefore, she touched Hu Chen's back and said to her, "Be careful. "One and a half is listening to our class in the back." Hu, a girl with black eyes and not white skin sitting in front of her, turned back and began to giggle. However, the head-teacher began cross despite Weiying's low voice. It turned out that he had been noticing her actions. After class, he told her in a strict tone, "Qiu Weiying, stay here to write a review after today's class. I know you like give nicknames to teachers. You are too impolite!" Weiying came across trouble finally for the bad habit of giving nicknames.

After class that day, she stayed in the classroom on the second floor and write the self-criticism alone. The head-teacher locked both the front door and the back door, saying, "Don't go home without finishing the review." Weiying, who liked talking and laughing with other girls, was quite disappointed at that time, but she had nothing to do but to write it. When she finished it, the teacher had not come, and she could not go out to look for him. It became quite silent outside, so she began to feel nervous. She stood up and looked out of the window. There was not a single soul in sight, and it gradually became dark. She became anxious and depressed. She was afraid that her parents might be worried about her, and thing jump out of the window…

At this moment, she heard some sounds outside the classroom and turned back to look, the head-teacher opened the door and walked directly towards her with a questioning expression. He asked,

"Why are standing here without writing the written self-criticism?" "It's done. Look. It's on my desk." She fetched the review to him, who browsed it over and said, "It's not profound enough. Go home and write another one. Hand it to me tomorrow."

When she went back home, mother eased, "I'm going to your school to look for you. Your dad and I feel strange, why didn't you come back till so late? What's up today?" Weiying described the whole thing briefly. Shao reproached her, "You go to school to learn from teachers. Who will you learn from without them? You should not have given nicknames to them. It's reasonable for them to be angry with you. Write another self-criticism after dinner and hand it to your head-teacher tomorrow, please forgive him."

The next day when Weiying handed the written self-criticism to the teacher, she said, "My mother criticized me yesterday. I should not have given nicknames to teachers. I made a mistake. Please forgive me." "OK. This review is all right. It's good to recognize your mistake and correct it." He answered after browsing the review. Since then, Weiying had not called teachers nicknames any more. Later when a school composition competition was held, the head-teacher asked her to choose a long composition which had got 98 points to participate in the contest. As a result, she won a certificate one award and stationeries.

That day, her parents felt pleasant for her. Aunt Liao said, "Miss Weiying, I'll cook more dishes for you today." Weiying, who had received education of proletariat thought and ideology, was unhappy to hear others call her "Miss", "Why do you call me 'Miss'? 'Miss' refer to children of families of exploiting class. My parents are doctors and so don't call me 'Miss' anymore." Aunt Liao replied, "Sorry. I'm wrong. But in the old society, 'Miss' are more popular than children of laborers." "But now we are in the new society where laborers are masters and more popular. If I was born of a family of exploiting class, I will be affected negatively in entering high school. Scores are

"Why are standing here without writing the written self-criticism?" "It's done. Look. It's on my desk." She fetched the review to him, who browsed it over and said, "It's not profound enough. Go home and write another one. Hand it to me tomorrow."

When she went back home, mother eased, "I'm going to your school to look for you. Your dad and I feel strange, why didn't you come back till so late? What's up today?" Weiying described the whole thing briefly. Shao reproached her, "You go to school to learn from teachers. Who will you learn from without them? You should not have given nicknames to them. It's reasonable for them to be angry with you. Write another self-criticism after dinner and hand it to your head-teacher tomorrow, please forgive him."

The next day when Weiying handed the written self-criticism to the teacher, she said, "My mother criticized me yesterday. I should not have given nicknames to teachers. I made a mistake. Please forgive me." "OK. This review is all right. It's good to recognize your mistake and correct it." He answered after browsing the review. Since then, Weiying had not called teachers nicknames any more. Later when a school composition competition was held, the head-teacher asked her to choose a long composition which had got 98 points to participate in the contest. As a result, she won a certificate one award and stationeries.

That day, her parents felt pleasant for her. Aunt Liao said, "Miss Weiying, I'll cook more dishes for you today." Weiying, who had received education of proletariat thought and ideology, was unhappy to hear others call her "Miss", "Why do you call me 'Miss'? 'Miss' refer to children of families of exploiting class. My parents are doctors and so don't call me 'Miss' anymore." Aunt Liao replied, "Sorry. I'm wrong. But in the old society, 'Miss' are more popular than children of laborers." "But now we are in the new society where laborers are masters and more popular. If I was born of a family of exploiting class, I will be affected negatively in entering high school. Scores are

Age of rapid change

The head-teacher of Weiying's class was a man teaching philology. One of his ears was left half perhaps because he was pressed when being born or because he encountered a doctor without outstanding skills. Weiying called him "one and a half" (a figure in math), which became quite popular in the class.

Once in physics class, Weiying wanted to speak with a classmate in the last row. But when she turned around, she found their head-teacher siting by the back wall and listening to the class. Because his two ears were not symmetrical, his glasses were slant hung on his ear, unparalleled. And Weiying felt funny also at his expression. Therefore, she touched Hu Chen's back and said to her, "Be careful. "One and a half is listening to our class in the back." Hu, a girl with black eyes and not white skin sitting in front of her, turned back and began to giggle. However, the head-teacher began cross despite Weiying's low voice. It turned out that he had been noticing her actions. After class, he told her in a strict tone, "Qiu Weiying, stay here to write a review after today's class. I know you like give nicknames to teachers. You are too impolite!" Weiying came across trouble finally for the bad habit of giving nicknames.

After class that day, she stayed in the classroom on the second floor and write the self-criticism alone. The head-teacher locked both the front door and the back door, saying, "Don't go home without finishing the review." Weiying, who liked talking and laughing with other girls, was quite disappointed at that time, but she had nothing to do but to write it. When she finished it, the teacher had not come, and she could not go out to look for him. It became quite silent outside, so she began to feel nervous. She stood up and looked out of the window. There was not a single soul in sight, and it gradually became dark. She became anxious and depressed. She was afraid that her parents might be worried about her, and thing jump out of the window…

At this moment, she heard some sounds outside the classroom and turned back to look, the head-teacher opened the door and walked directly towards her with a questioning expression. He asked,

Age of rapid change

not as important as family background. So, don't call me 'Miss' any longer."

During the second semester of Grade Two, she met a young man called Wang Tianliang at home. He was about 178 centimeters high and on his handsome face were two heavy eyebrows, a high nose between a pair of black eyes, as well as two sliced thick lips. He was Shao's patient and was now at Grade Three of high school in No.1 Middle School. It was said that his family were engaged in business in Changsha County, so he lived in the school's dormitory. Sometimes when he came to Qiu's home, he talked with Weiying's younger sisters and brothers. And Weiying, who was not used to getting in touch with boys and was at a girls' school, was reserved since childhood. Whenever Wang came, she always attempted to escape his eyes and never talked with him. Later she did not see him for several months and thus gradually forgot him.

One day after class, she felt weird while sitting in the chair. She stood up and turned around, only to find blood on it. What was wrong? The trousers got dirty; how could I go home? Yang Runzhi who sat after her and was two years older than her, looked at her chair and comforted her, "Don't worry. I'll help you after class. Come to my home and I'll find another pair of trousers for you."

After class, she took off her relatively long coat for Weiying to cover the dirty part of her trousers, but the result was not quite good. So, she called two elderly classmates to accompany her to her home to change another pair of trousers. In the street, Shao asked one girl standing in front of Weiying and the other behind her. When home, she found a pair of trousers which was suitable for Weiying from an old, red-colored closet. In this way Weiying dare go outside and went back home, feeling as if relieved from a heavy load.

Shao did not realize what happened when her daughter came back. She asked curiously, "I remembered that you wore a pair of grey wool trousers I have given you (The grey trousers had been

63

Shao's, but she became thin later and it was no longer suitable. But she was reluctant to throw it away, so she gave it to her daughter because clothes must be bought with planned tickets in the then not developed China.). Why did you change another pair?" Weiying, filled with embarrassment, described the whole thing. At this Shao began to find her another underwear and trousers and sanitary pads, while she started shedding tears as if a disaster was about to come. Seeing her reaction, Shao smiled, "Why are you sobbing? This is necessary for every woman. If not so, a woman will not give birth to children and mother will not have you." She stopped here, had a look at her, and continued, "But you must know that your body is given by parents, so you have to love and protect it and don't let other men touch it. Or you will probably be pregnant before getting married, which will damage your reputation and make you hard to marry the man you love." Weiying nodded at her mother's words. Though confused about being pregnant and giving birth to children, she always felt that things between men and women could not be neglected because they were concerned with one's lifelong happiness, for girls. She carved her mother's words into her head.

The final examinations of the second semester of Grade Two were drawing near. Soon after dinner one day, Weiying, in a short-sleeved dress of flowers' pattern, went outside to buy an ice-lolly before reviewing lessons. It became dark when she finished eating the ice-lolly. When passing the lane, she saw in dim light Mr. Han, an engineer, sitting beside the big pagoda tree. He stood up suddenly when seeing her walking near and grasped her arms quickly, "Go upstairs to my home." Weiying thought him abnormal, so she asked directly, "Is your wife in?" "No, she brought the children to her parents' home." Thinking up of her mother's words, Weiying felt that he didn't have a good intention! Such a senior intellectual became a low-level reptile out of a sudden. The two characters of "scum" bumped into her head, but she did not curse him. She escaped his grasp and walked to her home.

Han looked at her pushing open her family the big door that stood ajar and shutting it again. He fell in the sleeping chair with an upset mind...It turned out that Shao's in-time and beneficial education help Weiying who was still in her adolescence get rid of the attack of a lecher.

The year 1964 when Weiying was in the first semester of Grade Three was the 15th anniversary of the founding of the People's Republic of China. The school was preparing various art performances and a series of celebration activities. Weiying not only rehearsed sword dance with several other students to perform in the street but also joined "Red-scarf Singing and Dancing Group" to participate in contests on behalf of the school. Thus, she became busy and often stayed at school for rehearsal after class. One day the teacher of the "Red-scarf Group" said to her, "Qiu Weiying, you don't have to rehearse since you have remembered clearly the lyrics of <Sing the small child cowherds>. So, go back home early." But she thought there was no homework today and the nanny had not prepared dinner ready, so she walked to the basketball playground to watch the team's practice.

When she was leaving after the game ended practicing, a student of medium build back from Indonesia walked towards her. Slightly grasping her by the arm, she introduced herself, "I'm Wu Yunzhen. I have noticed you several times and want to make friends with you. What's your name please?" "OK. My name is Qiu Weiying." "Then how about having a seat in my dormitory?" "OK." With this, she followed Wu Yunzhen to her dormitory on the second floor. During that period, Indonesians have carried out anti-Chinese start riots, so there's a lot of ethnic Chinese girls lived in student dormitories returning from Indonesia.

Weiying Qiu joined her and went inside the big room where she lived. In Wu's big room, she took out a thick photo album brought back from Indonesia to show Weiying. After a while, the dinner bell for students living on campus rang and a specially groomed girl from Indonesia walked by slowly. She wore curved hair, which was bundled high behind her head, a pair of long golden earrings which swayed around while she was walking and several golden rings on her fingers. She was in a pair of tight trousers of flower pattern, an unbuttoned coat, and a pair of flip-flops. But she looked naturally while walking around. Seeing Weiying sitting on the bedside and browsing Wu's photos, she lowered her head and looked at, saying to Wu, "Do you have a guest?" Then she stood by Wu and murmured something to her in Indonesian. Finally, she briskly walked to Weiying, "My name is Zhuang Ruiying, friend of Wu Yunzhen. Welcome to our dormitory." "OK. I'll come when I'm free." Several minutes later, Wu said, "Now we're going to the canteen to have dinner. Come with us since I have meal tickets." Putting down the album, Weiying said, "Thank you, but I have to go home, or my parents will be worried about me. The nanny has prepared the dinner." She stood up and said goodbye. Zhuang Ruiying smiled to her, "Come here often." Weiying agreed happily.

At the art performance of "Celebrating the 15th Anniversary of the Founding of the People's Republic of China" held by the school, Weiying, while changing clothes in the backstage, saw a pretty girl who was white in skin and tall from another class in the same grade playing the piano. She was fascinated by the music and wanted to make friends with the girl. After class one day, she came across her in the alley and greeted her, "You played the piano so well. Could I learn how to play from you? But I heard that people must learn it since childhood." The girl answered, "Yes. I began learning playing the piano when I was just several years old in Shanghai. Now I often practice at home." "Then can I go to your home to watch you play the piano some day?" The girl agreed with readiness and wrote her name and address to her. Her name was Tang Na, living in Liu Fang Ling.

Age of rapid change

One Sunday after the National Day, Weiying found Tang Na's home according to the address. She knocked the iron bell on the gate with a mailbox. After a while, an amicable old man opened a small door on the gate and let her in. He brought her to pass the room in the middle of the house and then to one of the small rooms in the back, where Tang was sitting by a round crimson table. It seemed that she was waiting for her after having milk. Based on the then conditions, Tang lived in such a favorable environment. She got to know from their first conversation that the man who opened the door for her was Tang's uncle and that they came here from Shanghai not long ago. Her father's penname was Ke Lan, whose hometown was Changsha. She received education in a five-year middle school in Shanghai, so she was in the same grade with Weiying but one year older than her. Bothe her parents were revolutionary writers and joined the CPC in Yan'an in early years. Weiying was quite pleasant about this visit because she made friends with the daughter of revolutionary writers.

One day, Weiying went to the students' dormitory to chat with Wu Yunzhen and Zhuang Ruiying after class. She did not leave until they went to the canteen. Back home, Shao said, "You come back a little late today." "I've made friends with two girls back from Indonesia, who like me very much. I came to their dormitory after class, so I'm back late." "Overseas Chinese back from Indonesia? Invite them to have lunch at home on Sunday. I'd like to see what they look like." "OK. I'll tell them."

On Sunday, Weiying put on a new coat, and she found a little change in her breasts, thus feeling uneasy and embarrassed. Therefore, she took out underwear which was a bit small tight-fitting clothe and put it on.

Dr. Shao made several dishes to receive the two girls. China at that time was poor and Wu Yunzhen and Zhuang Ruiying did not expect that Weiying lived in such a large house and such favorable conditions. Wu looked around admirably and Zhuang opened eyes widely curiously… They were glad to have a rich lunch at Weiying's home and stay for several hours.

After dinner one afternoon, Shao suddenly took out a letter from the drawer. She unfolded it and showed Weiying a one-or-two-inch photo, "Look. This is the letter and photo from Xiao Wang who is now in college of Xi'an Aviation Army. Before leaving, he came here and called me "nominally adoptive mother". I thought I have several children and there was no need to have a godson, so I did not show my attitude. But he was so sincere that I sent him. Now he calls me "nominally adoptive mother" again in this letter, I don't know what he means…" Casting a glance at the photo, she saw the bust of Wang Tianliang in army uniform smiling. At that time, she had no other thought and therefore said nothing. So, shao put the letter and the photo back into the drawer and Weiying did not take it seriously.

Soon Tang Na's family moved to Yuanjialing and lived in the dormitory of Hunan Association of Literature and Art, where several prestigious writers of the province were living. Each of them was given an independent two and a half-storied building with a balcony. Once when Weiying was chatting with Tang at the latter's home, Tang's mother said to her amicably, "I heard that your mother opens a private clinic at home. You can learn medical skills from her!" "I don't like that profession. It was embarrassing to mix men and women together!" Tang Na's mother smiled gently and said, "You are still quite feudal, when a doctor treats people, why do you distinguish between men and women? Weiying answered immediately. "You are reserved. Men and women are not separately treated." "But my mother said that with these skills one can go everywhere and live better. I think that's right!" Tang's mother approved, "Of course. It's good if one has skills."

The first semester of Grade Three ended and Weiying was awarded "Outstanding Student Leader" of young pioneers. Her father had happily and seriously said, "Go on with your study carefully widely curiously… They were glad to have a rich lunch at Weiying's home and stay for several hours.

After dinner one afternoon, Shao suddenly took out a letter from the drawer. She unfolded it and showed Weiying a one-or-two-inch photo, "Look. This is the letter and photo from Xiao Wang who is now in college of Xi'an Aviation Army. Before leaving, he came here and called me "nominally adoptive mother". I thought I have several children and there was no need to have a godson, so I did not show my attitude. But he was so sincere that I sent him. Now he calls me "nominally adoptive mother" again in this letter, I don't know what he means…" Casting a glance at the photo, she saw the bust of Wang Tianliang in army uniform smiling. At that time, she had no other thought and therefore said nothing. So, shao put the letter and the photo back into the drawer and Weiying did not take it seriously.

Soon Tang Na's family moved to Yuanjialing and lived in the dormitory of Hunan Association of Literature and Art, where several prestigious writers of the province were living. Each of them was given an independent two and a half-storied building with a balcony. Once when Weiying was chatting with Tang at the latter's home, Tang's mother said to her amicably, "I heard that your mother opens a private clinic at home. You can learn medical skills from her!" "I don't like that profession. It was embarrassing to mix men and women together!" Tang Na's mother smiled gently and said, "You are still quite feudal, when a doctor treats people, why do you distinguish between men and women? Weiying answered immediately. "You are reserved. Men and women are not separately treated." "But my mother said that with these skills one can go everywhere and live better. I think that's right!" Tang's mother approved, "Of course. It's good if one has skills."

The first semester of Grade Three ended and Weiying was awarded "Outstanding Student Leader" of young pioneers. Her father had happily and seriously said, "Go on with your study carefully

Age of rapid change

One Sunday after the National Day, Weiying found Tang Na's home according to the address. She knocked the iron bell on the gate with a mailbox. After a while, an amicable old man opened a small door on the gate and let her in. He brought her to pass the room in the middle of the house and then to one of the small rooms in the back, where Tang was sitting by a round crimson table. It seemed that she was waiting for her after having milk. Based on the then conditions, Tang lived in such a favorable environment. She got to know from their first conversation that the man who opened the door for her was Tang's uncle and that they came here from Shanghai not long ago. Her father's penname was Ke Lan, whose hometown was Changsha. She received education in a five-year middle school in Shanghai, so she was in the same grade with Weiying but one year older than her. Bothe her parents were revolutionary writers and joined the CPC in Yan'an in early years. Weiying was quite pleasant about this visit because she made friends with the daughter of revolutionary writers.

One day, Weiying went to the students' dormitory to chat with Wu Yunzhen and Zhuang Ruiying after class. She did not leave until they went to the canteen. Back home, Shao said, "You come back a little late today." "I've made friends with two girls back from Indonesia, who like me very much. I came to their dormitory after class, so I'm back late." "Overseas Chinese back from Indonesia? Invite them to have lunch at home on Sunday. I'd like to see what they look like." "OK. I'll tell them."

On Sunday, Weiying put on a new coat, and she found a little change in her breasts, thus feeling uneasy and embarrassed. Therefore, she took out underwear which was a bit small tight-fitting clothe and put it on.

Dr. Shao made several dishes to receive the two girls. China at that time was poor and Wu Yunzhen and Zhuang Ruiying did not expect that Weiying lived in such a large house and such favorable conditions. Wu looked around admirably and Zhuang opened eyes and I'll send you abroad for further study." Qiu Weiying marveled and said, "go abroad to study? That will cost a lot when I live and study there." Qiu's father said, "Now that I say so, parents have certain means. You just focus on your study, and you'll accomplish a grand cause in the future." Though not understanding what her father meant by saying "a grand cause", she knew, "There was gold in books." If she studied hard and became outstanding, she would be a useful person in society.

2.6 Under the route of Liu and Deng

In the autumn 1956, After Shao Guizhen followed her husband Qiu Zhongyuan after join to the Changsha Southern District United Hospital and the hospital was by him take the lead invested and formed.

She gave her twin sons Damao and Xiaomao as well as her youngest son Juele a foster mother and a nanny and did not keep them by her side.

The nanny she invited at home mainly looked after Juecong and helped cook. Weiying began to receive elementary education and Xiaodong entered junior middle school. In the spring of 1957, the Qiu's family moved from Pozi Street to Laozhaobi.

At the 2nd session of the 8th conference of the CPC in May 1958, the CPC central committee proposed the general guideline, "Many, Fast, Good, Save Build Socialist". Chairman Mao called on all the Chinese people to hold high the three red flags of "the General Line, the Great Leap Forward, and the People's Commune" and to carry out economic revolution throughout the nation. Slogans such as "overtaking the U.S. in 10 years and exceeding the U.K. in 15 years" were being created and repeated all the time. To implement the "Great Leap Forward", the nation was engaged in smelting and refining iron and steel and taking any iron no matter whether it could be reused and calling on people to have meals in collective canteens. And even iron pans used for cooking and iron shovels were contributed to the nation go back to the furnace to make steel and iron.

Since the latter half of 1958, grassroots leaders in both rural areas and factories were all concerned with "proneness to boasting and exaggeration" under the impact of ultra -Left trend of thought. In rural areas, peasants were working hard in order to "produce tens of thousands of grains from each mu" and in factories, workers were trying their best to "produce iron and steel that can send a satellite". All these were frequently seen at that time.

Peng Dehuai, the then Minister of National Defense who had defeated enemies for many times, wrote a letter to point the phenomenon that had caused people to live further poverty to Chairman Mao. Nevertheless, at Lushan Meeting in July 1959, this letter was criticized publicly to be the poison of that combat the party. Since then, Peng encountered devastating attack and unexpected catastrophe until he was persecuted to death in the Cultural Revolution.

A lot of everyday essentials could hardly be bought with money during the most severe period of natural disasters from 1959 to 1962. People must buy them according to restricted plans, every adult had quantitively food coupon_of 10 kilograms per month and must use food tickets when going to restaurants and buying biscuits, fish, meat, and chicken. And the amount per person was allowed to buy was quite little. If people wanted to buy cloth or clothes, they needed cloth tickets; if they wanted to buy quilts, they needed cloth or cotton voucher and if they were to buy oil, salt, sugar, bean products, bean curd and vegetables, and even coal used for fire, they needed a few planned tickets, or they had to pay a price several times higher than voucher to buy them in so-called "black markets".

Before reform and opening-up, ordinary people earned a low salary, most of them tens of Yuan per month. The monthly salary for an apprentice was 18 Yuan, not enough to buy a chicken. Only old

Age of rapid change

revolutionaries or talents like senior leaders could have more planned discount coupon, but they did not abuse their power for personal gains or live a more luxury life.

During that period, Qiu Zhongyuan and his wife worked in the hospital and then brought home the twins who were beginning elementary schooling and Juele.

Ever since 1960, serious political conflicts appeared between the Soviet Union and China. After the two parties broke up, the Soviet Union tore the cooperation agreement, drew their experts back and asked for debt, all of which added further poverty and pain to Chinese people who had suffered enough for several years when living essentials were insufficient. People in urban areas had 10 kilograms of quantitively food supply and such limited materials would never make people think of the two words "losing weight". Most people got either dropsy or skinny because of hunger. And people in the rural areas had to dig potherbs and grassroots everywhere and even peel barks when there were no "meal from a big pot" in collective canteens. Under such circumstances, the national economy was on the brink of collapse.

Since the latter half of 1961, China began to implement the policy to "streamlined administration", each ministry and department must reduce working staff to lessen the financial burden of the state. There was no doubt that this policy was implemented in enterprises, institutions, factories and mines all over the country. The South Union Hospital where the couple worked was no exception. Therefore, many people felt nervous and scared that they would be cut off and no one was willing to submit one's resignation.

At the critical moment of food disaster, Qiu Zhongyuan earned more than the general public and he had the investment made in the hospital, it was returned at an arbitrary discount in the previous two years ago.

So, the Qiu 's family who attached great importance to eating well and maintaining good health but not to clothes had never carried out something like "quantitively meals" for their children who were growing up. Therefore, the children did not suffer from poor health. On the other hand, the family invited nursemaid to look after the several children. But the saying "poverty breeds thieves" had its own reason. Some small valuable things such as the bronze iron and the copper spittoon suddenly disappeared, and sometimes even food would get lost.

Once Shao Guizhen just asked the home maid, "Why did we have only half of a bag of rice?" This maid from the countryside began to cry hard. Shao tried her best to persuade her, who, however, held onto her braids and raised her mouth without a word. Weiying was then at the sixth grade of elementary school. When she saw the scene back home, she asked her mother, "What's up, mom?" Shao replied quietly, "Aunt Wu the next-door told me, 'I saw her relatives from the village taking something come out of your home.' I have doubted her before but did not ask her anything. We have hired a maid but could not ask her when something got lost, so it is troublesome to have stranger working at home."

One day, Shao told it to her husband and said at last, "Now almost everyone in the hospital feared losing jobs. Although Xiaodong was sent to the secret factory in Zhuzhou for college, you and other children needed to be looked after. If we hire someone, those from rural areas do not have planned food, so we must buy high-priced rice to feed her, who steels our things so that my salary could not afford her. Thus, I'd better quit the job and look after you and our children and do some housework at home. I think the hospital would agree as they wanted to cut off workers, but no one is willing to leave." As soon as she finished, Qiu Zhongyuan said in approval, "It will be better for you to stay home to care children and me than to go to work just for a monthly salary of dozens of yuan. In this way we will not have to worry about the nurse stealing things. And my salary is enough to afford all of us." With Qiu's support and under the circumstance of "Streamlined administration", Shao proposed demission to the hospital and got approval very soon. Meanwhile the hospital felt quite pleased that she responded actively to the call of central government.

Qiu Zhongyuan was in more favor of boys than girls, which was his deeply rooted belief, and Xiaodong was not his own daughter, so he asked a friend from North China who worked at the Survey and Design Institute of Changsha to introduce a boyfriend for Xiaodong who had not graduated from college then. The boy, over 10 years older than Xiaodong, was named Li Zhimeng and was from Changchun, capital of a northeast province. He joined the army at 16 and rendered many meritorious services on the battlefield in Korea. After coming back to China when the 10-year task of "opposing America and assisting Korea", he was also assigned to work in the Survey and Design Institute. He was a handsome guy, 20-odd centimeters higher than Xiaodong, so Xiaodong always ran following him when they went out together. Perhaps because Xiaodong lacked fraternal love since her childhood, she quickly fell into love. Shao thought Li Zhimeng was a good guy and did not oppose their relations, so they got married soon. But not long after that, Wu was assigned to work in distant Ningxia Hui Autonomous Region, which might have been triggered by Wu's unsmooth relationship with his superiors. Since then, he went back to Hunan to have home leave once a year.

The policy of "streamlined administration" made many people lose their jobs and face difficulties in life, and the national economy did not turn better, either. Therefore, in 1962, Vice Chairman Liu Shaoqi and his permanent pursuers Deng Xiaoping and Deng Zihui began to carry out the policy of working on one's own. In cities, people were allowed to be occupied with private business and in rural areas, farmland was allocated to each family.

That summer, some leaders of the streets and the administrative committee of medical of Medical Organizations went to Qiu's home, persuading Shao Guizhen, "You have the techniques but don't serve the general public, what a pity!" Although Shao explained the reasons deliberately, they tried their best to persuade her repeatedly, in hope that she could "engage herself in medical practice by opening a clinic in home". During the first two to three months, Shao always refused. But later, she was enlightened by their words that she should open a private clinic to serve patients. And then she would hire a nursemaid to help with housework, and that would become a good way. She told the plan to her husband and won his support.

Thus, in the autumn of 1962, Shao went to the medical administrative committee to apply for opening a clinic at home. Under the current circumstance, her application quickly won approval. Shao thought, we should hire an older nursemaid as there was no hard work at home. Therefore, she hired Aunt Liao. It happened that aunt Liao was unhappy living with her son and daughter-in-law, so she would rather come here as a nursemaid.

Sometimes Shao would ask Qiu Weiying when coming back home after school to rub cotton balls and cutting gauzes and cotton. Nevertheless, when Weiying was in her summer holiday after Grade One of junior middle school of 1963, a non-native woman who was very ill came. Shao could not handle it by herself, so she asked Weiying, "Weiying, the patient is quite ill. And I cannot do the operation on her without an assistant, so come and help me." It was the first time that Weiying saw her mother holding forceps and scissors and she felt somewhat uncomfortable at such blood and flesh. When the operation went half-way, she said, "Mom, I can't go on…" Shao slowed down and peered at her. Seeing her pale face, she knew that she was allergic to blood, and thus asked her, "Go and lie on the bamboo bed for a while." After this incident, Shao thought, there will be more and more patients and I can't do without an assistant. Great trouble would be caused once a medical accident occurs. But where to find a proper assistant? Just several days later, Qiu Xiaodong who was in the second year of college came home from Zhuzhou for the summer holiday.

One day another seriously ill patient was sent there, and Shao again needed an assistant and therefore asked Xiaodong to help.

that she could "engage herself in medical practice by opening a clinic in home". During the first two to three months, Shao always refused. But later, she was enlightened by their words that she should open a private clinic to serve patients. And then she would hire a nursemaid to help with housework, and that would become a good way. She told the plan to her husband and won his support.

Thus, in the autumn of 1962, Shao went to the medical administrative committee to apply for opening a clinic at home. Under the current circumstance, her application quickly won approval. Shao thought, we should hire an older nursemaid as there was no hard work at home. Therefore, she hired Aunt Liao. It happened that aunt Liao was unhappy living with her son and daughter-in-law, so she would rather come here as a nursemaid.

Sometimes Shao would ask Qiu Weiying when coming back home after school to rub cotton balls and cutting gauzes and cotton. Nevertheless, when Weiying was in her summer holiday after Grade One of junior middle school of 1963, a non-native woman who was very ill came. Shao could not handle it by herself, so she asked Weiying, "Weiying, the patient is quite ill. And I cannot do the operation on her without an assistant, so come and help me." It was the first time that Weiying saw her mother holding forceps and scissors and she felt somewhat uncomfortable at such blood and flesh. When the operation went half-way, she said, "Mom, I can't go on..." Shao slowed down and peered at her. Seeing her pale face, she knew that she was allergic to blood, and thus asked her, "Go and lie on the bamboo bed for a while." After this incident, Shao thought, there will be more and more patients and I can't do without an assistant. Great trouble would be caused once a medical accident occurs. But where to find a proper assistant? Just several days later, Qiu Xiaodong who was in the second year of college came home from Zhuzhou for the summer holiday.

One day another seriously ill patient was sent there, and Shao again needed an assistant and therefore asked Xiaodong to help.

hospital felt quite pleased that she responded actively to the call of central government.

Qiu Zhongyuan was in more favor of boys than girls, which was his deeply rooted belief, and Xiaodong was not his own daughter, so he asked a friend from North China who worked at the Survey and Design Institute of Changsha to introduce a boyfriend for Xiaodong who had not graduated from college then. The boy, over 10 years older than Xiaodong, was named Li Zhimeng and was from Changchun, capital of a northeast province. He joined the army at 16 and rendered many meritorious services on the battlefield in Korea. After coming back to China when the 10-year task of "opposing America and assisting Korea", he was also assigned to work in the Survey and Design Institute. He was a handsome guy, 20-odd centimeters higher than Xiaodong, so Xiaodong always ran following him when they went out together. Perhaps because Xiaodong lacked fraternal love since her childhood, she quickly fell into love. Shao thought Li Zhimeng was a good guy and did not oppose their relations, so they got married soon. But not long after that, Wu was assigned to work in distant Ningxia Hui Autonomous Region, which might have been triggered by Wu's unsmooth relationship with his superiors. Since then, he went back to Hunan to have home leave once a year.

The policy of "streamlined administration" made many people lose their jobs and face difficulties in life, and the national economy did not turn better, either. Therefore, in 1962, Vice Chairman Liu Shaoqi and his permanent pursuers Deng Xiaoping and Deng Zihui began to carry out the policy of working on one's own. In cities, people were allowed to be occupied with private business and in rural areas, farmland was allocated to each family.

That summer, some leaders of the streets and the administrative committee of medical of Medical Organizations went to Qiu's home, persuading Shao Guizhen, "You have the techniques but don't serve the general public, what a pity!" Although Shao explained the reasons deliberately, they tried their best to persuade her repeatedly, in hope

During the operation, Xiaodong did not show any allergic reaction to blood; she seemed willing to learn medical skills as she witnessed carefully the whole process of the operation. Shao asked Xiaodong, "Do you want to learn medical skills?" Xiaodong answered smiling, "Of course, I see you and father not only making money but also being respected as doctors." Because of Shao's elaborate techniques and responsible attitude, she became more and more prestigious, and more and more patients visited her. She needed an assistant and now Xiaodong wanted to learn the skills. In addition, Xiaodong was pregnant, and Shao was worried about her if she continued her schooling in Zhuzhou alone as Li Zhimeng came back once a year. After judging and weighing, Shao decided to let Xiaodong drop school and come back home. For one thing, she could serve as her assistant; for another, she was able to learn some medical techniques that could afford her life; and moreover, she could look after her child at home. Then Xiaodong hurried up to Zhuzhou to move her temporary home to Changsha.

Qiu Zhongyuan originally intended to marry Xiaodong to someone and keep her staying outside by introducing a boyfriend for her; however, now she, as a pregnant woman, came back and lived with them. Xiaodong looked more and more like her father Jiang Jianming when grown up. Sometimes when Shao Guizhen was at leisure and saw Xiaodong, she would think of her ex-husband.

Once she said to Weiying at will, "Xiaodong came from the village to Changsha and was admitted to the Second Middle School. She was good at study and even skipped grades. And she looked like her father who had never lost his temper to me, unlike him (referring to Weiying's father) who often got angry at me furiously." Seeing Weiying replied nothing, she did not go on explain clearly.

At that time, she was pondering about a secret no one knew, including of current husband Qiu. She put the jewelries and gold bricks Jiang Jianming left for her and Xiaodong in a round iron canister which used to contain talcum powder for children. To cherish the memory of her ex-husband and the original love deep in her heart that had never been hurt by her current life, she never spent any of the property even when she lived in poverty. And now that Xiaodong was pregnant, she thought, if Jiang was here and knew that he was going to be grandfather, how happy he would be! Xiaodong's child would be the offspring of Jiang's family. Subject to the thought, Shao secretly gave that canister which was about 7 centimeters in diameter and 10 centimeters in height to Xiaodong at her 20th birthday and let her hide it beneath the big camphorwood chest.

She felt subconsciously that Jiang Jianming is long gone from the earth! At least, he would not come home from the underworld to collect the debt from Qiu Zhongyuan. Because the only person who use Jiang Jianming money is his daughter - Xiaodong alone.

Nonetheless, Xiaodong, who was still quite young, began to spend money like water, totally unlike her mother who was thrifty all her life. She never considered the price of something she liked so that Weiying who was just entering into adolescence and did not understand the reasons started to detest her. And the twins did not like her, either.

In the winter of 1963, weather was so cold that water became ice once dropping down. Back home from school, Weiying saw, through the window of the kitchen, Aunt Liao cooking and her mother washing a garment of Xiaodong's child with a washboard beside the granite corridor outside the patients' room. At that time there were no washing machines in China. When free, Weiying would take off her shoes and socks and step into a big basin to help her mother wash beddings. More than often the clothes of the baby boy and Xiaodong's bed sheet filled the wooden basin. Weiying felt sad when seeing Shao's hands swelling like steamed stuffed bans with chilblains. After putting her bag down in her room, she ran to Xiaodong's room where she saw Xiaodong lying in bed and playing with her baby who was several months old. She asked her angrily, "Why don't you give a hand to mother? The basin was full of your clothes and mother was washing them alone." Lying in bed with her face up and seeing her cross, Xiaodong seemed unhappy, "Are you jealous because mother is in more favor of me?" She became more furious at that and said intentionally while walking outward, "That' funny! Do you have any advantage over me that is worth my jealousy?" But Xiaodong lifted, drawn her coat from the back and began to quarrel with her. Weiying threw off her hand and they started fighting. Shao fell into a rage when hearing them fighting and immediately strode up to blame Weiying, "What's wrong with you today? Why did you run to Xiaodong's room and quarrel and even fight with her?" At the same time, she defended Xiaodong and fight against Weiying. The twins saw the scene but dare neither come up nor say anything.

Weiying made use of an opportunity to run outside the gate, when the director of the street was walking beside the locust tree and looking into the direction of Qiu's house. Seeing Weiying run toward, she murmured, "How could it be that mother and daughter fought against one girl?" Weiying used to hear Xiaodong cursed her at home, "She lived on by being a prostitute in the old society. She was just jealous of us as she was not able to earn money." At this, Weiying did not greet her. What's more, this is the only one time that her mother beat her ever since she was born.

At that exact moment, Qiu Zhongyuan turned into the lane by bicycle, and seeing Weiying shedding tears standing there, got off his bike at once and asked, "Why are you standing here and wiping tears?" The dean came up immediately. Weiying said, "I quarreled with Sister Xiaodong for a while and mother beat me together with her." Qiu frowned his brows, "Your mother has been in more favor of Xiaodong. Let's go home. Don't let others know this." He entered the gate, followed by Weiying. She doesn't understand that these little things would hurt her parents' relationship. Soon she clearly forgot the hatred towards Xiaodong.

"Good wine sells well even deep in an outlying lane,", although Shao's clinic was located far in the lane that it could not be seen in Lao Zhaobi Street at all, many nonlocal patients came here owing to their friends' introduction. However, patients who had undergone an anorectal surgery were not able to walk immediately and needed observations for days in of postoperative infection, dropsy and even blood loss. In the beginning, Shao asked such patients to rent a room in hotels or to sleep on the operating table for a night if they could not rent one. But with more and more patients, the operating table was not enough for them to stay temporarily. Some patients stayed overnight on the bench in the living room serving as the waiting room. And still some directly asked, "Doctor Shao, I have no alternative. Could I rent a bed at your home?" And gradually, more and more patients proposed the same question. Looking at the pitiful faces, Shao could hardly refuse them.

In the summer of 1964, after Qiu Xiaodong's mother-in-law who came from the North and lived in Changsha for months left, Shao sent Juele and the twins to their wet nurse and foster mother again so that she could have two empty rooms to accommodate nonlocal patients. The residence permit system was quite strict during those years. In accordance with related regulations, all non-natives, despite age and gender, must register at local police stations if they were to live here.

Shao adhered to the regulations, on receiving next patient, she would ask Xiaodong to bring his or her household register to the police station and register name, address, age, gender, hometown, family background and unit there. And each month she would report all these to the administrative committee of medical of Medical Organizations, which would also send someone to check sometimes.

Once, Cheng Tianliang who oversaw the committee came here to check Shao's work and the patients' room she had set publicly in her house at lunch time. Seeing each patient having meat, vegetables and a bowl of broth, he praised, "You have arranged such a good meal for your patients?" Shao answered, "I like to prepare dishes such as stewed meat with nuts and eggs boiled with longyans. Anyway, patients would have the same meals with us." Cheng had read her monthly report and knew she charged less than hospitals, but she prepared nutritious meals for patients, so he continued to praise her in a few sentences. Finally, he said, "A relative of mine wrote to me and said it was so cold now in the North and wanted to live in Changsha for a period. But we have no more space for him at home, so could you let him live here?" Shao replied, "We do not have adequate planned coal for fire and usually I have to buy white charcoal. And sometimes the two patients' rooms are not enough for accommodation. So, you'd better think of another way." Cheng's face suddenly became dark at this; he left without another word.

Although Shao thought it was a little improper, she could do nothing because his requirement was in fact difficult to meet under that circumstance. Moreover, the room for Juecong and Juele was being used by male patients and Juecong had to sleep in a single bed by the side of the wall in his parents' room.

Doctor Shao left a very good impression to almost everyone thanks to her outstanding medical skills, strict working style and sincere attitude. During the three years since she opened the clinic, many patients wrote her letters expressing their thanks after they went back to their working posts or sent her exquisite red silk banners to extend their appreciation and gratification when they recovered. Almost every patient looked much healthier when leaving than before treatment. No one was unsatisfactory with her, and no superior criticized or gave suggestions to her. The trend of working on one's own initiated by Liu Shaoqi, Deng Xiaoping and Deng Zihui not only benefitted Shao and patients but also helped the unemployed in cities and peasants suffering from starvation in villages, thus improving people's living standard in the whole society to a certain degree. However, it did not last long…

2.7 Trumped-up charge

At one dark and gloomy noon with fierce wind and heavy snow at the end of 1963, one Jiangsu living in Changsha who had been cured of Seriously ill patients by Doctor Shao came to Shao's home, depressed. With frowned brows, he walked came through the gate of Qiu's house while Shao was leaving the consulting and going to the kitchen for lunch. She was surprised at the sudden arrival of her fellow-townsman, he walked towards her, "Doctor Shao, my wife has got pneumonia as she does not get in-time treatment after having cold and coughing for a long time. She is now in a coma, with the body temperature of more than 40 degrees. I have sent her to hospital and the doctor said, 'Her disease may easily cause complications like emphysema without immediate treatment, and the consequence will be disastrous.' But I cannot afford the fees, so could I pawn my gold ring to you at its original price? I will redeem it when I have money in the future; but I will sell it to you if I cannot earn any." As soon as he finished, Aunt Liao held her dish on a plate and urged, "The patients are already having lunch, but you are still busy. It is so cold that the dish will become cold very soon. So be quick." Shao replied immediately, "Wait a moment. His wife's life is more important than my lunch." Then she turned to say to the townsman, "All right. It is not necessary for you to explain too much." Finished saying these words, she handed the money at the price he cited of the ring." After that, she asked Aunt Liao to prepare a dish and a bowl of hot broth for him, who had the meal leaving. He is with enormous gratification for Dr. Shao's to pay for the fees. However, the Jiangsu never redeemed his ring later and Shao did not visit him to mention it, either.

Nonetheless, Dr. Shao done this one good deed of "take pleasure in helping people ", it became another cause for Qiu's family of properties to be confiscated several months later, buying gold from someone belonged to "speculation and profiteering". And they did not suffer only immense property loss but also uncalculated negative

2.7 Trumped-up charge

At one dark and gloomy noon with fierce wind and heavy snow at the end of 1963, one Jiangsu living in Changsha who had been cured of Seriously ill patients by Doctor Shao came to Shao's home, depressed. With frowned brows, he walked came through the gate of Qiu's house while Shao was leaving the consulting and going to the kitchen for lunch. She was surprised at the sudden arrival of her fellow-townsman, he walked towards her, "Doctor Shao, my wife has got pneumonia as she does not get in-time treatment after having cold and coughing for a long time. She is now in a coma, with the body temperature of more than 40 degrees. I have sent her to hospital and the doctor said, 'Her disease may easily cause complications like emphysema without immediate treatment, and the consequence will be disastrous.' But I cannot afford the fees, so could I pawn my gold ring to you at its original price? I will redeem it when I have money in the future; but I will sell it to you if I cannot earn any." As soon as he finished, Aunt Liao held her dish on a plate and urged, "The patients are already having lunch, but you are still busy. It is so cold that the dish will become cold very soon. So be quick." Shao replied immediately, "Wait a moment. His wife's life is more important than my lunch." Then she turned to say to the townsman, "All right. It is not necessary for you to explain too much." Finished saying these words, she handed the money at the price he cited of the ring." After that, she asked Aunt Liao to prepare a dish and a bowl of hot broth for him, who had the meal leaving. He is with enormous gratification for Dr. Shao's to pay for the fees. However, the Jiangsu never redeemed his ring later and Shao did not visit him to mention it, either.

Nonetheless, Dr. Shao done this one good deed of "take pleasure in helping people ", it became another cause for Qiu's family of properties to be confiscated several months later, buying gold from someone belonged to "speculation and profiteering". And they did not suffer only immense property loss but also uncalculated negative meal for your patients?" Shao answered, "I like to prepare dishes such as stewed meat with nuts and eggs boiled with longyans. Anyway, patients would have the same meals with us." Cheng had read her monthly report and knew she charged less than hospitals, but she prepared nutritious meals for patients, so he continued to praise her in a few sentences. Finally, he said, "A relative of mine wrote to me and said it was so cold now in the North and wanted to live in Changsha for a period. But we have no more space for him at home, so could you let him live here?" Shao replied, "We do not have adequate planned coal for fire and usually I have to buy white charcoal. And sometimes the two patients' rooms are not enough for accommodation. So, you'd better think of another way." Cheng's face suddenly became dark at this; he left without another word.

Although Shao thought it was a little improper, she could do nothing because his requirement was in fact difficult to meet under that circumstance. Moreover, the room for Juecong and Juele was being used by male patients and Juecong had to sleep in a single bed by the side of the wall in his parents' room.

Doctor Shao left a very good impression to almost everyone thanks to her outstanding medical skills, strict working style and sincere attitude. During the three years since she opened the clinic, many patients wrote her letters expressing their thanks after they went back to their working posts or sent her exquisite red silk banners to extend their appreciation and gratification when they recovered. Almost every patient looked much healthier when leaving than before treatment. No one was unsatisfactory with her, and no superior criticized or gave suggestions to her. The trend of working on one's own initiated by Liu Shaoqi, Deng Xiaoping and Deng Zihui not only benefitted Shao and patients but also helped the unemployed in cities and peasants suffering from starvation in villages, thus improving people's living standard in the whole society to a certain degree. However, it did not last long…

Age of rapid change

influence in terms of politics as they lived in an age when social strata and class were too emphasized.

The year 1964 is also still in progress of another political motion called the "Four Clean-ups", <See App. 1. F> the purpose of which was to clear thoughts, account, warehouses and money earned every day in each people's commune. To be more specific, it aimed at identifying such harmful behaviors as embezzlement, thrift, and possession of more than one should have got. In such a movement, some leaders assigned by their supervisors worked together as a "Working Group of Four Cleanups" to conduct ideological education for socialism at communes in rural areas. Shao often heard that from the talks among her patients.

One day at the end of 1964, one patient said, "Our village has begun to rectify the behaviors of the cadres and will make investigation into their properties if they live a relatively better life." Shao, at hearing that, felt a bit upset and uneasy and did not sleep until two or three in the morning. She thought, how much would the rural leaders have even if they lived a better life? The Kuomintang once advocated to the general public, "The Communist Party is coming. Private properties are not protected., the wealth of the rich will be confiscated by the Communist Party." Will they find an excuse to confiscate our properties since we have more than others?

At that moment her husband has been asleep, but she lay in bed and tossed and turned, never able to sleep. Qiu waking up and saw wife staring at the ceiling with her eyes wide open, and asked, "What's up? Why haven't you fallen asleep after so long?" She told him her anxiety, "As doctors, we earn more than those village cadres, so I wonder whether the work group of "Four Clean-ups" will cause us trouble. Qiu, however, answered, "You are just worrying yourself without reason. This motion aims at eliminating corruption of those cadres. We make a living by our own techniques, so how could they do so? Sleep well".

In January of 1965, the CPC central committee issued "the 23rd item", the main purpose being tackling the contradiction between socialism and capitalism. Therefore, the motion gradually spread to cities.

One Sunday noon, Weiying's father and some patients were sleeping at theirs rooms. Qiu Weiying said to her mother, "Mom, Juecong is on good terms with his classmate Ma Jianping. Juecong said, 'Ma's father is a leader while in the Long March <See App 1. A> like Zhang Tairan's father. Ma lives in Fuzheng Street at the turning point of Laozhaobi.' Now Juecong is going there and asked me to accompany him. I'll just have a look at his door and soon come back." Shao just nodded, "Ok" Aunt Liao was sent to buy subsidiary foodstuff by Shao either intentionally or unintentionally. Shao was thus left alone, cutting absorbent cotton and gauze in the clinic.

Now upset by the propaganda of Kuomintang before liberation, when suddenly she came up with an idea. She stood up and walked into the kitchen where she found a broken basin and put all the mixed coal in a groove into it with a shovel (at that time people mixed coal with yellow mud and water to start fire).

Then she started to dig a hole via the groove while Qiu Zhongyuan was walking through the kitchen towards the toilet in the lane. Peering inside, he felt surprised and asked, "Why did you put all the coal into the basin?" Shao had to explain, "I'm afraid somehow, so I want to hide all our gold and silver jewelry under this groove......" Qiu interrupted her, "Are you sick? How can people live on with such suspicions like you?" We have always been abiding by laws and regulations and have done nothing wrong, so does this motionhave anything to do with us? We've been working as well-behaved doctors to cure and save our patients, so there is no reason to confiscate our legal property. I have said it will be OK, but you refuse to believe." Finishing his words, he stared seriously at Shao, who was worried and afraid that he might lose his temper again. Moreover, she had not committed any crime. Therefore, she put the coal back into the groove, washed her hands and left the kitchen. From then on, she never intended to hide these gold silver and jewelry elsewhere again.

However, there was this is the right thing to do in Shao's anxiety. Soon, in the name of "Changsha Administration Committee of Medical Organizations", Chang Tianqing, the dean and Secretary Zhao as well as Chang Wanmin of Changsha Public Security Bureau and Feng Bin of Changsha Bureau of Public Health formed the so-called "work group of Four Clean-ups of the Administration Committee of Medical Organizations in response to "The Massive Socialist Education Movement". At the very beginning of the movement, Qiu, as one of the most prestigious doctors in treating anorectic diseases, who had the highest salary in all hospitals of this city and whose wife started a private clinic at home has, became one of their key targets. There is a proverb, "the person in the limelight bears the brunt of the attack". The Qiu's family, however, had not been informed of anything. At first, Wang Huijun, the head of the hospital where Qiu worked supported the work group quite actively as she intended to revenge Qiu who looked down his leaders. As a result, they did not find any fault with him. On one hand, he did not make any fault in operations and had got recognition of many patients with outstanding medical techniques. On the other hand, Qiu was upright and honest and had not taken anything in the hospital to his wife's clinic. He had not helped his wife treat patients at home, either. Therefore, the work group that had to start with Shao's patients investigated and collected evidence of crime. They tried their best to find patients for relevant materials from Changsha to other places and from cities to villages. In fact, nevertheless, they were just forcing the patients to write stuff to frame Qiu up. A woman patient who was a communist thought there was something wrong with it, so she expressed her appreciation of Qiu to them. Consequently, they got outraged and criticized her, "That is not the position a communist should have." And an overseas Chinese from Singapore named Liu Pofa also extended his gratification for Doctor

Sao who had cured his serious disease. So, he was reluctant to say something to the group, and felt upset for Sao, why should such a good doctor who was responsible for his patients encounter such unfairness? Liu had been living in Shao's home while getting treated and seen her conducts in person. Since the group could not find any evidence, they began to think up of other means.

One morning when Qiu Weiying left home for school, it was drizzling with snow. Weiying was reluctant to go home at noon, and when the rain stopped a little, she went to a small restaurant called "He Ji Rice-noodles" not far from her school to have a bowl of rice-noodle that was one of her favorites. She returned to the class before it began, only to find her teacher sitting on her chair and staring at her with a strange and serious expression, saying to her in a low voice, "A man from the municipal public security bureau wants to talk with you. He is now waiting for you at the headmaster office." Weiying, totally confused, followed her teacher, thinking, why does someone from the public security bureau want to talk with me? Do they want me, a 15-odd-year-old middle school student, to help solve a or arrest spies…? While thinking, she walked into the school office.

A man who looked more than 40 years old recognized her and strode towards her at once, "I'm Chang Wanmin, from Changsha Public Security Bureau. I have something to talk about with you. Please have a seat." Her teacher cast at Qiu with a complicated look and left. Chang began, "I heard from your teacher that you are very smart and do very well in your study. The school plans to directly recommend you to the teacher's college.

If you get credit for reporting your parents, and that will be quite easy after you finish school. So, do you know where your parents' property and gold and silver jewelry are?"

As soon as Chang finished, Weiying just wants to curse him by her instinct. At that moment, a strong sense of being offended overwhelmed her, "I thought you intended to let me help you arrest

Age of rapid change

spies! Why to report my parents? I just know they are upright and honest. They have never committed any crime and will never do so in the future. And I don't know of any place where jewelry is hiding." At this, Chang fell into a rage, "Your parents are occupied with speculation and profiteering and have opened an illegal underground clinic. How comes it that they did not commit a crime?" Though Weiying felt warmer after walking through the playground with a kind of sunlight shining on her, now a cold flow crushed her so that she almost began to tremble. She learned from her political lesson that "speculation and profiteering" referred to illegal conduct in which private businessmen earned price difference of commodities from long-distance transportation by buying at a low price and selling a high price and they were being seriously cracked down by the socialist country. However, Weiying had never seen her parent's doing business; instead, they were treating patients day and night. And it was impossible that her father's hospital was illegal. Her father was working in the union hospital established by himself, and her mother had received a license from the administration committee in starting the clinic. Each time a patient visited, she would get registered at the police station and she also helped them do this. But she did not how to reply to this "law enforcer" in front of her.

She cast her eyes to Chang's smiling but not smiling face with a surprising expression. Chang asked her again severely, "Do you know where your parents hide the property gold and jewelry?" Weiying answered, "I have only received pocket money from my mother and don't know where their property is at all. Moreover, my parents are quite well-disciplined, busy with treating patients, so they do not have time to do anything speculating. And I couldn't understand at all why you said my mother opened an illegal underground clinic, for she has received a license from the medical establishment administration committee and the patients living at home have all been registered at the police station." She gazed at him for whom she showed great antipathy. And Chang might be able to sense her outrage from her glaring eyes so that he suddenly realized that he could not get anything useful from her and that it would a waste of time if he continued asking. What's more, he had another plan. Therefore, he waved to Weiying, "Go to have your class."

Weiying returned to her class, but all eyes were on her and some of her classmates looked at her and were full of misunderstanding. Because they could not understand, "why she had to go between the class and the teacher's office during the class. "That afternoon, she is absent-minded in class and could hardly make sense of what the teacher said in the classroom.

In the same afternoon, Qiu Xiaodong, Weiying's half-sister (they have the same mother but different fathers), was called to the administration committee of medical organizations by a staff there. The committee was near Qiu's family in the Yuquan temple street near the Chang Zhi Road where the family often went to buy vegetables. Shao became anxious when Xiaodong did not go home after Weiying came back. Shao said to Weiying who had just put off her bag, "I have something to deal with at Zong Weikang's. And when your father come back, have your dinner. Don't wait for me." She thought then, do I need to hide the canister (which used to hold talcum powder) of gold bricks and jewelry that have been locked in Xiaodong's? Nevertheless, at that exact moment, she seemed to see her husband's angry face and hear him shout, "is it need?" Furthermore, Shao knew it would not be easy to pull the canister out because Xiaodong had put that canister in a large made of camphorwood chest at the bottom. Therefore, she decided that she should go first to Zong Weikang house to consult with them. Shao went to Juecong who was playing horizontal bar, saying to him, "Do not go outside. It's almost time for dinner." Then she walked out of the gate.

When she arrived at Zong Weikang, the old nursemaid working there had put dishes on the table. Zong Weikang wife, who worked in the same hospital as Qiu Zhongyuan, immediately stood for Shao. To prepare her to dinner. Shao said what happened today and the Zong Weikang thought that they should act at once the next morning if Xiaodong would not go home tonight.

Weiying felt anxious since her mother went out. Although she was quite certain that her parents were upright and did not do anything illegal, she had a feeling of inauspiciousness and confusion. These were what were in her view, her younger brother Juecong was playing horizontal bar in the sandpit in the front yard; Aunt Liao was cooking in the kitchen; her father did not come back yet.

She walked to her parent's sleep room automatically. Standing in the middle of the room, she stared blankly around and found nothing wrong. It was totally different from what she saw in the movie, the mountain cave that was gleaming because it was full of gold and silver. She gazed into a deep-red small leather chest, it is about 60-odd centimeters long, 30-odd centimeters wide and 15 to 16 centimeters high was quite delicate. the small leather chest was together with a big cabinet. The small suitcase was placed on top of the large cabinet and together close to the wall. Weiying knew that it meant a lot to her father as in it there were such certificates as property ownership license, medical practitioner and a few materials as well as cash. She happened to see her father open the chest twice and he pointed to several slices of paper and told her, "You see. These are all receipts for a borrow, some belonging to the pre-liberation period. Some borrowers are nowhere to be found now." But Weiying had never seen any gold or silver items. The chest was locked by two locks with small openings to keys on both sides so that she could not see what was inside.

However, once her father, after receiving a monthly salary of 184 Yuan, put it at one corner of the chest together with a big envelope containing the salary of that month and it happened that he did not lock that side. And instigated by a street rascal who was 10-odd years older than him, Juecong put his hand into the chest by the unlocked side and took the money out, and moreover, he spent almost all of it with some ill-behaved boys.

At that time, an apprentice only earned 18 yuan; it is because her father invests formed Southern Region Hospital of Changsha and had outstanding medical techniques that he had a higher salary than others. When father recognized that the money was stolen by Juecong who even spent it all, he became quite outraged. Binding Juecong hand behind his back, he lashed him with a leather belt. Weiying, who was afraid of seeing that, followed her mother and pled. Nonetheless, her father did not pay attention to them at all, "Go!" Scared to silence, the two of them dare not walk closer. Although her father was known for "treating girls as inferior to boys" and had lavished so much on Juecong, at that moment the boy became the one he disliked most. Though thinking of that event, Weiying still wanted to open the chest to identify whether there was gold and silver stuff. But she could do nothing since it was locked on both sides, and she had no courage to break it. She did not ever think of hiding the important, for she was young and simple after all.

At this time, she heard her father stopping his bicycle at the gate. Looking out, she saw her father with the same expression as usual. Knowing it was time for dinner, Juecong ran to the kitchen. Qiu, looking at his back, smiled as before. Weiying stopped what she had wanted to say, seeing her father's easy look. Then Aunt Liao said loud, "Miss Weiying, please help with the dinner." Weiying came into the kitchen, and while helping Liao take bowls and chopsticks and fill rice, she complained, "Why do you call me 'Miss' again? I have said that my parents are doctor who make a living by their techniques. This belongs to free occupation; they are not capitalist. So, please don't call me that again." Then with a still confusing mind, she held the dishes to the room.

Not long after the Spring Festival, there were just two patients, one of whom had gone home temporarily, so Aunt Liao had her meal with the only woman patient. Qiu heard that Shao went to Zong Weikang home and after dinner, he, as usual, placed the imported gramophone he bought years ago on the dinner table and put a disc recoding Yu opera sang by Chang Xiangyu into it. Then he inserted into the small round hole at one side of the gramophone the hand shank that twirled several times. While listening to the rhythmical music, Qiu made beats with his fingers and sang together with the disc. Seeing the pleasant look of her father, Weiying had tried to speak out on several occasions but decided against it in the end. normal times, she did not talk with her father much, so this time, she held <How the Steel Was Tempered> the novel of Former Soviet Union and lay on bed to read it. She fell asleep while reading.

Shao came back and asked her husband, "Haven't Xiaodong come back yet?" Qiu replied, "I had intended to ask you. I thought she had gone to Zong Weikang home with you." "No, some leaders of the Administration Committee of Medical Organizations called her there this afternoon. I must go to the committee to have a look." With these words, Shao opened the gate, quite anxious, and then turned to close the gate to let Qiu bolt it. Under the dark sky, Shao strode to the committee alone.

About two hours later, Shao returned and said to Qiu who was standing beside the wooden bolt, "It was strange that the gate of the committee was shut. I shouted for quite a while, but no one answered. The committee might have been off duty today, but where has Xiaodong gone? She should be either in the committee or at home now. Shall we go to the police station to report it?" "Now that the administrative committee of medical of Medical called her there, it's impossible that she has got lost. Maybe she went with one leader or one of our acquaintances and played too late to come back. Wait till tomorrow. It's time to sleep." Qiu then turned to step into his bedroom. Shao, at that time, thought with contradiction, "Xiaodong has never stayed overnight outside because of play. But even if the committee wants to cause me trouble, they should not detain my daughter.

She could not fall asleep because she could hardly reach a conclusion while there was obviously something wrong. Of course, if she had talked to Weiying and heard her say such unexpected things as "your parents' illegal clinic; speculation and profiteering; the place to hide properties" which were meant to identify their inexistent crime, the problem would become clearer. She would not develop a prompt_even in a dream---It was decided in advance when the Medical Management Committee was prepared to start doing with her. Inexistent accusation had been defined before the committee prepared to investigate into her. She felt drained and a drowsiness gradually invaded her organism ......

2.8 Unexpected disaster

In fact, after the administrative committee of medical went off work on Mar. 29th, not only Secretary Zhao Fusheng and Li Ke and Peng Fuzhen of the committee but also Chang Wanmin of the municipal public security bureau was there. Zhao and Cheng Tianqiang, in the name of the committee, invited Chang and Feng Bin of the municipal health administration to form the so-called "work group of Four Clearings "of the Changsha Administrative Committee of medical Organizations. The purpose of the group was to crack down and rectify all private clinics throughout the city in response to the call of "Massive Socialism Education" in 1965; however, it aimed at supporting the attack against the Single dry wind of capitalism. It was a false supporting force for the "Four Clearings", viz., clearings in terms of policies, organizations, economics and thoughts surrounding the people's communes as well as a superficial demonstration of the conflict between the two routes within the Communist Party. The Single dry wind was a product of the routes of Liu Shaoqi and Deng Xiaoping, who were not being criticized as representatives of capitalism at that time.

Changsha was the capital as well as the largest city in Hunan province, and it was reported that there were 100 tens of private clinics throughout the city and its adjacent towns and counties. This work group, therefore, decided to conduct key investigations and

Age of rapid change

try to make breakthroughs on well-known and high-income private clinics. At a result, the clinic of Doctor Shao and several others with relatively good business including "Brightness Ophthalmology" became the major targets of this movement. What's more, their relationship with the "Changsha Administration Committee of Medical Organizations is only average, and they have even offended those in power, so there are hidden dangers.

When Shao shouted outside the gate of the administrative committee of medical, Secretary Zhao and several other cadres, and even Qiu Xiaodong who was very nervous then, all heard her voice. Seeing no one going to open the gate for her mother, she wanted to do it herself, but was stopped by them who said, "The gate has been bolted. If you do not tell us where your family's property is hiding, do not go outside the gate." Xiaodong said, "It's so late. You have had your dinner, but I haven't yet. I'm hungry now, could you let me go home for dinner and I'll come tomorrow." Among them someone to her rant, "You can't even if you are hungry. You must tell us clearly where the property of your family is, or you can't go home this evening."

Xiaodong thought among the gold and silver jewelries in the iron canister which used to contain talcum powder below the big chest, most were left by her father. And her mother was frugal, putting them in her big chest together with all her savings, let alone use them. Neither she nor her mother had ever done anything illegal, so she would not easily tell them so that they might take the jewelries away. She decided to keep silent. The peoples then went downstairs to have midnight snack, but she was too hungry to move… Just after 12 o'clock, these cadres became so furious and violent. They asked Xiaodong to stand up and not to doze off, without regard to her murmuring, "I'm hungry. I'm thirsty…" But Xiaodong refused to say anything about the property. Zhao Fusheng, at last, forced her, "Your father whose last name is Jiang is an officer of Kuomintang. And Chiang Kai-shek's hometown is somewhere in Jiangsu and

Zhejiang, so who knows if your father came from Chiang Kai-shek's family." Seeing Xiaodong tremble suddenly, Chang Wanmin clapped the table and chair, "You should try to make clear your relationship with your family and be more active, or we'll detain you." Xiaodong was quite anxious and exasperated at what they uttered, for she had never heard her mother say that they bore any relations with Chiang Kai-shek. As they just intended to threaten her, she felt so wronged, lonely and helpless that she could not stop her tears...

A moment later, Feng Bin of the health administration said, "I can't support it anymore. I'll go downstairs to sleep for a while and call Wang Huijun to replace me." After these, she walked downstairs. Soon a storm began out of a sudden as if all evil spirits and monsters ran out from darkness... The remaining three men started slapping the table and chairs and growling at her. The storm beat the windows ruthlessly and cold wind came inside from slots between the windows... Xiaodong felt nervous, cold and starving. Suddenly she felt so dizzy that she fell on the ground. Coming towards her almost simultaneously, the three men lifted up her collar and grasped her by the arm, yelling, "Stand up! No pretending! Tell up where is your mother's property?" At that time, Xiaodong was too hungry, thirsty and cold to sustain herself, so she had to say with no alternative, "There is some property under the big chest in my room…" Then they let the hold of her. Someone by the way pushed her, who stumble and fall sat on the cement floor at the corner of the room and lied on the wall. Her mind was totally blank, completely forgetting what she had said just now.

Wang Huijun came over at this exact moment. Chang Wanmin said to her with excitement, "Qiu Xiaodong has told us where her mother put the money and property. We have to go there as soon as possible, or we will not make it when her mother began to doubt and taking measures."

These men started to set off when Wang said, "We should be quick now that the rain is lighter. Laozhaobi is very near; let's go." Zhao continued, "Let Qiu Xiaodong stay here. We just lock the gate

Zhejiang, so who knows if your father came from Chiang Kai-shek's family." Seeing Xiaodong tremble suddenly, Chang Wanmin clapped the table and chair, "You should try to make clear your relationship with your family and be more active, or we'll detain you." Xiaodong was quite anxious and exasperated at what they uttered, for she had never heard her mother say that they bore any relations with Chiang Kai-shek. As they just intended to threaten her, she felt so wronged, lonely and helpless that she could not stop her tears…

A moment later, Feng Bin of the health administration said, "I can't support it anymore. I'll go downstairs to sleep for a while and call Wang Huijun to replace me." After these, she walked downstairs. Soon a storm began out of a sudden as if all evil spirits and monsters ran out from darkness… The remaining three men started slapping the table and chairs and growling at her. The storm beat the windows ruthlessly and cold wind came inside from slots between the windows… Xiaodong felt nervous, cold and starving. Suddenly she felt so dizzy that she fell on the ground. Coming towards her almost simultaneously, the three men lifted up her collar and grasped her by the arm, yelling, "Stand up! No pretending! Tell up where is your mother's property?" At that time, Xiaodong was too hungry, thirsty and cold to sustain herself, so she had to say with no alternative, "There is some property under the big chest in my room…" Then they let the hold of her. Someone by the way pushed her, who stumble and fall sat on the cement floor at the corner of the room and lied on the wall. Her mind was totally blank, completely forgetting what she had said just now.

Wang Huijun came over at this exact moment. Chang Wanmin said to her with excitement, "Qiu Xiaodong has told us where her mother put the money and property. We have to go there as soon as possible, or we will not make it when her mother began to doubt and taking measures."

These men started to set off when Wang said, "We should be quick now that the rain is lighter. Laozhaobi is very near; let's go." Zhao continued, "Let Qiu Xiaodong stay here. We just lock the gate try to make breakthroughs on well-known and high-income private clinics. At a result, the clinic of Doctor Shao and several others with relatively good business including "Brightness Ophthalmology" became the major targets of this movement. What's more, their relationship with the "Changsha Administration Committee of Medical Organizations is only average, and they have even offended those in power, so there are hidden dangers.

When Shao shouted outside the gate of the administrative committee of medical, Secretary Zhao and several other cadres, and even Qiu Xiaodong who was very nervous then, all heard her voice. Seeing no one going to open the gate for her mother, she wanted to do it herself, but was stopped by them who said, "The gate has been bolted. If you do not tell us where your family's property is hiding, do not go outside the gate." Xiaodong said, "It's so late. You have had your dinner, but I haven't yet. I'm hungry now, could you let me go home for dinner and I'll come tomorrow." Among them someone to her rant, "You can't even if you are hungry. You must tell us clearly where the property of your family is, or you can't go home this evening."

Xiaodong thought among the gold and silver jewelries in the iron canister which used to contain talcum powder below the big chest, most were left by her father. And her mother was frugal, putting them in her big chest together with all her savings, let alone use them. Neither she nor her mother had ever done anything illegal, so she would not easily tell them so that they might take the jewelries away. She decided to keep silent. The peoples then went downstairs to have midnight snack, but she was too hungry to move… Just after 12 o'clock, these cadres became so furious and violent. They asked Xiaodong to stand up and not to doze off, without regard to her murmuring, "I'm hungry. I'm thirsty…" But Xiaodong refused to say anything about the property. Zhao Fusheng, at last, forced her, "Your father whose last name is Jiang is an officer of Kuomintang. And Chiang Kai-shek's hometown is somewhere in Jiangsu and

and go to confiscate the property of her family first." His words reminded Chang Wanmin; he opened the brief of drawing one of the blanks "the search warrant" taken from the public security bureau from his brief. He folded the license to make the marking words "the search warrant" outside and said to them, "It is not filled and sealed yet but reporting to the head of the bureau for approval is a complex process. But if we have these two words and I'm an employee at the public security bureau, so the Qiu's dare not protest." Zhao said, "We are contributing to the exchequer. So, is there anything wrong with that? It's impossible." He turned to close and lock the door, leaving Xiaodong alone in the room. Those people thought it was time for rendering meritorious services, so no one opposed. After they went downstairs, Xiaodong of crouched at the corner and lifted her eyes at the roof with a blank and powerless look at a loss…

Under the dark and dim sky in the night, By the faint light of a large flashlight, under the flickering and ghostly blinking streetlights, the five of them rushed towards walk with big strides Qiu's house. Beside the huge locust tree after they passed the turning point of the lane, Wang Huijun pointed to Qiu's house with his finger and said to Chang Wanmin, "Look, the Qius live inside that gate with two big bronze doorbells in front." In the darkness, the two doorbells, each of which had a diameter of about 20 centimeters still gave out shining radiance, serving as a foil to the wealthy host of the family.

Feng said with jealousy and hate, "It is rare to see such a splendid house in such a dilapidated lane, so he who could afford this house must be quite rich. Thus, don't leave until we get something valuable." Chang said full of hope, "Qiu Xiaodong has told us that there is property in the box in her room." With this, they reached the steps outside the gate. Chang could not help slapping furiously the bronze rings of the doorbells. And the clear and irregular sound broke the silence of the scaring night and passed onto the room of the Qiu couple.

While worrying about Xiaodong in her shallow sleep, Shao was woken up by the rude noise. Suddenly she realized that something she had been worried about would really happen. She pushed husband and immediately went out of bed before talking to him. She walked out via the back door through which she could reach the backyard, turned right, passed through the door of the small room, and turned right again into Xiaodong's room. When Xiaodong was in her college years in Zhuzhou, Weiying lived in this room alone, and when Xiaodong lived in the small room when back home temporarily. After getting married and coming back from Zhuzhou, Weiying changed the room with her. Now Xiaodong's two sons had been asleep in bed in this room. Standing there anxiously, Dr. Shao glanced over that big orange camphor chest wood which was put at the bottom. Since no one came to help, she could not move the above two camphor chests by herself. With no alternative, she immediately returned to the backyard and wanted to call her husband to give her a hand. While passing the backyard, she darted a look at the windows of their neighbor Ms. Wu and thought shall I take out and put it in her house…? She was on good terms with Wu and thought she was honest and kind. However, it's too late!

Qiu Zhongyuan was also woken up by the unceasing noise on the gate. Opening his eyes, he found Shao was not beside him. But the doorbells were still being knocked… He climbed up from bed and took on his slippers before Shao came back to see what happened. He passed through the close male ward where only Juecong was sleeping because no patients just after the Spring Festival, and then walked towards the gate. Qiu thought that some patients might come to Shao for a visit, so he opened the gate without even asking. Nevertheless, as soon as the gate was opened, Secretary Zhao and several workers rushed in. Only Wang Huijun, with an exciting look, stayed at the gate, reluctant to enter. Pointing to Chang Wanmin, Zhao said to Qiu, "He's from the public security and now is going to search your house!" Hearing this, Qiu thought there was something wrong with his ears! Meanwhile, Chang waved "the search warrant" before his eyes, and the four of them burst into directly towards Qiu's couple room...

At that moment, Qiu Weiying was woken up by the noise of the doorbells and gate-opening sound. She thought that her sister might come back home till that time. Soon she, who was easy to sleep and to have dreams, fell asleep again. That night, she dreamed the following scene, she drew her younger brother Juecong by the hand and walked on the road towards Yuelu Mountain. When they reached the cross of Wuyi Road, it suddenly began to roar and passers were flustered to cover their eyes with their hands, but she was worried about Juecong. She was blurred by the floating dust of the furious wind and felt so painful that she could barely open her eyes, and thus she lost her way with tears falling. And the gale also made her more and more cold all over...

The next morning, Qiu Weiying woke up much earlier than usual. It turned out that she was woken up by the coldness. She did not know why the door was entirely open as it had been closed last night. She climbed up and put on her clothes quickly. While passing Xiaodong's room, she suddenly found: Oh, how come Sister Xiaodong hasn't come home by now? She had a sense of inauspiciousness. Then she walked to the middle of the living room which also served as a waiting room, looked at the round clock hung on the wall and found it was time for school.

Full of doubt and unease, she walked into her parents' room. On entering her parents' room, Weiying was stunned by what she saw, both of her parents had swelling eyes, but they continued crying and wiped tears with a pillow cover... Ever since Weiying was born, she had never seen her father weeping nor anyone crying with so much pain like her parents...

About one minute later, her father sighed full of indignation, "I always go to work on time and treated patients with my heart and soul. What crime did I commit so that they confiscate all the property I have earned so hard?" Her mother said in a miserable tone, "They are just bandits and robbers, who have no reason to argue with you." Without finishing her own words, she began to shed tears again…

Weiying had no idea as to how to cope with such an unexpected accident. She was so strongly infected that she could not help but feel a pang of sorrow that who felt grieved with tears welling from her eyes. Walking out of her parents' room, she thought it was not the right time to ask her parents what happened down to the earth, but she could guess that the terrible scene might be related with Chang Wanmin of the public security bureau and his search for her family's property. She looked up at the cloudy sky desperately, for she could not make it out what took place in her home as both of her parents were upright doctors who worked hard to treat patient's day and night. That was horrible. She did not know how to comfort them.

Realizing it was time for school, she went into the kitchen, and Aunt Liao said to her, "Today, your mother hasn't given me the money for vegetables. I'm afraid…" She stopped. Weiying hurried to soak some leftovers with hot water and had it with some salted vegetables. She had no courage to have another look at the pathetic scene in her parents' room, and therefore went to school after putting on her bag.

Sitting in the classroom, Weiying could not comprehend what the teacher was talking about and could hardly turn to the pages to which the teacher referred. In the noon, Weiying did not ask her parents for money for lunch and bought a cheap pancake near the school. The last lesson in the afternoon was scheduled for students themselves and she did not want to stay here anymore. So, she put on her bag and went home.

On the road back, she felt uneasy because she was not clear what happened. It was just so terrible. Why were her parents so sad? Her heart was covered with a black shadow.

Age of rapid change

Full of curiosity for the truth, Weiying walked into her parents' room. She had never seen her mother like that. As usual, when she came back, her mother was either talking gently with her patients or busy with something in the treating room. She walked directly into her parents' room, only to find her mother lying in the purplish red sofa and weeping and wiping at the same time.

Weiying sat down in the sofa and asked her mother, "What happened, mom? What made you cry unceasingly?" Shao choked with sobs, "God! What kind of crime have I committed so that all our property has been confiscated?" She repeated these words over and over. At her mother's miserable cry, Weiying felt quite wretched on mother, with no idea as to how to comfort her…

A moment later, her father came back from work, unexpectedly he did not ride on his bicycle. Entering the room with a completely disheartened look, father said with anger after a moment of silence, "Last night, I opened the gate when hearing the noise. When they said they would search our house, I did not agree at first. They followed me, pushed me into this room, and forced me open my small chest or they would break it. or they would break it. I asked, 'why do you confiscate my property?' They are overbearing replied, 'your wife has opened a private clinic at home and is engaged in speculation and profiteering. Furthermore, we have the search warrant'. At that time, I argued, 'Embark on the capitalism road? It is you who have forced us to do so! Didn't you go here repeatedly to prompt my wife to open a clinic? And the business license issued by you is now hung on the wall in our living room.' After all, they intended to confiscate our money and treasures, so they could do whatever they wanted as long as they would achieve that purpose." He continued furiously, "I told them, 'Even if my wife has something to do with capitalism, I'm working in a public-owned hospital I have nothing to do with capitalism. Why would you confiscate my property?' After telling them so, I insisted, 'you can't confiscate my money and gold, silver, diamond ring! And property title certificate.' But they stickled, 'you are a couple, so what she does, of course, has something to do with you.' They still forced me to open my chest and after I unlocked it, they turned it over randomly and took away all valuable stuff, including my salary this month and not kept a little money for our to meal."

After a while, mother said, "They accused us that, "Now that you have several patients living in your house, your clinic is illegal of course. You bought a gold ring from someone, so you are selling what one has bought at a profit the gold. It is belonging to speculating and profiteering." I asked them angrily, 'an illegal underground clinic? I am not sneaking around, even the walls of the main street have the address of the clinic.

I have reported the registered temporary residences of all patients to the police station. Submit tax to the administrative committee of medical in proportion to my income. What's more, you have investigated to patients for many times at my house. When did you say it's not Ok? As for the gold ring, the man found me for money himself because his wife needed hospital fees at once. I did not earn his money and I said that he could redeem it at the original price at any time. So how could you call that speculation and profiteering?' But they refused to say anything reasonable with you. What they did was actually plundering." After these words, Shao began to weep again, "They are bandit, bullies!" She shouted herself hoarse... Weiying had never saw her father painful in the, but now he put his hands his and said to Shao, "Don't cry any more. These things have been taken, it's no use crying. What could we do when they came here to rob us of our property?!" As soon as he finished, he could not stop his tears from falling... His wife said pathetically, "Later, they went to the small room and confiscating valuable things in the middle of the night without giving us a receipt. Who knows whether they have got anything into their own pockets conceal?!

During the day today, Peng Guangxian from the committee came to my house, she gave me some receipts for the confiscated items.

are a couple, so what she does, of course, has something to do with you.' They still forced me to open my chest and after I unlocked it, they turned it over randomly and took away all valuable stuff, including my salary this month and not kept a little money for our to meal."

After a while, mother said, "They accused us that, "Now that you have several patients living in your house, your clinic is illegal of course. You bought a gold ring from someone, so you are selling what one has bought at a profit the gold. It is belonging to speculating and profiteering." I asked them angrily, 'an illegal underground clinic? I am not sneaking around, even the walls of the main street have the address of the clinic.

I have reported the registered temporary residences of all patients to the police station. Submit tax to the administrative committee of medical in proportion to my income. What's more, you have investigated to patients for many times at my house. When did you say it's not Ok? As for the gold ring, the man found me for money himself because his wife needed hospital fees at once. I did not earn his money and I said that he could redeem it at the original price at any time. So how could you call that speculation and profiteering?' But they refused to say anything reasonable with you. What they did was actually plundering." After these words, Shao began to weep again, "They are bandit, bullies!" She shouted herself hoarse… Weiying had never saw her father painful in the, but now he put his hands his and said to Shao, "Don't cry any more. These things have been taken, it's no use crying. What could we do when they came here to rob us of our property?!" As soon as he finished, he could not stop his tears from falling… His wife said pathetically, "Later, they went to the small room and confiscating valuable things in the middle of the night without giving us a receipt. Who knows whether they have got anything into their own pockets conceal?!

During the day today, Peng Guangxian from the committee came to my house, she gave me some receipts for the confiscated items.

Age of rapid change

Full of curiosity for the truth, Weiying walked into her parents' room. She had never seen her mother like that. As usual, when she came back, her mother was either talking gently with her patients or busy with something in the treating room. She walked directly into her parents' room, only to find her mother lying in the purplish red sofa and weeping and wiping at the same time.

Weiying sat down in the sofa and asked her mother, "What happened, mom? What made you cry unceasingly?" Shao choked with sobs, "God! What kind of crime have I committed so that all our property has been confiscated?" She repeated these words over and over. At her mother's miserable cry, Weiying felt quite wretched on mother, with no idea as to how to comfort her…

A moment later, her father came back from work, unexpectedly he did not ride on his bicycle. Entering the room with a completely disheartened look, father said with anger after a moment of silence, "Last night, I opened the gate when hearing the noise. When they said they would search our house, I did not agree at first. They followed me, pushed me into this room, and forced me open my small chest or they would break it. or they would break it. I asked, 'why do you confiscate my property?' They are overbearing replied, 'your wife has opened a private clinic at home and is engaged in speculation and profiteering. Furthermore, we have the search warrant'. At that time, I argued, 'Embark on the capitalism road? It is you who have forced us to do so! Didn't you go here repeatedly to prompt my wife to open a clinic? And the business license issued by you is now hung on the wall in our living room.' After all, they intended to confiscate our money and treasures, so they could do whatever they wanted as long as they would achieve that purpose." He continued furiously, "I told them, 'Even if my wife has something to do with capitalism, I'm working in a public-owned hospital I have nothing to do with capitalism. Why would you confiscate my property?' After telling them so, I insisted, 'you can't confiscate my money and gold, silver, diamond ring! And property title certificate.' But they stickled, 'you

All these years, I have not checked these gold, silver and jewelries, and they did not let us refer to the list last night. I couldn't believe it: They took the stuff one handful after another and don't they put the gold and silver jewelry in their private pockets!?They said, 'we'll prepare a list and record the stuff and then freeze them up. After make the result than wait for our notification.' If so, why did they search our home in the midnight stealthily? And after that they said, 'Don't tell anyone this matter. If you do, you'll be accused of a more serious crime.' Your father and I were made so angry that we felt could never make head. How could we be clear regarding, how much we have of gold and silver treasure confiscated?"

Qiu Zhongyuan said sadly, "I could not risk one's life with the group ruffians confront, or our whole family will be in great trouble if someone was injured or dead of this." Looking at her father's indignant expression, Weiying knowing that he must have, suppressed his anger. She knew that her father had known something about Kung Fu; he took part in wrestling competitions and ordinary men were not his rivals. He was practicing Taiji and Qigong every morning for a long time. And Juecong thought that he had learned something from his father since his childhood. For example, once he wanted to check how much strength he had on his feet at six or seven years old, he kicked a pig running from a neighbor's home to death. And this incident nearly caused a big trouble.

Weiying asked her father with tremble and fear, "What have they confiscated from your chest?" father told her, "Besides the gold and silver jewelries, pearls and crystals in my chest, my Omega and your mother's Innage watches have all been taken away. Overall, all the cash, property, and savings we have made through our medical technique_have been confiscated. What's more, they did not even leave any money for our living. They came again before dawn and took my imported stainless-steel famous brand bicycle.

I snatched it with them and argued, 'I can't do without the bicycle for work.' They said instead, 'you can go by bus!' They finally took it away." Dr. Shao said angrily, "They threatened us not to tell it to anyone else, or we're committing a more serious crime. They are just crueler than bandits!"

Weiying thought for a while and told her parents regretfully, "Then there is no doubt that Chang Wanmin of the public security bureau came to my school and asked my head-teacher to let me go to the teacher's office. He required me to tell where your property is hiding. He also said, 'you should separate yourself from your parents.' I thought his words were just unfounded, and thus immediately satirized him, 'I thought the bureau needed me to help capture spies!' and then argued, 'I have never seen my parents' gold and silver jewelries and I don't know at all what kind of crime they have committed. What I know is that both are upright and honest doctors!'"

Shao asked, "Why didn't you tell us that yesterday afternoon?" Weiying replied, "you went out to cousin's home before I had the chance to say anything. And I thought the public security bureau made a mistake, so I did not take it quite seriously. When father came back, he had dinner and play the gramophone as happily as usual, or I would have considered hiding the small leather suitcase in the gap under the bathing pond in the courtyard. I don't know it contained so much property. I'm so regretful." Qiu said, "If you had done so, it would be just great! Our valuables property would not have been confiscated total all at once." Shao said, "How could a 15-year-old girl think so considerately? I think used to hide the stuff away, but you just scolded, 'what crime have you committed to hide them?' If Weiying did so, she had no idea how you would treat her after work. The children are afraid of you." Qiu after a moment of silence, continuing said, "I don't know your mother had put so many good silver and jewelries in the room of Xiaodong'! Xiaodong was lock up by the administrative committee of medical organizations and forced to tell all out. And we have no time to hide the stuff away. Even if the stuff is collected, she has already said it, and it will not work if we don't hand it over." Looking at the unexplained pain in her father's face, Weiying had no alternative but to sit beside her mother in silence. After a while, Shao said in desperation, "Could it do if Xiaodong did not tell them? She had got crazy by their torture. If she doesn't say anything, I'm afraid she will be forced to die by them! How can she live?" Speaking of here, she began to her tears again…

At this time, Weiying listened to her mother, she quickly ran to her sister's room. Quietly pushing open the door, she saw Xiaodong sleeping in bed tiredly. There were bruises on her pretty face and several parts of the skin on her cheeks and forehead were scraped and was covered with mercurochrome. Looking at her sister's dull expression, she thought of the time when Xiaodong brought her to see the performance while the former was in the Secondary Key Middle School of Changsha, though Xiaodong was only 150-odd centimeters, she was fluttered her hands vividly on the stage and conducted the chorus with great vigor, totally different from now. When Qiu Xiaodong opened her eyes weakly and saw Weiying looking at her quietly, she asked, "Who are you?" Weiying answered in a low voice, "I'm Weiying. Don't you recognize your sister?" Xiaodong opened her eyes wider, "Wo…". Weiying felt that she might have intended to say something but did not and fell asleep again.

She left and closed the door quietly, walked into her own room and hung her bag behind the door. Then she went to the toilet. While passing the kitchen, she looked inside. Aunt Liao said to her, "Now no one will call you 'Miss'. You have become the proletariat in the real sense! Your mother does not even have money buy for planned supply bean curd of this month. I must buy back a pile of the cheapest vegetable slices. And I'll go back to village to avoid increasing the burden for your family." Not knowing how to answer Liao, Weiying remained silent and a gloomy and forlorn sense for the current circumstance overwhelmed her.

The day after their house was searched, Weiying found a lot disappeared when she came back home from school. In her parents' room which was put near under the window on the side of the backyard and the big chest and camphorwood chest one in Xiaodong's room both disappeared. Before dinner, she asked her parents, "Were the in your room and the one in Xiaodong's room also confiscated?" Shao sighed, "When they came the second time today, they put all the imported goods, relatively valuable stuff and higher-quality clothes into the chests. They even take our daily necessities including the imported woolen blanket away and filled them in two push carts" Qiu said full of sorrow, "My woolen tunic suites and your mother's silk floss coat have also been taken away. They take whatever they want from our home. It is even more serious than fire and water disasters! They just want to move our whole house away. This evening they forced me to submit the property ownership certificate meanwhile. They said, 'we are just freezing up those properties temporarily.' But who knows what they are thinking about?!"

After a moment, mother told Weiying powerlessly, "In the morning after the confiscation of family property, I thought, our properties have all been confiscated by them in pre-dawn today, so why hasn't Xiaodong come back until now? Therefore, I went to the administrative committee of medical after they got to work, planning to call Xiaodong back home." As a result, I saw a crowd of people were standing near the grocery market on the Chang Zhi Road and was wondering what they were looking at and talking about. I walked towards them to give a look, oh my God! It turned out to be Xiaodong! She, with her hairs down in a mess, kneed on the ground like a lunatic, kowtowing to those surrounding her, murmuring 'Chairman Mao, I'm guilty. Chairman Mao---'. I hurried up to squat beside her and hold her, 'My Xiaodong. poor girl…' However, she dodged and shouted as if she did not know me, 'go! go away---!' I held her and cried, 'I'm your mother. I will not hurt you. Come with me; let's go home, OK.' Some warm-hearted people who were sad at this scene helped me to lift up Xiaodong who was covered with mud all over. And two of them accompanied us home. On the way back, they told me, 'after burning joss sticks in Yuquan Temple, we two saw her kneeing on the ground nearby, kowtowing and murmuring repeatedly, 'my father is not Chiang Kai-shek. Don't bully me! My father is not Chiang Kai-shek.' We knew that she must is deranged. 'Therefore, we said to her, 'Chiang Kai-shek has fled to Taiwan. Who said he was your father? No one bullies you. Shall we take you home?'

She wept continuously, 'you don't allow me to go home the night over. You forbid me to eat, to go to toilet. You locked me in the room. Now will you take me home. Go away! Away from me!' She was crying and shouting to exhaust herself. We have no alternative but to follow her. on the way, whenever seeing someone, she just murmured, 'Chairman Mao, I have committed crime---' Then we found that when she saw one who wore the badge of Chairman Mao, she would kowtow to him or her, as what you have seen just now. Does she behave like that before or because of the torture last night?' I am totally clear, Yuquan Temple is just across the street from the Medical Management Committee. So Xiaodong must be driven too crazy by them! There is no reason to argue. Though quite bitter in heart, I dare not say anything at will but to answer them, 'No, such a phenomenon has never happened to her.' I knew clearly, it was the result of what those 'beasts' have done."

Qiu Xiaodong was driven to insane by those people's exacting a confession though they had no "warrant of arrest" from their supervisor. She was starving, cold and was forbidden to sleep, and the sudden attack and torture on her spirit added to her burden. For the so-called are "awarded for the merits one has performed" and "contribution to the country", they, without superior approval and a legal "confiscation of family property license", rob the properties of the general public willfully during the midnight by abusing the authority of the Communist Party and the power they owned. Their conduct could equalize and even go beyond what bandits and robbers did, couldn't it? Because they were the minority who had made their way into the Communist Party, just like the "Gang of Four" later. If they were allowed into the party or even to have certain power, they must not only damage the public's trust in the party but also the economic benefits of victims and devastate their "political life"! What's more, the then carry out class route was, if one committed a crime, his or her whole family would suffer! Qiu Weiying felt her mother was pitiful because she was such an industrious and frugal woman! She would sew the silk banners presented by her patients as gifts into cotton-padded jackets for her daughters; she would cut some worn clothes into pieces of cloth, paint them with watery flour paste, put them on a thin board under the sunshine and made them into cloth shoes for the children to wear. Thus, her mother was so busy every day that she seldom saw her resting. Now however, all the properties her parents had saved through hard work were confiscated cruelly and ruthlessly overnight. Why had she been so thrifty? Frugality was an adorable quality which the general public should possess, but the older generation was so austere!

Qiu Weiying had further felt, all signs indicate that the "comer is not good", this is terrible! Not only had her parents been economical and industrious for their whole life; Especially conscientiously Serving patients and worrying about most of the patients recover one's health. But they of family property after they are taken away by the blank "the search warrant" this group of bandits show, they are likely to be accused of "trumped-up charge"? Under a social system that strictly implements the class line, this will also lead to endless disasters for the whole family! After she became the child of 21 kinds of people <see Appendix, 1. D>, she will also be shrouded in the shadow of no bright future for her life!

One day, introduced by friends, a patient went to Ms. Shao's clinic come with admiration, being refused politely by Doctor Shao. From then on, Doctor Shao was unwilling to treat new patients at home. When Qiu Weiying went back home after school dropping her backpack, she went to her mother's room silently and sat beside

Age of rapid change

all over. And two of them accompanied us home. On the way back, they told me, 'after burning joss sticks in Yuquan Temple, we two saw her kneeing on the ground nearby, kowtowing and murmuring repeatedly,' my father is not Chiang Kai-shek. Don't bully me! My father is not Chiang Kai-shek.' We knew that she must is deranged. 'Therefore, we said to her, 'Chiang Kai-shek has fled to Taiwan. Who said he was your father? No one bullies you. Shall we take you home?' She wept continuously, 'you don't allow me to go home the night over. You forbid me to eat, to go to toilet. You locked me in the room. Now will you take me home. Go away! Away from me?' She was crying and shouting to exhaust herself. We have no alternative but to follow her. on the way, whenever seeing someone, she just murmured, 'Chairman Mao, I have committed crime---' Then we found that when she saw one who wore the badge of Chairman Mao, she would kowtow to him or her, as what you have seen just now. Does she behave like that before or because of the torture last night? I am totally clear, Yuquan Temple is just across the street from the Medical Management Committee. So Xiaodong must be driven too crazy by them! There is no reason to argue. Though quite bitter in heart, I dare not say anything at will but to answer them, 'No, such a phenomenon has never happened to her.' I knew clearly, it was the result of what those 'beasts' have done."

Qiu Xiaodong was driven to insane by those people's exacting a confession though they had no "warrant of arrest" from their supervisor. She was starving, cold and was forbidden to sleep, and the sudden attack and torture on her spirit added to her burden. For the so-called are "awarded for the merits one has performed," and "contribution to the country", they, without superior approval and a legal "confiscation of family property license", rob the properties of the general public willfully during the midnight by abusing the authority of the Communist Party and the power they owned. Their conduct could equalize and even go beyond what bandits and robbers did, couldn't it? Because they were the minority who had made their

103

way into the Communist Party, just like the "Gang of Four" later. If they were allowed into the party or even to have certain power, they must not only damage the public's trust in the party but also the economic benefits of victims and devastate their "political life"! What's more, the then carry out class route was, if one committed a crime, his or her whole family would suffer! Qiu Weiying felt her mother was pitiful because she was such an industrious and frugal woman! She would sew the silk banners presented by her patients as gifts into cotton-padded jackets for her daughters; she would cut some worn clothes into pieces of cloth, paint them with watery flour paste, put them on a thin board under the sunshine and made them into cloth shoes for the children to wear. Thus, her mother was so busy every day that she seldom saw her resting. Now however, all the properties her parents had saved through hard work were confiscated cruelly and ruthlessly overnight. Why had she been so thrifty? Frugality was an adorable quality which the general public should possess, but the older generation was so austere!

Qiu Weiying had further felt, all signs indicate that the "comer is not good", this is terrible! Not only had her parents been economical and industrious for their whole life! Especially conscientiously Serving patients and worrying about most of the patients recover one's health. But they of family property after they are taken away by the blank "the search warrant", this group of bandits show, they are likely to be accused of "trumped-up charge"? Under a social system that strictly implements the class line, this will also lead to endless disasters for the whole family! After she became the child of 21 kinds of people <see Appendix, 1, D>, she will also be shrouded in the shadow of no bright future for her life!

One day, introduced by friends, a patient went to Ms. Shao's clinic come with admiration, being refused politely by Doctor Shao. From then on, Doctor Shao was unwilling to treat new patients at home. When Qiu Weiying went back home after school dropping her backpack, she went to her mother's room silently and sat beside her mother on the sofa. Lifting her head from depressing, mother glanced at her daughter and said, "ever since the confiscation of family property, your father realized that we had no money for food. So, when someone invited him to dinner, he nods to show agree. In the afternoon, I went to the Doctor Management Committee to ask for the living expenses. But they asked back, 'what kind of living expense is it? Although your property was confiscated, we never forbid you resort to we have never forbid you continue treating patients. So, you can treat patients at home.' As I said, now that it is illegal to run a private clinic at home, why should I continue to violate the law? "Doctor shao Finish talking uttered a deep sigh.

Qiu Weiying knew that her mother was weak in appearance but strong in disposition. Her mother usually mentioned that "You see, the tiger is dead, He fell to the ground also is awe-inspiring. To be a person should be like a person. 'I would rather die standing cannot kneeling survive. I will not go to these people of be more to request and say unnecessary words." Those government officials who would utilize their power at hand for their own good or even use the power for private revenge. It's vain to reason argue with them within an unsound social law system.

On the second day morning after the property was completely confiscated, the Qiu's family is became poor and wretched overnight. Under such circumstance, after search Qiu's house and confiscate Qiu's property, the Qiu family only have dry sweet potato, porridge, and homemade salted vegetables for dinner.

While having dinner, Doctor Shao spoke to Liao Dama, "if you want to leave, I won't persuade you to stay. Since I won't treat patients at home, I can handle the housework by myself. However, the salary I owe you cannot be paid until my husband got his salary. But I will pay you some extra money to buy gifts for your family." But Liao Dama hoped to leave as soon as possible, and she was unwilling to stay long. When Mr. Qiu went back and finished dinner, Qiu Weiying heard the conversation between her parents while Liao Dama washing the dishes in the kitchen.

Ms. Shao wished her husband to borrow some money from his colleagues. Mr. Qiu replied gloomily, "Some colleagues even wished me to lend them some money once they had difficulties. Considering that I had many kids, they never voiced their wish. So how could I borrow money from them? How could I explain to them? I get the highest salary in my hospital so that Wang Huijun was jealous and deliberately pick my mistakes. Therefore, I displeased Wang Huijun by constantly quarrelling with her. I heard that Doctor Management Committee once turned to Wang Huijun and Yan Liqiu to investigate me. Although they failed to pick my mistake in the hospital, they went to my hometown to collect my information. They asked my hometown to issue a birth certificate that I was a landlord's family, but the township cadres in my hometown refused and said, "A few years before liberation, Qiu Zhong yuan's mother was a widow and dragged a large group of children. How can it be a landlord? They want to punish me to death; they are of white-eyed wolves bite the hand that feeds! I was sure that the confiscation of family property of our property was supported by the evildoers in our hospital."

"It was all because you displeased your leaders at the meetings." Ms. Shao said. Mr. Qiu repined angrily, "Fuck, I invested and organized a hospital and hired her to be the leader, but she turned back persecution against me. She envied me about my relatively high than her salary so that she was often like to deliberately find my fault..." Ms. Qiu mentioned, "In my opinion, there were personal factors for sure. But since he was the leader, you had to succumb to her." Mr. Qiu said with resent, "if I could know her before, I wouldn't recommend her to be cleaner in the hospital and promote her to be the leader. Now she bullied me, her fucking"

Paused for a minute, Ms. Shao said to her husband and daughter, "one of my patients told me that she once heard Liao Dama talking with the members of the Doctor Management Committee, saying "many patients visited Doctor Shao, so she must have made a lot of money. I think the Medical Board heard this rumor must be uncomfortable. Also, I did not establish personal relationships with them. Suppose Liao Dama wants to leave, just let her go. Later, we should hire a casual laborer carefully. Since I won't treat patients at home anymore, after you get the salary this month, I'll get Damao, Xiaomao, and Juele home to look after you and the kids." Noticed that her husband is still annoyed about his leaders, Ms. Shao didn't mention money-borrowing issue again.

Several days later, Li Zhimeng, husband of Xiaodong, mailed the board fee of her family to solve the pressing need for the Family. Upon getting the salary, Ms. Shao paid Liao Dama off and let her leave immediately.

While the leaders of Doctor Management Committee and Residential Committee knew that Doctor Shao wouldn't treat patients anymore, they came and harped on the same thing to her, "you are specialized in medical care. Nevertheless, you didn't serve for our people. It's really kind of waste for you to stay at home doing nothing..." She argued with great again aversion, "As I said, now that it is illegal to run a private clinic at home, why should I continue to violate the law?"

Several days after she dealt with several old patients, Doctor Shao took Damao, Xiaomao, and Juele home from the nannies. Damao, Xiaomao, and Weiying was accommodated in female wards while Juele, Juecong lived in male wards next to their parents' bedroom and the living room was no more consulting room.

Qiu Zhongyuan and his wife still shared one room; Qiu Xiaodong and her three kids shared one. From then on, Doctor Shao and Xiaodong took care of her husband, the five children who were studying at school and Xiaodong's three children (two boys and one girl).

Although Doctor Shao's license to practice medicine remained valid and she was able to keep running the clinic, she firmly refused to carry on with the treatment patients at home in any case after that.

Under that circumstance, Doctor Shao's did the right thing. Otherwise, her family would be harried endlessly! Since then and not until ten years before the reform and opening, the private economy in china has long been under harder hit and discrimination.

After the commencing of the Great Culture Revolution, Liu and Deng were criticized in public.

Things originated from that, it was the vice chairman Liu Shaoqi of the country and his followers, Deng Xiaoping who advocated the individual economy in 1962 that made it be. At the same time, Liu Shaoqi met his waterloo in his career.

In January 1969, during the Great Culture Revolution, Liu Shaoqi was criticized as a "big traitor, big enemy agent and big worker thief" and had all his posts inside and outside the Party removed.

So, Shaoqi fell into depression after the setback. What's more horrible, Liu Shaoqi was suffered tortuously from a disease under an assumed name to death in kai Feng prison. Even his families were not informed his of the death.

Before the 1980, provided that the individual economy was regarded as the product of "capitalism line" leading by Liu Shaoqi and Deng Xiaopin, its development was hard in those times. "Individual economy" was recognized in August 1980, more than a year after Deng Xiaoping's after resumption of his post, when the Chinese government announced, "We should encourage and support the appropriate development of individual economy. All law-abiding individual workers should be respected in the society." However, the so-called working group in the Medicine Management Association broke into people's houses at night, illegally searched and confiscated their property. It in fact trampled the constitution and was a criminal act which infringed people's rights.

Sadly, at that time, advocators of "individual economy" who achieved prosperity through diligent work had been criticized and stricken down. Common people following "individual economy" were excluded from the protection of laws. Moreover, the then legal system was not sound at all, lawyers were not widespread, and people had little awareness of the concept of the rule of law.

Therefore, it provided convenience for those who didn't have professional ethics to abuse power given by the Communist Party and the people, damaging the Party's credibility and people's benefits. More unfortunately, under strict implementation of the "proletariat line", prospects of victims and their relatives were easily ruined by them…

CHAPTER 3

The golden age was ruined

3.1 The days' time of fix the earth

It was spring, 1965, and Qiu Weiying was in the second term of junior grade 3, the Qiu family was raided in the middle of the night by the "Changsha Medical Institution Management Committee" in cooperation with Chang Wanmin of the city's Public Security Bureau, who presented a "blank raid warrant" to search Qiu Weiying's home and confiscated her parents' property.

It was only three or four months before her graduation. The teacher-in-charge of a class never again mentioned the previous intention of school authority to send her to teacher's university. She herself never asked about it anymore. Instead, the teacher continuously reminded her of "having one red heart and two different prepare". For it was possible that she be dispatched to the countryside to be reeducated by the middle, lower and poor peasants.

As a matter of fact, Chairman Mao had already put forward in 1955, as a proposal to tackle the problem of the jobless urban youth, that "The rural region is a large platform for the young to make huge differences." <See App,1. G> Seldom had it been advocated to the urban students before; however, one could tell the idea was given

CHAPTER 3

The golden age was ruined

3.1 The days' time of fix the earth

It was spring, 1965, and Qiu Weiying was in the second term of junior grade 3, the Qiu family was raided in the middle of the night by the "Changsha Medical Institution Management Committee" in cooperation with Chang Wanmin of the city's Public Security Bureau, who presented a "blank raid warrant" to search Qiu Weiying's home and confiscated her parents' property.

It was only three or four months before her graduation. The teacher-in-charge of a class never again mentioned the previous intention of school authority to send her to teacher's university. She herself never asked about it anymore. Instead, the teacher continuously reminded her of "having one red heart and two different prepare". For it was possible that she be dispatched to the countryside to be reeducated by the middle, lower and poor peasants.

As a matter of fact, Chairman Mao had already put forward in 1955, as a proposal to tackle the problem of the jobless urban youth, that "The rural region is a large platform for the young to make huge differences." <See App,1. G> Seldom had it been advocated to the urban students before; however, one could tell the idea was given system was not sound at all, lawyers were not widespread, and people had little awareness of the concept of the rule of law.

Therefore, it provided convenience for those who didn't have professional ethics to abuse power given by the Communist Party and the people, damaging the Party's credibility and people's benefits. More unfortunately, under strict implementation of the "proletariat line", prospects of victims and their relatives were easily ruined by them…

more and more attention to through a series of governmental plans and policies, which were designed to solve the rapid growth of urban population, backwardness of domestic economy and inefficiency in settling the millions of unemployed young students and citizens. Such ideological education had been imparted to Qiu Weiying ever since she was admitted to this key middle school, for example, "The frontline before liberation was Yan'an, and now the frontline is the countryside", and "A geed man should have lofty aspirations", and so on. Those educated youth s who had already gone to the mountainous areas and the countryside, such as Dong Jiageng and Xing Yanzi, were the role models for the graduates. Qiu Weiying used to think she was so young that she needed to seek further education to become a person of value. Meanwhile, her young age and inadequate no social experience deterred her from leaving her parents and go to the countryside and settle in the communes. What's more, life in the rural area had nothing to do with the future she planned for herself.

But later, the teacher's theories about "revolution" began to take on their effects on her. She began to form a vague idea that her family was proved rich in the confiscation of family property, and "rich" somehow equaled "guilty". She was obliged to go to the countryside to be reeducated by the lower-middle and poor peasants, to eat with them, live with them and work with them, and totally wash herself of the bourgeois ideologies that she was born with. In order to construct the new socialist countryside depicted as "two-story houses equipped with electricity bulbs and telephones", Qiu answered the Party's call and signed up for the "Down to the Countryside" motion the day before her graduation. The teacher-in-charge set her as an example, and said to the whole class, "Qiu Weiying's father has a very high salary. She could have lived a cozy life at home. But now, she gives the coziness up to response the call of our Party, to go into the mountainous areas and the countryside, and to be reeducated by the people there and exercised by labor. My dear students, you should really learn from her!" Hence, her "revolutionary act" influenced seven or eight of her classmates to sign up for the movement.

Even though she still took her high school entrance examination after graduation, she soon found out that year was the "entrance examination" become just a name.! The past score "admission line" has been thrown to the sky!

In fact, this was a complete implementation of the class line. Premier Zhou once replied in private: "Revolution is to cut off the grass and eliminate the roots." Punished the parents of these children will also implicate these unfortunate children in losing their future. Although these children often in their studies school records do better than they!

At that time, the Cultural Revolution did not officially start, and neither did the Down to the Countryside Motion of the educated youth s swept across the country as it later did. As a matter of fact, those who got to continue their education are from families of lower-middle and poor peasants, laborers and revolutionary leaders. Those so-called family origins bad class the children of so-called "twenty-one kinds of people" and have of family problems became principal force of the down-to-the-countryside educated youths.

It was one day at noon, during the turning of fall in 1965. Qiu Weiying, who was of the same age as new China, got the notification paper from her school by the front door of her house. She was to be dispatched to the mountainous area in Chen County, Hunan. Holding the notification paper in her hand, she entered her parents' bedroom and told the news to her mother, who had just gone to bed and was about to take her napping. Mother took over the notification paper by her trembling hands and read it twice in silence. Then suddenly the notification paper fell on the quilt. She held Weiying in her arms and burst into silent tears. She seemed to have thousands of words to utter, but none of them could break out of her lips. Tears welled up in her eyes and ran down her face.

Weiying supposed her mother was sad and stagnant, with hidden opinions, her family had already been deprived of all the valued – but the economic loss could be not put aside now – same time now the future of her children was ruined, no college, down to the countryside. (At that time, people in the countryside were not only poorer than those in the cities, but also had no food rationing. What's worse, they could not commute by means of transportation between one's the countryside and one's city freely among cities. If they wanted to leave the village for a while, they had to bring certificates with them.)

However, "Go to up the mountains and down to the Countryside" was a noble policy put forward by the Party; no one dared to oppose that in public; not to mention that Qiu's a family courage and confidence were greatly frustrated after the confiscation of family property, and that she had "a shameful political question". She had can't go to choose but to live with the unjust arrangement of fate, and to get everything prepared for her daughter's go and work in rural areas.

The day came when educated youths were to set out. The train station at Wuyi Road, which was near downtown, was crowded by so many young students and their family and friends, that it was almost impossible to penetrate through them. It was a gloomy day, but the train station was in heated atmosphere, decorated with red banners of slogans, such as "farewell educated youth go and work in rural areas "; "Construct the socialist new countryside"; "A good son and a good daughter have lofty aspirations "and other similar red banners.

Qiu Weiying's mother is at the scene say goodbye reluctantly, she is speechless. Everywhere there were crowds of people banging drums. Drums, gongs were beating loudly and sending off young students and their families with big red flowers on their chests. The young and innocent faces radiated with the glow of youth, and complicated feelings, unwillingness to leave their hometown, confusion about their future, pride of their contribution to the socialist new countryside… Qiu Weiying stood by her mother together on the platform for a while.

Qiu Weiying's mother is at the scene say goodbye reluctantly speechless. Person in charge is the students were divided into groups according to their destination and then were led on trains. The train slowly set in motion in gongs and drums and the bustle.

Qiu Weiying extended her neck and waved to her mother, who looked melancholy on the platform. Qiu Weiying upon seeing mother wiping the corners of her eyes with a handkerchief, sorrow took control of her. Qiu Weiying involuntarily tears welled up… The train speeding up in its clatters. Mother and the city of Changsha where she had spent sixteen years, soon fade away from her horizon…

The night was approaching, and the vision out of the window started to grow obscure. To Qiu Weiying's surprise, there was a girl named Xie Chun on the train. She used to be the mathematics class prefect of their class and ranked top in almost every total examination result. It was said that her biological father committed suicide to escape punishment because he was beaten as a rightist. <See App 1. D)>

But her stepfather was a primary school principal and her mother a teacher. Qiu Weiying was totally aware that it was the "family problem" that stopped Xie Chun from furthering her education.

She turned her eyes to the seat in face-to- face of her, and saw a quiet, gentle girl of her age looking back. Qiu started a conversation, "I think I saw you pass by me at the station. But I didn't see your family." She answered, "My parents went abroad when I was little. I was brought up by grandma. Most of my relatives are abroad, and grandma is too old to see me off." It suddenly dawned on Qiu that this smart girl's "oversea relations" got in the way of her education, for at that time, having foreign relatives and acquaintances equaled contacting spies. The country doesn't trust you and no bright future.

So, Qiu Weiying shut herself up and asked no more. Exhausted, she slept for a few hours seated. Finally, the train brought the choiceless but passionate young students to their destination – Chenzhou.

Qiu, along with other young students who were also dispatched to Chenzhou, carried their pieces of luggage off the train, and then followed the guide teacher out of the station. It was pitch dark outside; only a few unstable streetlights were blinking their slip sleepy eyes to these young students, as if playing jokes on them... The teachers who came along shouted on the way, "Watch out! Don't fall behind! We have neither adequate light nor cars to pick us up. It will be of great trouble if anyone falls behind..." Hearing the words, some students turned on their flashlights.

Once the group arrived at the square outside the station, a man and woman, who were both local officials, turned up to lead the way to the guesthouse of the Party Committee of Chen County. Everybody signed up and was given rooms to rest. The girls gathered and found out that they were all graduates of the year from No. Four Middle School of Changsha. (a key middle school for girls) They got themselves washed up and then attended a welcome ceremony, had a meal, and stayed for a couple of hours in the hotel. Then, the head of Siqing Water Reservoir management office, Li Bingxiao, came along with a peasant to pick them and the boys from No. Three Middle School of Changsha (a key middle school for boys) up. Altogether there were a dozen or so educated youth s to go to "fix the earth" in the mountains of Siqing Water Reservoir of Chen County.

They took a coach to the station at Huatang commune, Chen County. Some peasants came and helped get their luggage to the mountains. Hence, the educated youth s travelled easy and arrived at the reservoir within the day. It was located at the shoulder of a mountain, surrounded by endless up-and-downs and thick forests. Had there been not the reservoir, the veil of this mysterious place could never have been revealed to the be in the public eye.

According to Li, Siqing Reservoir was built when Siqing work team of the Party Committee of Hunan was paying their examining visit to Chen County. A stone curve of twenty-centimeter thick, thirty to forty-centimeter width and about a-hundred-centimeter length was fixed to the stone bridge over the reservoir, facing one side of the roof of the operational room where the floodgate control was. The name was curved into marble and colored by red paint, written by the top official at that time, Tan Zhenlin (Senior General of the Chinese People's Liberation Army, native of Youxian, Hunan). It could be seen clearly even from a kilometer away. Outside the operational room was a cement bridge, connecting the embankment and a 150-square-meters-or-so cement ground. Right in front of the reservoir was the great dam of Siqing Reservoir, which paralleled with the upper operational bridge that stretched to the middle of the reservoir. There was a line of newly built houses in front of the management office, directly facing the cement ground. The houses, the cement ground, the operational bridge and room were the only artificial works at the shoulder of the mountain, and made an outstanding scene in the unfrequented place along with a row of staff residence by the mountains. The square house in the center of the line of new buildings was the office of Li and the accountant; to the left of which were two rooms, one for the male educated youth s, and the other for the rest single male employees. There was a rectangle room to the left of the management office, which functioned as the boardroom. Close to the window of the boardroom was the canteen in the corner. Behind the boardroom and not far from the canteen were two connected cement wells, the upper one supplied drinking water; the lower was for daily use and could be collected by basins and buckets. They were not very deep, but the water was clean and fresh, for it was spring water in the mountain. The water kept flowing to the wells all year round, providing the employees with an abundant water resource. As for the back mountain, where the spring originated, it was rarely visited. Apart from the splashing of the spring water, the silence in the back of the mountain is frightening. Trees, wildflowers and grass grew everywhere. There was not even a narrow meandering footpath, not to mention buildings or residence. Right to the office was the storehouse for food.

The golden age was ruined

Right of the management office was another large rectangle house for Qiu Weiying and the other four femaleeducated youth s. Each of them was given a wooden board bed and a tiny space to lay their suit. Under the left window by the door was an unpainted white desk. Looking out of the window, one could see a comparatively even path leading to the staff residence, of several minutes of walk away. Pedestrians there needed not worry about traffic danger, for there was no traffic at all. Qiu Weiying had never seen any vehicle on the so-called driveway – and no vehicle was needed at that time. About seven families, including directors general Li and his wife, lived in the one-story staff dormitory standing by the driveway, its front door facing the road and back door the excavated mountain feet. By the entrance of the driveway were two public lavatories for male and female staff respectively, build by wooden board and sewali. At the joint of the cement ground and one side of the dam was a flight of stone steps leading down a slope. Left of the slope, to the edge of the cement ground against the feet of the mountain, was a ditch of ten kilometers or so, leading the water from the reservoir all year round to the hundreds of square meters of farmland. Not far from the right of the slope was a short and narrow path to the reservoir's bullpen. In which the young and old buffalos and scalper were kept in numbers of about eight or nine.

The educated youth s spent their first days at the reservoir reclaiming the wasteland near the barn with the peasant workers. Growing up in the city, Qiu Weiying had barely done any housework before; She heaviest work experience used to be queuing up in line for her family ration of vegetables.

Now every time when she held the pickaxe or harrow high to dig into the unimaginably tough land under her feet, she felt like she was going through some sort of penalty, her arms ache from the rebound, and the flesh between her thumb and index finger was almost torn. It was impossible to reclaim the virgin land if she did not gather every bit of her strength; usually she could only leave a shallow trait or a few tiny pits on it. Blisters appeared on the hands of everybody, and the situation only got better when they got thick callus instead. Qiu had particularly tender skin, and consequently suffered endlessly from the emerging and breaking of the blisters. She wondered what would become of her hands if she had not brought enough mercurochrome and gentian violet with her. After some days the skin thickened, and she started feeling better. With the guidance of a few peasants, they made it at last and had a large farmland by the barn, where they planted vegetables or raised fish and they grew sweet potatoes, jicamas, peanuts and cotton.

The task that terrified Qiu the most was transplanting rice seedlings in the field, when her shanks were under water, and leeches would stick on them from time to time if she was not cautious enough. Leeches would cling their soft bodies to human skin, prick it with their heads and feast on the blood. Whenever Qiu saw a leech moving towards her, she would lurch in panic to the dam. However, she was not allowed to escape such labor. When it comes her turn to work in the paddy field, she had no choice but to gather her courage and step into it and planting seedlings with fingertips.

One night, she thought to herself in bed, "My household register in the city has been cancelled. Am I bonded with such labor forever? In what way does such work contribute to the mankind? Can it save two-thirds of thebe downtrodden people of the world?" She couldn't figure out what her future would turn out to be. As a result, she buried herself in quilts and had a good cry…

However, there were different kinds of job in the reservoir. They also undertook tasks such as carrying mud to build the fishpond, dredging up the grass down the ditch to feed the fish, mowing in the mountains and carry the grass back for fish or lumbering in the forest, storing the wood or sending them to the canteen to make fire. There was a rusty iron stick fastened to a large wooden pole in the center of the cement ground. Every morning someone beat it, and upon hearing the sound, the educated youth s should get up immediately. They hasted to get themselves tidied up and all ran to the cement ground in time for morning exercises, moving their bodies to the rhythm along with the staff. The exercises were introduced by two ex-serviceman thirty-something veterans. At first it was taken seriously, but as the labor got heavier, they became sluggish. At last, the morning exercises were totally abandoned.

At times, the educated youths would spare some time and climb over a mountain to the town of Baohe, which was about 2 kilometers away, where the market was held. There they could use the money sent from their families to buy some necessities, snacks, meat, sweets, vegetables or potherb like bamboo shoots. At that time, food pressure was a bit lessened than before. Sometimes, Qiu saw some Miao women wearing beautiful silver bracelets and hand-sew clothes with gorgeous patterns on them. They sold herbs and invigorators. But few people came to buy their merchandise, for the top concern at that time was merely to keep oneself fed. However, life could be hard without the fair, for only rice and sweet potatoes were guaranteed at the reservoir canteen. Sometimes they went without any dishes except for some chili peppers. Even though Qiu grew up in Changsha, spicy food did not agree with her; especially the tiny, needle headed pepper that could got her insane, but it was the only food to go with rice. They did not have vegetables, and meat was rare. But in summer, opportunities came when they open the floodgate for irrigation. They would fix a large fishing net by the brake, and then rolled up their pants to step in the water and collect the fish. The fish they caught were sold to bring revenue to the reservoir. They could use cash or meal coupons to buy some fresh fish at market price. So, occasionally they got to experience the fun of idyllic life, If only you could settle down and not think about your future.

As time went by, head Li of the reservoir realized that the educated youths knew little about how things worked in the countryside and lacked adequate knowledge about agriculture. In order to enhance production, he matched each educated youth in pair with an experienced employee as master to take care of the problems in production and life. The employees did not complain, but secretly they were somewhat unhappy. Once Qiu Weiying heard an employee murmuring by her in the boardroom, "Those farm works are no problem for our own kids. But the city young student, they came here straightly after graduation. They can't even manage to fit in the life here, not to mention the farm works! They are only occupying our land, wasting our time and energy! Where are we going to settle our own children when they grow up?" He was speaking in a low voice, so Li did not hear him. Even if he had, he would have pretended hearing nothing, for Down to the Countryside Motion was not a decision of his own, but a national policy.

Qiu's master was a middle-aged woman named Li Jinyu. She was nice to Qiu. She lived in the staff dormitory with his husband, who was also a peasant at the reservoir. They did not have children.

Later, head Li divided the educated youth s and his employees into agricultural, fishing and water group. Qiu was in the fish group. There were three masters in her group, all males. One of them had his wife in the group also. It was a lady with a golden tooth, who always had a feminine smile on her face. She liked chatting with Qiu. There was another young, educated youth in her group, the shortest and youngest (one year younger than Qiu) boy among the educated youth s. He was a quick-minded, joking kind of person who would even make jokes about Qiu. It seemed that he had no sorrow at all. Their task was to lead water to the reclaimed land to get orderly fishponds. Instead of putting large fish in, they raised tadpole-sized fish fry only. They would coop the fish fry up with china spoons when they grew to one or two centimeters, then, according to the kind and size, put them into basins of 80-centimeter diameter with smaller rim and larger bottom. Using a shoulder pole and four ropes made from bamboo, the masters would bring the fish fry to the market to sell.

Then, manager Li reset the base work points. Work points were gained through everyday hard work. Their wage was not paid by month; instead, at the end of a year, their work points would be calculated, and their salaries would be given accordingly. The more points one gets, the more money he earns. Qiu Weiying has a big loss, because of for her base point was changed from 5 to 3 while other girls all got 5 or 6. There was a girl named Yang Aizhen, who was the most productive and had 7 points. Boys usually got 7 or 8. Zhou Gong Jian, the boy in her team was given 5. Being friends with Li, Xie Chun was assigned to the Canteen, with literally no labor and a base point of 6. Zhu Daji, a tall young man with the greatest strength and productivity among the boy, was given 10, the same as the local peasants. Sie, the chef, defended Qiu against the injustice, "No matter how physically weak she is, there's no way she gets only half the points of the others. How can she manage to live with such few points?" Li answered, "Why, she won't be starved anyway! It is said that her father has a salary that is several times more than others!" Sie was not convinced, "She's in the countryside now. No matter how rich her parents are, they could not possibly support her for her whole life!" He seemed indignant after the words.

However, Li was the decision maker, and no one could reverse his mind. Qiu was silent about what was happening. She secretly admitted she was not as competitive, especially on rainy days, when she was so afraid of falling that she almost couldn't walk on the muddy road. The incidents her family went through also slackened her pursuit of money, the money her parents got had perished overnight! In the mind of young Weiying, she kept thinking, can money be the most important thing in this world? Isn't there anything else of greater value? At present, all she cared about was her future.

They were given a few days' break during the Spring Festival in 1966. Some of the educated youth s gathered in the cement ground and used a huge steelyard with a sliding weight attached to weigh themselves. Xie Chun held tight to the string to which a hook was fastened, bending her knees into a 90-degree angle. Sharing the same height with Qiu, her weight was sixty kilograms, about 10 kg heavier than Qiu Weiying, which was to everybody's surprise. She laughed and said half-jokingly, "You grow faster than pigs!" Instead of being angry, Xie smiled. Qiu remembered seeing her eat a lot of boiled sweet potatoes in the canteen and seemed to enjoy a lot no matter if they were hot or cold. So, she said, "She ate too much sweet potatoes!" Sweet potatoes contain much starch and sugar, directly contributing to weight. Qiu continued, "The educated youth son Huatang Farm do not have enough food to eat. They don't have so many sweet potatoes, and definitely have no way to gain weight." So, someone proposed, "Why don't we go and have a visit sometime?" Qiu said, "Let's make it tomorrow. They are also on holiday recently. I know someone there." The others agreed immediately, "Deal! Let's go while the weather's well so we won't be troubled by road condition. It'll be nice to look at Huatang."

There had not been snow or rain for some days, so it was easy for them to travel. But the cold wind blew so heavily that they were almost frozen. Yang Aizhen, Xie Chun, Li Xiaosi and Qiu Weiying had to quicken their steps to keep their bodies warm. When going by the toll station for the water rent in Huatang region (a site affiliated to Siqing Reservoir), which was at the foot of the mountain where the reservoir was, Qiu said to the chef there, "Master Xia, would you please cook the meal for us? We are going to visit our classmates on the farm and will return for lunch." Then they each had a glass of water and continued their way.

It was their first visit to Huatang Farm, but they had been to the marketin Huatang Commune, Chen County, a few times. It was five kilometers away from the reservoir, more than twice the distance of that to Baohe, so they didn't go there a lot.

Both Farm No.1 and 2 of Huatang were near the marketand the community hospital. Walking along the ditch to the feet of the mountain, they arrived at the farms, where hundreds ofeducated youth s from Changsha lived and worked. The farms were also five kilometers away from the reservoir. The educated youth s was from than Qiu Weiying, which was to everybody's surprise. She laughed and said half-jokingly, "You grow faster than pigs!" Instead of being angry, Xie smiled. Qiu remembered seeing her eat a lot of boiled sweet potatoes in the canteen and seemed to enjoy a lot no matter if they were hot or cold. So, she said, "She ate too much sweet potatoes!" Sweet potatoes contain much starch and sugar, directly contributing to weight. Qiu continued, "The educated youth son Huatang Farm do not have enough food to eat. They don't have so many sweet potatoes, and definitely have no way to gain weight." So, someone proposed, "Why don't we go and have a visit sometime?" Qiu said, "Let's make it tomorrow. They are also on holiday recently. I know someone there." The others agreed immediately, "Deal! Let's go while the weather's well so we won't be troubled by road condition. It'll be nice to look at Huatang."

There had not been snow or rain for some days, so it was easy for them to travel. But the cold wind blew so heavily that they were almost frozen. Yang Aizhen, Xie Chun, Li Xiaosi and Qiu Weiying had to quicken their steps to keep their bodies warm. When going by the toll station for the water rent in Huatang region (a site affiliated to Siqing Reservoir), which was at the foot of the mountain where the reservoir was, Qiu said to the chef there, "Master Xia, would you please cook the meal for us? We are going to visit our classmates on the farm and will return for lunch." Then they each had a glass of water and continued their way.

It was their first visit to Huatang Farm, but they had been to the marketin Huatang Commune, Chen County, a few times. It was five kilometers away from the reservoir, more than twice the distance of that to Baohe, so they didn't go there a lot.

Both Farm No.1 and 2 of Huatang were near the marketand the community hospital. Walking along the ditch to the feet of the mountain, they arrived at the farms, where hundreds ofeducated youth s from Changsha lived and worked. The farms were also five kilometers away from the reservoir. The educated youth s was from month; instead, at the end of a year, their work points would be calculated, and their salaries would be given accordingly. The more points one gets, the more money he earns. Qiu Weiying has a big loss, because of for her base point was changed from 5 to 3 while other girls all got 5 or 6. There was a girl named Yang Aizhen, who was the most productive and had 7 points. Boys usually got 7 or 8. Zhou Gong Jian, the boy in her team was given 5. Being friends with Li, Xie Chun was assigned to the Canteen, with literally no labor and a base point of 6. Zhu Daji, a tall young man with the greatest strength and productivity among the boy, was given 10, the same as the local peasants. Sie, the chef, defended Qiu against the injustice, "No matter how physically weak she is, there's no way she gets only half the points of the others. How can she manage to live with such few points?" Li answered, "Why, she won't be starved anyway! It is said that her father has a salary that is several times more than others!" Sie was not convinced, "She's in the countryside now. No matter how rich her parents are, they could not possibly support her for her whole life!" He seemed indignant after the words.

However, Li was the decision maker, and no one could reverse his mind. Qiu was silent about what was happening. She secretly admitted she was not as competitive, especially on rainy days, when she was so afraid of falling that she almost couldn't walk on the muddy road. The incidents her family went through also slackened her pursuit of money, the money her parents got had perished overnight! In the mind of young Weiying, she kept thinking, can money be the most important thing in this world? Isn't there anything else of greater value? At present, all she cared about was her future.

They were given a few days' break during the Spring Festival in 1966. Some of the educated youth s gathered in the cement ground and used a huge steelyard with a sliding weight attached to weigh themselves. Xie Chun held tight to the string to which a hook was fastened, bending her knees into a 90-degree angle. Sharing the same height with Qiu, her weight was sixty kilograms, about 10 kg heavier

The golden age was ruined

different schools in Changsha, but those from No. Four Middle School for Girls were the largest in number. Upon arrival at the simple, or rather, vacant farm, the girls directly entered the place where Qiu Weiying's friends and her classmates lived. It was even worse than the temporary residence in the construction sites nowadays, it was a large shed built by wooden boards and pillars, and bamboo pieces. Each shed contained dozens of educated youth s. Cracks were everywhere, even on the roof which let light in. The floor was uneven, tough soil.

Qiu asked a female educated youth who lowered her head to weave a sweater, "How can you manage to spend the winter in such a place?" She answered without stopping the work at hand, "We put two or three beds together and share the quilts when it gets too cold." Their single-sized wooden beds were probably purchased by the farm with the "settlement allowance". Qiu continued her questions, "How's the food here?" Another answered, "We have meat once a month. Any food given will do. When there is no vegetable, we add soy sauce to the rice." An educated youth beside the classmate interrupted, "You raise a lot of fish, don't you have fish?" Xie Chun said, "Fish and water are the major income of our reservoir, we don't raise them for food. But once or twice in autumn we can buy the fish with our own money." The educated youth said, "My parents don't have much money, and they had to raise my younger sisters and brothers, so they can't send me any money. I haven't even had dried or salted fish for a long while. How I envy you!"

Another educated youth sitting on the bed beside said, "My sister was dispatched to Jiang Yong. She lived on her own, collected her own firewood and cooked for herself. Sometimes when she couldn't get any firewood, she burned the leaves. The smoke brought her into tears and coughs. I spent like four days with her and could not stand it anymore. She is a high school graduate, but her household residence permit in the city was cancelled, so she cannot go back. A year later it brought her to the edge of breaking down, so she married the leader of her production team." Qiu said, "She is really combined with the poor, lower and middle peasants…" Qiu interrupted, "Many of the peasants are nice people. They do whatever their women tell them to."

Qiu turned to Chen Yi, who was contemplating beside her, "What kind of jobs do you do?" She answered, "Reclaiming the wasteland, carrying the pond mud, planting rice and vegetables…" Qiu asked, "Are you tiring?" Chen said, "Tiring? Definitely! But what choices do we have? We have family problems." Chen and Qiu are from the same grade in the same school. It was learnt by Qiu that Chen's father was a high navy officer of Kuomintang and had escaped to Taiwan or the US before the Communist Party came into power. No doubt Chen was the child of one of the "twenty-one kinds", just like Qiu. She could not further her education either.

It was lunch time on the farm. Chen Yi proposed, "Stay here for lunch!" Some educated youth s volunteered to borrow bowls for them. The girls told Chen Yi, "No, thanks. We have already ordered meals at the toll station. Just go get your meal, we'll stay for a while and then go back."

The educated youths sat together to share their meals and the self-made chili-radish. Qiu Weiying said, "How sweet! You share everything you have with each other in such tough situations. What close friendship must that be!"

Yu Mingchi, a girl of Qiu's age, answered, "It does take really great friendship. When I was in grade one in primary school, there were two classmates on very intimate terms who on very intimate terms as sisters. Later, one of them went move to a new house to another school and never came back. Before long, the other girl's father was transferred of work to Beijing, and her whole family had to move. Before she left, she came to school to deal with the procedures, with eyes puffed and red. Our teacher asked her, 'What's wrong? Did you cry?' She answered, 'I can never see my best friend again.' I wonder how they could love each other so much!" Qiu reflected on her words for a short while and asked, "Which primary school did you go?" She answered, "Pozi Street." Qiu was asked anxiously, "Oh! Was that girl named Zhang Tairan who moved to Beijing?" Yu

The golden age was ruined

answered curiously, "Yes. How did you know that?" Qiu said bitterly, "I was that best friend of hers who moved away. What a coincidence! But how come I don't remember you?" Yu said, "I did not go to Pozi Street Primary School until the second term of first grade. You had already left by that time, so we haven't met before. I've seen Zhang Tairan though, but not much. She was only there for a few days, and then left for Beijing."

Qiu was overwhelmed by sorrow and excitement. The conversation brought the friendly and innocent face of Zhang Tairan back to her memory... She thought to herself, Tairan must be in Beijing, while I was enrolled in the Down into the Countryside Movement, in this rural area of Chen County not far from Guangdong. Am I going to see her face again in this life? When can my days of fixing the earth come to an end?!

3.2 The cow herding girl

Before the confiscation of family property, Qiu Weiying had been enjoy a rich and comfortable lifestyle living in a family environment with closed doors and barely had any chance to be exposed to the society. Meanwhile, her personality was greatly influenced of her parents, she was never apt to fawn, nor was she an ass-kisser. She herself never had any opinion with her unjust distribution of low base points in Siqing Reservoir. It was Master Sie's disapproval that made Li feel uneasy. Consequently, he dispatched Qiu and a local girl who was two years younger to pasture the buffalos. Qiu thought it was an interesting task, for her Chinese zodiac was bull, too. What's more, she had been required to dredge the grass from the ditch as a task in the fishing group, and as a result of standing in cold water, she suffered from arthritis, which gave her unbearably sore joints in rainy days. She would set her jaw and hit her joints with her fists, which, however, never worked. So, she gladly accepted the mission. Pasturing the cattle could save her from the stimulation of cold water, and consequently from the physical pains. Ever since then, Qiu become being a "buffalo girl" along with the girl cowherd.

They were to take care of three big bulls and five buffalos, four grown and one young. Every morning when the bell rang, they would rush to the shed even before the dews dried and drive the cattle to the mountains nearby to graze. The task seemed easy but contained huge responsibilities, if they had carelessly lost one buffalo, they would never have been able to pay for it. What's worse, they might be criticized in a moral level as being deliberately sabotaging. The cattle seemed loyal and poor to Qiu, They would gather all their strengths in the field, pulling the plough one step after another with head lowered. Behind them was the soft, ploughed soil. Without their cooperation in the under-modernized countryside, how tough must it be for the peasants to grow rice! However, people tended to forget about their contribution. Should they go a bit slow, they would have to suffer the whips from their owners. In winter days, they slept in sheds with no walls, but only a ceiling and hayed ground. Sometimes they also caught cold. They had life, senses, voice and even sentiments, too. But because they could not speak, they would not be able to protest to human, and could only silently live with whatever arrangement human made for them. The only moment of joy for the hard-working animals was when they were in the mountains, leisurely wagging their tails and grazing on the grass. Ignoring the existence of people, they ate on and on and on. If one patch of land was almost cleared, they would move to another automatically. They seemed to be aware that if they don't feed themselves, they won't be able to shoulder the back-breaking farming work. Sometimes when the farming is busy, except for the little buffalo who is locked in the cattle pen, the other cattle have "tasks."

When Qiu and the country girl would be distributed to the mountains to mow and to carry two dustpans of grass back to the reservoir to feed the fish. The fish all got good eyesight and hearing, upon hearing the grass falling onto the water, they would gather at once in shoal, waving their bodies and carrying the grass away by their mouths. Some acted like sportsman, they jumped out of the water upon the grass, their scale shinning. Then, they would drag the grass with their lips and dive into the water.

Before long, the country girl thought the base points for pasturing were too few, and the extra task of fish feeding added to their workload. She wanted to go to the agricultural group and learn farm work from her father, so she quitted.

So Qiu was alone with the cattle. Li said, "There are only two or three buffalos to graze in busy days. Let's just leave the work to Qiu alone". So even if there was one person less, Qiu's work points did not increase. She expressed no objection still, and gladly became the "cattle commander". Usually, people would whip the bulls that don't obey, in order to teach them how to behave. To these animals' comfort, Qiu never pulled the string on their nose when letting them out of the shed, nor did she whip them with anything in hand; she thought that would make the silent animals feel intimidated and scared, and in order to protect themselves they would get angry, which makes it even harder to manage. So Qiu would often have a strong, mature bull to take the lead; the rest would follow it on the crooked mountain roads. She taught them to listen to her commands, when she wanted them to turn left, she would order "left" in the local language. If she wanted them to turn right, or to keep on going straight, she would also order in dialect. Occasionally there would be someone that wanted to leave the team and graze by itself. Qiu would hit the road or the rocks with a twig, to warn it with the sound. This usually worked – the bull would obediently go back to the line and move on. If it dared to be so stubborn as to leave the team and munch on the grass by the road, Qiu would give it a few whips on the back, for the sake of the group; but she would not be too hard on the whipping – her purpose was to warn it of the disciplines and interest of the collective. The most robust bull was also the most modest and docile one, which at the same time had the greatest strength. If the cattle marched too slowly after the go-home bell rang, Qiu would loudly quicken the drumming of her feet. As a result, the cattle followed one by one in trotting on the path ahead of Qiu, all the way back to their shed. Sometimes the scene would chuckle the peasants who witnessed it. Occasionally, when Qiu was chatting at her master Li Jinyu's place, they could hear the cattle mooing. Master Li would smile and say, "Listen, the cattle are calling for their commander." So even if Qiu was to attend to all the cattle, she did more than just managing. The cattle were docile to her command. Every morning when the bell rang, she would hold a twig and drive the herd to the mountains. She would first check around and pick out the grassiest place for her cattle to graze.

Hot summer came, which was neither season for plowing and seeding, nor for harvest, lessening the burden of the cattle, but adding to the task of Qiu. Every morning, she had to drive the herd to a grassy spot in the mountains where they could feast. The blazing sun at noon shone like fire in the sky, tossing its scorching heat to the ground. The rocks burnt from the sun, leaving Qiu Weiying no place to sit; she had to stand with the herd in sweat and exhaust, the cattle usually graze on the juncture of plain and slopes, for they wouldn't enter the thorns, vines and undergrowth hidden behind the trees.

The buffalos got especially naughty in hot weather. When it came the time to return, they would usually ignore Qiu's direction to the path, and instead, suddenly run away from the team by the col near the two wells of the reservoir, or by the water. They would evade the rocks and run into the reservoir for a swim with high spirits. They were smart, knowing not to swim too far or where the water was deep; but they would always go out of Qiu's reach. Showing only the part from their nose up above the water, they were totally obsessed with their "free style swim" with mouths half open. They would ignore the bell indicating end of the day and keep on swimming and swimming. No matter if Qiu lost her temper and shouted at them, or threw stones at them, they would just ignore her and enjoy themselves. On such occasions, Qiu usually had nothing to do but sit on the rocks by the reservoir and wait for them to finish. It was only after they got back to land could she take them home. Consequently, it was usually when the others finished dinner or even took their bath did, she arrive at her residence.

In fine days when she was in lighter mood, she sometimes couldn't help singing, "How fun it is to pasture, on the hills when the day is new..." However, it would not be of too much fun for a city-grown girl like her to pasture day after day in the mountains, especially after one horrible incident. One day, upon hearing the ending bell of the day on the hill opposite to the dam, she walked to the largest, strongest and most competent bull, and patted it on the bum to indicate their return. In the first days Qiu was quite afraid of it; if it happened to blow its nose when grazing by Qiu, she would step backward from it. But later they got along. Qiu wanted it to take the lead, for it could act the leader and take the rest home. When it started walking, the herd would follow in an obedient manner, slowly going on their way back home. But for this time its reaction seemed a bit abnormal. It suddenly raised its head, twisted its neck a bit and glared at Qiu with its large, round eyes. There was still unfinished grass hanging by its mouth. It was not until then did Qiu notice a large snake extending its body off the grass nest down some branches, not far from where the bull just grazed, and waving and raising its triangle head. Mother's instructions immediately came into her mind, a viper! She lost her cool in shock and had nobody to turn to. At this moment, a female buffalo not far behind mooed in prolonged voice, probably calling for its child to come back. The snake, as if scared, laid down its intimidating body, and soon crawled across the path and grassland on her left, and quickly hidden into the other side of the hill.

From that day on, Qiu never sang again when she was pasturing the herd in the mountains alone. On the contrary, she was quite afraid. She knew it was but lucky for her to survive from the viper's attack. If she had got hurt by the snake, there wouldn't have been anyone else to know it, and the chances of survival would have slight. But as an educated youth under reeducation by the lower-middle and poor peasants in the countryside, she had no other choice, not to mention that without her city household residence permit, she could neither get a job nor the food rations. Even the hope of being recruited back to the cities was dim. Sometimes, when she was **the cow herding girl** standing on a rock in the hills, looking over the successive mountains and the sparse huts emitting kitchen smoke, she would wonder, what would the socialist new countryside be like? How long will it take for it to be accomplished? At school the teacher said, "We have a responsibility to rescue two-thirds of the world's suffering downtrodden people. "My own city hukou was cancelled and I had to produce a certificate to go home. Otherwise, there would be trouble checking the hukou, and where would be the means to rescue people in other countries! She was raised her head, gazed vague and boundless sky…. She couldn't help feeling lost about her future…

One autumn day in 1967, Wang Tianliang and Mother suddenly arrived at the reservoir. Qiu Weiying had no idea before at all. After driving the herd to the shed, when she was walking up the hill, she saw her mother and Wang standing on the cement ground in front of their dormitory, by the road to staff resident. Mother was twisting her neck and checking around, looking happy. Maybe it was because the accommodation and situation were better than she had anticipated. Qiu Weiying remembered once when a delegate of her teachers came to visit, a female teacher looked at the surroundings and commented enviously, "Ah! Living at mountainside like this is just like living in paradise!"

Mother had a tender smile on her face, staring at her daughter with delight. Meanwhile, Qiu saw Wang Tianliang standing beside in his casual clothes, which made her a bit embarrassed, and she suddenly stopped by the stone steps by the cement ground, as if her feet were glued to the earth. At this time, the wife of manager

The golden age was ruined

Li, who had just finished her work, came to Qiu. She is standing by and asked by her ear, "Is this your fiancé?" Qiu immediately explained in bashfulness, "No way! He is the nominally adoptive son of my mother." Mrs. Li asked, "So she has a nominally adoptive son?" Qiu added in rush, "I have never engaged him! He used to be the patient of my mother. Besides, why would I be engaged at such an early age?!" Mrs. Li grinned, "It is a fine age to marry in the countryside. Oh, what a handsome boy!" Qiu did not deny the compliment. Wang's appearance could be defined as perfect, about 179-centimeters in height, thick, black eyebrows, large, glowing eyes. His lips were large and thick though, but her father once said, "Men with large mouth have the eat four sides". However, she never had any chemistry for Wang, probably because she was too young and innocent. After a while, Qiu moved her feet directly to her mother, who said excitedly, "It is not a bad place, with the lovely mountains and clear water!" Before she finished, Qiu carried her luggage in hand and said, "Mom, I'll get your things settled first. After dinner, they will arrange a place for you to sleep." With these words, Qiu put their luggage by her bed in dormitory, and then then ran to the door, for it happened to be the fish catching day in the reservoir, and she had just seen the employees carrying a fishing net with jumping fish in it, all the way up the stone slope under the dam. Her mother was glad to see the big fresh fish; the two of them chose a satisfying fish and Mother immediately paid for it. Qiu took it to the canteen, had Master Sie cook it with all her best. Then, Qiu Weiying, her mother and Wang Tianliang had a nice meal together.

After dinner, Qiu accompanied them in having a walk along the dam. The three of them left the residence, walked over the cement ground toward the dam. Down the stone slope right to the dam was the water reservoir, right to it were the farmland and fish pool, and the water gate at the hillside, and the ditch stretching to the mountain feet faraway. The mountain at the end of the dam was where Qiu often pastured and where she saw the viper. The terrible memory of the restless snake came back vividly to her. Looking at

Mother's easy, delightful face, she gave up the idea of mentioning it, for she didn't want the incident to mother. Mother told her, "I was dispatched to the East Hospital not long after you left. It is near Fu Zheng Jie Primary School where you used to go. It was once a church before liberation, and now it is a hospital. I am now a doctor there." Qiu said, "I know that place. It used to be the Methodist Church. I had a classmate who lived there, and I had been there a few times." Mrs. Qiu said, "The people who used to live there have probably moved to behind the church." The three of them chatted over the walk. They rested for a while after the stroll, and then Qiu took the two to the temporary bedroom.

The weather was fine the next day. Up in the clear, blue sky hanged the glowing sun, not only decorating the skies with a bountiful of colors, but also giving the sceneries below an especially lovely luster. Qiu asked Manager Li for a day's leave, for she wanted to show mother and Wang Tianliang around and talk with them. Li seemed displeased, but he had no reason to object. Qiu learned from the talk that Wang had just been transferred to civilian work in Changsha, and upon his return, he was given a job as a technician in a radio factory in the city. Qiu Weiying was shy, and listened without a word, while Mrs. Qiu constantly moved her sight between Wang and her daughter. She didn't speak much, as if having something on mind… So, the three of them talked and walked, as the morning time flew by. Qiu heard the ending bell rang, and said to the two, "It's lunch time now, let's go back." After lunch, Mrs. Qiu said, "I'm feeling sleepy now and would like to take a nap." So Qiu took her to the bedroom and left after Mother lay down. She saw Wang standing outside the door, who said, "Let's sit down somewhere. I have some words for you." Hearing this, Qiu stood still in hesitation. Some people went by and looked over curiously. Qiu felt a bit uneasy from the sight, so she promptly answered "Ok". Then, she took him to the back of the residence, and searched for some large rock for seat.

There were some stones and rocks of all sizes in the vacant land back of the management office. At the mountain feet by it was a cliff about one meter high, devoid of any vegetation. One could tell from the sight that the people used dynamite to create a plain out of the mountains to build the reservoir. It was an unfrequented place, but not far from it was a relatively broad and even road leading to the staff residence. The two young people sat on a smooth, irregular shaped rock side by side. At first Wang twisted his body a bit and stared at Qiu for a while, which made Qiu a bit nervous and uncomfortable. Then, he said to her in composure, "Your mother and I have to go back for work tomorrow. There is one thing that I want to ask, Will you be my fiancé?" With these words, he suddenly got hold of her hands. It upset Qiu Weiying who had no romantic experience before and made her ears burn. She drew her hands back instinctively from his hot palms, tried her best to cool down and reply, "We've known each other for some years, but we've not known much about each other in person. Marriage is a major event in life, so I cannot make such decision in haste. Let's take our time to know about each other before we decide! After all, we are still young." Then, she twisted her neck to look at Wang, and found the latter to be speechless, with an almost disappointed look.

At the same time, she saw over his left shoulder that Manager Li was coming near the Management office. There was an elusive look in his goldfish eyes, which were casting their sight over them. He pouted his lips a bit, which made him look rather serious.

Qiu suddenly realized it was improper for them to sit there for so long. It had not been long She came to the countryside for the "reeducation by the lower-middle and poor peasants", it had not been long. If she has being eager to start a love relationship, it is means being eager to get away. She was silent for a while and then stood up and said, "Let's go back. My mom has probably regained consciousness, don't leave her alone." Wang could not refuse; he could only follow Qiu and go back to her mother.

As Wang had told, they were leaving the next day. Qiu Weiying asked leave from Manager Li to see them onto the bus station in Huatang.

They walked along the ditch for about ten miles of mountain path along the ditch and arrived at the station. There, Qiu Weiying paid for two tickets with the money her mother gave her, and then they bought some simple food nearby. After the bus came, Mother and Wang Tianliang got on a bus to the city of Chenzhou and were to take a train there back to Changsha. As the engine started, Mother and Wang forced themselves to smile and wave goodbye to Qiu Weiying. The bus left for Chenzhou. Looking at it is disappearing, Qiu Weiying was brought to tears by the sudden attack of loneliness.

On her way back, she came by some lately harvested farmland near the ditch, with piles of hay by the side. There, she saw two buffalos having a fierce fight head-to-head, horn to horn. It seemed that they would never quit unless one of them were to be defeated and dead. A farmer hasted to set fire to the hay, used an iron fork to hold the burning hay, and wove it between the buffalos. He seemed to be attempting to scare them apart to avoid dual loss. Qiu Weiying was eager to get back before dark, so she did not stay to watch.

On her way, she thought to herself, The two buffalos should have known that they were of the same species. Why couldn't they live in peace, but rather, devoted themselves to a life-or-death fight? She suddenly felt her fantasies about life which had accompanied her ever since childhood began to fade away…

3.3 A Trip to Changsha and Wuhan during in the Cultural Revolution

<See App, 1. H> The Great Proletarian Cultural Revolution in China started in the second half of late 1965, when Yao Wenyuan published his criticize against the theatre play "Hairui dismiss". Intellectuals who were regarded as bourgeois reactionary academic

Qiu Niao

As Wang had told, they were leaving the next day. Qiu Weiying asked leave from Manager Li to see them onto the bus station in Huatang.

They walked along the ditch for about ten miles of mountain path along the ditch and arrived at the station. There, Qiu Weiying paid for two tickets with the money her mother gave her, and then they bought some simple food nearby. After the bus came, Mother and Wang Tianliang got on a bus to the city of Chenzhou and were to take a train there back to Changsha. As the engine started, Mother and Wang forced themselves to smile and wave goodbye to Qiu Weiying. The bus left for Chenzhou. Looking at it is disappearing, Qiu Weiying was brought to tears by the sudden attack of loneliness.

On her way back, she came by some lately harvested farmland near the ditch, with piles of hay by the side. There, she saw two buffalos having a fierce fight head-to-head, horn to horn. It seemed that they would never quit unless one of them were to be defeated and dead. A farmer hasted to set fire to the hay, used an iron fork to hold the burning hay, and wove it between the buffalos. He seemed to be attempting to scare them apart to avoid dual loss. Qiu Weiying was eager to get back before dark, so she did not stay to watch.

On her way, she thought to herself, The two buffalos should have known that they were of the same species. Why couldn't they live in peace, but rather, devoted themselves to a life-or-death fight? She suddenly felt her fantasies about life which had accompanied her ever since childhood began to fade away…

3.3 A Trip to Changsha and Wuhan during in the Cultural Revolution

<See App, 1. H> The Great Proletarian Cultural Revolution in China started in the second half of late 1965, when Yao Wenyuan published his criticize against the theatre play "Hairui dismiss". Intellectuals who were regarded as bourgeois reactionary academic

The golden age was ruined

There were some stones and rocks of all sizes in the vacant land back of the management office. At the mountain feet by it was a cliff about one meter high, devoid of any vegetation. One could tell from the sight that the people used dynamite to create a plain out of the mountains to build the reservoir. It was an unfrequented place, but not far from it was a relatively broad and even road leading to the staff residence. The two young people sat on a smooth, irregular shaped rock side by side. At first Wang twisted his body a bit and stared at Qiu for a while, which made Qiu a bit nervous and uncomfortable. Then, he said to her in composure, "Your mother and I have to go back for work tomorrow. There is one thing that I want to ask, Will you be my fiancé?" With these words, he suddenly got hold of her hands. It upset Qiu Weiying who had no romantic experience before and made her ears burn. She drew her hands back instinctively from his hot palms, tried her best to cool down and reply, "We've known each other for some years, but we've not known much about each other in person. Marriage is a major event in life, so I cannot make such decision in haste. Let's take our time to know about each other before we decide! After all, we are still young." Then, she twisted her neck to look at Wang, and found the latter to be speechless, with an almost disappointed look.

At the same time, she saw over his left shoulder that Manager Li was coming near the Management office. There was an elusive look in his goldfish eyes, which were casting their sight over them. He pouted his lips a bit, which made him look rather serious.

Qiu suddenly realized it was improper for them to sit there for so long. It had not been long She came to the countryside for the "reeducation by the lower-middle and poor peasants", it had not been long. If she has being eager to start a love relationship, it is means being eager to get away. She was silent for a while and then stood up and said, "Let's go back. My mom has probably regained consciousness, don't leave her alone." Wang could not refuse; he could only follow Qiu and go back to her mother.

133

authorities and stinking ninth grader were widely criticized and persecuted. They are becoming the target of being primarily beaten down. But it did not officially begin until the Central Party Committee criticized "The capitalist road" of Liu Shaoqi and Deng Xiaoping.

On August 18, 1966, Chairman Mao, wearing a Red Guard's armband, met with millions of young students at Tiananmen Square, Beijing. Since then, the spark of the Great Cultural Revolution had developed into fires spreading through the country by the Mao-worshiping Red Guards and their revolutionary big linking up.

With the slogan "The revolution is not guilty", "Rebellion is justified" sounding universally, on January,1967, the Rebel faction's faction in Shanghai successfully seized the power from the municipal government, and other cities and provinces soon followed suit and established local revolutionary committees.

The fire of Cultural Revolution started burning fiercer than ever before, in a way no man could stop, and it kept on developing. Chairman of the state Liu Shaoqi, among the ten marshals have Peng Dehuai and He Long, and Tao Zhuo a member of the Standing Committee of the Political Bureau of the CPC Central Committee, they were killed by the revolution.

It was summer, 1967 when Qiu unexpectedly got a telegraph from her aunt in Wuhan, saying, "The marriage between me and your uncle is in crisis; he was seduced by a female patient of his. I don't want to see my family crack up, but I have nothing to do about it. I have been informed that, young as you are, you are natured with eloquence and intelligence. I'm looking forward for your trip to Wuhan upon receiving my words. You are my only hope."

Qiu Weiying felt a bit awkward with the telegraph, thinking, "Aunt has all her trust and hope on me, but I have never even had a boyfriend. Am I able to deal with family issue of this kind?" But her five cousins in Wuhan were almost ten years younger than her, so if she did not step up, the problem will be left unsettled. A happy family breaking into pieces was the last thing she wanted to see, so she decided to ask for leave immediately and go to Wuhan.

Head of the reservoir Li widened his goldfish eyes at her request, but there was nothing he could say. So, she easily got the permission. Probably it was because he had heard something about the Cultural Revolution, though it had not really started in the mountainous district. The core of Cultural Revolution was to overthrow the Capitalist Roaders in power within the Party and to break down "Destroy of Four old's" (old thinking, culture, customs and habits). Li was not only a Party member but also the only man in power at the reservoir, making him a target of mass campaign. Qiu had been away from home for two years already, so she decided to take a train from Chenzhou to Wuhan and drop first by Changsha to visit her home.

Changsha was hot as fire in July. The entire city was steaming with heat as if it were a superb boiling pot, soaking its citizens with sweat. Men on street worn vests and shorts only and walked in their slippers. However, Qiu saw many young and mid-aged men and women wearing thick green uniforms of the Red Guards in the unbearable heat. On their rolled-up sleeves were armbands of various rebel groups, for example the Red Guards. They were rushing here and there in the streets for revolution acts they defined as "justified". Qiu was not interested in what they were doing. Getting off the train, she carried her luggage out of the train station near the city center and hired a tricycle through downtown to her house in Lao Zhaobi.

Entering the gate late, she saw the twins Damao and Xiaomao, who were age for junior high school, and her little brother Juele all at home. She asked curiously, "Isn't it time for school? Why are you still at home?" Her brothers and sisters were surprised at her question, and replied, "Don't you know that we haven't had class for almost a year? This is what happens in the whole country. The Capitalist education is to be overthrown. If teachers make any mistakes in class, they will be repudiated by the students." Qiu Weiying said, "How am I supposed to know that among the mountains? I was almost secluded. I could never have imagined that the schools in the cities would change so much!" They added, "The peasants in the suburbs of Changsha have also had their rebel organizations…"

At noon, father and Mother came back from work. Seeing Weiying, Mr. Qiu Zhongyuan asked, "What brought you back?" She answered, "I've got a telegraph at the reservoir from Aunt, saying…" She retold the telegraph to her parents. Mr. Qiu said, "You are too young to intervene in grown-up business! What's more, you don't have any relevant social experiences to be of help."

Mrs. Qiu said, "Let her go if her aunt asks her to." She turned to Weiying and said, "How about visiting Eastern Hospital where I now work at tomorrow?" Weiying said delightfully, "Sure! How is the new place?" Mother said, "Not bad. You'll know when you see it." Weiying asked, "How's the salary?" Mother said, "Forty-something. Plus, the food allowance, I get about fifty." Weiying said, "How miserly! Why do you get so little? You must be the chief doctor there!" Mother said, "Oh, I don't care as long as there is a job for me! The wages are calculated based on length of service. I'm a newcomer. All the organizations value seniority." Weiying said in disapprove, "That doesn't make sense. Working for one patient only could get you more than that." Mother said indifferently, "I can do with both high and low. There are a lot of people out there who have harder times than us!" Weiying said, "That's true, but it's a different thing."

The next day, Qiu Weiying went to Eastern Hospital where her mother worked, when a patient had just finished his surgery and left the operation room. Weiying entered the operation room directly and saw her mother cleaning the equipment with latex gloves by the sink. Mrs. Qiu saw her and said, "Sit down for a while. I've almost finished." Weiying walked over and asked, "Don't you have any assistant? And you clean the tools yourself? Where do you sterilize them after cleaning?" Her mother replied, "I've got a girl apprentice, but she has asked for sick leave today. I can do it on my own, only it's a bit trouble. Ms. Dong in the kitchen helps to sterilize." Weiying was surprised, sterilizing in the kitchen? She went to the white desk where the apparatus was and uncovered the rectangle enamel lid. The instruments were washed clean, but all very old and it Is out-of-date medical apparatus and instruments. She inspected the room and said, "Mom, it's much worse than Southern Hospital!" Mrs. Qiu replied, "Southern Region Hospital was established long before this one, when your father first called for collectivism. It has greater fame and income. How can they be the same? Eastern Hospital was built after the Cultural Revolution, the year when I joined in. We started from nothing. The Eastern Hospital of Liuzheng Street was established several years before but was small and bad equipped. That's why we constructed this one. The administrative group runs the two hospitals at the same time."

After work, Mrs. Qiu and Weiying went home. During lunch, Weiying asked, "Mom, do you still remember my best friend in primary school, Zhang Tairan, when we were living at Pozi Street?" Mrs. Qiu said, "Yes, of course. She came over a few times, and her mom came once and asked me to have you stay in theirs." Weiying told Mother what she heard from Yu Mingchi at Huatang Farm, and added, "I want to go to Pozi Street to find out her new address in Beijing this afternoon." Mrs. Qiu said, "Is it possible, for she had been gone at ten years?" Weiying said, "I'll try asking the new dweller or the police office." Mrs. Qiu said, "Go have a try then!"

That afternoon, Qiu went to the former house of Zhang Tairan's at Pozi Street. It had already been changed into government office. She asked the old doorkeeper, who said, "It was another office before. I haven't heard of any cadre in the Long March, not to mention his new address in Beijing." She said, "So I can only count on the police office!" The old man said calmly, "It's been such a mess in the Cultural Revolution. If you go and ask about a high-ranking revolutionist, and you without any official certificate, they won't even bother to look at you." Weiying was convinced, thinking, "That's true. I'm not even a registered resident of Changsha now. Who am

I to ask for Tairan's address in Beijing?" As a result, she could only put the innocent friendship of childhood in a cherished place of her memory.

The next day, Qiu Weiying went to visit Tang Na. Before leaving home, an idea came to her. She thought, "We've be confiscated for running 'underground hospital' and 'speculation' in the mass campaign, and still haven't been overturned. It must be a wrong verdict! The parents of Tang Na are senior party members and revolutionary writers; they must know the policies well. Why don't I show them the documents about our confiscation of family property and seek for advice?" So, she collected all the documents, and before leaving home, she took six-year-old Wu Di, the eldest son of Xiaodong along, for Xiaodong was dispatched to Eastern Hospital almost the same time as Mother, and thus was too busy to take care of the children. What's worse, she became a bit mentally abnormal since the night of confiscation of family property in spring, 1965 for being pressed for confession. Instead of being a doctor, she served as an ordinary nursing at Eastern Hospital.

Qiu Weiying's arrival at the dormitory of Literature Association, Yuanjialing where Tang's family lived, made Tang Na very happy. Tang's mother complimented Wu Di, "He is very pretty and a cute boy!" Qiu said, "He takes after his father. I've seen the childhood picture of his father; they are the same!" Hearing these words, Mrs. Tang seemed thoughtful and walked away. So Qiu turned and asked Tang Na, "You're graduating next year. Going for college?" Tang said, "It's hard to say. Even if I enter college, it won't make much difference. There aren't many classes offered during the Cultural Revolution. There's nothing much to learn, the capitalist education is repudiated; the teachers are disdaining become bourgeois intellectuals. A lot of students joined the Red Guards and Rebel organizations, breaking down The Gang of Four and repudiating Capitalist Roaders everywhere. I heard that Zhang Tie Sheng handed in a blank paper in the exam, got a zero and was honored as a 'hero in overthrowing the Capitalist education', and was picked as a delegate to visit Japan. The Japanese gave him a pair of chopsticks as presents. When he came back, he said to Premier Zhou, 'How miserly the Japanese are! I can't believe they should only give me a pair of chopsticks!' When he left, Premier Zhou sneered, 'What does he know except eating?' I have no idea what the school is going to do about me after graduation." Hearing the words, Qiu began to feel less pitiful about not having continued her education.

After a while, Qiu took the documents out of her bag and said, "Here's the document about our confiscation of family property, and some detailed description I wrote. Changsha Medical Institution Management Committee that takes charge of the hospital said, 'Don't say anything to the others about the confiscation of family property, or you'll be more guilty. The properties will be frozen until the decision is cleared.' But two years have gone by, and we don't see any verdict or property returned. Your parents are experienced party members and writers. They must know more than my parents do. Can you show them the document and see if they can return the properties? Let alone the properties, we are also affected inestimably politically. My eldest brother and I cannot go to school anymore. A few months before my entering high school, people from the security bureau came to my school; and my brother found his files marked with an 'L'. His class adviser said, 'I suspect that you were confiscated family possessions for holding back the fact of being landlords.' My parents have had enough of bullying, but they don't dare to say anything. But I'm not the timid kind." Tang took a lot at the documents and said nothing, so Qiu put them on the table beside.

After some talking, she stood up and said, "My aunt in Hankou telegraphed me saying she's going through a divorce with my uncle and needs my help. I must go and buy tomorrow's ticket. I'll come and see you when I return." Tang asked, "She has her own children, why does she send for you?" Qiu said, "They are too young; and they might be afraid of Uncle." Tang said, "Aren't you afraid?" Qiu said, in the exam, got a zero and was honored as a 'hero in overthrowing the Capitalist education', and was picked as a delegate to visit Japan. The Japanese gave him a pair of chopsticks as presents. When he came back, he said to Premier Zhou, 'How miserly the Japanese are! I can't believe they should only give me a pair of chopsticks!' When he left, Premier Zhou sneered, 'What does he know except eating?' I have no idea what the school is going to do about me after graduation." Hearing the words, Qiu began to feel less pitiful about not having continued her education.

After a while, Qiu took the documents out of her bag and said, "Here's the document about our confiscation of family property, and some detailed description I wrote. Changsha Medical Institution Management Committee that takes charge of the hospital said, 'Don't say anything to the others about the confiscation of family property, or you'll be more guilty. The properties will be frozen until the decision is cleared.' But two years have gone by, and we don't see any verdict or property returned. Your parents are experienced party members and writers. They must know more than my parents do. Can you show them the document and see if they can return the properties? Let alone the properties, we are also affected inestimably politically. My eldest brother and I cannot go to school anymore. A few months before my entering high school, people from the security bureau came to my school; and my brother found his files marked with an 'L'. His class adviser said, 'I suspect that you were confiscated family possessions for holding back the fact of being landlords.' My parents have had enough of bullying, but they don't dare to say anything. But I'm not the timid kind." Tang took a lot at the documents and said nothing, so Qiu put them on the table beside.

After some talking, she stood up and said, "My aunt in Hankou telegraphed me saying she's going through a divorce with my uncle and needs my help. I must go and buy tomorrow's ticket. I'll come and see you when I return." Tang asked, "She has her own children, why does she send for you?" Qiu said, "They are too young; and they might be afraid of Uncle." Tang said, "Aren't you afraid?" Qiu said,

I to ask for Tairan's address in Beijing?" As a result, she could only put the innocent friendship of childhood in a cherished place of her memory.

The next day, Qiu Weiying went to visit Tang Na. Before leaving home, an idea came to her. She thought, "We've be confiscated for running 'underground hospital' and 'speculation' in the mass campaign, and still haven't been overturned. It must be a wrong verdict! The parents of Tang Na are senior party members and revolutionary writers; they must know the policies well. Why don't I show them the documents about our confiscation of family property and seek for advice?" So, she collected all the documents, and before leaving home, she took six-year-old Wu Di, the eldest son of Xiaodong along, for Xiaodong was dispatched to Eastern Hospital almost the same time as Mother, and thus was too busy to take care of the children. What's worse, she became a bit mentally abnormal since the night of confiscation of family property in spring, 1965 for being pressed for confession. Instead of being a doctor, she served as an ordinary nursing at Eastern Hospital.

Qiu Weiying's arrival at the dormitory of Literature Association, Yuanjialing where Tang's family lived, made Tang Na very happy. Tang's mother complimented Wu Di, "He is very pretty and a cute boy!" Qiu said, "He takes after his father. I've seen the childhood picture of his father; they are the same!" Hearing these words, Mrs. Tang seemed thoughtful and walked away. So Qiu turned and asked Tang Na, "You're graduating next year. Going for college?" Tang said, "It's hard to say. Even if I enter college, it won't make much difference. There aren't many classes offered during the Cultural Revolution. There's nothing much to learn, the capitalist education is repudiated; the teachers are disdaining become bourgeois intellectuals. A lot of students joined the Red Guards and Rebel organizations, breaking down The Gang of Four and repudiating Capitalist Roaders everywhere. I heard that Zhang Tie Sheng handed in a blank paper

"No if it's his fault." Then she said goodbye to the Tangs and took Wu Di to the train station.

She bought a ticket to Wuhan the next day without much trouble, for the Cultural Revolution covered the whole country, and the Red Guards could free get on any transportation with their armband and certificate, so no one would queue for a train ticket in the national cascade.

The next afternoon, Qiu Weiying arrived at Changsha Station with her big green canvas bag. The station square was crowded with people, and there was a comparatively vacant space. There are several Xinjiang men clapping tambourines, surrounded by a beautiful Xinjiang girl in a long skirt, face like a red apple, dancing there is quite a national flavor of Xinjiang dance. Although Qiu Weiying grew up loving Xinjiang dance and appreciating the Xinjiang girls who can sing and dance well. But now Qiu was not in the mood watch. She went directly to the platform. The ticket inspector there only took a random look at the ticket.

Having gone to the countryside before the Cultural Revolution broke out and stayed there for two years, she was unaffected by the crazy revolutionary 'passion'. So, as the train arrived, she was hoping to get on as usual. It turned out that all the fervent Red Guards all came up swarming for entrance even before the door opened, pushing her far behind. As she finally dragged her green canvas bag to the door, she was shocked at the scene, the door was blocked by crowds of Red Guards with not even a slit left. How could she manage to get on? Despite that people were sweating like pigs, everyone was trying his best to strike his way on. Meanwhile, Qiu saw some people climbing through the windows. Those who had got on even stretched their hands out to pull the others in. As Qiu was totally at lost, a mid-age male attendant came close, blowing his whistle and trying to force the door closed. Qiu was uneasy, if she couldn't make it immediately, she could never have to get on. The train was leaving!

Suddenly, the courage of revolution fell on her, as well as the fervor. Qiu Weiying, in her green years, was no longer the girl before going to the countryside who could not fulfill any physical labor. After two years of hard farm work in the countryside, she was endowed with extra strength that could come to her if she set her mind to make it. Stepping one foot on the stance, she grasped her bag with one hand and held the door with another, and at the same time got the other foot on. She made it the last to get on the train, as the door was closed hard, and the train started moving. She had trouble breathing in the car crowded by Red Guards occupying even the passageway, and the train was burning under the sun. She suspected that she would pass out in heat if the train had not left sooner.

Holding her ticket in hand and pushing through the crowd, she finally found her seat, which, however, was taken by a mid-aged Red Guard, who was not wearing uniform but only the armband. She showed him the ticket with seat number on, and he left without a word. Qiu found a place barely enough for her bag on the luggage shelf behind her, and then sat down. Beside and in front of her were some boys staring at her friendly. They were student Red Guards. She smiled and began chatting with them after the train started. She learned from the conversation that two of them came from Beijing, and two were from Tianjin. They grouped to visit the former residence of Chairman Mao in Shao Shan and planned to join the train station from Changsha to Wuhan and then go home. Qiu, who was never a liar in nature, told them that she is now a rural resident, and saw the sorry look on their faces. Though they still treated her nicely, she could sense that she was somehow disdained in their heart, for only those from good families, for example children of Party leaders, workers and poor and lower-middle peasants, could join the Red Guards. As for those who went to the countryside before Cultural Revolution, they were mostly from families of landlords, rich peasants, anti- revolutionists' criminals, right wings or issued families. Even though they were not performing any worse than the other classmates, they were still left behind by those from better families, for class line was implemented in school too. Feeling bitter, she became less willing to talk.

The train went pass small cities and hamlets, as wasted farmland came into horizon every now and then. The remains of crumbled walls were decorated with big-character posters and slogans such as "Crash the brazen attack of right-wing Capitalism"; "To rebel and revolute is justified"; and "Long live the Proletariat Cultural Revolution". As the train stopped at some rural way stations, Qiu saw some peasants staggering with their luggage on shoulder poles and streaming with sweats, who were trying to get on train. But crowded with Red Guards on cascade between metropolises, it was almost impossible even to open the gate. A bare-handed person would have to go through tremendous efforts to get on, not to mention the peasants with luggage on shoulder. So, they could only stare at the mercilessly leaving train and sigh. Despite that it was severely overloaded, the train kept going from stop to stop, spilling the combative Red Guards all over the country, and meanwhile spreading the great hope of their top leader, Chairman Mao, as well as the spark of Cultural revolution from Tiananmen Square, Beijing, to every corner of China.

After long hours of toil, the "train of Revolution" gradually lowered its puffing and brought the bustling Red Guards with burning spirits to Hankou. Looking outside the window, Qiu saw endless Red Guards planning to head north and a few ordinary passengers. She stood up almost at the same time with the Red Guards by her, so as to get off the train as soon as possible. But to her surprise, she looked back at the luggage shelf only to find her bag missing. She flustered, "My bag! It's gone!" At the same time, she saw the man who had taken her seat before, pushing his way to the passageway near the door in panic. She shouted at him, "Thief! Stop!" At this moment, the tallest and eldest Red Guard who was sitting in front of her dumped his luggage into his companion's hands, saying, "Hold this for a second." Then, he pushed a way in the crowd and ran after the thief. Qiu Weiying hurried to follow him off the train. The thief was about to run away but was held by the collar and almost stumbled.

The tall Red Guard asked him, "Why did you steal her bag? Give it back to her!" The thief said, "What's the big deal? See, she's not even wearing an armband. She must be from a bad family." Qiu was annoyed by the words. She said, "Who are you to judge my family? I can't be worse than a thief!" If she had been a boy, she would have smacked him hard on the face. As she snatched her bag back, the other Red Guards came over and said to the tall one, "Hurry up! The Revolution Committee is waiting for us." So, he let go of the thief, who left at once. Qiu Weiying thanked him with a grateful smile, and waved goodbye to his congenial companion. Then they went separate ways, and Qiu hired a tricycle to her uncle's home.

It was July in the midsummer. Hankou, known as one of the four "stoves" of China, was burning already from the rising sun in the morning, and even the tree trunks cracked in thirst. Qiu saw the so-called "the evil people of all descriptions" be forced by Red Guards and Rebel factions in streets, wearing tall hats and no shoes and walking showing crowd in the street. She was not interested in watching the unprecedented street show; all she desired was to hide away from the scorching sun and arrive at uncle's home as soon as possible. It was only when she got there that she knew her aunt had moved to a nearby house in the same street.

Her uncle Qiu Zhonglin seemed a bit displeased at Weiying's unexpected visit when he came back at noon. Having guessed her purpose, he said, "Your aunt asked you to come, didn't her?" Weiying said calmly, "Yes." She held back her real thought, "I came to stop your family from falling apart. I have to do aunt the favor, even if you're angry with me, for your bunch of kids are still so small." Her eldest cousin had no class in the afternoon and was especially happy. He held Qiu Weiying's arm intimately and said, "My dear old sister, finally to have you here!" With two silk handkerchiefs in hands, he imitated the walks of emperor's maids, which he learned from the then repudiated film <Secret History of the Qing Palace> twisting his waist in a feminine way. Weiying chuckled and screamed, "Xiaomao, you walk better than women!" Before supper, Weiying went to her aunt with all her cousins who didn't go to school, leaving her uncle alone at home. The two-story house uncle bought was a nice place. For a long time, the parents of her aunt had lived with them, and her aunt's mother cooked for the family, but then they moved away with aunt. So, Weiying and her cousins went to aunt's new place for supper.

As Weiying and her cousins stepped into the living-dining room, she saw a nice, benign face man in his sixties. He and aunt were talking, each sitting in a single sofa with a tea table between them. Aunt stood up as she saw them entering, and said to the old man, "This is Qiu Zhonglin's eldest niece." Then, she turned to Weiying, "Mr. Chen is your uncle's best old mate. He'll tell you about the woman who is now getting hot with your uncle." Mr. Chen gladly said, "Alright! I used to be his patient, and we've known each other for some decades. I know him quite well. Look how a happy family gets ruined by an outsider! I can tell you're smart from your look. I believe you can work it out." He told Weiying to sit down before talking further. At this time, Aunt said, "Dinner's ready, let's talk over the meal." So, she served the table and the family gathered by it. Mr. Chen started eating and talking, "The woman is also a patient of you uncles. She is a few years younger than your aunt, divorced, and has two children. Her neighbors said that she is lazy and hedonic and dresses up all day. She never cooked after work, but only went out to have fun. She never catered to the family, and often quarreled with her husband over the routines. When he became fed up, he divorced her and took the two kids away. Later, when she went to the hospital, she was informed that your uncle is an expert doctor with good fame and high salary (about 160 yuan per month), so she played a few tricks to hook up. Your aunt is a well-educated, polite doctor. She moved here for the incident, but she dares not argue with her. That's why she asked you for help." Weiying said, "How senseless! My uncle is married already with so many kids. Does she have any moral? How can she ruin a family like this! Why doesn't Aunt go and tell it to her leaders?" Mr. Chen said, "The leaders are too busy catering to their own businesses. Who gives a damn?" Weiying said, "I see. I'll go look at her workplace tomorrow. Do you know the address?" Mr. Chen said, "Of course. Your uncle has invited me once to dinner with her. But when I tried to persuade him out of the affair, he not only ignored my words but also stopped contacts with me. I've never seen him close to women before. What a vixen she must be to seduce him so easily!"

Weiying's cousins didn't have school during the mass campaign, so after breakfast the next morning, she took them to the woman's workplace. She first sought for the leader's office, but there were only offices of the Rebel factions' organizations. She entered one and explained her purpose, but the man in charge said, "We deal with Capitalist Roaders only. If you want to solve such kind of personal issue, go for her." They showed her a room on the second floor, where she went directly. The woman was not surprised at seeing them, and said indifferently, "Why do you come for me? I have nothing to say to you!" Weiying said, "Why? Ask yourself! You have nothing to say, but I do!" The vicious woman was prepared for such words, and responded shamelessly, "Your uncle said that you have no position to intervene in his private live!" Weiying did not give in, "Well, I came here for my aunt! If it had not, been you, they could have made a perfect family. If they are not divorced, I'll see this through. If you don't quit, we'll see who stays till the end!" Hearing such a speech, the woman grabbed her handbag without a word and headed for the door. Weiying warned, "Alright! If you choose to do it the hard way, let's see who's got more guts!"

The sun of Hankou in late July hung high in the sky, tossing its flaming light to the ground. Regardless of people's complaint "It's hot like hell!" it kept rising higher and burning harder. The big-character posters on the streets wrinkled from the sun, some even curled up and almost fell. Qiu had no interest in the content of them, but she can she ruin a family like this! Why doesn't Aunt go and tell it to her leaders?" Mr. Chen said, "The leaders are too busy catering to their own businesses. Who gives a damn?" Weiying said, "I see. I'll go look at her workplace tomorrow. Do you know the address?" Mr. Chen said, "Of course. Your uncle has invited me once to dinner with her. But when I tried to persuade him out of the affair, he not only ignored my words but also stopped contacts with me. I've never seen him close to women before. What a vixen she must be to seduce him so easily!"

Weiying's cousins didn't have school during the mass campaign, so after breakfast the next morning, she took them to the woman's workplace. She first sought for the leader's office, but there were only offices of the Rebel factions' organizations. She entered one and explained her purpose, but the man in charge said, "We deal with Capitalist Roaders only. If you want to solve such kind of personal issue, go for her." They showed her a room on the second floor, where she went directly. The woman was not surprised at seeing them, and said indifferently, "Why do you come for me? I have nothing to say to you!" Weiying said, "Why? Ask yourself! You have nothing to say, but I do!" The vicious woman was prepared for such words, and responded shamelessly, "Your uncle said that you have no position to intervene in his private live!" Weiying did not give in, "Well, I came here for my aunt! If it had not, been you, they could have made a perfect family. If they are not divorced, I'll see this through. If you don't quit, we'll see who stays till the end!" Hearing such a speech, the woman grabbed her handbag without a word and headed for the door. Weiying warned, "Alright! If you choose to do it the hard way, let's see who's got more guts!"

The sun of Hankou in late July hung high in the sky, tossing its flaming light to the ground. Regardless of people's complaint "It's hot like hell!" it kept rising higher and burning harder. The big-character posters on the streets wrinkled from the sun, some even curled up and almost fell. Qiu had no interest in the content of them, but she

The golden age was ruined

you walk better than women!" Before supper, Weiying went to her aunt with all her cousins who didn't go to school, leaving her uncle alone at home. The two-story house uncle bought was a nice place. For a long time, the parents of her aunt had lived with them, and her aunt's mother cooked for the family, but then they moved away with aunt. So, Weiying and her cousins went to aunt's new place for supper.

As Weiying and her cousins stepped into the living-dining room, she saw a nice, benign face man in his sixties. He and aunt were talking, each sitting in a single sofa with a tea table between them. Aunt stood up as she saw them entering, and said to the old man, "This is Qiu Zhonglin's eldest niece." Then, she turned to Weiying, "Mr. Chen is your uncle's best old mate. He'll tell you about the woman who is now getting hot with your uncle." Mr. Chen gladly said, "Alright! I used to be his patient, and we've known each other for some decades. I know him quite well. Look how a happy family gets ruined by an outsider! I can tell you're smart from your look. I believe you can work it out." He told Weiying to sit down before talking further. At this time, Aunt said, "Dinner's ready, let's talk over the meal." So, she served the table and the family gathered by it. Mr. Chen started eating and talking, "The woman is also a patient of you uncles. She is a few years younger than your aunt, divorced, and has two children. Her neighbors said that she is lazy and hedonic and dresses up all day. She never cooked after work, but only went out to have fun. She never catered to the family, and often quarreled with her husband over the routines. When he became fed up, he divorced her and took the two kids away. Later, when she went to the hospital, she was informed that your uncle is an expert doctor with good fame and high salary (about 160 yuan per month), so she played a few tricks to hook up. Your aunt is a well-educated, polite doctor. She moved here for the incident, but she dares not argue with her. That's why she asked you for help." Weiying said, "How senseless! My uncle is married already with so many kids. Does she have any moral? How

145

was inspired by them somehow... As soon as they got back, Weiying saw Mr. Chen and Aunt waiting for them. Aunt stood up and poured her a glass of cold boiled water, and asked, "Have you seen her?" Qiu said, "Yes. She started talking before I did, saying that Uncle said I had no right to intervene. Then she left without any further talk." Aunt said, "Sounds tough! What do we do then?" Qiu said, "People put up big-character posters in the Cultural Revolution. Chairman Mao's first big-character poster 'Bombardment the Headquarters' has dragged the vice President Liu Shaoqi down. It does work well! We should do this to the vixen! I'm going to write a big-character poster and put it up in her workplace to give her a good blast. Let's see if she still has face to seduce my uncle. She avoided quarreling with me, for she doesn't want her colleagues to know about it. It seems that the people in her unit still don't know." Aunt turned to Mr. Chen, "What do you think of my niece's idea of putting up a big-character poster in her workplace?" Mr. Chen laughed and said, "Why not? Sounds like a good idea to me! Your niece truly is a smart cookie. Her idea can work nowadays!" So, the afternoon and the next morning when Uncle went to work, Weiying worked on the big-character posters on the scarlet, foldable table at his house. She remembered the woman was tall and skinny and had a pale face. So, she entitled the big-character poster "White Skeleton Demon (a character in the novel Journey to the West, which is an evil demon that can change shapes to deceive people.), Please Stay Away from Others' Family!" Then she included every detail on the issue and her criticism in the big-character posters.

On the third day straightly after she got up, Weiying took her big-character posters and a bucket of glue to the woman's workplace with a son and a daughter of her uncle's. As soon as they stepped into the gate, some people started twittering and following her. It seemed that they had heard something about it. Then Qiu Weiying saw the woman standing by her office window on the second floor of a nearby building, looking at her furiously. Qiu took a glance at her, and then unfolded her big-character posters elatedly. She found a ladder in the corner by the big-character poster wall and put it by the spot she picked. She painted the backside of the big-character posters with glue and started putting them on the wall one by one. Her cousins helped her in passing the bucket and the big-character posters. She was sure that the woman did not dare to come down and argue, not to mention tear the big-character posters down, for big-character posters were protected during the Revolution. One could run into trouble for tearing big-character posters down at his or her own will. While Qiu was putting up the big-character posters, people started to gather around her and read. Some discussed while reading, and even inquired her cousins. Some looked at Qiu with respect. Qiu thought, "The big-character posters may not work, but at least people will criticize her after reading it, giving her some hard times!" Happiness of revenge lighted her after the job. She immediately went back to Aunt and described the scene in high spirits. "The big-character posters can work as propaganda there. She will watch out for her own behavior."

Some days later, Qiu Zhonglin rode a bicycle back home after work. He entered the room, looking furious, and shouted at Weiying's cousin Xiaosi, "Xiaosi, hand me my slippers!" Xiaosi did not hear clearly, or she was being dissatisfied with him, and did not respond. Weiying saw him fetched them himself, took his leather shoes off in the sofa by the door, and changed into the slippers. Then, he grabbed a shoe in his hand and walked to Xiaosi, holding the shoe high to hit her. Xiaosi was scared to running around the big round table in escape. Seeing the scene, Weiying walked up and hide Xiaosi behind her back, saying, "Uncle, how can you beat her for such a trivial?" With these words, she began feeling bitter. She remembered her mother once said, "Your uncle is not so selfish like your father. He eats only the food his children do not like. In the end, he has all the leftovers dumped into his plate." It was because food was offered as rations at that time, and he did not want to waste. How could her caring uncle change so much! Was it because a man's love for his children changes as with the love for his wife? Qiu couldn't help saying, "Uncle, do you blame me for taking them to vixen? If you do, just put the blame on me. My cousins did nothing wrong; I took them there." Qiu Zhonglin said, "Sure! Why is my niece trying to intervene in my private business? It has nothing to do with you! Does your father know what you're doing? Don't you know you aunt is very ill-tempered? I've given in too much, and I don't want to give in anymore!" Weiying said, "Aunt is a knowledgeable and sensible person, and after all, she is your wife. And, you shouldn't have been with such an immoral person any way! A woman who seduces a married man is no way a good woman. I heard she's into coxcombry and doesn't even care to look after her own children. You won't be happy with her, and my cousins will have to suffer. I can't just stand by." Qiu Zhonglin said, "I'm not so eloquent to argue with you." Weiying said, "Uncle, I'll listen quietly to whatever reasoning you have." Qiu Zhonglin was speechless, and so the argument did not proceed.

Some days later Qiu Weiying got a letter from Tang Na, saying, "I wish to go to Beijing with you. We don't need a ticket during the cascade for no one inspects. If you have no place to live, you can come live with me and my aunt." Qiu thought, "That's not bad. I've never been to the Beijing, except for once when Dad took me to visit his cousin Wang Xinglin in Xi'an when I was little. I've never been to Beijing before! If I go, I can drop by and visit old sister Weifen." So, she asked her aunt for permission.

Aunt did not urge her to stay, and agreed at once, saying, "I heard that your uncle has stopped contacting the woman for some days. And I bet she's too ashamed to mess with him after being criticized by her colleagues. Anyhow, stay some more days before you go!" Qiu agreed, and toured Hankou, Wuchang and visited spots like Changjiang Bridge. Before she left, Aunt gave her a white Dacron (which was then a trendy and expensive fabric) blouse with light patterns on, and said, "I can never thank you enough for doing me such a big favor. I can't afford precious gifts, anyway, so just keep the blouse as a memorial." Qiu said, "I don't see any need to thank me; we are family. Just keep it yourself." Aunt said, "I had the tailor made it for your size." Qiu could not refuse any longer, so she said, "Thank you" and took the gift.

The next day, Qiu Weiying got on a train again be packed in like sardines with a lot of passionate Red Guards. Many among them were to visit the village of Shao Shan in Xiangtan, Hunan, where Chairman Mao was born, and they are now also taking the train to Beijing. The train is not clear direction to loaded with these people groggy in sleep. It is following the unfolded old track, dragging them in the dark to the unknown future…

3.4 Beijing, the elegant demeanor of blood dye

To fulfill her promise of accompanying Tang Na to Beijing, Qiu Weiying went back to Changsha from Wuhan. The land of Changsha in late July was burning under the sun, making the city almost as hot as the stove city Wuhan. It seemed to Qiu that the big-character posters had increased in number, but she did not bother to read the harsh and mean content of them, for it was unbearably hot in the street and all she desired was to find somewhere cooler. Even the furniture at home turned hot from the heat.

It was Sunday when she arrived at home. She saw mother and Xiaodong, but father was not there. She asked, "Mom, I saw Dad's domestically made bicycle behind the front gate, but I don't see him at home. Where could he be in such hot weather?" Mrs. Qiu replied, "He's in the bathtub, hiding in cold water!" At that time, no household was furnished with air conditioners. Her father could not stand the heat, but their imported electric fan had been confiscated. So, when it got too hot, he could only resort to a bath in cold water at their small yard.

Weiying wiped away her sweat and found that Mother had finished cooking the green bean porridge and thin pancakes to go with vegetables rolled inside. At dinner, Mrs. Qiu said, "How's your uncle and aunt?" She replied, "They're fine..." when Mr. Qiu came over and interrupted, "It's very likely that Zhonglin has got angry with me!" Mrs. Qiu defended Weiying, "It was for his own family good! His children become single-parent families. It will be a great tragedy for family. Saving a family is always a virtue." Mr. Qiu became silent. After dinner, Weiying secretly asked her mother, "Has Ms Li (Mr. Qiu's ex-wife) been living with grandma and Weizhen, Weidi, Weifen in the north since you married father? When did they go to Beijing?" Mrs. Qiu said, "We left Jiangsu and bought a house at Pozi Street in Changsha. Then once Ms Li took your grandma and the girls to us, and we lived together for a while. Weizhen used to go to school in Changsha before you went to kindergarten. Later, Ms Li blamed your father for favoring me, and Grandma thought it was too crowded for the big family to live together in Changsha; she had always preferred Caiyuangou. So, they went back to the north; only Weizhen stayed for school. When she graduated from middle school, you father sent Ms Li and her three daughters to Beijing, while Grandma stayed in Caiyuan Gou until her hard life came to an end. Thanks to your father and your uncle, she was never starved. The relatives all say that she was lucky to have never been through any toil." At the end of their talk, Weiying said, "Mom, Tang Na asked me to go to Beijing with her, and I can stay in her aunt's place. Is it alright?" Mother said, "Of course, you are best friends, and her parents are both writers. I have no worries at all."

The next day Qiu Weiying took a bus to Tang Na's place at Yuanjialing. The bus was quite crowded. She held the bus ring with one hand and faced the window. While the bus was passing by Provincial Military, she saw the wall marked with huge slogans like "Drag out the handful within of the military" and "Bring down Wu Zili". She had learnt that Wu Zili had been a top commander in Provincial Military, just like Chen Zaidao in Hubei, but suddenly, he became a target to be brought down. She was puzzled, Don't they say the PLA is the steel iron Great Wall of China? If their lives are not guaranteed, how can the security of China be guaranteed? She observed that the other passers seemed accustomed to such unbelievable slogans, all facial expression they appeared for not be surprised by anything unusual with the propaganda and agitation.

Qiu Weiying got off the bus at her destination, and it did not take her long to arrive at the gate of the dormitory of Provincial Literary Federation. As soon as she entered the gate, she noticed a big-character poster aiming at "Kelan", which was the penname of Tang Na's father. The big-character poster attacked his personal life and criticized his work the <Beat bronze Gong> ugly poor and lower-middle peasants, and that <Mending the Pot> was a modern version of the praises gifted scholar and market lady, which were all poisonous weeds of Revisionism. Qiu knew that the two plays had won prizes in that Central-South adapted into movies and praised by the top Secretary of Central South district, Tao Zhu. As Tao Zhu became a key target and was brought down, the works of Kelan were affected and repudiated. Kelan had taken part in the revolution in Yanan and when he was young, and was an experienced Party member and writer, playing quite many essential roles in the literary circles of Shanghai, Hunan and nation-level groups. Qiu also noticed that the four most famous writers in Hunan were all attacked in the big-character posters. She did not read them in detail and direct headed for Tang Na's home.

She noticed it was a bit disordered at Tang Na's home. Tang Na was glad to see her, and yet seemed heavy minded. After Qiu Weiying took her seat, Tang said, "Isn't it ridiculous? Dad wrote <Beat the copper gong> when he was in the countryside for the 'four clear-ups (Clearing up the work points, accounts, storage and properties)'. It was based on the true story of a rural woman, whom he characterized as Lin Shiniang. The play has been praised and awarded before, but now it's the poisonous weed of Revisionism!" Qiu immediately said, "Things have stopped making sense already. It's been two years since we were confiscated. They said, 'We'll freeze your properties until they say the PLA is the steel iron Great Wall of China? If their lives are not guaranteed, how can the security of China be guaranteed? She observed that the other passers seemed accustomed to such unbelievable slogans, all facial expression they appeared for not be surprised by anything unusual with the propaganda and agitation.

Qiu Weiying got off the bus at her destination, and it did not take her long to arrive at the gate of the dormitory of Provincial Literary Federation. As soon as she entered the gate, she noticed a big-character poster aiming at "Kelan", which was the penname of Tang Na's father. The big-character poster attacked his personal life and criticized his work the <Beat bronze Gong> ugly poor and lower-middle peasants, and that <Mending the Pot> was a modern version of the praises gifted scholar and market lady, which were all poisonous weeds of Revisionism. Qiu knew that the two plays had won prizes in that Central-South adapted into movies and praised by the top Secretary of Central South district, Tao Zhu. As Tao Zhu became a key target and was brought down, the works of Kelan were affected and repudiated. Kelan had taken part in the revolution in Yanan and when he was young, and was an experienced Party member and writer, playing quite many essential roles in the literary circles of Shanghai, Hunan and nation-level groups. Qiu also noticed that the four most famous writers in Hunan were all attacked in the big-character posters. She did not read them in detail and direct headed for Tang Na's home.

She noticed it was a bit disordered at Tang Na's home. Tang Na was glad to see her, and yet seemed heavy minded. After Qiu Weiying took her seat, Tang said, "Isn't it ridiculous? Dad wrote <Beat the copper gong> when he was in the countryside for the 'four clear-ups (Clearing up the work points, accounts, storage and properties)'. It was based on the true story of a rural woman, whom he characterized as Lin Shiniang. The play has been praised and awarded before, but now it's the poisonous weed of Revisionism!" Qiu immediately said, "Things have stopped making sense already. It's been two years since we were confiscated. They said, 'We'll freeze your properties until go with vegetables rolled inside. At dinner, Mrs. Qiu said, "How's your uncle and aunt?" She replied, "They're fine…" when Mr. Qiu came over and interrupted, "It's very likely that Zhonglin has got angry with me!" Mrs. Qiu defended Weiying, "It was for his own family good! His children become single-parent families. It will be a great tragedy for family. Saving a family is always a virtue." Mr. Qiu became silent. After dinner, Weiying secretly asked her mother, "Has Ms Li (Mr. Qiu's ex-wife) been living with grandma and Weizhen, Weidi, Weifen in the north since you married father? When did they go to Beijing?" Mrs. Qiu said, "We left Jiangsu and bought a house at Pozi Street in Changsha. Then once Ms Li took your grandma and the girls to us, and we lived together for a while. Weizhen used to go to school in Changsha before you went to kindergarten. Later, Ms Li blamed your father for favoring me, and Grandma thought it was too crowded for the big family to live together in Changsha; she had always preferred Caiyuangou. So, they went back to the north; only Weizhen stayed for school. When she graduated from middle school, you father sent Ms Li and her three daughters to Beijing, while Grandma stayed in Caiyuan Gou until her hard life came to an end. Thanks to your father and your uncle, she was never starved. The relatives all say that she was lucky to have never been through any toil." At the end of their talk, Weiying said, "Mom, Tang Na asked me to go to Beijing with her, and I can stay in her aunt's place. Is it alright?" Mother said, "Of course, you are best friends, and her parents are both writers. I have no worries at all."

The next day Qiu Weiying took a bus to Tang Na's place at Yuanjialing. The bus was quite crowded. She held the bus ring with one hand and faced the window. While the bus was passing by Provincial Military, she saw the wall marked with huge slogans like "Drag out the handful within of the military" and "Bring down Wu Zili". She had learnt that Wu Zili had been a top commander in Provincial Military, just like Chen Zaidao in Hubei, but suddenly, he became a target to be brought down. She was puzzled, Don't

The golden age was ruined

conclusions are made'. But the country is in a big mess now, and the Red Guards confiscate without receipts. The hope of getting our belongings back looked bleak." They talked for a while, and Tang asked, "Have you set your mind about going to Beijing?" Qiu said, "Yes. I've talked to my mom, and she agreed. When are you leaving?" Tang said, "A few days later. Is it ok for you?" Qiu said, "Sure. I came back from Hankou just to join you. Should we buy the tickets first?" Tang said, "Who would to buy a ticket during in the big series?" Qiu said, "You've joined the Red Guards in school, but I haven't." Tang said, "It's alright. No one will know about it, and nobody inspects. A lot of students travel around the country by train. They even go to red areas like Yan'an and Jinggangshan. Maybe we can go there sometime." Qiu Weiying replied, "Don't count me in. I've had enough about mountainous areas."

On the day of leaving, they met at the train station. The train came from the Guangzhou along Jingguang line, and the terminal is Beijing. Before it even came into the station, Qiu Weiying saw a lot of heads reaching out the window. As the train approached, Qiu saw their faces flushed from the revolutionary passion. Before the train completely ceased moving, the people waiting started rushing towards it. This time Qiu was quicker in action and ran by the door. As soon as the door opened, she stopped right by it. People on the train were pushing their way off, while those behind her were also pushing to get on. Tang Na was two centimeters taller than Qiu. Qiu saw her standing behind, so she held tight to the door and got her feet on train. Tang Na followed her on train. For they got on earlier, they were both able to find a seat. Before long, the scorching train in sun whistled and started moving. Qiu began to feel excited. The wheels rolled restlessly, taking Qiu's heart already to the heart of China – She's never been to Beijing, a place where the Party Central Committee and Chairman Mao were, and the entire Chinese people as well as world's proletariats dreamed of.

The train arrived in Beijing. Qiu Weiying and Tang Na walked out of the station, and each with their own a travelling bag. They headed straight for the bus station to get on a bus to Tang Na's aunt – Aunt Mei's home. The asphalt road almost melted from the sun. Cars dashed by, raising the dust behind, informing them of the dryness of the north. Getting off the bus, they circumvented a wall to an unsheltered gate leading to the dormitory of China National Radio, where Aunt Mei lived. Mei's husband worked at CNR, which was the media of supreme authority then, no matter if it was domestic or foreign news, if it was broadcasted by CNR, it would be taken for granted.

Mei auntie couldn't stay at home at that time, because she was the chief and party secretary of the Central National Orchestra that who was the focus criticism object of the motionat that time. The Rebel factions detained her in the office and forbade her to go home.

There were only Tang's uncle, a kind veteran revolutionist whom Qiu met with every day in the following two months and sincerely respected, and Mei's youngest daughter, Xiaomei. Mei auntie had two sons, one at Shanghai Conservatory of Music, whom Qiu had never met but only heard of from Tang Na; and the younger one called Junjun, who studied at the high school attached to Beijing Music Academy and was about to graduate. He lived at school, and only came back occasionally during Sundays.

The first time Qiu Weiying saw him was on a Sunday when she came back from shopping. As she walked inside the front door, she saw a young lad with a unique look. He was tall, and had dark eyebrows, mysterious eyes and a noble nose, which made him look handsome and gentle. He was sitting on a small stool by the door, bending down to wipe the black leather shoes on his feet. He raised his head as he heard the door, and saw Qiu Weiying coming in. He smiled at her in a gentle manner, and she smiled back coyly. Both had been informed of each other, but they were too shy to say hello. Qiu went pass him a bit bashfully, strolled into the house, put down the groceries and entered the living room.

The golden age was ruined

Tang's uncle was sitting in the couch, writing something by the table. He saw Qiu coming in, smiled and said at ease, "Here you are. And so is my younger son, Junjun." Qiu replied to Uncle (she followed Tang Na in addressing him) in a blush, "Yes, I've seen him." He added by the way, "You're a year younger than Nana, right? Junjun and Nana were born in the same year." Being young and naïve, Qiu did not sense his purpose immediately. Feeling shy, she changed the topic on purpose, "Where is Nana?" He replied, "She's out to handle some business." Later, Junjun had some casual conversation with his father, and then left for school without having dinner. Qiu had never seen him dine at home anyway, probably it was because Mei did not live and eat there, so the family only bought their meals from the canteen. However, she never asked why Tang Na did not eat at home either. Tang usually went out for things she never told. Qiu guessed it was for her parents. One day when Uncle left for work and Xiaomei was playing with some neighbor kids in the yard, Qiu wrote a letter to her sister Weifen, saying that she had arrived in Beijing. But she did not get her reply in time.

Some days later, Tang Na told Qiu Weiying, "My parents have arrived at Beijing. They are staying at their old friend, Mr. Luo Gongliu's place, whom they have known since the days in Yan'an. How about visiting them with me tomorrow?" Of course, Qiu immediately agreed. The next day they took a bus to a major street, and then turned into alley nearby. There was a wide gate in a long alley, which Tang came close to and pushed the doorbell button on. Soon, a gentle, smart and with short hair mid-aged woman came for the door. She was Mrs. Luo. Qiu followed Tang into their living room, as Mrs. Luo was smiling and looking at her while making tea. Mr. Luo greeted them friendly and asked Qiu to sit. However, Tang Na's mother, Wang Wenqiu was trying to pull herself together and greet her. She looked worried. Qiu asked in surprise, "What's wrong? Are you sick?" She replied weakly, "I'm not sick. It was the Rebels factions…" She told Qiu Weiying to roll up her clothes to see her back. It almost took Qiu's breath away, there were countless of scars and blacks and blues on her back; not an inch of fine skin could be found. Qiu said with a mixture of feelings, "How cruel must they be to do this to someone who has never done them wrong?" Mrs. Luo sighed and said, "Alas, it's inevitable in the motion." Mrs. Tang had already dried all her tears. She said, "It's not over! I was to scare of them coming again and did us the 'jet plane' (a kind of physical punishment during the Cultural Revolution. The victims were bent into a 90-degree angle or even more, as if in a bow, and the arms were forced straight behind as if the wings of a plane. A big black board was hung on the victim's necks). I can't stand it any longer, so Nana's father and I hid into your family house. If we hadn't, we would have been tortured to death. After some while, your mother took the whole family to your father's hometown. She asked me if we wanted to come along, but we didn't want to trouble them any longer, so we came to Beijing." Qiu felt a bit gratified and said, "They did the right thing."

Altogether there were seven people at Mr. Luo's dinner table, Mr. and Mrs. Luo and their son, Mr. and Mrs. Tang, Tang Na and Qiu Weiying. Qiu Weiying liked the family, their son studied at Central Academy of Fine Arts and was gentle and quiet by the table; Mrs. Luo was kind and amiable with great hospitality; Mr. Luo was knowledgeable and talkative, for he had participated the revolution in Yan'an, studied in Soviet, played crucial roles at Central Academy of Fine Arts and Chinese Artists' Association and joined in big event for example the design of RMB. What's more, his most famous paintings were odes to Civil War, revolution and Chairman Mao, which have nothing to do with the Gang of Four, Feudalism, Capitalism or Revisionism. That was probably why Mr. Luo was not affected by the Cultural Revolution. So, his house was the safest place for Tang Na's parents.

After lunch and some rest, Qiu thought it was time for the elders to take their nap, so she said to Tang Na, "I'd better get going now." Tang said, "Alright, I'll walk you to the station." On the way, Tang

The golden age was ruined

Na told the stories of their family, "Mom was born in Shanghai. Grandma was rich when she was young, but she gave up the cozy life and joined revolution in Yan'an. There she met Father and married him. Aunt Mei had gone to Yan'an first, and then she wrote a letter and had my dad and the other aunt at Changsha go to Yan'an. It was a tough place to be and a lot of people quitted. But my mom held on and became a Party member there. Now they call her a Capitalist intellect trying to sneak into the Party. They were so young at that time. My father was only 16 when he joined the revolution; people called him the "Red little one". How on earth could they know anything about 'sneaking into the Party'?" Qiu asked, "How's your father now?" Tang replied, "Repudiated, but they didn't beat him. Probably because his teacher was Xu Teli, Chairman Mao's teacher. They call it 'the mass movement', but it is 'the motion mass! 'How could the mass ever figure out what's on the authorities' minds?" Tang Na was right somehow. How did Japan manage to launch invasive wars in China and other Asian countries? How did German Nazi manage to invade some European countries and slaughter the Jews? All massive acts must be based on the mass. Even though Hitler, the leader of Nazi committed suicide in 1945 at the complete failure of his invasion, and that the Chinese people finally won the Anti-Japan War under the leadership of Chairman Mao and Chinese Communist Party after eight years of struggle, isn't it because of the Gang of Four had taken advantage of the inexperienced young students that the Cultural Revolution could develop so widely in China? Some evil forces within the society also took advantage of the chance to let off their rage and revenge, or to get some political benefits, making the situation even worse.

Qiu thought, "Remember when I said your mother looked like Jiang Qing? You nodded and said, 'Sure she does! People all tell us so.' Now Jiang Qing is having her day on the political stage while your mother has to hide away and is deprived of her normal life." But she did not utter her black humor, for at that time the Gang of Four had deceived Chairman Mao into absolute trust in them. They had the utmost power and were able to play the entire country in the palm of their hands. How did she dare to make jokes about them? The bus came as they were talking. Tang Na said to Qiu Weiying, "Go. I'll be back in a few days. Tiedan and Tang Di are coming to Beijing soon." Hearing that Tang's brothers were coming too, Qiu realized that Tang's family could not manage to stay in Changsha any longer.

The next afternoon Qiu Weiying was washing her clothes in a basin put in the bathtub near the front gate, while Xiaomei was at her neighbor's home playing with other kids. She suddenly heard some noise from the front door and saw Uncle coming in with his bicycle. Behind him was a young girl of middle size. She had a delicate face, short hair and was wearing a pair of gold-rimmed glasses, which made her look like an intellect. She observed Qiu, who was a stranger to her, and asked Uncle in a quiet voice, "Who's this?" Uncle replied in a voice that Qiu could hear, "She's Nana's classmate. She's here to be with Xiaomei. We're all happy to have her!"

After Tang Na arrived at Aunt Mei's home the next day, her first words with Qiu were, "Do you know who the young woman is yesterday?" Qiu replied, "No. She followed Uncle in the living room, and they talked. Every day after work, your uncle is indulged in writing or checking documents. I've never seen him free, nor have I ever asked him anything." Tang Na told her, "She's the girlfriend of Aunt Mei's elder son at Shanghai Conservatory of Music. Her name is He Xiaoqiu, She He Luting's daughter. She cannot be convinced for her father being convicted as 'big black ghost' and came to Beijing to appeal to the authority. Aunt Mei's elder son was Xiang Yansheng; the name was given by Chairman Mao, for he was born in Yan'an." Qiu uttered a "wow". She had learnt that He Lùting was the most famous composer in China. Later one day, He Xiaoqiu came again. She looked depressed, had some small talks with uncle and then left in a hurry. Qiu Weiying did not expect that was the second and last had the utmost power and were able to play the entire country in the palm of their hands. How did she dare to make jokes about them? The bus came as they were talking. Tang Na said to Qiu Weiying, "Go. I'll be back in a few days. Tiedan and Tang Di are coming to Beijing soon." Hearing that Tang's brothers were coming too, Qiu realized that Tang's family could not manage to stay in Changsha any longer.

The next afternoon Qiu Weiying was washing her clothes in a basin put in the bathtub near the front gate, while Xiaomei was at her neighbor's home playing with other kids. She suddenly heard some noise from the front door and saw Uncle coming in with his bicycle. Behind him was a young girl of middle size. She had a delicate face, short hair and was wearing a pair of gold-rimmed glasses, which made her look like an intellect. She observed Qiu, who was a stranger to her, and asked Uncle in a quiet voice, "Who's this?" Uncle replied in a voice that Qiu could hear, "She's Nana's classmate. She's here to be with Xiaomei. We're all happy to have her!"

After Tang Na arrived at Aunt Mei's home the next day, her first words with Qiu were, "Do you know who the young woman is yesterday?" Qiu replied, "No. She followed Uncle in the living room, and they talked. Every day after work, your uncle is indulged in writing or checking documents. I've never seen him free, nor have I ever asked him anything." Tang Na told her, "She's the girlfriend of Aunt Mei's elder son at Shanghai Conservatory of Music. Her name is He Xiaoqiu, She He Luting's daughter. She cannot be convinced for her father being convicted as 'big black ghost' and came to Beijing to appeal to the authority. Aunt Mei's elder son was Xiang Yansheng; the name was given by Chairman Mao, for he was born in Yan'an." Qiu uttered a "wow". She had learnt that He Lùting was the most famous composer in China. Later one day, He Xiaoqiu came again. She looked depressed, had some small talks with uncle and then left in a hurry. Qiu Weiying did not expect that was the second and last

Na told the stories of their family, "Mom was born in Shanghai. Grandma was rich when she was young, but she gave up the cozy life and joined revolution in Yan'an. There she met Father and married him. Aunt Mei had gone to Yan'an first, and then she wrote a letter and had my dad and the other aunt at Changsha go to Yan'an. It was a tough place to be and a lot of people quitted. But my mom held on and became a Party member there. Now they call her a Capitalist intellect trying to sneak into the Party. They were so young at that time. My father was only 16 when he joined the revolution; people called him the "Red little one". How on earth could they know anything about 'sneaking into the Party'?" Qiu asked, "How's your father now?" Tang replied, "Repudiated, but they didn't beat him. Probably because his teacher was Xu Teli, Chairman Mao's teacher. They call it 'the mass movement', but it is 'the motion mass! 'How could the mass ever figure out what's on the authorities' minds?" Tang Na was right somehow. How did Japan manage to launch invasive wars in China and other Asian countries? How did German Nazi manage to invade some European countries and slaughter the Jews? All massive acts must be based on the mass. Even though Hitler, the leader of Nazi committed suicide in 1945 at the complete failure of his invasion, and that the Chinese people finally won the Anti-Japan War under the leadership of Chairman Mao and Chinese Communist Party after eight years of struggle, isn't it because of the Gang of Four had taken advantage of the inexperienced young students that the Cultural Revolution could develop so widely in China? Some evil forces within the society also took advantage of the chance to let off their rage and revenge, or to get some political benefits, making the situation even worse.

Qiu thought, "Remember when I said your mother looked like Jiang Qing? You nodded and said, 'Sure she does! People all tell us so.' Now Jiang Qing is having her day on the political stage while your mother has to hide away and is deprived of her normal life." But she did not utter her black humor, for at that time the Gang of Four had deceived Chairman Mao into absolute trust in them. They

meeting with the young girl. Before long, Xiaoqiu was gone forever…
<See App, 2. A) 2. B)>.

The following day Qiu got the reply from Weifen, saying, "I had been to hometown to visit mother and sister Weidi, so I didn't get your letter in time. I will soon graduate and be arranged for job by school. I'm having a get-together with my classmates at the Temple of Heaven this Sunday. Come to my school by 9 and join us."

In Sunday morning, Weiying took the blouse her aunt gave her in Hankou to Beijing Business Administration College where Weifen studied, as she was informed. She entered Weifen's dormitory and saw the fine bamboo mat on her bed, which was bought by her mother when she was in junior high and Weifen came to Changsha to visit them. She also noticed a book by her pillow; it was <Morning Glory Piccolo> Weiying told Weifen, "The author is my friend's father. I'm now living in her aunt's place." Weifen said, "Really? A lot of college students in Beijing are fond of this book of prose poetry. It's really well-written!" Weiying added, "He's the president of Prose Poetry Association. But now he is in Beijing with his wife to escape the persecution." Weifen sighed. Weiying gave the blouse to Weifen and said, "It was given by Aunt, and I've never worn it. Keep it as my gift." Weifen said, "Keep it yourself for she gave it to you!" Weiying said, "No. I'm a rural dweller now and don't need decent clothes. You're a college student in Beijing, and I don't see you with many good clothing, so please keep it. Don't be so ceremonious with me!" Weifen said no more, so Weiying put the blouse by her pillow. They went for a stroll on campus and left for the Temple of Heaven.

The Temple of Heaven was located at Chongwen District, Beijing. It was where the emperors of the Ming and Qing dynasty offered sacrifices to gods. The north sides of the buildings are round, and the south are square, for ancient Chinese believed that the sky is round, and the earth is square. The students sat on a grassy land surrounded by trees, with only one path leading in and out. Weifen introduced Weiying to her classmates as "sister of the same father". They commented, "What a nice sister you have…" After all their classmates had arrived, they started clapping their hands to ask Weifen to sing. Weifen was not shy at all. Her voice was magnetic, loud and clear, "O my dear horse, walk slowlier and take no rush…" Her voice resounded above the grassy land of sunshine and happiness, temporarily wiped away the depressing influences of Cultural Revolution from their minds… Soon after Weifen graduated from college, she was dispatched to a state-owned factory in the mountainous district of Guizhou.

The next day Tang Na came from Mr. Luo Gongliu's home and told Weiying, "My parents and I came yesterday when you were visiting your sister. Junjun was also back from school, and Xiaomei and Aunt were all here. Junjun said, there was one day when he came back and saw no one in the living room. He heard someone playing the piano and thought it was Xiaomei. When he looked inside the room, he saw you. He said the way you played the piano was adorable. My father said, 'You can teach little Qiu.' But he said he had never taught anyone before and did not know how. So, we all laughed at him." Qiu remembered Tang Na's uncle used to say to her, "If there weren't the Cultural Revolution and do away with four old customs, we would have you as our nominal daughter and send you to a music academy for further studies." Qiu was silent for quite some time after Tang Na's words. She began to have a vague idea that ever since the confiscation of family property, the god of luck had never favored her, while on the contrary, stood in her way from time to time…

Some days later, Tang Na told Qiu Weiying, "I'm going to the Luo Gongliu's to be with my parents this Sunday. You can go to the Summer Palace with Aunt's family. She's got a day's sick leave and can join you. They may take pictures, so wear the blouse your aunt gave you. It's a nice blouse, but you've never put it on." Weiying said, "I've given it to my sister." Tang blamed her, "It was your only decent clothes, why did you give it to her?" She replied, "It suits her better;

she's a college student in Beijing." Tang said, "You really should have considered more for yourself!"

The next day Weiying and Xiaomei got up early. Junjun and Aunt Mei came to join them in the trip to Summer Palace. Before leaving, Aunt Mei asked Qiu Weiying, "Can you swim?" She replied, "No, but I have my swimsuit with me." Aunt Mei said, "That's alright, we can teach you. We all can swim, including Xiaomei. Let's put on the swimsuit inside, for it will be inconvenient to change in the boat." Qiu Weiying agreed and did as Aunt Mei said. When everybody was ready, they set out together. Junjun and Uncle rode bicycles, while Weiying, Aunt Mei and Xiaomei took a bus. The bus took them to the gate of Summer Palace at the feet of West Mountain in Haidian District, Beijing. Then, they went to Kunming Lake in the Palace to meet with Uncle and Junjun.

The Summer Palace was built in 1750, and it covered an area of about 300 hectares. It was the residence of the emperors in the Ming and Qing dynasty, and where Emperor Guangxu and his mother Cixi dealt with domestic and foreign affairs. It had been adapted several times after Liberation to a place for the laboring people to relax. However, in the Cultural Revolution, the Red Guards would destroy every historical relic as an act to break the Gang of Four". So, some with stronger sense of responsibility closed the spots of key protected cultural relics and stored the so called "feudalist" articles in museums. The relics which people could appreciate at ease were then gone completely. But still lots would like to come in sunny summer days to breathe some fresh air and relax. So, boating on the Kunming Lake became one of the most favored activities. The warm breeze by the lake had blown away the tension and fierceness of Cultural revolution. Weiying, Aunt Mei and Xiaomei arrived at the lake, and saw uncle had already queued up for the ticket to rent a boat. The sun rose high up in the sky, giving off its glories that made people dizzy. Weiying went to him and said, "Let me do this." Uncle refused at once, "No, you just wait under the shade. I can handle it by myself."

He took a pair of sunglasses out of his pocket and put them on, Qiu followed Aunt Mei in the shade await.

After a while, Uncle rented a boat for six. They gladly got on boat, especially Xiaomei, who jumped on delightfully. Uncle and Junjun each held a paddle and rowed the boat towards the other bank of the lake to have a swim down Wanshou Hill. After paddling for a while in the large lake, Junjun said, "It's so hot!" Aunt Mei said, "Take off your clothes then. You'll have to take them off anyway." So Junjun took of the clothes outside his swimsuit, exposing her long legs and kept on paddling with his strong and agile arms. Xiaomei said in the boat, "I feel hot too." She also took off her clothes. As the heat became unbearable, courage fell on Qiu, who was conservative in nature. She took off the outer clothes with only swimsuit on; but she felt uncomfortable at once. So, she turned her face to Xiaomei and asked, "Do you have the big towel with you?" Xiaomei asked, "Why?" She replied immediately, "I want to cover my body." Uncle heard it and said to her, "What a nice and healthy body! Don't cover up, let me take a photo first." He handed the paddle over to Aunt Mei and held up his camera. Qiu found the family smiling at her, which made her even more embarrassed. She turned her body and said, "Oh, please! Taking a photo in swimsuit? That's too edgy for me!" She made them all laugh. Xiaomei's eyebrows bent, and she said loudly, "Qiu Mi Mi, True feudal…!" Anyhow, Qiu found the big towel in their bag as quickly as possible and used it to cover her body.

At this time, a warm breeze swept over the lake, decorating it with golden glow and rippling wavelets. Qiu felt warm inside. She suddenly thought that she had been so close with the family… As the paddles rowed on, the boat took the five people to the other bank of green shades… In order to survive the many campaigns during the Cultural Revolution, Aunt Mei and Uncle was deprived of the normal, ordered life. As the Gang of Four became more rampant and more veteran cadres were brought down, the trip of friendship with Aunt Mei's family became one that Qiu could never forget.

The golden age was ruined

Some days later, Tang Na told Qiu Weiying, "Tiedan and Tang Di are coming to Beijing; it will be too crowded if we all live at Aunt Mei's, so I'm moving to Mr. Luo's to cater to my parents and can't stay here with you any longer." After Tang Na took her luggage away, Qiu began to feel uneasy. When Uncle came back, she said, "Nana has moved to Mr. Luo's house; it'll be of too much trouble if I still stay. I'd better go back to Changsha." Uncle replied immediately, "Why? Did your parents ask you to return? It's no trouble at all to have you! By the way, Xiaomei is so young that she needs to be accompanied. Isn't it better for us to have you stay and help?" Qiu said, "My parents know I'm with Nana and they are not worried at all. It was all my idea to go back." Uncle was relieved and said, "Alright then. We'd be glad to have you with us. What do you say?" She said, "Ok. It won't be any difference if I return or not anyway." Uncle pointed to the drawer where he put the meal coupons of their canteen and said, "If you are home alone, you can take the coupons to canteen to get your meals." He also gave her keys to their house and a bankbook, saying, "Aunt Mei is segregated now and can't come back. Please help get her salary back from her workplace and send her the food ration coupons."

On the salary day, Qiu took the coupons and bankbook and arrived at the informed time and location, which was in an alley behind Aunt Mei's workplace. Aunt Mei came from the back door to meet her. Qiu gave her the coupons and took over her salary of the month. Aunt Mei reminded her, "Tell Xiaomei's father that the situation's getting tough, he shall take care." Qiu said, "Ok, I will." As she went past a bank, she took out the bankbook and deposited Mei's money.

Qiu gave the bankbook to Uncle when he returned from work, saying, "I've put the money in." Uncle looked and said, "That's quick!" Qiu said, "I had the bankbook with me when I went there. After she gave me the money, I put them in when I went by a bank." Uncle seemed satisfied, and said, "You can keep the bankbook in you need money. You can have her seal and the bankbook to draw

163

cash from banks." Qiu replied, "There's no need. I already have meal tickets, and I have some money that Mom gave me, which I have barely used."

One morning later, Tang Na came. Upon entrance, she said in indignation and bitterness, "Aunt Mei was beaten by the Rebel faction sat her workplace! Did you know she came back at midnight?" Qiu was surprised, "Are you sure? I didn't have a clue!" Tang said, "She did not come through the front door to avoid waking you, Xiaomei and the neighbors. She opened an unlocked window behind the bush and crawled in. she was repudiated and beaten to nose blood. She said those attacked her were the people who had behaved ill at work, whom she had neither trusted nor given important positions. She only had a few words with Uncle and then went to the hospital before dawn. She was afraid that she had fractures. She had to leave before dawn, for the neighbors all know that she was in power at work and could not go home randomly. As long as one reveals her return, she could never go to hospital and will have to suffer from harsher attacks." It sounded unbelievable to Qiu, for she had viewed many photos of Mei showed by Uncle, in the photos, Mei had been leader of Chinese artists' delegates and traveled to different countries; she was wearing ethic-featured cheongsams, shaking hands with foreign leaders and smiling. What's more, she had joined the revolution in Yan'an and became a Party member long before. How could she possibly become a key target within the Party and suffer ill-treatment tortures in the motion?

Before long, Tang Na's brothers, Tiedan and Tang Di also came to Beijing. Tang Di also lived at Mei's auntie home, while Tiedan lived somewhere else, but he came occasionally, to kill time. He would draw a kitten on the little blackboard on the wall every time, which Xiaomei liked very much. Tiedan was 22, very gifted in drawing, and had been directed by a famous artist. When he was 16 years old, he won the first place in the national youth drawing competition. He would personify the kitten, Qiu Weiying think he was deliberately drawing their own. So, she would try to erase the picture while Tiedan was drawing. In the end, Tiedan noted by the picture, "This is Qiu Mi Mi." Innocent Xiaomei would laugh and scream, clapping her hands, "Little Qiu! Little Qiu…" Qiu would stand on her tiptoes and try to erase it, but she always failed. As a result, she became angry, and never looked at Tiedan when he came again. Tiedan felt snubbed and never drew again. Tang Na was unhappy to know about it, and said, "My old brother was only making a joke with you. Why should you be angry with him?" Qiu replied, "I wasn't really angry. Only, I was unhappy that he gave me a cat face with mustache and noted 'this is Little Qiu'." Tang felt funny, raised her eyebrows and said, "What's the big deal? My families also call me Na Mi Mi." The two friends were silent for a while and argued no more.

There was one night when Tang Di, who was about 13, lay on the bed opposite to Qiu's and started talking. Qiu did not interrupt; she listened attentively and thought, "No wonder he knows so much at such young age! His parents are all veteran revolutionist and writers." In the end, Tang Di told her, "Uncle could have been further promoted. But he made some Right-leaning mistakes, and he has foreign relations which made a suspect of spying…" Qiu could hardly believe it. She had read On the Cultivation of a Party Communist Member by Liu Shaoqi at Xinhua Bookstore, when she was in middle school. After her days of contact with Uncle, she thought he met every standard of a typical good Party member with noble morals and strong sense of social responsibility. What's more, he had joined the revolution in Yan'an since 1937, and had been a Party member for almost 40 years. How could he possibly make "errors of route?" after liberation? How could the Party possibly suspect him of making such mistakes? She was lost in thought and by confusions.

Later Qiu mentioned her puzzles to Tang Na, who said, "Tang Di really trusts you to have told you all these. Uncle had been investigated before he joined the Party in Yan'an. There's no way that he's a spy! Some people are trying to set him up! As to the Right-leaning errors, who could say for sure? There are a lot of veteran Party members brought down out there!" Deep in thought, Qiu said, "That's true. There is not even one-Party member in my family, making it even harder to understand the policies."

Qiu Xiaodong arrived at Beijing in September, and Weiying went to the guest room in the petition office of State Council to meet her. Xiaodong told Weiying, "The headquarters of Xiangjiang Fenglei (Xiangjiang Fenglei Advancing Column of Maoist Red Guards, the largest mass organization in Hunan during the Cultural Revolution) had written me a letter of introduction to appeal. With the letter, I can get a place to live here with the help of the State Council. But I can't stay here for too long, for Mother has asked leave from the hospital and took the family to Father's hometown. I was the only one left at home, for Father goes to work every day. Before leaving, Mother asked Mrs. Tang to go with them, but she refused. She said she could go to her friends' or relatives in Beijing. Before she came here, Mother asked her to tell you if it's inconvenient for you to stay for too long, you can go to hometown too. Some days after Mrs. Tang left, I got a letter from Tang Na's uncle, saying everything's fine with you, so we don't need to worry…" Weiying said, "Really? I have no idea that he wrote to my family!" Xiaodong continued, "The main reason I came to Beijing this time was because of the "raid-the confiscated of our family property. It's been two years and a half since our properties were 'frozen', but no conclusion has been given yet. You and Juecong cannot continue school; Father and Mother are really upset." Weiying said, "I think they purposely did so. All they wanted was to confiscate all our properties, hand them over to the national treasury as their personal contribution to the country. They have never thought of giving us a conclusion. But let's see what the Central Revolutionary Petition Office says about it. We can't let them take all the properties away and live with a political stain for all our life."

The golden age was ruined

They arrived at the Petition Office and saw two long lines of people queuing. It seemed rather crowded in the front, for the windy lines but did not move for a long while. Later they heard people quarrelling about queuing and were even about to put up a fight. At that time, a man pushed out of the front crowd, shouting, "It's no use coming here! No one gives a damn about the old case! Tell me to seek help from local authorities? Why do you think I came here? I've put all my hope on the central committee, sold all our properties to come here!

You want me to go begging from door to door my way home?!" Hearing him, Weiying and Xiaodong looked at each other, knowing there wasn't much hope for them. Standing in the bustling crowd, looking at the anxious faces anticipating help, they realized that a lot were like them, hoping that the Central Committee and Chairman Mao could offer justice and solve their long-stuck case. But the reality in front of them are all hopes were dashed.

How tough it is for you to survive in this world! Weiying contemplated for a while, and said to Xiaodong, "Sister, our house is empty when Dad goes to work with no one to cater to it. The petition thing seemed tough! Tang Na's uncle likes me a lot, so I can stay longer. You can leave the documents to me, and I'll mail them to Central Revolutionary Committee and wait for their response at Aunt Mei's." Xiaodong said, "Alright. I'll return after visiting Weifen tomorrow. I'm quite worried for leaving Juecong alone. He may wander all day long and not at home!"

After Xiaodong left Beijing, Weiying over the whole situation and decided that she should take her chance in the visit by the complaint by letter or visits office and have their problem solved. If not, the thing would be even more complicated as time proceeded. So, she immediately wrote a report about their confiscation of family property and mailed it to the Petition Office of Central Revolutionary Committee and People's Daily together with relevant documents.

While she had nothing to do at Mei's, Qiu Weiying would go to the streets to read the big-character posters. She hoped to figure out what was going on about the campaign. From the big-character poster entitled Capital Red Guards, she learnt that the August 5th persecution of "jet plane" on Liu Shaoqi at Zhongnanhai was favored and praised by Jiang Qing, Kang Sheng and Chen Boda. Liu Tao, the daughter of Liu Shaoqi and his ex-wife was encouraged by Jiang Qing into writing the big-character poster "A Look into Liu Shaoqi's Ugly Soul", which started a series of political attacks on Liu's personal life. Meanwhile, his wife Wang Guangmei became a sacrifice along that was consistently ugly and assaulted. Jiang Qing was jealous of her travelling abroad with Liu Shaoqi several times, stealing her thunder as the First Lady. In the comics satirizing them, Wang was wearing a cheongsam that did not fit and a long necklace made of big round pearls… Even the president of Indonesia, Soekarno, who expressed his welcome to them, was attacked in the comic, president Soekarno is a local bullies and loafers.

The most incredible thing for Qiu Weiying was that from 1962 to 1965 before their confiscation of family property, the time when her mother ran a personal clinic, she could see the picture of Chairman Mao and Liu Shaoqi hung side by side almost everywhere. But now, despite it was the same Party in power, Liu Shaoqi was under key repudiation as "the Capitalist headquarters under Liu Shaoqi and Deng Xiaoping" became the major political target. There should only have been one headquarter under one administrative party; however, the situation was totally different according to the contemporary mindset! Her mother was first encouraged into opening a legalized personal clinic and then was deprived of everything her parents earned in life – this was a social miniature of the fights between two mindsets within the party. This, Qiu Weiying did not get thoughts straight for the moment.

Qiu waited for a dozen of days without any reply from the petition office of Central Revolutionary Committee, and she wanted to visit father's hometown to see how her family was living there.

She told her thought to Uncle, who did not object but only asked quietly, "Have you really decided so?" She replied, "Yes. And as the National Day is approaching, there will surely be a check on the household occupants. I don't have any certificate, which could bring you troubles." Uncle said, "It's a state-owned house, so there won't be any problem." Seeing Qiu being silent, he asked, "When are you leaving?" She replied, "September 30th." He asked at last, "Do you need us to buy the ticket for you?" She replied, "No, you're too busy. I'm ok. I still have the money mom gave me."

In the morning before she left, Uncle went to work as usual. She went to the stores at Wangfujing alone and bought some specialties of Beijing, for example haw jellies. She returned and found Xiaomei waiting for her at home. Xiaomei gave her a notebook with blue plastic cover and said, "Mom dropped by purposely while going to the hospital. She waited for you a long while and had to leave. Otherwise, the Rebel factions find faults with her." Qiu opened the new notebook for her and saw a letter written by Uncle, saying, "Little Qiu, Sorry I have no time to see you off. Do you need anything, or shall we buy something for your parents…?

All in all, you've been an understanding and helpful girl. You've caused no trouble; on the contrary, we've troubled you a lot. We should say thank you! After you arrive at Changsha, tell us about the situation and we'll see when it will be proper and safe for Nana's parents to return.

You are still young, and the matter is quite big, but I believe, small will be able to do great things! So, entrust this to you at ……. Welcome you to come back to Beijing and stay with us when you have the chance! Auntie, Xiang Yu"

After reading, she put it between the plastic layers of the notebook carefully. She thought it was a precious souvenir, in which Uncle showed his sincere trust and hope on her. Particularly, he had a high opinion!

She looked at the clock while putting the book in her bag. Then she told Xiaomei, "I'm leaving." Xiaomei was unwilling to part, and said, "Let me see you off." Qiu said, "No, it's not safe out there. When I went to the station yesterday, I saw the station crowded with Red Guards and Rebels. You're too young to walk home alone. I can't put you in danger." Xiaomei said, "Alright, so I stay. If you come to Beijing again in the future, remember to stay here. I like being with you." Despite she was unwilling to, Qiu carried her bag and waved to Xiaomei, "Alright, I'm leaving now. See you, Xiaomei! Say goodbye for me to Tang Na and her parents, for I have no time to farewell them. But I can see them again when they go back to Changsha; meeting you again is not that easy." Xiaomei looked at her quietly. There was a mixture of sorrow and innocent smile on her round, adorable face.

To Qiu's surprise, within a year's time it became impossible for her to see Uncle and He Xiaoqiu again! Not long after she arrived at Changsha, Tang Na told her the astonishing bad news, "He Xiaoqiu committed suicide! <See. App. 2. (B> She wrote a last letter, saying her life was hopeless as her father was imprisoned in the cowshed and she was dispatched to a small city in Guangxi after graduation. She wanted to leave the world, and she said sorry to Yansheng…" He Lùting, Xiaoqiu's father, was born in Hunan. Before Liberation, he was the first Chinese artist to have won the first and second prize in international competitions in Soviet; his works were popular in Europe and America as early as 1935, among them were The Piccolo of the Shepherd Boy, and works like Vagrant Song-girl and Seasons Song has passed on for generations till today. He joined the revolution in Yan'an before Liberation and used to be the dean of Shanghai Conservatory of Music after Liberation and worked in essential positions in Central Music Association. But ever since the Cultural Revolution, he had been repudiated and persecuted, and was imprisoned for five years until January of 1973. This was all due to his criticism against Yao Wenyuan, the leading figure of the Gang

She looked at the clock while putting the book in her bag. Then she told Xiaomei, "I'm leaving." Xiaomei was unwilling to part, and said, "Let me see you off." Qiu said, "No, it's not safe out there. When I went to the station yesterday, I saw the station crowded with Red Guards and Rebels. You're too young to walk home alone. I can't put you in danger." Xiaomei said, "Alright, so I stay. If you come to Beijing again in the future, remember to stay here. I like being with you." Despite she was unwilling to, Qiu carried her bag and waved to Xiaomei, "Alright, I'm leaving now. See you, Xiaomei! Say goodbye for me to Tang Na and her parents, for I have no time to farewell them. But I can see them again when they go back to Changsha; meeting you again is not that easy." Xiaomei looked at her quietly. There was a mixture of sorrow and innocent smile on her round, adorable face.

To Qiu's surprise, within a year's time it became impossible for her to see Uncle and He Xiaoqiu again! Not long after she arrived at Changsha, Tang Na told her the astonishing bad news, "He Xiaoqiu committed suicide! <See. App. 2. (B> She wrote a last letter, saying her life was hopeless as her father was imprisoned in the cowshed and she was dispatched to a small city in Guangxi after graduation. She wanted to leave the world, and she said sorry to Yansheng…" He Lǜting, Xiaoqiu's father, was born in Hunan. Before Liberation, he was the first Chinese artist to have won the first and second prize in international competitions in Soviet; his works were popular in Europe and America as early as 1935, among them were The Piccolo of the Shepherd Boy, and works like Vagrant Song-girl and Seasons Song has passed on for generations till today. He joined the revolution in Yan'an before Liberation and used to be the dean of Shanghai Conservatory of Music after Liberation and worked in essential positions in Central Music Association. But ever since the Cultural Revolution, he had been repudiated and persecuted, and was imprisoned for five years until January of 1973. This was all due to his criticism against Yao Wenyuan, the leading figure of the Gang

She told her thought to Uncle, who did not object but only asked quietly, "Have you really decided so?" She replied, "Yes. And as the National Day is approaching, there will surely be a check on the household occupants. I don't have any certificate, which could bring you troubles." Uncle said, "It's a state-owned house, so there won't be any problem." Seeing Qiu being silent, he asked, "When are you leaving?" She replied, "September 30th." He asked at last, "Do you need us to buy the ticket for you?" She replied, "No, you're too busy. I'm ok. I still have the money mom gave me."

In the morning before she left, Uncle went to work as usual. She went to the stores at Wangfujing alone and bought some specialties of Beijing, for example haw jellies. She returned and found Xiaomei waiting for her at home. Xiaomei gave her a notebook with blue plastic cover and said, "Mom dropped by purposely while going to the hospital. She waited for you a long while and had to leave. Otherwise, the Rebel factions find faults with her." Qiu opened the new notebook for her and saw a letter written by Uncle, saying, "Little Qiu, Sorry I have no time to see you off. Do you need anything, or shall we buy something for your parents…?

All in all, you've been an understanding and helpful girl. You've caused no trouble; on the contrary, we've troubled you a lot. We should say thank you! After you arrive at Changsha, tell us about the situation and we'll see when it will be proper and safe for Nana's parents to return.

You are still young, and the matter is quite big, but I believe, small will be able to do great things! So, entrust this to you at ……. Welcome you to come back to Beijing and stay with us when you have the chance! Auntie, Xiang Yu"

After reading, she put it between the plastic layers of the notebook carefully. She thought it was a precious souvenir, in which Uncle showed his sincere trust and hope on her. Particularly, he had a high opinion!

of Four. As a result, Shanghai Conservatory of Music became "the foundation of the attacks against the Proletarian headquarters", and he was targeted as the leading opponent.

There was no doubt that her father's tragedy in the Cultural Revolution remained a shadow over He Xiaoqiu's head. She failed in her attempt to appeal for him in Beijing, and was faced with an unsatisfying job after graduation, all of which she could not live with, and made her terminate her own life. As a talented girl with good cultivation, she could have had a bright future! But even if the thousands of millions ofeducated youth s is not excluded, there were still many talents like He Xiaoqiu who were be physically and spiritually tortured in the Cultural Revolution. Countless intellects were ruined before they realized their value...

One day in 1968 (the second year since Qiu Weiying came back from Beijing), Tang Na's uncle felt indignant when he was writing his "confession" papers after supper. Liu Shaoqi was treated as the leader of Right-leaning trend and was expelled from the Party in the beginning of the year. Those who made Right-leaning mistakes like him were also repudiated at a more serious level. Truth was forbidden within the Party, and he could not admit that he was wrong in any sense. It was late in the night, and he was not making any progress with his confession. Annoyed, he lay down, wondering what troubles would come to him if he could not hand in a satisfying confession tomorrow. Around midnight, he suddenly began feeling heartaches and sweating. He was upset and grew more uncomfortable, but there was only Xiaomei at home, and she was sleeping tight... Later, the pain grew so strong that he sensed something abnormal. He pulled himself together and turned on the light, and then knocked heavily with his fist on the wooden wall to inform his neighbor, who heard the sound and came, and found it an emergency... In the Cultural Revolution, the "Capitalist academic authorities" were also repudiated. The people on the ambulance had not any basic knowledge about first aid and had him walked on the car by himself.

He passed away even before the ambulance arrived at the hospital. By then, he was only 56, and had never even been sick before.

Mr. Xiang Yu was born in Changsha, Hunan. In 1937, he joined the revolution in Yan'an directly after his graduation from Shanghai Music College. He became a Party member there and started organizing the early revolutionary cultural and artwork of the Party. He had taken part in the production of opera The White-Haired Girl and many revolutionary songs. Early after liberation, he became dean and secretary of Party branch of Shanghai Conservatory of Music. Later, he was dispatched to Beijing for the post of secretary of Central Music Association and other positions in music organizations. He was an energetic person before Cultural revolution, who used to spare time from work to swim in winter days. Was it not for the exhaustion from Cultural Revolution and the stupid first aiders, he could have lived on for many, many years…?

Ever since different opinions with those of the "three red flags" and the then economic policies came into being, represented by Vice President Liu Shaoqi and general secretary Deng Xiaoping as well as other party members like Deng Zihui (who was in charge of agriculture), the conflict of two different roads rose and the situation went harsh. Liu Shaoqi used to say to Chairman Mao, "If the people are starved, some even starved to death, the history will never forgive you and me…" Liu Shaoqi, a noble leader that thought of his people all the time, was defined as a Capitalist Roader and attacked in the Cultural Revolution by the Gang of Four, who made Mao's Proletarian theory as their excuse.

As the Cultural Revolution started, Liu Shaoqi sensed the cruelty of the political storm. At the early stage, he said to Chairman Mao at the Great Hall of the People, "It was I that put forward the wrong line, please set the veteran cadres free as soon as possible. I am willing to quit my post and go back to Yan'an or my hometown to undertake farm work." But his request was not permitted. It was not just power in the party that he lost – it was every basic right as a human! Liu Shaoqi, a veteran Party member that used to be in crucial positions like the vice president, central secretary of Party Committee and chairman of PRC before the Cultural Revolution, became a big scab, traitor and hidden enemy within the Party for divergence with Mao Zedong in ideologies and economic theories. At that time, Chairman Mao's only standard for evaluating people other than Lin Biao and the Gang of four, was whether they listened to and followed his directions.

Think of it, had it not been the Cultural Revolution, reform and opening could have started since Liu Shaoqi, Deng Xiaopin and Deng Zihui put forward policies of free market, private plots, self-responsive profit and loss, and fix farm output quotas for individuals. However, these were regarded by Chairman Mao as "Revisionism" and "return to Capitalism", which were vital threats to the country! The Red Guards who idolized Mao invented a slogan, "Whoever that is against Chairman Mao is anti-revolutionary and should go to hell", which was made use of by the Gang of Four, – they even did more than that – they secretly sent Liu Shaoqi to the prison in Kaifeng, Henan, tied him in bed and finally tortured him to death in November, 1969, without even informing his family (he was given a pseudo identity as "Liu Weihuang, unemployed" when he was cremated). This is a classic for lack of complete judicial system and respect for human right then, casting a chill on people and is well worth deep reflection.

The Gang of Four took chances in the Cultural Revolution launched and led by Chairman Mao himself and took advantage of the worship of him by the Red Guards to fool and agitate them into assisting the Gang to snatch power from the veteran revolutionists. A lot of cadres were persecuted to death near Chairman Mao in Beijing, where the Party Central Committee was. The unprecedented disaster continued for ten years on the land of China. Beijing, the heart of the country, was seriously wounded in the trauma, bereft of normal blood circulation and spreading its pain all over. As Lin Biao and the Gang of Four waved their flag of Cultural Revolution while appealing for a thorough campaign, workers were carried away from producing, peasants became lazy in their fields, and students could not go to school, not to mention the private merchants who would risk their lives if they dared to do business. It was only after the Gang of Four was brought down that the bloody skies in Beijing cleared up finally.

3.5 A trip to fathers' hometown

Qiu Weiying took a train alone from Beijing to Zhengzhou, which was still dozens of miles from her father's hometown Caiyuangou. Despite that she was born in Jiangsu, she spent her childhood in Changsha. So, it was the first time in her memory to have been there. She took a bus to a minor stop near Caiyuangou, and had trouble making out the direction.

When she was about to ask some passersby, she saw the twins creaming excitingly nearby, "Sister Weiying!" as they ran to her. They had a small fight for the right to help with her luggage. Weiying asked curiously, "How did you know I would take this bus?" They answered, "We got your telegraph yesterday and knew you would arrive today. Weidi said, 'The time is appropriate for Weiying to get off the train and take the bus. It's also the only bus in the day.' So, we are sure that you will take it." Damao (the girl in the twins who was born before the other one minutes earlier) looked at her face and said, "Sister, your skin is much lighter than when you just came back from the reservoir!" Weiying said, "Sure! When I was working in the reservoir, sweat went down like streams in summer days, and I could not hide in the shade. Though I worked with my hat on, it did not work about 40-something degrees weather! How could I not get tanned?" She twisted her neck to look around. Except for some corn fields nearby, there was only light-yellow soil, which looked like smashed rocks and was not fertile at all. The three sisters talked over the walk, and soon approached Caiyuangou, where home was near. Qiu found residence down the ravine, which brought her to the memories of Mr. Luo Gongliu's paintings about Chairman Mao in the caves of Yan'an.

She said to the twins, "Aren't the people actually living in caves? Except that they open doors and windows in the front of the caves…" Xiaomao said, "That's two different things. Such houses are cool in summer and warm in winter; I've been in it once." Weiying said, "Take me for a visit when I settle down, I'm really curious." Damao and Xiaomao said "Ok!" almost at the same time. Then they told her, "People in Caiyuangou have given us a lot of red dates, dried persimmons and pomegranates." Weiying asked, "People here seem poor. How can they afford them?" They explained, "They don't need to buy them; the fruits grow in trees." Weiying was curious, "The soil here doesn't look fertile. It's a surprise that fruits are yielded." They talked for a while, and then Damao and Xiaomao suddenly pointed to right front, "Look, that's where we live." Weiying looked to the direction and saw a big locust tree in a yard surrounded by a wall of big cyan rocks. Weiying had seen a photo of her father and uncle by the tree, taken when they returned there to condole with Grandma. Right behind the tree was a two-story stone house made also of big cyan rocks, which seemed rather luxurious in the countryside. All of these remained unchanged from the photo father and uncle took ten years ago.

The three of them entered the gate in the middle of the yard, and saw mother standing on a stone step by the door of the house, smiling and looking at Weiying.

Xiaodong's two sons, both around ten, were also there. The younger one, Wu Jian's hand was in his maternal grandmother, and the elder, Wu Di, held by maternal grandmother's her pants. They looked as her with eyes opened wide, curious as if looking at a stranger. Weiying hurried to the door, and called out happily, "Mom!" Then, she followed her mother indoor, and saw Juele sleeping in an old cane couch from their home in Changsha. There used to be no furniture at all in the house; the few old pieces, including the big wooden bathtub, were all transported from their former house at Changsha.

Now, Juele greeted her, rubbing his eyes, "Sister, you're back?" She replied, "Yes. Did I wake you up?" He said, "No, I wasn't asleep." Mother asked in tender voice, "You must be tired after the train ride! Are you hungry? I've got millet and sweet potato porridge ready." She went to fetch the bowl as talking and handed the porridge to Weiying. Weiying took the bowl over and started eating immediately. Mother smiled, staring at her lovingly. Then, she served Xiaodong's two sons each with a bowl of porridge. Everybody started eating the porridge with some steamed corn bread and pickles. After finishing her bowl, Weiying said, "Mom, I want some more. The sweet potato is so delicious, I like it very much." Mother was very glad, "If you like it, have more!" She took over Weiying's bowl. Weiying asked, "Why don't you have some?" Mrs. Qiu replied, "I'm not hungry yet..." Weiying looked into the pot and found there was not much remained, so she said, "Mom, have some! I've had enough!" Mrs. Qiu said, "Don't worry, I can make some more. The production brigade has given us enough millet and sweet potatoes, and do not charge at all. The team leader said, 'We've been using your house to store food for more than ten years, since Grandma Qiu died. You've never charged us. This is a solid house that can do with mass storage. We're just giving you a little food as payback; we don't need your money.' I replied, 'When we return to Changsha, you can still use the house for free.' They were very happy! Look at the house, it's made of large stones and has thick, solid floor. It can solve their problem of storage very well!" Weiying said, "Of course they are happy to have such a good storehouse for free. I bet people here are even too poor to buy the daily necessities!"

Then, Weiying carried her luggage to the second floor to put it in the bedroom. Just like the first floor, the second one had no separated rooms, for it had been storehouse for more than ten years. So, the whole family all slept on the second floor, on beds made of thick wooden boards, which was a fun experience! After she put down her luggage, her two sisters followed her downstairs. Mother had just finished her lunch and was cleaning the table. Xiaomao

The golden age was ruined

went over and said, "Let me take care of it." After lunch, Juele took Wu Di and Wu Jian to hang out, while Weiying sat in the middle of the yard and talked with Mother and Damao. She looked at the yard and the big locust tree, and then looked to the house and said, "Even if the house is made of cyan stones, it looks very luxurious in the countryside."

Mother said, "Your aunt in Hou village said that your grandpa used to come first in the literary examination of the county. He rode a horse home, with a big red flower on his, very eye-catching. Later, he was hired by the county mayor as his clerical assistant. For he could write very good articles, he became famous around the county. People all came to him for writing articles or plaint documents, and so he made a lot of money. He did not gamble and visit prostitutes. He spent all his money in purchasing land…" Weiying interrupted and asked, "Mom, who's the aunt in Hou village? I've never heard of her." Mrs. Qiu answered, "She's the daughter of your grandpa and his first wife. She is to your father what Weidi is to you." Weiying understood and said, "Oh, so Grandpa used to have two wives too? So, dad and she were born by different mothers?" Mrs. Qiu replied, "It was legal for a man to have several wives before Liberation. But the new government does not allow so." Damao said, "The villagers say that Grandpa used to be a peculiar landlord who is very well cultivated. A lot of land around here used to belong to him." Weiying said, "Watch your words! If Grandpa had been a landlord, then we would all be screwed in the new society!" Mrs. Qiu said, "Your grandma used to say that he had a lot of land. But after his death, she sold them all to raise the children. So, after liberation, she was classified as upper-middle peasant." Weiying said, "That's a good thing! I heard there were some landlords who saved all their money to purchase land, which turned out to be big trouble. Father said, 'The class division in countryside after Liberation was according to the quantity of land owned by a family.' Grandma did a great thing to sell the land and had lessened much trouble. I learned from the books that a lot of capitalists went abroad before liberation; they were

177

further-sighted than the landlords. The landlords it hard to part from one's, their land."

After breakfast the next day, Weiying asked the twins to stay home with the two kids of Xiaodong, while she and her mother went to visit her second sister who had just returned from Beijing. They walked along to a slope and saw a scary basin down the mountain to their right. The basin was about 20 meters deep and wide. There was no plant, nor was there any water, but only dry, light yellow soil. There was no plant around the slope either, which made the surrounding rather gloomy. Weiying said, "Mom, I wouldn't dare to walk here alone." Mrs. Qiu said, "Neither do I. Your father and the villagers have told me that your senior uncle was pushed down here and died. He was a kind man of knowledge and could write good articles. A hooligan here lied to him, saying he wanted to do business and borrowed a lot of money from him. He thought the hooligan had decided to be a good man, so he lent him without any hesitation. Later, people told him, 'He's a liar.

He spent your money on gambling, indulge in sensual pleasures and playing with the prostitute' So, your senior uncle went to the hooligan to ask his money back. The money did not come back, nor did he. Your grandma was up all night being worried about him. She got up before dawn to search for him. Someone told her, 'I saw your son yesterday afternoon with the hooligan in town. He bought your son some buns. How can he be missing today?' Grandma sensed something wrong and set out in tears to search for the hooligan. She went to his house and cried for her son at his door. It was not far from town, and the villagers all gathered and discussed. At last, someone found your senior uncle dead down the ravine. There were congestions around his eyes, and the eyeballs sank. The hooligan ran away the next morning, and no one ever saw him again." Weiying asked, "Why didn't the KMT government sent people to catch him? He wouldn't have run away if he had done nothing wrong! It must be him who killed Uncle!" Mother said, "It's a vast land with sparsely populated areas and no government agencies." Upon the talked, they arrived at Weiying's second sister, Weidi's house.

Weiying followed Mother in Weidi's house. Weidi was glad to see them. Putting down the needle work at hand, she came to greet them and said, "I was feeling quite boring before you came!" Mother gave her a bowl of Jiangsu-styled braised pork which she made by herself. Weidi smiled and said, "Oh, it's already a big pleasure to have you here! You don't have to be so courteous as to bring gift to me! Aren't we family?" It was the first time for Weiying to see Weidi (she had only seen a picture taken in Beijing of Ms. Li and her three daughters before), but they felt as if they had known each other long. They mentioned the of senior uncle being murdered. Weidi said, "It was early after Liberation, and there was no witness at all, so it's difficult to sue him. Grandma went to the hooligan, but he said, 'He fell down carelessly himself. Why do you blame me?' And later he escaped, making it even harder to prosecute." Weiying said in a certain voice, "It's impossible! I saw the path is of some distance from the ravine. Why would uncle give up the safe path to choose the dangerous ravine side? And he ran away after Grandma's inquiry. He must have been scared! We can't just forget it. If I had been there, I would have investigated the until truth was revealed. We can't let senior uncle die just like this and allow the criminal to walk away from it!" Weidi replied, "If people had been like you, the killer would have been caught already. Father and Uncle had asked people to look for the hooligan, but he was nowhere to be found. It's likely that he had died somewhere." Weiying said, "His death can't make up for it! An evil person like him would hurt more people if he had not died. All that's evil will get what they deserve. By the way, one really needs to be cautious before lending people money. The nature and background of the borrower must be taken into consideration. There are still receipts for loans in our father's little suitcase, still have IOU of before liberation someone else borrow money not returned."

With these words uttered, Weiying heard the door. She turned her sight to the door, and saw the curtain rolled up. There was

Weidi's husband coming inside, whom Weiying had only seen in photo. Weidi said, "Mother and sister are here to visit us." He looked at them and smiled nicely. Weidi said, "Can't you say anything? All you can do is simper!" Weiying asked her, "You used to be with your mother and sisters in Beijing. Why are you back in the village?" Weidi answered, "I have always been weak physically, and have to attend to my two sons, who kept me from work. My husband used to be in the army in Beijing, but then he returned here after demobilization. So, I took the two boys back, too." Then Weidi turned to her husband and said, "Go and cook for us while we talk." Weiying interrupted, "Don't cook for us; we have eaten before we left. I'm not hungry at all. I just want to talk with you, and later we'll go to the ravine and have a look." After a while, Mother and Weiying were to take their leaves. Before they left, Weidi gave them some dried persimmons, fresh dates and pomegranates. She said, "These grow in our tress. You can come along anytime. We don't have nice food to treat you, but there's no way we leave you hungry." Mrs. Qiu said, "You can also come visit us." Weidi smiled and agreed, but she claimed, "I hope to, but my mother has gone to my sister in Qingdao together live. If I go, there's no one here to cook for my boys and husband." Weiying said, "That's alright. Women have been busy with house works throughout history."

The family were sleeping on the second floor that night, when Weiying suddenly remembered Xiaodong's words at Beijing and asked, "Why isn't Juecong here?" Mother said, "He's the one that worries me most! The commander of 'Red Flag Army' likes him for being handsome and tall, and took him away when he was fifteen, to be his bodyguard. Last month before Tang Na's parents came to us, an opposing organization came for the commander. They shouted at the gate, 'The commander of RFA and the bodyguard, get the hell out of here, or we'll come inside and kill the whole family!' I shouted to the gate, 'The commander is not here.' But they shouted back ferociously, 'Open the gate first! we need to talk to your son!'

Your father was scared into the big water vat and had it half covered. I was anxious like a cat on hot bricks, afraid that they would rush in and kill us all. The police do not help at all nowadays. Having no other choice, I hit the window glass of Xiangzhong Printing House next door. My hand was bleeding, but whatsoever! I told Xiaodong to take the kids to the other side of the window, and I went into the room to get myself mercurochrome and gauze, and then ran to the gate while wrapping the wound and keeping an eye on the door. The door was thick and solid with two big bolts. They found a wooden pillar somewhere and hit it on the door, but the door was too solid. Later I heard people shouting, 'Go get a ladder and climb over the wall into the yard.' I was scared and lost when the noises suddenly stopped. After a while, I heard Xiaodong calling, 'Mom, open the door. It's safe now.' It turned out that Xiaodong took Xiangjiang Fenglei next door over and drummed the mob out. I invited them in gratefully. They said if anything happened, we could go to them, and they were willing to protect us. But I was anxious all the time, for Juecong likes to play with guns, which I was afraid would incur other troubles. Later when Tang Na's parents came over, I was afraid that people would come to investigate, which could make things worse, and everybody will be in danger. So, I decided to come here for a while. I asked them to come with us, but they refused. After making decision, I consigned the luggage from Changsha to Zhengzhou, and dropped by you uncles in Hankou while passing Wuhan. However, Juecong wouldn't come long, saying it's boring here. He stayed in Hankou for two days and insisted on going back to Changsha. Your uncle said when he was seeing Juecong off at the station, Juecong raised his arms and called out, 'Bring down the Million Lions!' He incurred a group of people wearing armbands of 'Million Lions' with big knives in their hands to chase him, which made your uncle so scared as to drop the bananas in hand. A train happened to be starting, so Juecong grasped the handle on the train, jumped on and got away. I heard that the Rebel factions in 'Millions of Lions all used to be butchers! Juecong truly is the one that worries me the most!"

Weiying was quite scared and said, "Oh! He might have learnt from the movie Railway Guerrillas! Why is Changsha and Wuhan in such a mess? Beijing is the capital, and the campaign against the major characters was fierce. But surface it's not so disordered there. Juele said, "Disordered it is here! I heard the guns in Shaoyang Military had been robbed. There are opposing organizations fighting everywhere, just like in war…"

Weiying gradually started to feel sleepy, and dreams fell on her. In her dreams, she was alone on a mountain top, and it started to flood. Everything around was swallowed by sea water at her feet. Then wind started blowing and it went dark. The heavy swell of the sea kept swelling and becoming blurred with mud…All sceneries were blocked by it. She couldn't see who was it that started all the mess in this vast land, even to block out the sun and heaven on earth.

But she was not panicked, nor was she afraid, for she was the only one left in the world. Neither would, so she would ever get to experience the fun of life anymore. As the water was only about fifty centimeters from her feet, a huge dragon showed half its head and parts of its body above the nearby waters. It opened its sleepy eyes, behind which hid its spirits, and twisted its body to swim by her. It looked like a dragon that had slept under sea for thousands of years and was about to leave the water and fly away. Its face seemed ruthless, but Qiu Weiying was especially calm; she stared at it without a move…

Suddenly, she woke up, confused of what the dream might mean. Influenced by the myths she heard the dragon was but a kind of animal that looked ferocious. It could turn the sea where it lived upside down, and even show off its strengths in the sky make threatening gestures. But its former times never attacked people… So, What will happen in the future?

Weiying and Mother walked over some distance the next morning to visit her second aunt. As she followed Mother into the front yard, she saw the two roosters raised by Aunt jumping and

Weiying was quite scared and said, "Oh! He might have learnt from the movie Railway Guerrillas! Why is Changsha and Wuhan in such a mess? Beijing is the capital, and the campaign against the major characters was fierce. But surface it's not so disordered there. Juele said, "Disordered it is here! I heard the guns in Shaoyang Military had been robbed. There are opposing organizations fighting everywhere, just like in war…"

Weiying gradually started to feel sleepy, and dreams fell on her. In her dreams, she was alone on a mountain top, and it started to flood. Everything around was swallowed by sea water at her feet. Then wind started blowing and it went dark. The heavy swell of the sea kept swelling and becoming blurred with mud…All sceneries were blocked by it. She couldn't see who was it that started all the mess in this vast land, even to block out the sun and heaven on earth.

But she was not panicked, nor was she afraid, for she was the only one left in the world. Neither would, so she would ever get to experience the fun of life anymore. As the water was only about fifty centimeters from her feet, a huge dragon showed half its head and parts of its body above the nearby waters. It opened its sleepy eyes, behind which hid its spirits, and twisted its body to swim by her. It looked like a dragon that had slept under sea for thousands of years and was about to leave the water and fly away. Its face seemed ruthless, but Qiu Weiying was especially calm; she stared at it without a move…

Suddenly, she woke up, confused of what the dream might mean. Influenced by the myths she heard the dragon was but a kind of animal that looked ferocious. It could turn the sea where it lived upside down, and even show off its strengths in the sky make threatening gestures. But its former times never attacked people… So, What will happen in the future?

Weiying and Mother walked over some distance the next morning to visit her second aunt. As she followed Mother into the front yard, she saw the two roosters raised by Aunt jumping and

Your father was scared into the big water vat and had it half covered. I was anxious like a cat on hot bricks, afraid that they would rush in and kill us all. The police do not help at all nowadays. Having no other choice, I hit the window glass of Xiangzhong Printing House next door. My hand was bleeding, but whatsoever! I told Xiaodong to take the kids to the other side of the window, and I went into the room to get myself mercurochrome and gauze, and then ran to the gate while wrapping the wound and keeping an eye on the door. The door was thick and solid with two big bolts. They found a wooden pillar somewhere and hit it on the door, but the door was too solid. Later I heard people shouting, 'Go get a ladder and climb over the wall into the yard.' I was scared and lost when the noises suddenly stopped. After a while, I heard Xiaodong calling, 'Mom, open the door. It's safe now.' It turned out that Xiaodong took Xiangjiang Fenglei next door over and drummed the mob out. I invited them in gratefully. They said if anything happened, we could go to them, and they were willing to protect us. But I was anxious all the time, for Juecong likes to play with guns, which I was afraid would incur other troubles. Later when Tang Na's parents came over, I was afraid that people would come to investigate, which could make things worse, and everybody will be in danger. So, I decided to come here for a while. I asked them to come with us, but they refused. After making decision, I consigned the luggage from Changsha to Zhengzhou, and dropped by you uncles in Hankou while passing Wuhan. However, Juecong wouldn't come long, saying it's boring here. He stayed in Hankou for two days and insisted on going back to Changsha. Your uncle said when he was seeing Juecong off at the station, Juecong raised his arms and called out, 'Bring down the Million Lions!' He incurred a group of people wearing armbands of 'Million Lions' with big knives in their hands to chase him, which made your uncle so scared as to drop the bananas in hand. A train happened to be starting, so Juecong grasped the handle on the train, jumped on and got away. I heard that the Rebel factions in 'Millions of Lions all used to be butchers! Juecong truly is the one that worries me the most!"

fighting with each other while the other hens were busy seeking for corns on the ground, paying not even a look. Weiying was carried away by thoughts, even animals fight when enraged, not to mention human! If so, how did the ruthless fights among factions in the Cultural Revolution start?

While Weiying was contemplating on the question, her second aunt rolled up the curtain on the door and stepped out. Weiying commented at once, "Oh, Aunt looks like Uncle so much!" Mrs. Qiu said, "Exactly. And you first aunt looks like your dad." Weiying followed Mother in the house, which much resembled Weidi's, except that there was a brick bed. Out of the side door were the kitchen, stock corral and toilet. Before Weiying could observe more closely, she heard mother talking to her aunt, who was a tall woman with bound feet and had trouble walking, "Don't get yourself busy treating us, I just want to take my girl here to visit you." Weiying added, "Auntie, we're just here to see you, so don't trouble yourself! Come and visit us when you're free." Her second aunt replied, "Fine. I'll go with your aunt in Hou village."

The next afternoon Weiying and her mother went to visit a family down the ravine. Before they entered the door, the old lady inside saw them from her only window by the door. Weiying also saw through the broken window that the lady dropped the needle work at hand and moved her body off the brick bed, and then dragged herself to the door. She was about sixty, with grey hair set at the back of her head. Her 170cm body seemed to be in good state, except that her bound feet made it a bit difficult for her to walk. Weiying followed her mother into the cave. It was at the end of summer while the weather was still hot, but it was a bit chilly inside the cave. Weiying looked at the room dug out of the cliff and shivered, it brought back her memories of the newly built residence among the mountains of the reservoir, which were heaven compared with the cave house. The old lady noticed Qiu Weiying's being uncomfortable, and immediately lighted a kerosene lamp in the corner, in the dim light of which Weiying could make out everything in the cave… She felt as if she was in a cave of the primitive society, except that the furniture, if not modernized, belonged to evolved human. They stayed for a while and then said goodbye to the old lady. Weiying asked Mother outside the cave, "If they shut the door and window in winter, wouldn't they suffocate from lack of air?" Mrs. Qiu said, "Haven't you seen the door and window? They won't be that close! It'll be market enough if they can keep the room warm in winter, for people in the countryside don't have fireplaces. If one was born in this world, he will have to do with whatever he was born to."

Weiying asked puzzled, "Why do women like to bind their feet before liberation? Especially women in the north who was born taller than those in the south; their feet are bound into slender, sharp, narrow and thick shape, and the toes are bent to the sole. I see them walk in pain. Why would they do it?" Mrs. Qiu said, "It's not that they like it; it was the society that liked it. Men would consider large feet not elegant but too masculine. While a woman was seeking for a husband, the male side would pay priority to the size of her feet. Some women were ashamed of their large feet and would try to hide them down the chairs when sat down. I used to bind my feet when I was little, but later I could not stand the pain and used to cry in bed at night. Your grandmother felt sorry for me, and never forced me to bind my feet again. Later Sun Zhongshan became president and forbade women to bind their feet." Weiying said, "No wonder your feet are elegant but still in normal shape." Mrs. Qiu said, "How dare you jokes on your mother!" Weiying said, "Mom, it's been three months since I left the reservoir. I wonder what it's like there. I can't be out for so long. I hope to go back to Changsha and then to the reservoir." Mrs. Qiu said, "Let's go back together then. I'm also worried about home in Changsha." Weiying said, "That'll be perfect!"

On the day they left, the brigade sent out a villager to drive a coach pulled by two horses to take them to the station. It had rained the day before, and the horses were going through some difficulty pulling the coach with people and luggage on the muddy road. Mrs. Qiu said to the villager, "My friend, take your time, don't whip the horses. Let them walk slowly. The horses are so thin; it's no easy job for them." Sitting on the slow coach, looking at the desolate, yellowish land, Weiying thought it was fortunate for Father to have studied medicine and left here, or else, they would have had to suffer a lot living in a place like that. Even though they were confiscated, her parents had an expertise that could sustain a decent life. She remembered the old stories told by Dad, "When I was young and still in the countryside, my father died early, and my mother sold our land to sustain her three sons and two daughters. I said to one of my friends in the village, 'We don't have much land left. I want to go to Xi'an and learn medicine from my aunt's husband, Wang Xinglin.' My friend said, 'You are too naughty. If you become a doctor, I shall put a dining table on my head and serve you with a feast!' I knew he meant that I could never make a doctor, so I replied, 'Alright! If you don't trust me, I'll prove it to you.' Later I did learn the medicine and became a doctor. When I went to ask him for the feast, he said, 'You should feast me instead! You were such a naughty boy at that time. If I had not prodded you into action, you wouldn't have become a doctor.' In the end, it was I that paid and treated my childhood friends."

The scattered corn fields by the roadside were left behind the coach. Mrs. Qiu was having some small talks with the villager. Weiying thought Mother was really a hard-working lady who knew clearly what she was to do. She had only studied for three or four years at her brother and ex-husband's home, which equaled the first three years of primary school, and she had a lot of children; but she set her mind into learning medicine and became a doctor. She never gave up learning and serving her patients, even when she was pregnant with the twins. Now she is burdened with a groundless crime, but she never gave in to life though feeling much wronged, and she tried her best to make her life meaningful. Looking at Mother's gentle face, her heart was filled with respect. It did not seem long before the horse-drawn left the rural area of Zhengzhou and arrived at the train station in the tiring steps of the horses and the rolling of the wheels.

There were more Red Guards at the station than those who traveled on business. The Qius was not in the mood to observe those passionate rebel factions called Red Guards; all they wished was to arrive home as soon as possible. The villager stopped the horse-drawn near the consignment place, and the Qius got off. He helped them to carry the luggage down, and then tied the horse-drawn to a nearby wood pillar of streetlight. When he finished helping with every detail and said, "Madam, it's time for me to leave." Mrs. Qiu stopped him and said, "Please wait here with my children for a while. I need to buy something and will return soon." Then she ran to a food store and bought a lot of candies and pastries. She had a string of three paper bags, on top of which covered a piece of red gift paper, and handed it to the villager, which made him very happy. Then, she took some money out of her pocket for him. The villager refused at the beginning, saying, "No way, no way. It's my mission from the brigade to send you here. I've already taken your gift; how can I charge you?" Mrs. Qiu insisted, "It's hard to make money among the mountains. These are my personal offer and have nothing to do with the brigade. You've done a lot for us!" He took the money and gift gratefully, thanked the family and said goodbye. Then he got on the horse-drawn, whipped and yelled at the horses to drive back to Caiyuangou.

It was early for the train, so Mrs. Qiu took the family to a restaurant nearby. As soon as they sat down, a thin old woman with grey hair reached her dirty hands to them, when waiter was coming over to drive her out… Mrs. Qiu looked at the wrinkled, sorrowful face, opened her wallet and gave her a ten-yuan bill without a word. The old woman took the money at once and staggered out gratefully. Juele was sitting beside Mother, he asked, "Mom, you have the change. Why did you give her ten?" (At that time, an apprentice's monthly wage was only 18.) Mrs. Qiu replied, "Hey, the most terrible thing is being old with no one to help and having to leave home to beg. There are tens of thousands of kinds of people, but they are all human being. No matter how hard the days are, most people still struggle to survive." Weiying said approvingly, "Mom, I also think we should give money to those people in need. If it were a young and healthy beggar, we can leave him alone, for he could think of ways to earn by his own hands."

The family had noodle in the restaurant, and then Mrs. Qiu bought some cakes and a delicious Luo He roasted chicken. They took some rest at the station and headed for the train. They went through much trouble to get on the crowded train full of Red Guards, which took them away from Mr. Qiu's hometown and she boarded the already overloaded train heading south to Changsha

3.6 Hazy first love

After she left Beijing and stayed at Father's hometown near Zhengzhou for a dozen of days, Qiu Weiying returned to Changsha along with Mother, the twins and Xiaodong's two boys. Qiu Xiaodong started complaining the minute she saw Mother, "I've seldom seen Juecong since I came back from Beijing. He usually spends nights at the headquarters of Red Flag Army. The boy is only 15, so inexperienced that he himself need to be protected by adults, how can he be someone else's bodyguard? He only wants to have fun among those people, and he especially likes to play with guns. It's most prominent and unsafe to live at the Rebels' headquarters, so if he does not come back, I shall ask people to take me on the motorcycle of Xiangjiang Fenglei to search for him. I usually searched into midnight and could not find him. Sometimes he keeps me searching late into the night without even a slightest trace."

Mother replied in front of Weiying, "Alas, he's the only one in our family that has kept me worrying! Juecong is your father's favorite kid, but no matter if he was sick or had problems with his studies, your father never bothered to help. One day when Juecong was little, he ate some canned food at supper and cried at midnight for stomachache. He had diarrhea and a fever. I woke your dad and asked him to send Juecong to hospital. He only went back to sleep, and murmured, 'Let's leave him till tomorrow...' But Juecong was crying loud, and I thought it would be too late to put until the next day. I pushed him again, but he would not wake up. So, I had to carry Juecong on my go to the hospital. It was chilly in the middle of autumn, and I did not see any tricycle in the street. I forgot to bring the quilt, so I could only take off my overcoat to cover him. It turned out that he had acute gastroenteritis. If it had been put off, it might have developed into peritonitis, which could be vital!" Weiying thought, "How absurd father was! Life is full of incidents. A couple should shoulder all the responsibilities of family. My future husband must be one who can share the happiness and sorrow and all the responsibilities with me." Mrs. Qiu added, "Juecong did not choose to be sick himself back then. But now, we've suffered so much for him when he is out every day in such turmoil – what a troublemaker!" Weiying noticed her frowning and looking rather upset, which made her think that too many children can really be a great burden to parents, especially those naughty kids...

A few days after she arrived at Changsha, Weiying remembered Tang Na's uncle's letter, "...After you arrive at Changsha, tell us about the situation and we'll see when it will be proper and safe for Nana's parents to return. It is an important task, but young as you are, we can totally depend on you." She knew it was a letter of trust, and collected some information, During the National Holiday, Hunan had taken over many of the arms and ammunition robbed from the militaries. At least she had not seen any more public gunfire, which made Changsha much more peaceful than two months before. She reckoned it would not be a convenient and lasting plan for Tang Na's parents to live on at their friend's place, so she wrote to Uncle studies, your father never bothered to help. One day when Juecong was little, he ate some canned food at supper and cried at midnight for stomachache. He had diarrhea and a fever. I woke your dad and asked him to send Juecong to hospital. He only went back to sleep, and murmured, 'Let's leave him till tomorrow…' But Juecong was crying loud, and I thought it would be too late to put until the next day. I pushed him again, but he would not wake up. So, I had to carry Juecong on my go to the hospital. It was chilly in the middle of autumn, and I did not see any tricycle in the street. I forgot to bring the quilt, so I could only take off my overcoat to cover him. It turned out that he had acute gastroenteritis. If it had been put off, it might have developed into peritonitis, which could be vital!" Weiying thought, "How absurd father was! Life is full of incidents. A couple should shoulder all the responsibilities of family. My future husband must be one who can share the happiness and sorrow and all the responsibilities with me." Mrs. Qiu added, "Juecong did not choose to be sick himself back then. But now, we've suffered so much for him when he is out every day in such turmoil – what a troublemaker!" Weiying noticed her frowning and looking rather upset, which made her think that too many children can really be a great burden to parents, especially those naughty kids…

A few days after she arrived at Changsha, Weiying remembered Tang Na's uncle's letter, "…After you arrive at Changsha, tell us about the situation and we'll see when it will be proper and safe for Nana's parents to return. It is an important task, but young as you are, we can totally depend on you." She knew it was a letter of trust, and collected some information, During the National Holiday, Hunan had taken over many of the arms and ammunition robbed from the militaries. At least she had not seen any more public gunfire, which made Changsha much more peaceful than two months before. She reckoned it would not be a convenient and lasting plan for Tang Na's parents to live on at their friend's place, so she wrote to Uncle thing is being old with no one to help and having to leave home to beg. There are tens of thousands of kinds of people, but they are all human being. No matter how hard the days are, most people still struggle to survive." Weiying said approvingly, "Mom, I also think we should give money to those people in need. If it were a young and healthy beggar, we can leave him alone, for he could think of ways to earn by his own hands."

The family had noodle in the restaurant, and then Mrs. Qiu bought some cakes and a delicious Luo He roasted chicken. They took some rest at the station and headed for the train. They went through much trouble to get on the crowded train full of Red Guards, which took them away from Mr. Qiu's hometown and she boarded the already overloaded train heading south to Changsha

3.6 Hazy first love

After she left Beijing and stayed at Father's hometown near Zhengzhou for a dozen of days, Qiu Weiying returned to Changsha along with Mother, the twins and Xiaodong's two boys. Qiu Xiaodong started complaining the minute she saw Mother, "I've seldom seen Juecong since I came back from Beijing. He usually spends nights at the headquarters of Red Flag Army. The boy is only 15, so inexperienced that he himself need to be protected by adults, how can he be someone else's bodyguard? He only wants to have fun among those people, and he especially likes to play with guns. It's most prominent and unsafe to live at the Rebels' headquarters, so if he does not come back, I shall ask people to take me on the motorcycle of Xiangjiang Fenglei to search for him. I usually searched into midnight and could not find him. Sometimes he keeps me searching late into the night without even a slightest trace."

Mother replied in front of Weiying, "Alas, he's the only one in our family that has kept me worrying! Juecong is your father's favorite kid, but no matter if he was sick or had problems with his suggesting Tang Na's parents come back. Before long, Tang Na's parents did return.

Weiying spent some days at home, and then said to Xiaodong one day, "I should go back to the reservoir some days later. It's been months since I left, and I wonder what it's like there." Xiaodong said, "Forget it! The whole country is in a mess now. Students stop going to school, workers stop going to factories and peasants stop going in the fields. Why go back to the countryside? It'll be fine to stay home until the Spring Festival finishes. Or you can find a boyfriend here and you don't have to go back anymore." Weiying was uncomfortable with her words and said, "What boyfriend?!" Xiaodong replied, "Now comes the time when 'the laborers take the lead'. There is a smart guy in the printing house next door, tall and handsome. He's in charge of Xiangjiang Fenglei. Probably three or four years elder than you...", Qiu Weiying replied in an unpleasant manner, "I don't know him. I haven't even seen him!" Xiaodong replied, "He has seen you a few times through the window when he was at work. If you say yes, he'll have no problem. I can take him here for you to have a look." Weiying answered, "I'm a rural resident now. If I have a baby after marriage, it will have to follow me in the countryside and become a rural resident too. I don't want to pull its leg." Xiaodong said, "He's a leader of the Rebels. He will figure out a way to get your household residence permit back." Weiying was not moved, "Marriage is something for once in a lifetime. I'm not interested in trading it for a city household residence permit!" Xiaodong looked at her, contemplated for a while and said, "Alright, I won't force you to do anything, in you regret one day and blame me for it. You are still young any way." However, judging from the situation, Weiying found Xiaodong right in some way, so she decided to stay for the Spring Festival.

The letter Weiying wrote to the Central Revolutionary Committee requesting exculpation for their groundless confiscation of family property got no reply at all. However, a letter came from People Daily arrived some days after her return, saying they had no right to handle such problem, but she could take their letter to Changsha Revolutionary Committee and demand for proper disposition according to policies. So, she took the letter there with a little remained hope. The receptionist said to her, "There are millions of illegal confiscation of family property's during the Cultural Revolution, which we've been unable to handle already; you took place before the Revolution, so your properties are either handed in to the State Treasury or lost. Now you come to sue, but it's too difficult for us to figure things out. The government can't compensate for your loss, and it's a bill that could never be made clear. But you can leave the documents here, and we will inform you once there's helpful information." Hearing these words, Qiu lost all her hope. She knew that the day of rehabilitation could never come to them. Desperate and helpless, she went back home.

About a month after she left Beijing, she got a letter from Tang Na's uncle. In the letter, he wrote, "…Were it not the Cultural Revolution, we would have you as our nominal daughter… We've decided to have you back in Beijing, and you can live with us forever… As for when to come, just wait for our next letter. Uncle, Xiang Yu. Dec 1967, Beijing." The letter was written in the voice of a loving father, which made her feel warm inside. She took the letter to Mother and said, "Mom, Tang Na's uncle asks me to live in Beijing with them and let me wait for their notice." Mrs. Qiu smiled and asked, "Really?" She took over the letter, read it through carefully and said gladly, "My daughter is going to have a nice marriage! There's no doubt! I'll get things ready for you…" Mrs. Qiu had already had some knowledge about Mei's family. What's more, Tang Na was Weiying's one and only best friend.

Hearing her mother, Weiying recalled Junjun's gentle smile, and was overwhelmed by a happiness that she had never felt before. Two days later, Mrs. Qiu sent for a tailor to make some clothes for each season, especially a satin silk cotton-padded jacket for the winter. She reminded the tailor, "It's especially cold in Beijing, so please make the jacket thicker." The tailor had someone send the sewing machine to them, and measured Weiying's size. Then, Mrs. Qiu went to buy the cloth needed to make new clothes. Weiying thought she should tell it to Tang Na immediately, so she went to her straightly after lunch.

She arrived at the Tang's in the afternoon, and told Tang Na, "Na Mi Mi, your uncle wrote to me and asked me to stay with them in Beijing. I forgot to bring the letter here. But as to the exact time, I shall wait for their next letter." Tang Na was quick in response, "Really? Is it appropriate? Junjun has a girlfriend at school, and they've been together for quite some time. If they come home and see you there, his girlfriend must be mad!" Her words hit Weiying straightly on the face and made her silent.

Tang Na looked at her face and said, "What's more, your mother said that she had a nominal son, who is your boyfriend." Weiying felt a bit strange and said, "He's, her patient! I was only around fourteen when he came to us, and we've barely talked. After Mom cured him, he insisted on calling her 'Mom'. He joined the army in Xi'an and studied at aviation academy after graduation from high school, and we had no contact since then. He has been to the countryside once and asked me to be his girlfriend, but I knew nothing about him, so I did not agree." Weiying was silent for a while and felt like leaving, so she said, "I'm going to buy something from the department store at Yuanjialing. I'm leaving." Tang Na said, "Alright, I'm not going, for I have nothing to buy. Come to me again when you are free." They made their farewells, and Qiu went to the store alone. She strolled in the first floor and was not in the mood for going to the second and third. She originally planned to buy something for Mei's family, but as a result, she went home melancholy with empty hands.

Weiying arrived home, put her handbag down and entered her parents' room. She said to Mother, who had just bought much cloth, "Mom, I didn't see the tailor at the living room." Mrs. Qiu said, "She went to buy the black frogs for your cotton-padded jacket." Weiying said, "Mom, don't make clothes for me. I'm not going to Beijing. I can do with the worn clothes while doing farm work at the reservoir." Mrs. Qiu was puzzled and asked, "Why? What stopped you from going to Beijing?" Weiying replied, "Tang Na said her cousin had a girlfriend. They are classmates and have been together for a long time. If I went there, I would harm their relationship. Aunt Mei already has a daughter; she was only being courteous when asking me to be their nominal daughter." Mrs. Qiu said, "It was Tang Na's uncle that told you to go; he must have discussed it with his son. Even if Junjun has a girlfriend, he still has the right to choose again as long as he is not married!" Weiying replied, "I had no idea until Tang Na told me today. Everything has been fine between Junjun and his girlfriend, and I have no interest in being the third parties. What's more, being in a storm of jealousy is the last thing I desire. It is probably only his parents' wish to have me in Beijing. I think true love is about the one and only." Mrs. Qiu thought the decision might be inappropriate, for her daughter had got alone quite well with Mei's family. So, she asked, "Are you sure that you're not going to Beijing?" Weiying replied, "Tang Na talked to me today; how could she be wrong about her own cousin? I've made a decision."

The next afternoon, she wrote to Mei's family, saying, "Dear Uncle and Auntie, hello! … I heard from Nana that Junjun has already had a girlfriend in his class. I don't want to be a clown who destroys the happiness of others! So, I've decided that I'm not going to Beijing." She went to the post office and mailed the letter at once. Within ten days, she got a reply from Aunt Mei, saying, "Junjun has been classmates with Qu Xiaodi since primary school, and they fell in love in middle school. If you think it's improper to come in such situation, we respect your decision… You're a nice girl, and we're sure that you'll get a nice husband in the end." After reading, Weiying felt somewhat disappointed, for Tang Na was speaking the truth. The things in this world are usually unpredictable, especially for Qiu Weiying, who was especially conservative and passive as regard as love. Her real feelings, which had not been given a chance to evolve into first love, was buried deep in her heart and faded away…

The golden age was ruined

One Sunday, Father told her, "Your uncle is coming today…" Mrs. Qiu gave her some money and said, "Your uncle likes the preserved meat of Hunan. Go to the shop near the department store to buy some." Weiying took the money and left. She knew Mom was right, when Uncle took her cousins to Changsha in the past, he would buy a lot of cured food back to Wuhan. She almost spent all the money at the store. When she took the food back into their gate, she saw Uncle coming out in his slippers, going across the living room to the direction of toilet. She greeted him, "Uncle." But he only turned his face and answered indifferently while walking on. Weiying felt that he was still angry with her, but she didn't care and went directly into the kitchen. Mother was there, covering the dough in the basin on the hearth with gauze. She called out, "Mom." Mrs. Qiu raised her head and said, "Here you are. We're having dinner early tonight, so that let your uncle can have a good rest after meal."

After supper, Wang Tianliang came unexpectedly on his bicycle. He saw Weiying passing by the front yard, and greeted her before his bike even fully stopped, "Weiying, you're back? You had been in Beijing for two months!" Weiying replied, "Yes, I stayed at my friend Tang Na's aunt's place." Wang Tianliang stopped his bike and said while walking the stairs, "I was told in July that you had come back, so I came to visit you on Sunday, but you had gone to Wuhan then. I didn't expect that you would go to Beijing soon after you returned. You've got away so quickly twice!" In the following weeks, Wang came almost every day after work and supper at his factory to chat with his nominal brother and sisters at the Qiu's.

One Sunday, Wang had breakfast and came in the morning. He told Weiying, "I'm now a technician at a local radio factory. How about coming to my factory to have a visit?" Weiying agreed informally and then added, "Not recently. I have to treat my uncle." Qiu Zhonglin happened to enter the living room, so Wang said to him warmly, "Uncle, here you are! May I talk with you?" Qiu Zhonglin smiled and nodded, "Why not? I'd love to have someone as company!" So, wang started chatting with him at Weiying's home, and later her sisters and brother also joined in their talk. It got late, but he did not feel like leaving. Weiying said, "It's late now, and you have to work tomorrow. Aren't you going back to the factory?" Wang said, "I want to talk with you tonight, may I?" Being innocent, Weiying replied without much thought, "Talk? Alright if you hope to." Wang waited until the others went to bed and only the two of them remained in the living room, and then said to Weiying, "I'm afraid it'll be noisy for them if we talk here. How about going to the yard?" Weiying felt a bit shy, but she could not refuse, so she said, "Alright." They each grabbed a chair and left the living room to the passageway.

They walked down the steps and put down the chairs at the middle of the yard and sat side by side. After some random talk, it went darker. The moon hung up high in the sky, with some twinkling stars surrounding it, as if blinking their eyes. Later, the moon suddenly hid into the clouds, leaving the whole yard in a dark and misty atmosphere. It was the first time for Qiu Weiying to be that close to a man, which made her shy and timid. After a while, the moon came out of the gauzy clouds, tossing its elegant light to decorate the yard with a mysterious color. Weiying looked a bit to her right; it was hard for her to see the facial changes of Wang, but she sensed that he was grinning with his thick lips and looking at her through his large eyes. She did not know what to do except lower her head in embarrassment. After some silence, Wang complimented her, "You're gorgeous. Arched eyebrows, large eyes, double eye lids, noble nose, tiny mouth, dimples when you smile, nice body and an oval face. You're really like a fairy!" Weiying did not lose her sanity over the compliment. She smiled coyly and started her doctrine, "When I was in primary school, there was a text called The Fox and the Crow. The crow was standing in a tree with a piece of meat in its mouth, while the fox down the tree desired the meat but could not reach it. So, the fox raised its head and complimented the crow, 'I heard that you are a fabulous singer, but I've never really heard you sing. Can and later her sisters and brother also joined in their talk. It got late, but he did not feel like leaving. Weiying said, "It's late now, and you have to work tomorrow. Aren't you going back to the factory?" Wang said, "I want to talk with you tonight, may I?" Being innocent, Weiying replied without much thought, "Talk? Alright if you hope to." Wang waited until the others went to bed and only the two of them remained in the living room, and then said to Weiying, "I'm afraid it'll be noisy for them if we talk here. How about going to the yard?" Weiying felt a bit shy, but she could not refuse, so she said, "Alright." They each grabbed a chair and left the living room to the passageway.

They walked down the steps and put down the chairs at the middle of the yard and sat side by side. After some random talk, it went darker. The moon hung up high in the sky, with some twinkling stars surrounding it, as if blinking their eyes. Later, the moon suddenly hid into the clouds, leaving the whole yard in a dark and misty atmosphere. It was the first time for Qiu Weiying to be that close to a man, which made her shy and timid. After a while, the moon came out of the gauzy clouds, tossing its elegant light to decorate the yard with a mysterious color. Weiying looked a bit to her right; it was hard for her to see the facial changes of Wang, but she sensed that he was grinning with his thick lips and looking at her through his large eyes. She did not know what to do except lower her head in embarrassment. After some silence, Wang complimented her, "You're gorgeous. Arched eyebrows, large eyes, double eye lids, noble nose, tiny mouth, dimples when you smile, nice body and an oval face. You're really like a fairy!" Weiying did not lose her sanity over the compliment. She smiled coyly and started her doctrine, "When I was in primary school, there was a text called The Fox and the Crow. The crow was standing in a tree with a piece of meat in its mouth, while the fox down the tree desired the meat but could not reach it. So, the fox raised its head and complimented the crow, 'I heard that you are a fabulous singer, but I've never really heard you sing. Can

The golden age was ruined

One Sunday, Father told her, "Your uncle is coming today…" Mrs. Qiu gave her some money and said, "Your uncle likes the preserved meat of Hunan. Go to the shop near the department store to buy some." Weiying took the money and left. She knew Mom was right, when Uncle took her cousins to Changsha in the past, he would buy a lot of cured food back to Wuhan. She almost spent all the money at the store. When she took the food back into their gate, she saw Uncle coming out in his slippers, going across the living room to the direction of toilet. She greeted him, "Uncle." But he only turned his face and answered indifferently while walking on. Weiying felt that he was still angry with her, but she didn't care and went directly into the kitchen. Mother was there, covering the dough in the basin on the hearth with gauze. She called out, "Mom." Mrs. Qiu raised her head and said, "Here you are. We're having dinner early tonight, so that let your uncle can have a good rest after meal."

After supper, Wang Tianliang came unexpectedly on his bicycle. He saw Weiying passing by the front yard, and greeted her before his bike even fully stopped, "Weiying, you're back? You had been in Beijing for two months!" Weiying replied, "Yes, I stayed at my friend Tang Na's aunt's place." Wang Tianliang stopped his bike and said while walking the stairs, "I was told in July that you had come back, so I came to visit you on Sunday, but you had gone to Wuhan then. I didn't expect that you would go to Beijing soon after you returned. You've got away so quickly twice!" In the following weeks, Wang came almost every day after work and supper at his factory to chat with his nominal brother and sisters at the Qiu's.

One Sunday, Wang had breakfast and came in the morning. He told Weiying, "I'm now a technician at a local radio factory. How about coming to my factory to have a visit?" Weiying agreed informally and then added, "Not recently. I have to treat my uncle." Qiu Zhonglin happened to enter the living room, so Wang said to him warmly, "Uncle, here you are! May I talk with you?" Qiu Zhonglin smiled and nodded, "Why not? I'd love to have someone as company!" So, wang started chatting with him at Weiying's home, you sing a song for me now?' The stupid crow was overwhelmed. It opened its mouth, but the meat fell to the ground where the fox was standing. The fox immediately carried the meat in its mouth and ran away. Now you're complimenting me like the fox due to the crow. Are you planning to…" Weiying stopped, for she did not know what to say, while Wang Tianliang suddenly turned and held her head, covering her shivering lips with his thick ones and started kissing her passionately…? It was like an electric current passing through her body… Wang held her waist with his left hand, while his right hand moved inside her clothes to release the back buckle of her bra… Being startled, Weiying put a hand on the back of the hand moving towards her breast, but she lost all strengths to push it away. Wang was trying to make a further step. He moved his hands down to her belt while kissing… Suddenly a chilly wind started blowing, which made Weiying felt a bit cold and brought her back to sanity, This is so awkward! I haven't married him yet! She blushed, heart pounding, and pushed him away. She moved her body further and said calmly, "I'm going to bed now. You can sleep in the living room." Wang looked at her confusedly. He did not say anything, nor did he move. Later, he said, "I'm not tired." Weiying said quietly, "It's already midnight and you're not tired? I'll stay a few minutes then, but not too long."

At that time, her uncle suddenly opened the door to the passageway. He turned his face slowly and took a glance at them, and then kept on going as if he had seen nothing. Weiying waited until he passed the kitchen door and went to the alley where the toilet was, and said to Wang, "Lucky that he didn't come out earlier, or I'll be ashamed to death!" Wang did not approve, "Whatsoever. You think he doesn't do it with Aunt?" Weiying said, "That's two different things! Humans are not lower animals that can make out in public!" Soon, Qiu Zhonglin returned from the alley. Weiying immediately stood up and said, "I must be going now." Tianliang also stood up and said, "Me too."

The next morning Juecong opened her door while she was sleeping and said loudly, "Sister, Wang Tianliang is going to work." Weiying, who had always been a sound sleeper, did not open her eyes or turn her face from the ceiling. She murmured, "Well, I see. I went to sleep too late last night, and I'll get up later." As she was about to fall asleep again, the thick lips of Wang felled trembling on hers again. She opened her eyes in the touch and saw Wang's face and bent body slowly moving back. She stared at him quietly, while he said, "I'm going to work. If you are free tomorrow, come and see me at the factory." She answered him blurrily, as if she had just wakened from her dreams. He gently touched her face with the palm of his hand, and unwillingly shut the door and left. The phrase "true love's kiss" suddenly came into her mind. She felt that she neither liked him nor hated him. If kiss is the token of love, she had admitted her relationship with him. So, she could only wait and see where the kiss could take them to.

The next day, she had her supper early and took a bus to the address Wang Tianliang gave her. The doorkeeper at the gate sent for someone to call Wang over. He was glad to see her, smiled and said, "Here you are!" She replied, "Right. Didn't you ask me to come?" He said, "Yes, I did. Of course, you should come. Have you had your supper?" She replied, "Yes, right before I came. Which workshop are you in?" Wang said, "I'll show you." She followed him, passed some workshops and short old buildings where the workers lived, bypassed a pond and finally arrived at two-story newly built in the back of the factory, where Wang worked. He took her into the door, and she saw a woman sitting on a stool at the workshop right to the stair, who was inspecting the products. She asked him, "Why is there only one person at work?" Wang replied, "It's the examining workshop, and she is the inspector. She is from a Hui (an ethnic group in China) family." The woman saw Qiu Weiying coming inside and fixed her eyes on her until she went to the second floor with Wang. Qiu asked him on the stairs, "What's the biggest difference between Hui people and us Han?" He replied, "They are Islamic and eat beef instead of pork." Over the talk, they arrived at the second floor.

It was about 300 square meters, and no one was there except some spare parts of radios. There was a single bed by the window, and a large, rectangle desk with drawers. There were many books and spare parts on the table. Wang said, "I work and sleep here." Qiu commented, "That's quite convenient!" They sat on the bed, and Wang opened his drawer to get himself a pack of cigarettes, which made her move a bit away from him. He smiled and said, "You don't want me to smoke?" Then he put the cigarette which he had just taken a few smokes in the ashtray. He stared at her for some while, and then suddenly hugged her and pushed her in bed, while gently covering her body with his. His thick lips fell passionately on hers again… She felt her blood running fast, and allowed him to feel and explore her, all the way down to her secret part… She was overwhelmed by something she had never felt before. As if being shocked by electricity, her body started trembling… Suddenly she remembered Mother's warning, "Don't let a man touch you before marriage, or else…" She also remembered once when Father was making dumplings with her and Mother, he said as if talking to himself, "One's body is bestowed by parents, and should be cherished by oneself." A defensive wall of sanity was built inside; however, she was too weak to resist. She almost begged him, repeated to his face in a quivering voice, "No, please don't, we're not married yet…Please…" Her tender and pitiable request worked somehow. Wang suddenly sat up. He frowned and picked up a match to light the cigarette again. At the same time, Qiu also sat up. She quickly tidied her clothes and combed her hair with her hands. She was glad that she did not lose her virginity before marriage, which was a relief.

In that time, having sex before marriage will remain a stain in one's personal file for a lifetime. If a woman was pregnant before getting married, she would be considered as a dirty and obscene woman. Even be expelled from work if this person has a job. That had probably occurred to Wang Tianliang, too.

Later, when two people walked together downstairs, the inspector had already left. As Qiu went near the pond, she heard the rolling and rumbling of machines in an opposite workshop. She asked, "Why are people still at work at such a late hour?" He replied, "We have three shifts, and that's the third shift. There are only two shifts in the examining workshop." She asked, "When does the last bus leave?" He said, "Eleven o'clock. I can take you home on my bicycle." She said, "No, you have to go to work tomorrow, and you need to rest early. The bus hasn't left yet, you can just walk me to the station." As they approached the cement slope by the gate, Wang bend down and picked up a long, round wooden stick of the workers' picket and said, "Who dropped it here? If people happen to step on it, they may fall." Then he threw it away by the wall with the slogan of "The working class leads everything" on. Before long, they arrived at the bus station. Qiu Weiying raised her head to investigate the sky. The veiled moon was like a sickle; some sparse stars were blinking their sleepy eyes nearby. The moon was not bright, leaving of blurry shades on the land. Qiu felt a cold wind blowing on her…

The new year came soon. One gloomy day in 1968, Qiu Weiying did not feel like going anywhere, and she stayed home as usual, absorbed in a novel. Later she began to feel tired, so she went to the passageway outside the living room and wanted to breathe in some fresh air in the front yard. There she was surprised to see Tang Na's old brother, Tiedan, looking at her while walking into their front yard. Next, he stepped on the stairs to the passageway, as if he had something to say. Qiu had known him when she was in Beijing, and she knew he was a well-behaved person. Except for drawing a kitten to make fun of her, he would never intrude in other's house without any reason. Except when his parents for avoid rebel faction's criticism struggle, the short-term lived outside her home. at the Qiu's, Weiying had never seen him come to her place. She didn't know what was it that he wanted to tell. She took the silent boy into their living room. He sat down politely and contemplated for a while.

The golden age was ruined

Qiu sensed something wrong. She went to make a cup of tea for him, put it on the tea table and then sat down in a chair opposite him. As soon as she sat down, Tiedan said directly without even touching the cup, "Uncle is dead..." She knew who he meant by "Uncle", and she almost couldn't believe her ears! She asked astonishingly, "What? Uncle's dead? Are you sure?" Tiedan confirmed, "Yes, he died of miocardial infarction. He was cremated and buried at the Babaoshan Revolutionary Cemetery." Tiedan's words were like a bolt from the blue. Uncle's loving face appeared immediately in her mind, and soon faded away. The astonishing bad news brought her into endless tears. Tiedan looked at her speechlessly, not knowing what to do. After a while, when Qiu began to calm down, he slowly stood up and said quietly, "I'm leaving." Qiu could not say other words; she nodded and replied "Ok" with a lumpy throat. Tiedan walked out of the gate, his head lowered, his footsteps muted...

The twins entered the living room scarcely when he left. One asked, "Sister, why don't you see him off?" while the other asked, "Sister, you're crying. Did Tang Na's brother make you angry?" She immediately answered in grief, "How could he make me angry? He is such a nice person! Oh... Tang Na's uncle in Beijing died. I bet he was only in his fifties, too early for him to pass away. When I was living at his house, he never treated me like an outsider; he was like a father..." Tears welled up in her eyes again. Xiaomao repeated, "Oh, but there's nothing we can do about it..." Damao said, "I know he is nice, or else why would you stay so long in Beijing? And they even asked you to go again..." The twins comforted her for a while, and then left in quiet grief, leaving her alone in the living room. She was somewhat regretful, for it might not have happened if she had gone to Beijing. Xiao Mei is not yet ten years old; it is difficult to deal with this crisis... But many things happen independent of people's will!

About three days later, Qiu Weiying went to visit Tang Na when Tang's brothers were not at home. Tang Na greeted her and put a glass of water by her side. Mrs. Tang saw her, smiled and said, "Little

Qiu is here!" Then she entered her room to talk with her husband. After some silence, Qiu started talking, "I heard from Tiedan that Uncle is dead." Tang said, "Yes. I blamed him, 'Why did you tell it to little Qiu? You made her cry!' He did not answer." Qiu did not approve, saying, "You can't blame him for telling me the news. He knows that I've lived at Mei auntie's house about two months and know them very well; it was necessary to tell me." Tang Na said, "That's true. That day Aunt Mei was at her workplace and could not go back; Junjun was at school; Xiaomei was too little. Probably Uncle did not want to wake her up. In the end, he knocked at the wooden wall to inform his neighbor, who sent for an ambulance. He had miocardial infarction, but the first aiders had him walk on the car by himself. As a result, he died even before arriving at the hospital…"

Qiu did not hear the rest of Tang's words. She raised her head in contemplation, and said slowly, "Around December last year, I got a letter from Uncle. I was planning to go to Beijing, but you said Junjun had been with a girl for a long time, so I wrote to Uncle and said 'I don't want to be a clown that intrudes in others' happiness'. Later, Aunt Mei wrote to confirm what you had said. So, I did not go to Beijing." Tang Na replied at once, "It was true that he had had a girlfriend for quite some time, but they've broke up, for the girl was seeing a son of a high-ranking official. Junjun was angry and asked her to quit that relationship, but she refused, so they broke up." Qiu asked, "Aren't your uncle and aunt already high ranked?" Tang said, "They would be if they were here, but there are many central officials in Beijing, which made them nothing special." Qiu said, "A man cannot live with his parents for a lifetime. It's himself personalities and the love that matter." Tang said, "But that girl wanted a boyfriend of high-ranking parents, the higher the better. What does she know about love?" At that time, Qiu realized Uncle's intention of writing her the letter, and felt somewhat regretful. But what could she say? They were silent for a while, then Qiu sighed, "If I had gone to Beijing, I would have been there and might have saved him. When I was in Beijing, I saw him writing every day after

Qiu is here!" Then she entered her room to talk with her husband. After some silence, Qiu started talking, "I heard from Tiedan that Uncle is dead." Tang said, "Yes. I blamed him, 'Why did you tell it to little Qiu? You made her cry!' He did not answer." Qiu did not approve, saying, "You can't blame him for telling me the news. He knows that I've lived at Mei auntie's house about two months and know them very well; it was necessary to tell me." Tang Na said, "That's true. That day Aunt Mei was at her workplace and could not go back; Junjun was at school; Xiaomei was too little. Probably Uncle did not want to wake her up. In the end, he knocked at the wooden wall to inform his neighbor, who sent for an ambulance. He had miocardial infarction, but the first aiders had him walk on the car by himself. As a result, he died even before arriving at the hospital…"

Qiu did not hear the rest of Tang's words. She raised her head in contemplation, and said slowly, "Around December last year, I got a letter from Uncle. I was planning to go to Beijing, but you said Junjun had been with a girl for a long time, so I wrote to Uncle and said 'I don't want to be a clown that intrudes in others' happiness'. Later, Aunt Mei wrote to confirm what you had said. So, I did not go to Beijing." Tang Na replied at once, "It was true that he had had a girlfriend for quite some time, but they've broke up, for the girl was seeing a son of a high-ranking official. Junjun was angry and asked her to quit that relationship, but she refused, so they broke up." Qiu asked, "Aren't your uncle and aunt already high ranked?" Tang said, "They would be if they were here, but there are many central officials in Beijing, which made them nothing special." Qiu said, "A man cannot live with his parents for a lifetime. It's himself personalities and the love that matter." Tang said, "But that girl wanted a boyfriend of high-ranking parents, the higher the better. What does she know about love?" At that time, Qiu realized Uncle's intention of writing her the letter, and felt somewhat regretful. But what could she say? They were silent for a while, then Qiu sighed, "If I had gone to Beijing, I would have been there and might have saved him. When I was in Beijing, I saw him writing every day after

Qiu sensed something wrong. She went to make a cup of tea for him, put it on the tea table and then sat down in a chair opposite him. As soon as she sat down, Tiedan said directly without even touching the cup, "Uncle is dead…" She knew who he meant by "Uncle", and she almost couldn't believe her ears! She asked astonishingly, "What? Uncle's dead? Are you sure?" Tiedan confirmed, "Yes, he died of miocardial infarction. He was cremated and buried at the Babaoshan Revolutionary Cemetery." Tiedan's words were like a bolt from the blue. Uncle's loving face appeared immediately in her mind, and soon faded away. The astonishing bad news brought her into endless tears. Tiedan looked at her speechlessly, not knowing what to do. After a while, when Qiu began to calm down, he slowly stood up and said quietly, "I'm leaving." Qiu could not say other words; she nodded and replied "Ok" with a lumpy throat. Tiedan walked out of the gate, his head lowered, his footsteps muted…

The twins entered the living room scarcely when he left. One asked, "Sister, why don't you see him off?" while the other asked, "Sister, you're crying. Did Tang Na's brother make you angry?" She immediately answered in grief, "How could he make me angry? He is such a nice person! Oh… Tang Na's uncle in Beijing died. I bet he was only in his fifties, too early for him to pass away. When I was living at his house, he never treated me like an outsider; he was like a father…" Tears welled up in her eyes again. Xiaomao repeated, "Oh, but there's nothing we can do about it…" Damao said, "I know he is nice, or else why would you stay so long in Beijing? And they even asked you to go again…" The twins comforted her for a while, and then left in quiet grief, leaving her alone in the living room. She was somewhat regretful, for it might not have happened if she had gone to Beijing. Xiao Mei is not yet ten years old; it is difficult to deal with this crisis… But many things happen independent of people's will!

About three days later, Qiu Weiying went to visit Tang Na when Tang's brothers were not at home. Tang Na greeted her and put a glass of water by her side. Mrs. Tang saw her, smiled and said, "Little work, except when he was eating and reading newspapers. He was still writing when I and Xiaomei went to sleep… Probably it was all because the Rebel factions forced sap him energy and spirit too hard and made him exhausted both physically."

Qiu Weiying had already become Wang Tianliang's girlfriend by then, and it was improper for her to ask about the other details about Mei's family. Uncle had died. The story in Beijing when she was eighteen could only remain an unforgettable past. It was hard for her to tell – who was really her first love?

3.7 The tumultuous years

The children had heard Father complaining about Mother several times, "If she had not opposed to move to Guangzhou or Hong Kong, the confiscation of family property would never had happened. I have a relative in Hong Kong, who is also a doctor. He wrote to me saying he was making much money there and asked why I didn't go there too. He said Li Jiacheng started from nothing in Hong Kong, and later became a big man of means! I heard he had sponsored all the PLA's rubber shoes in the war to resist US aggression and aid Korea. He has never been searched house and confiscate property for being rich! We are not native Changsha people, and have no social relationship here that can save us from the disaster."

But Weiying thought, "There are also many old revolutionists who had contributed greatly but also going to die at any time in the mass movement launched by Chairman Mao. Aren't Liu Shaoqi, Peng Dehuai and He Long the country fellows of Chairman Mao? How did they end up falling victim to the Cultural Revolution? They cannot protect themselves, what could we do about the confiscation of family property? All in all, the nation is in a total turmoil now. Everything seems so desperate…" Usually she would like to stay at home, and think of random questions at leisure, such as why can the birds both walk on land and fly in the sky so far and wide and not fall down? Why are some people so mean and evil as to harm and persecute people all the time, even to kill others? Aren't their hearts human hearts too? Aren't they made of human flesh? She bought a book named A Hundred Thousand Whys from Xinhua Bookstore, but it only covered subjects like physics and chemistry. How could she possibly figure out that it was the Gang of Four that was conspiring for power in the capital and causing all the turmoil? She only felt, at that time, those who should not have died, while those should have survived and remained a hazard to social stability… She couldn't figure out what contribution she could make to "the salvation of two thirds of the world population" by going to the countryside; on the contrary, her own survival was tough there. She would even envy a cleaner in the street, for he had a registered permanent residence in the city, food rations and income, which she did not. But she could not possibly depend on her parents forever!

The children also know that when Father was ill treated at the hospital, he would curse the top manager Wang Huijun when arrived at home, saying, "Who the hell does she think she is? An ungrateful bad person! I hired her as a cleaner, but once she became the dean, she bullies me…" He also cursed a woman named Huang Qi twice since the Cultural Revolution, "Shit! What a shameless! She will sleep with any one if he pays! A whore! Now even she can play tricks on me for just because I show no respect for her…" Once when Qiu Weiying saw him cursing madly, she asked, "Dad, who is that Huang Qi?" He replied angrily, "She's a nurse who got the job here for some under table friends and relationships in the Revolution. She has been unreasonably jealous of me, playing dirty tricks and writing big-character posters against me ever since she came. If it had not been me, the hospital wouldn't have been established, and she would never have got the job!" Hearing his words, Weiying decided to go to the hospital the next day, but she did not tell her plan to anyone.

The next day after breakfast, she walked to South Huangxing Road (the present pedestrian street downtown) where Southern

Region Hospital was. It was then the oldest, longest and most prosperous business street in Changsha. It was wide and straight, stretching all the way from the central square at Wuyi Road to Nanmenkou, covering several bus stations and countless shops of various kinds. The Changsha Southern Region Hospital established by Qiu Zhongyuan was an outstanding grand building on the road. It was then the largest and busiest hospital (later it changed its name to Changsha Traditional Medicine Institute) among the four districts. Qiu Weiying purposely took that road, for she wanted to mend her old watch at the clock shop at Bajiaoting, which was near Wuyi Road. She walked by two bus stops, passed a branch of China Bank at Wuyi Road to Changsha Police Office, and saw big-character posters and slogans on its walls, for example "Crash the public security organs, procuratorate, court of law". She was confused, for if there were no longer public security organs, who would be there to deter the criminals? Who would be there to make laws that rule the country? She was totally at loss about what the political aim of Cultural Revolution was, and which direction the country was going into.

Contemplating, she crossed the road and reached the timepiece shop, where an old shop assistant came up smiling. He bowed down and asked quietly, "Excuse me, what kind of watch do you prefer?" She replied, "I don't need to buy any; I came here to repair watch." She took out of her pocket the old watch Mother gave her, which had already stopped going, and gave it to the assistant. He took it over, put a piece of round glass between his eyelids, and then opened the watch and said, "A nice watch it is, but it's too old. Even if I get it running this time, it may stop soon, being a waste of labor. I suggest you buy a new one." Qiu said, "A new one? I can't afford it." The assistant said, "I don't sell that. Look at you; you don't seem poor at all." She replied, "Am I not dressed normal? I'm an educated youth and have no money." He said, "Well. Ask your parents then; they must be rich." She said, "I don't really need a watch when working in the countryside anyway. Thank you!" She grabbed the old watch from the counter, put it back in her pocket and walked towards the hospital, thinking, "Rich people? My parents are deprived of all their properties. Even I need the support from my parents; I wonder what will become of my siblings?" Mother has a legal license for running personal clinic, but now it's called underground hospital. But Father works at a public hospital, why did they take away all his money, and even the decent clothes and daily necessities? Now the only comfort is Father has relatively higher salary than others, but that incurred jealousy and oppression. But it was he who invest started the hospital! He had made great contributions and been through tough efforts, but people attacked him in big-character posters only because he had higher salary.

She recalled in great sorrow that in the morning of spring, 1965, her parents cried bitterly over the confiscation of family property; and before she went to the countryside, Mother shed helpless tears… The series of misfortunes kept her low. She glimpsed at the titles of the big-character posters in the street, also saw, "hail the big worker scab, a traitor Liu Shaoqi expelled from the party forever." and the big-character posters such as "Step on one foot again, so that he will never turn over".

Complicated feelings welled up in her mind. Liu Shaoqi, Peng Dehuai and a lot of Hunan people who joined the revolution with Chairman Mao had been brought down, as well as other old revolutionists who made great contributions. They were either disabled or dead. Compared with them, the mistreat the Qiu's family received was nothing special. She walked and thought, and soon arrived at the hospital.

As soon as she entered the gate to the residence permit office and outpatient department, she noticed the wall on the right which used to be blank was then filled with big-character posters. There was an especially large and prominent big-character poster with comics on, titled with bold black characters Look at the Ugly Face of Qiu Zhongyuan, the high-income Capitalist Roader. On the left of these big-character poster, Mr. Qiu, who was tall in figure, was depicted as a seated stout ancient man. He has a large circle drawn on his chest witch the character "Qiu" in it. Above his head was a sentence marked with break line, "How can I get back my lost paradise?" Weiying held back her anger and read on. The general idea was, "Every salary day, Qiu Zhongyuan would count the money in hand greedily... To make what he gets in a month, I must sweat myself for half a year, and I'm much more tired than he is. Isn't he a modern capitalist? However, he is not satisfied with what he gets and still dreams of recapturing his lost paradise." The signature read "a member of the Revolutionary Rebels, Huang Qi".

Weiying was pissed off after reading it. She stands on her tiptoe to tear these big-character poster down while cursing, "What member of revolutionary rebels? You're a whore who sells both body and soul!" To her left there were rows of traumatological and hemorrhoidal patients waiting on chairs, who all looked at her in surprise. Hers the anger grew stronger, and so she scolded in exceptionally high voice, "Even I have no right to work at the hospital my father established. You sneaked in by some under table trade. How dare you envy my father for earning more than you do! Who the hell are you to envy him? You heartless brutes!" She pulled these big-character posters down and threw them into the dustbin.

Then she crossed the road to the specialty store and bought some snacks and local treats such as peanut cakes, sesame slices and animal crackers. Then she went to Wenhua Theater at Jiefang Road to see if there were any play her parents would like. But for the costume dramas telling love stories about scholars and beauties were "poisonous", there weren't many tickets on sale, except for Li Weikang's piano accompanied revolutionary model operas such as The Red Lantern and Shajiabang. So, she decided to go home first and then go to Xinhua Cinema near her house to watch The Red Lantern, in which Li Weikang played Li Tiemei. She learnt from the big-character posters on the street that the rise up in rebellion organization "East red" used to have fierce gunfire here with other groups, and did not stop until papers came from Beijing commanding all arms be handed in.

Weiying came home and she asked about the use of weapons to engage resort to violence in Changsha during the previous period, "Where did they get the guns and ammunition?" Xiaodong replied, "I heard the Rebel factions attacked Shao Yan Military and seized many arms. Later, Chairman Mao also made a speech supporting them." Xiaomao said, "Once I went shopping during that time. When I was just about to enter the street, a bullet flew by my ear. I was so scared, and I immediately ran home." Damao said, "In the street where our nominal mother lives, there were two brothers who took a car to join the violent clash. A grenade fell on the open top van and they both died. Later when their mother saw others took guns to join the violent clash, she cried and kowtowed to them, saying, 'Give me back my sons! Give me back my sons…' The woman used to be a single mother, and now she is all alone. The deaths of her sons were too much for her to handle, so she became insane. The neighbors often shed tears at the sight."

Weiying thought, isn't it the same as war to fight with arms in time of peace? Good heavens! Would a civil war break out? How would Cultural Revolution end up like? According to statistics, From July 1967 when Shaoyang Military District was robbed to September in the same year, there were about five million guns robbed from militaries all over the country, especially in Hunan and Jiangxi. Later, Premier Zhou had to stand out and convene all the leaders of Rebel groups to discuss about terminating gun fights…

Later father came back from work. Weiying widened her eyes on the passageway outside the living room to observe him, as he was putting his bicycle by the wall near the gate. He walked up smiling, pass her some pot-stewed meat served cold and said, "Go to the kitchen and cut them up, I'll eat and while I drink." Weiying sensed

The golden age was ruined

he was feeling good and knew what she did at the hospital did not bring him trouble. At dinner, father said happily, "Today I was on duty at Fanxixiang (the inpatient department) when Zhousi (the old woman at the reception office) came in panic and said, 'Emergency! Doctor Qiu, your daughter has tear off the all big-character posters. Go, or she'll have to suffer!' As I arrived, the big-character posters were gone. Doctor Cao from traumatology department told me, 'Your daughter had gone when Huang Qi took people here. She has done a great job for you!' So, I immediately returned to the outpatient department. Later Huang Qi took some rebel factions to me and blamed me for not having stopped you. I said, 'You were just there upstairs and too late to stop her.

I'm in the inpatient department, how could I make it?' She had nothing to do and left." Weiying said, "Dad, if she comes to you again, tell her 'My daughter is waiting for you at home!' If she really comes, I will say, 'What kind of member of revolutionists are you, you bitch who sells both body and soul?!"

Some days later, Qiu Weiying told the incident to Tang Na when visiting her. Tang Na was surprised and said, "How brave you are! Now whoever pulls down a big-character poster is anti-revolutionary and will be attacked. See the many big-character posters defaming my father here? I don't dare to pull them down. If I do, they will surround our house." Weiying smiled and replied, "That won't be a problem for us. We have a large and strong front door with two good bolts; there is a window connecting the printing house in the front yard; the terrace above the kitchen connects with a large area of roof; and there is a window in the back yard that leads to the neighbors. But I've done the right thing! If it was wrong, I wouldn't have done it. Since I've done it, I won't be scared!"

The only thing Qiu Weiying worried about was her future. She envied Tang Na somehow, for her parents were both old revolutionists and Party members. She still had a chance to go to university anyway and would have a brighter future than she would. Tang Na said,

"When will the Cultural Revolution come to an end? What will China become of? The Revolution is also launched in schools. If teachers are not cautious enough in class, they will be repudiated by their students. And due to the big link up, there aren't many lessons in school. My two years in school didn't teach me more than you have been taught." In the end, she said to Qiu, "Aunt Mei said Junjun ate a lot, and their rations were not enough." Qiu said nothing, but she thought she should mail enough food coupons to them, for she had been lived for about two months at theirs home.

On her way back, a chilly autumn wind blew, pulling some yellow leaves down to the ground. It indicated that the nature ignores all human politics and evolves in its own way. Qiu remembered clearly when she was at No.4 Middle School before going to the countryside, her teacher once said, "The frontline before liberation used to be Yan'an, and now it is the countryside. In order to rescue the suffering who, take up two thirds of the world's population, we should devote every bit of our energy..." Qiu thought, "Now our country is in such a mess. I don't even see my own future and wonder how I should move on! What energy do I have to rescue the suffering people?" Such noble ideals were too impractical to the educated youth s and could only remain legendary stories! Entering the alley, looking at their front door, she thought, "It's been months since I left. I wonder what it's like in the reservoir. It's probably time to go back; I can't always stay home and consume expensive "black market food" like this, which can't get me any future."

She went home and said to mother at dinner, "Mom, Tang Na said her aunt 'didn't have enough rations. I've spent two months with them; shall I mail them the food coupons?" Mother replied without hesitation, "Your friends. Friends should help each other, even if you have not lived with them. I have some national food coupons. How much do you need?" Qiu Weiying said, "How about 500 grams a day for two months?" Mother immediately opened her box and gave her coupons for 30 kilograms of rice, which Weiying mailed all the 30 kg food stamps to Aunt Mei the next day.

In October 1968, files came from Beijing that cadres should go to the countryside or "May Seventh" Cadres' School to be exercised by labor and reeducated by poor and mid-lower peasants. Tang Na's parents went to the countryside one after the other. Before long, Qiu Weiying said to her parents, "It's been more than a year since I left the reservoir, and I wonder what it has become of. I want to go back some days later." Mother said, "It's all up to you." while Her father said, "Alright. You can't stay here forever anyway." Weiying asked him, "Dad, how are things going in your hospital?" He replied, "No one writes big-character posters against me again. I've done nothing wrong! I've never harmed anyone; only some try to harm me. They envy me of my high salary, so I've asked to lower it from 240 to 184, and I will never give in again. It was I who established the hospital; The hospital I founded has merit and hard work. Mainly by me, plus the money borrowed from your uncle, with silver dollars bought the hospital a house that big. In the hard time, for a building of more than one thousand square meters, only two thousand yuan was refunded to me, but I never argued. Now all my properties have been confiscated, and they are still jealous and take revenge me.

Because I have for earning a bit more than they do and try to play me – shit!" Weiying said, "Yes. Chairman Mao said, 'When drinking the water, never forget those who dug the well', but your colleagues are treating the well digger as their enemy!" Mr. Qiu said, "Only Wang Huijun and Huang Qi do. They are trying everything to lower my salary; the others respect the fact that I deserve the money. Even my own child has gone to the countryside instead of working at my hospital; how ridiculous they are to bully me at my place!" Weiying said, "Right. I have neither a job nor a city household register. I shall again go back to the countryside after Moon Festival."

3.8 Among the quiet mountains

The Cultural Revolution has spread all over the country, of course it also involves the Siqing Reservoir in Chen County, where Qiu Weiying is located. On her return reservoir, Qiu Weiying noticed some changes had taken place in the management office. There was a routine after getting up in the morning, all the employees in the reservoir, each holding a small, red book of Chairman Mao's quotations. The eldest of the educated youth s, Zhu Daji would take the lead while the others follow him in waving the book and shouting out loud, "Long live Chairman Mao! Long live Chairman Mao! Long, long live!" Even vice- commander Lin, who later conspired the "571" (homophone of "armed uprising") military coup, was wished long life along with Chairman Mao. As the next procedure, everybody sat down and read the book in hand. Such routine was not a peculiar custom in the Reservoir; it was a common practice in the whole country and had even become a culture. After the reading, Zhu would elaborate the "commands from higher authorities" on the contemporary movement, and then came the time for discussion on the quotations. Sometimes director general Li was sent in to be criticized.

It was noticed by Qiu Weiying every time that even if Li was forced to lower his head, his goldfish eyes glared at all the others like searchlight examining its objects by turn. His anger only showed in his face, and never came out in words. He seemed to think that his self-esteem as top director of the reservoir was sabotaged. Yang Baohui, a newly come girl educated youth from Hengyang, always sat by Qiu during the gathering. One day, looking at Li's face, Yang Baohui lowered her voice and said, "Look at him, as if he is not intimidated at all." Qiu answered half-jokingly, "Seems to me that he's trying to intimidate and remember hatred us…" then she suddenly sensed Li's wary eyes on them. Obviously, he was aware that they two were talking and making fun of him. When Qiu noticed his expression, he quickly turned his eyes to elsewhere. Yang Baohui did not catch the scene and kept on talking, "The educated youth s at the reservoir is really mild. This is too formalistic. Those repudiated in Hengyang, they walk on sun-heated streets on bare feet. They wear tall hats and strike the gong in their hands, shouting, 'I'm a monster, I'm a demon'." Qiu answered, "In such a mountainous place? Apart from us in the reservoir, only a few dozens of families live here. Who's there to watch the pillory?"

One afternoon when Qiu Weiying rose from her nap, she heard a loud scream "Oh my goodness!" of a woman from the cement ground outside. Hearing this terrible sound, Qiu rushed to the door, where the scared educated youth almost ran into her. Then, Qiu saw a poor black, mid-size dog with broken, bloody chin, quivering and slowly moving across the cement ground to the opposite direction of the dam. It was the time when the educated youth s and some of the single employees living in the reservoir management office left for work. Many of them noticed the seriously injured dog running down the dam.

They all widened their eyes and looked at it in shock; some cried and shouted in complete panic voices. The dog was running in pain towards the mountains opposite the dam. Everyone was trying to get their bit in at the same time. Two or three who had seen more clearly declare, "It must be the explosion. Look at the burns on its chin." Qiu Weiying observed the path the dog walked past and did not see much blood; it was likely that the burns got too serious, and the blood coagulated! She questioned, "How can there be an explosion?" Someone answered, "Don't you know? There are landmines near the reservoir ground in people come and guard against steal our fish." The words are like a thunder from a clear sky – she did have no idea about that! Li had never warned her of that before! What if she had accidentally stepped on the mine when she was grazing the cattle? She is feeling tremble with fear.

After reading Chairman Mao's quotations the next morning, Li was sent in to be censured as usual. An old farmer from the agricultural team rose, and being quick tongued, uttered, "How can you bury landmine by the reservoir just for fear of people coming to steal the fish? Yesterday it was a dog. What if a man was injured and become handicapped? Would you blow a man disable just because he wants some fish? What an evil nature you have!" Another young employee stood up and continued, "You yourself are a member of the poor and mid-lower peasant group. Do you think you have been admitted to the Party and given a title, so you can forget about where you're from? Those people steal fish because they don't have money. Why would anyone go stealing if they had money?" These words reminded Qiu Weiying of an ancient Chinese saying, "Poverty produces thieves." She couldn't decide whether this young man was right or wrong, does poverty authorize a man to steal? people are poor, but still have but still have high aspiration. It was also said that "a man may have lack of money but never of a backbone". Before she could figure these things out, another young man with red cheeks got up from his chair, pointed at Li and said, "Where did you get the powder? You'd better be honest!" The other seated employees followed suit, shouting, "tell it! Be frank!" Li had no choice but to answer. In a quivering voice he said, "It was spared from the dynamite we used to blow the mountain to build the reservoir." Hearing the confession, Qiu commented with disgust, "How could a man be so evil?" Meanwhile, Zhu Daji, who was standing by Li, couldn't help waving his fist and shouting, "Long live leadership of the proletariat! Bring down the evil Li Pinchuan!" Others took up his words and joined in the shouting. However, a revolutionary committee was not established even months later, and Li was not brought down. Because of the Cultural Revolution in the remote mountainous areas, there were no Red Guards collaborators and no outside help. Since no one in the reservoir wanted to take over his position, Li remained the head and was allowed to keep on doing whatever he wanted.

After reading Chairman Mao's quotations the next morning, Li was sent in to be censured as usual. An old farmer from the agricultural team rose, and being quick tongued, uttered, "How can you bury landmine by the reservoir just for fear of people coming to steal the fish? Yesterday it was a dog. What if a man was injured and become handicapped? Would you blow a man disable just because he wants some fish? What an evil nature you have!" Another young employee stood up and continued, "You yourself are a member of the poor and mid-lower peasant group. Do you think you have been admitted to the Party and given a title, so you can forget about where you're from? Those people steal fish because they don't have money. Why would anyone go stealing if they had money?" These words reminded Qiu Weiying of an ancient Chinese saying, "Poverty produces thieves." She couldn't decide whether this young man was right or wrong, does poverty authorize a man to steal? people are poor, but still have but still have high aspiration. It was also said that "a man may have lack of money but never of a backbone". Before she could figure these things out, another young man with red cheeks got up from his chair, pointed at Li and said, "Where did you get the powder? You'd better be honest!" The other seated employees followed suit, shouting, "tell it! Be frank!" Li had no choice but to answer. In a quivering voice he said, "It was spared from the dynamite we used to blow the mountain to build the reservoir." Hearing the confession, Qiu commented with disgust, "How could a man be so evil?" Meanwhile, Zhu Daji, who was standing by Li, couldn't help waving his fist and shouting, "Long live leadership of the proletariat! Bring down the evil Li Pinchuan!" Others took up his words and joined in the shouting. However, a revolutionary committee was not established even months later, and Li was not brought down. Because of the Cultural Revolution in the remote mountainous areas, there were no Red Guards collaborators and no outside help. Since no one in the reservoir wanted to take over his position, Li remained the head and was allowed to keep on doing whatever he wanted.

not catch the scene and kept on talking, "The educated youth s at the reservoir is really mild. This is too formalistic. Those repudiated in Hengyang, they walk on sun-heated streets on bare feet. They wear tall hats and strike the gong in their hands, shouting, 'I'm a monster, I'm a demon'." Qiu answered, "In such a mountainous place? Apart from us in the reservoir, only a few dozens of families live here. Who's there to watch the pillory?"

One afternoon when Qiu Weiying rose from her nap, she heard a loud scream "Oh my goodness!" of a woman from the cement ground outside. Hearing this terrible sound, Qiu rushed to the door, where the scared educated youth almost ran into her. Then, Qiu saw a poor black, mid-size dog with broken, bloody chin, quivering and slowly moving across the cement ground to the opposite direction of the dam. It was the time when the educated youth s and some of the single employees living in the reservoir management office left for work. Many of them noticed the seriously injured dog running down the dam.

They all widened their eyes and looked at it in shock; some cried and shouted in complete panic voices. The dog was running in pain towards the mountains opposite the dam. Everyone was trying to get their bit in at the same time. Two or three who had seen more clearly declare, "It must be the explosion. Look at the burns on its chin." Qiu Weiying observed the path the dog walked past and did not see much blood; it was likely that the burns got too serious, and the blood coagulated! She questioned, "How can there be an explosion?" Someone answered, "Don't you know? There are landmines near the reservoir ground in people come and guard against steal our fish." The words are like a thunder from a clear sky – she did have no idea about that! Li had never warned her of that before! What if she had accidentally stepped on the mine when she was grazing the cattle? She is feeling tremble with fear.

The golden age was ruined

Down the mountains, between the reservoir and the town of Baohe, one to one-and-a-half kilometers from where they were, stood Baohe Primary School. At that time, it was devoid of people. One day in October 1970, Li gathered the staff and had a meeting in his office, where he announced, "The Water Conservancy Bureau of Chenzhou Organizational Department of the CPC has given the site of Baohe Primary School to our reservoir. The school moved away during the summer vacation. Now we have some empty classrooms and some orchards to take care of. I'm going to dispatch Qiu Weiying and Yang Baohui to live there and look after the trees. If accountant Qiao were not occupied during the day, I would send him and a young male employee to help you plant and attend to the orchards…"

So, on November 1st, Qiu Weiying and Yang Baohui moved to the site Baohe Primary School and lived on to attend to the orchards. Baohe Primary School had its one side next to the reservoir, the other three closes to mountains. Its ground level was a big higher than the reservoir. Its east side faced to the water conservation and its west to an unfrequented primitive forest. There was a steep path to its south, leading to Baohe Town over the mountain, where a market was held every five days; and there was a winding path to its north, leading to the reservoir management office in the middle of the mountain. The school was located near mountains and waters, surrounded by charming natural sceneries, but it was almost secluded from modern life. There was no transportation nor shops, and not even a household. All they could see there was the waters of the reservoir and the continuous mountains. Let them know schoolchildren that stretch for miles are going to school, must overcome how much difficulty and not have personal security.

By the time the weather turned chilly, the orchards had already been taken care of by Baohe Primary School. Qiu Weiying and Yang Baohui would take the Qin, a plucking instrument which they bought from Chenzhou, when there's nothing better to do on rainy days, and play and sing songs like, "On the west the sun is to set…", "The sun comes out and light is all around..."; "The sweet Osmanthus blooms all over the August land..." Sometimes Qiao, the accountant in the reservoir, would come along with a young farmer to help plant the orchards, or grab the chopper and take them to the mountains to collect firewood, which were needed for cooking, boiling water and keeping them warm in winter days.

By the reservoir there were two rooms, one of which was the kitchen; the other room was where Yang Baohui lived. Between the two rooms there was a door that connected the two rooms. Qiu Weiying's bedroom was beside the opposite of Yang Baohui. It also derived from two connected classrooms but connected by a doorframe only. These two rooms were at the feet of two mountains which formed a 90-degree angle. The inner one, having two walls against the mountains and four small, wood lattice windows through which came only dim lights, was connected to the outside only by the doorframe to Qiu's bedroom. Qiu's room was about ten meters away from Yang Baohui. Between their rooms, near the northern mountain, there was a granite stair of about ten steps, leading to two Toilets without doors one for men and one for women. There was also a path down the left of the lavatories which went by the kitchen near Yang Baohui's room. It was the only way to the reservoir management office and Baohe market. It extended from the back of the office and winded down from the waist of the mountain all the way to the flatlands in the valley, and then climbed over the other mountain to the town of Baohe. It was such a quiet path that during the non-market days one happened to walk by its emptiness and silence may be very frightening.

It was a gloomy and chilly day in late December 1969. When Qiu Weiying and Yang Baohui returned from picking firewood, the day started turning dark. Yang Baohui was boiling water in the kitchen next to her bedroom, while Qiu doing the number one job in the toilet, facing the outside. Now, she noticed a shadow outside the kitchen moving towards the window...! She lowered her head warily and observed more carefully – she was right! There was a sneaky man creeping under the window! Seemed that he wanted to peep inside! She became nervous, and quickly finished her "job". She shouted while belting, "Yang Baohui, watch out for the bad guy!" Then she immediately went out of the toilet and ran down the stone steps, carrying in hand a brick she removed from the wall between the men's and women. But to her amazement, At this time, the sneaker shadow had disappeared at an astonishing speed! She ran to the kitchen and looked inside and saw Yang Baohui standing up panicked. She asked in puzzle, "Why? What did you see? Where's the bad guy?" Qiu told her what she saw, and then asked, "Haven't you seen anyone peeping inside from the window?" Yang Baohui widened her frightened eyes and said, "No. Are you sure?" Qiu said, "Yes. I did saw the shadow of a man by the window! How could he disappear so fast?" She dropped the brick in hand, and grabbed two hoes from the corner, giving one to Yang Baohui. She said meanwhile, "Let's search around the school, if we find him, strike the iron bell for class. The management office is not far; if people hear the abnormal bell they will come and save us." Yang Baohui agreed in shivers and followed Qiu outside. They checked Yang Baohui's bedroom from inside out and found nothing.

Night fell, so Qiu went to her room and find a flashlight from her green canvas bag. She stood in the middle of the school yard to inspect the slopes, mountains and paths, and still found nothing. Yang Baohui said, "Maybe you've mistaken." Qiu felt strange, Mistaken? But she did see a man's shadow. Could she possibly have made a mistake? As a result, she could only return to the kitchen with Yang Baohui doubtfully. They cooked and had dinner together, cleaned the kitchen, and then boiled some water for washing. After all the routines, Yang said to Qiu, "I'm a bit scared. Let's shut the door and go to bed early." Qiu thought calmly for a while. The ghost-like shadow came into her mind again, making her rather afraid; her courage had faded away. It was already dark, and she could not strike the bell without finding the bad guy. Being afraid, she said, "Can I sleep at your room tonight? I don't dare to sleep alone!" Shao said,

"Couldn't be better. I'm also scared of being alone!" Qiu said, "I'll go to lock my door first." Yang Baohui nodded, "Be quick!" Qiu ran to the opposite side and locked the door without even entering her room, and immediately ran back. She and Shao bolted the kitchen doors, including the one leading to the room next to Yang Baohui's. At last, they made sure that the door to the outside in Yang Baohui's room was bolted. In addition, Qiu fixed a hoe between the floor and a traverse on the door to make it safer. After all these works, she went to Yang Baohui's bed and slept on the side by the window. After some time in bed, she asked, "Why don't you put off the kerosene lamp?"

Yang Baohui replied, "I'm still scared about the shadow you saw. I want to leave the lamp on, in he came, and we can't see him." Qiu said, "It'll be even more dangerous! The room is lighted by the lamp, so he could see us through the latticed window from outside, while he is in the darkness, and we can't see him." Yang Baohui contemplated for a while and said, "You're right!" She sat up at once and blew out the lamp on the table next to her.

Lying in bed, Qiu recalled a big-character poster by an educated youth back in the city, reporting a story of a femaleeducated youth being raped in the countryside. Feeling uneasy, she looked outside the window, where the moon was blocked by dark clouds, and the mountains and woods blended in darkness. Wind blew, rustling the trees, as if some monsters had left their mountain habitant to hunt for people. Qiu was overwhelmed by some terrible hunch, which kept her awake and tossing over in bed. She opened her ears to the winds, trying to recognize any abnormal sound. After some nervous hours, sleepiness took over her. Just as she was struggling not to fall asleep, some strange noise came from outside the bedroom door, which was constantly cheeping. She immediately became wary, got up a bit and listened carefully – obviously it was not a mouse – someone was doing something with the door! She tried her best to calm her fast-beating heart, and pushed Yang Baohui, who was sleeping tight and made no response. The noise was going on, so Qiu pushed a

The golden age was ruined

bit harder and finally woke Yang Baohui. asked in a sleepy voice, "What's up?" Qiu whispered, "Listen. Someone's handling the door." Yang Baohui immediately became sober and aware of the situation, and she listened closely… What was trouble to Qiu was that once Yang Baohui made sure somebody was trying to get in, she became so panic-stricken that she couldn't help trembling and repeating "Oh my god". No matter if Qiu shook, beat or even pinch her and pull on her ears, Shao just could not stay sane. After some while, the noise suddenly stopped. When Qiu held her breath and listened again, she heard something from the door by the kitchen, which made her a cat on hot bricks. She thought to herself, "Now the two doors are sounding. If there are two bad people, then we are doomed; even if there is only one, Yang Baohui won't be of help, and I'm not odds-on fighting alone; and it's impossible to go out and ring the bell, what's more, people in the management office are sleeping and can't get here in time…" She was worried and did not know what to do, while Yang Baohui only trembled by her. The noise went on and on, which confused Qiu – were there two people each at one door, or was there only one? All in all, it seemed that he or they would not give up. She thought it was only middle of the night, and she wouldn't be rescued by anyone if she was not to help herself out. She wasn't sure whether it was a rapistor or robber, or both, but she was sure it was absolute not a good person in such a late hour. As long as he or they got in, she and Yang Baohui would have to suffer! She had to calm down and do something… So, when the bedroom door sounded again, she gathered all her power to make a big cough, pretending she was a man. Her voice was loud, for she used to practice treble in her middle school choir. Then she got off her bed to grab a large hook and gathered all her strengths to bump its back against the old desk by Yang Baohui. It was an extraordinary bump at night, with which the kerosene lamp fell to the ground and smashed. Fortunately, it worked! The noise stopped from then on. She remained wary for a while, but it was all quiet; even the wind stopped too.

Qiu went back to bed. After a while, she noticed that Yang Baohui had not recovered yet, so she pulled at Yang Baohui ear and said comfortingly, "It's alright now. The noise has stopped." Yang turned her body to the ceiling, stared outside the window and said after long, "Oh my god! It was so scary!" However, Qiu did not give up her wariness, and only had some light sleep during the latter half of the night, following every tiny noise outside. When dawn came, she heard the steps and talking of people coming by their house to the slope, who were going to the market in Baohe, she guessed. She felt as if she had returned from a visit to Death, and finally was saved. She rejoiced for having made it through the horrible night. Soon she fell asleep in extreme tiredness and the survive a disaster.

When she opened her eyes, the morning glow was tossing its gentle light on their quilt, which, however, did not bring any warmth, but only reminded her that it was winter already, and she could not stay there anymore! She turned to look at Yang Baohui, who was staring at the ceiling. Qiu asked, "How long have you been awake?" Yang Baohui said word by word, "Quite some while. I don't dare to open the door and go to the toilet." Qiu said, "It's daytime now, and there is a market in Baohe, so lots of people come by here. The bad people don't dare to come in day. But let's forget about the fair; we shall go to the management office and ask Li to send two men here. It's too dangerous for us two girls to live here. Bad things can happen!" Yang Baohui said, "Right, right. I'll go with you after breakfast." They got up. Yang Baohui opened the door between bedroom and kitchen, and then the kitchen door to go to the toilet. Qiu made her bed and went to the opposite direction. She opened the bedroom door to go to her room and fetch her towel and toothbrush.

When she stepped out Yang Baohui's room, she immediately noticed her door was wide open! She was shocked, and thought, "Oh, my god! Someone got inside my room last night!" Still scared, she went to the door, only to find the bolt had been removed, and the door leaned against the wall. She looked inside the barely decorated

The golden age was ruined

room. She used to hang her straw raincoat on the wall, and her canvas bag with loads of clothes and a new sheet in by her bed – both were gone, stolen! It was obvious that someone got in the last night! Qiu called Yang over, who had just left the lavatory, and said, "See? I was right. Someone came last night! My door is damaged, and things are stolen. Fortunately, I did not sleep here, or I would have died in a fight!" Yang Baohui was scared, widened her eyes and thrust her tongue. She followed Qiu to examine the room, which was against the mountains and barely lighted, almost vacant then. Qiu recalled the last night when she came to lock the door – At that time, she did not check the room connected behind. Did the bad guy suddenly disappear, is in the back of this room to hide over?

After the frightening incident, they almost flew to the management office after breakfast. They told Li about what happened, and Qiu asked, "Can you send two male comrades there?" They thought Li would take it seriously, but he understated the issue, "It has already happened, and he did not find that many valuables. He won't come again." His unexpected indifference pissed Qiu off – Li is trying to dodge away! She asked, "If you won't send more people there, how about letting us move back here?" Li replied, "I can't leave their unguarded." Qiu said, "You can send some men instead." Li said, "That'll be a waste of good labor. There's nothing much there to do." Qiu said, "But it's not safe for two girls to be there." Li said, "It's not that dangerous! Well, I'll think about it." Qiu insisted, "For how long? I need an answer today. We are too scared to spend the night there!" Yang Baohui added slowly, "Yes, I'm too scared." Li widened his goldfish eyes, and he was not mind one way or the other, "I can't give you any answer today."

During the morning break, Qiu told the incidents to the staff. Two single men and a brave femaleeducated youth said they would like to go to accompany them after the day's work, for there was no vacant place left in the management office for Qiu and Yang to settle, if Li were not to make some arrangements. Before leaving, Qiu said to Li, "Manager Li, I'll come tomorrow morning for your reply." Li did not say a word. That night, the femaleeducated youth Yang Aizhen and Accountant Qiao together came to the orchards. When day came again, the four of them returned to the management office. There the daughter of a country cadre (who was the colleague of Li) told them, "Li has gone to Chenzhou Water Conservation Bureau for a conference and will stay there for some days." They were angry and anxious, for they knew Li did not care about their situation at all. Qiu was furious, "This man treats our life as ants'!" They sat in trance for some while and then Qiu said to Yang Baohui "I'm going to Baohe Town to telegraph my family. I won't stay there anymore!" Yang Baohui said, "I'll go with you and contact my boyfriend to ask him to pick me up. Neither do I want to stay any longer!" Qiu smiled at Yang Baohui, who was two years older than her, and said, "Well, you've found a boyfriend before you came." Yang Baohui gave a goofy smile and said nothing. That morning they went to the orchards, had a hasty lunch and then went to the post office in Baohe Town to send their telegraphs.

It only took one day for Yang's boyfriend to come and get her. Yang Baohui told Qiu happily, "he said we'll go back and get married! But we shall wait until Li came back." Qiu was rather glad, "Great! Congratulations to the bride!" But Qiu found some changes has occurred to the once bubbly girl – her eyes looked dull, and her smiles were sometimes unreasonable, which made Qiu worried, was it the incident the other night scared her too much and had some bad influence on her nerves? But Qiu would not speak out, in order not to spoil her marriage. "I wish her a happy marriage life." Qiu thought to herself, for she believed the minor wound could be cured by a happy life after marriage; but things could also get worse if her marriage were not a satisfying one. To some extent, Qiu worried about are Yang Baohui sorting to marriage as an escape. The only reason why Qiu could manage to calm herself down in danger was that she realized she herself was the only one to help. Giving up trying was giving up her own life; only when one tries could one find hope.

Soon Qiu got reply from her family, saying, "Come back as soon as possible and leave the rest after your return and make other plans." It was signature by sister Xiaodong, but Qiu knew it was mother's idea. When Li came back some days later, Qiu went to inform him and farewell the staff. Mrs. Li asked, "Are you going to get married? Will you come back?" Qiu said, "I'm only 20, too young for marriage. Will I come back? No if I am to stay at the orchards and wait to be killed. I'd rather stay home and be unemployed."

The next day she had breakfast at the orchards and waved goodbye to Yang and her boyfriend. Then she would take a bus to Chenzhou from Baohe Town and get on a train to Changsha. Before leaving, Yang said, "Let me see you off." Qiu said, "No, thanks. Just stay with your boyfriend! It's only a few miles over the mountain, and I don't have much luggage left. It's a market day, so it's safe to walk the mountain path with people coming by." Yang said, "My boyfriend and I are going shopping anyway." Qiu was glad to have company, and the three went to Baohe together. There, Qiu bought some mountain-grew bamboo sprouts and other local specialty products. Finally, she said goodbye to Yang Baohui and her boyfriend and boarded a long-distance bus. When she arrived in Chenzhou, she was easily paid for a train ticket to Changsha that day. Qiu Weiying boarded the train and with a long, heartbreaking whistle, the old train took her to Changsha, her destination.

Along the way, she saw bountiful of destroyed scenes, all due to the Cultural Revolution. There were barely any new buildings, and almost all FCR (feudal, Capitalist and Revisionist) buildings were torn down, which made Qiu even more depressed. She had been in Chen County for over five years, lost her city household residence permit and gained literally nothing. Sixteen to twenty- one years old was the best ages for acquiring knowledge and expertise, but her golden age was wasted! In the silence of the mountains and even life is almost ruined!

3.9 Mother and daughter's anxiety

Relaxed and yet confused go home, Qiu felt like a lost lamb, having no idea of which way to go or what kind of fate was awaiting her. She responds to a Party's call and volunteers to go the countryside, making herself a role model in class. But in the end, she realized that, even if the purpose of going there was to be "reeducated by the poor and mid-lower peasants" and construct socialist new country, the fact was that she used to be a more innocent and aggressive girl before. What's more, the poor and mid-lower peasants had no time and energy to educate them, and socialist new countryside was not to be built by primal mode of production. Unpaired with modernized means of production, mere passion and heavy labors could only leave "Construct socialist new countryside" as a hollow slogan. The only benefit for the educated youth s in going to the mountains and countryside was they could be more industrious and thrift, but most people had already possessed those qualities through hard life and ideological education before the Cultural Revolution. Qiu used to read the Soviet novel <How is steel made?>. The protagonist in the book a famous quote is deeply engraved in her mind. People's life should be spent like this, when he looks back on his past, he would not be regretful of wasting his years." Qiu deemed it one hundred percent truth! She even had the idea that she should burn her own life to offer light and heat to the course of human progress! But in that environment, she had no idea how to. No one could show her a way, nor would any offer her the opportunity.

She arrived at Changsha, and as soon as she stepped on the stair outside the gate, Xiaodong, who was on the passageway, noticed her and called out happily, "Weiying! You're back!" Then she twisted her neck to inform Mother, "Mom! Weiying is back!" Mrs. Qiu was about to go to work. Upon hearing Xiaodong, she put on her coat come down the aisle. She looked at Weiying in love and sorrow, and said, "You're much skinnier. I'm so glad to have you back! I couldn't eat or go to sleep, for I was worried about your safety. Go have some food and rest; I have to go to work now." After Mother left, Weiying put down her luggage and asked Xiaodong, "Sister, has Dad already gone to work?" Xiaodong replied, "He took some Tai-chi exercise in the garden, had his breakfast outside and then went to work, just as usual." Weiying asked, "Why don't you go to work today?" Xiaodong said, "I'm now a nurse in the obstetrics and gynecology department, and I'm on the afternoon shift today. Go to the kitchen and have some breakfast. We have some dumplings left from last night; I'll go and fry them for you." Weiying said, "Let me do it. You can talk with me while I cook." She put the cold dumplings in the frying pan, heated them and put them on the table. Then she said, "Sister, it's too much for me. Join me in eating." Xiaodong said, "Alright. I've not had my breakfast yet, and there's some hot porridge for us." Weiying asked, "Where are your three children?" Xiaodong said, "Asleep. The youngest girl is only three months old, an adorable baby. Wu haven't seen her yet, but he can see her during the spring festival." Weiying said, "I shall go to see her after breakfast."

The sisters talked over the breakfast. Weiying said, "Where are Damao and Xiaomao?" Xiaodong said, "Damao was sent to the countryside, and Xiaomao is now a driver in a provincial department. It's lucky for her to get the job as a middle school graduate. Damao said that those graduated in 69' are dispatched to the countryside, mines, grass-root public serving positions or frontiers, there are four aspects.

Their class advisor said, 'It's unreasonable for both of you to go to the countryside,' Damao was dispatched to the countryside and Xiaomao to the State-owned enterprise work unit." Weiying said, "Oh, this is like the different fate of 'Kim Hee and Eun Hee' (North Korean film)." Xiaodong said, "We got your telegraph by the time of the New Year and were all worried. Mom almost broke down. A twenty-year-old single girl could be damaged if bad things happen! I work at the department of gynecology and obstetrics, and once a young girl came with her mother for abortion. The doctor asked, 'Why?' She cried in pain and said, 'I don't want a child of a rapist!' She explained in despair, 'One day when I was passing a construction site after my night shift, someone came from behind the walls in darkness and blocked my mouth with a towel so I could not scream. I was too panicked to see his face, and he dragged me to a torn down house and did the evil thing and left me in blood and pain. I had neither strength nor courage to chase him. But I did not expect to have his baby. I can't have this baby!' We all felt pity for her." Weiying was furious, "How could such evil creatures exist in this world! If it were me, I would crash a brick against his head and kill him if I could! Did the girl go to the police?" Xiaodong said, "So did we ask. Her mother said helplessly, 'that'll be of no use; where to find him? If we let the baby be born, it'll be a huge shame for my daughter, and we don't know what to do with it. Her father said that if he knew who the criminal was, he would have him killed.' But she could not recognize his face in the dark." Weiying commented at once, "It'll only add to their trouble if her father kills him. Wouldn't it be better for him to be punished by law? All those who commit murder, fire, robbery and rape should be severely punished! They are much guiltier than political offenders!" At that time, Xiaodong's two boys walked in. Weiying said, "What cute boys!" Xiaodong said, "The girl is even prettier. She has delicate skin and a cherry mouth, just like a Barbie. After waiting for the boys to finish their meal, we went inside and looked."

Qiu Weiying returned home, two or three days after New Year's Day in 1970, one day she was talking with Xiaodong and her children and said, "Sister, when I went by Guangming Ophthalmology on my way to the grocery this morning, the eldest girl asked me to go inside, and we had a chat. She asked, 'It's been years since you went to the countryside, but you look so good and energetic, just like an athlete! I had nothing to eat in the countryside and had to collect firewood and cook for myself. I look so pale now.' I told her, 'I was dispatched to the reservoir, so the food is probably a little better. We had no vegetables there, but we could use our own money to buy some meat and other food during market days. In the past I did not eat any hot chili, but sometimes that was the only thing the canteen serves to go with rice, so I didn't have any choice.' I also wonder why the peasants in the market could tell that I am an urban educated youth, despite that I was wearing patched clothes." Xiaodong said, "They could tell from your presence." Later Xiaodong said, "Do you know that the Guangming Clinic was also searched house and confiscated property? Their eldest daughter had just graduated from high school then, so she could not enter college either. She's now in her twenties, and she hope to find her a husband in the city." Weiying said, "I don't think it's rewarding to be a housewife in the city. But it must be hard for her to be in the countryside alone in Jiangyong, too."

Upon the talk, they heard the street director calling at their door. Weiying wondered when their Qiu's family brass doorbells were stolen. She ran to the door and saw the street director with one envelop in hand. The street director said, "So you're back." Weiying said, "Yes. What brings you here?" She knew it was not at a random call, for the street director had never, and would never enter their gate, even if she lived right in the neighborhood and seemed to have got along with them not well. In her eyes there was some trace of jealousy, probably for the Qiu's family had a large house and decent salary even after the confiscation of family property, and were not small talkers; especially Qiu Zhongyuan, who rode his new bicycle to work and barely greeted her when coming across in the alley. The street director gave the mail to Weiying and said, "tell your parents to bring you brother to street's office after the Lantern Festival, to sign up for going to the countryside. If you don't cooperate, his household residence permit will be cancelled anyway." Then she went down the stairs and went back to her own house. Xiaodong walked along the steps of the living room passage to the middle of the yard at home, and said, "To send Juecong to the countryside? Our family had two already going to the countryside! Mom and Dad have always ignored her."

That day when Mrs. Qiu returned from work, Weiying gave her the notice from the residential committee. Mrs. Qiu had always been concerned with the issue. During dinner, she frowned and barely ate. Weiying put some braised pork in her bowl, but she put them back in the plate and said, "I will get my own food." Xiaodong said, "Mom, don't hurt yourself." Then Xiaodong made some complaints about the street director. Tears welled up in Mrs. Qiu's eyes. She said, "We've already suffered from the confiscation of family property, and now my children's future is also damaged. Weiying and Juecong had just graduated from school and could not further their studies. After Weiying left, Juecong went out every day. It was so messy outside, and I worried a lot. Once he spent a whole night outside, and did not return for lunch, so I had to go and look for him in the heat. I saw him and the other two boys buying tickets at the Martyrs Park and called him. But he turned and saw me, pretended not knowing me and sneaked into the park. I bought a ticket to go in, but they had already disappeared. I was so angry that I almost passed out. I did not feel like eating anything that day, and only had some heat stroke medicine before going to work. He just won't be tamed! How can I let this naughty boy go to the countryside? He's only 17!" She almost cried. Qiu Zhongyuan looked at her and said worriedly, "My colleagues all say I 'treasure boys more than girls', for I have more girls than boys. If we had seven boys and two girls, I would probably treasure the girls more. It's probably that I spoiled Juecong when he was little. But how can we object to the policy? It's all because you wouldn't go to Guangzhou. We wouldn't end up like this if we were in a bigger city. There would be more rich people, so we won't suffer any confiscation of family property! It would also be easier to go to Hong Kong if we were in Guangzhou. Now we've lost everything, and the children suffer." Mrs. Qiu frowned, as if in regret. She had a little food and then sat aside and sighed, "I don't think he'll get down to business even if his household residence permit is canceled.

The golden age was ruined

He will run into big trouble someday. And boys are not like girls; girls can marry an urban man if she wants to leave the country. But would any urban girl marry a country boy? Juecong whole life will be ruined!"

Weiying thought that she had already gone to the countryside and couldn't support herself if she could not get her residence back. If Juecong went too, their parents would have to raise him forever. An idea came to her, so she said, "How about hiding him in Father's hometown? It takes the certificates from production team, brigade, commune and the county to transfer his residence, but I think the people there are nice to help. Once the team and brigade agree to accept him, the director cannot force him to go any more, the residence is where the person is." Mrs. Qiu said, "But who will go there for the procedures?" Weiying said, "I will. Father has to work every day; he has bountiful of patients. You and sister also must work and take care of the children. I'm the one who's free." Mrs. Qiu said, "It's snowing in the north, and it can be very cold." Weiying said, "I have to go even if it's freezing; this concerns Juecong entire life. The Lantern Festival is within a month!" Mrs. Qiu said, "That's true. When are you leaving?" Weiying said, "I'll go to buy the ticket tomorrow, the sooner, the better. There's no time for us to hesitate." Mr. Qiu immediately agreed and gave her the money for ticket. The next morning, Weiying went to the station and bought a ticket to Zhengzhou two days after.

After buying the ticket, Weiying took a bus to Tang Na's place. It had been days since she came home, and she hadn't seen Tang yet. The bus took her to the terminal in Yuanjialing. She crossed a wide flat street, and soon arrived at the dormitory of provincial literary federation. It was a bit messy in Tang's house, but Tang Na was glad to see Weiying back. She said, "My parents have gone to the cadre school, and I'm now an educated youth, too. But I was dispatched to a very near place, Changsha County, where my eldest uncle is. You can go and have a look if you are free! I'll go after spending the

Spring Festival here with my parents." Weiying said, "Maybe next time. I must go to my father's hometown the day after tomorrow to transfer my brother's residence. The street director urges him to go to the countryside after Lantern Festival; if he doesn't go, they will cancel his residence. By the way, why do you go to the countryside instead of going to college?" Tang said, "Almost all the middle school graduates in 68' have gone to the countryside, except the few from worker's or poor and mid-lower peasant's families. People can hardly get down to business and study. Due to the Cultural Revolution, classes were often not held. It was hard for people to get down to work and study. I didn't learn anything more than you did these years. And nothing much can be learned, for Capitalist education is being repudiated. Who knows when would all these come to an end? What will become of the country?" The best friends chatted about politics and their family, but the talk only made them even more confused. But in the time of the Gang of Four, who could have any idea of what was in Central high-level was going on?

After a sleeting night, the temperature fell sharply. The next day rain and snow stopped, but the road was still wet. Qiu Weiying hadn't informed Wang Tianliang of her return, so she went to his factory after lunch. Getting off the bus, she soon arrived at the janitor's office. She said, "I'm here for Wang Tianliang." The old man took a glimpse and immediately said, "Oh, you're his girlfriend." Qiu was a bit shy. She smiled and said, "How do you know that?" The old man said, "Who doesn't?" Qiu thought, "I don't come here often; he must have been spreading the news himself." The old men asked a worker to send for Wang, and Wang came before long with their Party branch secretary, who was wearing short hair, had big thick lips just like Wang's and a masculine voice. She smiled at Qiu in a rather queer way, and her eyes were examining Qiu all the way, both of which made Qiu very uncomfortable. Qiu stood up and followed the two into the factory. As they went by a pond between the plant and the dormitory, Qiu uttered her misgiving, "it is work time, so I'd

The golden age was ruined

better keep off in order not to interrupt your production." Wang said, "Many factories nowadays are very easy; but our secretary is strict on both revolution and production. If you don't want to go inside, I can take you to the female dormitory where you can chat with the girls, and I'll come to see you after work."

So, he took Qiu to the dormitory, knocked on the unlocked old wooden door. Soon a chubby young lady came out, pulled the door half-open, and then beamed on them and said, "Oh, it's Wang, the technician! What brings you here?" Wang said, "My girlfriend is here to visit me, but I have to work now. Can she come in?" The lady said with a fawning smile, "Sure! I've just finished my work and am free until tomorrow." She took Qiu inside, while Wang gladly went into the plant to inspect the wireless. There were two other female workers sitting in their quilts, weaving and chatting. They seemed happy to see Qiu, and said, "Great, new member to join in the gossip!" Qiu sat down, and soon couldn't help exclaiming, "My feet are frozen! How come you don't have any heating here?" The lady who opened the door said, "Take your shoes off and get in bed; sit opposite to me." Qiu reckoned that Wang won't be back in some hours, so embarrassed as she was, she could not deny the kindness, and at last took off her outer pants and shoes and got in bed. She leaned against the bedside and went on chatting. Suddenly the door was open, and two girls came inside, chuckling. One of them was skinny and comely, around 26 years old. She went to Qiu directly and said, "Excuse me. You're Wang Tianliang's girlfriend, right?" Feeling rather shy, Qiu confirmed with a smile. The girl stood by the bed and said, "My name is Zhang Manru. I've just finished my work, and Wang asked me to accompany you. I live just across the street, so why don't you come have a visit?" At that moment, the secretary came inside, took a glimpse at Qiu and said, "Looks like had the baby in a confinement." Qiu was rather uncomfortable with her words. She thought, "I'm not even married! How rude are you to say that!" So, she immediately got off the bed and told Zhang

Manru, "Let's go." The secretary felt she asked for a snub and showed herself the way out.

Qiu and Zhang crossed the street, walked over a slope and turned to a line of houses, where Zhang lived. It was a two-floors dormitory with a gate in the middle. dormitory with a gate in the middle. Zhang lived in a room on the second floor, right to the stairs, which faced her kitchen. She had one large and one small room and shared the bathroom with all the residents on the floor. It was then a very nice apartment. They entered the room, and Zhang said friendly, "My husband will be back soon. Let's talk for some while and let him cook for us." Qiu replied, "No, thank you! I have to go back and pack my bags, I'm leaving for Zhengzhou tomorrow…" She briefed Zhang on her purpose, then rise and one's gone home.

The next day Qiu Weiying got on the train to the north, as an act to lessen Mother's sorrow and guard her young brother's city household residence permit. As she walked out of the Zhengzhou station, she saw thick snow and wheel traits on the street, as if it had been snowing for days. Snowflakes were still flying in the air, like a handful of petals scattered by fairies. As they fell on her face, her temperature soon melted them. However, the freezing wind that blew them soon numbed her. There weren't many people in the streets, for one would not volunteer to suffer the cold, unless for work or emergency.

Qiu Weiying saw an inn nearby and wanted to hide in for a while before going to the country, but she weighed and thought that would be a waste of money. Even though Father had a comparatively high salary, their expenditure was not a slight sum. Father was a heavy smoker, and his cigarette expensed per month could reach dozens of yuan, which equaled the salary of a common worker. mother's salary was given on the basis of length of service, which meant she could get only tens of yuan for she was a newcomer in East Hospital. She can only which means a few dozen yuan a month. One night in the inn could cost mother a week's hard work. She and Juecong had to depend on their parents; Damao was in the countryside and busy catering to herself; Juele would graduate from junior high in a few months and weren't likely to get a job. She walked and weighed, passed the inn and arrived at the ticket window. A nice looking mid-aged woman asked in a local accent, "Gal, where are you going?" Qiu replied, "Caiyuangou, Yuzhai brigade, Xiaoqiao Commune." The ticket seller said, "In such a day? It's dozens of miles from here." Qiu said, "I've just got off the train from Changsha." The seller opened her booklet and said, "Sorry, the bus is suspended today." Qiu was worried, for she could not walk that far even if it was a fine day. But she soon remembered Aunt's place, which was only a few miles from town. So, she asked, "Excuse me, is there any bus to Shibalihe?" The woman seemed to be released too, and said, "Shibalihe? No problem! There's a bus today." Qiu was glad to hear that. She originally planned to visit Aunt after the business, so she had the address with her. She is the big aunt, a few years ago she came to Changsha, lived at home.

The bus arrived at her destination. The hamlet and paths were covered with thick snow, making the tramping very difficult. She got off the bus and stepped toward a half-opened door. As she was about to ask for directions, she heard the host seeing off some guest, and dodged aside. But the door soon was open, and she was seen, leaving her no choice but to speak up first and make her inquiry. The host seemed to know her aunt well, and after knowing Qiu was her niece, he pointed to a large bungalow on the plain and said amiably, "See, that's her house, not far from here. But it's been snowing for days so it'll take some trouble to get there." But in order to carry out her mission, Qiu had to walk against the wind and stagger on her way, which was a path, snow covered it.

Qiu Weiying knocked at the door of Aunt's quadrangle, and a man around his thirties, whom she had never seen before, came to open the door and examined her curiously. She made self-introduction, and Qiu learnt that he was the eldest son of Aunt, namely her eldest cousin. He took Weiying to the central door in the quadrangle and said, "My mom is inside by the fire." Then he opened the door. Weiying saw her aunt as soon as she stepped into the house; she looks very much like her father and was sitting on the brick bed. Aunt recognized her at once and was lighted with pleasure, "Weiying! I did not expect you to come on such a freezing day! Come on my girl, come to the fire." Weiying's leather boots were already soaked with melted snow, inflicting unbearable pain on her toes. She put down her luggage, took off her shoes and socks, got on the brick bed and sat by her aunt. She asked, "Aunt, where does Cousin work?" Aunt replied, "He's a technician in Luo Shao Tractor Factory." Weiying said, "Well, not bad!" Aunt smiled kindly, investigated her face and said, "My girl, what brings you here under such bad weather?" Meanwhile, she took up Weiying's numbed hands to warm them. Weiying briefed Aunt on her coming, which made Aunt sighed, "Alas, I just can never figure out why they want to send the city kids to the countryside!" Weiying was amused, and added, "Neither can I, and farmers in the countryside do not welcome young people from the city to come to the countryside. It's said that there are already more than 500 million peasants out of China's 700-million population. Why do they still ask the educated urban youth to go to the countryside?"

In fact, the key issue at that time was the construction was stagnated, especially during the Cultural Revolution when the national production was almost paralyzed from the persecution of the Gang of Four. Students had nowhere to work after graduation and had no choice but to be sent to the countryside, where production facility was rather backwards, leaving their knowledge wasted. Thus, the urban youths lost the chance to bring out their larger potentials! Those young people could have entered high school, university or vocational school, which can lay a solid foundation for their entire life and at the same time contribute to China's prosperity even ten folds more than what they end up doing!

Later her cousin came in, sat on a stool by them and said, "I was quite young when you lived at Pozi Street. I have always envied your father, for he has the expertise that can earn big! I had no job after graduation and wanted to learn medicine from him, but he denied, saying, 'I only pass my expertise to my son; even my own daughters are excluded.' I was worried to tears, feeling that my whole life was to be doomed. But later I heard Zong Weikang had learnt medicine from your mother and lived a decent life ever after." Qiu said, "That's true. He is now the attending doctor at Changsha Northern District Hospital, and his wife is a doctor at Southern District Hospital I've heard about him from my parents. It was after grandma's death that Mom took him to Changsha. Father was not pleased at first, but he could not send Zong back and had to let him stay. Finally, he became a doctor." Her cousin said, "Alas, I can only blame my fate." Weiying said immediately, "Fate? Mine's even worse! Aunt says you are a technician at Luo Shao Tractor Factory. I heard it was a large state-owned factory when I was back at school. Now comes the time of the laborers! We were search family's house and confiscate my property parent's afterwards, and I am now a child of one of the "twenty-one kinds" who has no right to further education. When the policy of going to the mountains and countryside came, I became an educated youth and lost my urban household residence permit! Even the food I eat must be bought from the black market, and I even must rely on my parents' support. Aren't you luckier than me?" Aunt frowned and said, "I don't get it. You grew up with your parents in the city. Why do they take away your household residence permit?" Qiu said, "National policy. The residence is where the person is. Once I am in the countryside, my residence goes there too. I come here just to maintain Juecong residence." After Weiying made everything clear, Aunt said, "There is no bus in such bad days, and my girl, you can't go there alone. Stay here for some days, and if the bus still doesn't come, I'll have your uncle send you there by our carriage." Weiying said, "All right." Her Uncle returned by lunch and met her for the first time. Even thought he was at his fifties; he was a vigorous man with red about his tanned gills. Weiying greeted him and asked, "You still work in such a bad day?" He smiled and replied,

"Just helping the commune." Her cousin's wife saw him come back and immediately served the table with a steaming pot filled with millet porridge, some steamed corn bread and a mixture of fried pickles and meat and carrot slices. The whole family, including the two children of Weiying's cousin, sat around a square table by the brick bed and started having their lunch. Weiying said, "Uncle looks younger than Aunt." The wife of her cousin said, "He is a few years younger than her. My parents all say that my mother-in-law used to be the prettiest girl in town. And my father-in-law was a decent young fellow. He owned a shop in Zhengzhou city, and business was quite good. People beat a path to his door, trying to set him up with dates. But he wanted no one except her." Uncle said, "It wasn't only because of her beauty; she is the nicest person in the world." Weiying turned to look at Aunt and saw a happy smile on her still rosy cheeks, as if chewing on the sweet memories. Weiying reckoned from the harmonious scene that they had never even had a fight, and she was possess feelings of admiration!

The next morning the snow stopped, and the sun came up. Qiu got up rather late, and it was almost noon after she finished her breakfast. She opened the door and saw the red sun shining gloriously on the snow-covered land. The snow in the street had started melting, whereas that in the farmland remained in shadows. It was still chilly in wind, and the paths leading to highways were still covered with snow. As she stood by the door in a daze, Aunt walked over slowly by the wall, looked outside and said tenderly, "My girl, stay until tomorrow when the snow melts from sun, so it'll be easier for the carriage to go. The people in Caiyuangou are very nice, if you find the people, they will get things done in a day or two." Weiying said, "Ok. I've seen cars going that way already, and tomorrow I can go there by bus."

There was still snow in the cornfield the next morning, but it was fine on the ways and paths. So even though reluctant to part, Qiu left cannot but the family after breakfast. Her cousin walked her to the roadside, where she took a bus to Caiyuangou.

The golden age was ruined

Upon arrival, Weiying settled down at Weidi's place. That day Weidi took her to the head of the production team. The next day the team leader brought Weiying the credential with all the seals of team, production brigade and commune straightly after his return from meeting. Weiying was overjoyed for such a smooth day, and even if Weidi asked her to stay longer, she couldn't wait to go back to Changsha the following day.

Her parents were both happy to see her. Mr. Qiu said, "Even if Juecong residence has to go back to hometown, we'll be consoled for people will take care of him, and he will come back one day." Weiying gave the credential to the street director and said, "My brother will go back to hometown after Lantern Festival." The director looked and said, "Not completed. I don't see the county seal." Weiying said, "I grew up in Changsha and am not familiar with my hometown. And it's too cold in the north for me to complete it. My father will get it done when he takes his leave and visits my brother there." The director could not argue for the moment, and Weiying looked at her and immediately turned and left. Hence, Juecong did not have to cancel his household residence permit.

Soon after the Lantern Festival, Juecong left for hometown. Before long, he wrote home and said, "Dad's ex-wife has come back from Qingdao, and she's taking good care of me… I have a friend here, Qiu Shuangbao, who is a teacher in the town middle school. He takes me to work every day so I can take the high school course…" After reading the letter, Mrs. Qiu was relieved, and the whole family was happy for a supposed disaster turned out to be a nice deed.

Later as Deng Xiaoping's intellect policy was carried out, Juecong became an excellent doctor at father's hospital, which was later baptized under the name of "Changsha Traditional Medicine Institute". Without the experience in hometown, Juecong could never have accomplished this!

CHAPTER 4

Lose one's bearings

4.1 Between the people

The day after Qiu Weiying got the credential for her younger brother in father's hometown and came back to Changsha. She went to Tang Na's home and decided that they would go together to Tang Na's hometown in Changsha County to see tomorrow.

On their arrival, Weiying found that Tang Na's room was spacious there were such simple pieces of furniture as a bed, a big wardrobe, an old desk and two chairs. She said to Tang Na, "It is better for you to live in your father's old house than to be arranged by the government. This room would accommodate at least 10 people if it had been in a farm." Tang said, "I have no relatives here now and I was not able to cook, so I went to next door---an old woman's home ---to have meals. And she was glad about it as she was a lonely old woman with no children. Although she was more than 60 years old, she's much stronger than me. I had once tried to shoulder what she carried but could not even make my back straight, let alone walk. But she could walk easily with such heavy things on shoulder." Weiying said, "It was the result of exercise! When I first went to the village, I could hardly walk on with nothing as my burden when it rained, and the paths became slippery. But after exercising for a period, I could do it while shouldering dozens of kilograms without so much effort." Tang answered, "I would not grow stronger than those villagers even if I do exercise every day." Weiying agreed, "Of course, we could not be compared with those born and growing up in rural areas." Tang continued, "If I have to stay in the village for the rest of my life, I could not even afford myself. What should I do?" Weiying replied, "We have to 'go on tolling the bell so long as one is a monk- do the least that is expected of one (follow a routine)' as the country is undergoing such turbulence! Now I dare not continue staying in the reservoir and my household residence permit was not implemented. I don't know what to do, either." Tang asked with a depressed tone, "Shall we take a walk outside?"

Soon after they walked out of the room, they saw a white-haired granny wending on with a bundle of firewood on her shoulder. Tang said to Weiying, "You see, precisely that's the old woman. On her shoulders carrying heavy burden, who walked faster than we." Weiying felt surprised, "Even if we exercise for several decades, we could not do it at her age." Tang became dejected, "Since we were born in cities but sent here. Why?" Weiying answered, "for building new socialist rural areas and responding to the call of the communist party. The government has spent a lot arranging for the intellectuals to go to villages. It is a loss of life and finance." They talked while walking in the silent village. Weiying asked, "Aunt Mei had written to ask another aunt of yours to take part in the revolution in Yan'an, so what she is doing right now?" Tang Na answered, "She is the director of Higher-Education Bureau of Changsha, and her husband is the principal of Hunan University." After a while, they went into the kitchen to help the granny cook. On during the dinner table, the old granny said, "Though I'm living a hard life in village, I could do with it anyhow." Tang said, "Now we are called on to trust in and rely on. lower-middle and poor peasants" the granny said, "I myself am Wu Bao Hu (household enjoying five guarantees) and have nothing to rely on." Weiying smiled, "Such an old-aged is still collecting firewood?" The granny said again, "The five guarantees can't cover everything. So, I'd better do something within my ability." Tang said, "She is too thrifty to take the money I've given her to buy firewood. I have no alternative." Weiying said, "Certainly. Villagers have no income in cash. Some people are diligent and like working. She is healthy and she will feel bored if she just sits at home and does nothing."

Tang Na and Weiying talked for such a while before falling into sleep that night. Weiying had a dream, under bright sunshine, she and a group of intellectuals are going to pass a forest to buy something in a shop in the town ahead. As they walked through a path in the middle of the forest, it became darker and darker, and the path gradually disappeared. Therefore, they turned back, but it was also dark and dim. Dead silence overwhelmed them all. The dream made Weiying feel nervous as if being pressed on the and she opened wide her eyes… As wind went into the room, Tang Na covered two quilts on them and Weiying put her own cotton-padded jacket on her. And so, she threw the jacket and other clothes to a big chair beside. When she fell asleep again, she put her hands that used to be on her on her stomach. During the latter half of the night, she slept to the morning and got up with Tang Na. When they got up off bed, Tang asked her, "How did you sleep last night?" Weiying answered, "Well. I sleep well everywhere but I just like dreaming." Tang said, "OK, then stay here for two more days." Weiying said, "I just have a look at the place you live in. I want to go back this afternoon. As the Spring Festival is drawing near, I need to queue up to buy some planned stuff." Tang said, "Then I'll go together with you. My parents will go back home from the May 7 Cadre School for the festival." When the granny heard that Tang was going back for holiday after breakfast, she gave her some pieces of sweet potatoes planted in village and dried by herself. Tang gave half of them to Weiying to let her family have a taste.

Lose one's bearings

Back home, Weiying fried the potatoes and let her mother taste them. Mother had some and smiled, "Villagers have little money, and it is inconvenient for them to buy something. These specialties have their particular taste."

After two or three days since she came back to Changsha with Tang Na, Weiying suddenly thought that she had not been to the factory where Wang Tianliang worked since she went to her father's hometown to for Juecong. She felt Zhang Manru who also worked there was friendly, amiable and talkative, so it was all right to chat with her when she shifted work. Weiying arrived at the factory and sat in the lodge for a while before Zhang Manru got off work. Passing the lodge, she smiled to Weiying, "I heard from Wang Tianliang that you wanted to talk with me. Let's go. My husband has rest today, so he can cook and we just chat." Weiying walked out of the lodge and went with her happily.

When entering her home, Weiying saw her husband, who saw Weiying for the first time and asked Zhang, "Guest?" Zhang answered, "She's Wang Tianliang's girlfriend." A technical worker in a steel factory, Zhang's husband appeared polite and amicable though high and strong. The couple talked and smiled from time to time, and Weiying felt they were quite affectionate. Almost four hours has passed. Then Zhang smiled to her husband, "Xu, go to prepare for the dinner. I'll talk with Weiying." Xu replied, "Well, you are good at commanding me", and then go to the kitchen. Zhang said to Weiying, "Someone in the factory said that a Hui woman worker is chasing Wang Tianliang. But he is unlikely to accept her because she is nothing when compared with you…" Weiying did not pay much attention to her words, nor did she take that matter seriously because she thought, anyhow I did not marry him. Our love will be worth nothing if he accepts another woman. Unmarried women thought Wang Tianliang was an ideal boyfriend, for he was high and handsome, and he graduated from an aviation college and became a technician in wireless radio. And a thick-faced woman would chase after him actively. But she thought Wang was reliable!

After dinner in Zhang's home, Wang came over and Zhang said to him, "Why not come earlier for dinner?" Wang answered, "I have bought her something in the canteen, but she came here to have dinner." Zhang said, "That's Ok. I asked her to stay here. Food cooked by us tastes better. Come here next time. I often cook with Xu after work and thus a meal is easy to prepare." Weiying asked, "Do you have children?" Zhang said, "We have a three-year-old son. Xu's parents are free at home and are willing to bring him up. Then we won't be occupied. When you two have a child in the future, you can send him or her to Wang's parents." Weiying replied immediately, "I don't want to get married so early. When a child is born, I could do nothing. What's more, my household residence permit is in rural areas, so the child will follow me. I'm afraid that will harm my child for his or her whole life." Zhang turned to Wang, "What do you think of it?" Wang answered, "That's a matter in the future. She has thought too much and do not want to get married now." Weiying was quite direct, "I'll become your burden and I have to be a housewife for my life long if we get married now." After a while, Weiying said, "It's time to go home and I have to go to catch the last bus today." Wang said, "Shall I go back to the factory to fetch my bicycle to take you home?" Weiying replied, "There is no need. I can take bus home. You will work tomorrow." She stood up with these words. Zhang said then, "Wang will take you home." Wang followed Weiying and said to her, "The communist party secretary of the factory said that you are like a capitalist lady without any deposition of laboring people. She also said that she wanted to introduce a girlfriend for me, but I didn't show my attitude." Weiying became unpleasant, "Must laboring workers have high voice and look strong? She would certainly set me up since she wants to introduce a girl for you." Wang said, "Not exactly. But I'm really looking at a salted fish and only having rice." Weiying answered unhappily, "I'm not a salted fish!"

With these words, she saw an embarrassing expression on Wang's face. Wang looked at her getting on the bus and they said goodbye.

Tang Na went to Weiying's home before the Spring Festival of 1970 and asked her, "I plan to pay a visit to my aunt who works in the education bureau. Would you like to go with me?" Weiying agreed, "Good idea. Your aunt lives in the bureau, doesn't she? I haven't been there before." Tang answered, "Just behind the Youth Palace, near your home." On the way there, Tang told Weiying, "My uncle, the principal of Hunan University, was persecuted to death several days ago, so my aunt is now in very bad mood." Weiying was quite surprised, "Ah! How was he persecuted?" Tang answered, "The Rebellion Group of his University locked him up in a multi-storied teaching building and forbade him to come and go freely. That day, he fell out of the window and was found blood all over his body and bone fractures. He died immediately. Our family all think that he was pushed out by the rebellion group, but they said he "committed suicide." That was totally impossible. My uncle never thought he had committed any crime. When Xiaomao (Tang's cousin) sent him something, he said, 'I have participated in revolution for dozens of years but never done anything wrong. So, don't worry about me!' He was very strong in character, so there was no reason that he committed suicide. Rebellion group's slandering is unfair. Isn't that irritating? He was very knowledgeable and knew several foreign languages. He was reading German books when locked and did not show any abnormal reaction. The noon when he died, Xiaomao, his favorite daughter, sent him food and clothes. If he intended to committed suicide, he, as an educated person, would be sure to write a posthumous paper and notify his family!" Qiu Weiying could not agree more. She nodded, "Of course." Soon they arrived at Tang's aunt home. The woman greeted them and then sorted out the materials on her desk without a word. She was heart-broken…

During the Spring Festival, Aunt Man---a far relative of Wang Tianliang---came to Qiu's home from Changsha County and insisted to invite Doctor Shao and Weiying. With a round face, Aunt Man appeared amiable. She sat down together with Shao and Weiying and said, "Doctor Shao, if you do not agree to go to Tongguan, it'll be hard for me to talk to my relative. She said that her son's hand would have been cut off but for your treatment. And you did not ask for a cent, so they were very grateful to you and hope you can go there anyhow during the Spring Festival. Could you accompany your mother, Weiying?" Weiying turned to her mother and asked, "Mom, could you cure one's badly hurt hand?" Shao smiled and took it for granted, "That boy played with combustive fireworks and did not walk away in time, and thus hurt his hands. But he did not go to hospital immediately for sterilization and treatment, so his hands became seriously infected by bacteria. And then when they arrived there, the hospital cut off the fingers of one hand in order to keep his wrist.

Later the hospital told his family, 'The fingers of the other hand have to be cut off because they were also infected', which made his parents quite anxious. Aunt Man brought him here and I found his hand was almost decayed and turned black. It was severely infected by bacteria, so the fingers must be cut off according to western medical theory. Therefore, I put smashed Chinese medicine powder that could eliminate toxins on his wounds. Finally, the inflammation disappeared and therefore his hand remained." Aunt Man smiled while Shao was explaining and then said, "Yes, so you should accept their invitation. Weiying, will you accompany your mother to Tongguan to have a look and play around?" Smiling and looking at Weiying, Shao agreed. Therefore, that day the three of them went to Tongguan where Shao and Weiying had never been before.

They boarded the ship at Changsha dock by the Xiangjiang River and set off to the town of Tongguan. Shao and Weiying stayed overnight at Man's home. The next morning, Man prepared eggs boiled with longans for them as breakfast and then brought them to that boy's home. They embarked on a winding slope on the mountain not far from the town. On the hillside, what Weiying viewed was an open and wide but not that flat peak with several small trees with scattered leaves. Some houses are located up there and heaps of yellowish earth, which should be used to make pottery. Aunt Man said to them, "Those living on the mountain peak are engaged in making pottery. It is convenient for them to 'get materials. Soon they reached the door of that family. Aunt Man stepped into the half-opened door and the hostess who was a little bit plump stood up at once and strode outwards very happily. She greeted, "Doctor Shao, you come finally. Please sit down. Then she was busy preparing a kind of tea containing sesames, beans and gingers for them to eradicate the cold. She said to Shao full of gratitude, "Doctor Shao, we must thank you for your wonderful medical skills that could keep my son's right hand. Now he's able to look after himself. He can eat, read and write on his own. I just care for him when I'm free. I was quite anxious when learning that his right hand might not be kept. What could he do without both hands after I pass away? You did not charge me, either. You are such a warm-hearted doctor. We will not forget your favor." Shao smiled with modesty, "You have several children who are all at school and you have to spend a lot on them. It did not cost me much to treat your boy. I just used some Chinese medicine. So that cannot be called 'DA EN DA DE' (big favor)!" The hostess said, "No, definitely not. That could have been an easy matter for you but for my son, a task of lifelong destiny." Seeing the woman's gratitude and respect for her mother, Weiying thought being a moral doctor with outstanding medical techniques was also a good occupation! Doctor could be viewed as "the engineer of human body". But why did mother encounter so much launch a tough crackdown just by opening a clinic at home…?

While the hostess was cooking, Aunt Man guided them to visit this relatively spacious family workshop. In the largest room, they saw rotatable earth machines used to make pottery and some already made or half-made potteries such as flower plant, broth kettle and medical kettle, all of which were spread around the room and had similar colors with the earth on the mountain. People living on the peak had dug the earth so much that it became uneven. It could be a simple way of living to "take advantage of the mountain while living there". The hostess prepared a variety of delicious dishes for lunch. She and her husband were both about 50 years old and had one boy and two girls who were all at school. They were engaged in the production of ceramics in their own workshop and submitted all potteries to the collectives. Though Weiying did not inquire about their income, she could see that if they had not spent all their savings for their only son's treatment and operation, they could have been living a decent life with their diligent. After lunch, at the hospitality of the couple, Weiying, her mother and Aunt Man walked around and chatted with them and then had dinner there. The hostess said to Shao after dinner, "Doctor Shao, you and your daughter just stay here overnight, and I have prepared a room for you. You live here until the Lantern Festival." At this, Shao said immediately, "I know your gratitude, but we can't bother you for too long. Moreover, I have to go to work after the Spring Festival."

Back the Man's auntie home, Shao and Weiying went to bed soon. After breakfast the next day, Man accompanied them to walk around the town and bought some meat and vegetables by the way. When they started to go back, Shao said to Weiying, "Shall we go to the dock to buy tickets tomorrow? We have bothered Aunt Man here so much." Weiying just uttered, "OK" when Man interrupted, "I haven't told you yet. My husband has gone to my daughter's home to visit our grandson, and I'll accompany you to Tianliang's home tomorrow." Shao said, "I'm afraid we'll cause trouble for them, so we'd better go back." While dragging them back home, Man said, "It's the Spring Festival, a good time for visits. And you hardly come here." Shao asked Weiying, "Would you like to go there?" Man said again, "Tianliang's parents had talked with me about it before the

Spring Festival. Tomorrow his younger brother will come here to bring you to their home." Weiying said, "It's all right to have a look at his family." Then Man was very happy, "That's a deal!"

The next morning, Wang Tianpu, Tianliang's brother, came to Man's home to bring the three of them. Seeing him for the first time, Weiying felt he looked like a young scholar with the heavy makeup in an ancient drama. On his red face, below his two black and almost vertical brows were two big and black eyes with raised tails. He was above 180 centimeters tall. If there could be a selection of models in ancient times, he could become a top model without makeup. Therefore, if one was born out of the right time or the right place, he or she would lose the opportunity to give play to his or her real value!

Wang Tianliang's home was in a village about four kilometers from the town. Walking out of the street where Aunt Man lived, they embarked onto a mudded path with luxuriant bushed and short trees on both sides. As there had been no rain during those days, or it would be difficult for them to walk on because it was uneven with some obscuring footprints and irregular trails of vehicles. When they covered one fourth of the whole journey, Weiying saw a family connected their old house to a canopy in a depression beside the path, in which passers could have a rest, have some water and chat with each other. Wang Tianpu put down the burden on him in which there lied the everyday stuff he bought for Shao and Weiying in town. Then he said, "Shall we have a rest and some water here?" Shao answered, "OK!" They sat down and began to talk. The host of teahouse asked, "Ms, are you guests from Changsha city?" Shao replied with native Changsha accent, "Yes." And Weiying who was straightforward added, "My household residence permit was in rural areas, so I can be regarded as a villager." The host then said, "Then you must be an intellectual youth. There are such young people in our town. We do not understand what the people's government is doing; however, urban residents have enough food, but we don't. We have less food than you, so why the government called on youths to come here?" At that moment, one interrupted, "I remember that while Liu Shaoqi was implementing his policy of 'San Zi Yi Bao' (the private plot; be responsible for their profits and losses; a free market; the practice of fixing farm output quotas on a household basis and allocating farmland to each family', we began to have food to eat and live a better life. But just after two or three years, Liu Shaoqi 'became viewed as a capitalist and our farmland has been expropriated by the production team. Now that Liu has no right to speech, we cannot expect our land to return." After that, he sighed in disappointment. Another person continued, "At that time, we have strength and enthusiasm to work and have superfluous food to sell…" The host turned to Wang Tianpu, "Where is your home, old bro?" he said, "He Tan Ao." As soon as he heard that, he asked, "There was a well-known workshop making sweet wine balls a few years ago. Their balls were sweet and delicious, and I had bought them. But in recent years I haven't seen the balls sold. Why?" Wang Tianpu blinked and answered him, "Grandpa, that workshop was ours, but later private business was forbidden. If we had carried on with that, the cadres of the village would have caused trouble to our family." It could be heard that he felt that was a great loss. After a period of silence and thinking, Wang Tianpu said, "Shall we go? They are waiting for us to have lunch." Shao paid for the tea in advance and the four of them set out again and after a while reached Wang Tianliang's home finally.

In front of the house there was a proper-sized pond, a little far from where several families of production team lived sparsely. A few trees were standing scattered round the pond. And a place which covered an area of a single bed was put up with wood boards and blocks for the family to wash clothes and vegetables, and on the right side of the pond was the place for them to have and use water. At that moment, Wang Tianliang's father, a 50-year-old tall man, was sitting in a chair against the wall. He held a copper smoking kettle and smoked. Seeing the four people walking towards to the

Lose one's bearings

door, he immediately put down the smoking kettle and stood up to welcome the guests. Weiying followed the other three people and entered the house. Wang Tianliang's mother appeared to be an astute and capable woman. She had a red face on which there was a pair of blinking black eyes and two black and curved brows. She came out from the cooking stove on the right side of the kitchen, full of smiles on her face. Wang's father waved his right arm and said with hospitality, "Please have a seat in the room." Weiying followed her mother and Aunt Man and turned right to walk to the living room whose one side was facing the courtyard.

When she walked through a door on the right side of the living room, she heard a girl's laughter. Aunt Man brought them to that room and Weiying saw a young woman tailor cutting clothes on a wood board like a door. The girl put down the clothes at once and shouted clearly, "Oh! Aunt, you finally came. She must be your daughter, my brother's girlfriend, Weiying?" Then she quickly praised Weiying to an old granny who was sitting on the bedside and smoking with a copper kettle, and asked, "See? What I said is true, isn't it?" The granny with a wrinkled face looked at Weiying and smiled, "Yes, of course, you're right…" And Man asked Shao and Weiying to sit down. A relative, who had been holding a child and looking at the girl tailoring walking out of the room with a smile on her face. It turned out that this smart woman tailor was Wang Tianliang's younger sister Huihua. Looking strong, she wore a long braid which almost reached her legs, had a spot like a green bean beside her left twinkling black eye, and had a pair of black brows. When she raised her head and laughed, people in another room could hear her voice. Her appearance made an impression on others that she must be a sharp girl. After a while, Wang's father came in and said, "It's time for lunch, Doctor Shao. Please sit in the living room with your daughter." And then he walked to the bedside and said to the granny, "Let's go for lunch, mom." He escorted his mother to the best seat in the living room. Then he seated himself beside her and asked Shao and Weiying to sit down beside the granny on the other side. The living room was in the middle of the house, its back against a low mountain, its two sides opposite to two doors and its front facing a 20-odd square meters' courtyard. At lunch, Wang's father said, "Tianliang is on duty in the factory and will be back in two days, so please stay for a few more days." Shao hurried to refuse, "No, I'll begin to work the day after tomorrow, so we have to go back tomorrow. Maybe we'll come here someday in the future." Weiying saw Wang's two other younger brothers and little sister who was just several years old. This youngest sister had a pair of black and watery eyes under her long willowy brows, with long and raised eyelashes. She looked very lovely when blinking eyes. On her oval-shaped face which was naturally red like putting on rouge were an upright nose and a small pretty mouth like a cherry. But she appeared a bit thin and weak. Weiying could not help appreciating her, "This little girl is very pretty!" Huihua said to her immediately, "She and another sister were twins, and that girl was even more beautiful. Everyone liked her and regarded her as a flower. But it was a pity that our food was insufficient after we were search house and confiscated property, fined so that she began to undergo malnutrition. We did not send her to hospital in time and she passed away due to anemia." Wang's mother said, "Born in the village, our children have suffered too much. We have no planned food, and it is inconvenient to visit a doctor." Weiying said immediately, "Though I was born in the city, my household residence permit is in the reservoir of a village in Chenzhou county." Then she said regretfully, "What a pity! If we were living in ancient times, she would have the opportunity to be selected into the palace to be an empress. And has your family ever been confiscated?" Huihua asked, "Don't you know? Hasn't my brother told you that?" Weiying answered, "I don't know. And I haven't heard that from your brother. Why was a rural family search house and confiscated property? For what?", Huihua said immediately, "For making sweet wine balls. Even urban wine-making factories liked buying our balls. But making money is also a kind of crime."

Wang's father said to Shao, "We can take you to have a look at the workshop after lunch."

At the upper right edge of the kitchen was a door which seemed open all the year round. Walking out of that door, they could see a pig-raising farm and that unoccupied workshop. In the middle of the workshop was a three-storied round mill which related to a long and thick handspike. The handspike was pushed by livestock and only one person could hardly move it. Wang's father said to Shao, "A few years ago, they said our making wine balls belonged to capitalism. They took away all the tools making balls besides confiscation of family property and fining. Only the mill was fixed here so that they could not move it. We did not know what the people's government was doing, but who knew making wine balls was a kind of crime?"

Shao doctor continued, "In my family, there are too many children, so I quit from the hospital in 1962 in order to look after them. Later the administrative committee of medical of Medical Organizations came home several times and persuaded me, 'You should serve the general public with your medical skills…'After the confiscation of family property, they still asked me to go on with the clinic at home. But I would not do that anyway since it had caused us so much launch a tough crackdown."

Hearing such a conversation, Weiying thought Liu Shaoqi and Deng Xiaoping implement capitalism by initiating the trend of working on one's own and Chairman Mao has advocated the Cultural Revolution to oppose capitalism and anti-revisionism. We live in a world led by the CPC that has split apart into two routes, but what has that to do with the general public who don't know at all whose route is right and whose is wrong? Didn't the so-called "capitalist road" by Liu and Deng aim at lifting more people out of poverty and improving our living standard? Is asceticism, right? Is it the correct socialist road when we cannot buy anything with money but can with planned tickets? Nevertheless, Chairman Mao and Liu Shaoqi were fellow townsmen of Hunan and there seemed no personal conflict between them. Both joined the revolution at an early age and cooperated with other revolutionaries to create the new China, but they split apart in this conflict as to choose which route 21-odd-year old Weiying was at a cross of her life amid this torrential political battle, she could neither know the political direction of the country and the objectives of this motion nor understand what kind of crime her parents and others committed for conducting legal business. She was unable to predict her own future. She felt like sitting in a large ship full of passengers on the sea, without an idea where the helmsman would take it amid furious waves in the darkness…

4.2 Heavy cross

Li Zhimeng did not go back home during the Spring Festival of 1970. Both Shao and Qiu Xiaodong felt strange, why didn't he send letters and life expenses for the children for months and even did not go home for the Spring Festival? Was he too busy or sick? Just after the Lantern Festival, Xiaodong sent a telegraph to her husband, but did not receive any reply.

Not long after that she suddenly received an air letter from Wu's mother, and the letter indicted that she had not received living expenses or letters for consecutive months son's and during the Spring Festival, so she wondered whether he was back to the institute after staying in Changsha for the Festival. And she hoped that he could send some expenses back. Therefore, Shao and Xiaodong felt it quite unusual, but they could not make out the reason. Wu's mother once came to Qiu's family and lived for a period after Xiaodong gave birth to the second son Wu Jian. From the talk with her, Shao knew that her husband had passed away before the liberation and that she currently lived with the family of another son in a village of Shangdong, but she did not rely on that son because the latter could just sustain his own family. So, she had to depend on the expenses Li Zhimeng sent her to make a living. Shao, who always thought of other people in the first case, accompanied Xiaodong to a post office, transferred 50 yuan by telegraph to Wu's mother to help her out, and then sent an urgent telegraph to the revolutionary committee of Wu's institute to inquire about the reason why he did not come back home for the Spring Festival and lost contact with his family.

One day at the end of February, the sky was dark and gloomy with light rain and snow. Shao and Xiaodong did not come back from work, and Weiying, with a plastic umbrella, went out to buy bean curd, refined white sugar, etc. supplied by the planned tickets of this month. While walking through the door of a coal store which she had to pass, she saw someone walking out with planned coal on shoulders. As the floor was wet, the door of the store and its surrounding area was made dirty by sprayed coal scraps. That reminds Weiying of one Spring Festival when Li Zhimeng came back home and went out to buy something together with Xiaodong. He fell over himself and his trousers got dirty, so he had to return home to change another pair of trousers first. And Xiaodong laughed even with tears in her eyes, "I have told him, 'Watch out as the floor outside is slippery!' and he said loudly, 'Is this slippery? Not at all'. With these words, he fell, with his face upward." Then Xiaodong continued laughing.

However, the Spring Festival and the Lantern Festival had passed for 10-odd days, but he did not come back, which made her mother and old sister worried. Walking up the stairs to the gate, Weiying saw the big and heavy wooden door without the bronze doorbells which had been stolen was ajar and wondered who did not lock it after going back. She pushed the door and walked in, only to find the whole house quite silent. Juecong went to their father's hometown just after the Lantern Festival; Damao was in the village where she was sent as an intellectual youth; Xiaomao worked and lived in her workplace; Juele might have gone to school; Xiaodong's two sons were in Grade One and junior middle school respectively; her two-month-old daughter Wu Sha was lying in bed quietly and whoever was at home would look after her. Weiying entered the kitchen directly opposite to the gate of the courtyard, stood in front of the window by the right side, and saw that the small door through which they could reach the balcony. Nevertheless, she did not see anyone as it might be blown open by wind. She put down the stuff in hand, walked up to the door and locked it, and then walked towards her parents' room. While passing across the living room and entering her brothers' bedroom, she suddenly heard her mother's bitter cry. She knew that her mother was a strong woman who would not easily cry and often said, "Be a person should be like a person! 'The tiger is dead, but the spirit not down,' you see the tiger is dead, fallen to the ground is also a majestic!" In her memory, she only heard mother's such weeping sounds when their family was confiscated property in the spring of 1965. Therefore, upset and restless, she walked into mother's room.

What surprised her was that her mother was lying in bed with her face up, tears falling like a breaching dike. And her hairs beside her ears were dipped by the bursting tears. There were two special envelopes and a torn one lying on the bedside near the sofa. Weiying knew immediately that mother's abnormal circumstance must be caused by the letter, so she walked towards her with big curiosity, asking lightly, "What's up, mom?" Shao began wailing loudly at her inquiry, "My God! How could it happen? How could he become an anti-revolutionary? I can't make it out…!" Weiying quickly took up the letter and a black bold word entered her eyes, "court verdict" which shocked her greatly. The court verdict that the existing anti-revolutionary born of a rich farmer's family, had been sticking to the reactionary position, hating proletarian leadership, attacking the Cultural Revolution, and eavesdropping "Voice of America" during the period when he was held, so he had to begin with transform labor. He was sentenced to be imprisoned for 10 years starting from Nov. 1st, 1969. It was the final decision and any appeal to higher courts would be rejected. It is signed by the revolutionary committee of Intermediate People's Court of Ningxia Autonomous Region. And there was a paper generally describing Wu's crime, As he was born of a rich farmer's family, he hated socialism all the time, and he attacked this unprecedented Cultural Revolution in public, "What's it for?" In addition, he eavesdropped "Voice of America" and radios of Hong Kong and Taiwan to intend to coordinate with reactionists abroad to overthrow the dictatorship of proletariats… Therefore, he must be suppressed hard.

With grave scare, Weiying looked over the court verdict. Her heart fell out of a sudden and could not find proper words to comfort her mother. She realized that it matters a lot, not only would her brother-in-law lose his freedom, job, and income, but Xiaodong's family and their three children would become "family member of anti-revolutionary", which meant that the whole family was going down to the hell! Xiaodong, whose salary was not high, had been forced to abnormality to some degree by the administrative committee of medical during the night when their family property was confiscated, so it would be impossible for her to bring up a two-month-old girl and two boys both of whom were under 10. And she could not expect her mother-in-law who was living in the rural area to offer some help. Thus, Xiaodong had to rely on her mother for her whole living! What was more depressing was that Qiu's family was again covered with a more darkened and gloomy political shade in that socialist country where family background and politics were emphasized too much! And Weiying did not, either expect to be employed back to the city. She had no idea as to how her mother and old sister would confront such a cruel fact! Her sister would witness endless hardships and her mother would also be tugged to a bottomless abyss!

When Xiaodong came back home from work and heard that her husband was identified as an anti-revolutionary and sentenced to 10 years in prison, she broke down out of a sudden. Weiying saw all the terrible scenes, Xiaodong dropped the letter of judgment she had just browsed, ran to the center of the courtyard and cried "God! How could it be? Why does he become an anti-revolutionary?" At this, Mother out of her room quickly and looked at her nervously and desperately while standing on the steps. Weiying tugged Xiaodong into the room to have a rest but was rejected by her hands. Mother walked down the stairs with her brows frowned and stood by her side together with Weiying. They can do nothing about it.

After crying and shouting for a while, Xiaodong ran into her room, took out a big jewelry box Weiying had never seen, and put it in the middle of the courtyard, "God! Have a look at the medal this anti-revolutionary had been awarded with on the Korean battleground…" Without finishing these words, she sat on the ground and continued crying. Shao strived to pull her up and Weiying saw that her trousers had been wet with urine. Seeing that, too, Shao handed her up to the room to have a rest and changed another pair of trouser for her. Weiying followed her mother but found Xiaodong could not settle down anyway. Mother talked to Weiying, "Go to find two tables of diazepam and some water." While mother was feeding Xiaodong with the pills, Weiying went to the yard to pick up those several medals and put them into the jewelry box. She was reminded that Xiaodong once told her very proudly, "Your Brother Wu had been a scout on the Korean battleground, rendered several meritorious services and won many medals." She walked into the room with the box in hand, finding Xiaodong asleep and her mother wiping out the tears on her face. Then out of the room, mother sighed and said to Weiying, "I could not make it out, either. He enlisted in the army at 16 and rendered several meritorious services in the war to resist America and help Korea. So why did he become an anti-revolutionary out of a sudden?" With these words, Shao closed the door of Xiaodong's room. Wu Sha, who was only two to three months old, slept in a small bed beside her mother. Since then, her father could never bring her up besides exerting negative influence on her. So, a road filled with hardships and pains began to wait for this lovely and pretty little girl …

Weiying followed her mother to walk into her parents' room and sat down in the sofa. Xiaodong's two sons came back from school and could not understand what happened to their family, so they ran to the yard to play after staying for a while with worried looks there. Shao said to Weiying, "Your Brother Wu can write good articles but doesn't know how to communicate with other people, that is, he is unwilling to greet others. Although he enlisted in the army at an early age and rendered several meritorious services, he had absolutely no power in his institute. And I heard that he was assigned to Ningxia because he offended the leaders of his unit." Finishing these words, Shao fell into painful meditation and Weiying felt a miserable and desperate atmosphere overwhelming her family and the whole house…

At that time, Qiu's family were not very clear about the fact, the war to resist America and help Korea was a glorious and great victory of the Chinese People's Volunteer Army guided by Peng Dehuai under the strategic leadership of Chairman Mao Zedong against America on the Korea battlefield. It was impossible to succeed without the soldiers' persistence to fight when they lacked clothes and food and it was 20-odd minus degrees! Even Americans themselves admitted that this is the most terrible war they had ever experienced, and beyond their expectation. <See App.1. B>

Nevertheless, at the Lushan Mountain meeting of the CPC central committee in 1959, Peng was identified as a right-leaning anti-Party elements deviator just because he criticized some of the policies and guidelines of the communist party though he had served as the commander of the volunteer army, the Minister of National Defense, etc. Then he was oppressed to death in 1974 during the Cultural Revolution. So even the political fight within the communist party was very cruel and brutal via the operation of the "Gang of Four", for Li Zhimeng, who was neither a party member nor had an important position, his situation was no better. Therefore, it is not something that could not be understood if compared with the miserable destiny of Peng Dehuai! And the Cultural Revolution was initiated and led Chairman Mao. Wu just claimed that it "Wat was making the mischief!". Looking at such political movements and wronged judgments as anti-righteousness after the liberation, what he said was just improper, so it is goes without saying that that he was sentenced to be imprisoned.

During the 10 years while Li Zhimeng was identified as an anti-revolutionary, not only did he lose freedom, but his wife got seriously insane as she could hardly bear such a grave strike. Therefore, Shao had to take over the responsibility to bring up the three children. In the beginning, someone said to Shao, "Now that your daughter is still young and good-looking, you can persuade her to get divorced and find her another husband. It is easy for her to get divorced if she clearly divides the line with an anti-revolutionary, or 10 years will tire you out since her three children are too little." Kind-hearted and selfless Shao rejected this idea immediately, "He participated in the war to resist America and goes without saying that help Korea just after graduation from high school, worked in the Survey and Design Institute after going back when he was over 20 years old, and then was assigned to work in Ningxia. He must be quite depressed to have been identified suddenly as an anti-revolutionary. Life in prison is hard, so if my daughter proposes divorce, he may not stand the strike one by one in succession and the three little children may lose their father. If my daughter can wait 10 years for him to come out, the children will have grown up. At that time, they have their father and a complete family." Shao was fully show deep sympathy for and pathetic for her son-in-law, this anti-revolutionary. She more than once told Weiying personally, "It is quite probable that your brother Wu did not know how to communicate with others in his institute, so he was just set up by somebody. And we have no reason to argue. This is a society where people oppress each other!" During the Cultural Revolution, many communist party members did not understand that it was the CPC central committee that committed a serious mistake, so how could Shao make it out and get a correct conclusion? Therefore, she had only attribute this to a highly irrational social phenomenon ...

Mao Zedong once said, "Political power is developed from the guns", but the most powerful vice commander -in-chief then, Lin Biao, betrayed our country and defected fell from a plane to death in Mongolia. At that time, there were many unjust, framed-up and wrong s and criminals could be more and more unscrupulous due to the severe incomplete legal system! Since Shao had undergone the pain and misery of being confiscated and forced to commit an "inexistent" crime, she would rather sacrifice herself to do everything for her anti-revolutionary son-in-law and the whole family...The then grain and oil, pork and refined white sugar, etc. were supplied by means of tickets, but almost every month Shao sent Li Zhimeng a parcel containing fried noodles she had parched wheat flour with oil and white sugar and dried pork.

She became more frugal so that she did rarely buy new clothes for herself and had meat on dinner table. Whenever seeing that, Weiying would clip fish that was Shao's favorite food to her bowl with chopsticks, but she would clip it back to the bowl with an unpleased look and said, "Do not clip it for me. I'll eat what I want." Weiying knew that Shao did not dislike meat but just save it for others and that she never looked after herself but just consider how to care for the children of the family. One day, Weiying went to a nearby rice noodle restaurant to look for her mother, finding she was having a bowl of rice noodles without any meat or vegetables but a little oil, salt and soy-bean sauce. She said to her, "Mom, why didn't you order a bowl of rice noodles with slices of meat?" Shao said, "I have to pay twice that price just for those several slices. It's OK since I'm full of that."

One morning, Weiying needed to meet her mother for something, so she went to the hospital where Shao worked without breakfast, only to find that she was eating portage and a steamed bun. But when she learned that her daughter did not have breakfast yet, she bought two salted eggs besides a bun and portage for her. While having breakfast, Weiying asked, "Mom, why didn't you buy some salted vegetables which just cost two or three cents? Is it OK with a bun and portage?" Shao answered, when people have money, they pursue something good to eat, but when not, they just expect to fulfill their stomach." In fact, however, the couple had an income of over 240 yuan every month. If not for Li Zhimeng, his insane wife and their three children, they would have lived a much better life than the general public do. Nevertheless, she was sacrificing herself for her daughter's family and she was becoming weak and declining owing to malnutrition and excessive overwork oneself…

Weiying never knew or asked how the salary of her parents was distributed? But she never heard that her father had any criticism about the life arranged by her mother. But because of his idea of favoring boys more than girls, he would spend more money to bring his sons to restaurants if he thought a meal was not satisfying. He said to Weiying twice, "This is because there are more girls than boys in our family. Think about it. We have seven girls but only two boys. If the opposite is true, I'll attach more importance to girls." But Weiying thought her mother was also right to some degree, if father had supported Xiaodong in finding a boyfriend after graduation from college, she would not have encountered such a terrible matter which even exerted influence on the whole family! What was particularly horrible was that since Li Zhimeng was identified as an antirevolutionary, Xiaodong became more severely insane, her monthly salary of 30-odd yuan often disappeared before she brought it home. Neither Shao nor the hospital staff knew what she was doing, and she would not tell them the truth when being asked. It was until a somewhat upright communist party member returned a cover side of a quilt made of Hunan embroidery to Shao, "Doctor Shao, I'm quite grateful to you for curing my disease. I had not given you anything, but your daughter gave it to me. It is just embarrassing." Later Shao inquired after Xiaodong, "Why didn't you ever buy some clothes for your children with your salary but buy something for others for no reason?" Xiaodong replied, "The reason why Li Zhimeng was set up as an anti-revolutionary was that he was reluctant to spend money to buy something for party members." No matter how much effort Shao made to persuade her, she would not accept and did that repeatedly. Once, Shao got so angry that she tried to pick the money out of her pocket, "What will you do with all this money? Above all, I'll arrange everything for you and your children." However, Xiaodong did not give it to her mother, but she also shouted and cursed her, "Go away, Shao Guizhen!" At that time, Shao got quite irritated. Now even if Shao wanted her to get divorced and then remarried, she thought that everyone, including those living in poor mountain villages without any techniques, would fear and not accept her. Under such circumstances, Shao did not give up the burden brought by her daughter's family, her son-in-law was identified as an anti-revolutionary and it was impossible to expect some help from his mother who was then leading a hard life in a village. Every Spring Festival, Shao would send some money to Wu's mother out of sympathy. Shao bore such a burden not only economically but also physically. Ever since the Qiu's family got confiscated property, Qiu family never hired a nanny again. The children of the Qiu family often saw their mother scrubbing clothes or sheets for Qiu Xiaodong and her three children in the front yard on the porch. Even in the winter when it was a few degrees below zero, had the even hired a few degrees below zero when her hands are frozen, swelled like steamed buns!

Once when Xiaodong was resting, Weiying walked into her room and wanted to scold her, why do you let mother alone wash such a big basin of clothes and sheets? But when she saw Xiaodong lying in bed and staring up at the ceiling, she felt somewhat sympathetic, she could not require her to do something like a normal person as she had already gone insane! Sometimes, she just poured away some of the cold water in the wooden basin and added some hot water from a jar beside the coal stove. Then she took off her shoes and socks and stamped on the clothes to help her mother wash them. But how much help could she offer? Very little, Li Zhimeng was sentenced to 10 years in prison because of anti-revolution, but her innocent mother-in-law would also be suffering for 10 years both spiritually and physically! She was pressed by this burden too hard to take a breath and be in an inextricable situation …

Weiying found her father still smoking "Da Qian Men", a kind of premium cigarette under such circumstances, but the quantity was less. He might even resort to liquor sometimes when he was in bad mood. Mother said to Weiying, "Occasionally, he fell to sleep after drinking liquor, which is one of his advantages, unlike some other men who just shouted, cried and even beat their wives after getting drunk. If a woman marries such a man, she will suffer for the rest of her life!"

However, Weiying thought that her father was quite subjective and once a kid advises something to him, he would begin to curse no matter whether the opinion was right or not, "how can you dare to oppose my view?" because he felt that it harmed his dignity as a father. He thought children would do what he said and abide by him in any situation. Sometimes he even beat those who dare to oppose him, but that often happened when he was not drunk. Weiying thought that he was "Tiger's butt cannot to the touch", without any democratic thought. It was proper that this kind of people did not serve as the Chairman of the country, or who knew how many people would put behind bars by him because of holding opposite opinions! Nevertheless, he would never consider your point of view.

Sometimes the children heard their father say with great interest at home, "There's always someone saying I looked like Chairman Mao and sometimes senior provincial leaders send their drivers to pick me there to deal with their illness. When coming back to the hospital, some doctors who are on good terms with me ran to the gate to welcome me and shake my hand. If passers saw me there, they would stop and looked at me, 'Here comes Chairman Mao!'

and stamped on the clothes to help her mother wash them. But how much help could she offer? Very little, Li Zhimeng was sentenced to 10 years in prison because of anti-revolution, but her innocent mother-in-law would also be suffering for 10 years both spiritually and physically! She was pressed by this burden too hard to take a breath and be in an inextricable situation …

Weiying found her father still smoking "Da Qian Men", a kind of premium cigarette under such circumstances, but the quantity was less. He might even resort to liquor sometimes when he was in bad mood. Mother said to Weiying, "Occasionally, he fell to sleep after drinking liquor, which is one of his advantages, unlike some other men who just shouted, cried and even beat their wives after getting drunk. If a woman marries such a man, she will suffer for the rest of her life!"

However, Weiying thought that her father was quite subjective and once a kid advises something to him, he would begin to curse no matter whether the opinion was right or not, "how can you dare to oppose my view?" because he felt that it harmed his dignity as a father. He thought children would do what he said and abide by him in any situation. Sometimes he even beat those who dare to oppose him, but that often happened when he was not drunk. Weiying thought that he was "Tiger's butt cannot to the touch", without any democratic thought. It was proper that this kind of people did not serve as the Chairman of the country, or who knew how many people would put behind bars by him because of holding opposite opinions! Nevertheless, he would never consider your point of view.

Sometimes the children heard their father say with great interest at home, "There's always someone saying I looked like Chairman Mao and sometimes senior provincial leaders send their drivers to pick me there to deal with their illness. When coming back to the hospital, some doctors who are on good terms with me ran to the gate to welcome me and shake my hand. If passers saw me there, they would stop and looked at me, 'Here comes Chairman Mao!'

for your children with your salary but buy something for others for no reason?" Xiaodong replied, "The reason why Li Zhimeng was set up as an anti-revolutionary was that he was reluctant to spend money to buy something for party members." No matter how much effort Shao made to persuade her, she would not accept and did that repeatedly. Once, Shao got so angry that she tried to pick the money out of her pocket, "What will you do with all this money? Above all, I'll arrange everything for you and your children." However, Xiaodong did not give it to her mother, but she also shouted and cursed her, "Go away, Shao Guizhen!" At that time, Shao got quite irritated. Now even if Shao wanted her to get divorced and then remarried, she thought that everyone, including those living in poor mountain villages without any techniques, would fear and not accept her. Under such circumstances, Shao did not give up the burden brought by her daughter's family, her son-in-law was identified as an anti-revolutionary and it was impossible to expect some help from his mother who was then leading a hard life in a village. Every Spring Festival, Shao would send some money to Wu's mother out of sympathy. Shao bore such a burden not only economically but also physically. Ever since the Qiu's family got confiscated property, Qiu family never hired a nanny again. The children of the Qiu family often saw their mother scrubbing clothes or sheets for Qiu Xiaodong and her three children in the front yard on the porch. Even in the winter when it was a few degrees below zero, had the even hired a few degrees below zero when her hands are frozen, swelled like steamed buns!

Once when Xiaodong was resting, Weiying walked into her room and wanted to scold her, why do you let mother alone wash such a big basin of clothes and sheets? But when she saw Xiaodong lying in bed and staring up at the ceiling, she felt somewhat sympathetic, she could not require her to do something like a normal person as she had already gone insane! Sometimes, she just poured away some of the cold water in the wooden basin and added some hot water from a jar beside the coal stove. Then she took off her shoes and socks

That's interesting!" Weiying thought that Chairman Mao was an idol of people throughout China and even the world as a whole and people who yearn for a communist society bow down and worship him very much. But how about your situation? And you did not keep your property you had earned from medical practices for dozens of years, which affected the political life of the whole family and the destiny and future of the children. At the same time, she felt that her father wanted to get rid of the burden brought by Xiaodong, so he asked someone to introduce a boyfriend for her before her graduation, which, as a result, did harm to him and forced the whole family bear a heavier burden! Since Li Zhimeng was identified as an anti-revolutionary, his parents-in-law were bullied by others in the hospital. Furthermore, this anti-revolutionary's wife and children were living in Qiu's house. Although Shao was kind and did what she was supposed to do in the hospital, she had to suffer from another inhibiting matter. At that time, if there was an anti-revolutionary in a family, all other family members would suffer a lot in terms of politics, which was more serious for the Qiu's who not party members were and had been confiscated. This was true during the Cultural Revolution when one would be criticized and denounced if he or she was identified as an "academic authority of capitalism". At the same time, to a great extent it will increase the crime.

One day, when Xiaodong was relatively sober-minded, she told Weiying quite sadly and indignantly, "The hospital pays mom salary based on her length of service instead of her techniques and merit. Despite the low salary, she works carefully and diligently, and rendered excellent treatment. But the hospital has never praised her. Instead, it once criticized her for not conducting serious sterilization or for other reasons at a meeting because a patient got tetanus. Someone even insulted her, 'You have done that out your class of retaliation because that patient was a communist party member.' At that meeting, I sat beside mom and wanted to declare, my mother was also born of a poor family, and the tetanus was probably caused by not strict sterilization to the medical facility, which was not carried out by my mother and thus she should not take all the responsibility alone. However, when mom saw me standing up, she kicked me and asked me not to speak. So, I had to sit down with my temper restrained and looked at some people criticizing mom imprudently and violently. Later someone even began to call, 'Down the wife of the Kuomintang officer'! I intended to declare that my current father is not a Kuomintang member, but mom just kicked me to prevent me from saying anything. I was so angry that my tears almost fell. Then, they deducted mom's salary for half a month to give it to the patient as nutrition fees. They were so evil-minded without analyzing the real cause for the accident and just putting all the responsibility to mom alone. I was furious." Xiaodong's eyes were full of sparkling tears.

Weiying said disappointedly, "Sister, I have seen those medical facilities that are easy to trigger tetanus because of the rust caused by long-time use. If you don't tell it to me, I'll never know it since mom hasn't mentioned." Xiaodong said, "I have more contact with mom and know more about her than you. If she has something unpleasant or depressing, she will never tell them to the children. She just bears all the difficulties without revealing them to us because she wanted us to live a happy life." Indeed, every time Weiying went to the hospital to visit mother, she always smiled. It happened only once when Weiying heard mother sighed, "My God! Who can stand all this…?" while talking with the woman cook at the door of the canteen. Weiying thought she was talking about Xiaodong's behavior of buying and giving others something at random with her salary. She did not inquire after why mother sighed but just felt she had too much pain in her heart. Weiying was shocked by what Xiaodong said. She knew that mother was strong and did not shed tears easily as a woman. But above all, she was a human being with flesh and blood. Who knew how inexhaustible pain she was suffering in her heart alone with these endless disasters surrounding her?

Lose one's bearings

Later, Weiying asked her mother, "Mom, you have said that these rusted medical facilities were in the charge of the kitchen staff disinfect at high temperature. So, she was them that should take the responsibility for any accident. So why did you decide to be responsible for the tetanus without explaining the reason?"

But Shao, who was not a communist party member, sighed, "The person responsible for the sterilization of medical instruments is a worker that who with several children in a poor family. If she lost her job, it would have been more disastrous!" Weiying once heard from young sister Damao, "Once I saw mom looked down on the ground with her waist bending and a biscuit on hand. I wondered what she was doing and therefore asked, 'what are you looking at, Mom?' she answered, 'ants are strange. They can climb very fast with things several times heavier than their own weight. As winter is drawing near, I feed some biscuits to let them move into the hole.' You see mom is so kind-hearted that she is even sympathetic for ants."

Thinking of that, Weiying said, "You are so kind, Mom! The hospital staff did not have any reason. How can you suffer all this?" Shao replied with deep feeling, "Is there any reason to argue? When our family was confiscated, they said that they would first freeze up our property and then deal with them after the is settled.' Now several years have passed, and we still see no hope to get it solved." Weiying replied immediately, "Mom, when I was studying politics at school in Grade Three, the teacher said, 'the Four Cleanups Movement refers to the clean-ups of thought, account, warehouse and work credits in communes and production teams in rural areas. It also aims to investigate whether rural cadres commit s of corruption, theft and possession of more than what one should have.' How did they count your opening up a clinic legally as a kind of crime and even confiscate our property with such an excuse?" Shao sighed, "That's why I say, they would not argue with you. They are just bandits!" Weiying said, "Bandits rob people publicly, but they robbed us stealthily at midnight and prevented us from telling it to others. You and my father are just too honest." Mother replied, "We have no choice! Could we fight with them? This society was too dark!"

In fact, even at that time when the legal system was not complete, it was illegal for those to confiscate people's property with a blank "certificate of confiscation of family property" at midnight. But without an improved legal system, people's awareness of laws was too weak, and the couple were indeed too honest.

After their property was confiscated, father said to Weiying several times, "That can also be attributed to your mother's reluctance to leave Changsha. We are not native and prone to being envied and set up by others. We heard that the administrative committee of medical of Medical of Medical Organizations consulted the hospital for advice before confiscating our property. Wang Huijun supported their idea. If your mother's property should be confiscated as she was operating a private clinic at home, they should not confiscate mine because I was working in my own established hospital. They did not even leave money for our meals. I gave up being the president of the hospital and let a cleaning lady be the dean. She bullied me like that, bitch!" Weiying could feel that cursing them was the only way for her father to complain.

One evening, Weiying told her mother, "Mom, today I encountered the son of a doctor, and his father also operated a private ophthalmology clinic in Xueyuan Street. He told me, "I heard that of your family of all property had been confiscated, but they just took away a little of ours. Because my father was very polite to Director Cheng, and their relationship is very good. He divulged the information to us before the confiscation of family property and we did our property into a safe place in advance.' You see, there was no one informing us of anything, but they just bullied us more."

Mother said to Weiying, "It seemed that I offended the leaders of the administrative committee of medical of medical and they retaliate me in excuse of the movement. If I had agreed with Secretary Zhao's demand to let his relative live in our home, they would not have confiscated our property. Your father is totally careless about socialization; he just thought it was he who invested in and established the hospital, and that he earned money by his own techniques. If the leaders irritate him, he will express his opposition directly. So, there was harbor a deep resentment to him and avenge him with any chance. They are vicious." Weiying said, "Father sad that was because he was not a native…" Mother said, "He has never reflected on himself. Secretary Zhao is not also native, either so how could he become the secretary of the committee? If your father did not intend to get rid of the burden brought by Xiaodong, he would not have introduced a boyfriend for her before her graduation. If Xiaodong had not got married after graduation, she might not have encountered such a matter.

Li Zhimeng was identified as an anti-revolutionary bringing our whole family down. Now once Xiaodong saw the matchmaker, she would curse him. Not only Li Zhimeng himself suffers…" With these words, mother seemed to shed tears and sighed.

She was thinking what the Wu's family would look like in 10 years. It was hard to imagine as the three children were little and Xiaodong became insane. Confused by all these problems, she began to doubt whether she could sustain the whole family for another 10 years both mentally and physically. She felt a tremendous pressure on her spine coming down from the sky, binding her tightly and making her feel heavier and heavier, and compressed her so hard to breathe…!

4.3 Touchstone of love

During the Cultural revolution, the central government sent many cadres and leaders to rural areas to labor in the Five-Seven Cadre School (Party and Government officials into re-education during Cultural Revolution) and much medical staff participates in the countryside Circuit Medical Team.

Everybody did not know whether that would be permanent or temporary. However, a certain number of cadres did not go back after several years in the Five-Seven Cadre School. The situation did not change until the "Gang of Four" stepped down. Since it was the general trend of that time, no one could predict the result.

At the beginning of 1970, Qiu Zhongyuan was sent to Fulin Regional Hospital in Changsha County to carry out the tour of medical treatment. Before the Lantern Festival, he wrote a letter to his family, saying that he felt cold at night and that it was inconvenient to buy things in the village, so he hoped they could send another thick blanket. The next day Weiying took a coach there with a blanket.

There were no guest rooms in the hospital, so Weiying slept on the operating table in his father's consulting room that night and prepared to go back to Changsha the next day. At midnight, she was woken by the light and noise outside the room. Jumping down from the table, she put on her clothes and went out to see what happened. It turned out that a patient needing emergent treatment came. She was a woman of advanced paternal age on fertility and pregnancy, and it was said that this is the first time for her to give birth though she and her husband had been married for dozens of years. Since she was suffering from dystocia, the man doctor of the department of gynecology and obstetrics got quite anxious as there were not enough medical facilities there. He made great efforts but still failed. Although it was cold, he was sweating all over. The hospital worried that the woman and her unborn child would encounter something unfortunate after such long time, so they decided to send an ambulance to take her to a better hospital in Changsha immediately.

On hearing this decision, Weiying walked up to the driver who was pacing about outside the treating room and asked, "Comrade, I live in Changsha. I came here today to send a blanket to my father who was touring the medical treatment here. So, could you take me there later together with them?" The driver answered with a smile, "Certainly. I also live in Changsha." Weiying ran to her father's sleeping room quickly and told it to him. Qiu said, "It's OK. Then I don't have to see you off." Weiying replied, "The ambulance is parked at the gate. As you must work tomorrow morning, do not see me off."

After Weiying got on the ambulance, some doctors and nurses took the woman onto it quickly. There were no hospital staff there but Weiying and the woman's husband who looked quite worried. The woman lied on a thick pillow and was covered with a quilt made of cotton brought from home. Lying upwards in the stretcher in the middle of the ambulance, she looked painful. Weiying and her husband sat opposite to each other. And affected by this situation, Weiying could not fall asleep as she was worried about her.

It was sunny in Changsha, but the road was still wet because it drizzled with snow during the past few days. The remaining snow and the melted water froze during the night so that it was somewhat difficult to drive on the surface of such a rural road and the ambulance jolted around. The driver was striving to control the steering wheel and drive more stably. But the reality made it impossible and shocked the woman's body from time to time. Hearing the continuous moan of the woman and feeling the progress of the ambulance, Weiying began to ponder about the urgent problem. While standing beside the department of gynecology and obstetrics in the hospital, she heard the doctor sigh, "The baby in the woman's body is horizontal, so only by putting it vertical can we help her give birth to it. Now the biggest trouble is that it is too difficult to put it vertical. I can't take such a grand responsibility if death threatens her when I drag her too much." Weiying thought, if so, if the baby lied vertically, it might come out without much effort. If she slept to one side, then the baby might turn vertical with jolts of the ambulance. Therefore, she stood up and said to the woman, "I think you can lie on the other side of your body, which may be good for the baby." The woman then changed her position with the aid of her husband and Weiying. It really worked soon, in less than half an hour, the woman became anxious and upset. Weiying looked at her expression from time to time and comforted her, "Hang onto it. We will get to Changsha soon." After a while the woman shouted suddenly, turned back to lie on her back and meanwhile separated her two legs a bit, indicating her husband that he should take a heap of yellow paper under her body quickly. At that exact moment, Weiying saw a flow of red and black blood from her body. Surprised at that, she shouted loudly, "Driver, she can't stick to it. She may be going to give birth to the baby. Is there any hospital nearby?"

Hearing Weiying's threatened voice, the driver turned back and answered, "There is a small commune hospital." At the same time, he turned the ambulance back to a cross he just walked through and drove towards a narrower street on the right side. He quickly parked the ambulance on the square in front of the hospital, jumped out, and ran to the gate in several steps. Then he shouted, waking up the hospital staff, who had been asleep, and someone opened the gate. At that time, the dawn was coming. Weiying could see that the commune hospital was not too small in scale. She also saw some doctors and nurses standing inside the gate and taking on their white work clothes gowns while waiting for the pregnant woman. When the stretcher was taken off from the ambulance, they hurried to follow it to walk into the consulting room. And the woman's husband also entered. Weiying and the driver sat in the dim patient-waiting room, waiting for news. Soon a woman nurse walked towards them, smiling, "She just gave birth to a red-faced boy. She does not have to go to Changsha and can get out of the hospital after staying here for a few days. And you can leave now." They said goodbye to the nurse and got on the ambulance that directed to Changsha. When the ambulance arrived in Changsha, the dawn came. The driver drove Weiying to Laozhaobi and then she thanked him said, "Thank you" and walked into the lane go home.

Back from Fulin Regional Hospital where her father worked, Weiying suddenly realized that she should let Wang Tianliang know she had already been home. It was sunny the next day and the road seemed dry. Having dinner earlier than usual, Weiying took her sister Damao, who had just come back from a village for holiday, to the factory where Wang Tianliang worked. On the way there, she thought under the current circumstances, not only not could she share her parents' sadness, but instead she became their burden. Although she turned 21 and identified her love relationship with Wang Tianliang, she thought that she could not get married because her household residence permit was not in the city. But she was young anyway and Wang Tianliang was about 24, so they could get married several years later in a time when the government advocated "late marriage".

It was already dark when Weiying and Damao got off the bus after several stations. She took Damao directly to the wireless factory. She greeted the old man who had known her at the entrance guard and then walked to the two-storied building where Wang Tianliang worked and lived. When they reached somewhere not far from that building, they saw him standing in front of the door, which was unexpected to Weiying. Wang, with a calmer attitude, led them to a laboratory on the first floor. Weiying felt a little bit strange, why didn't he take us to the place where he worked, it is lived upstairs when I took my sister here? But she was without saying anything, she sat down in the chair while Damao seated herself separately in a chair about 10 meters away from them.

After a moment of silence, Wang told Weiying directly, "I'm a demobilized army man and will go to battlefield sooner or later, you would become a widow. So, let's be brother and sister and put an end to our relationship in this respect." At this, Weiying suddenly felt confused and said slightly, "Go to battlefield? That's OK. I'm still young and willing to wait for you." However, Wang said without any sympathy, "But I don't know when to go to battlefield and when to come back." Weiying shed tears depressed, hearing such words. But she stopped crying at once as she felt something abnormal. Both remained silent for a few minutes and Weiying stood up slowly, very calm, "It's time for us to go back home." Wang did not have any intention to let them stay and said, "Then I'll send you out." Weiying replied, "There is no need. My sister will accompany me." But Wang still insisted on seeing them off at the gate of the factory.

Out of the factory, Damao asked immediately, "Why did you cry just now? What did Wang Tianliang say to you?" Weiying repeated Wang's words to Damao who was surprised, "How could it happen? It's unbelievable. Although he was somewhat handsome, he always gave me a feeling of being uncomfortable." Weiying said, "Do you refer to his disposition? He can't be compared with Tang Na's cousin in Beijing! But I heard Tang said that he had a girlfriend, so I can't get in between."

During that night, Weiying thought in bed about why Wang Tianliang should make such a change. She had seen such slogans as "digging holes and store food", "making preparation for wars and disasters and doing everything for the people". But there was no news that Wang Tianliang would go to battlefield. And even if he would, he would just be engaged in astrological techniques instead of shedding blood. So why was he afraid of me becoming a widow? I'd better ask him for clarification and help eliminate some of his unnecessary misgivings.

In the evening of a sunny day, Qiu Weiying went to Wang's factory by bus after dinner. Although in the past Wang often went to Weiying's home when he was free, Weiying also came to the factory several times so that the old man in the lodge had already known her. Therefore, Weiying greeted him while passing the lodge and then directly walked to the building where Wang Tianliang worked. At the stairway exit, she saw some products put at random waiting for inspection on the first floor. But no one was there, including the inspector, so Weiying went to the second floor, full of doubt.

Reaching the stairway exit at the second floor and looking into where Wang used to work, she was stunned by the scene before her eyes, which completely smashed her innocent and unswerving emotion deep in her heart, Wang suddenly stood up from his bed, with a somewhat panicking expression while the woman inspector was looking at her with her head lowered. There was not a single sign of shyness on her square face, but an expression of complacency. Meanwhile, she stretched her hands to her head to flatten her messy hair. And Wang opened his mouth with two thick lips and smiled reluctantly to Weiying who was amazed by the newly discovered secret.

Weiying's strong self-esteem made her realize that she could not walk closer to Wang any longer and that their love had lost the value of existence. No one needed to explain anything to her, no sound is better than have sound here! She turned around and ran downstairs at once. When she walked out of the building, she heard Wang shout from the window of the upstairs room, "Weiying, wait a minute!" Pretending that she did not hear him, she walked out of the factory as fast as possible.

While waiting for the bus at the bus station, she did not feel sad, but instead, she thought she was lucky because she did not have sex with Wang and now, she discovered his secret! At that time, the love seed planted by Wang fell off suddenly before being able to give blossom to a flower. He had just cheated her by saying that he had to go to battlefield as a demobilized army man. Although she heard that first love was the most unforgettable, she felt that she could not go on with such a man and that the man who could be in love with another woman was not worth her love any more. Thus, Wang's image was totally changed, and he was eliminated forever in her heart.

Weiying felt a little bit cold when a gust of wind in the early spring blew through her. The bus light was becoming brighter from afar, but she thought that the time was still early and suddenly realized that she would not come here again, so she had better go to Zhang Manu's home to say goodbye. Reaching the second floor of Zhang's house, Weiying saw her washing bowls in the kitchen at the stairway exit. Seeing Weiying, she smiled and greeted her,

"You've come, Weiying. Sit down, please. I'm finishing washing the bowls." The she stretched her head out of the door of the kitchen and shouted to her husband in the room which was diagonally across the aisle, "Liu Dahan. Here comes Weiying. Prepare a cup of tea!" When Zhang walked out, she asked Weiying, "Why didn't Wang Tianliang come with you?" Weiying told her what happened just now to them. Liu Dahan said immediately, "Wang's that much into you and that woman is not pretty at all. How would that happen? You must have made a mistake." Weiying said directly, "I saw it in person. I did not hear it from others, so it is impossible that I have made a mistake. She is an urban registered permanent resident, and she has got a job, while I'm just an intellectual youth without residence cards or work." Zhang smiled, "There's no doubt that the rumor that he is in love with that Hui woman is spreading. It turns out to be real. I heard that that woman's parents and relatives are very fond of Wang. But they do not have pork and have differences with us in customs. If Wang lives with her, how can he adjust himself to such a life? You two were on fine terms, so why would you break up? Did you quarrel?" Weiying replied at once, "No, I have never quarreled with him. We didn't have much contact and thus there is little that worth quarreling about." I have neither urban household residence permit nor work, and my brother-in-law was identified as an anti-revolutionary. Now that we haven't got married, he can change his mind as early as possible, or it would cause great trouble to divorce after we get married and have children." Zhang said, "You are so honest that you didn't curse her?" Weiying answered, "What qualifications do I have to curse her? I did not marry him, and even so, he would be self-conscious and pay attention to his own behaviors. If a couple must restrict each other's conduct, it will be too boring. And they do not have enough energy to do so as while living together." Liu asked, "Do you hate to lose him?" "He has already given me up, so why not hate to leave him? People have mutual feelings for each other. I will not fall in love with a man who did not love me in the first place. If a man does not love you, you will torture yourself if you chase after him and harm yourself if you marry him and have his children. Any man who can fall in love with someone else is not worth my love."

Zhang gave a signal to Liu to stop talking and said to him, "It's not hard for Weiying to find a lover." Then she asked her with a smiling face, "We have a friend working in Changsha Public Security Bureau. He is very handsome and matches your figure. He has just graduated from the medical school and was appointed to work as a forensic doctor at the Bureau. Shall we introduce him to you?" Weiying answered, "Such a man must be the target of many girls. It's OK that you do not make the match since I have no urban household residence permit and have no interest in developing a love relationship. Even when I get married, I'll just cook and care for children at home. If Wang Tianliang did not begin to be fond of me when I was in my elementary school, I would not go on a love relationship with him. I don't like getting married at an early age as I can do nothing after I have children. Furthermore, children registered permanent residence follows that of their mother, so I'll harm my own children in the future." After talking for a while, Weiying thought it was time to go back and then said goodbye to them.

The next day, Damao asked Weiying, "Sis, do you really end your relationship with Wang Tianliang?" Weiying answered, "Of course. Love and marriage matter life-long happiness. He has been on terms with another woman of the factory, so is there any value in it if I still love him?" Damao said, "I know he's unreliable. He has seldom come to our home since the "Sep. 29th" incident last year. Mother said that Wang had gone to the police station only once and had never come here ever since she got captured by rebel factions. Weiying felt strange and asked, "Why was mother captured by them? Why didn't I know that?" Damao told her, "Peasants from Changsha County came to city to stage a protest on Sep. 29th last year. One afternoon, several rebel factions rushed into our house and said that the green iron-covered radio given by our uncle was a telegraph transmitter. They did not hear what mother was saying at all, but instead, they pushed mother outside the gate from the courtyard very fiercely. They also forced mother to hold the radio and brought her to streets. At that time, Juele came back home from school and saw kind mother bullied by them in such a way, he hit the ceiling! As soon as putting his bag down, he ran to the kitchen and then out of the gate with a knife in hand. He followed and tried to fight with them. Aunt Yan, our next-door neighbor was frightened at the scene and thus hurried to drag Juele, 'My Goodness! You can't do this! That will cause greater trouble!' They detained mother for several days before letting her out."

Later when Weiying asked Juele about the incident, he said, "I know what uncle gave us is a radio as all of us had been using it to listen to programs. But the rebel factions said it was a telegraph transmitter, seized mother and pushed her outside the gate to demonstrate to the masses. Father and mother are not spying but doctors. I was so angry that I'd like to hack at them with the knife." Weiying said, "If Aunt Yan had not stopped you and they had seen you, or you had actually killed someone, then our family would have encountered greater trouble." Juele replied, "I did not think of that much with such indignation." At that moment, mother told Weiying, "Then I was asking for a conclusion from the liberation army man who oversaw military control. I said, 'Why was I detained several days without a reason? And the radio was taken away as a telegraph transmitter. Why don't you send it back?' The man said, 'It is a public movement, and we have no alternative. We don't know where to find back the taken stuff.' The rebel factions are engaged in beating, smashing and robbery. Even if they made a mistake, the stuff they took away have never been returned if not confiscated."

Weiying began to doubt now her brother-in-law was identified as an anti-revolutionary and her father was sent to the village. Was Wang Tianliang afraid that our whole family would go to the village? And I, without registered urban permanent residence or work, would probably become his burden economically. So, if I had lived in a village and been born of a rich farmer's home, then it would have been impossible for him to pursue me. Therefore, I will never be with him even if he breaks up with that Hui woman. True emotion can only be felt amid great trouble, and he failed to pass such a test. There are so many false, ugly, and unauthentic things in this world. If a couple do not have true feelings for each other and cannot work together to overcome hardships, how could they face each other every day with their mind unchanged?

That Sunday, while Shao was having a rest at home, Weiying told her at the dinner table that she had broken up with Wang Tianliang. Looking at Weiying with an examining expression, mother felt that her daughter did not take the whole thing very seriously, so she was assured. Then she told Weiying, "Wang insisted on being my adopted son after getting treatment in our home before he joined the army. I could not reject him. Anyway, you two were not married, so he can love anyone as he likes. If you feel unhappy after getting married, you must get divorced all the same. When I was operating the clinic at home years ago, a woman tried to seduce your father with every means because he earned a high salary. When she was playing Mahjong here, I even treated her with a meal. I did not realize her abnormal relationship with your father until I saw she touch your father's leg with her foot. I did not quarrel with your father and made myself sad in the end. 'Couples with love for each other feel happy even when they live in hardship.' So, you must be happy when living together, even if you do not have enough money." Weiying asked, "Mother, who is so shameless? Have I ever seen her?" Shao answered, "She's Uncle Zhang's wife." Then Weiying was reminded the time when mother was operating the clinic at home. One day she walked into her mother's room, only to see her wiping tears in the sofa. When she tried to ask what happened, her father came in, looking very angry and saying to her mother without a pity, "Don't cry any more. I've explained that I have nothing to do with her, but you refuse to believe me." Shao was refuting to him, 'I saw you kicked each other with your feet under the dinner table. Doesn't that demonstrate something?"

At that time, Weiying was in her elementary school, so though she felt sorry for her mother, she still walked out of the room immediately since she knew nothing about affairs between a couple. But that her mother got cross and shed tears for those affairs made a lasting impression on her, which prompted her to make up her mind to take her marriage seriously to avoid an unhappy family life. Now that she had gone through a love relationship and got some experience, she thought it was not that simple. She has later inquired, "Did Uncle Zhang know it? Didn't it affect their family life?" Shao said, "He should have known it. She is his wife and has several children with him, so he must be clear about what kind of woman she is. But there are men who do not care about emotion between husband and wife. In the old society, if a woman married a good-for-nothing man, she had to serve as a prostitute in order to make a living foe both. There are also men who just like his wife flirting with him every day but will kill another man with whom his wife hangs out. There are also men who are furious towards others but very kind to their wives and men who are just the opposite. If a woman encounters such a man, she will suffer for the rest of her life. Nevertheless, many men are kind to their wives, or they will not get married." Weiying thought, how many men are like this? There are good-for-nothing men and good men. So, women must open their eyes wide to find a good one. And she would rather not get married for her whole life than find a good-for-nothing man, or she will suffer for a lifelong time. She also thought that Aunt Zhang still came to their home occasionally, sometimes with her husband. She felt she was a woman without any self-respect as she just wanted to rely on her father's high salary and did not realize that she was married and had several children. She came here to influence my family life, so I had to do something to help prevent her from doing so.

After lunch that day, Weiying went to Uncle Zhang's home where she had never been according to the address and intended to talk about the whole thing to the couple. Seeing Weiying when opening the gate, Uncle Zhang asked her with great hospitality, "What's up, Weiying?" I'm just leaving for the hospital since my wife was hospitalized for illness." Standing outside the gate, Weiying said, "Since your wife was sick, I do not want to bother you. But would you please tell your wife that for the happiness of two families, we will never welcome her to our family! Bye!" with these words, she left without looking back.

Back home, Weiying did not mention it to anyone because her father was on good terms with Uncle Zhang and her mother was honest so that she could hardly predict what would happen if she told them. But since then, she had never seen Zhang's wife or the couple coming to their home to play mahjong.

Although someone said that Weiying looked like her father, she was more like her mother in character. It was unlikely for her to fall in love with two men at the same time and to accept that her beloved man had a love relationship with another woman, which constituted the fundamental reason for her to break up with Wang Tianliang and never to recall him with nostalgia. She was innocent and faithful as for love and was unable to accept cheating or impure behaviors, especially in critical moments to test his heart!

4.4 Be born at the wrong time

It has been cloudy and drizzly for days on end, which made Qiu Weiying more depressed. One day after lunch, it was still gloomy though it stopped raining. Qiu thinks that Tang Na should be home and decided to visit her. At that time, telephone had not been popularized, so friends would not notify each other before visiting. Arriving there, Qiu found that Tang was unhappy as the latter just smiled to her reluctantly and said, "Why haven't you come for such a long time?" Qiu answered, "It rained so much that I was unwilling to come out. Furthermore, I did not know where you were, Chang Sha or your hometown?" "My residence permit is in my hometown, but I'm free to choose in the team. If I labor in the rural area, it is impossible to live on. So, I often go back home. Pang Zi = Fatty (Tang Na's younger brother) went to village after graduation from higher middle school. However, it is better for boys than for girls to go to the rural area. But Pang Zi knows nothing about farming. If boys are too honest, it will be difficult for them to be given a job in the city; but it is easier for those naughty ones to find a job because peasants tend to think that they would cause trouble." Tang Na replied.

Qiu Weiying thought in rural areas, most educated youth are in this situation. She asked, "Two of your family members have been sent to village, so your old brother will not be sent there, will him?" Tang sighed, "He has got nephritis, and lives in my aunt's home in Higher Education Department as it is located near Hunan Medical College making it easier for him to see a doctor. He got such this disease, because of the rebellion organization in my parents' unit lead to serious consequences. He debated with them because he was angry, but they refused to reason with him and said he was a member of the Royalists in the black bang and imprisoned him instead. The room was too damp, to live several people together. He could not even go to toilet if it was not exercise time. Someone just peed in the corner while my old brother felt it was so shameful that he would try to suppress the urine, caused him to suffer from severe nephritis. In order to save his life, my mother prepared to transplant one of her own kidneys to him." Tang frowned and sighed deeply.

Qiu Weiying felt that Tang's whole family were worrying about her brother's disease amid this Cultural Revolution. Tang Na wanted to go to her aunt's home in the Department behind Youth Palace to have a look at her brother. And Qiu's home was near the Youth Palace, so she accompanied Tang there. In the house of Tang's aunt, Qiu saw Tie Dan lying in a single iron bed, with dropsy around his eyes. There were no vigor young people were supposed to have on his face. When the dinner was ready, Qiu left for home. Since then, Qiu also made acquaintance with Tang's two younger female cousins, Xiao Mao and Xiao He, Qiu has also out with Xiao He to go for a swim.

How time flies! It has been several months since Qiu Weiying left the reservoir for home. Though she learned the prophecy, an inch of light is an inch of gold. she had no work nor planned food as she did not have a municipal registered of residence. So, she had no alternative but to help in housework and read books and newspapers to kill time. Fortunately, her father had a high salary, which can be used to buy some high-priced food if the planned food was not enough." But she can't stay at home like this forever, because she has no registered permanent residence and future.

One day, Wang Tianliang's father came to her home and said to her mother, "Doctor Shao, you have not only cured my son's disease but also saved one hand of my relative. We are deeply grateful. But we are sorry to hear that your daughter encountered something unpleasant at the reservoir. And we have discussed and decided to let Weiying live with us. If you agree with that, we can immediately assist her report to the local authorities for change of domicile. What is your opinion?" Mrs. Qiu answered, "I have been worried that her residence permit at the reservoir has caused much trouble to us. I agree with your idea. And Weiying can live here but put her residence permit in your family. But I heard that your son had a new girlfriend, so will he oppose to it?" Wang's father said, "The boy has no conscience, all of us are angry with him. Weiying is so good that he should not have fallen in love with anyone else." Weiying interrupted, "I have neither urban registered permanent residence nor a job, so I'll become a burden of my future husband and our children will have no residence cards. If your son is married to a girl with a job and residence cards, things will be much better." Wang's father said to her and her mother, "That's not it. Don't care about

Tianliang. He's now working in the city and not living at home. Since he has regarded Doctor Shao as his nominally adoptive mother, he will definitely not oppose it and he has no power to object to our decision." Shao said, "If so, it's OK to let Weiying's residence be in your family. We'll think of alternatives in the future. I can't bear her residence going back to the reservoir again." With these words, she turned around to ask Weiying, "What do you think of it?" Weiying said, "Then that's the only choice. Anyway, it's just dozens of kilometers away from home. If there's any inconvenience, I can come back." Mrs. Qiu extended her heartful thanks to Wang Sandie. Then Weiying continued, "Uncle Wang, please handle a four-level accept certificate. of the production group, production brigade, commune and county government. Then I'll come to the reservoir to move my household residence permit." Wang's father said, "OK. I'll handle it as soon as I go back home"

Several days later, Wang's father completed relevant procedures and brought the household transfer procedures to Qiu's family. Weiying rushed to the reservoir as quickly as possible with these Household transfer procedures. Soon she successfully transferred her residence from Siqing Reservoir in Chen County to Wang Tianliang's family in Changsha County. At the reservoir, she witnessed the marriage between Xie Chun and He Xianshu, an intellectual youth from Chenzhou. She felt both pleased and sad for Xie Chun. She was pleased because Xie had a family of her own at the reservoir and her husband who liked her very much could look after her; she was sad because she, in charge Class Representative of mathematics, was good at study and achieved wonderful scores at school. But such a promising intellectual youth suffered severely in her destiny just due to her father's "commit suicide". Now that she got married here, she would probably stay here forever without development opportunities.

Entrusted by Xie Chun, Weiying went to visit her mother when backed to Changsha. Xie's mother was a teacher at Ruyijie Elementary School and her stepfather was a principal of that school.

When speaking of Xie Chun's marriage, her mother said to Weiying with tears in her eyes, "She's my only daughter, but she'll never come back now that she has got married in the village." Weiying comforted her, "He Xianshu is a man of knowledge and good temper. It seems that he loves your daughter very much, so there is no need to worry about her." "But I'll not go to live at the reservoir after retirement because I'll not be used to the life there after living so many years in Changsha. And when they have children, whose registered permanent residence will be in the village without planned food and work in the city, it will be impossible for them to come here to live with me. I'm not in good health in my 50 years old. I don't know what to do while growing older." Weiying could not come up with better words to comfort her as she was uncertain about her own future. How could she reach a conclusion for Xie Chun's future? But she was sure about one thing, she doesn't dare get married and have children before having residence cards and work in. Because her children had also no planned food and residence cards. After a while, she said goodbye to her mother and left.

In the spring of 1971, when Wang Tianliang's brother Wang Tianpu, came to invite Weiying to live in his home after all relevant procedures were settled. Before starting out, her mother bought a lot of food and snacks for them to express her thanks and because it as inconvenient to buy things in the village.

Wang's family had prepared a room beside the sitting room and to the left corner of the couple's bedroom for Weiying. A double bed and a closet which were not new, but delicate was put inside. Weiying had meals there too. Wang's family was an extended one, with his parents, grandmother, three younger brothers, two younger sisters and an unmarried aunt called Aunt Wan living together. The more than 10 family members sat by two tables when having meals, adults by one and children by the other. Although Weiying used to live in the village in Chen County, she lived at the reservoir and therefore had a different life from native peasants. As a result, she could do nothing but help Wang's mother cut vegetables and add firewood. Sometimes she felt uncomfortable when working in the group because she was regarded not as an intellectual youth but as Wang's wife. Once a middle-aged man said to her jokingly, "Weiying, does Tianliang's mustache hurt you?". She was quite angry, "He does not live at home, why do you ask me that?"

One day a 50-odd-year-old man who seemed a little mad but quite honest walked into Wang's home. Aunt Wan made a cup of tea for him, who, however, ignored that and left immediately. Aunt Wan said to Weiying, "He looked a bit giddy, but he's highly intellectual. He used to be a teacher. He once said, "the big red flag was swinging, not fixed; Yangge - Wu (A folk dance) is difficult to advance or to retreat." which was regarded as reactionary, and he was identified as a "right-winged" person and sentenced to prison for seven years. Nevertheless, he smoked in a warehouse while in prison, so he was said to put fire to the warehouse on purpose and received another three years in prison. When he came out, the school refused him to be a teacher again. After all these sufferings, he became a little mentally deranged. So, he's so unlucky, isn't him?" "Of course, he has been ruined all his life. He is smart since his poem, though a little bit anti-revolutionary, has rhymed." Weiying was sympathetic towards him in heart but did not show it.

She knew that the big red flag he mentioned in the poem referred to the general line, the great leap forward and people's commune. Weiying could not comprehend one thing, people's commune used to eat big pot meals and threw their private iron and steel cooking tools into iron-smelting pots. Was getting all families to have meals together the mode of transformation from a socialist society to a communist one? Most right-winged people were intellectual, and that was why they could see the times more clearly and speak and write something useful. They could also propose public and straightforward opinions on the economic policies of the CPC. Was that unacceptable? They did not commit killing, arson, robbery and threatening social security; instead, they had good intentions. Weiying began to doubt herself, if she had grown mature during that era, she might have been identified as a rightist owing to her straightforward character. <See Appendix 1. C> And these people of insight are probably also be born at the wrong time, right?

On a Sunday during the hot summer, Weiying went to have a nap in her room after lunch. Since it was suffocating, she only wore a small sleeveless garment and a pair of short pants. She did not lock the door because an empty room was opposite to hers and thereby no one would see her sleeping. When she just fell asleep, she suddenly felt something heavy pressing her. She had opened her eyes, she saw Wang Tianliang's face close to hers and his big and black eyes staring at her with doubt? They glared at each other for a while like strangers. Weiying did not know when he came back, so she felt she was in a dream. He touched her "forbidden area", attempting to… At this moment, a sense of parched as well as thirst overwhelmed her, which drove away her sleepiness. They began in each other's eyes, striving to find a certain answer. Nonetheless, before Wang Tianliang found the answer, he needed from Weiying's expression, she ceased looking at him. The former familiar face became very strange at this moment.

She began to persuade herself; he had changed his heart and had another girlfriend in the factory. But I don't have urban registered permanent residence or a job. She became cold at this thought and her blood flow seemed to be stopped. She turned her head to another side as though this face close to her was totally strange. She tried to avoid his body and moved away when he was hesitating. Her body involuntarily to avoid his further actions, under his uncertain body, she moved resisting away. Her once-emerging desire in her body was overwhelmed by her reasonable and strong sense of objection. Wang Tianliang, who dare not do anything to her, could only see her escape under his body. Neither of them said anything. He sat up unhappily and walked out of this room after standing by the bed for a minute.

Not knowing whether to pity him or herself, Weiying got off bed and locked the door which Wang Tianliang left ajar. Then she went to lie in bed again, but she could hardly fall asleep. Wang Tianliang before joining the army, Wang Tianliang when in first love with her, and especially Wang Tianliang who suddenly changed his attitude, as well as Wang Tianliang nowadays kept appearing before her eyes... She wondered whether Wang regarded her as his first lover, or sister, or both, and someone else. Overall, she thinks that her heart has been destroyed by him, would never give out flowers, let alone fruits. He had become a piece of floating cloud by his earlier coldness, drifting farther and farther away from him...

Since Weiying could not fall asleep, she put on clothes and walked out of the room, only to find Wang Tianliang sitting in a chair beside the wall opposite to the well and smoking hard with a pair of frowned brows. His mother who also frowned was making efforts to shovel the rice crispy crust out of the big iron pot. Impressed by a certain unharmonious atmosphere, she felt uneasy. Wang left by ship for Changsha before dawn the next morning.

For the next several days, Weiying felt more and more upset in Wang's home. Since her 22nd birthday was drawing near, she said to Wang's family, "I've been there for several months, so I wanted to go back home for my birthday." Before starting out, Wang's parents said to her, "We have two cats. Bring one for your mother." Weiying thought a cat could catch mice and that her mother would like it, so she accepted and brought the cat put in a bag onto ship.

Onboard, she put the bag under her seat, but she did not notice that cat had come out and ran to the end of the ship quickly.

And it jumped onto a thick board vertical to beneath the wooden pole through a hole. The waves kept tumbling and the cat, standing on the deck, looked at her without moving. She stared at it, full of fear so that she burst into tears. She had to knee on the board and looked down at it with anxiety. She didn't know how to swim,

Not knowing whether to pity him or herself, Weiying got off bed and locked the door which Wang Tianliang left ajar. Then she went to lie in bed again, but she could hardly fall asleep. Wang Tianliang before joining the army, Wang Tianliang when in first love with her, and especially Wang Tianliang who suddenly changed his attitude, as well as Wang Tianliang nowadays kept appearing before her eyes... She wondered whether Wang regarded her as his first lover, or sister, or both, and someone else. Overall, she thinks that her heart has been destroyed by him, would never give out flowers, let alone fruits. He had become a piece of floating cloud by his earlier coldness, drifting farther and farther away from him...

Since Weiying could not fall asleep, she put on clothes and walked out of the room, only to find Wang Tianliang sitting in a chair beside the wall opposite to the well and smoking hard with a pair of frowned brows. His mother who also frowned was making efforts to shovel the rice crispy crust out of the big iron pot. Impressed by a certain unharmonious atmosphere, she felt uneasy. Wang left by ship for Changsha before dawn the next morning.

For the next several days, Weiying felt more and more upset in Wang's home. Since her 22nd birthday was drawing near, she said to Wang's family, "I've been there for several months, so I wanted to go back home for my birthday." Before starting out, Wang's parents said to her, "We have two cats. Bring one for your mother." Weiying thought a cat could catch mice and that her mother would like it, so she accepted and brought the cat put in a bag onto ship.

Onboard, she put the bag under her seat, but she did not notice that cat had come out and ran to the end of the ship quickly.

And it jumped onto a thick board vertical to beneath the wooden pole through a hole. The waves kept tumbling and the cat, standing on the deck, looked at her without moving. She stared at it, full of fear so that she burst into tears. She had to knee on the board and looked down at it with anxiety. She didn't know how to swim, and threatening social security; instead, they had good intentions. Weiying began to doubt herself, if she had grown mature during that era, she might have been identified as a rightist owing to her straightforward character. <See Appendix 1. C> And these people of insight are probably also be born at the wrong time, right?

On a Sunday during the hot summer, Weiying went to have a nap in her room after lunch. Since it was suffocating, she only wore a small sleeveless garment and a pair of short pants. She did not lock the door because an empty room was opposite to hers and thereby no one would see her sleeping. When she just fell asleep, she suddenly felt something heavy pressing her. She had opened her eyes, she saw Wang Tianliang's face close to hers and his big and black eyes staring at her with doubt? They glared at each other for a while like strangers. Weiying did not know when he came back, so she felt she was in a dream. He touched her "forbidden area", attempting to… At this moment, a sense of parched as well as thirst overwhelmed her, which drove away her sleepiness. They began in each other's eyes, striving to find a certain answer. Nonetheless, before Wang Tianliang found the answer, he needed from Weiying's expression, she ceased looking at him. The former familiar face became very strange at this moment.

She began to persuade herself; he had changed his heart and had another girlfriend in the factory. But I don't have urban registered permanent residence or a job. She became cold at this thought and her blood flow seemed to be stopped. She turned her head to another side as though this face close to her was totally strange. She tried to avoid his body and moved away when he was hesitating. Her body involuntarily to avoid his further actions, under his uncertain body, she moved resisting away. Her once-emerging desire in her body was overwhelmed by her reasonable and strong sense of objection. Wang Tianliang, who dare not do anything to her, could only see her escape under his body. Neither of them said anything. He sat up unhappily and walked out of this room after standing by the bed for a minute.

Lose one's bearings

but she was worried that it would be patted down by the waves and fell into the Xiangjiang River.

Several people shouted to her, "Danger! Don't go down" while calling crew to save the cat. Later a crew member came, jumping by her side swiftly and stooped on the wooden pole. Finally, he caught the cat and brought it back to Weiying who thanked him for his bravery with tears in her eyes, she took the cat back cabin.

Back home, Weiying told the adventure of the cat to her mother who was scared to almost breathlessness. She said, "If you had jumped down following the cat, I could not have seen you, let alone it." Weiying thought her mother was right and decided to think twice when encountering dangerous things again!

The next day she came back, she decided to visit Tang Na since they hadn't met for several months. Before starting off, she brought a plastic umbrella since the sky was grey. During while on bus, it began to pour with fierce there was a heavy downpour. She felt it got cold immediately after getting off. The storm was invading into the earth and the people…

At Tang Na's home, Weiying found that there were grey hairs on her head, feeling quite surprised, why would a 23-year-old girl have so many grey hairs in just several months? And Tang's attitude towards her was quite different from before. She did not smile at all; instead, she looked painful as if her heart had been stricken hard. Not knowing what happened, Weiying remained silent for quite a while. Out of a sudden, Tang said, "My brother died!" Weiying was startled at her words! What! Tiedan had died!? She had been feeling herself wasting time and youth, but Tang's old brother, who was so young, lost his life!? She could not believe her ears! She asked with a tightened nerve, "What---your brother died? How could it come since he's so young?" Tang Na said, "Yes, my brother died---due of the revolt party. If they had not closed my brother in the private prison without a toilet, he could not have got nephritis. He argued with them for my parents, so they hated him and did not release him in time for treatment and furthermore, put some false accusations on him, which made his illness more serious. As a result, his kidney went out of gear, his hands and feet grew swollen, and did not have appetite at last. Although my mother had given him herself kidney of transplant, that was failed to save his life. My mother cried several days and nights for him. She is saying, 'I have never thought that he survived in the warfare but lost life during the time of peace.' The reason why he was called Tiedan was because at the beginning of the war, my mother gave him this nickname in hope of not letting him be bombed to death by enemy's planes. When the planes were hovering in the sky, my mother pressed him under her body to protect him, not consider of her own security."

After hearing what Tang said, Weiying sighed, "Oh, your family is even more miserable than mine. Both your dad and two aunts have lost a family member respectively during the Cultural Revolution. Although our family's properties have been confiscated before and during the Revolution, our family members were not hurt. My father often said, 'As long as people are alive, there is hope'. But there's no alternative now that people are gone." Tang Na went on, "Of course. My parents would rather lose all their properties than lose my brother. He survived in the warfare but died now." Tang took on a sad expression. Weiying knew that she was in deep sorrow for her brother's death and Weiying was sympathetic towards that, so she did not stay long and left soon.

Back home, Weiying told the news to her mother and meanwhile said, "Mother, only our properties have been lost, but we all saved our lives." Weiying's mother expressed her sympathy to Tang's old brother and said, "Your brother-in-law Wu was an upright person, but he has been identified as an anti-revolutionary. It is hard in prison since he is like a living dead man. It also destroyed his whole family, and I must worry about him. I've been expecting him to come back as soon as possible so that he could take over the responsibility of caring for the whole family. His three children are so young, and I can't stand seeing them wander from place to place about…" Weiying thought that both her sister and brother-in-law were intellectuals, but they encountered such a thing, and their children follow also suffer, meaning that they were really "born at a wrong time".

When the National Day of 1971 was drawing near, the street director in charge of the street said to Weiying, "We'll examine the registered permanent residence soon. It won't do if you, with a rural residence, always live here." Weiying felt very disgusted, "I live at my own home. Is there any problem?" "Your residence is not at home and thus you are counted as 'contravene a regulation, stop in the city'." Understanding this policy, she did not want to cause trouble for her family, so she brought her two younger sisters who were eager to see the environment where she lives in the village to Wang's home with some gifts.

Arriving in Wang's house, she gave the gifts to Wang Tianliang's parents. But she found it a little strange this time. Huiye, Wang Tianliang's younger sister, looked unhappy. Weiying regretted bringing her two sisters there and she thought that they just lived here for two or three days. That evening, her two sisters slept together with her. Waking up the next morning, she had a stomachache and her sisters persuaded her to lie down for another while. However, she felt more and more painful so that she began to roll in bed. But she had nothing to do as it was inconvenient to visit a doctor in village. Her sisters were sitting on the bedside, at a loss as to what to do.

After a while, she heard clearly Huiye's furious voice from the kitchen, "It's late. They are so lazy as not to get up for breakfast." Weiying knew that Huiye was targeting at her. Later her pain in the stomach abated a bit, so she got up and brought her sisters out of the room. Outside the kitchen, she saw Huiye cleaning up the table and washing bowls and chopsticks. Weiying pretended not to see that and began to wash up the things calmly. However, Huiye became more and more angry, patting the bowls hard. Her sisters could say nothing but to stand aside. It was obvious that Huiye targeted at her but no one in Wang's family came out to blame her. And Weiying, with strong self-esteem, felt more uncomfortable. Therefore, she said to her sisters, "Be quick to wash up. I'm taken a coat and bringing you to the production group."

After finding the leader of the production group, Weiying described the whole thing to him. Then she asked, "Could you please arrange another family for me live in?" He replied, "The group will not settle the family chaos for you. Go to tell Tianliang." She is feeling a little strange and argued that "I came here not to be Wang Tianliang's wife. I have said that before. If I had not encountered the security problem, I would not have transferred my residence to their home. Now there occurred such a contradiction between them and me, why can't you arrange another family for me?" He said, "You are not assigned here by the government, so we have no means to settle you. And even if the government needs employment from intellectuals one day, you will not be one of them." Weiying was so anxious as to shed tears, "Then is my for whole life done?" Seeing such a situation, her two sisters began to sob, too. Since Weiying did not take Wang as her lover any more by that time and she encountered such a dilemma in his family, she suddenly felt desperate as for her future.

She had heard from her father several times, "If you cannot live on in one place, you may see hope again if you move to another place because 'People move place to rebirth, tree move place to death'." Therefore, after the National Day, she packed her stuff and went back to Changsha with two sisters. She decided to stay in the city where she had lived and then began to hunt for jobs after doing housework at home for a while.

The first thing she did when back to Changsha was to go to hospital to have examinations to see why she always had serious stomachache. And the results showed that roundworms were in her tripe. She thought this phenomenon must be caused by drinking raw water which she often had after work at the reservoir in summer.

Lose one's bearings

After the National Day and the Mid-autumn Day, it was in October when the weather was nice with little rain. One day the sun was shining up in the sky. Tang Na came to Weiying's home and told her, "The Guangzhou Military Region Soldier Song and Dance Ensemble is enrolling students in Hunan. Shall we go to register? I can play the piano and you can sing." At this, Weiying was very glad and agreed immediately. Singing was one of her favorite activities. She once participated in the school red scarf song and dance troupe, represented her middle school in the singing competition and won. When she was in good mood at home, she would also sing go on uninterruptedly for two hours. In particular, she expected that once admitted she could get rid of the rural registered permanent residence and have a job to her like.

Several days after they sign up, Tang came to Weiying's home and then they together went to a yard of an institution near the Teenage Palace. Where Tang entered a room to play the piano while Weiying sang in the open air. The yard was crowded with people, some came for the invigilate, some in company of them, and still some just for visit. Weiying saw two amicable women examiners in army uniform standing in the middle and called names according to the name list. Then they said a few words and wrote down something after each examinee.

Tang came out after playing the piano, appearing not quite happy, "I have finished. Hasn't your turn come?" "No." Weiying replied and then asked Tang in a low voice, "What about your examination?" "I hold no hope." "Why? You started to learn playing the piano at an early age and you play so well!" "I don't know why I'm so nervous today. I'm just began trembling at the beginning and thus the whole piece of music was in a mass. So, it is impossible for me to be enrolled." "Oh! What a pity!" With this, she heard an examiner calling her name. She walked to the center of the yard and sang an interlude of movie "Who doesn't say that my hometown is good" in soprano. Finishing the song, she saw the two examiners smiling to each other and nodding at her with satisfaction. And the crowd also looked at her with an expression of approval, so she walked happily to Tang who said, "Shall we go home? The examination is coming to an end." "OK." While turning around to leave, she noticed that the examiners were looking at her attentively and waved to her "Goodbye". She waved back to them.

Entering the door, she told her mother happily, "Mom, I think I can be admitted. The two examiners were quite friendly to me and waved to me goodbye after the examination, but they didn't do so to other examinees." Mother approved, "I think you are likely to be enrolled. Your voice often sounds high and pointed." Weiying was more confident at her mother's words, waiting for good news. At the age of 22, she was longing for a bright future at the army…

Several days later, Weiying was making dumplings with her parents in the big room where Juecong and Juele lived. The door of the room was opposite to the alley, and it was beside the front yard and the gate, so they could clearly see whoever came in. That day they saw a 40-odd-year-old man with a pair of glasses walked into the gate with push a bicycle. Weiying went out at once to meet him. "Are you Qiu Weiying?" The man asked affirmatively. "Yes." She felt a bit strange because he who she never met knew her name. The man continued, "The results of the Guangzhou Army Song and Dance Ensemble have come out. Even though you are good at singing, you can't be admitted if you failed the political review!"

Hearing this, Qiu Weiying's mother understood what happened immediately, but she had not mentioned it to Qiu Zhongyuan who did not react at the time and was still making dumplings with his head lowered. Shao began to explain in anxiety, "We were wrongly judged when our properties were confiscated. And they said, 'We'll freeze your properties first and then handle them after the reach a vindicated is settled.' Politically, we have never made any mistakes." That man turned angry at once, "But there is an anti-revolutionary in your family who is now in a prison of another province." Shao did not know how to explain it. When signing up, Weiying wrote her looked at her with an expression of approval, so she walked happily to Tang who said, "Shall we go home? The examination is coming to an end." "OK." While turning around to leave, she noticed that the examiners were looking at her attentively and waved to her "Goodbye". She waved back to them.

Entering the door, she told her mother happily, "Mom, I think I can be admitted. The two examiners were quite friendly to me and waved to me goodbye after the examination, but they didn't do so to other examinees." Mother approved, "I think you are likely to be enrolled. Your voice often sounds high and pointed." Weiying was more confident at her mother's words, waiting for good news. At the age of 22, she was longing for a bright future at the army…

Several days later, Weiying was making dumplings with her parents in the big room where Juecong and Juele lived. The door of the room was opposite to the alley, and it was beside the front yard and the gate, so they could clearly see whoever came in. That day they saw a 40-odd-year-old man with a pair of glasses walked into the gate with push a bicycle. Weiying went out at once to meet him. "Are you Qiu Weiying?" The man asked affirmatively. "Yes." She felt a bit strange because he who she never met knew her name. The man continued, "The results of the Guangzhou Army Song and Dance Ensemble have come out. Even though you are good at singing, you can't be admitted if you failed the political review!"

Hearing this, Qiu Weiying's mother understood what happened immediately, but she had not mentioned it to Qiu Zhongyuan who did not react at the time and was still making dumplings with his head lowered. Shao began to explain in anxiety, "We were wrongly judged when our properties were confiscated. And they said, 'We'll freeze your properties first and then handle them after the reach a vindicated is settled.' Politically, we have never made any mistakes." That man turned angry at once, "But there is an anti-revolutionary in your family who is now in a prison of another province." Shao did not know how to explain it. When signing up, Weiying wrote her

Lose one's bearings

After the National Day and the Mid-autumn Day, it was in October when the weather was nice with little rain. One day the sun was shining up in the sky. Tang Na came to Weiying's home and told her, "The Guangzhou Military Region Soldier Song and Dance Ensemble is enrolling students in Hunan. Shall we go to register? I can play the piano and you can sing." At this, Weiying was very glad and agreed immediately. Singing was one of her favorite activities. She once participated in the school red scarf song and dance troupe, represented her middle school in the singing competition and won. When she was in good mood at home, she would also sing go on uninterruptedly for two hours. In particular, she expected that once admitted she could get rid of the rural registered permanent residence and have a job to her like.

Several days after they sign up, Tang came to Weiying's home and then they together went to a yard of an institution near the Teenage Palace. Where Tang entered a room to play the piano while Weiying sang in the open air. The yard was crowded with people, some came for the invigilate, some in company of them, and still some just for visit. Weiying saw two amicable women examiners in army uniform standing in the middle and called names according to the name list. Then they said a few words and wrote down something after each examinee.

Tang came out after playing the piano, appearing not quite happy, "I have finished. Hasn't your turn come?" "No." Weiying replied and then asked Tang in a low voice, "What about your examination?" "I hold no hope." "Why? You started to learn playing the piano at an early age and you play so well!" "I don't know why I'm so nervous today. I'm just began trembling at the beginning and thus the whole piece of music was in a mass. So, it is impossible for me to be enrolled." "Oh! What a pity!" With this, she heard an examiner calling her name. She walked to the center of the yard and sang an interlude of movie "Who doesn't say that my hometown is good" in soprano. Finishing the song, she saw the two examiners smiling to each other and nodding at her with satisfaction. And the crowd also parents' workplace, so she thought the hospital had said something destroy. Looking at the man in enormous depression, she didn't know how to make the explanation. He immediately walked down the stone steps to in front yard and said, "Then that's it. I have to notify other examinees."

Looking at his back, Qiu Weiying's mother said while entering the room, "What a society it is! Why should my children future be taken away too after our properties were confiscated? What is an anti-revolutionary? I can't make it out." Weiying said to Qiu Zhongyuan who was still making dumplings without moving, "Dad, if I can go to the Troop Song and Dance Ensemble, it'll be good to our family politically. So, they must have to your hospital for a family class status survey and your leaders must have said something bad about us family." "There is no doubt. Wang Huijun has always attempted to damage my reputation, so she is unlikely to let my daughter to join the army. What's more, our family have been destroyed like this, but she's not resigned to see my salary higher than hers. Why didn't she think, without me asking her to be a cleaner at the hospital and then be the director, what would become of her? What a bitch!" Weiying went on, "So many leaders of the CPC central committee have died to suffer a lot in the Cultural Revolution. Thus, it is no wonder that our family is of trumped-up charge and hurt. I was born at the wrong time!"

4.5 Returning to the city and my resist

Before Cultural Revolution, Deng Zihui, who used to be deputy premier of the State Council and the Minister of the ministry of agriculture, was participating the motion of the "four cleanups" in the first half of 1965 year.

He discovered in the people's commune, "Farmers set out like a dragon; Working is a swarm; close the work they are mount a charge against." In conclusion, he decided that private-owned economy was more practical and more effective in boosting production.

However, he, along with Liu Shaoqi and Deng Xiaoping, was declared as embark on the following the capitalist road people in power for the right deviation, and consequently deprived of political rights. At last, he died in the Great Cultural Revolution from continuous persecution and lack of proper treatment.

convene of the tenth plenary session of the ninth CPC central committee in April 1969, the Gang of Four sent large groups of there be close to and trust sb and followers to central and local Revolutionary committees, bringing ultra-left trend of thoughts be very much. Back then, private-owned economy which was regarded as capitalistic had no market, no social status and no government support.

So, even the urban residents were having trouble finding a centrally planned job, not to mention Qiu Weiying, who did not even have planned food and other stuff for her household residence permit was in the countryside. The only way for her to go was report to the local authorities for change of domicile back to the city. Get her household residence permit back first. It was not an easy task, or else she would not have agreed to transfer her residence to the Wangs and ended up in such big trouble. She had to turn to someone for help.

But the Qiu's a family and Qiu Zhongyuan – a famous Doctor of Professional skill best in the united hospital of Changsha south zone, were never apt at pleasing ask sb for help.

Qiu Zhongyuan liked to work out in the morning and took Taichi exercises. Except for snowy and stormy days, it was a routine in the morning for him to go to the Youth Palace, Tianxin Pavilion or the Martyr's Park to work out. He met a man named Liu Pingan in Tianxin Pavilion, who used to be a crosstalk comedian. Liu's former workplace was cancelled in the Revolution, and he became a leader of a rebel group. For he was funny, optimistic and often

Lose one's bearings

gave impromptu performances at the Qiu's place, he brought much joy to Mr. Qiu, releasing the tensions he got from the hospital. Qiu Weiying also liked his performances, so Mr. Qiu was glad to have this interesting friend.

One day when Liu was chatting with the Qiu's family after meal, he asked about Weiying's situation. She answered, "My priority for the moment is to settle my household residence permit. Without a city residence, I can't even have my food rations and must rely on my parents to buy me the expensive black-market food, not to mention finding a job." Liu said, "It's very likely that I can solve it for you." Mr. Qiu was glad to hear that and said, "Great! I'll have you as my nominal son if you can do me the favor." Liu was very happy and replied immediately, "Good! My father died early; you're just the person I need." Weiying followed, "It's a big family now. There are already so many of us, plus the nominal son of Mom and now you." Liu almost laughed his eyebrows off and said, "Well – sure it is!" Weiying thought both his look and his character were quite funny, and his words plus his facial expressions added even more to his fun – that was why she did not take him for granted. Probably to make the Qius believe his bragging, he began his oration, "In the Revolution, I was interviewed by Premier Zhou in Beijing as the leader of "East red" rebel organization. He shook hands with me! There I met the first-class Peking Opera artist Li Weikang..."

Weiying had watched the piano accompanied opera "Red Lantern", in which Li Weikang played the role of Tiemei. She liked both her vocal and her look. She did not know until later that Li's father lived in Changsha too and was Weiying's father patient. Once she met Li at her friend's place – a delicate, well behaved lady. During the Cultural Revolution, women were not allowed to wear makeup, not to mention take plastic surgeries, but natural beauty was even more attractive. Li smiled and said to her, "If you ever come to Beijing and want to watch Peking Opera, feel free to contact me." Weiying sensed that life goes on its own mysterious way. She did not know when she would ever be able to go to Beijing again, to watch Li's opera and to mourn by Tang Na's uncle's tomb.

That Sunday Weiying and her parents cooked a lot of food to invite Liu Pingan and the other two who Liu claimed could help with Weiying's of city residents remained for dinner. That morning Wang Tianliang also came and was displeased upon seeing that many young men at her house. He did not even enter the living room; instead, he stood in the front yard gazing at the goldfish. The dishes were sent to the table, so Liu went to him and said, "Mr. Wang, it's at dinner time, eat together! Come along and join us!" To Liu's surprise, Wang replied without even looking at him, "I don't feel like joining the hooligans!" Its annoyed Liu into silence. Weiying was walking over with a dish in her hands. Wang's rudeness to her guests incensed her. She thought, "Liu and his friends are here to help me. They are all polite, well-behaved people. How dare you call them hooligans?" At the same time, another guest from Provincial Physical Cultural and Sports Commission came to the door and said, "Come on in, Mr. Wang." Weiying was afraid that Wang would utter more rude comments, so she glared at him. Wang lowered his head in silence and kept on watching the goldfish. The shrewd guest sensed something was wrong and went back to the dining table without saying anything to Wang. As everybody gathered around the table, Mrs. Qiu went outside to bring Wang in, only to find he was already gone.

Things grew unexpected. A few days later, when Liu was talking about the permanent household residence permit and the following procedures with Weiying and Mr. Qiu in their living room, Wang came again. He entered the gate, put his bike by the wall under a window, and then immediately walked on the corridor to Weiying, who was crossing the passageway. He took a primary school student's notebook, gave it to Weiying and left without a word. Weiying opened it while walking to the living room. On the first page was, "Weiying…" following up all the way to the end was filled with his complaints about their relationship and how he could not bear any third people. Most shockingly, he wrote in the end, "Hand up, knife down, long live!" That was unbelievable! She closed the book restlessly. Liu asked, "What engrossed you so much?" She gave him the book. After reading, Liu frowned and said, "He's so in love with you that he would even kill a person for you!" Weiying denied, "So in love with me? If so, why would he be in a love relationship with that woman from work? I don't call that love! If I'm in love with someone, I won't care for someone else in the meantime. And it only freaks me out when he mentions the knife and I want to leave him farther!" Liu said, "Really? I wonder what's on his mind. You'd better be careful!"

The next day was Monday, so Wang would go to work instead of staying at home in the countryside. Weiying was not sure if Mother had told Wang that she was about to transfer her household residence permit from the Wangs; all she knew was she had to quicken her steps and do it.

So, she got up early in the morning and took a ferry by Xiang River to the Wang's. The Wang's could not force Weiying to stay, so the production team easily gave her the certificate she needed. The brigade was not far from the production team. People there heard about her things and helped her with the certificates. But when she came to the commune, two cadres objected, "You're not our intellectual youth, why do you need our credentials?" Weiying knew that the country gave money to the countryside for accepting the intellectual youths, and her money must have gone to the reservoir. So, she converted the topic, "The new society does not allow arranged marriages, not to mention I and Wang are not married yet. I did not transfer my residence here for marriage…" She explained why she wanted to return to her own home, and then said, "If you don't approve, then please recommend me as long as any city job is available or settle me somewhere else. Or what shall I do stick in the middle of nowhere? Please consider my request!" They were finally touched and seal the documents by the end of day accomplish. Weiying was exhilarated, and hurried home before it turned dark.

She had to go to the Revolutionary Committee of Changsha County for the move from the country to the city final procedure. Which was a strange place for her, and she did not know anyone there. Back then, central and local revolutionary committees were mostly in the hand of the rebels.

Lin Biao, who had become the number two figure in the Chinese Communist Party, gradually broke down due to the power struggle with the Cultural Revolutionaries factions and his relationship with Mao Zedong. who on September 13, in 1971 and died in an air crash on his escape did the rebel factions become less rampant.

Lin Biao, the man Mao trusted the most, betray him was a huge shock to the Chairman. Liu quitted the rebel organization after Premier Zhou met with these rebel factions of heads, but he still knew those people who worked and, in the committee, who helped him handle the last procedure for Qiu Weiying. Before long, Qiu smoothly transferred her permanent household residence permit back to Changsha, and finally got to stay home legally.

Year in and year out, in her golden years from 16 nearly to 23, Qiu Weiying was deprived of her right of further education due to the confiscation of family property that made her one of the children of the "twenty-one kinds". She used to think of leaving her so-called capitalist family to go to the countryside, to be reeducated by the poor and lower-middle peasants and to construct socialist new country. But her seven years in the countryside proved all those lofty ideas to be hollow slogans. The confiscation of family property and the fact that her brother-in-law was declared anti-revolutionary took away her only chance to join the Guangzhou Soldiers' Song and Dance Troupe. Ruthless real life in no way resembled her innocent wishes in the past. The silver lining was that her household residence permit came back the city!

Being a city resident all over again, she felt as if she found a way in the endless desert, which was quite relieving and pleasing?

At least she had the chances to seek for a job, her parents could not support her to the end. A girl of her age should get down to business and think about her own future. But it was not easy finding a job back then. Except for thousands of young intellectuals who are in the golden age who are still repairing the earth in the mountains, countryside and border areas. There were also loads of young people in the city staying at home, couldn't find a job.

Later Juecong wrote home saying he had gone to his uncle in Jiangsu, but his household residence permit in Changsha for incomplete move procedures. Juele was in junior third year. Mr. and Mrs. Qiu as well as Xiaodong were still working at the hospital, and Xiaodong's two sons were in primary school. Weiying was jobless for the moment, so she stayed home and accompanied the kids, or read some novels or other books to broaden her mind. But her main task was to cook for the family, so that when everybody came back, they were immediately having hot food to eat.

One day after new year 1972, it seemed to snow with grey clouds heaping up in the sky and freezing wind blowing from the empty front yard to the passageway. Weiying had a clear perspective of the yard and the gate from the kitchen. That day before the rest of the family came back, she left the gate ajar as usual. Outside their kitchen window, in the corner down the passageway, there was a square garden of about six square meters. Back then, it was almost a deserted land with no tending at all. Before their confiscation of family property, Mother who was industrious and always had a passion for life and flowers, used to planted things there. But after the confiscation of family property, she fired their nanny and no longer had the leisure for the flowers. Instead, she set up an easy trellis and planted pumpkin. But the barren field barely nourished the vine into blooming, not to mention to bear fruit. As a result, they had to pick the flowers to make soup.

That was how most things work in the world, they never go as you wish, and sometimes even go against your hope! They were just like the fruitless winter vine, dry and broken, twisting around the unsteady trellis, leaving people profound sorrow...

That noon Weiying finished cooking all the food, left the soup warming on slow fire and other dishes by the fire, so that when the family came back, they would have hot food to eat at once. Suddenly she heard the big door was pushed open, so she went to the cabinet for the bowls and chopsticks. But when she through the glass window of the kitchen against the small garden, looked at the door, she saw about seven ferocious strangers, wearing the armbands of the workers' pickets and carrying sticks, who were pulling handcarts into the gate. She sensed that they did not come on nice purpose, and hurried down the stone stairs and asked, "What are you doing here?" Someone answered bossily, "To get you move!" She had never heard from her parents about moving, and asked in confusion, "Who told you to move?!" Somebody pushed on her hard and said, "Get out of the way! The house is no longer yours! It's a decision made by the medical establishment! The hospital your father works at has already approved of it!" The group of people broke into their house and started moving things onto the handcarts. Weiying realized that they were treating the Qiu's a family as enemies and were about to force move them out of the house they bought legally and had been living in for outdo 15 years! Sorrow took over her.

She is felt especially greatly distressed for her parents, who have been serving countless patients from the old society to the new, bringing them hopes of health and the opportunity to go back to work again. Her parents have received broad compliment as well as many silk banners of gratitude and thank-you letters. And not to mention father had been set up the Southern District Hospital and made this great contribution. Her parents had never done anything bad. Just because Mother opened a of legal means of clinic. Her family became a victim of the struggle between the two lines of the Party. And were declared "speculation and profiteering" who ran an "underground hospital". They had been constantly being persecuted before the of their "property freeze" even not have to conclude that is innocent law. Someone was trying to send them to hell, plunder the sole legitimate of permanent residence to stay away from their normal life.

Along with Feng Bin from Changsha Health Bureau and Chang Wanming from the Public Security Bureau, they came with a blank confiscation of family property illegally took away all their properties her family had earned over thirty years in the name of medical establishment, and even took away all their nice furniture and clothing with handcarts.

In the Culture Revolution, her parents were also influenced at work, followed by a couple of confiscation of family properties by the rebel groups. Now, their private house – the only thing remained— was going to be taken away too! Where are those bastards moving them to?

To stop them, she stood on the stairs in the front yard and read a passage entitled Dealing with the Contradictions within the People in Reasonable Ways from People's Daily loudly. Later, she read Chairman Mao's quotes on differentiating friends and foes. By then, some workers at the printing house next door stopped the work at hand to look over through the window on the wall by the garden next to their kitchen. As Weiying was denouncing them with Chairman's quotes, they were still moving the things to the handcarts. Embarrassed as they were, they did not run away; on the contrary, two men ran to the kitchen while the others were sealing the doors. Weiying followed the two and saw one of them move the soup from the fire. She said calmly by the door, "My family is about to come back. Please let us move after lunch; it's such a cold day!" But the men said, "Eat in your new house!" Upon these words, they continued moving.

Weiying was incensed, "New house? God knows if there is any hearth! Let's say there is – that still takes a long while for us to make fire! You mean we have to have a cold supper there in such a day?" A man replied ruthlessly, "That's your own business.

We don't care!" Hearing such cold reply, Weiying almost exploded in fury. She murmured, "This doesn't' make sense! What have my parents done wrong? Why treating us like enemies? You're trying to kill us!" By then, the two rooms by the passageway and the living room were already sealed. The kitchen was almost cleared, making it impossible for the family to have their meal before moving. Fire of anger was scorching her heart, burning away her carefulness. She said, "This is too excessive! What have my parents done to be treated like this?" and ran to the doors to tear down the strip seals and then throw them to the ground. Two men came, shouting, "You're boost morale of bourgeoisie, deflate of proletariat aspirations!" She replied at once, "Both my parents are doctors who save lives, and have never exploited anyone. I'm from a family of freelancers, not capitalists!" A man who looked like a leader said, "You're sabotaging the Proletarian Cultural Revolution! I'll take you to the police station!" He came close and tried to grab her collar. She shouted, "No violence! Peaceful revolution!" and stepped off the stairs and said, "I have feet of my own. There's no need to push!"

As she walked out of the front yard, down the stairs outside the gate, she saw Xiaodong coming close. Xiaodong noticed her sister being crowded by people wearing armbands and carrying sticks and knew something was wrong. Before she figured out what was going on, she was sober that Weiying was in trouble. She came up with a battered-body trick. She walked up to Weiying and gave her a slap on the face. Weiying was confused and annoyed, but she said nothing and kept on walking out of the alley, for it was the group of mobs that she should deal with, not Xiaodong. In her mind she was angry with Xiaodong, for even those men did not dare to smack her, why did Xiaodong hit her on the face?

She walked out of the alley, all the way down Laozhaobi and came to the cross with Fuzheng Street, and then went directly into a grocery store. Those men who followed her had to stay outside and wait for her. To show her contempt for their illegal atrocity, she bought a cake and put it in her mouth casually and started eating as if they did not exist.

This group of men followed Weiying (who had grown less ferocious) came to Fuzheng street Police Station, which was under military control. The PLA at the gate said nothing and let them in. Weiying was pushed into an office where two soldiers in charge looked up and asked, "What's up?" A man pointed to her and said, "She pulled off the seals on her house, sabotaging Proletarian Cultural Revolution!" Weiying said fearlessly, "My parents bought the house back in 1957. This has nothing to do with the Cultural Revolution! We were confiscated for a made-up offense before the Revolution, and now they are still jealous of our only house. They want to take our house away and kick us out. Why shouldn't I pull of the seals?" Another man from the rectification team immediately said, "What an articulate girl! Ten men together might not be able to win over her in a debate." Another man said cruelly, "Eloquence does not help! Let's put up a ten-thousand-people Struggle Assembly!" Weiying knew that meant wearing tall hat, being beaten into blacks and blues and doing "the jet-plane", still she said nothing. However, the man in charge said, "Off you go. I shall ask her some questions." When the men left, Weiying told the PLA what happened in a helpless voice. He listened carefully and then said, "If what you said is true, then go on appealing!" Then he stood up and Weiying walked out the police station.

Weiying quickened her steps home. She was worried that the bastards had turned their house into a total mess. As she walked into the alley, she saw a notice as large as a newspaper on the street-side wall that read, "Turn down the speculator Shao Guizhen who runs underground hospital!" "Bullshit!" Weiying said angrily. She paid no further attention to the content and hurried home.

As soon as she turned to the big pagoda tree, she saw father pushing his bike out of the gate. On the back seat of his bike was a tapestry of the West Lake in a glass frame. It was a gift from a patient to thank Mr. Qiu, and it used to hang on his bedroom door. Now the glass was broken, and the frame also cracked. She had already been used to seeing the silk banners, certificates of merit and thank-you letters from the patients. She asked Father, "Why are you carrying this broken thing?" He said, "Why shouldn't I? I hid my money behind the tapestry!" "Well, right." Weiying said. She felt sorry for Father. Before the confiscation of family property, they had many jewelries and money, but he was unwilling to put them away because they were his legal belongings. When Mother suggested they should keep them carefully, he was angry with her. But now he had become so wary that he even hid his normal salaries. Now they not only lost their properties, but also lost their house. Weiying took a last look at the gate to the empty house, and then followed the bike of her poor father, who looked angry, painful and pathetic, silently went to their new place at Wujiajing.

It is an old street near the main road, not far from Laozhaobi. The so-called new house was a terribly old rectangle house. It was already deep winter, but there was not put in a pane of glass on the latticed wooden window. The floor was made of hard black earth, and the lime on the wall had begun to come loose and fall. The house was dark and damp, with no water pipe or toilet. There was a well outside the house in the left, and a public lavatory was just near it.

In front of theirs by street near, was occupied by another family; whose hostess was a doctor in Eastern Hospital. She lived with her two daughters and two sons, all of whom were grown-ups, but three of them seemed to be jobless. Going down the passageway between the two houses was the kitchen of the Qiu's. The so-called kitchen was a small room with a stair above it.

Upstairs was a worn room of less than 10 square meters with only one window facing the courtyard. The room was given to Xiaodong's two little boy and the little girl. Under the room downstairs was a room of about 8 square meters, it was Weiying's bedroom, but also served as the living room and dining room. There was also a passageway between her room and the opposite room. There was a small courtyard on the right of the passageway, where the family washed their face and brushed their teeth. There was no furniture, nor any place to put things, for it was an open-air cement ground with a draining hole, most of the time is wet. Down the passageway was the room of Mr. and Mrs. Qiu, about 10 square meters. Apart from the door and a small window facing the courtyard, there were only three blank walls, making the room stuffy, damp and dark. It was like a ghetto, or rather, a prison cell! Weiying had never thought they would have to live in such conditions. She even doubted if she would shoot the bastards who took orders from the evil and made them move, if she had been a boy and had a gun. Force them to move to an old house, the house is the wall, and the room is both in a dilapidated condition. It's a gang of rob houses gangsters!

The family soon affected with diseases such as cold, cough, fever, vomit and diarrhea after moving out in a freezing day.

Weiying's bed was under the glassless window, so with the cold wind constantly blowing on her, she had almost all the symptoms and was very sick. She did not tell her parents about her illness, for they were both ill and unhappy and had to work. She bought some medicine from the pharmacy, but later had to go to the hospital for the pills did not work. It was only after the wind slowed down, and the sun came out for some days that she started to get well. The stairs were so small and steep that Xiaodong's elder boy Lidi fell and rolled all the way down one day when he was about to go to school. Luckily there was a narrow and small corner between the stairs and the wall, so the boy stopped rolling further and was not hurt seriously.

Across the street was a dormitory of Hunan Foreign Trade, where lived a couple who used to live in Singapore. The couple both worked at the trading company and had no child. They liked Wu Sha a lot, for she had rosy cheeks and an adorable face. They knew her father was in prison and her mother had to raise three children, leading a very hard life. So, they offer to adopt Wu Sha, and pay the Qius some money. But Mrs. Qiu firmly refused the suggestion. She said, "This is like the old society all over again, where the poor can't raise their children and sell them in the streets; we are only selling kids at home. I would never sell my children. I shall have them with me even if I go begging."

In this world, a kind-hearted person does not necessarily bring good results. Qiu's mother would rather tighten her belt for her daughter's family not to be scattered. But in the end not only she suffered, but the anti-revolutionary family background also influenced the mental and physical wellbeing of the children, as well as their future... One day around 10 o'clock in the morning, Weiying saw Wu Di coming down the stairs, looking rather blue. Back then the schools were "resuming the classes and making a revolution". She asked him, "Why are you still home in school hour?" Wu Di said with a woeful face, "They bully me at school, call me 'little anti-revolutionist'. If I talk back, they will hit me. I don't dare go to school anymore." Weiying asked, "Didn't your teacher help you?" He said, "Sometimes yes, sometimes no. He has no respect for me any way. He is nicer to others than to me." Weiying was unable to help, for it was a common social phenomenon back then. She said nothing, but secretly complaint, "They not only torture my brother-in-law, but also persecute his children!" Wu Di often skipped classes, making Mrs. Qiu rather angry and scolded him. But Weiying could say nothing to help.

It had been months since Weiying transferred her household residence permit to the city home, but still had no job. It was no better staying at home all day than being in prison. Her only pastime was reading all kinds of book to enlarge her knowledge. One day she went to the near Xinhua Bookstore to read and saw on a large table with many books about tailoring. She picked up a thick one with illustrations, carefully read the words and pictures, and found out that no matter if one wants to make a blouse or a dress, there was certain proportions of the body for one to cut the cloths. Putting the pieces of cloths together, one can get a nice garment. She thought the books were very easy for her, and she could follow the instructions and make clothes. So, she picked a thick book about tailoring, paid for it and went home. She said to her mother, "Mom, it's too hard finding a job, maybe I can learn to make clothes. Everybody must eat and dress. If I can master the skill, I can at least make clothes for the family." Mrs. Qiu asked, "Can you manage to do that?" Weiying replied, "There is detailed instruction about cutting and sewing, not difficult for me. I think I can do it." Mrs. Qiu was glad and said, "That's a good idea. I'll tell your father to buy you a sewing machine."

Before long, certain person had a brand new "Butterfly" sewing machine sent to the house. Weiying was very confident. She soon cut for a Red Guard uniform and a pair of grey Dacron pants according to her own size, sent them to a tailor processing to refine the rough selvedge seams. Then, she followed the instruction of the book and started sewing at home. At last, she put on the clothes made by herself for the first time. Mother complimented her gladly, "What a surprise your first work fits so well!"

One Sunday, a very dignified-looking PLA officer around thirty to forty came to visit. He used to be a patient of Mrs. Qiu. While talking to Weiying and her mother, he took off his jacket and said while smiling, "The house is a little bit too stuffy and hot." He was only wearing a shirt inside, so Qiu saw a small pistol on his belt. Later, he came a few times, sat in their couch very casually and chatted with them.

One day after he left, Mother said to Weiying, "It seems that he is of some high rank and probably ten years older than you. It's very possible that he likes you. If you can end up with someone like him, that'll be of help for you and our family; at least we won't be discriminated politically." Deep in her heart Weiying has some feelings for him too, but she replied, "Mom, I can't even pass the political censor for Guangzhou Soldiers' Sing and Dance Troupe. He works in the army and be a Party member and cadre. I can't consider being with him even if he likes me, the army has the strictest political censorship, and it won't work out any way. I am very aware of whom I am…" It made sense to Mother, who said no more. The officer never showed up anymore, and Weiying never asked about him.

Even though Weiying did not like Wang Tianliang anymore, especially after Wang Tianliang gave her a book filled with bullshit, he wrote at their house in Laozhaobi, she still had gratitude for his parents, and Wang Tianliang still dropped by every now and then and called Mrs. Qiu mother. So Weiying made him a blue Dacron shirt as instructed by her notebook, which made Wang very happy. He could not help complimenting, "I didn't expect an amateur tailor like you can make such good clothes with the mere help of a book! Our Party branch secretary used to say, 'Even if Qiu had been to the countryside, she still looks like a capitalist lady. There's nothing laborer about her at all!' She even tried to set me up with a girl from her street." Weiying said, "Nothing is difficult to a willing heart, that's why I found making clothes easy. She wants to set you up with someone and so certainly will not speak nice of me! Why don't you just go and see her girl!" Wang was displeased, which Weiying did not care at all. This made Wang even more resentful. He had no idea that Weiying was not the jealous kind of girl! What's more, she had already considered their relationship finished.

Weiying's old arthritis recurred in the dark, damp and stuffy house, which was so painful that she could hardly eat and fall asleep. She spent her 23rd birthday in the house, forgotten by both her gloomy parents. She was not in the mood of celebrating either, so she only went to a photo studio and took a picture. Some days later she bought a photo frame and put the picture in it. The family's health was greatly affected in the lousy environment. Mr. Qiu often murmured, "No way! This is unbearable! We have to move!" But he did not like to ask for help, and never turned to any one or any authority, even if his patients were from various occupations.

Lose one's bearings

One day Weiying was making a dress for herself on the sewing machine when a young couple suddenly came to see their house. The man was tall and thin, and the woman was pregnant. They said their workplace was quite near and the woman is about to be in labor, so the man's mother wanted to move in and help take care of the baby. If the Qius agree, they were willing to exchange places with them. So Weiying went to their place, which was located far from the city center, but close to the old park, Tianxin Pavilion. It was an old house with red brick walls and a wooden floor, standing by a road called Shiziling. It was shared by two households, had altogether two large rooms and one small room. The other family occupied a large and a small one. There was a living room and kitchen behind the door up on the stairs, which was shared; the back door was on the other side of the passageway by the small room; behind the back door there was an earthen ground of about one meter in width and five meter in length. There was a slope by the ground, covered by small trees and wild grass. The couple owned only one room in the house, about twelve square meters in area and had a window facing the earth ground. There was no water pipe and toilet either; they had to fetch the water from the hill opposite the house, and there was a double-floored public lavatory down the hillside on the left. Up the hillside was the street; down it was a line of one-floor houses.

When her parents got home, Weiying told them, "A couple came today and took me to see their house at Shiziling. The light and ventilation were both good and there was a kitchen to share with another family. But they only have one room, how should the three of us live in it?" Mr. Qiu said, "I'll go and take a look tomorrow after the work."

The next day he came back and said, "I have agreed to switch houses with them. The room was okay, at least better than the one I'm in now. It's closer to my hospital, and I can go work out and have breakfast in Tianxin Pavilion in the morning." Weiying asked, "Where shall I sleep?" Mr. Qiu replied, "You're already in your twenties. Now that your household residence permit is back, you won't stay with parents for too long. The room I'm living in now is totally sealed up when I close the door and is too damp and moldy. I can't stand it anymore. I have to move."

Upon hearing his words, Weiying was filled with speechless, indignant grief. Both her parents were bite the hand that feeds one by their leaders, who take the campaign as an excuse to political persecute them with the power in hand. Especially the leader in Father's hospital, they not only did they obliterate his huge contributions for investing and establishing the hospital. When they were forced to move out their legal house in Laozhaobi and her revolt, she had no idea what misfortune would fall on her if there had not been the compassion of the PLA officer at the police station!

4.6 The future, be enveloped in smoke

As Qiu Weiying packed up her things to leave Wujiajing to Shiziling, she suddenly found that her photo taken at her 23rd birthday and its frame disappeared, and she felt confused that no one in her family stored them. What made her feel more helpless is that the sewing machine in her room was nowhere to be found after she came back. Her father said, "We have got only one room, so there is no space for those unnecessary things except for two beds, a desk and a cabinet." Weiying nodded as only one room was too small. She had no alternative but charge herself with knowledge to improve her quality so that she could find more job opportunities in the future.

One day after they moved to their new home, their neighbor's son who lived in the factory chatted with Qiu Weiying, asking curiously, "I heard that your father has first-class medical skills, he has cured the anorectal disease of several acquaintances of mine. So why don't your family have an independent house?" She answered with a bitter smile, "We used to have our house and have a whole building not just an apartment. Later, my mother has opened a private clinic at home at home, and though it was legitimate, our property was confiscated unreasonably, including our property ownership certificate. Then our house was occupied forcefully. We have two rooms in Wujiajing, but my father could not endure the environment in there and thus change two rooms with other people in here. And we have another room upstairs for my sister and her three children. My father has been engaged in medicine for 20-odd years in Changsha and knew a lot of people. But he has never asked them for favor, which has become one of his habits." The boy said, "Oh, then your whole family is really encountering meet with a have a large impact tragic" However, what the Qiu family never expected was that was not the end of their suffering. Property loss and political suffering were not the only problems. Although Qiu Weiying found a job after moving here, however the Qiu family's misfortune is still not over...

One day when Weiying came back home from an occupational school, she saw her father lying in bed, uncomfortable. While he was passing the T-cross at the end of a downhill path on his bicycle after work, a granny with a basket in hand was rushing out from the right side of the turning point and was to cross the street straightly forward without looking around. Mr. Qiu braked suddenly with all his strength to avoid knocking her down. However, the granny walked across the street slowly without being hurt while. He separated from the seat and he was thrown down rapidly to the ground. He was too painful to make a move. At that time, the boy at next door and two of his friends saw the crowd gathering there and went into them to see what happened, only to find that the man who had fallen on the street was their neighbor, Doctor Qiu. Then they spared no effort to send him who was high and heavy home, and then to hospital for injury examination and treatment. And he was seriously injured in his spine from the photo, so he had to lie in bed for at least one month before being able to go to work. Therefore, Qiu Weiying had to take over the work of caring after her father.

One day about half a month since Mr. Qiu began to stay at home, Qiu Weiying bought something back and found him sitting on the bedside sadly and full of anguish. So, she asked him worriedly, "Wat is up?" He replied with a long sigh, "Wang Huijun cut my salary to 87 yuan. How dare she?" Qiu Weiying felt so confused, "Then about 100 yuan was cut off. Why could she do so?" He answered, "The man who sent the salary here said, 'all those who received a high salary have been treated like this. So do Doctor Cao and Doctor Shen (the most well-known doctor dealing with bones in Changsha who has the same reputation as Qiu)'." Weiying asked, "How much of their salaries has been cut? Did you know?" "they have 110 yuan and over 120 yuan left respectively." "That's much better than your situation. Their salaries used to be 160 yuan and 170 yuan, so they were cut by 50 yuan only." (Qiu knew that the three of them had the highest salary in the hospital). Her father said, "Because I'm older than them and will retire in a few years, so the hospital leaders do not expect me to earn much. What's more, I have to ask for leave for rest at home now." At this, he cursed Wang Huijun and expressed his regret once more, "I arranged her to be a cleaner in the hospital in the beginning and let her to serve as the dean. But she has always been envious of my salary. This bitch has finally reached her goal." After that, he was still quite cross and cursed her once more. Weiying could understand that Wang had endless jealousy and retaliation for his father though the Southern Region Hospital set up by her father became a Chinese Medicine Research Institute in Changsha. She also heard that the hospital sold the house bought in her father's original name to Financial Department of Hunan province in several hundred times more than the original price when house price was on the rise. However, the hospital leaders always set his father political frame-up instead of showing gratitude. In fact, at that time when the "Gang of Four" was so rampant, a society lacking in democracy and legality facilitated outlaws to retaliate anyone they hated with their power. Thus, it is market to say that that was a tragedy not only for the Qiu family but also for the whole nation.

Lose one's bearings

At one Sunday evening after Qiu Zhongyuan recovered and got back to work, Qiu Weiying stood in the yard and chatted with her mother who was resting in a chair. Suddenly Wang Tianliang came on a bicycle, and said to Qiu's mother, "I have found a job for Weiying in a factory which is not far from mine. I'm quite familiar with the CPC secretary of that factory. Weiying can go there next month if she agrees." At this, Mother said to her, "Heard that? What do you think of it?" She was then hesitating and therefore did not give an answer immediately. Seemed somewhat uneasy at Weiying's reaction, Wang Tianliang said to his nominally adoptive mother, "just let Weiying make the decision" and left. Watching Wang riding away, Mother appeared angry. Weiying felt a little embarrassed and thus explained to her mother, "Wang found me the job through personal connection so that I'm afraid of negative consequences." Her mother said with depression, "He loves you for all these years. He is handsome and engaged in the radio technical work. Isn't that, OK? If you break up one day in the future, you can still make friends. And it is good for him to find you a job." Mother lowered her head again as if thinking of other problems, and Weiying forgot to tell in detail to her that Wang had once fell on love with another girl. Given their housing problem and her father's cut salary, she explained to her mother, "I'll go to ask him to see whether the factory can provide accommodation, if so, I'll work there."

The next day is Monday. Weiying did not want to go directly to Wang Tianliang's factory, so she went to Zhang Manru's home since she knew that Zhang's husband had a rest every Monday and Liu Dahan was home when she came. He accompanied Weiying to the gate of the factory where his wife worked and walked alone into the gate to call Zhang out. Seeing Weiying standing there, Zhang smiled, "Oh, Weiying, you are here coming! I haven't seen you for such a long time!" Weiying told her why she came and then asked her whether he could help inquire after Wang Tianliang. Zhang said,

"OK, I'll ask him about it. Please come to my home to have a rest, I'll be back soon."

When Zhang came home, she said to Weiying, "Wang said it was not a difficult problem, and that he would help you ask in two days. So, you two just broke up like this? You did not come into the factory and he always showed your picture to others, "See, this is my ex-girlfriend, so don't introduce someone for me. I won't take a girl at random." Weiying felt strange at hearing that, I had never given my photos to Wang, so where did he get mine? Thus, she asked Zhang, "What kind of photo is it?" Zhang answered, "A color photo with words "23rd birthday." She realized at once, "It's no wonder that the photo I had put in the corner was missing. Why didn't he tell me when taking it away?" The couple burst into laughter at what she said and felt it quite interesting. The next Sunday, Wang Tianliang went to Qiu's house by bicycle and told Shao very gladly, "That factory can provide accommodation for Weiying." Therefore, Weiying accepted this job, report for duty at the factory at the designated date and lived there. Not long after that, Juecong went back to Changsha from the village to live at home temporarily.

This factory was called "Changsha Northern Region's Cold Working Plant" was in the northern part of the city---Shangdalong---through the Martyr's Park. It was near Wang's factory, only a few minutes' walk. In the plant, there were three sites and workshops responsible for production separately, the largest factory building with two workshops that mainly produced boilers and their spare parts were opposite to the dormitories of Changsha Automobile and Appliance Plant; the factory building of lathe workers' shop producing spare parts of boilers and processing raw materials was beside Hunan Silk-making Factory; there was also a galvanized iron sales department engaged in producing and selling hand-made galvanized iron products.

The sales department of plant was in the downtown, and the house the Qiu's family bought in the past was in an alley on the left of the road near the sales department of the plant. It is less than five minutes' walk from forcibly occupying Qiu's house by force.

The plant was not large without a formal dormitory. When you entered the gate of the lathe workers' shop not far away from the Silk-making Factory, passed not-very-large empty grassland and walked to the end, you would see two connected rooms, one for a young monitor of the lathe workers and the other for his sister and another apprentice and Weiying together live. Weiying did not ask about when his sister came to live here, but she only knew that their parents had passed away and they seemed to be on good terms with the secretary of the plant.

All these girl apprentices came into the plant at the same time. And 23-year-old Qiu Weiying was the oldest among the ten apprentices. Their monthly salary was 18 yuan and their apprentice period varied from two to three years in accordance with their type of work in production. In the beginning, they were digging air-raid shelters that might have been dug out by workers in big factories nearby in response to the call of "digging shelters and storing food" by the CPC central committee. Because in the first half year of 1965, China went into the period of emergency preparation for warfare and began to dig air-raid shelters in the latter half of that year. In 1972, Mao Zedong put forward the idea of "digging deep hole, accumulating more grain, and not claiming hegemony" in the light of the foreign situation facing China and the socialist nature of the country. The meaning of "digging deep hole" was especially the construction of protective works for large and medium-sized cities. At that time, the danger of a world war was overestimated. By this time, the air-raid shelter was almost dug, and the size of the inside was not small. Whenever Weiying entered the shelters, she was reminded of the film "Tunnel Warfare".

The apprentices needed to put the loose soil left in the shelters into bamboo baskets and then use rotating robes to lift the soil to pour it out. These young men were often working while chatting with each other, so they would not feel tired. Among them, Weiying had a girlfriend named Chen Youying who was on the best terms with Weiying. Chen lived in the dormitory of the nearby Appliance Plant; her father worked there as a technical worker and her mother was responsible for housework at home. Although her parents had several children, they were very kind and amiable to Weiying and sometimes invited Weiying to have dinner with them.

In one hot morning of July or August, Chen Youying came to Weiying's room and asked her to go swimming. Weiying said, "Neither of us is able to swim, so will it be safe?" Chen replied, "No problem. I know a place with shallow water, and it will be safe to swim there." Therefore, after having lunch at a nearby small restaurant and a short rest, Weiying went to Chen's home and put on her swimsuits inside her clothes, just like Chen. Then they said goodbye to Chen's parents and left for that place.

After getting to that place, they took off their clothes on the beach and walked into the water in swimsuits shoulder by shoulder. Under the summer sunshine, the water opened its arms to them. At that time, Weiying saw clearly two young men wearing sunglasses who were lying on the beach, with some clothes beneath their heads and arms. She felt that their eyes followed them closely. So Weiying, who were always quite conservative-minded, said to Chen, "You see those two men. They are staring at us all the time. How boring they are." Chen looked to the direction where Weiying pointed and smiled, "They just do whatever they like, which has nothing to do with us."

But it turned out that it mattered a lot. If not for them, they would probably have lost their lives. When they swam for a while in the water, Weiying saw Chen Youying stretching her hand out suddenly and shouting to Weiying who was several steps away, "Qiu Weiying! ..." Weiying realized that she must encounter some trouble. Without making clear what happened, Weiying hurried to cross the water to walk to her side, stretched her right hand to her and grasped her sinking fingers. However, Chen hugged Weiying out of a sudden, thus holding her rigidly. It turned out that what was beneath them was a deep and big hole! A sense of fear was overwhelming her and a desire for living prompted her to tread on where they got down into the water. But consequently, she was drawn into the water by Chen before standing firmly. After making the same efforts repeatedly, she felt that she could not bear it and that she was dying without clearly seeing the scene before her eyes.

At this exact moment, she felt someone seizing her hand and dragged her and Chen out. Standing on her soft feet in the water that reached her, she saw that the men who had saved them were just the young men looking at them on the beach. They left after looking at the two girls. It was never expected that they were saved by them! Probably because they paid attention to them, they could discover that they were in danger just now. Later, Weiying asked Chen, "Since you know that I could not swim either, why don't you shout 'Help' while at risk?" But Chen answered, "I'm afraid of being ashamed by doing so." Weiying could barely understand, "Why did you feel ashamed since you were on the brink of being drown to death? That was not something worth shaming." Several days later, Weiying suddenly began to regret that she had lost contact with the two men, who, after all, saved her life!"

After cleaning up the air-raid shelters, the apprentices were engaged in temporary ideological and educational study and then were assigned to different types of work in production. The two girls living together with Weiying worked in the lathe workers' shop while Weiying and a young man who lived in downtown worked in the sales department of galvanized iron products. So, she had to take bus through several stations to reach the place. At that time, it was not easy to catch a bus especially during rush hours, for there were too many people but too few buses. Whenever a bus comes, passers just crowd each other to get on it and those who were more arbitrary could usually make it. But Weiying who was too shy who was not very accustomed to squeezing with others, so she always waited until the rush hour passed to get on the bus. She should have been assigned to work in the plant since she was living in the dormitory. Thus, she felt such an appointment somewhat created more difficulties for her, but she could say nothing as the plant Luo, with a big belly, seemed ignorant of her. This job was provided by Wang Tianliang, so she was embarrassed to ask him for more requirements.

Besides the long and crowded journey away from the workplace, there was no canteen there. Other workers of the department lived in nearby places, so they could go home for lunch and have a rest. Weiying always went to a store of preserved meat and fish on Zhongshan road about one station away from her workplace and then passed another station to go to Xiaodong's home. Because the hospital where the mother works was not far from Wujiajing where Xiaodong lived and she was worried about Xiaodong's and her three children, she went there almost every noon to help her cook. Therefore, Weiying went there to have lunch with them together.

In a day for rest in the spring of 1973, Weiying was thinking about whether to come back home after breakfast or at noon after washing the clothes when the sky suddenly turned dark, and a downpour came with horrible thunder. The rain became heavier and heavier so that she realized that she could not go out for that moment. Without alternative, she poured some water in the cup and ate some biscuits. Then she took out all the clothes needing washing to the public bathroom. It was still raining when she finished washing, so she began to read the French novel "The Count of Monte Cristo". At noon, it was just drizzling a little and she took bus back home with an umbrella. It stopped raining when she got off the bus.

Weiying Walking into the house, she greeted the granny next door who was sitting in the joint kitchen. Then, as soon as she stepped into the room. She was so stunned when seeing her mother lying in bed with her face up, a quilt beneath her neck, and her head and face being wrapped with gauze all over but her eyes and nose, she wanted to shed tears instead.

Mother opened her eyes weakly and saw Weiying standing there with an astonished expression, she asked, "You come back?" Weiying said hurriedly, "what's wrong with you, mom?" Mother sighed and explained in weak voice, "I wanted to walk through the shortcut from the back of the house when going to work. After passing the railway and walking up to the opposite hillside, I was thinking about Xiaodong's family with my head lowered. Thus, I did not notice that a worker walked out from the bypath beside the butchers with a cart full of goods. It happened that the goods fell off on the hillside and I did not have enough time to hide, thus hurting my head. At that time, a kind-hearted neighbor saw me and found Juecong there as soon as possible. Juecong went to the hospital immediately and sent me there with a stretcher and a car. Juecong was going to hit that guy, but I stopped him as the guy had not meant it. It was a hard job for him to drag a cart full of stuff on the uphill path. Like that, Juecong must take the responsibility for wounding others."

After listening to her mother's explanation, Weiying sat on the bedside indignantly, "The guy was so stupid. He should have fastened the stuff! If they had felled off on the road, an accident would have happened even if it did not hurt passenger. At least Juecong should have cursed him and for injuring you like this...!" She finished these words, looked at her mother sadly and could not speak for quite a while when. Mother said to her in a feeble voice, "Help me write a letter to Li Zhimeng's family, asking his brother to take Xiao Sha and Xiaojian to the village of Shandong and live with their grandma. I will send life expenses for them each month so that Wu's mother will have some money to live. When Wu Jian grows at a school age, I'll bring them back. I don't know when the wound in my head will recover, and I'm afraid that Xiaodong could not look after well her three children. It will be too bad if to have them wander from place to place about..."

Weiying thought her mother's concern was rational, so she wrote a letter to her brother-in-law's hometown in Shandong in accordance with what her mother had said. Several days later, Wu's younger brother came. He looked very much like Wu, a typical strong man from Shandong, a tall and thin figure over 1.8 meters and a tanned face. As there was no room for him to live in and nobody to care for him, he took Wu Jian and Wu Sha back to Shandong by train the next day.

No long after that, Shao gradually recovered and there was little scar remaining on her face, which had been mostly covered by the wound that was not quite deep. Her skin was born well, so it might have been easier and quicker to recover. However, human is not a piece of iron, but a body with flesh and blood. Whoever was strong physically and psychologically could hardly stand endless mental tortures, which could indirectly harm health severely…

Then, she came across Wang Yi, a classmate of Juele. She helped Weiying solve the big problem of having meals on weekdays by ask her to eat at the canteen of an institution nearby. After lunch, she would go upstairs of the department building and sleep in a bamboo board bed without feet on the wooded floor where galvanized iron products were piled up. When it was cold, she would put an old blanket on the bed and a quilt on herself. Since Mother had recovered, she usually went back to the plant to have dinner as if she went home to have dinner; it would be too late to come back because there was no space for to sleep at home. Furthermore, it was not quite safe around Martyr's Park.

What Weiying feared most at work was soaking the burnt iron with hydrochloric acid before welding the seams with melted tin sticks. Whenever she did it, she was always made cough to breathlessness by the pungent hydrochloric acid smog though wearing a gauze mask. The galvanized iron department was engaged in producing and selling galvanized iron as well as undertaking its processing. It was a galvanized iron production group. Workers were beating the iron with hands while working there. The main products included, ice-cream modes for cold drink factories, galvanized tins, kettles to water flowers, pumping units and funnels. Weiying was mainly responsible for making pumping unit which was composed of three parts, a long and round tin, a round directors general Like a funnel and a curved choke. A woman worker once joked to her, "Pretty girls make pretty products." This was because the units made by Weiying sold quite well. However, her respiratory tract was negatively affected during the process because iron which was soaked in hydrochloric acid after being burnt hot would cause smog, seriously stimulating people's respiratory tract and making them cough unceasingly. Sometimes Weiying coughed so hard that she could not even breathe and felt headache. Although the factory would give her several yuan as nutrition subsidy for doing this job, she really suffered from it. Nevertheless, she must accept it in order to make a living, for she felt that Mr. Luo was not friendly towards her as if he was discriminating her politically. And she was like her father in this aspect, she was neither good at making up to nor resorting to others. As a girl with strong self-esteem, she was afraid of being rejected.

Once, a male worker with the surname of Xia said to another worker in front of her, "the prettiest worker in our factory is doing the worst job and the ugliest worker is doing the best one." An apprentice who began working in the factory at almost the same time with Weiying was assigned to the office as secretary of youth league branch because her father was a worker and member of the CPC. Later, the girl knew what Mr. Xia said about her and therefore lost her temper before Weiying, "I would rather become the one who has a beautiful face but does the worst job." Weiying comforted her, "Why are you so serious? Our factory is small without many people, so there's no big difference between the prettiest and the ugliest." The girl remained silent at her words. She just took something favorable for granted and didn't understand that being trusted and given the full play was a kind of happiness itself. It was such a bad feeling to be discriminated by others and suffer in both life and work just owing to so-called family's political problems!

The rest day fell on the same dates in both Weiying's and Wang Tianliang's factory. One day when Weiying was at home alone while her parents went to work, Wang Tianliang walked in from outside. He asked Weiying with grudge, "You will never be on good terms with me, will you? If so, you will be on this job forever!" Weiying knew that their factories shared one party branch and that the two-party branch secretaries often met with each other. She became more get angry, "I did not think that much. What I know is that when my father was make the circuit of medical tour in the countryside, you changed your mind because you thought our whole family might go to the village. You even had a romantic relationship with another woman of the factory, so the love tie between us has disappeared." Wang said, "That's a rumor." Weiying replied immediately, "I saw it myself, with my own eyes. And you told me that we'd better be brother and sister. The most important thing as a couple is to be able to not only share happiness but also overcome hardships together! But at the critical moment, you just lied to me that you might need to go to battlefield as a demobilized army man, which made me cry."

At this, Wang suddenly kneed down beside Weiying, who, remained aloof and indifferent to this. She walked to the kitchen to fetch a knife. This moment, Juecong came back and followed his old sister to the room. Weiying threw the knife before Wang's knees, "Kill me! I'll never fall in love with a chameleon!" She did not know clearly why she was so firm for this moment. Wang stood up, took a cigarette out of his pocket, put the one end with fire into his mouth on purpose and shut his mouth. Then he fell onto the ground. Juecong gave an indication to Weiying to let her leave. After that incident, nothing seemed to have happened between Weiying and Wang Tianliang.

In fact, there were some men who "Only himself set the fire, not allowed the women to light the lights." When he changed his mind in love, he didn't care, but when a woman wanted to leave him after losing her heart, he resented her and even took revenge on her…

The rest day fell on the same dates in both Weiying's and Wang Tianliang's factory. One day when Weiying was at home alone while her parents went to work, Wang Tianliang walked in from outside. He asked Weiying with grudge, "You will never be on good terms with me, will you? If so, you will be on this job forever!" Weiying knew that their factories shared one party branch and that the two-party branch secretaries often met with each other. She became more get angry, "I did not think that much. What I know is that when my father was make the circuit of medical tour in the countryside, you changed your mind because you thought our whole family might go to the village. You even had a romantic relationship with another woman of the factory, so the love tie between us has disappeared." Wang said, "That's a rumor." Weiying replied immediately, "I saw it myself, with my own eyes. And you told me that we'd better be brother and sister. The most important thing as a couple is to be able to not only share happiness but also overcome hardships together! But at the critical moment, you just lied to me that you might need to go to battlefield as a demobilized army man, which made me cry."

At this, Wang suddenly kneed down beside Weiying, who, remained aloof and indifferent to this. She walked to the kitchen to fetch a knife. This moment, Juecong came back and followed his old sister to the room. Weiying threw the knife before Wang's knees, "Kill me! I'll never fall in love with a chameleon!" She did not know clearly why she was so firm for this moment. Wang stood up, took a cigarette out of his pocket, put the one end with fire into his mouth on purpose and shut his mouth. Then he fell onto the ground. Juecong gave an indication to Weiying to let her leave. After that incident, nothing seemed to have happened between Weiying and Wang Tianliang.

In fact, there were some men who "Only himself set the fire, not allowed the women to light the lights." When he changed his mind in love, he didn't care, but when a woman wanted to leave him after losing her heart, he resented her and even took revenge on her…

responsible for making pumping unit which was composed of three parts, a long and round tin, a round directors general Like a funnel and a curved choke. A woman worker once joked to her, "Pretty girls make pretty products." This was because the units made by Weiying sold quite well. However, her respiratory tract was negatively affected during the process because iron which was soaked in hydrochloric acid after being burnt hot would cause smog, seriously stimulating people's respiratory tract and making them cough unceasingly. Sometimes Weiying coughed so hard that she could not even breathe and felt headache. Although the factory would give her several yuan as nutrition subsidy for doing this job, she really suffered from it. Nevertheless, she must accept it in order to make a living, for she felt that Mr. Luo was not friendly towards her as if he was discriminating her politically. And she was like her father in this aspect, she was neither good at making up to nor resorting to others. As a girl with strong self-esteem, she was afraid of being rejected.

Once, a male worker with the surname of Xia said to another worker in front of her, "the prettiest worker in our factory is doing the worst job and the ugliest worker is doing the best one." An apprentice who began working in the factory at almost the same time with Weiying was assigned to the office as secretary of youth league branch because her father was a worker and member of the CPC. Later, the girl knew what Mr. Xia said about her and therefore lost her temper before Weiying, "I would rather become the one who has a beautiful face but does the worst job." Weiying comforted her, "Why are you so serious? Our factory is small without many people, so there's no big difference between the prettiest and the ugliest." The girl remained silent at her words. She just took something favorable for granted and didn't understand that being trusted and given the full play was a kind of happiness itself. It was such a bad feeling to be discriminated by others and suffer in both life and work just owing to so-called family's political problems!

Several years later, transferred from the Ministry of Foreign Affairs to the of Hunan Province foreign affairs office, Mr. Zhang, Mr. Zhang, who works as a translator. When he applied to the provincial Leader to marry with Weiying, her political censorship did not pass. And this the results showed that Wang Tianliang further Qiu Weiying's family political problem in front of the leaders of the factory.

Meantime, the secretary of the factory branch thought, although Qiu Weiying had been in village for several years, but she had not temperament of village working people. Therefore, he often, while touching his shaven head, examined her with a proletariat point of view. However, a woman cooks with the surname of Mo had a totally different opinion, "You look delicate but actually you are not at all. Although sister Ying looks not delicate, it is hard to make up to her. She's just a nuisance!" However, Ying's elder brother was monitor of lathe workshop and they had a certain special relationship with the party branch secretary, who, Weiying felt clearly, held a different attitude towards them in almost every aspect, take care of this brother and sister. Under a certain circumstance, interpersonal relationship could totally affect one's destiny severely, especially in an era of stressing political conditions and lacking democracy and freedom. Whoever possessed power could not only use their power to favor their friends and relatives but also use it to take revenge on you.

One day before her registered permanent residence was returned to the city, Weiying encountered the son of a doctor, his father had also opened a private clinic at home. He told her, "On the eve of the confiscation of family property of our family's properties amid the "Four Clean Movement's" Movement, Chen Tianxiang (dean of the Medical Administration Committee) went to my home to tell my father, 'The medical institution management committee decided is going to confiscate properties of the families who are operating private clinics. Make preparation quickly!' My father hided our properties immediately and thus they just superficial damage took some worthless stuff. Later my father thanked him a lot..." Thereby

Qiu Zhongyuan who only had a good mastery of medical skills without considering interpersonal relationships were set up; (Shao Guizhen was no better than her husband in this aspect and just won't lose temper easily). So, it was natural that she become the target of the committee. Sometimes he also thought of that point, but it was his nature. The fact that he often offended the leaders caused his relationship with them to be always in vicious cycle...

One day at work in the galvanized iron sales department, a woman worker asked her, "Girl Qiu, both your parents are doctors, and I heard that your father is quite famous and highly skilled. So why don't you ask them to find you a better job?" Weiying answered, "My father would not resort to others for help, which is his nature. I have no alternative!" She dared not reveal to her colleagues that her family's properties' being confiscated, and her brother-in-law's being identified as an anti-revolutionary and how they seriously affected her future. But the worker's question reminded her of the past time full of endless sadness. Now they were living in Shiziling, and her parents encountered misfortunes in a row.

After work that day, Weiying crossed the street and walked to their former private house which was less than five minutes' walk from her workplace. She wants to look at, what it looked like now and who lived there.

Reaching the big pagoda tree in the lane, Weiying saw the big door wide open and thus she stepped up into the courtyard as usual. But she saw nobody there, so she stopped at the step. Then a forty-odd-year-old woman with short yellow hair walked out of the sitting room. She saw a young woman who had never seen it standing in front of the steps under the corridor and was stunned, so she asked in a strange but mild tone, "Who are you looking for?" "I come for a middle school classmate. I came here before." Up the steps, she scanned the house her family had once lived and found, the former floor became cement floor in the opened door on the left. The woman asked her in doubt, "What's the surname of your classmate?" Weiying was sure that she didn't know who she was, so Qiu Weiying replied, "She is surname Qiu." The woman seemed to see the light suddenly, "Oh, this house was confiscated. The former owner's surname was Qiu. They have moved away for over one year." Weiying pretended not to know it, "Confiscated? Then who are living there now?" "All are upright people. My husband works in Bureau of Public Security. Another family are working in real estate. There's another family I'm not very familiar with." Weiying was angry, "My classmate's parents are both upright doctors." The woman looked at her full of suspicion and Weiying did not know whether her husband was Chang Wanmin. Exactly at this moment, her husband came back, and he was not Chang!

On the way back, she thought, Her parents took the take great pains of decades of effort, mother is even pregnant with twins about to give birth to them and still treating patients! The outcome, deprived of their only residence by violence and all their family property come to naught. Her whole family was forcibly live a life of fall apart. Also, there is a huge pressure on the political! "There is no place complain of an injustice against oneself"! She felt sad for her current situation. Even more for parents feel wronged and pitiful!

Why the floor had been changed. It was ridiculous since they must have doubted that we had hided gold and jewelries under the ground. So, they just dug it up... She thought of her father's words, "After the confiscation of family property I came back to my hometown where I heard, 'Someone from your hospital in Changsha once came here to investigate you and intended to change your family into landlord but met firm opposition of us!' Look. Wang Huijun is so bad that she always takes advantage of every opportunity to me proceed political persecution and uses every chance to take revenge on me." Weiying said to her father, "I heard from mother, 'You patted desks and beat chairs at meetings of the hospital, so she has every reason to hate you!' There are good and bad people in CPC members. Didn't she become the director from a cleaner?" "Yes!

They had asked me to serve as the director of hospital, but I refused because I just wanted to focus on medical work. But I would not have recommended her if I could forecast the current situation." Weiying thought, if her father has become the director of the hospital, her family might not have been so unfortunate!?

Zhuang Ruiying, Weiying's good friend in middle school, graduated from No. Four Middle School and was assigned to work in Changsha Chinese Medicine Factory after returning from Indonesia based on policies as regards returned overseas Chinese. She got to know Mr. You back from Myanmar while working in the factory. They got married and had a girl.

When Weiying had a rest, Zhuang Ruiying brought her to Chen Dao's home. Chen, also an overseas Chinese back from Indonesia, lived in Beizheng Street near her workplace. Chen and his parents came back to China when Indonesians were carrying out anti-Chinese activities. Chen got married not long ago and had no children yet. The newly married couple lived together with his kind parents. Whenever Weiying and Zhuang Ruiying went to their home, they were very hospitable to them and interested in talking with them. Therefore, she often went there after work, making her feel happy.

Qiu walked to other places at the city proper sometimes. Once when passing Fuzheng Street, she wanted to have a look in the Xinhua Bookstore to see whether there were books in her interest. At the cross, she came across Zhou Xiong, one of her close classmates in elementary school, at the time of which Qiu Weiying liked to see her drawing ancient beauties at her home. Now Qiu asked her, "Where are you working?" Zhou replied, "Drawing in Xinhua Printing Factory." Qiu said, "That's great. You liked drawing since childhood, and you are engaged in what you are really interested in. I am not that fortunate, for I have to beat galvanized iron like a monk." She said that with a deep sigh and a little pain in heart.

Zhou Xiong asked her with doubt, "Since you used to be quite active and love singing and dancing in elementary school, why are you satisfied with such a job?" Weiying answered, "I have no alternative. Our family's properties were confiscated when I was in middle school. At that time my younger brother was graduating from Fuzhengjie Elementary School and the character "land" was written into his archive as the teacher said, they doubted that his family were a landlord!" Then Zhou asked, "Are you married?" "Married? I don't even have a boyfriend." "I don't believe it!" "Why?" Weiying questioned, feeling strange. "Because you have all that a man loves." Weiying blinked her eyes, but she was still quite pure in mind and thus could not understand what aspects a man loved of a woman. However, she had never considered that she should have had a boyfriend since she was already 24. She only thought her job was not promising at all. She felt that emerged in front of her be everything enveloped in smoke…

4.7 Love, cannot set foot into two boats

One day during the summer of 1973, Qiu Weiying went to Chen Dao's home in Beizheng Street to have a chat after dinner. Chen's family were having dinner then and Chen's young wife stood up to take a bowl of rice for Weiying who said, "Thank you, but I have had dinner." Chen Dao asked her, "If you are free on your day off, you can come to visit my factory with my wife." "That's nice. Won't we affect your work?" "It doesn't matter, I'll be relatively free when working in the repair workshop and so visitors will not affect my work." Weiying said, "ok, I will go there on Tuesday with your wife." Chen just married his wife for a short time, and they had no children yet. Hearing their talk, his wife agreed with a smile to visit Changsha Thermos factory.

That morning, Weiying had a bowl of soybean milk, and two deep-fried dough sticks near her dormitory and caught a bus to the downtown. She got off and walked to Chen Dao's house. Chen's father, who wore a pair of metal-rimmed glasses, greeted her warmly and his wife turned to call their daughter-in-law in the kitchen. Chen's wife stretched her head out of the kitchen and said to Weiying, "Please have a seat and I'll finish with these bowls and plants."

Chen's father asked her with kind and pleasant countenance, "I heard that you and my daughter-in-law would visit my son's factory today?" "Yes." Weiying answered gladly. He then asked, "You have been in village for several years, haven't you?" "Yes." "Then have you transplanted rice seedlings with your fingers? Did you feel pain in your figures? Can you stand that?" Chen's father asked while pretending he was transplanting the rice seedlings. Weiying answered, "That which was not so terrible, but what I feared most was leeches that would climb onto my legs to cling to me and sucked my blood. Moreover, it was easy to catch arthritis because legs were soaked in cold water. I used to be so naive that I thought we were assigned to the village to build up our ideology and help establish new socialist rural areas. However, I became more complicated in thought and did not witness any changes in the village during those six or seven years. It was not easy to realize that objective, so it was just a waste of time for intellectual youths to practice there. Agriculture depending on hands instead of mechanics will always make us backward. Peasants were not quite welcome us; instead, they contended that we occupied their land because they thought intellectual youths who had grown up in cities knew nothing about agriculture and could not adapt to their life." Chen's father smiled, "It's reasonable." At that moment Chen's wife came out of the kitchen and Weiying said to her, "You are lucky enough not to be assigned to village." She replied, "If not for the policy of giving favorable treatment to overseas Chinese and my in-time marriage, I would have gone there." Then she changed her clothes, "Now we can go."

It was a day in July. When Weiying and Chen's wife got off bus at a station near the thermos factory where Chen worked, the downtown. She got off and walked to Chen Dao's house. Chen's father, who wore a pair of metal-rimmed glasses, greeted her warmly and his wife turned to call their daughter-in-law in the kitchen. Chen's wife stretched her head out of the kitchen and said to Weiying, "Please have a seat and I'll finish with these bowls and plants."

Chen's father asked her with kind and pleasant countenance, "I heard that you and my daughter-in-law would visit my son's factory today?" "Yes." Weiying answered gladly. He then asked, "You have been in village for several years, haven't you?" "Yes." "Then have you transplanted rice seedlings with your fingers? Did you feel pain in your figures? Can you stand that?" Chen's father asked while pretending he was transplanting the rice seedlings. Weiying answered, "That which was not so terrible, but what I feared most was leeches that would climb onto my legs to cling to me and sucked my blood. Moreover, it was easy to catch arthritis because legs were soaked in cold water. I used to be so naive that I thought we were assigned to the village to build up our ideology and help establish new socialist rural areas. However, I became more complicated in thought and did not witness any changes in the village during those six or seven years. It was not easy to realize that objective, so it was just a waste of time for intellectual youths to practice there. Agriculture depending on hands instead of mechanics will always make us backward. Peasants were not quite welcome us; instead, they contended that we occupied their land because they thought intellectual youths who had grown up in cities knew nothing about agriculture and could not adapt to their life." Chen's father smiled, "It's reasonable." At that moment Chen's wife came out of the kitchen and Weiying said to her, "You are lucky enough not to be assigned to village." She replied, "If not for the policy of giving favorable treatment to overseas Chinese and my in-time marriage, I would have gone there." Then she changed her clothes, "Now we can go."

It was a day in July. When Weiying and Chen's wife got off bus at a station near the thermos factory where Chen worked, the

Zhou Xiong asked her with doubt, "Since you used to be quite active and love singing and dancing in elementary school, why are you satisfied with such a job?" Weiying answered, "I have no alternative. Our family's properties were confiscated when I was in middle school. At that time my younger brother was graduating from Fuzhengjie Elementary School and the character "land" was written into his archive as the teacher said, they doubted that his family were a landlord!" Then Zhou asked, "Are you married?" "Married? I don't even have a boyfriend." "I don't believe it!" "Why?" Weiying questioned, feeling strange. "Because you have all that a man loves." Weiying blinked her eyes, but she was still quite pure in mind and thus could not understand what aspects a man loved of a woman. However, she had never considered that she should have had a boyfriend since she was already 24. She only thought her job was not promising at all. She felt that emerged in front of her be everything enveloped in smoke…

4.7 Love, cannot set foot into two boats

One day during the summer of 1973, Qiu Weiying went to Chen Dao's home in Beizheng Street to have a chat after dinner. Chen's family were having dinner then and Chen's young wife stood up to take a bowl of rice for Wciying who said, "Thank you, but I have had dinner." Chen Dao asked her, "If you are free on your day off, you can come to visit my factory with my wife." "That's nice. Won't we affect your work?" "It doesn't matter, I'll be relatively free when working in the repair workshop and so visitors will not affect my work." Weiying said, "ok, I will go there on Tuesday with your wife." Chen just married his wife for a short time, and they had no children yet. Hearing their talk, his wife agreed with a smile to visit Changsha Thermos factory.

That morning, Weiying had a bowl of soybean milk, and two deep-fried dough sticks near her dormitory and caught a bus to the sun had given off glaring light though it was just 10 in the morning. They walked into the gate of the factory. After greeting the janitor, Chen's wife led Weiying to the repair workshop. Seeing them coming, Chen asked, "It's very hot, isn't it?" Then he bought two glasses of cold drink for them. After a short rest, Weiying asked, "Could we have a look at your production workshop to see how the thermoses produced?" "OK, but you have to wait till noontime. It's just tens of minutes, so have lunch at my workshop first."

Near noontime Weiying saw a man of medium build at the age of 26 to 30. Wearing a pair of glasses, a pair of deep-grey trousers and a vest, as well as a Rolex gold watch, he swaggered out in flip-flops. He seemed to reveal a cynical attitude towards life from behind his glasses. Looking at Weiying, he smiled to her as if he was her acquaintance and showed two gold-covered teeth. Weiying also smiled to him. At that time Chen Dao walked close and said to Weiying, "This is my colleague, Shu Fuhua, an overseas Chinese returning from Singapore." "Oh." Weiying looked at him unintentionally. Shu looked very excited, but Weiying had no further reaction and turned around to continue talking with Chen's wife. After a while, Chen Dao said, "It's time for lunch in the canteen and I'm going to buy it." Shu said immediately, "I'll go with you." Chen did not refuse him, and they went together. Back they put the food on a round table and the four people of them began to have lunch.

As it was hot summer, the blazing sun was hanging in the sky, shining everyone be dripping to sweat. Despite the big fan in the repair workshop, they still sweated on face. Weiying took out a small handkerchief from the pocket of her short-sleeved shirt to polish her face when Shu put down his bowl at once and walked to her side to fan the wind for her with a big paper fan. She blushed in the face by his sudden intimate behavior and wanted to escape but feared that would make him embarrassed. Therefore, she just ate more quickly, pretending to ignore what he was doing. Then she walked to wash the bowl and chopsticks and washed up her face with cool water.

Then they went to the production workshop and returned to the repair workshop thereafter. When the sun declined a little, Weiying said to Chen's wife, "Shall we go?" The latter agreed immediately, and they walked out of the factory, followed by Shu who said, "I'm going home. I lived near here. Welcome to my home if you are free." Chen's wife agreed with a smile, but Weiying didn't say anything. The earth was still giving off suffocating heat so that the road was sticky to walk on…

Soon, Weiying had dinner at the usual place and went to Chen's home to have a talk. Chen's parents were hospitable and asked her to have dinner together. She thanked them, "I have had dinner." Then she took a magazine. After dinner, Chen's wife put a cup of tea on the table for her and Chen, sitting on the other side of the table, said, "Shu Fuhua wants to make friends with you." Weiying declined immediately, "No, that man is too frivolous. He dared to fan the wind beside me the first time we met, making me quite embarrassed." Chen laughed and didn't continue.

On another day off, Qiu Weiying went to female friend Li Yongni's home at the provincial exhibition hall and her husband was an oil painter. Qiu told her that matter, Li said, "If I were you, I would agree without hesitation. Anyway, you have no promise with the current job, so you'd better be with a returned overseas Chinese to go abroad." Weiying explained, "Both food and clothes are for spiritual happy. If he's frivolous, it will be easy for him to have relationships with other women. So, if a couple are not happy together, money can't do anything. 'The loving husband and wife bitter also sweet.!'" Li didn't deny her opinion.

Half a year passed. One day when Weiying was in Chen Dao's home, Chen mentioned Shu Fuhua again. But she said, "I don't like frivolous person, be it man or woman, for such a kind of people are not reliable." Chen said, "He's not like that towards others who many think him hard to talk with. Since you went to our factory last time, he has never worked." Chen's father smiled at this, "Hey, he's caught lovesickness." Weiying asked, "Does your factory allow a half year's leave?" "It implements favorable policy towards returned overseas Chinese, so no one supervises him. The factory deducts his salary while he's away. He has become casual in work and always asked for leave for two or three days since his mother came to visit him from Singapore two years ago. But he has never been away for several months consecutively. Anyway, he has money for food." Weiying thought, Did he fall in love with me at the first sight? So, she was a little touched, and said to Chen Dao, "OK. I'll try making friends with him. But I have to let my parents know that first." At this, Chen's family smiled. Then Weiying wrote her address to Chen and asked Shu to come there on Sunday afternoon to let her parents have a look at him. She also asked leave for half a day.

On Sunday Weiying's parents rested at home, Shu Fuhua went there with some fruits and candies. But it seemed that parents did not attach much importance to this matter and took similar attitude to Shu as to other guests. Perhaps Shu thought it uninteresting, he said goodbye to them and rode on his high-quality bicycle. After seeing him off, Weiying returned to ask her parents, "Dad, mom, what do you think of him?" Mother answered, "He doesn't look good in appearance. Maybe he's just rich." Qiu Zhongyuan said, "'A girl will choose a potential talent with merits if she has prospects but will choose a man with wealth if she is not good at making a choice'. But it is you who will spend the rest of your life with your future husband, so you make the decision. We will not force you if you don't like him in you blame us in the future." After these, Qiu Zhongyuan said to wife, "Do you agree?" Shao said, "I take a moderate attitude towards him. Make the decision yourself." Weiying told her parents' opinion to Chen Dao, who said, "As long as your parents do not oppose, there will be no problem." At that time, Weiying was 24 years old.

Shu Fuhua's factory gave him a low-storied apartment with two bedrooms and a kitchen. The doors of these rooms are open to each other. Beside the right corner of the kitchen was a backdoor, near which a public toilet

Used by the staff of the factory was located. A family, with the surname of Liu, of an old couple, their daughter, son and daughter-in-law, lived to the right side of Shu. A piece of hard cement land before he dormitory with several scattered big trees was on a slope of about one meter high. Under the slope was a level ground on one side of which weeds, and woods grew, and the other side was lay by a small path where the staff as well as Weiying would pass when going to the dormitory.

It had not been long since Shu Fuhua and Weiying identified their romantic relationship. One day, Weiying found it still early after dinner, so she took a bus to Shu's dormitory directly. And it happened that Shu also finished his dinner after work. She sat by the desk beside his bed while he on the bedside. He told her, "My parents and me used to live in Singapore, but they broke up due to quarrels when I was young. Later my father took up business and went to Canada and my mother served as a steward at the home of my father's rich friend. I was unhappy with this situation, so I came back China." Then he took out some photo albums from the drawer of the desk. They talked and looked at the photos while it was getting dark. After browsing the last album, she looked at the clock hung on the wall above the desk and said to Shu with surprise, "I have to go, or I won't catch the last bus." Exactly at this moment, Shu stretched out his arms and hugged her out of a sudden, kissing her wildly and passionately… Though realizing it was late, she could not move her feet, let alone stand up. He was just sucking her lips as if he was quite thirsty…

After a fit of dizziness, Weiying cast a glance at the clock and said to him with a tone of shyness, "It is you who made me miss the last bus." Shu unfolded his arms and said in a quiver, "I… don't want you to leave." Weiying sat up, "Then where will I stay tonight?" He answered, "There's a bed in that bedroom. My mother bought it when she came to visit me. Quilts are in the closet, so you can sleep

there." There are several far-off routes on her way back, so it was impossible that she walked back alone. But since Shu had to work the next day and he was reluctant to ask him to send her back. Therefore, she said, "Then only that will do." She locked the door before going to bed and nothing happened during that night. However, she had regarded herself as Shu's girlfriend since then.

Weiying often came to Shu's dormitory since that day. One day off, she went there again. Shu, knowing that she would come, did not go to work yet. Before leaving for work, he opened the door of the closet in his room and took out a pretty and delicate gold watch, "It's brought by my mother from Singapore. She asked me to give it to my future girlfriend." With these words, he passed it to Weiying, who then put it on. She had no idea whether a watch was famous or not, but she was in favor of such an exquisite lady's watch, and in particular its dazzling gold color which made it look noble around her wrist. Shu told her, "The ten boxes in these two rooms are filled with clothes and cloth-like objects that my mother brought me when she returned home, so you can pick whatever you like to wear" After he left, Weiying opened four or five s and was immediately attracted by the beautiful clothes for ladies, children and men, for at that time clothes were quite monotonous both in color and style in China. But the dresses were so pretty that she dared not wear them outside, or people would think she wore stage attire in the street.

The next day off when Weiying came to Shu's house, Shu said, "I'll go to the workshop for a while. If there's nothing to do, I'll be back soon. Weiying said, "Then shall I go to buy some vegetables to cook?" Shu said, "It's troublesome to cook at home and there are meals in the canteen. But if you want to have it at home, you can just cook some rice and there are a lot of canned food under the bed." After he left, Weiying looked at what was under the bed curiously, seeing various tins in a big, opened pack and several other packs beside. Then she walked to the kitchen, only to find an electric rice cooker and a few bowls and pairs of chopsticks. There were few tools for frying or ingredients, so Shu must seldom cook by himself except having some rice and canned food, the latter of which, however, was regarded as something good to eat at that time. Having nothing to do in the kitchen, she looked around and found a sewing machine beside the door. She thought that Shu had said to her, "There's cloth besides clothes in the leather s." Thereby she moved two s onto the bed and opened them. Shu once said, "You can do anything with the clothes." But they were just too beautiful, and she only saw similar coats, trousers and dresses on the stage. She was clear that she must draw people's attention if wearing them in the street, but it was a pity to let them "sleep" in the s. Thereby, she chose two sweaters suitable for her and two pairs of trousers for her mother. And she thought that she could make ordinary clothes out of some pieces of cloth in accordance with tailoring books. Then she took a piece of grey nylon cloth with tiny pink flowers on it, preparing to make a cotton coat. Finally, she saw two largest s lying on the tall closet in Shu's room which she had not seen but she was not interested in getting them down. So, she stood on a higher chair and investigated the s, finding out that they contained Shu's suits and trousers. Jumping down from the chair, she heard someone talking outside.

She opened the door and found Ms. Liu and her daughter-in-law cleaning up vegetables, so she went to talk with them. The young woman said to her, "It's easy for him to find a girlfriend since he's rich. All his girlfriends are pretty." Weiying thought oh, he had several girlfriends already. The woman's mother continued, "His mother says that she has only one son and hopes that he can marry a suitable girl as soon as possible. But he's nearly 30 after all these years. Maybe he's a little eccentric. When his mother came back from Singapore, she brought a lot of stuff in a truck. And she said that she would be back again when he got married. It seems that he likes you very much, so there will be no obstacle for you to get married."

At that moment, Shu walked towards them, asking laughingly, "What are you talking about? It seems so interesting." Weiying responded, "Just talk casually. I can't cook since there are no cooking tools." Shu said walking into the room, "No need to cook. Just boil some noodles and eat canned food." He took out two tins from under the bed. She looked at the date, they were not yet out of date but near. So Shu really didn't know how to arrange his life without a wife. However, Weiying, who was strongly self-esteemed and reserved, would never take the initiative in proposing marriage because in her mind, it was natural that men pursue women, and a woman would suffer herself if she pursued a man who didn't love her. It would be full of misery especially after having children. She had no courage to seek after a man even if he was perfect and rarely seen in the world. Weiying was on normal romantic relationship with Shu Fuhua for three to four months and no twists and turns occurred, no sex.

On the May Day of 1974, both Weiying's factory and Shu Fuhua's gave two days off. Shu accompanied Weiying to Zhuang Ruiying at her dormitory of Changsha Chinese Medicine Factory in Shazitang. Zhuang was her good friend in middle school. Weiying and Zhuang cooked the lunch together while Shu talked with the latter's husband. After lunch, Weiying played a while with Zhuang's daughter Youqian.

Then she and Shu went to Martyr's Park, ate something in a nearby food store, and took a bus to his dormitory finally.

They talked in the room for quite a while till Weiying said, "I'm sleepy." With these words, she walked back to her bedroom, locked the door and went to bed.

A short while after she went to bed, she heard some noise between the room and the other bedroom of Shu. So, she turned around and found Shufu's arms were on the door frame, under the movable window that had been turned up. He was peering at her from above the doorframe, smiling at her and his facial expression appeared somewhat ridiculous from behind the glazing glasses. Smiling back to him, she didn't move and stared at him in a daze. After a while, Shu disappeared from the doorframe, and she unconsciously fell asleep.

The next evening, Shu climbed on to her bed before she locked the door, hugging and kissing her... After a while he sat up, attempting to have sex with her, who, nevertheless, controlled herself calmly, said to him nervously, "No. I'm still in my apprenticeship, so I'll be fired by the factory if I have sex with you before the wedding." Shu laughed, "Are you afraid of having no income?" He still wants to do that, but she avoided him, saying mildly, "We are not married. What will we do if I'm pregnant? So please don't..." (At that time, a woman who had sexual relationship before wedding and got pregnant would be recorded in her archives or even be work unit fired, i.e., she had stained all her life.) Shu laughed, "You are lovely in this way. I won't force you..." He went off the bed and back to his room to sleep, full of unpleasantness. However, after this, he didn't have as much passion to Weiying as before, but she didn't care too much. She, who didn't have enough experience in love, was unable to understand what men thought in this aspect.

One day Weiying went back to her dormitory in the northern region from the galvanized iron sales department in the city proper. Then she went to the sink beside the boiler to wash her face with warm water as usual because she always felt the hydrochloric acid on her face uncomfortable. But to her surprise, the wristwatch that she put under her pillow before washing up had gone. She was totally scared; it had become a custom for her to take off the watch and put it under the pillow before washing up and going to bed. Why had it disappeared today? Her salary rose from 18-yuan last year to 24 this year as an apprentice, which could hardly afford an ordinary watch, let alone one of a precious gold watch. And it was inconvenient for her everyday life. Furthermore, Shu gave it to her, so how could she tell it to him? More anxious, she became more confused, was it stolen on the crowded bus? But she remembered clearly that she saw it while holding onto handrail and didn't found it lost before washing up. She felt muddled, whether it was stolen while getting off bus or from beneath the pillow. But the staff of the factory had gone off work.

Lose one's bearings

At that moment, Chu Fen, her roommate, came in and stared at her, "What's wrong?" She worked in the workshop outside the dormitory and thus it was easy for her to come in and out. Weiying said, "My watch is lost. Have you seen it?" Chu blinked her eyes, "Why should I see it?" Weiying looked for it somewhere else and realized that there was no hope to find it. Then she walked to Chu's side, "It was either squeezed off while I was getting off bus or stolen from under my pillow." Chu Fen said, "That must be when you got off the car. yourself didn't pay attention and it got squeezed dropped!" Weiying looked sad, "Then there is no hope to find it." Chu Fen said, "Nowadays there are many thieves on buses. Where do you expect to find it? I have acquaintances in the thermos factory and heard that Shu's mother is very rich. So just ask her to bring another one famous brand watch from Singapore." Weiying criticized herself, why should she have been so muddled that she could hardly judge whether the watch was stolen from underneath the pillow.

On the next day off when she entered Shu Fuhua's dormitory, she told the whole matter to him. Shu didn't reproach her but just frowned, "Then lost is lost." Impressed by his attitude. Weiying thought he didn't blame me for losing the delicate watch, so he was indeed sincere to me. If he proposed marriage later my apprenticeship ended, I would agree. Nonetheless, she came to such a conclusion too early…!

One day when she was having breakfast at the canteen before going to work in the galvanized iron sales department, she found her purse lost. She felt so strange, the purse was yesterday there when she got on the bus and showed the driver the monthly ticket attached to it. Now, she rummaged her bed and under of pillow, but couldn't find it. She was beginning to doubt her roommate, she poured out all her stuff in her backpack in front of Chu Fen on purpose, murmuring, "It's strange. Why is my purse lost?" But Chu seemed to hear nothing but only glanced at her. She had to look under the bed but found nothing. However, when lifting her head, she saw her purse lying under Chu's bed! She asked her angrily, "Why is my purse under your bed?" The young worker answered, "How do I know? It's you who are too careless." Weiying was about to hit the ceiling, "If I had been too careless, it would have fallen under my bed. How could it turn around to fall under yours bed? Does it have wings?" With this, she walked out in a rage and became more suspicious about who stole her watch.

As time goes by, Weiying felt tiny changes in Shu Fuhua's attitude towards her. On a day off, she went to Shu's dormitory and sat in the chair beside the bed. When she wants to sit close to him who sat on the bedside to kissing her, he avoided her, "Since you don't love me, why do you act like this? If you love me, you will not consider going through the procedure of a marriage certificate!" Weiying knew that he was unhappy with her refusal last time, so she objected with a little bit irony, "Then those who have sex after getting married don't love each. But other while prostitutes have the most favorite, right?" Shu sat onto the middle of the bed and began to smoke. He was a little mad, "That's your view. You always do what you want." He then went to work.

Weiying thought he was different from the usual. After he left, she opened the drawer of the desk in distraction, tidying the stuff while looking at his photo albums which she had not carefully seen last time. Suddenly, an envelope which lay under the right corner jumped to her eyes. The small characters seemed to come from a woman's handwriting and the receiver was Shu Fuhua. Half of the letter was revealed out of the envelope. Seeing "Dear Shu Fuhua" at the lower left corner of the letter prompted Weiying to see the two pieces of paper. She noticed that the date was within the week. And throughout the letter, there were full of sickeningly disgusting words she would never such say to men as well as the time and place to meet next month. Weiying was so unpleasant with this letter! She could not tell whether she was jealous of this woman, but she hated the most to fight for one man with other women. Furthermore, she thought, if a man loved you while falling in love with another woman,

Lose one's bearings

the love between them was not worth existing. Then reminded of Shu's changed attitude towards her, she felt bad about betrayal. She thought his neighbor's words, "Shu Fuhua is rich, and his girlfriends are all pretty." So Weiying decided to find the girl herself---to see how pretty she was and why Shu would fall in love with her. It happened that the address was written on the back of the letter. She put it into her pocket without hesitation, and left Shu's room for the girl's house in Jinggang Town. She came to the ferry terminal of Changsha and took a ship to the town.

The ship started off in a siren and the waves beside it turned into two flows as it accelerated its speed. When the ship was near Jinggang dock, the flows became waves again. Weiying found the house according to the address. The old, wooded gate without being painted stood ajar. Weiying knocked on it several times, but no one answered. Then she patted a little bit harder, and soon a 50-odd-year-old man who was a little humpbacked came out. Holding the letter in hand, she asked politely, "Are you Tu Runzhi's father?" He cast a look at the letter and seemed to realize something, "Yes, what's wrong?" Weiying said, "I'm Shu Fuhua's girlfriend, but I can see from the letter that your daughter is also his girlfriend. So, I just want to see her to understand the development of their relationship. I'll quit if necessary." "OK." He said and let her in. A granny poured a glass of water for her, and Mr. Tu said, "This is my mother. Runzhi's mother has passed away for several years. She is my only daughter and she's now 22. So how old are you?" "She's two years younger than me. She is not home?" "She went to a neighbor's home." "I wonder when your daughter began the romantic relationship with Shu Fuhua." "On May Day last year they met each other through a matchmaker. Since then they had met several times but later, they broke up. It's until recently that they began to correspond." Weiying came to know that they began romantic relationship before she knew Shu. Mr. Tu asked again, "When did you start making friends with Shu?" "At the beginning of this year." "Then you started after that, so you can't

337

blame my daughter." "I don't intend to blame your daughter. Didn't I declare it at first? If I hadn't found the letter, I had no idea that your daughter and Shu Fuhua were lovers…"

At that moment, Tu Runzhi stepped in. Seeing the letter and hearing Weiying's last sentence, she wants to take the letter back. Weiying said to her, "It's no use if you take it back, but it can explain why I will break up with Shu." Mr. Tu was pleased, "That's reasonable. Are you sure you will break up with him?" "Probably, but I have to tell the matchmaker first." After these words, Weiying looked at Tu Runzhi carefully, about 160 centimeters high, she was slim, with two long braids hanging down to her arms. Although she was already 22, she seemed under nutrition and unattractive as she had thought. At the same time, she looked not like a pure girl in disposition, but more like a sophisticated and mild-tempered housewife. Weiying felt it unnecessary to continue sitting there and therefore stood up to say goodbye to them. Tu Runzhi followed her, "I'll see you off." Weiying turned around, "You are good at writing love letters. I can't compose such words and sentences under any circumstances." Tu put on a false smile, "My father teaches me to write them." "Your father cares you so much that he teaches you how to write love letters." "I'm his only daughter, so he's concerned with everything of mine." "I have several brothers and sisters. My parents, especially my father, never ask about my marriage." They reached the bank of the river while talking. Weiying said, "You can go back. Goodbye!" Then she ran into the ship, which left Jinggang dock in a siren. It was getting dark.

When Weiying came back to her dormitory, the sun had totally set down. She opened the big iron gate of the factory with a key. Passing the open space behind the gate and walking into the quiet workshop, she saw the door of her dormitory still locked, so Chu Fen was not in. And apprentices of the dormitory never stayed there on days off, except when she was on night shifts, and it was inconvenient for her to go home. Weiying put down her backpack and lay in bed for a while. Feeling her legs drooping along the bed obstructed in blame my daughter." "I don't intend to blame your daughter. Didn't I declare it at first? If I hadn't found the letter, I had no idea that your daughter and Shu Fuhua were lovers…"

At that moment, Tu Runzhi stepped in. Seeing the letter and hearing Weiying's last sentence, she wants to take the letter back. Weiying said to her, "It's no use if you take it back, but it can explain why I will break up with Shu." Mr. Tu was pleased, "That's reasonable. Are you sure you will break up with him?" "Probably, but I have to tell the matchmaker first." After these words, Weiying looked at Tu Runzhi carefully, about 160 centimeters high, she was slim, with two long braids hanging down to her arms. Although she was already 22, she seemed under nutrition and unattractive as she had thought. At the same time, she looked not like a pure girl in disposition, but more like a sophisticated and mild-tempered housewife. Weiying felt it unnecessary to continue sitting there and therefore stood up to say goodbye to them. Tu Runzhi followed her, "I'll see you off." Weiying turned around, "You are good at writing love letters. I can't compose such words and sentences under any circumstances." Tu put on a false smile, "My father teaches me to write them." "Your father cares you so much that he teaches you how to write love letters." "I'm his only daughter, so he's concerned with everything of mine." "I have several brothers and sisters. My parents, especially my father, never ask about my marriage." They reached the bank of the river while talking. Weiying said, "You can go back. Goodbye!" Then she ran into the ship, which left Jinggang dock in a siren. It was getting dark.

When Weiying came back to her dormitory, the sun had totally set down. She opened the big iron gate of the factory with a key. Passing the open space behind the gate and walking into the quiet workshop, she saw the door of her dormitory still locked, so Chu Fen was not in. And apprentices of the dormitory never stayed there on days off, except when she was on night shifts, and it was inconvenient for her to go home. Weiying put down her backpack and lay in bed for a while. Feeling her legs drooping along the bed obstructed in the love between them was not worth existing. Then reminded of Shu's changed attitude towards her, she felt bad about betrayal. She thought his neighbor's words, "Shu Fuhua is rich, and his girlfriends are all pretty." So Weiying decided to find the girl herself---to see how pretty she was and why Shu would fall in love with her. It happened that the address was written on the back of the letter. She put it into her pocket without hesitation, and left Shu's room for the girl's house in Jinggang Town. She came to the ferry terminal of Changsha and took a ship to the town.

The ship started off in a siren and the waves beside it turned into two flows as it accelerated its speed. When the ship was near Jinggang dock, the flows became waves again. Weiying found the house according to the address. The old, wooded gate without being painted stood ajar. Weiying knocked on it several times, but no one answered. Then she patted a little bit harder, and soon a 50-odd-year-old man who was a little humpbacked came out. Holding the letter in hand, she asked politely, "Are you Tu Runzhi's father?" He cast a look at the letter and seemed to realize something, "Yes, what's wrong?" Weiying said, "I'm Shu Fuhua's girlfriend, but I can see from the letter that your daughter is also his girlfriend. So, I just want to see her to understand the development of their relationship. I'll quit if necessary." "OK." He said and let her in. A granny poured a glass of water for her, and Mr. Tu said, "This is my mother. Runzhi's mother has passed away for several years. She is my only daughter and she's now 22. So how old are you?" "She's two years younger than me. She is not home?" "She went to a neighbor's home." "I wonder when your daughter began the romantic relationship with Shu Fuhua." "On May Day last year they met each other through a matchmaker. Since then they had met several times but later, they broke up. It's until recently that they began to correspond." Weiying came to know that they began romantic relationship before she knew Shu. Mr. Tu asked again, "When did you start making friends with Shu?" "At the beginning of this year." "Then you started after that, so you can't

Lose one's bearings

blood, she climbed up and went to wash her face with cold water. Though it was getting cold at night, her heart was burnt like fire. She felt soberer after washing up. Sitting on the bedside, she again lay in bed with her face up. Lying alone in this cold and cheerless room, she had no one to talk with and to concern about her. At that time, Shu Fuhua who had once loved her so much was totally denied by recent changes and current facts. Her heart that had been almost conquered by him was jumping up and down inside her body. After a moment of meditation, she felt that her romantic relationship with Shu lost its due value.

Suddenly she decided to go to the thermos factory on the next day off and expressed her attitude to Shu Fuhua in front of the matchmaker that she would end her relationship with him since then. After making this decision, she felt much easier and till then she felt hungry as she had not had lunch or dinner. Therefore, she ran to a nearby food store to have a big bowl of rice noodles.

Weiying had not been to Shu Fuhua's dormitory for one whole week. She only went back home after work once and had dinner with her parents. She told them after washing up bowls, "Shu Fuhua has another girlfriend, and I would not like to continue with him." Mother said, "I don't think he is suitable for you, either. 'Love husband and wife bitter also sweet.' He was on terms with another girl when you are not married. But if he does so after you get married, it will be no use also on eat ginseng." Qiu Zhongyuan said, "You're good-looking and you should be on better and better terms with your boyfriend, but why do you always break up with them? What's more, if you have children, your love towards each other will be deeper." Then he turned to wife, "Don't you think so?" mother looked at her daughter and didn't say anything. Afraid that she couldn't catch the bus, Weiying did not explain more to her parents.

On the next day off, Weiying went to the thermos factory with the letter by Tu Runzhi to Shu Fuhua. After greeting the janitor, she walked directly into the repair workshop where Chen Dao the matchmaker worked. It happened that both Chen and Shu were there. Seeing her come in, they looked at each other. Weiying walked towards Chen and said, "I decided to break up with Shu Fuhua because he has another girlfriend. I hate most fighting for a man with other women, so this is the end of our romantic relationship. Please call Shu and your monitor here to witness this for me." Chen called them mildly and they sat together. Then Weiying read the letter word by word and said, "Now that you haven't ended your romantic relationship with her, don't take me as your girlfriend; and when you began making friends with me, you should not have any relation with her. I cannot bear any man having two girlfriends at the same time, so I'd like to break up with you!" With these words, she handed the letter to Shu who put it into his pocket. It seemed that he wanted to explain something but finally didn't say anything. Maybe it wasn't until then that he realized Weiying was sincere to their love, but it was too late. Weiying stood up and Shu followed her to the gate of the factory. She returned to cast a glance at him with a resentful expression, feeling painful in heart. She saw Shu glaring at her through his glasses in a very complicated expression, wondering whether he was regretful or reluctant to let her go or had a mixed feeling of love and hate. After all, for her, he was not worth her love any more. Thereby she walked farther and farther away firmly. Since it was in the afternoon, Weiying could return to her factory after going back home. But after eating something at a nearby food store, she went directly back to the dormitory. She went to bed unhappily after washing up in the bathroom but didn't fall asleep until midnight.

In the evening of one day off, Weiying and Chu Fen returned to the dormitory from outside to sleep. Chu said to her, "Today I went to visit my acquaintance at the thermos factory. He told me that their dean of security department knew Wang Tianliang who told him, "Since you got the residence cards residence permit of city, you changed your mind and broke up with him!' Therefore, Shu Fuhua had a certain view to you." At this, Qiu Weiying heard her say this, and said angrily, "Fart! "Damn it! He once changed his mind when my residence permit was in the village. And I left his home before my residence permit of city is settled. I broke up with Shu because he has another girlfriend at the same time!" She associated it with the fact that Wang Tianliang distorted facts and slandered her. She could barely understand why he didn't examine his own mistake and was unable to stand the test and why he didn't think that she couldn't bear his sister's attitude so that she left his home in a rage before getting a residence cards residence permit. Weiying lay in bed with great grievance and fell asleep.

In her dream, she saw a demon with a mask chasing after her with a bright-colored knife in hand. There were a lot of people around, but they were just standing there, without offering any help. She attempted to escape but her feet were stuck firmly by something. In order to protect herself, she had to stop to pick up a big stone. However, before throwing it to the demon that was holding up the knife over her head, she woke up with a scream. Until then did she know that she came across a demon in a dream....

4.8 True love falls into Xiang Jiang

The factory had several days off when the Spring Festival of 1974 came. Qiu Weiying and her parents stayed at their small home for the New Year's Eve. After that evening, Qiu Zhongyuan began riding to the home of her twin sisters' or his friends and colleagues alone relieve boredom; Juecong stayed at his girlfriend's home; Juele was in Junshan Farm in Yue Shao for several months without coming home for the festival; Shao Guizhen went to Wujiajing every day to accompany Xiaodong and her eldest son; and sometimes Weiying went there to have dinner or chat with them.

The weather was not nice during the Spring Festival in Changsha. It often rained and snowed, and when it stopped raining, some sparrows would shout on barren branches. Their weak sounds reminded Weiying of her childhood. She thought of the much warmer and more interesting atmosphere during the winter when living in Laozhaobi, her mother would always take time to make lovely animals out of flour (She used beans as animals' eyes and tugged salty or sweet filling into their bellies, and then steamed them.) And she would lift a round lantern, cross the sitting room with four doors in each side, and run about through the bedroom and courtyard. When she was extremely happy, she would let go of the lantern, sing and dance, as well as make some funny expressions to the laughter of her parents. Nevertheless, everything became the past. Now, they would not have enough space to put dishes or even sit down if all family members gathered. Under such circumstances, no one was willing to stay in a rented public room, and neither did Weiying want to stay home alone. Thus, she went her friends' or colleagues' home. Naturally, since she lived in the dormitory of the factory, she become a person who acts alone.

On the third day of the Spring Festival, Weiying thought that she should go to visit two families in Beizheng Street because they had always been friendly and welcoming to her. One of them was Chen Dao's family and the other was that of Chen Biyun, a woman worker responsible for producing spares of radios in Wang Tianliang's factory. She met her not long-ago near Chen Dao's house and the latter asked her, "Would you like to go to my home? It's just around the corner." She lived in a two-storey dormitory in a street beside Chen Dao's home, so Weiying followed her to have a look at her home where she met her husband Wen Yinxin who was an overseas Chinese back from a South-east Asian country and now worked in Changsha Hardware Electronic Device Co., Ltd. While talking, Chen Biyun asked, "Don't you have a new boyfriend after breaking up with Wang Tianliang?" "No." Weiying answered. And Wen Yinxin said, "How about I am introducing an overseas Chinese back from Japan?" "I can't decide if I don't see the person." "If you see him, I'm sure that you will like him. He's a classmate of my

Lose one's bearings

friend and was born and grew up in Japan. He may be two years older than you, matching you in both stature and look. "I heard that the Japanese are shorter than our Chinese in stature." "He is not short. He is more than 170 centimeters high. His parents are from Guangdong. So, would you like to meet him?" Finally, Wen told the man through his friend Xiaoliao and made an appointment to let them meet after dinner on the seventh day of the festival at Chen's home. Later when Weiying came to Chen's to pay a New Year call; they welcomed her and to ask her to have dinner together.

According to Chinese tradition, the Lantern Festival was the last day of the Spring Festival, which therefore had not been ended since only a week passed by. The galvanized iron sales department closed door earlier than usual on the seventh day, and Weiying went home to have dinner with parents. She mentioned that someone introduced a boyfriend for her before taking bus and getting down in Zhongshan Street.

People should have started work since that day usually, especially under the guidance of "grab revolution and promoting production", but the Cultural Revolution made them less regulation-abiding than before, worker finished work early and shops by the road closed. It was not so cold as the sun appeared for some time during daytime. So Weiying didn't feel chilly while walking in Beizheng Street by dusk. She came to Chen Biyun's home after taking a turn at a crossroad.

While walking in up to the second floor of the residents' dormitory lightened by weak streetlamps, she found Chen's door ajar and heard the gentle voice of a strange man and a fit of laughter. She stopped there. She is in her heart thinking, He must be the man Mr. Wen intended to introduce for me. She calmed down a little and knocked the door. Hearing Chen shout, "Come in", she pushed the door open slightly and saw a young gentleman sitting inside, with his side facing the door. He turned around and looked at her. She walked in by his side with shyness and sat down in his opposition. Wen Yinxin smiled, "This man is called Lu Gengwei, an overseas

Chinese back from Japan. What do you think of him? Very good, yes?" Chen looked at Lu smilingly and then at Weiying to observe her reaction. Weiying glanced at him rapidly, only to find that he was watching her mildly, so their sights became two parallel lines. She blushed immediately and looked somewhere else in embarrassment. She dared not look at him but lowered her head. But it was such one look that made her clear about Lu's appearance, with dense black hair, he had a rectangular and relatively white face, a pair of black brows under which blinked a pair of big eyes. His broad shoulders made him look muscular, but his behaviors were gentle enough. He was the type of man to Weiying's like. Although she seemed to be listening to them talk, she could not calm down in heart. The room was full of warm atmosphere, and she felt the love god had come to her. For a long while, she only felt excited and shy, without knowing what they were talking about till she heard the clock on the wall ring. She looked up and found it was already half past 10. She stood up at once, "It's time for me to go back, or I'll miss the bus." Win said, "Let Xiaolin accompany you back." Lin Jingji stood up and walked out with Weiying.

At the foot of the stairs, Lu said to her like an acquaintance, "Wait. My bike's here." While walking in Beizheng Street, Lu who was over height one meter seven a few and trust to her. He introduced himself, "I was born in Japan and came back to China at 16. Because I have an older brother attending in Japan the local Communist Party. He was hunted down by the government; my parents brought the whole family back. One of my sisters married an overseas Chinese from Indonesia and they have gone to America; another two brothers have been married, one in Tianjin and the other here in Changsha. I work in Hunan Daily Stuff Factory and live with my parents." And Weiying also introduced briefly her family background. When they reached the bus station at the end of the street, Lu looked at Weiying, "I live near your workplace. Just walk towards Xiangjiang River. I will pass your department when going to and back from work, so you can

Chinese back from Japan. What do you think of him? Very good, yes?" Chen looked at Lu smilingly and then at Weiying to observe her reaction. Weiying glanced at him rapidly, only to find that he was watching her mildly, so their sights became two parallel lines. She blushed immediately and looked somewhere else in embarrassment. She dared not look at him but lowered her head. But it was such one look that made her clear about Lu's appearance, with dense black hair, he had a rectangular and relatively white face, a pair of black brows under which blinked a pair of big eyes. His broad shoulders made him look muscular, but his behaviors were gentle enough. He was the type of man to Weiying's like. Although she seemed to be listening to them talk, she could not calm down in heart. The room was full of warm atmosphere, and she felt the love god had come to her. For a long while, she only felt excited and shy, without knowing what they were talking about till she heard the clock on the wall ring. She looked up and found it was already half past 10. She stood up at once, "It's time for me to go back, or I'll miss the bus." Win said, "Let Xiaolin accompany you back." Lin Jingji stood up and walked out with Weiying.

At the foot of the stairs, Lu said to her like an acquaintance, "Wait. My bike's here." While walking in Beizheng Street, Lu who was over height one meter seven a few and trust to her. He introduced himself, "I was born in Japan and came back to China at 16. Because I have an older brother attending in Japan the local Communist Party. He was hunted down by the government; my parents brought the whole family back. One of my sisters married an overseas Chinese from Indonesia and they have gone to America; another two brothers have been married, one in Tianjin and the other here in Changsha. I work in Hunan Daily Stuff Factory and live with my parents." And Weiying also introduced briefly her family background. When they reached the bus station at the end of the street, Lu looked at Weiying, "I live near your workplace. Just walk towards Xiangjiang River. I will pass your department when going to and back from work, so you can friend and was born and grew up in Japan. He may be two years older than you, matching you in both stature and look. "I heard that the Japanese are shorter than our Chinese in stature." "He is not short. He is more than 170 centimeters high. His parents are from Guangdong. So, would you like to meet him?" Finally, Wen told the man through his friend Xiaoliao and made an appointment to let them meet after dinner on the seventh day of the festival at Chen's home. Later when Weiying came to Chen's to pay a New Year call; they welcomed her and to ask her to have dinner together.

According to Chinese tradition, the Lantern Festival was the last day of the Spring Festival, which therefore had not been ended since only a week passed by. The galvanized iron sales department closed door earlier than usual on the seventh day, and Weiying went home to have dinner with parents. She mentioned that someone introduced a boyfriend for her before taking bus and getting down in Zhongshan Street.

People should have started work since that day usually, especially under the guidance of "grab revolution and promoting production", but the Cultural Revolution made them less regulation-abiding than before, worker finished work early and shops by the road closed. It was not so cold as the sun appeared for some time during daytime. So Weiying didn't feel chilly while walking in Beizheng Street by dusk. She came to Chen Biyun's home after taking a turn at a crossroad.

While walking in up to the second floor of the residents' dormitory lightened by weak streetlamps, she found Chen's door ajar and heard the gentle voice of a strange man and a fit of laughter. She stopped there. She is in her heart thinking, He must be the man Mr. Wen intended to introduce for me. She calmed down a little and knocked the door. Hearing Chen shout, "Come in", she pushed the door open slightly and saw a young gentleman sitting inside, with his side facing the door. He turned around and looked at her. She walked in by his side with shyness and sat down in his opposition. Wen Yinxin smiled, "This man is called Lu Gengwei, an overseas

Lose one's bearings

go to my home when free." Weiying nodded smilingly. Therefore, Lu wrote her his address after leaning his bicycle on a lamp pole.

When arriving at the post office in Zhongshan Street, Weiying said, "I have to cross the road to take a bus back to the dormitory." She didn't mention to him something about the confiscation of family property of her family's properties and the occupation of her family's private house of more than 200 square meters which was just located in the lane opposite to the office, for it would only make her sad besides feel sorry for her parents' being wrongly treated.

At that moment, Lu said to her like an old friend, "Sit on the back seat of my bike and I'll ride you there." Without saying more, she agreed. This was the first time she sat on the backseat of a man's bike, so she, who was a little conservative, dare not move closer to his body but kept some distance from him. But Lu said, "Sit closer in you'll fall off." At this, she laughed and sat closer to him.

When they arrived at the gate of Changsha Auto Factory which was near the crossroad of Hunan Silk Factory, Weiying said, "Please stop. My dormitory is just across the Silk Factory." Lu stopped immediately and she jumped down briskly. When she walked towards him, Lu stretched out his hand, "Let's shake hands." Weiying said with shyness, "What's that for?" Lu burst into laughter, "You are embarrassed to shake hands, what will you do if I kiss you?" At this, she walked towards the direction where her dormitory was located with her face blushing and her heart beating. Lu shouted behind her, "When will you come to my home, Weiying?" Looking back at him, she still replied with a heartbeat, "Tomorrow after get off work and after dinner." In the dim lamp light, she saw Lu's smile which seemed to indicate you are so shy and so feudal!

Back to her dormitory, Weiying went to the sink to wash face and brush teeth and to the bathroom to have a shower before going to bed immediately. She fell asleep soon and dreamed that she entered a colorful garden with a bright-colored guitar. She was so pleased while singing and dancing with the guitar which was glistening under the sunshine. To the direction of the sun, she stood on her tiptoes and rotated around like an actress in a ballet play of the Soviet Union, which she liked very much. Suddenly a gust of storm came with the sky becoming dark. It turned out that she was almost involved in a cyclone that made her rotate faster and faster so that she couldn't stop. Her feet began to cramp, and tiptoes ached. She was rolled up by the cyclone, feeling very dizzy, and finally dropped on the ground heavily, losing consciousness. When she opened her eyes again, she found herself in a dream…

After work the next day, she had dinner at the usual place before going to Lu Gengwei's home. She found the dormitory which belonged to his father's institution easily according to the address. It was near the bank of Xiangjiang River and just several minutes' walk from her workplace. Entering the gate, she was in an empty rectangular courtyard where she asked a woman who was walking out for her house and the latter pointed to a door on the right side. When she walked into the door, Lu and his parents were having dinner beside a square table. Seeing Weiying come, Lu ate the rest food in his bowl quickly and said smilingly, "You had dinner so early." Weiying answered, "After get off work, I ate in a company dining hall near my work, I don't need to cook." "Come here to have dinner from now on." "No, that will bother your mother." "My mother has to cook anyway, and four people just fit the table." His mother smiled gently when hearing that. His father was a man of few words. Lu was almost as high as his father but looked stronger, for he had broad shoulders like a gymnast. His handsome face took on a gentle expression when he smiled. This was the second man who Weiying thought was outstanding in both appearance and disposition after Junjun. Her feeling of love developed faster because this time the boy was introduced formally by a friend. What was more; she was not 18-year-old girl six or seven years ago; she is now a woman at the age of 25. She felt firmly that Lu fell in love with her at the first sight and so did she. When Lu's mother stood up after dinner, she, with a stature of over 170 centimeters high, looked even taller than his father. She looked a little like a Russian and Lin Jingji like both his parents. After cleaning up the table, he made a cup of tea for Weiying, who sat down for a while after taking the tea. Then Lu said to her, "Shall we take a walk to the Xiangjiang River?" Weiying agreed and stood up. Saying goodbye to his parents, they walked towards the riverbank.

It was a sunny February day. Scattered stars hang in the sky, the changes of which were unpredictable, twinkling to the young couple who were immersed in the ocean of love instead of observing the surrounding environment. When they reached the end of the bridge, they found the piers underneath became short dry tunnels because the riverbed had been dry. Lu proposed out of a sudden, "Shall we take a walk under the bridge?" Weiying agreed at once. But when they walked to the piers, she stopped involuntarily as she could see nothing in the darkness. Lu lowered his head to ask her slightly, "Are you afraid?" Weiying looked far into the distance across the piers and saw indistinct streetlamp light by the riverbank as well as passers and scenes. She involuntarily one arm inserted in his arms and said softly, "I'm not afraid now that you are here. But I dare not walk here alone."

Later Lu unfolded his arms and put them around Weiying's head, kissing her wildly. Leaning on the pier so as not to fall, she put her hands on his shoulders without any intention of resistance. Though she looked calm but had a feeling of addicted intoxication. Lu said, "Oh, it's comfortable" and continued kissing her... Weiying seemed to get an electric shock which spread throughout her body quickly... After a while, Lu stood straight and held her up by the way. Then he held her hand to walk out of the piers. They got to the surface of the road after taking a left turn and walking up a slope. They felt a burst of soft wind while strolling on the pavement, sobering Weiying up from a "drunken" state.

Suddenly she felt so shy as not to lift her head while walking. She just heard Lu say at her ears, "I love you so much! If you have a change of your heart, I'll jump into the Xiangjiang river." Though she didn't say anything, but she said in her heart, I loved you too. Why could I change of my heart? Reserved Weiying would be reluctant to express her wonderful feelings for love under any circumstance.

She has no courage to praise each other's strengths, which she thought was an unsuitable behavior to please men. In her view, for women, true love was implicative and hard to describe in words because it originated from the bottom of heart. Therefore, a man was likely to misunderstand her; he might think that she was just a woman loved by him but didn't take him seriously. When they were in peaceful romantic relationship, a man would not have such a wrongful judgment. But once there was interference from the outside, twists and turns and even breakups might occur.

The cold spring passed, and they became passionate lovers in just three months. Before the May Day, Lin Jingji said to Weiying, "Shall we go to Yuelu Mountain during the May Day festival?" She agreed with pleasure. That morning Weiying had some sweet wine and two fried pancakes nearby and took a bus to a station near Lu's home. Lu was waiting for her after breakfast and saw her enter the door with a smile. They said goodbye to his parents and started off. Looking at each other, the old couple saw them walk off smilingly.

The lovers went on a bus at the end of Xiangjiang River Bridge and soon arrived at Rongwanzhen---the foot of Yuelu Mountain. At that time, the sun appeared through clouds, hanging high in the sky as clear as a blue ocean and giving off dazzling light. The two hearts began to fly even before they climbed the mountain. They wished to fly to the summit at once to enjoy the great nature. When they climbed to Aiwan Pavilion by the road built of cement and stones, the sun gave off bright light under which green and luxuriant trees were full of the fascinating atmosphere of nature. Birds flew about and sang briskly on the treetops. Brooks nearby flowed like a melody without sound. Weiying and Lin Jingji stopped for a while and then climbed to the summit via a narrow path. They had intended

Lose one's bearings

to go the summit, but Weiying wanted to have a rest because the road was difficult for people to walk on. Later Lu held her hand and they walked off the path to a relatively broad area on the top of the mountain. Then they went to the tomb of Huang Xing and visited the motto on it (Huang Xing from Hunan, was a democratic revolutionary who had studied in Japan and once been an assistant to Sun Yat- Sen's.) While standing on the stone steps surrounding the tomb, Lu suddenly turned around and began to kiss Weiying…

After one minute, Weiying, who was not superstitious, was occupied by a sense of fear, would that mean our love would be ruined and buried in a tomb? She was immediately moved her feet from the stone steps of the tomb with anxiety. She walked down, stepped on the grass next to her, and left Lu Gengwei's kiss. So, Lin Jingji glanced at Qiu Weiying at a loss. At this moment, Qiu Weiying's heart was tumbling!

She thought of an article in a magazine, Li Xiao long, the famous Chinese Kung Fu star who was prestigious in the U.S. once took a photo on a tomb at about 24 years old; later he regretted as he predicted that he would not live a long life. Because he stooked pictures on the grave. On July 20, 1973, he suddenly died when he was 32 years old! At that time, he was at the home of actress Ding Pei, discussing the script for filming the movie "Game of Death". Tens of thousands of people in Hong Kong saw him off but no one could make out the reason why he died suddenly!

Now Weiying also had an inauspicious prediction that her romantic relationship with Lu would encounter something unfortunate. When they left Huang Xing's tomb, she had no intention to climb to the summit and said to Lu with a bit of anxiety, "Shall we go back? Since the beginning of the Cultural Revolution, temples have been regarded as feudal, capitalist and revisionist symbol and thus they've been smashed or closed. There may be nothing beautiful on the top." Lu glanced at her, and they went down without saying more. At that time the sun disappeared into clouds and the sky became dark though it was not too late…

Qiu Weiying and Lin Jingji together, after have dinner at Lu's home, he rides a bicycle send her back to the factory. Lu said, "Would you like to sit on the front of the bike?" "The front? It's embarrassing if others see us. What's more, if we two fell on the road when I obstructed your sight, we'll be laughed at." Lu smiled and said nothing. Sitting on the backseat, Weiying said, "tell you a story. A couple once were riding a bicycle and the woman on the backseat said to the man, "When we were in romance, you asked me to sit on the front row, but when we get married, you ask me to sit on the backseat, and when we have a child, you will throw me onto the ground'…" Hearing this, Lu smiled, "You made up this story, didn't you? When you give birth to a child, I'll not throw you onto the ground but will attach more love to you." Weiying felt so sweet in heart at his words. In a while they reached the dormitory of the factory. It was quiet there and she looked at Lu leaving quickly after they kissed each other passionately.

Lin Jingji worked on three shifts at that Factory. He must work the night shift this week, work from 12 o'clock in the evening to the next morning. So Weiying went back home instead of going to Lu's after work that day also because she hadn't been home for two weeks. After having dinner and cleaning up the table, she went back to the factory. While she was passing a workshop, a woman worker told her, "Qiu Weiying, your friend came here to see you over two hours ago when I was engaged in auto spares. So, he didn't bother me and went to the dormitory directly. When not seeing you there, he seemed soulless and went to the dining hall to look for you. Your boyfriend looked handsome, like Miura Tomeka, the husband of the famous Japanese star Momoe Yamaguchi. It seemed that he is deeply loving you!"

Weiying felt comfortable at what she said, Lu's appearance, disposition and behaviors really satisfy her, and she loved him deep in her heart! The next day was a day off, and Weiying went to Lu's home after breakfast at the usual place. After getting off bus, she entered

Qiu Weiying and Lin Jingji together, after have dinner at Lu's home, he rides a bicycle send her back to the factory. Lu said, "Would you like to sit on the front of the bike?" "The front? It's embarrassing if others see us. What's more, if we two fell on the road when I obstructed your sight, we'll be laughed at." Lu smiled and said nothing. Sitting on the backseat, Weiying said, "tell you a story. A couple once were riding a bicycle and the woman on the backseat said to the man, "When we were in romance, you asked me to sit on the front row, but when we get married, you ask me to sit on the backseat, and when we have a child, you will throw me onto the ground'…" Hearing this, Lu smiled, "You made up this story, didn't you? When you give birth to a child, I'll not throw you onto the ground but will attach more love to you." Weiying felt so sweet in heart at his words. In a while they reached the dormitory of the factory. It was quiet there and she looked at Lu leaving quickly after they kissed each other passionately.

Lin Jingji worked on three shifts at that Factory. He must work the night shift this week, work from 12 o'clock in the evening to the next morning. So Weiying went back home instead of going to Lu's after work that day also because she hadn't been home for two weeks. After having dinner and cleaning up the table, she went back to the factory. While she was passing a workshop, a woman worker told her, "Qiu Weiying, your friend came here to see you over two hours ago when I was engaged in auto spares. So, he didn't bother me and went to the dormitory directly. When not seeing you there, he seemed soulless and went to the dining hall to look for you. Your boyfriend looked handsome, like Miura Tomeka, the husband of the famous Japanese star Momoe Yamaguchi. It seemed that he is deeply loving you!"

Weiying felt comfortable at what she said, Lu's appearance, disposition and behaviors really satisfy her, and she loved him deep in her heart! The next day was a day off, and Weiying went to Lu's home after breakfast at the usual place. After getting off bus, she entered to go the summit, but Weiying wanted to have a rest because the road was difficult for people to walk on. Later Lu held her hand and they walked off the path to a relatively broad area on the top of the mountain. Then they went to the tomb of Huang Xing and visited the motto on it (Huang Xing from Hunan, was a democratic revolutionary who had studied in Japan and once been an assistant to Sun Yat- Sen's.) While standing on the stone steps surrounding the tomb, Lu suddenly turned around and began to kiss Weiying...

After one minute, Weiying, who was not superstitious, was occupied by a sense of fear, would that mean our love would be ruined and buried in a tomb? She was immediately moved her feet from the stone steps of the tomb with anxiety. She walked down, stepped on the grass next to her, and left Lu Gengwei's kiss. So, Lin Jingji glanced at Qiu Weiying at a loss. At this moment, Qiu Weiying's heart was tumbling!

She thought of an article in a magazine, Li Xiao long, the famous Chinese Kung Fu star who was prestigious in the U.S. once took a photo on a tomb at about 24 years old; later he regretted as he predicted that he would not live a long life. Because he stooked pictures on the grave. On July 20, 1973, he suddenly died when he was 32 years old! At that time, he was at the home of actress Ding Pei, discussing the script for filming the movie "Game of Death". Tens of thousands of people in Hong Kong saw him off but no one could make out the reason why he died suddenly!

Now Weiying also had an inauspicious prediction that her romantic relationship with Lu would encounter something unfortunate. When they left Huang Xing's tomb, she had no intention to climb to the summit and said to Lu with a bit of anxiety, "Shall we go back? Since the beginning of the Cultural Revolution, temples have been regarded as feudal, capitalist and revisionist symbol and thus they've been smashed or closed. There may be nothing beautiful on the top." Lu glanced at her, and they went down without saying more. At that time the sun disappeared into clouds and the sky became dark though it was not too late...

directly the door of his house. And Lu said to her immediately, "We've been in touch for several months, but I haven't seen your parents yet. I'll go to work at 12 at night this Sunday, so shall we go to see your parents during daytime since they'll rest at home?" Weiying thought now that they had identified their relationship, they should let her parents know, so she agreed with pleasure at once.

Though it was hot, there had been a shower during last night. So, it was not that hot, and the air was quite fresh. Asking leave for one day, Weiying led Lin Jingji to her home. Qiu Zhongyuan proposed after having lunch together, "Shall we go to Tianxin Pavilion for a walk?" Shao Guizhen continued, "It will be nice to have a walk there in such good weather, but I have a bellyache." "This is because you have never done any exercises and so are easy to get sick. How about I am bringing you there on the bike?" Qiu Zhongyuan said. They walked out of the door and Shao sat on the backseat of the bicycle. As it was an upper slope, Qiu pushed the bike for a while. At that moment, Lu said to Weiying, "I should learn from father. Will you sit on the backseat and let me push you?" Looking at him, Weiying said, "I haven't got a bellyache! I'll be embarrassed to sit there." They looked at each other and smiled simultaneously.

Tianxin Pavilion was a park built in old China and might be the second highest place in Changsha except Yuelu Mountain.

It was reputed that its ancient walls were built during the Taiping Heavenly Kingdom period. Inside the ancient city wall, there was a piece of quiet low open land, surrounding which there were several caves built up of bricks and some old cannons were put there. The Park also had some ancient architectures and pavilions with carved dragons and phoenix. In addition, there were flat and broad roads as well as narrow paths. Therefore, it became a favorable spot for Changsha people to do morning exercises, have afternoon tea and chat together. Weiying's father often went here to do Taiji and talk with others. The four of them went back home to have dinner and Shao boiled porridge, fried pancakes with onion, peeled some Songhua dan (process of eggs) and cooked several dishes. After dinner, Weiying and Lin Jingji said goodbye to her parents and left.

Out of the door, Lu, pushing his bicycle, smiled to Weiying, "Porridge saves food." Weiying didn't care, "Not on save food. My parents are used to have some porridge and flour food cook whether they had money or not." Then she walked and thought, "They did not consider saving food when we were in hard life. Our family has never rationed eaten and hungry."

However, Weiying had never told Lu that her family been a wealthy life at earlier times. Her family had a big house and that her father had earned a much higher salary than others. Furthermore, her home after an overnight "pillaged", have become as poor as a toiling mass! Furthermore, her family had been in utter destitution after that night not only of confiscation of family property. Moreover, the real estate certificate was taken away and the house was also taking by forced. So, that the members of this big family are not now living together. Now we were really like a poor family because we had just one room to live in, although both parents are doctors.

She thought boasting of these to her boyfriend would only reduce the real meaning of love. Young lovers should seek for the truth of love instead of the conditions added to love. Though one's family was quite wealthy, he would spend all if he was good for nothing, while though a family was very poor, he would top other people if he made great efforts.

At the crossroad of Sizzling and Liuchengqiao, Lu said to Weiying, "sit onto the bike. I have to take the night work up shift." At this time, Weiying jumped onto the backseat. The two sits of the same bicycle, when approaching the park, Lu decelerated to let her get down and they stood under a big tree beside the road and its there stood several scattered trees around, which were swaying in the dim streetlamp light and the night breeze. Lu, while holding the bicycle with one hand, touched Weiying's face with the other. Reserved Weiying said with a blushing face, "It's not good if pedestrians see us like this." Lu stopped with a smile and said with a tone of slight criticism, "You are my friend, so what's the matter?" Weiying said, "Then can we get married on the road?" "I'll not argue with you since I'm going to work." He riding a bicycle leave with smile.

On a day off in Weiying's factory, Lu was doing night shift that day. Daytime Qiu Weiying came to his home. He said, "Shall we take a walk to Wuyi Road?" She followed him without consideration. At Wuyi Road, he pointed to a company store and told her, "My father retired from this corporation." She said, "The nominally adoptive father of my twin sisters also retired from this company." "Do your sisters have a nominally adoptive father?" "It was when they were young, and my mother had work and didn't have time to stay home with them. The husband of the godmother who put them in foster care and took them." When she finished these words, Lu touched her shoulder with his arm, "Have you noticed that many people are watching us when we walk together?" She looked around and found it seemed so. Therefore, she smiled happily. But if a man watched her when Lu was not by her side, she would think that man was not decent person and would look down upon at him. After dinner at Lu's home, he rode her back to her dormitory.

There were few people in the factory on the day off. When they entered the dormitory, Weiying put her backpack in the corner of the bed and Lin Jingji closed the door naturally. He walked to her, held her head and kissed her. Then they fell in bed together. At this time, he hugged her and put her beneath his body as if she was a sheep, beginning to kiss her wildly...She felt burnt beneath his and strong arms, and his passionate kiss intoxicated her like a fit of electric flow spread through her whole body and heart. After a while, Lu held up his head and touched her body slightly, murmuring in a tone of pleading while looking at her face, "Let's have each other! Let me…" At that time, Weiying felt completely burnt down so that she was unable to refuse his requirement. She, at the age of 25, was also attracted by this…. Showing a shy smile, she looked at his eyes twinkling because of love, saying softly, "Shall we hold the wedding soon?" Lu nodded. She pushed him slightly and they stood up almost at the same time as they both wore clothes. She totally believed his promise to get married.

But when they were putting off clothes, Weiying suddenly heard "pa" of a door in the big wooden gate of the workshop nearby. Therefore, her desire for sex was put down by a basin of cold water. She calmed down and said to Lu calmly, "My roommate is back. We can't do it." Lu must also have heard that, so he said nothing but stared at her, who immediately opened the door. Looking outside, she found it was the vice director of the factory walking through the workshop with a lowered head. Normally, the vice director should have felt that she had opened the door, but he pretended not to notice and walked towards the office. When he took a turn, Weiying closed the door and said to Lu, "It was the vice director. But I don't know why he came here tonight. He may come from the boiler workshop. He must have seen your bicycle. But I think my roommate is coming back." In an instant, the fire of desire that was beginning to burn was doused by a shower of cold water that rained down on her head. By then, they had no desire anymore. It was late and she saw him off at the gate of the factory. She saw his back gradually disappearing into the darkness of the night.

On another day off, Weiying went to Lu Gengwei's home again. Lu smiled to her, "Shall we take a photo and send it to my elder sister? She wanted to see our picture. She has jewelry stores in America and Venezuela and hopes that we can go to America to help her with the business after we get married." Weiying agreed and told him, "The Oriental Photo Studio is opposite to Xingsha Food Store, where I took a photo at my birthday. It's clear." Therefore, they went there. While the photographer was adjusting the light, several acquaintances of Lu, whom Weiying had never seen, came in suddenly. They pulled Lu away to talk and laugh like discovering a new continent, embarrassing Weiying. So, she smiled unnaturally when sitting down and facing the strangers and the flash lamp. After that, Weiying felt a little uneasy, but she should have felt happy because she was in passionate love.

Weiying went to the photo studio directly after lunch to fetch the photo on the designed day. When she came back to her department, her colleagues were just beginning to work. One of them asked, "Where did you go?" "I went to fetch a photo." Then a woman worker whose surname was Fang said at once, "Let's have a look at it." So Weiying had to pass the photo onto them. Fang held up the photo and stared at it for quite a while, "Oh, it's lovely. You are born to be a couple. Is this your wedding photo?" Weiying said indifferently, "How could it be the wedding photo? It's what my boyfriend intends to send to his elder sister." Another woman worker leaned to the photo and complemented it, "It could be a wedding photo." With no reason to argue, Weiying took it back and put it into her backpack.

After work, she walked to Lu's home, "I have fetched the photo. It's not very good." Lu looked at it and said, "Why isn't it good?" Looking at it carefully, she found that although Lu was leaning close to her physically, but he looked to another direction, while she investigated the front. The photo is a little be seemingly in agreement, but at odds. Because they didn't focus one's attention on the same direction. But she did not tell out her opinion as she was worried that he would misunderstand her. Thus, she gave the two photos to him.

Weiying often had dinner at Lu's home and sometimes she brought some dried meat or vegetables there, when, however, Lu would say, "There's no need for you to buy vegetables. My mother knows what to buy, so it doesn't matter that you come here directly to have dinner." She said, "You mother has a lot to do at home, so I can bring some food."

One noon, she thought that Lu's parents stayed home all day without walking out relieve boredom. So, she bought two film tickets that evening at the nearby Xinhua Cinema after lunch. Before dinner, she gave them to Lu's parents, who left happily for the cinema.

When his parents left home afterwards, Lu smiled and said with jocosity, "You are so smart that you know how to make my parents leave with two film tickets." Weiying pounded his back and objected, "I haven't thought of that! I just think that I create trouble for your mother for usually having dinner here, so I just want to express my thanks." Lu's family lived in his father's dormitory, and they had just one room, which was relatively large. His parents' bed was put by the left-side wall and his the upper-left hand opposite to the door. An L-shaped curtain was hung to separate the two spaces. A desk was put horizontally beside the head of his bed and the only window of the room was above this table so that the room was not very dark during daytime. Lu was then sitting on his bed and Weiying in the chair beside the desk. She leaned towards him slightly, "My brother will get married at the National Day and he will live in her wife's home. He invited us to attend his wedding. What do you think of it?" Lu agreed smilingly, "It's a pity that we don't own a house so that we can't get married. But my parents said that if we're getting married, they can live in my brother's house in Tianjin." Weiying didn't express her opinion on this because she thought it would be a little cruel for his parents. Lu didn't continue with topic. She thought regretfully that if our private house had not been confiscated, we could have one room after the wedding of my family!

After a while of silence, Lu said softly while patting his thigh, "Come to sit here." She said, "I don't know when the film will end. It will be embarrassing if your parents come back and see us like that!" Lu stood up, pull up the bed curtain, and grasped her by the arm. She was ignited by the fire of love immediately and therefore sat on his thighs abidingly. When she leaned in his warm hug, he lowered his head to look at her and began kissing her. While rubbing his hands on her round breasts and feeling her smooth skin…he murmured, "You've got beautiful skin. I'll kiss you all over on our wedding day!" Weiying thought he said this just to prove someone's words, so she felt doubtful. However, she had totally lost herself as a kind of desire occupied her whole body. She felt a little nervous but also kind of

When his parents left home afterwards, Lu smiled and said with jocosity, "You are so smart that you know how to make my parents leave with two film tickets." Weiying pounded his back and objected, "I haven't thought of that! I just think that I create trouble for your mother for usually having dinner here, so I just want to express my thanks." Lu's family lived in his father's dormitory, and they had just one room, which was relatively large. His parents' bed was put by the left-side wall and his the upper-left hand opposite to the door. An L-shaped curtain was hung to separate the two spaces. A desk was put horizontally beside the head of his bed and the only window of the room was above this table so that the room was not very dark during daytime. Lu was then sitting on his bed and Weiying in the chair beside the desk. She leaned towards him slightly, "My brother will get married at the National Day and he will live in her wife's home. He invited us to attend his wedding. What do you think of it?" Lu agreed smilingly, "It's a pity that we don't own a house so that we can't get married. But my parents said that if we're getting married, they can live in my brother's house in Tianjin." Weiying didn't express her opinion on this because she thought it would be a little cruel for his parents. Lu didn't continue with topic. She thought regretfully that if our private house had not been confiscated, we could have one room after the wedding of my family!

After a while of silence, Lu said softly while patting his thigh, "Come to sit here." She said, "I don't know when the film will end. It will be embarrassing if your parents come back and see us like that!" Lu stood up, pull up the bed curtain, and grasped her by the arm. She was ignited by the fire of love immediately and therefore sat on his thighs abidingly. When she leaned in his warm hug, he lowered his head to look at her and began kissing her. While rubbing his hands on her round breasts and feeling her smooth skin…he murmured, "You've got beautiful skin. I'll kiss you all over on our wedding day!" Weiying thought he said this just to prove someone's words, so she felt doubtful. However, she had totally lost herself as a kind of desire occupied her whole body. She felt a little nervous but also kind of that, Weiying felt a little uneasy, but she should have felt happy because she was in passionate love.

Weiying went to the photo studio directly after lunch to fetch the photo on the designed day. When she came back to her department, her colleagues were just beginning to work. One of them asked, "Where did you go?" "I went to fetch a photo." Then a woman worker whose surname was Fang said at once, "Let's have a look at it." So Weiying had to pass the photo onto them. Fang held up the photo and stared at it for quite a while, "Oh, it's lovely. You are born to be a couple. Is this your wedding photo?" Weiying said indifferently, "How could it be the wedding photo? It's what my boyfriend intends to send to his elder sister." Another woman worker leaned to the photo and complemented it, "It could be a wedding photo." With no reason to argue, Weiying took it back and put it into her backpack.

After work, she walked to Lu's home, "I have fetched the photo. It's not very good." Lu looked at it and said, "Why isn't it good?" Looking at it carefully, she found that although Lu was leaning close to her physically, but he looked to another direction, while she investigated the front. The photo is a little be seemingly in agreement, but at odds. Because they didn't focus one's attention on the same direction. But she did not tell out her opinion as she was worried that he would misunderstand her. Thus, she gave the two photos to him.

Weiying often had dinner at Lu's home and sometimes she brought some dried meat or vegetables there, when, however, Lu would say, "There's no need for you to buy vegetables. My mother knows what to buy, so it doesn't matter that you come here directly to have dinner." She said, "You mother has a lot to do at home, so I can bring some food."

One noon, she thought that Lu's parents stayed home all day without walking out relieve boredom. So, she bought two film tickets that evening at the nearby Xinhua Cinema after lunch. Before dinner, she gave them to Lu's parents, who left happily for the cinema.

pleasure and yearning. At this moment, Lu said with great passion, "Take off clothes and get in bed. I can't stand it!" She stood up and took off her underwear and bra which had been loosened already while he took off his shirt quickly and opened his arms, "Come. Lie on me." They didn't take off their underpants but hugged each other tightly without noticing the time. They were just enjoying the moment of love…Later he put her under his body, with his hands touching her skin and his tongue kissing around her lips, making her feel befuddled. Her heart was completely conquered by him, and she was reluctant to part his love. Nonetheless, Lu lifted his head suddenly and stared at her face, seeming to meditate on something. So, she became not as passionate as before, smiling, "How about us getting up? Your parents may be home soon." Without saying anything, Lu sat up and put on his clothes.

Soon his parents came back. Weiying asked his mother, "Is the film interesting?" She answered happily, "Yes." Then Weiying said to Lu, "I have to go back to the factory." But he said in front of his parents, "It's too late and it seems to rain soon. So just sleep here with me." She was made laugh by his words, asking, "How could we do that since there's only one room?" He said seriously, "Why not? We can sleep opposite to each other without taking off clothes." She thought it would be impossible to sleep in one bed, but she did not say it out of embarrassment. So, she said, "Send me back, OK?" Lu nodded and took an umbrella for her. It was raining outside, so Weiying opened the umbrella and jumped onto the backseat. On the way there, it was raining harder and harder, making her wonder whether she was so strict because Lu had to go back on the way back alone without an umbrella.

The rain became lighter after about 20 minutes. She got off the bike and opened the door in the big gate with a key while Lu stopped his bike on the roadside and followed her into the factory, saying, "I'm reluctant to leave you!" She hugged him by the neck and welcomed his kiss. They clung to each other, making her feel shy and have an untold feeling so that she began to glide down. Lu felt this and asked with laugh, "I like you hugging my neck and kissing me, but why are you gliding down? Don't fall onto the ground!" With this, he walked out and rode on his bike, disappearing into the dark night.

On Juecong's wedding day, the dinner was held in an ordinary restaurant in Beizheng Street where Chen's family lived. Towards the end of the dinner, Lu didn't want to stay long, so he said to Weiying, "Shall we go?" Weiying stood up and walked to the outside. Passing a food store, Lu went in to buy some candies until when Weiying realized that he might hope to bring something for his parents so that he bought some candies back with his own money. According to customs, the bride and gloom should give each guest some candies, just to show joyfulness and extend thanks. It was the first time for her to attend such a wedding, so she didn't think of the general rules. Later her twin sisters told her, "Sister, when you stood up and followed Lin Jingji to the gate, the guests appreciated you so much. They acclaimed 'You are born to be a couple.' Now brother is married, what about you?" Reserved Weiying answered, "All marriages are proposed by men, which abides by the historical trend. If a man loves you, he will make a proposal, but if not, you can hardly maintain permanent happiness even though you require him to marry you. I'll listen to Lu Gengwei's arrangement since he should be clearer about when to get married. And I'll not take the initiative. What's more, we didn't have a house now, so how can we get married?"

Juecong's wedding was drawing near, so Lin Jingji bought a blanket and a clock with his parents' help, and together with Weiying sent them to the home of Juecong and his girlfriend. At the time when the material life was still not very rich, it's very polite to give such a gift.

Though Juecong learnt medicine from his parents, he didn't get a job in the hospital because of his family background. When national policies became easier after he had been married for two years, he began working as a doctor at Changsha Paper-making Factory. But rural areas were lacking in medicine and relevant treatment at that time, so he often went there to cure diseases. Moreover, his wife was good at making clothes, so it was not hard for them to make a living. Meanwhile, his wife's father used to be a General of Kuomintang before liberation and once studied in America. As he launches a revolt and surrendered to the Communist Party, he became a democrat after liberation. Thereby he was not so much affected by movements. He had a private house so that Juecong could live with them.

During that period, Chu Fen, Weiying's roommate, often told her rumors she heard at the thermos factory. She said that her acquaintances worked at Shu Fuhua's factory. In the evening of the day off, lying in bed opposite to Weiying, Chu Fen said, "The dean of the security department of that factory knows Wang Tianliang because his relative works in the factory Wang's. Wang said that you had been engaged with him and had already lived in his home, but when you got the urban household residence permit later, you changed your mind and lifted him." Weiying was disgusted at this, "What a ridicule it is! When was I engaged to him? And what gift he brought to me? I lived at his home because special circumstances occurred, and his parents let me live there. He worked in the city and lived in his factory. His parents lived in the village, and they said that it did not matter if I lived there as he was not there. When my household residence permit, was in village, I had broken up with him." Chu continued, "Someone in Shu's glasses (His alias) said before him, 'You deceived Wang Tianliang and left with money.' Shu did not say anything and went away with a laugh." At this, Weiying was quite angry, "I deceived his money? I haven't taken anything from him. In doing so, he did not mean default it?" Chu Fen agreed, "Of course." Weiying was in such indignation that she would rather jump out of bed and ran to the thermos factory to argue with him and reveal the truth for everyone.

When she said this, Qiu Weiying was tremble with rage and said, "What did I deceive of him? He himself gave me the watch over which I cried later for losing it, and he asked me to take at random clothes and cloth from the 10-chests his mother brought for him, but I took only a few. I'll throw total them back to him on tomorrow off."

When it came to the day off, Weiying found out the two bright-colored wool sweaters out of her. Although she had worn them and liked them very much, she thought of her mother's words, "People are poor and have high aspirations are not poor!" Thus, she tugged them into a bag. Then she took a bus home and found the two pairs of trousers which belonged to Shu Fuhua and later she brought to her mother. But she found only one pair and the other might be worn by her mother to work, and it was impossible for her to go to the hospital to ask her mother to take it off. So, she put this pair trousers into the bag and took a bus to Shu's dormitory in a rush.

At the door of Shu's room, the daughter of his neighbor asked, "Have you made up with each other?" Weiying denied, "No, I came to return his clothes." At the same time, she opened the bag and let her see the clothes. "You are too serious. He can't wear such clothes, so why do you return them?" "No, I have to return these to him in he will say anything unfavorable. I left him because he was getting back together with his girlfriend in Jinggang, but who did not know the details said I was a deceiver. I cannot stand this." The girl's mother heard their conversation and interrupted, "Since you left, that girl and her father came here several times, but she stopped coming later. So, they might have probably broken up. However, every time I saw her come out of Shu Fuhua' room, her hands were full of stuff, unlike you. You used to take nothing." She went on, "He has several girls friend because he thinks he has money. I'm afraid of such kind of person." Her mother said, "He did not go to work these days and got up late every day. I haven't seen him go out, so he must be home now." Weiying knocked his door and heard his voice, "Who?" "It's me. I come to return your clothes." The neighbor closed their door at that moment. After a long while, Shu did not answer the door. Weiying became angrier when thinking of her relationship being slandered by others under his permission.

She thought she would never come here again. Therefore, she turned around, stood on her right foot, and kicked the door open with her left foot. Seeing Shu sitting on the bedside and browsing something, she walked there and threw the clothes onto his bed, while Shu stood up to close the door rapidly. Then he took out a string from somewhere and said to her, "I'll bind you and you can escape nowhere." Weiying was so angry that she could not say a word. She squatted in a corner and cried to him out of a sudden, "You dare! I'll turn these all over and smash everything in your room." With this, she burst into tears with grievance...Shu was at a loss as to what to do, so he opened the door and stared at her. Knowing that she could go out, Weiying wrapped up her tears and walked out of the room full of sorrowfulness.

Later Weiying told Chu Fen's words to her mother, "Shu Fuhua started a rumor that Lin Jingji pushed him away by being my boyfriend and that he had sex with me." Therefore, Shao Guizhen accompanied her daughter to Shu's home on her day off, "You and my daughter are both unmarried, and you're not doing yourself any favors if you're not mindful of the repercussions of your rumor out there." Facing her mild criticism, Shu Fuhua blinked his eyes behind his glasses, saying nothing. Shao realized that she was just Play the piano against the cow. Therefore, she did not continue but took Weiying out of is room. They walked further away...

However, Lin Jingji told her later, "Shu Fuhua told my colleagues, 'You abandoned him in the beginning but later you came to beg his pardon." After hearing this, Qiu Weiying almost jumped up and said, "Have I done anything wrong to beg his pardon? Do you believe it?" Lu remained doubtful, "I don't believe it, for you look proud before me." Weiying felt uncomfortable at what he said because she didn't understand in what aspects she was proud in front of him. She was just a traditional and reserved woman who would never take the initiative in pursuing a man. And she thought that rumors had exerted influence on Lu.

Soon another event that made Weiying and her parents quite anxious and even shocked the whole city and the province at large took place. The "happiness gang" made up of almost all senior cadres' children in Changsha were seized as hoodlum gangs. According to the rumor, these young people had mainly committed face-to-face dancing, swimming without clothes on, seeing imported porn movies, doing something ungraceful to girls, etc. all of which belonged to capitalist behaviors and should be strictly punished and forbidden. Ordinary children could not join them because they could not afford such expenses. The reason why Juecong became a member of them was that his father's salary was no lower than that of provincial leaders. And he was introduced by his elementary schoolmate, Ma Jianping, whose father was a retired leader who had participated the Long March.

One Sunday, when Weiying went back home after work, she saw her parents crying sadly, with red and swollen eyes, indicating clearly something serious must have happened. Upset, she asked her mother, "What happened, mom?" "Juecong was arrested as a member of the "happiness gang" and could probably be sentenced to death penalty or life imprisonment…" Weiying had heard about the matter in the factory, but she had never thought that it could happen to her younger brother. The shocking news immerse them all in deep sorrow. Usually, in Sunday evening Weiying could hardly see her father at home as he would either play mahjong or poker in the park or at his friends' homes or be invited to have dinner. Realizing her parents did not have dinner, she went to the kitchen and found there were no vegetables. So, she stopped crying and ran to a grocery at the crossroad to buy some vegetables and meat.

On the way back, she saw a bulletin of sentence by the court and the procuratorate on the wall, reminding her of what her father said, he had a patient serving as the procurator who was quite respectful to her father. Some officials on important posts have moral and are amicable, while many others taking on tiny roles were quite arrogant...Her father was once regretful that he had not resorted to that patient for advice when their family's properties were confiscated as the district attorney should know how policies worked. Therefore, at the dinner table, Weiying reminded her father, "Dad, you are respected by almost all patients, so you have developed the habit of "so you have the developed a of ten thousand things don't request for other people help." Some families of my colleagues in the factory have a second or even third house. There should be someone working in real estate companies among your patients, but we still have only one public room just because you've never asked for help. But Juecong must receive the penalty if you don't resort to other people. I remember You once said..." Her words reminded Qiu Zhongyuan who patted his head, "Yes! Why haven't I thought of that? I'll ask for leave tomorrow to go for him." Still then, the whole family began to have dinner.

When Weiying went off work the next day, Lin Jingji was home. But she didn't go to his home as usual but directly went back home hurriedly, "Dad, what did your patient in the procuratorate say?" "He said he could not show his position at random but had to know the in detail at first." "Did you bring gifts to him?" "I brought two elaborate packs of cigarettes, but he refused to accept them. He said that he felt quite well after I cured his disease, so he was grateful to me and that he would help us as much as possible if it did not breach the law. He asked me not to give gifts. He was upright and would not accept gifts." Several days later, there was still no news about Juecong from the procuratorate, and the whole family became anxious again as there were various rumors in the society.

Weiying went home after work instead of going to date with Lu. And she felt that Lu was not as good to her as in the beginning. Once he said to her, "I'll not love a girl who doesn't love me no matter how pretty she is. I heard that even a prostitute will have more love to the man she loves than to others and she can quit doing such a job after getting married." Since then, Weiying was not quite happy and unwilling to ponder on what he meant also because Juecong encountered such a matter. But she thought unpleasantly, how could a prostitute have any emotion towards people? She could exchange her body and soul for money just like the public toilet! However, she didn't say it out especially when Lu said, "If I can't marry you, I'll go to America alone. Facts have proved the rumors…" He stopped here, making her so confused and uncomfortable. She was not in the mood to speculate about his words but felt that they are losing their profound friendship.

While going to work the next day, she sighed in the lane near the department, Oh, God! Why should our family suffer from so much misery? Why don't you save us? Thinking of the misfortunes right now and in the past, she couldn't help sobbing. The "happiness gang" incident had become the top priority in her mind so that she further ignored meeting with Lu and did not tell it to him. Meanwhile, she, who had was not much socialized, never predicted that pure and chaste love could be destroyed by secret conspiracy!

During that period, the "happiness gang" incident became a shocking piece of news in the whole city of Changsha, and it was rumored that every member of the group would be sentenced to death, which had been submitted to the central government. Qiu's family also heard that Ma Jianping's father was hospitalized because of his son's imprisonment and that Ma went to see his father with handcuffs on before his father death.

Therefore, Weiying went home after work almost every day and she had no time to meet with Lu's family. She and her parents were to upset and nervous to eat and sleep. Later her father's patient told them, "A pretty girl with the surname of Chen, who Juecong and Ma Jianping both knew acknowledged that she slipped into their room from the window and slept in their bed. So, they didn't commit the crime of rape in turns, but the girl herself was not self-loving. Then the nature of the incident has changed. It will not become so serious if they commit nothing else." Qiu Weiying felt sorry for Ma's father, when hearing that as he died from worrying about his only son Ma Jianping.

Till then did Weiying realize that she hadn't met Lin Jingji for a long time. Though losing a little confidence in his love to her, she still loved him, and after all, the two are still friends and relations. Therefore, she went to Lu's home after dinner. Entering the door, she felt something weird, different with the usual situation, his mother was washing bowls and chopsticks in the kitchen and showed a somewhat different expression when seeing Weiying; his father walked out without saying a word; and Lu was sitting by the desk unhappily. He held a cigarette, making Weiying wonder, when he began to smoke?

She did not ask him but went to sit in the chair as usual, "I rarely came here recently because something happened to my brother…" Lu interrupted her angrily, "Does your brother's incident have anything to do with you? He's not a little child anymore and he's been married. So, his wife can attend to him." Weiying recognized that Lu was cross about her not visiting here but didn't know how serious the matter would be as she did not understand the truth yet. Looking at Lu, she said, "What's wrong with you? You seem unhappy. Are you sick or engaged in something else?" Lu answered unpleasantly, "I don't know when we'll hold our wedding. I've sent the picture to my sister but received no reply until now. We can hardly get married without her support." Weiying opposed his opinion, "Then we can wait till we have the ability by ourselves." "When? Our salary only amounts to two digits, not even enough for everyday expenditure!" Weiying who had strong self-esteem hit the freezing point without carefully considering his words and she exploded like a firecracker, "What do you mean by that? You mean we can't get married if your sister does not send money? And I say, when we have our own ability, then the wedding. But you say doesn't work? If you have changed your mind, tell me immediately. Be straightforward, and I'll not cling to you. Take our photo out!" Lu realized the seriousness of the matter at that moment, saying doubtfully, "I've sent them to my sister…" She could not help her indignation and felt her love for him was turning into hate, "You just need to send one to your sister. I've given you two and the negative. Take them out!" Lu had to hand them to her, who saw there was a pack of matches on the desk and put fire to the photo and the negative which became dust in less than one minute and fell on the desk. Weiying was stubborn in appearance at that moment but cried in heart…She was being torn apart by enormous pain…as this is her first true love for the past 25 years, but it had to be forced stopped.

She made great effort to control her emotion and stood up, "I'm going." Lu, with tears in his eyes, said to her in a quivered voice, "Let me send you back." She did not decline because she was reluctant to leave deep in her heart. But at that moment, her self-esteem overwhelmed her emotion. She was pursuing pure and chaste love, which required her to do so, she would rather remain single than give herself to a man she did not love or who did not love her for a certain purpose. What she sought for was unremitting and invaluable love that would not change under any circumstances, so it was to say that most people were unable to be as rational as she was in emotion!

They stood up at almost the same time and walked out of the door one after another. Because of the unusual mood, she forgot to say goodbye to his honest and upright parents while passing them. The old couple looked at their son and felt there was something wrong, so they said nothing but to let such an atmosphere continue. Out of the door, Weiying sat on the backseat of Lu's bike.

They had nothing to say on the way and when arriving in the place where they parted the first time, she said, "It's near, so let me get down." He stopped immediately and prepared to accompany her for a while. But she suddenly felt a fit of dizziness as soon as her tiptoes touched the ground. When she stood on, she said, "I can't walk." Staring at her face, Lu patted the backseat, "Come, let me go a little way with you." However, unable to overcome her strong sense of self-esteem, she insisted, "No" and then walked onto the pavement and back against a tree squat. Lu was watching her, who just wanted to give it a cry. But it was not too late, so people might come around if she cried…Thus after a while of rest, she stood up, "Go back. I can walk by myself. The factory is over there."

Till then, the "born couple" reputed by everyone broke up forever---the couple who could love each other sincerely, share happiness and pain together parted due to a secret conspiracy and misunderstanding caused by coincidence. So far, everyone thinks that "Match made spouse in heaven, match made spouse in earth." They parted ways completely. The pair have been completely true love, lovers who can share joys and sorrows. It is being conducted conspiracy and the huge misunderstanding completely broken up due to coincidence.

Chu Fen did not come back when Weiying reached the dormitory. The next day was a day off, so no one was on night shift in the workshop. Throwing her backpack beside the pillow near the wall, she fell in bed and burst into tears. She took off the towel after using it to wipe off tears. Despite great effort to control her tears, she could not yet stop them, and the pillow got wet soon, she got down to wash her face but not brush her teeth. And she would not like to take a shower though the water in the boiler was hot enough. She went to bed, turned the pillow upside down and fell asleep. The dream-loving girl dreamed that several monsters following her while she was running, and the ground underneath began to descend. There was nothing and nobody around in the darkness and she could neither shout nor cry but felt suffocated…

Shortly after this Juecong and Ma Jianping were not sentenced to death and released almost at the same time, so Weiying and her parents felt relieved! She told Juecong, "Father said that you just play with Ma Jianping and haven't done anything wrong or immoral…" "Anything immoral? I have saved two lives from the artificial lake when playing in Martyr's Park in my childhood and I was 14 when I saved a boy for the first time. The boy who lived behind the Youth Palace was two years older than me." Weiying was reminded of the old saying that "Saving one life is better than setting up a seventh-level pagoda". She never knew that Jucong, about whom her parents were most worried, had saved two lives in his teens.

Chu Fen often spread various kinds of rumors to Weiying, who did not hide anything from her though not regarded her as a friend. Many things would not happen to her if Chu did not start rumors as she could hear her say something while lying in bed every night. Furthermore, Weiying could not bear others distorting the truths and slandering her. Measuring herself with traditional moral standards, she attached great importance to the purification of the soul and the reputation. One night, Chu said to her, "The last time you went to Shu Fuhua's home to return his clothes, someone called Zhang Qiukai living near him asked, 'Has the deceiver come?' They do not understand why you came there since you had broken up with him?" Weiying was indignant at this and wanted to go to Zhang Qiukai's home to ask for the reason. She thought that Lin Jingji might probably be affected by some rumor, and she seldom visited him due to the coincident "happiness gang" thing, which prompted him to doubt our love is happened questions.

At that time, the Cultural Revolution was not over yet, so Weiying thought that big-character poster might be of help, Liu Shaoqi, the vice chairman of the country, was killed by it and the detestable woman dare not harass her uncle thanks to it. Now that her reputation was distorted by others, she wanted the truth to be revealed by means of putting on big-character posters. Thus, she went to Xinhua Bookstore to buy some pieces of white paper and went back to the dormitory and moved the big on the chair onto

Lose one's bearings

the bed. Then she sat on the bedside and began to write the article with the title of "Please Look at the Truth." Finishing with the big-character posters, she rolled them up in two rubber bands, preparing to put them up outside Shu's dormitory. Pure Weiying insisted that the brightness of truth can't be hided, but she ignored that cloud might cover the sun's rays sometimes.

On the day off, Weiying got up very early. She combed washed finished, after eating breakfast at a nearby restaurant. She took the finished big-character poster and direct set off to Thermos factory. Though restless and whimsical on the way, she would not cancel her plan, which conformed with her character---she would stick to what she meant to do and never retreat. At the turning point of the path leading to Shu Fuhua's dormitory, she came across a young man who knew her and lived near Fu. Thus, she went to say, "Hello." That guy replied, "I haven't seen you for a long time. Are you coming for Shu Fuhua?" "No, I came for Zhang Qiukai. Do you know which house he lives in?" He pointed to a house with the door open, "Over there, the door on which there are chalk prints drawn by children." Seeing it clearly, Weiying thanked him and took a big- character big-character poster out to tag it on the wall outside Zhang's house nearby. While putting on the big-character poster, some people began to pay attention and walk towards her. Then she walked directly to Zhang's house entrance.

She thought naively that everything had a reason and "people could be convinced by reasons". But she, without much social experience, had not realized, someone had no morality in nature and would treat others mercilessly. Such a kind of people had no difference with animals in their inner heart though they wore beautiful clothes. This world was like a shift between day and night as it had light as well as darkness.

When Qiu Weiying walked to near the door of Zhang Qiukai's house, she saw Zhang Qiukai pouring tea beside the table close to the door. She stood side the door outside and said, "Mr. Zhang, I'd like to ask you to clarify something." He asked her unhappily, "For what?" "I heard that you said I'm a deceiver, so can you come with me to Shu's home to make sure whether I'm a liar?" Qiu Weiying's words just landed, Zhang pulled the door open and took out a wooden pole of about one meter in length and four centimeters in diameter. He shouted to Weiying is overbearing and insufferably arrogant, "You went to his home yourself, so why should I go there? Go away, or I'm going to hit you!" Weiying was reluctant to be slandered and threatened by him. So, she held a glass on the corner of the desk and said, "If you are to beat me, then I'll break your glass."

But Zhang Qiukai was fierce bellow, "You dare take my stuff." Then he began to beat her with the pole so that she had to drop the glasses fling on the ground. So, Zhang beat up her harder and more mercilessly. There were more and more people surrounding them and watch. But no one dared to support Weiying and curb this ruthless beat up. Because Zhang was a cadre and member of the CPC of the factory. Weiying fell from the high earth slope opposite to his house to the lower slope, and till then Zhang did this atrocity stop.

She choked with sobs so much that she couldn't get the words out. She stands up and walked onto the narrow path full of grass and thorns. She wiped off tears when reaching the road and walked to the bus station with depression, looking at a bus which she could have caught driving away. Then she got to the platform and waited until the next bus came. The driver had a glance at her face with a strange expression and it seemed that many people were staring at her to seek for an answer. Feeling a little uneasy, she went to the back of the bus and sat down in a corner.

Though she had another free afternoon on the day off. But she realized that her mother would be sure to sense her abnormal emotion if she went back home with the sadness. So, she decided to go back to her factory directly. However, she did not realize that she had passed the due stop and thus had to get off at the Martyr's

Lose one's bearings

Park and then walk back to the dormitory. From then on, she has left unforgettable trauma and excruciation both mentally and physically.

On falling asleep again, Weiying was woken up by Chu Fen's coming back, so she looked at the Chu after turning to the outside. The Chu asked, "You sleep so early?" "Yes, what time is it?" "More than nine o'clock."

Weiying did realize that she had not lunch and dinner until then as she felt so hungry and Pain all over her body to fall asleep. Thereby she got off the bed and poured a glass of water with and which she ate several biscuits. Then she went to the sink near the kitchen to brush one's teeth up and went to the bathroom with all the stuff she needed.

After that, while having the shower, she was surprised and scared to find bruises all over her body! She is going to bed filled with sorrowfulness.

Chu asked, "Weiying, did you go to the thermos factory today?" "Yes. How did you know that?" "I went there this noon and heard my acquaintance discussing with others. They said, your two younger brothers were naughty and would be bound to take revenge on Zhang Qiukai, who had brutally beaten you so hard?" Weiying did not respond, because she didn't want to involve her two younger brothers. But she was reminded that she should go to the office of the CPC branch secretary of the thermos factory to report Zhang's cruel behavior. She'd like to ask whether such a party member could serve as and cadre of the factory? Because of he would negatively affect the conducts of the workers. Was there any fairness in this society?

On Sunday, Weiying saw the dark sky after getting up. She considered that even though it would rain today, she must go to the thermos factory. She'd like to ask whether such a party member, the person could cadre of the factory as he would negatively affect the conducts of the workers. Was there any fairness and justice in this society? First, she called the sales department to ask for one day's sick leave. Then she started off to the thermos factory.

Arriving there, she is do things according to conventional practice. She said to the janitor, "I come to meet your factory manager to report Zhang Qiukai's brutal behavior, for he had beaten me unreasonably yesterday." The janitor said, "This is in the charge of the security department." With these words, he began to speak into a microphone. Soon she saw a tall and strong man, he swaggered walked come over. Qiu Weiying predicting that making a complaint would not do much. But she still reported the matter of yesterday. The guy interrupted her, "The security division in our factory must know that. Now that it has not interfered in it, how can we do anything to help you?" At this, Weiying was quite angry and anxious, "Then I'll meet your party branch secretary. He's a member of the CPC, so he must be responsible for it." "You're not our staff. We'll attend to it if you are, but you are not. So just go home." Such words without any humanity made her burst into sudden tears, but the cold- security section chief went off the janitor's room, pretending that he did not see that. Weiying's cries astonished workers around and more and more people surrounded her. The janitor said to her, "It's no use crying, for you are the one to suffer if you continue. It seems that the factory will not attend to this matter, so just go back." She had confirmed the factory branch party that it would not take responsibility for what happened. She continued to sob helplessly for a while, wiped away tears after. She dragged heavy steps to the bus station.

Since she had asked for one whole day's leave and had no intention to go to work at that time, she went home directly because her parents didn't have to go to work either on the public holiday. Arriving home, she saw her father making meat pies and mother boiling porridge and frying dishes in the kitchen. After calling "Dad and Mom", she really wants to cry before them, but she thought it would be of no use to tell them. They had nowhere to complain about the confiscation of family property of their properties, and they were neither members of the CPC nor cadres. Thus, knowing this matter would only increase their sorrow as they were honest and easy to be bullied. While thinking, she walked to the single bed and sat down, but felt painful like being stabbed by a needle. Therefore, she put off her shoes with feet, bended her knees and sat by the wall, looking right up to the blurring sky with a blank expression.

Qiu Weiying's mother suddenly appeared at the door, asking her with doubt, "How are you, Weiying? Are you sick?" At this, she could not help her sadness and miserable tears ran down through her cheeks. Mother became a little panicked and ran to her side, "Is there anyone who has bullied you?" "I've been beaten." She answered slowly in a quiver while showing the bruises to her mother. Mother was shocked, "How? Why have you been beaten like this?" She described the whole matter in simple words, and her mother stared at her injuries, unable to speak anything.

At this time, Qiu Weiying's father went in the room, "The pies are ready. Let's have lunch." Mother turned around to say to her husband, "Look. Weiying was bully, just for questioning Shu's neighbor. Shall we go to find the leaders of the thermos factory to make a complaint? Why should an upright girl suffer from such grievances? What has become of the society?" Qiu Weiying's father said, "People are good to be bullied, horses are good to be people ridden. Look. It was I who established the hospital, but the director always attempts to do harm to me just because I don't like to please Wang Huijun. We are honest people, but they have destroyed our whole family. So, there's no use being honest, kind and upright. What a world!" Shao said, "You patted the desk and beat the chairs when quarreling with the hospital's leaders, so it's natural they hate you." "It is legal to open a private clinic at home. Are you that an offend them? They even took away all our lawful income and properties. Now it's no use to argue about these things. Shall we go to the thermal bottle factory to meet their leaders?" "OK. I'll ask for one day's leave tomorrow and we'll go there the day after tomorrow."

The next day Weiying in after getting off at Zhongshan Ting and asked for a day's sick leave and went onto Northern Region Hospital Carry out medical examination and certification. She felt very aggrieved, and suffering is angered at the slander against one's reputation. The doctor said to her, "Bring the certificate to where you registered to be sealed and it will serve as the proof you can use to make the complaint." This reminded Weiying to register at the department of gynecology. Then she went there and required the doctor to examine her to prove that she had no sexual relationship with anyone. The woman doctor was serious and said, "I must make a careful examination because I'll be responsible to you in the future." She, finishing the inspection, wrote on the book, "Through careful examination, her hymen was complete, and she has had no sex with anyone…" Therefore, Weiying brought this doctor's certificate to be in safe keeping.

In the morning the next day, Weiying and her parents asked to the Work Unit respectively for leave and went to the thermos factory far from their home to make a complaint to the leaders. Weiying, full of grievances, also brought the doctor's certificate. As a result, the matter was not solved as expected as the leaders refused to meet the three. The janitor made a call to the security department. Nonetheless, none of the leaders of this department came out to meet them, and the janitor prevented them from going into the office. Weiying's parents were intellectuals and thereby unwilling to quarrel in the factory, so they went home, filled with unpleasantness and grievance.

Seeing that her parents could hardly eat anything for her, Weiying felt sorry for them as well as herself. Parents made great efforts for their children, who, however, made their parents worry every day, let alone pay back their child support payment.

Later, Qiu Zhongyuan told this matter to one of his patients who was the warden of the provincial prison and the latter also felt sorry for his daughter's encounter and thus asked his friend--

-head of a farm of labor reform---to go to the thermos factory. Later, the warden told Qiu Zhongyuan, "The dean of the security department was immoral. He dares ask me, what relations I have with your daughter. I could have sent him to labor reform before the Cultural Revolution. Now everybody ignores public security organs, procurator organs and people's courts, so it seems there's no way to settle the matter." Weiying felt strongly that the Cultural Revolution had destroyed the morality of the whole society and legal sanction…

She felt a fierce headache when waking up the next morning. On the day off, Chu Fen had gone out and no one was in workshops. She was sitting on the bedside alone, feeling deeply grieved for there was nowhere to complain. At that time, she seemed to have gone to a dead end and no one could save her so that she thought only death could help her out of personal attack and mental harm which were difficult for her to bear. She lost heart and felt desperate for this world, so she took out a pen and a piece of paper and prepared to write the letter of suicide on the big chest which had been moved on the bed.

Just writing the three characters "Letter of Suicide", she cries with grief again. She had never thought that she would be forced to end her life at the young age of 25! She loved life, but she felt that she had lost interest in living on. She lived such a hard and painful in the life. The world became insensitive and without a sense of justice, which was not worth her attachment!

Therefore, she decided to leave the cold world. She wrote in the letter of suicide, "Men and women, the old and the young in this world, I was born on this boundless land, but my miserable destiny forces me to leave it at such a young age because it has nothing deserving my nostalgia. I had a happy childhood and a beautiful youth. I once expected to become a useful person for the society to make contribution to the prosperity of the country and the world, but my future began to be affected ever since my family encountered the confiscation of properties… A series of cruel realities destroyed my ideal and even my life! Someone slandered me in public. I was suffered severe beaten and abuse so hard just for questioning Zhang Qiukai for the truth. There's nowhere for me to make complaints and tell reasons. What a painful life I am now leading! I really cannot understand where people's consciousness has gone, for no one stood out to help me under that circumstance. Do they fear an insignificant factory cadre? If there is no justice in the society, bad people will be more rampant, and we have no safeguarding of the basic live, and protect the rights and interests of the survive.

While writing, Weiying felt hungry. It was time for lunch, but she had not even had breakfast. Therefore, she went out to have food nearby. While passing the gate of Hunan Silk Factory at the crossroad on the way back, she came up with one thing that had happened there… She decided to write it into the letter. When she entered the quiet factory and the dormitory, she felt tired and thus fell asleep in bed.

After getting up, she ran to the sink to wash her face with cold water though autumn had come in order to keep cool head. Then she continued to write. Once I saw under a big tree near Hunan Silk Factory several strong young men beating a relatively weak man who was forced to hold his head and squatted by the tree, his face bleeding. I looked around with an expression of pleading for other, and murmured, "Why is there no one standing out to prevent or persuade?" At that time, some guys stood beside me but glared at me with obvious misunderstanding, appearing to say, "Does that have anything to do with you?"

And another once I stood at the end of a crowded bus. When the door opened, a man with just one leg got on with the support of a cane in enormous efforts, but no one gave their seat to him. When the bus started, it jolted around, and the man might have fallen if there were so many passengers. I'm uncomfortable to see this, so I could not help shouting, "Why are you all sitting there comfortably? Why did you ignore such a scene? Who could please offer a seat to him?" When I cried out these words, a woman beside me gave her seat.

In my sweet memory of my adolescence, people were moral and polite, respecting the senior and caring for the young. How about now? They have all changed. Fewer and fewer people attach importance to ethics. With deteriorating social norms, this world will become more and more horrible. I plead I'd like to wake up your consciousness with my blood and life as the expense, please save the world of degrading morality, or you will live on without warmth and humanity. Then what is the meaning of life?

Finishing this letter of suicide of fully filled one page, Weiying put it into her pocket and went to a nearby restaurant to have dinner. She ordered two favorite dishes and a soup and intended to meet the God after the delicious food. However, she, though quite hungry, was full of tears in her stomach and unable to eat the food. A middle-aged woman servant frowned at the leftovers while cleaning up the table perhaps she thought the guest had wasted too much. In fact, Weiying earned 24 yuan per month for the year after she completed the apprentice period. Adding food and nutrition expenses, the salary was just more than 30 yuan. Moreover, she knew the importance of saving food. Because she used in former times go to the mountains and the countryside, knowing the hardship of farmers. She never asked her parents for money and didn't like luxury and waste even if she had money. She walking to the bus station, and she went on a bus passing Xiangjiang Bridge. Arriving at the midst of the bridge, she went down the bus off in a spirit trance.

It was totally dark then. With bleak autumn wind, there was neither moonlight nor pedestrians. She walked a while on the pavement, and she thought of Lu Gengwei's words "If you change your mind, I'll jump from here" when reaching the part on the bridge where they strolled together. She talks to oneself said, "Now it's not you, but I'll jump from the bridge; it's me." With this, she stopped and leaned on the cement railing, looking down to the underneath water. In this night without the moon or stars, only dim lamp lights around the river brightened the world, which, however, seemed cold. She couldn't see the color of the water clearly, but felt it covered the river completely like a large black silk quilt. All appeared so ghostly and gloomy that she felt she was standing on the edge of the hell. She was unable to swim, jumped Xiangjiang Bridge off, she would leave the depressing world forever in just one minute.

Looking afar into the sky, she could not see the real scene of the mountain range at night, making it hard to distinguish clouds, mountains and forests. Then she turned left to gaze into the distant Yuelu Mountain which was asleep like a deep-colored ink and wash painting. Taking the letter of suicide out from the pocket, she didn't find any stone suitable to press it. So, she hesitated a bit, when a passerby stared at her while walking by her side. Weiying felt uncomfortable and so she gazed at the sky again.

This time she seemed to see her mother appeared in the sky and landed on the ground out of a sudden, hugging her dead body and bursting into tears so painfully, hover between life and death… At this moment, a cool breeze blew over, she saw her mother stand up again and stare at her without moving around…She began to sober suddenly, if I die this way, my mother who had already been very tired must unable to stand this a large hit …Would I end my life like this? No, I'm just 25 years old! A poem popped into her head, "The mountains and the rivers end at the end of one's rope; a sudden turn new hopeful prospect." She sudden realize that if she continued living on, there would be a possibility that she would come across some change in her destiny. So, the suicidal attempt suddenly disappeared. She tore up this page of suicide last words and throw it into the river. These shreds of paper down into the merciless water and went west as with the waves billowed goes on go away …

Because gossip is a fearful thing, Qiu Weiying, who has strong self-esteem and innocence, didn't see through the evil in the world. She was under the cruel and merciless tortured of the spirit and body, this nearly cost her life.

CHAPTER 5

Injured lonely bird

5.1 The counterrevolutionary of implicate all of one's close relatives.

The Chinese people who had suffered much from political movements since the criticism of Lin Biao and Confucius beginning in 1974 lost interest in such things. Moreover, it was rumored that the criticism of Confucius was originally targeted at Zhou Enlai. And what about Lin Biao? He almost became the successor of Chairman Mao Zedong. The masses felt more and more confused, losing not only interest in but also sensitivity of politics.

Qiu Weiying was shocked by the torture in her romantic relationship, so she lost heart in love. She spent most of her spare time reading after breaking up with Lin Jingji She believed that "there were ten thousand gram of gold in books.". She tended to fill herself with knowledge, especially medical expertise. Changes occurred in almost every aspect ever since Chairman Mao passed away on Sep. 9, 1976, and the "Gang of Four" were beaten down. Weiying thought that if she could learn more knowledge, she might have the opportunity to change her job. However, she would go shopping or go to the cinema occasionally in her spare time.

Affected by a cold and the hydrochloric acid smog from tin soldering one day, Weiying was coughing and even expectorating all day long. She even sometimes had a headache and felt sleepy. She doubted whether she had got pneumonia and thus went to a hospital to visit a doctor. Fortunately, she did not get the disease after a fluoroscopy examination. But the doctor gave her an injection and offered her a two-day sick leave when seeing her suffering so much from coughing. That day, after taking antiphlogistic pills at the galvanized iron sales department, she had lunch at the fixed place and then returned to the department to take a nap upstairs. Waking up in the afternoon, she felt much better and therefore went to the nearby Xinhua Cinema to see the movie. As soon as the movie was over, Weiying went out to the broad open square with the movie goers. While looking upper left at the film advertisement, she was hit on the right shoulder by someone intentionally. She turned around, only to find that guy was Lin Jingji! At this moment, Lu greeted a man in front of her. She wanted to ask, "Are you OK with everything? Do you have a girlfriend?" Nevertheless, she became dumb as if he hit the edge ball while playing Ping-Pong. If she was to receive the ball, she could have made it, but she did not because she wasn't sure about it. Therefore, she lost it.

Weiying was so conventional that it would be quite difficult for her to take the initiative to ask her ex-boyfriend something. She was like a bead on an abacus in that respect, and her move was completely decided by men. Therefore, when seeing Lu greeting someone else, and her tongue stopped at the incisors, and she couldn't move it but still stayed dumb. This accidental encounter was their split up last meeting between them both, and their future was like the tragedy in Qiong Yao's romance novels… Thus, it was obvious that in our real life, those who love each other truly and wholeheartedly might not get married due to various reasons…

Time flies! China witnessed remarkable changes during this period. Several shocking events took place in 1976, Premier Zhou passed away on Jan. 8; an unprecedentedly catastrophic earthquake hit Tangshan on July 28; Chairman Mao--an idol of Chinese and the people who had proletariat ideology throughout the world passed away at 00,10 on Sep. 9. The "Gang of Four" were beaten down and put into prison in October when they attempted to usurp the power, getting their due punishment. The Cultural Revolution, which had devastated China for ten years, came to an end. That shocked the whole the China and the world as much as the Tangshan earthquake. <See App 1. H>

Qiu Weiying who grew up with the vicissitudes of New China, did not get married until 28. At that moment, the Chinese government was advocated the policy of "late marriage and late childbearing". Whenever someone in the factory joked, "We should present an award of 'late marriage and childbearing' to Qiu Weiying," Weiying would just laugh it off. She would not casually marry someone merely because she was not so young anymore. She was born to this characteristic; she would be single rather than get marry due to her age or for a far-fetched purpose. She always believed that it was an unalterable principle that men should pursue women and women would seem somewhat disrespectful if the other way around; and meanwhile, if a woman took the initiative to purse a man, it would be hard for her to get a perfect marriage. Moreover, women would get pregnant and give birth to children after getting married, so it was they who would sacrifice more physically. Therefore, if a man did not love you, what was the value in it to get married just for its own sake?

While at home, Qiu Zhongyuan told wife more than once in front of Weiying, "Usually couples have better and better relationships as time goes by, and after getting married and having children. But she just goes the opposite, she always has a good beginning, then conflicts occur, and finally ends up being broken up. However, a man who marries such a girl can be void of worries no matter how far they go away from home to do business!" Qiu Zhongyuan left home after finishing these words.

Shao turned to Weiying and said, "Do not find a man who has a strong sexual urge. Since you may not be so desirable for that…" "Ah!" She was embarrassed to explain anything to her mother. But she was clear that when she was in relationship with her several ex-boyfriends, she did have sexual urge. But she did not want to look like a loose woman in front of men because on the one hand she had strong self-esteem and on the other she was afraid of pre-marriage pregnancy. So, she restrained herself. She was not devoid of sexual urge. It was just because she has so strong will power that she controlled her desire.

Weiying's workplace was not far from the hospital where her mother worked. She just needed to cross a road, go through a street by her original house and turned to the middle of another street to get to the hospital. So, when she got off work a little bit earlier, she would go to accompany her mother, or cook dinner together and chat before returning to her dormitory. One day when she went to the hospital and directly into her mother's clinic, a woman patient who appeared like a cadre got out of a bed. Hearing her voice "mum", she asked Shao, "Is this your daughter, Doctor Shao? How old is she?" Shao answered, "Yes, she is. 29." The patient replied, "She's so good. Is she married?" "Not yet." "Then could I introduce a boyfriend for her?" Weiying smiled without saying anything. She would never be initiative and generous in anything concerning marriage. Shao said, "OK. What kind of a boy is he?" "He's from Shanghai, a few years older than your daughter, working as a translator in the Foreign and Overseas Chinese Affairs Office of Hunan Province Party committee" Weiying remained silent, which showed that she approved of it.

Then Shao asked, "When will they meet?" "How about this Saturday evening at my home? If there is any change, I'll let you know." She gave her address and telephone number to Weiying before leaving. Shao said to her daughter, "You can call her Aunt Wang."

Injured lonely bird

Weiying was not listed informed of any change in Saturday evening, and she went directly to Aunt Wang's home after dinner. In Wang's house, Weiying saw not only Aunt Wang, her husband, and daughter, but also that medium-sized cultured man who was just over 30 and wore a pair of glasses. He looked like a senior intellectual just from his appearance. Weiying knew he was no doubt the boyfriend Aunt Wang introduced to her. At this time, she felt somewhat easy since she had had several relationships and was already 29.

After she seated herself in the chair, Wang's daughter who had an apple-shaped face told her, "This comrade is called Zhang Hao. I met him when he brought some foreign guests to pay a visit to Xiaoxiang Film Studio where I worked." With these words, she smiled to Weiying. Aunt Wang also looked at their expression from time to time, while Zhang Hao was staring at Weiying all the time when talking. Their first meeting finished in a harmonious, natural and friendly atmosphere. They sat there for a while till Weiying said, "It's time to return to my dormitory. I'm afraid if it's late, there will be no bus." Aunt Wang said, "Let Xiao Zhang see you off." Both stood up at almost the same time and said goodbye to the family.

Zhang took his bicycle downstairs where he had locked it and they walked to the gate beside the road. Under a big tree on the pavement, Zhang said, "I work and live in the provincial committee of the CPC. Would you like to visit the place where I live after work tomorrow?" Weiying answered, "OK. I'll go there after dinner." Zhang said, "I'll come to the gate to wait for you at eight. We can talk for about two hours and then I'll send you back."

Qiu Weiying said, "OK. But you don't need to come here. Just tell me your house number and I'll find it. One of my mother's patients oversees the cinema in the provincial party committee and I have seen several movies played only within the committee in recent years. The janitor may have already known me. Moreover, it is very near the backdoor to the factory by bus." Zhang was pleased, "That's all right. Then I'll wait for you at home. Now do you need me to send you back?" Weiying pointed to a bus station near the train station on the other side of the road and said, "No, I can take a bus back." Zhang said, "OK. When I go out to accompany foreign guests, the committee will assign a car and a driver, so I have little chance to ride a bicycle. And it's unsafe to ride you back with so much traffic." Then he told Weiying his house number before they parted.

Weiying arrived at the janitor's room of the provincial Party committee to fill a form before eight the next day. The janitor told her, "There's no movie tonight." Weiying said, "I know. I have a date here." She filled the form and handed it to the army man at the gate. She found Zhang's house easily and knocked at the door lightly. Zhang quickly opened the door and invited Weiying to sit down in a wicker chair beside a desk. He poured a cup of tea for her and said, "Just have a seat. I'm writing a report to my supervisor, and I'll finish it soon." Weiying nodded with a smile, looking at him writing in beautiful and smooth calligraphy in the light of a green lamp while talking to her.

This made her feel that he was talented and would succeed in the future. After a while, he said in an easy manner, "It's done. Now I have time to chat with you." He told Weiying about his own experience, "I was born and grew up in Shanghai and now my parents have retired and live there. I graduated from Shanghai International Studies University and was assigned to the Ministry of Foreign Affairs. I married a colleague in Beijing, but we ended up in divorce because we happened intense quarrel and adopted different views during the Cultural Revolution. But it's fortunate that we have no children. Soon after that I was assigned to Hunan Provincial Committee of the CPC. I have worked here for almost three years but remained single. I have known Aunt Wang's daughter for more than one year since the foreign guests took me to pay a visit to Xiaoxiang Film Studio. I'm very pleased that she introduced you to me. I felt you were quite pretty when you smiled yesterday…"

Weiying remained silent, but she knew that he liked her very much. Divorce? It was not his fault. She heard many couples ended up in divorce due to different views take part in different organization in the Cultural Revolution. Besides, she was satisfied with his other aspects. So, she just followed his feelings and let it freedom develop.

Later, Zhang Hao went to visit Qiu Weiying's mother. She afterwards told Weiying, "It seems that such a man will never make you angry if you live with him." Weiying believed there was some reason in her mother's remark as every time she dated with him, he always looked calm without any excitement or compulsion.

But one evening, they accompanied Foreign Ambassadors to China to watch a shadow play by the Provincial Puppet Art Group at Dongfeng Theater. After she went back to her dormitory, she received a phone from Zhang who was delighted and excited, "Just now I accompanied the Mexican ambassador back to the hotel and he asked me, 'Is the girl sitting beside you your girlfriend?' I said, 'Yes.' He praised that you are so beautiful!' And I'm very happy since even a foreign ambassador appreciates you…"

When they met again, Weiying told Zhang, "I think his wife is beautiful! She looks quite like Norodom Sihanouk's wife and is even more pretty. His two boys are lovely. How can they speak such good mandarin?" Zhang replied, "Because they grow up in Beijing." Weiying asked again, "I saw several policemen sitting around us. Were they there to prevent theft?" "No, to safeguard the ambassador. Our nation must be responsible for their personal safety. And thieves are clever in this aspect because they dare not steal from foreign guests for fear of being heavily punished." Zhang once said to Weiying not long after they met, "I do not want others to know our romantic relationship." However, soon after that, he brought her to the home of the office dean and applied for marriage after knowing each other for only three to four months.

Nevertheless, when they met again, Zhang looked gloomy and lost his usual smile. Seeing his expression, Weiying suddenly lost confidence and predicted that something bad would happen. Zhang told her after remaining silent for a long while, "The committee did not approve my application report for marriage. They said that your family had serious political problems according to investigation. Your father has once served as an army doctor in the Kuomintang; the family of your mother's ex-husband had been senior officials of the Kuomintang; one of your families had committed economic crime and your family property had been confiscated; and your brother-in-law who is an anti-revolutionary is still in prison. I was striving to be admitted by the CPC, but the provincial Party committee said that I won't be admitted if I keep touch with you and that they will fire me and assign me to an English teacher's post if I insist on marrying you. Now I feel so anxious and have to ask for your opinion." He gazed at her with pained and be at loss eyes.

How about Weiying at that moment? She was extraordinarily calm after going through so many ups and downs in life! And she became more and more reasonable in dealing with relationships after breaking up with several boyfriends. During the few months when she was with Zhang, he just touched her hair or kissed her face and did not do anything more intimate. So, they were just friends according to western customs. Furthermore, he did no harm to her feelings. Though she was surprised at what he said, it was also what she had expected.

She had failed the political examination when taking part in the examination of the Song and Dance Ensemble of Guangzhou Military Region because of her family's political problems. But it was false news about that her father had served as an army doctor for Kuomintang. Weiying said to Zhang sadly, "They are true about everything, but my father's does not service as an army doctor." Zhang frowned, "That your brother-in-law is an anti-revolutionary prevents our marriage from being approved. This is the most serious." "Yes, I know that." She turned to Zhang, "You love your job, don't you?"

"Yes." "Certainly, your work is interesting as you can often together with distinguished foreign guests. Furthermore, you earn a high salary and receive good treatment. If you with marry me, you will be assigned to a teacher's post. What a pity as you will lose interest. My job is so ordinary, so if neither of us is in a good department, it may not be conducive to our children in the future. Moreover, I don't want you to destroy your destiny for me. So, we may just be friends instead of a couple." Perhaps Zhang Hao did not think that Weiying would give him such a simple and short reply, so he just ended with "oh" and Weiying thought he approved of her view.

Back in her dormitory, Weiying thought quietly in bed, Wang Tianliang must have mongered a rumor about her father to the leaders of her factory because her father had once said to him that the guerrilla forces had wanted to seize him to serve as their doctor. But he pretended to tie his shoestrings and fled to a piece of corn land and then escaped to Jiangsu. So, wang must have distorted the fact. It was no doubt that there were always troubles in my romantic relationships, when I was with Shu Fuhua, Wang Tianliang did some harm; and when I was with Lu Gengwei, Shu made trouble. If such things continue, my love life will never get tranquil…

Several days later, Zhang chatted with Weiying again and told her, "These days leaders are participating in labor, so I do not have to think too much. Or I would be in a mass now and cause trouble in work." Feeling totally blank, Weiying did not know how to reply. Though she heard all his words, she was unable to react. Because a series of ups and downs and cruel realities impeded her romance from free development. And she became numb and more rational after undergoing such a complex life that she could control her complicated and stimulating thoughts with an extraordinarily calm appearance. Her romance with Zhang was over and drifted apart by then political environment. Thus, it was obvious seen, that time marriage without any political influence could not exist freely everywhere in China.

On the day of rest, Wei Ying returned home and told her parents that Zhang Hao's leaders had not approved their marriage. Qiu Zhongyuan said, "You don't want us to interfere with your marriage relationship, so you still haven't gotten married until now when you are almost 30 years old, so you can handle it at your own discretion. We'd better not interfere with your marriage because you won't live with us forever afterward anyway." Then he turned to his wife and asked, "Do you think so?" Mom looked at her daughter and said nothing; she seemed to be thinking about something. Wei Ying said, "Of course the advice of parents is important because you have more social experience than I do." Thus, they finished the talk about marriage.

Weiying felt, Family property was illegally confiscated at home and her brother-in-law's being labelled as counterrevolutionary. Affected not only her future but also her marriage. If so, her future would be forever covered with smog, and she couldn't see brightness anymore. She was so confused.

Although the Cultural Revolution ended in 1976. But the harm caused by the ultra-left trend of thought was not completely erased. However, the work of vindicating the counter-revolutionary and other wrongful cases in the Cultural Revolution by "bring order out of chaos" began a few months after the two men broke up completely in 1979.

Li Zhimeng had been sentenced to 10 years in prison as an anti-revolutionary for attacking the Cultural Revolution as "what a hell is going on!". And it was his upright and selfless mother-in-law who had suffered deadly impact. Not only Weiying's career and marriage had also been affected. At the same time, had his mother in a village in Northeastern China who had been praying for him every day. Later Wu Sha, who had lived with her grandmother in the northeastern village for two years, told Weiying, "Weiying aunt, the first thing grandma would do after getting up every morning was to burn joss sticks for the Buddha, praying for father's safe return.

Injured lonely bird

Every time when aunt prepared the breakfast, grandma would fill two bowls of porridge, take some steamed buns and salted vegetables for Wu Jian and me, while she herself would go to burn joss sticks and came back to have some leftovers." Weiying said, "Hey, your father's being identified as an anti-revolutionary has not only made our whole family suffer but also made his 80-year-old mother knee down and burn sticks for him. Who oversees the life expenses your maternal grandma sends?" Wu Sha answered, "Of course our aunt. She oversees the whole family. But whenever grandma needs money, she would give her." Weiying said, "That's OK. Villagers make no money. She is good if she has conscience. Your whole family might have collapsed without the help if not of your maternal grandma. And Your father is in jail without a paycheck, and your whole family is likely to wander when you follow your unhinged mother!"

Weiying understood though her mother was strong enough, her insane sister with three children would be a heavy burden if her brother-in-law was not discharged from prison. If her mother had not taken the responsibility to bear this burden, this anti-revolutionary's wife and their three children would have become an irremediable trouble. His mother in the northeastern village could do nothing but pray for him every day for 10 years in a row, hoping that he could come out safely. So, it was clear that no one would send him food and expenses except the kindhearted mother-in-law. Was Wu clear that he had such a good mother-in-law who lived a frugal life to care for him and the almost broken family instead of asking her daughter to divorce him in his most difficult days?

Under such circumstances, the political future of his children and the Qiu family was seriously devastated. What they had suffered even made Qiu's mom so worried about and devoted to Li Zhimeng 's family day and night that she even forgot own herself declining health. His mentally disordered wife and three young children had become a heavy mental burden that her mother-in-law was forced to burden.

Li Zhimeng --an anti-revolutionary attacking "the Cultural Revolution" and causing harm to his whole family. At the same time, Weiying's career and marriage had also been affected.

Though her mother was nature strong, and she was clench one's teeth, to face all the misfortunes in life and the injustice done to her. But her insane sister with three children would be a heavy burden if her brother-in-law was not discharged from prison.

If his mother-in-law had not taken the responsibility to bear this burden, this anti-revolutionary's wife and their three children would have become a be all broken up family.

His mother in the northeastern village could do nothing but pray for him every day for 10 years in a row, hoping that he could come out safely. So, it was clear that no one would send him food and expenses except the kindhearted mother-in-law. Was Wu clear that he had such a good mother-in-law who lived a frugal life to care for him and the almost broken family instead of asking her daughter to divorce him in his most difficult days? Under such circumstances, the political future of his children and the Qiu family was seriously devastated. What they had suffered even made Qiu's mom so worried about and devoted to Li Zhimeng 's family day and night that she even forgot own herself His mentally disordered wife and three young children had completely become pressed his mother-in-law on body's a heavy cross….

Li Zhimeng, a counterrevolutionary who was branded as an "attacker of the Cultural Revolution". The greater tragedy he caused was the "implicate all of one's close relatives", not only did his wife go insane, but his three children were deprived of a normal living and growing environment. Even his and his wife's parents were affected, and their family members lost their bright future!

5.2 The god bird fly to heaven

One day when Juecong came back home, Weiying said to him, "I heard that a blind person with the surname of Yuan in Yicha Pavilion is good at fortune-telling. Shall we go there to ask him to tell the fortune of our family as well as ourselves?" That time, Juecong worked as a doctor in Changsha Paper-making Factory and was unhappy about not allowed working going to his father's hospital. He agreed and immediately headed there with Weiying. Yuan's house was on a small slope beside the road.

When Weiying and Juecong came in, Yuan could not see but could feel them and asked, "Are you here for fortune-telling?" They answered, "Yes. Please tell the fortunes of our mother and ourselves." Asking for Shao's birthday, Yuan said, "Her birthday indicates that she would suffer. She was going to encounter a hardship at 56, Either her children might be injuring seriously, or she might go to the heaven."

Though they were not happy about his words, they didn't say anything. Then Yuan began to tell the fortune for Juecong, "…you will surpass the last five generations of ancestors." Juecong was quite pleased with that. Yuan told Weiying, "…You were born at noon in summer, a very hot moment. The boy needs noon, but he has no noon. If you were a boy, you would become the No.1 scholar in the imperial examination. But now that you are a girl, you should not get married too early, or you would be divorced. However, you will live a luxurious life in the future and be happier in your declining years." Weiying told him, "I haven't been married at 29, so I'll certainly have a late marriage." But she felt surprised to hear the words "live a luxurious life" because such life was far from her. She just earned 36 yuan a month, the money to buy a cheap watch is not enough. So, the fortune-telling became a riddle in her mind.

Soon a new Secretary of the Party Branch and director Mr. Bian came to the factory. He used to be a cadre retired early from the army. The new director, whose face was always glowing with health, was amicable and humorous, often helping workers in production assembly. He was totally different from the former director who was always assuming great airs with his projected belly and viewing Weiying from a proletariat perspective. Not long after Mr. Bian took office, he was quite confused about why Weiying lived in the factory but had to work in the downtown far away, so he assigned her to work inside the factory soon, making her feel much more convenient in work and life. During that period, the factory began to witness better performance and more profits, so Bian decided to purchase a piece of land of the farmers nearby and build a one-story dormitory in the form of a four-section compound near Changsha Auto Factory. Weiying moved there and it was a few minutes' walk to work.

In the beginning, Weiying was assigned to work in the paint group. She with a few girls together, who to the boilers remove rust and painted. Such a job, though not quite satisfying, would not make Weiying cough every day by smog of hydrochloric acid. She didn't need it from now on tremendous efforts, take a bus to go to work in a faraway city center.

That time the bus was too crowded that she had to wait for the next one, which would occasionally make her late for work and in a bad mood. Transferred here to work, she with young people often got together to talk in their spare time, seeming to bring her back to her middle school time. What was different was that in her school time, those who surrounded her to talk, and laugh were girls of school. But now they were workers and in particular young men. When hearing Weiying talk, they were delighted and always laugh, causing young women workers next to them laugh together. A girl on good terms with Weiying asked her, "Why do they like talking with you? Even if you lose your temper sometimes, they won't take offense." Qiu Weiying said, "It doesn't matter that we talk together, but I often say to them, 'Talking is talking. Don't put your feet on my body. Behave yourself!' I haven't seen anyone who got angry with me after I told them the words."

One day after lunch, while Weiying was going to drink a cup of tea, a technical worker said to her, "Qiu Weiying, Teacher Pan asked you to go to the warehouse." Mr. Pan, a friend of the technical worker, was a warehouse manager. Following the worker to the warehouse, Weiying asked, "Do you know why Pan asked me there?" Into the room, Pan was sitting on a chair. Weiying asked, "What do you want me to do, Mr. Pan?" But he took out a book and declaimed in a leisured voice, "I am a man and fall in love with you sincerely…" Weiying suddenly poured the cup of tea onto him before he could finish the poem, laughing loudly, "Your romance has exceeded the limit!" Pan was not cross at all. He even began to laugh, with his eyes squinted like a line. He was busy patting off the tea leaves and water without saying anything. Standing by Pan's desk, the technical worker rocked with laughter, "You are done, Mr. Pan. You bet on the wrong person." Holding the empty cup in hand, Weiying walked out of the warehouse, feeling his look funny.

On a day off, Weiying was hanging clothes to dry on the tranquil courtyard behind the kitchen when a man comrade came over. She asked him to help lift the bamboo pole. The man held the pole and smiled to her, "Sister Qiu, if I kiss you now, no one will know." She became serious, "You have a girlfriend. You are so dissolute by saying that to me. Don't hold the pole for me. Aren't you afraid that I will tell it to your friend?" He had to smile reluctantly, "Please forgive me. I'm just kidding!" "I can forgive you once but will never if you commit it the second time." He replied immediately, "There will be no second time."

As a result, he had more trust and respect in Weiying and introduced the son of his father's friend to her. He said, "The man is tall and handsome. He has a good master of German. Although he didn't receive college education, he is highly intellectual. And he must be very happy to meet you." Weiying asked, "Where did he learn German without going to college?" "He learned it from his father, who used to be a senior professor in the pre-liberation period, and his mother was a famous film actress then." Therefore, Weiying agreed to meet with that guy.

One day, Weiying followed the colleague to the guy's home after work. What she saw was similar with what he had described, his mother was in illness like Lin Daiyu, sitting beside to listen to their talk; his father was an amiable white-haired tall man, who was pleased to meet Weiying and talked a lot. Weiying looked over the room, simple and poor, but she felt comfortable with the favorable atmosphere of the family. She could also feel the mutual loving emotion between the old couple, which reminded her of her mother's words, "A couple will be happy together as long as they love each other even in hardships." After a while, as it was becoming dark, Weiying stood up and said goodbye. Her colleague and the guy also stood up to see her off. At a crossroad, the colleague said goodbye to them.

Alone with the guy, Weiying asked him, "Do your parents live on their pension?" "No, my father used to write books to sustain our whole family before the Cultural Revolution, after which our property was confiscated, and my father was prohibited from writing. Although I have a job, my poor salary cannot sustain my parents. My father has a lot of students in America, who can help them make a living." "They are so kind to help you. It may not be easy for them to support your family for a long time." "Several students asked my father to go to America to teach and said that he would earn a high salary as a senior intellectual. But he was reluctant to leave the motherland, as a result of which our family were confiscated several times and it's too late to regret. Now my parents have high expectation on me, hoping I can make a difference." While talking, they walked across two stations. Weiying said when arriving at the factory, "You need to work tomorrow. Please go back and I can walk back myself. Thank you." He stopped, holding back what he had intended to say, and bid farewell to her.

Weiying had a sound sleep that night and didn't wake up until the late morning. Two days later, the colleague asked, "How do you think of that guy, Sister Qiu? His parents are fond of you and intend to buy you a bicycle." "Buy me a bicycle? His parents are living a hard life. He is nice and honest. I'll come back to ask for my mother's opinion on the next day off."

When Weiying came back home, before she could tell her mom her colleague had introduced a friend to her, Shao who was in her sick leave at home asked her, "I often have a stomachache and diarrhea these days. Accompany me to the People's Hospital to have an examination.". She said, "Really? Why didn't you tell us earlier?" Mother said, "I have no time. I spent all my spare time looking after Xiaodong and her children. What's more, only my apprentice and me work in a room of hospital. So, I couldn't leave. And the health doctor in my hospital said I just caught diarrhea and would not let me transfer to another hospital. Without their approval, no expense will be reimbursed if I go to another hospital to get treatment. But several months has passed and I don't get any better, so she agreed."

It was then hot in late August or September. Weiying accompanied her mother to People's Hospital not far away from home after cleaning up the house. Although the sun had not risen much high, there was no breeze, making people feel almost suffocated. While in the waiting room, Weiying told her mother that one of her colleagues introduced a boyfriend for her. Shao said, "We have been embarrassed by our own economic and political problems and if you find a guy with similar issues, your future family will be full of trouble like Xiaodong's. Bothersome problems will always pop out." Weiying could words fail one but was unable to give her a correct explanation. Moreover, her mother was not good both physically and mentally, so she didn't insist on saying more.

When it was Shao's turn, the doctor asked about the situation and prescribed some examination sheets. It was almost noon after the colonoscopy was over. A nurse took out Shao's the medical record, asking Weiying, "Is Shao Guizhen your mother?" "Yes." Qiu Weiying let Shao sit on a bench outside and followed the nurse into the clinic to consult the results. In the clinic, Weiying sat down beside the desk. While looking at the medical record, the doctor asked, "Are you Shao Guizhen's daughter?" Weiying nodded. The woman doctor said slightly, "Your mother has got advanced intestinal cancer and may have only half a year to live." The words shocked Weiying like a thunder, prompting her to sudden tears. She turned around her hands, holding the side of the desk to in she would fall to the ground. Sitting in front of the desk, the doctor cast outside at Shao and said to Weiying, "Your mother is watching you." Weiying tried her best to hold back tears. "Thank you." She said in a quiver, taking the medical record and examination sheets on the desk. Outside the clinic, pretending nothing had happened, she said to her mother, "Just have a seat. There are not so many people in the hall and it's close to noon time, so I'm going to fetch your medicine." Waiting at the window for the medicine, she put the sheet on which there were words of "advanced intestinal cancer" into her pocket. Then she returned to her mother's side.

Buses didn't pass by streets and roads near the hospital, and if to a nearby avenue to take a bus they need to walk much farther. So, she holds the mother by the arm and help her across the street. She could not remember what she told her mother perfunctorily on the way back but felt unbearable pain in her heart. When they were waiting for the green light to cross the road down from the gate of Tianxin Pavilion, Shao asked her, "I've caught intestinal cancer, haven't I?" She heard it clearly and replied, "No, I haven't heard the doctor say so." After crossing the road, Shao asked, "Why are you looking so sad? Are you uncomfortable?" "Really? Maybe I've got sunstroke." "Then why don't you visit the doctor just now?" Weiying continued, "It's about noon. Too late. But it doesn't matter. I have had such a situation in the past. If I'm sick or uncomfortable in stomach, a bottle of Huoxiang zhengqi Liquid (a kind of Chinese medicine) will do. I saw there are some at home." At this point, Shaw was staring at Wei Ying's face with suspicion in gaze.

Back home, Weiying told the terrible news to every family member including her cousin Zong Weikang. She didn't tell her sister Xiaodong for fear that she could stand such a shock or a relapse of mental illness. Later she said to Juecong, "The blind Yuan was so accurate in telling mother's fortune." "Yes. So strange."

Zong Weikang went to see Shao several days later, "Aunt, now that you can't be cured by the current medicine, shall we go to 163 Military Hospital to have more examinations and treatment since I've known someone there? Military Hospital is better than local ones in equipment, which may be favorable for you." Shao didn't propose any objection and Zong connected a military hospital in suburban Changsha.

Two days later, Weiying accompanied mother to the hospital at the appointed time and Zong asked one of his acquaintances to send them to the hospital with a car. Shao appreciated the young driver very much, saying to Weiying, "I have rarely seen such a handsome and gentle young man!" Weiying did not express any denial for this 26 or 27-year-old guy of about 180 cm tall. It was said that his father was a senior cadre of a northern military region. He looked well-bred from appearance. Thanks to the driver's timely and selfless help, Qiu didn't need to pay for him. For the first time, the doctor asked Weiying to wait outside and her mother to come in alone to take the examination.

Afterwards, when the door was open, Shao walked out with extremely hard steps, looking extremely worried. Seeing her mother coming out, Weiying immediately rose to her feet and walked towards her mom to support her. Shao said to her daughter weakly, "I got cancer." Weiying heard that cancer patients would better be uninformed of their conditions, or they would collapse mentally, and the disease would worsen. So, she pretended not knowing anything, "How could it be?" Shao went on, "It's true. I asked the doctor, 'How serious is my cancer?' She answered, 'Quite serious.' So, there is no doubt that I caught cancer."

Weiying knew she could not conceal the truth any longer. Walking in silence for a while, she said in a mollifying remarks tone, "Don't be anxious, mom. We should take a positive attitude and get treatment as soon as possible." Shao was quite depressed and said, "I'm not anxious about myself. I'm just worried about Xiaodong and her family. Now I'm just a few steps from death and if Li Zhimeng doesn't come back before I die, what will she and her children do in the future since she is insane sometimes?" "We'll look after them." "They have their own families except you and will not have time to help them. And you must get married soon since you are not young." Not knowing how to answer her mother's question, she just fetched the medicine and accompanied her mother to get into the car.

Fortunately, the new leader was much better than the former one. Knowing Weiying's mother got cancer, he assigned her to do some "safeguarding" work, perhaps out of sympathy. Therefore, she began to sit in the janitor's room at the gate of the workshop of boiler production, ensuring that no one would take the factory's belonging out and letting others sign their names when coming into the factory. The best part of this job was that there were three shifts every day, from 8 a.m. to 4 p.m. and from 4 p.m. to 12 p.m. and Weiying was assigned to be on duty for the latter period so that she had time to look after her mother in the morning. Her younger brother could take turns to care for her mother after work.

At the beginning of the treatment of Shao's cancer, everything seemed not so terrible. When off work, Weiying spent almost all her time caring for her mother. Once she bought two tickets for the film "Three laughs" in a cinema near home. While sitting in the cinema, she saw her mother smile once and seem to have forgotten all miseries in life, which was so rare. And Weiying wished to see mother smile more. She deeply knew that mother had endless sorrowfulness and poignancy, but she had always been bearing them by herself. In the past she used to smile though in reluctancy in order to alleviate the sorrow of the whole family, but now that she knew she got cancer and felt dispirited about everything, she became unhappy even in appearance. She thought she had been "sentenced to death with a reprieve system" and could go away at any time before her son-in-law came back! What could Xiaodong's family that how to do!?

Weiying thought, her brother-in-law being identified as an anti-revolutionary was the top priority of all the miseries that her mother had to confront every day, even more seriously than the confiscation of the properties of her family. This was because Xiaodong was further stimulated by her husband's meet with a tragic death and went insane from time to time, under the circumstance of which mother had to take care of Xiaodong and her three children day and night. But the confiscation of family property of the properties came as a sudden shock and occasional pains. However, mother would never be tranquil in mind until Li Zhimeng came out of prison. Unwilling to see mother disappear from this mortal world at just 50-odd years old, Weiying expected to prolong her mother's life so that she could get spiritual compensation in later life; she yearned to see mother could sustain till a miracle in curing cancer in the medical arena occurred. Therefore, she ran to Hunan Medical College to ask Zhao Zhengrong---a classmate who was on good terms with her eldest sister with the same father but different mother during elementary school in Changsha---for help. It was established in 1913 in Changsha by the Hunan Yuqun Society in association with the American Yale Association, with the church stepping in, and is the best hospital in Hunan for nearly 100 years.

Zhao was surprised to hear that Shao got cancer! She frowned, "Your mother is such a kindhearted woman! How could she get such a disease? When your sister who is now in Qingdao was being schooled in Changsha, your family lived the life. Whenever we went to your home, your mother always asked us to have dinner. If you want your mother to have an operation, she'd better have it at an earlier date because this can ensure a longer survival. A person working in the library of our college who had an operation on intestinal cancer for more than a decade is living quite well now. But the difference is that she discovered the cancer and had the operation at a much earlier date. It was so poor to get such a disease. I've seen many patients suffering from advanced cancer die of unbearable pain. Since your mother is a doctor herself, why doesn't she get immediate examination and treatment?" Weiying replied, "She had to concern her patients at work and sister Xiaodong's family off work. Since the confiscation of our family properties, Xiaodong was imprisoned in the medical management committee and once went insane. Later my brother-in-law was identified as an anti-revolutionary, making her totally insane. My brother-in-law had no salary and his family in a northern village couldn't offer any help; furthermore, my sister often used her little salary to buy things for other people. So, if not for my mother, her family with two little boys and a girl baby who hadn't seen her father since born would collapse. Who will care for this anti-revolutionary family except my mother? Mother spent enormous time and money on her family and was very frugal to herself especially when father's salary was reduced by almost half. Thus, it's no wonder that she suffers from mal-nutrition and poor health. What's more, the two unjust s of the confiscation of family properties and my brother-in-law's identification as an anti-revolutionary makes her feel sorrowful and desperate. She bears much more mental pressure than anyone else."

Zhao frowned and said in a sympathetic tone, "It is unimaginable that your family which used to be so well-off that we all admire your eldest sister is that miserable now. If you did not encounter so much, ordinary family cannot overtake yours. And Xiaodong was also very smart and active. It's unbelievable that she would go insane." Weiying said, "Yes. We have never been as poor as now. When we were in hardship in the past, we have meat to eat, and our meals had never been quantified. Sister Xiaodong skipped grade in No. 2 Middle School. When the school held get-togethers, she looks quite impressive directed the whole team in singing, and high-and mighty, though she was not tall enough. Nevertheless, now my mother lives a much harder life than those times in the past and is depressed for a long time, which is called 'qi stagnation' according to the Chinese medical theory. I think the mental shock and stress constitute the main reason for her cancer." Zhao continued, "Exactly. I suggest your mother having an artificial anus as early as possible and I will try to find her a skilled professor." "Thank you so much. I'll try to persuade my mother to accept operation."

Several days later, Weiying accompanied mother to the hospital of an amiable white-haired professor at the appointed time. After looking over the medical record and making relevant examinations, the professor asked Shao to have an operation of artificial anus immediately. Weiying persuaded her mother to agree and signed the agreement on behalf of their family. The day before the operation, she accompanied Shao into the patient ward to have related examinations. She said to the professor responsible for the operation, "I will be off work tomorrow morning and can come here to accompany my mother." "It is stipulated that family members can't come in while patients are in operation. So, don't come here tomorrow. There will be nurses responsible for caring your mother. But you can come to the ward to visit her after the operation." Therefore, Weiying said goodbye to her mother and went back to her new dormitory in the factory.

It was dark and gloomy the next morning. Not knowing whether the operation would be successful, Weiying felt sad and repressed. After having breakfast in a nearby little restaurant, she decided to go to the hospital in the afternoon. She planned to go back home in the morning to clean up mother's room and bed so that she would live more comfortably when back home from hospital. When she arrived at the steps, she felt surprised to see the room door opened, father brought Juecong to Dalian Army Hospital to participate in the cooperation project of proctorial diseases. Damao and Xiaomao had never stayed at home. Who opened the door? To her surprise, she saw her mother lying in bed in the room. She felt strange, "What's wrong, mom? Why are you home?" Shao answered, "I'm not willing to have an artificial sphincter. What's the meaning of being a human if I always have a rubber bag below my waist to hold urine?" Weiying said, "How could that do? I have signed my name on the agreement." Shao answered, "The signature will lose effect now that I've fled. I heard that an old Chinese medical doctor in Heishidu is good at curing cancer." Weiying didn't believe that she speaks, "I don't believe it, or he has got the Nobel Prize. Perhaps he was a mountebank." Mother still insisted, "Anyway I'd like to have a try. I don't want an artificial sphincter!" At this, Weiying was quite anxious and sat down in a chair beside the dinner table. Not knowing how to persuade her mother, she told her about the fortune-telling by the blind Yuan. Consequently, mother said unswervingly, "I don't want child to become handicapped. I would rather die, for people were born to die anyhow." Weiying remained silent, feeling the gloom and fragility of life.

From then on, Shao began to look for the "charlatanism" in Heishidu. Knowing that Weiying doesn't believe him, Shao never asked her to accompany for fear that she would cause trouble. The Chinese medicine prescribed by the mountebank needed to be braised in crock two or three times a day, so Damao asked her mother to live in her home in the village. In this way she could look after her mother as well as her two boys. Later, Zong Weikang asked that driver again to send Shao to Damao's home with the accompany of Weiying. Damao's husband who was a villager did some small businesses, which were introduced by Juecong's wife. And Shao began to live in Damao's home.

But after two or three months, she did not get any better; instead, she felt more uncomfortable while taking the Chinese medicine. Weiying was learning by herself the medical theory of the "combination of Chinese and Western medicine to treat anus and intestinal tract disease." She thought cancer was malignant tumor which originated from benign tumor. Since cancer could pass on to other parts of the body, could I use the combination of Chinese and Western medicine to ligate the malignant part of the intestine and then inject and operate? But she had never practiced, so she went to Zong Weikang's home, asking, "Brother, can you use the method of combining Chinese and Western medicine to operate on my mother?" Zong refused at once, "I dare not do that, for I can't take the responsibility if there occurs any problem." Weiying said, "Mother is hard to escape her destiny anyhow. If we have a try, she might be saved. Who knows?" Zhong insisted, "I don't agree with you. So, let's go to persuade aunt to come back to Changsha and have an operation in hospital." Weiying nodded. Then Zong asked the young driver to come to Damao's home to persuade her and brought her back.

Shao did not notify the hospital staff last time she was going to have an operation, so Weiying was embarrassed to find Zhao Zhengrong again. Hunan Tumor Hospital, which was specialized in treating cancer, opened at that time. As all its facilities were new, they urged Shao to have the operation and change an artificial austere. Weiying got up early on the day her mother was to have the operation. It was cloudy and she felt nervous and gloomy as she was afraid whether the operation would be a success. After cleaning up and having breakfast nearby, she went back home and then went to the hospital alone, very upset. Mother was hospitalized the day before, and Weiying followed her movable sickbed all the way till she was pushed into the operation room. Shao looked much weaker and paler than last time she went to hospital. Weiying looked at nurses pushing her into the room and then sat down on the bench by the window. Although it was not very hot, she felt suffocated and therefore stood up to open the window. She saw the newly built wards were almost empty, with few patients and sickbeds. It seemed that this hospital was not ready for everything, and at this, she felt upset and anxious.

After a short while, the door of the operation room opened out of a sudden and two nurses pushed out the sickbed on which her mother was lying. Knowing that such a complicated operation could not be finished so soon, she became frightened and ran there, "What's wrong?" The nurses did not say anything but pushed her mother to the ward. Hearing her daughter's voice, mother opened her eyes and murmured with a quiver, "The power was off, they just finished injecting anesthetic." Weiying was so angry that her tears went down. She tried her best to stay calm and asked the nurses, "Why did the power go off during the operation?" A nurse answered, "Our hospital hasn't been equipped with full electricity circuits, so now we're using a generator to give power. During the operation, the generator stopped working." Weiying blamed them immediately, "Then you should have prepared two generators to ensure the smooth process of operations. You are irresponsible for patients." With these words, she could not stop her tears but could do nothing, and She could only feel sad for the poor mother. The next day the operation began and went smoothly. Shao continued to be in hospital for several days after the operation, then she left the hospital and went home to live.

National policies became easier after the "Gang of Four" was beaten down. In January 1979, the government formulated a policy of letting children under unemployment replace their parents' occupation after the latter retire. Therefore, Juele who was in Junshan farm in Yue Shao that spring began working in his mother's hospital and engaging in treatment of rectal diseases. In this way, when Weiying had to go to work, he could take care of his mother after four p.m.

Qiu Zhongyuan was unlikely to look after Shao though he had retired for two to three years. Because Juele could work freely after retirement, Therefore, some people who do not have a fixed job, and who have no reimbursement for medical treatment, and a few who even have a work unit, are willing to find him. because he has a reliable treatment effect. Therefore, he was much happier even though he just earned 87 yuan because he, in his own words, did not need to quarrel with Director Wang, whom he hated a lot. However, he was just straightforward and never attempted to revenge on her.

After the operation, Shao thought she must listen to the arrangement of destiny. She asked Weiying to remit money to Li Zhimeng's younger brother to send Wu Jian and Wu Sha to Xiaodong's home as Wu Jian was going to attend middle school. Seeing her children, Xiaodong was glad, "I thought they must have been quite thin and small because of hunger, but they aren't." Weiying saw lisha become stronger and thought full grained food was good for people.

During this period, after the cancerous rectal segment of Qiu's mother was removed and replaced with an artificial anus, didn't have any negative reaction during the first two months after the operation. One day Weiying came back home but didn't see her father. Juele, lying in the big bed he shared with his father, said, "Xiao liu and I are to get married, but father doesn't support me. He said he had brought us up and that both of us had jobs, so we could solve it by ourselves. After marriage, I'll live in her home. Her family has an apartment with three bedrooms and one sitting room, which is given by the Provincial Power Machinery Factory, and they prepared one room for us." Weiying said to Juele without hesitation, "It was inconvenient to live with our parents. And your wedding is no small matter, so I can provide help. I have saved more than 500 yuan these years. Is that enough?" Juele smiled immediately, "Really? Then that will be sufficient for my wedding." "My bankbook is locked in the chest in my dormitory. I'll draw the money out from the bank tomorrow and give it to you. Just wait for me at home." Listening to them talk, Shao smiled with comfort. mother who had been looking after Xiaodong's family for nearly 10 years was unlikely to have any saving in bank.

The next day, Weiying drew the money out from the bank near the galvanized iron sales department she had worked at before and then went to have a look at the situation of the department. One of her former colleagues called her, "Weiying, what do you come here for?" "My brother doesn't have enough money to hold his wedding, so I drew my savings of about 500 yuan out to help him." Another white-haired woman said, "Your mother has got cancer and you yourself are already 30. It's not easy to save 500 yuan. You won't have money to prepare dowries when you get married if you give all to your brother, will you?" Weiying objected, "Now I don't have a boyfriend, so it's unnecessary to consider getting married. Even though I have one someday, I'll not marry him if he emphasizes my dowries. He marries me the person not my dowries. It's meaningless to marry a man who attaches too much importance to a woman's dowries." At this, the colleague remained silent. Perhaps she thought Weiying was right. On arriving home, Weiying gave the money to Juele, who was quite pleasant and held the wedding soon. After the wedding, Juele's wife gave birth to a lovely girl. He really needed to get married, or his daughter might not be able to have a registered permanent residence. When Weiying was not home, he would come back to look after Shao, but he stayed overnight less and less. Usually only the parents stayed home at night.

Seeing his wife was the same with normal women from appearance, Qiu Zhongyuan who was still full of energy demanded sex sometimes. But because Shao was reduced to despair, so that she coldly rejected her husband. Thus, Qiu began to neglect his wife's illness more and more, and Shao had to be looked after only by Weiying and Juele.

One day when Weiying came home and saw her mother's painful expression, she asked, "Are you feeling uncomfortable, mom?" Shao told her, "Your father was totally inconsiderate. I've had an operation, but he even demanded to have sex at midnight. I said to him, 'I have no interest as the sex life doesn't accord with me.' He lost his temper to me, 'Then I'll have it with another woman. Don't blame me.' Perhaps he had a ligation, so he has much desire for sexual life though he is already more than 60." Finishing these words with tears, Shao seemed more sorrowful. Weiying who had never had sex couldn't think of anything to comfort her mother. She felt that her father was just too selfish for he never considered his wife's feelings.

Since 1978, the government China's work to redress unjust, false and wrong cases. By this time it had been going on for several months. Qiu Weiying who was born with values of justice and fairness felt strange as her brother-in-law's was not redressed. She knew that the wrongful judgment to him and the confiscation of family property of her family's properties were two burdens in the heart of her mother, who, however, did not mention them probably because she feels held no hope and got the incurable cancer. Weiying could do nothing as her brother-in-law had been identified as an anti-revolutionary in Ningxia. But she was clear about the confiscation of family property, so she took the receipt from her father and went to the Office of Letters and Calls of Changsha Committee of the CPC in Pan Zheng Street.

While waiting at the office, she made acquaintance with Xiaoliang, a gentle woman who was about the same age with her and she lived nearby. Talking with her, Weiying knew that her father's disease was cured by Dr. Qiu Zhongyuan. The woman's family was a of national capitalist, and she came here for the illegal confiscation of family property of her family's properties during the Cultural Revolution and visit the complaint by letter place or visits authorities to voice one's grievances and ask for help.

Weiying also told her family cases, but the working staff of the office responded, "There are so many properties confiscated illegally during the Cultural Revolution that the state cannot count and repay all. What it can do is not make enquiries politically any longer."

Weiying said, "Our properties were confiscated before the Cultural Revolution and our house hasn't been returned." "Then there's no alternative. The properties have been submitted to the state treasury. As for your family's private house, we can reexamine the case. And we'll notify you later."

After back go to the home, Weiying didn't mention her petition to her mother. Because she was unwilling to aggravate mother's poignancy before the problem was solved. Her single wish was that mother could live longer till the miracle to cure cancer in the medical circle occurred and at that time she would probably be able to make mother's. Live become better than now and which could be a compensation for her. Nevertheless, under the current circumstance, she could only buy some food her mother liked to eat. The mother's requirements are not high, it was very easy.

Qiu Zhongyuan submitted a report when he retired at the beginning of 1978, in which he wrote, "They confiscated our properties illegally…They took family Qiu's everything forces an entrance and including our daily necessities and food coupon, so that we had nothing to eat after the confiscation of family property… The Medical Management Committee said then, 'I'll keep them temporarily and return them to you when the case ended.' But they haven't returned anything till now. The central government has put in place the redress a grievance policy, but why can't you redress the miscarriage of justice?" Consequently, he didn't get any reply and became dispirited. Therefore, he and Juecong went to Dalian Army Hospital to work and returned to Changsha one year later.

After retirement, Qiu Zhongyuan had sufficient free time and thus had many things to do. Furthermore, he was well-known for curing diseases, so when he went to treat patients at their home, he would always receive warm welcome. Despite his age, he never looked old or clumsy. Instead, he was vigorous and spoke loudly, attracting those vainglory-adoring women who couldn't make money and especially young women. There was such a woman named Tu Hua who was just 20-odd years old and could be Qiu's granddaughter. Tu's father was sick with serious high complex anal fistula, with a large part of his ass rotten. It would take several months to recover if he accepted treatment, but if the operation failed, it would probably cause fecal incontinence because though the cut of high anal fistula was on the skin surface, it had a channel passing onto the anal. A complex anal fistula was formed by complicate channels like branches of a tree, so channels and rotten flesh had to be cut off to let new flesh grow. And a severe medical accident would happen without superior skills in operation. Tu Hua's family were peasants living in suburban Changsha, with no one making money in the city, so they could hardly afford the expenses of going to hospital. What's more, the hospital didn't agree to render treatment until her father got hospitalized. When in great anxiety, a friend who had been treated and cured by Qiu Zhongyuan recommended Qiu who could go to their home to treat her father, delighting the whole family very much. They welcomed Qiu warmly and put all their hopes on this prestigious doctor. And for Qiu, this was quite easy. As Tu's father was recovering well after the treatment, her whole family were grateful for him. Out of admiration for his superior medical skills and his ability to earn money easily, they let their daughter learn skills from him and keep in touch with him frequently.

One day when Weiying came back home, mother said to her sadly, "Look at your father. He's so annoying. He just wished me to die as soon as possible. The girl named Tu Hua ran here and slept in your father's bed, opposite to your father, who even asked me to put the mosquito-repellent incense beside her head. I said he shouldn't have done such a thing, but he lost temper to me. That girl got up the next morning, singing and dancing happily in front of me. Doesn't she feel ashamed?" With these words, Shao could not help her tears. Then Weiying felt so bad that she could not understand why his father could be so ruthless and cruel after living with her mother for decades and having several children. There was no doubt that must increase mother's endless pain. Weiying regretted that she didn't encounter Tu, or she would have cursed her seriously and then kick her out the door.

She wrapped her mother's tears with tissues, asking, "Mom, I can't understand why a girl who can be father's granddaughter would like him?" mother sighed indignantly, "There are various kinds of people. These shameless women just look for men who can benefit themselves. Though your father was old, he was a prestigious doctor with extraordinary medical skills. She may think that he is much better than villagers with neither skills nor money. If she marries a young villager, she'll have to do housework and cut vegetables feed the pigs every day and find it difficult to earn even changes. She will have money by staying around your father. I also saw your father bought her a pair of shoes and she fitted them before me, 'They fit my feet. I like it.' She kept smiling to your father all day long, singing with satisfaction." Weiying went on, "Anyway, she should find a man about the same age with her and owns a family. But now she interferes in our family affairs, does she want me to call her who is even younger than me 'mother'? It is ridiculous. Mom, you are too simpleminded, why didn't I hear you talk about it before?" Shao answered, "In the beginning, I thought I was going to go away, so I just let it be. But who knows they have gone too far, and your father becomes more and more merciless to me? I can't stand it anymore." Shao said with her tears running down her face. Weiying said, "Mom, this woman is so shameless, and you can't remain silent anymore. You should tell Juecong and Juele to let them intimidate her."

Juele came in just then. He knew earlier than his sister that Tu Hua was on abnormal terms with his father, but he didn't know that she dared to stimulate his mother so directly and furiously. He hit the ceilings, "Damn it! How dare she deal with mother? I'll kill her the next time I see her." Weiying said immediately, "Don't kill her. It's not worth losing your own life. What's more, it's not good to let others know you are imprisoned for that. I dare not visit you then." Shao said, "That's why I did not tell you in the first place." Weiying continued, "Don't worry, mom. Juele is just too angry. He will not do that." Juele turned around and watched his mother, "Of course not. I'll just kick her out of our house." Several days later when Weiying came home, Juele told her, "I came across that shameless woman before dinner yesterday. I found a hammer beneath the cement table in the kitchen and rushed into the room, shouting at her, "Go away! Are you waiting to be killed by my hammer?' Father ran to scramble for the hammer, and she was so scared as to run out. I chased her to the door and shouted at her with the hammer in hand, 'I'll kill you the next time I see you.' When I walked back into the room, father was pushing his bicycle outwards." Shao continued, "He must have accompanied Tu home located in the suburban area. He once said that the air was fresh in village and riding to her house was doing some physical exercise and that the whole family received him with great hospitality every time he went there."

When Weiying came back after a few days, Shao said with grievance, "Your father blamed me for instigating Juele and Wu Jian to steal his bicycle and quarreled with me furiously. As I did not attend him, he dragged me down from the bed. I can't bear such a man anymore. Accompany me to his hospital and I'd like to report his behaviors to his leader." Weiying felt sad at her mother's requirement, but it was so hard for her to do so. She objected with unwillingness, "Mom, that will not do. Director Wang has always been hating dad. If you tell her this matter, it will be spread all over, what can we children do in front of others?" Shao was angry, "I'm dying soon, but he still bullies me. What else should I consider?" Weiying was quite poignant but could not accept her mother's requirement. Shao did not mention it as she remained silent. But she felt that her mother was a little angry with her because of her disagreement.

Soon Shao brought Xiaodong's two sons to the hospital without telling Juele, and the hospital took this matter much more serious than Shao had predicted, Wang was expecting Qiu's family to report his scandal, which gave her a chance to take revenge on him. Therefore, she sent her staff to collect proofs of Qiu's crimes and attempted to use the scandal as a fuse. Nonetheless, Qiu Zhongyuan had not had any abnormal relationship with his women patients for decades. They asked him to go to the hospital and write a self-review. Qiu didn't admit that he was wrong in this matter and thus refused to write anything. So, the hospital sent someone to Tu Hua's home, threatening her, "If you cover up Qiu Zhongyuan, you are also committing a crime, for he will harm other people in the future." Tu Hua, though shameless, had some conscience then and insisted, "I'm willing to do that. How can you say he did harm to me?" Interpersonal relationship might have been devastated by mutual hatred in narrow-minded people who would be so delighted to push the other to hell. Despite the fact that Qiu Zhongyuan, invested in and set up the past Changsha Southern Region Hospital and made it earn millions of yuan by selling the buildings to Hunan Provincial Department of Finance when the hospital was renamed "Changsha Institute of Chinese Medicine" and moved, who could remember the history? And who would thank Qiu Zhongyuan? He let a cleaner be the director Part-time party branch secretary position of the hospital but did not expect that she hated him so much as to make use of every opportunity to revenge.

The next day, Shao became was be anxiety-ridden because Qiu Zhongyuan did not come home for lunch and therefore asked Wu Di to go to the hospital to see what happened. Wu Di came back, "Grandpa was in a room alone and there are pieces of paper and a pen on the desk beside him. He told me, 'The hospital forced me to confess my crime related with Tu Hua, but I have nothing to say.' Grandpa said he had lunch there." Later Shao told Weiying, "I was just trying to relieve my hatred and let the hospital leaders educate him …". At this moment, Qiu's mother's heart was like frying oil, she wanted to use the power of the hospital leadership to help her to dispel her sorrow, but now she is "even more sorrowful". The result went against her will and it is too late to regret it! She thought this world was merciless because a couple who had lived together for decades could become enemies! She couldn't control herself cried in front of her daughter.

Watching her mother bearing the agony both physically and mentally, Weiying was reminded of the series of tortures her mother had undergone ever since her childhood, sister Xiaodong told her experience of being forced to confessed to an inexistent "crime" after the confiscation of family properties in 1965, after which she became insane from time to time though awake most of the time; but she totally collapsed since her husband got identified as an anti-revolutionary. Under such circumstances, selfless and kindhearted mother took all responsibility to look after her and her three children, as well as Li Zhimeng and his mother in village. The 10 years during which Wu was imprisoned was also the period when she suffered a lot in the "prison" of the mortal world. She led such a hard life that she finally got the incurable cancer, and moreover, when she needed comfort most, she didn't get it but… (Weiying thought her care for her mother was insignificant, which could not abate her pain.)

In the first place, Weiying thought that most men like young women and her father should take the main responsibility for that matter. However, once when washing clothes for her father, she found in his pocket a letter which completely reversed her view. On her day off, she went home at noon and saw her mother sleep, so she took out the clothes to be washed. Meanwhile she found father's coat hanging behind the door, on which there was a layer of dust, so she took and prepared to wash it too. But she found a letter, on the two sides of which there were different handwritings. One side was her father's handwriting she was familiar with very much, but the other was handwriting like an elementary school student. Curious about this letter, Weiying unfolded it to read.

Her father wrote, "Dear Tu Hua," and then listed five items below, three of which were remembered by Weiying most clearly, it is impossible that I will marry you. Because our age is very different, my whole family will oppose.

If you want to learn medical skills out of admiration for me, I can teach you. If you have the patience to learn, I'll teach you by myself till you master all and get a doctor certificate. Although I can't marry you, I will not change my mind if you don't. You can be my nominally adoptive daughter forever. Finishing reading this side, Weiying began to read the other side, on which Tu Hua wrote in quite a ridiculous tone,

My love---Doctor Qiu,

I miss you so much since I haven't seen you for a long time. I'm so anxious that I can't eat and sleep. I'm happy to receive your letter but become when you say you can't marry me. I feel very back pain (Bèi Tòng). At this, Weiying felt angry but ridiculous as she knew that Tu must have written the wrong character. (Profound sorrow - Bēi Tòng).

What was more laughable was that in the blank space of the paper, Tu drew two hands, one big and the other small, clutching together. Weiying thought it seemed that Tu Hua yearned to hold her father tightly for fear that he would flee away and what she did might have been approved and supported by her parents. Therefore, it was her own dream to be together with father.

Weiying wondered whether they were playing or not, what degree they had reached, and what the result would be. But anyway, Tu never dared to come here since Juele intimidated her. After reading the letter, she decided to buy some vegetables for lunch and then wash the clothes. As she was heading out, mother woke up, "You're back." "Yes. I'm going to buy some vegetables. What do you want to eat?" "I'm not feeling well and have no appetite. Just boil some porridge." Weiying said, "I have bought you a pack of rice cake and peanut cake you like very much." "Then soak some rice cake for me." Weiying made that for her mother and then went out to buy some pork livers and vegetables.

Back home, she saw Juele sitting in the room in company of mother, who said to Weiying with enormous effort, "My cancer may have spread, causing pain to my whole body. Go to the Provincial People's Hospital to ask the doctor to prescribe some pethidine for me. But tell the doctor that anodyne no longer works for me and only injection of pethidine can work a little." Weiying said, "I heard from a skinny old woman say, 'she has been addicted to pethidine for killing pain, but the hospital rejected to prescribe it for her because it is poisonous to a certain degree. She has been very weak, and the hospital cannot take responsibility if any problem occurs. So, you'd better not use it." Shao said, "But anodyne can't alleviate my pain. Doctors did not often prescribe pethidine for me, so they will do so." Weiying believed that her mother was painful, for she had never sat up since she went to the hospital to report father to his leaders with the company of Xiaodong's two sons. If she wanted to eat something, someone must raise her head up and fed her with a spoon. Her hands, feet and belly began to swell. She was suffering from the unbearable sufferings both mentally and physically. Thus, Weiying had no alternative but to make some concessions.

Weiying went to the hospital after lunch and Juele was home to accompany mother. At the end of the downgrade path of Tianxin Pavilion, she saw Liu Pingan's mother sitting at the gate of their house and watching passers come and go through the lane. Seeing Weiying, she immediately called her, who walked there and began to talk. Liu's mother had known a little about her father and Tu Hua, so Weiying took out the letter to show her, "Look, from this letter, Tu Hua wished to marry my father. I can't understand why she would be interested in a man 40-odd years older than her. Look, my father is unlikely to marry her, which, in her words, makes her too sad. And she mistook the characters." The granny laughed, "Your father has a stroke of luck in adventures with women." Weiying pointed to the end of the letter, "Look. She even drew two hands, indicating that she wouldn't let my father go."

Seeing that, Liu's mother burst into laughter and her tears came out. While wiping the tears with a handkerchief, she said, "Weiying, I have lived in this world for decades and seen various kinds of people. You are not the same kind of person with that girl, so you can't understand her. Moreover, she's probably taught by her parents. Some parents only look for temporary interests instead of considering their children's future." Weiying replied, "Perhaps her parents are grateful to my father. Since your son is good at cross talk, you can ask him to turn this story into a comic monologue and there must be a lot of listeners." Liu's mother smiled, "No, he can't do that. He's your father's god son." Weiying said, "I just said it for fun." Then she said with a sad look, "My mother is now so painful all over that she could hardly bear it and sent me to ask the doctor to prescribe pethidine for her in the People's Hospital." The granny sighed, "Your mother is such a good woman. How could she get cancer?" Weiying stood up, put the letter into her pocket, and said goodbye to Liu's mother. After fetching pethidine, she thought on the way, it was urgent for the medical circle to cure cancer as so many good guys were killed by it. How she wished that her mother could wait for the miracle and have a happy life in her declining years and a get compensation.

It was dark as to rain in a morning of October. Weiying returned home and Juele told her in the kitchen, "Mother was aching quite severely yesterday so that she did not have dinner and couldn't sleep at night. I sat by her bed and kept awake all night. So, I want to come back to sleep a while and come here to take your turn before you go to work." After Juele left, Weiying went to her mother's side, seeing her lie in bed and stare at the ceilings with a painful expression. Knowing that her daughter came, she said, "Fetch the bottle of sleeping pills on the table and feed me all." Hearing that, Weiying knew what she meant. She felt miserable and scared, "Mom, I'll never do that!" Shao said powerlessly and intermittently, "You'll do a good…deed. I can't bear the pain… anymore. What's more, it'll be hard for you to look after…" "No, not hard." But Shao insisted, "You are already 30 and spent all your spare time…looking after me at home. If you continue like this, you can only marry a man whose wife has died. It'll be difficult for you to find an unmarried man… But you are unwilling to be a stepmother…if you marry a divorced man. There are few good ones among unmarried guys." Weiying didn't want her mother to continue because it was so hard for her to speak, so she interrupted, "It doesn't matter, mom. There are not few grateful to my father. Since your son is good at cross talk, you can ask him to turn this story into a comic monologue and there must be a lot of listeners." Liu's mother smiled, "No, he can't do that. He's your father's god son." Weiying said, "I just said it for fun." Then she said with a sad look, "My mother is now so painful all over that she could hardly bear it and sent me to ask the doctor to prescribe pethidine for her in the People's Hospital." The granny sighed, "Your mother is such a good woman. How could she get cancer?" Weiying stood up, put the letter into her pocket, and said goodbye to Liu's mother. After fetching pethidine, she thought on the way, it was urgent for the medical circle to cure cancer as so many good guys were killed by it. How she wished that her mother could wait for the miracle and have a happy life in her declining years and a get compensation.

It was dark as to rain in a morning of October. Weiying returned home and Juele told her in the kitchen, "Mother was aching quite severely yesterday so that she did not have dinner and couldn't sleep at night. I sat by her bed and kept awake all night. So, I want to come back to sleep a while and come here to take your turn before you go to work." After Juele left, Weiying went to her mother's side, seeing her lie in bed and stare at the ceilings with a painful expression. Knowing that her daughter came, she said, "Fetch the bottle of sleeping pills on the table and feed me all." Hearing that, Weiying knew what she meant. She felt miserable and scared, "Mom, I'll never do that!" Shao said powerlessly and intermittently, "You'll do a good…deed. I can't bear the pain… anymore. What's more, it'll be hard for you to look after…" "No, not hard." But Shao insisted, "You are already 30 and spent all your spare time…looking after me at home. If you continue like this, you can only marry a man whose wife has died. It'll be difficult for you to find an unmarried man… But you are unwilling to be a stepmother…if you marry a divorced man. There are few good ones among unmarried guys." Weiying didn't want her mother to continue because it was so hard for her to speak, so she interrupted, "It doesn't matter, mom. There are not few killing pain, but the hospital rejected to prescribe it for her because it is poisonous to a certain degree. She has been very weak, and the hospital cannot take responsibility if any problem occurs. So, you'd better not use it." Shao said, "But anodyne can't alleviate my pain. Doctors did not often prescribe pethidine for me, so they will do so." Weiying believed that her mother was painful, for she had never sat up since she went to the hospital to report father to his leaders with the company of Xiaodong's two sons. If she wanted to eat something, someone must raise her head up and fed her with a spoon. Her hands, feet and belly began to swell. She was suffering from the unbearable sufferings both mentally and physically. Thus, Weiying had no alternative but to make some concessions.

Weiying went to the hospital after lunch and Juele was home to accompany mother. At the end of the downgrade path of Tianxin Pavilion, she saw Liu Pingan's mother sitting at the gate of their house and watching passers come and go through the lane. Seeing Weiying, she immediately called her, who walked there and began to talk. Liu's mother had known a little about her father and Tu Hua, so Weiying took out the letter to show her, "Look, from this letter, Tu Hua wished to marry my father. I can't understand why she would be interested in a man 40-odd years older than her. Look, my father is unlikely to marry her, which, in her words, makes her too sad. And she mistook the characters." The granny laughed, "Your father has a stroke of luck in adventures with women." Weiying pointed to the end of the letter, "Look. She even drew two hands, indicating that she wouldn't let my father go."

Seeing that, Liu's mother burst into laughter and her tears came out. While wiping the tears with a handkerchief, she said, "Weiying, I have lived in this world for decades and seen various kinds of people. You are not the same kind of person with that girl, so you can't understand her. Moreover, she's probably taught by her parents. Some parents only look for temporary interests instead of considering their children's future." Weiying replied, "Perhaps her parents are unmarried good men and women and I'm not that significant. And I must listen to fate. Look at you. You have brought up several children and are tired all day, what about now? I'll not do as you said." Shao replied at once, "Men are doomed to die. What have the meaning… of living now for me? I suffer tortuously from a disease and live so hard and would rather die, which might be much better." Knowing that her mother had entirely lost confidence in life, Weiying couldn't find any words to comfort her. She was just choking and turned around to avoid her mother seeing her tears. She could understand her mother's requirement to end her own life because she could feel her circumstance and her thought. But in the then world, there was no euthanasia. Yan said those words to indicate that she could not bear the huge pain anymore.

On October 15th, 1979, Weiying returned to her dormitory after work at 12 o'clock at night and finished washing, she suddenly heard several distressing cries from a crow in the thundering silence of the night, making her feel scared, whether mother would…tonight? Should I come home now? Hearing a crow cry was unlucky according to the traditional saying. Moreover, her mother had been sick in bed for months and could not even turn over. And her body skin was full of cocoons. Weiying looked up into the sky, the dark sky seemed totally inert. But it was too late, and she was afraid to ride home along the silent path beside the Martyr's Park. She had no courage to take the risk and there was no suitable place for her to sleep at home, so she went to bed with a heavy heart.

Weiying woke up early specially the next day and saw the dark sky was full of clouds. The rain was coming not coming down and making people cause difficulty in breathing. She is having breakfast nearby, she rushed home. Entering the door, she saw her mother lying in bed alone and staring at the ceilings hopelessly. She called "Mom" and mother replied in so weak a voice, "Juele has gone…to take…medicine." Stammering these words, mother seemed to begin going to another world. Weiying thought that she must be tortured too much to have not a sound sleep last night, so she sat down at the door quietly and glanced over medical books. Later when she saw her mother's eyes half-closed, she shut the door in order not to disturb her and went to the kitchen to prepare lunch. After washing the vegetables, she pushed the door open and saw mother fall asleep.

Thus, she went to the kitchen again, preparing to fry the vegetables, before which she wanted to have a look at her mother first.

She had seen a big mosquito on her mother's pale face, she immediately ran to drive it away. She didn't hit vampires to death directly for fear of waking her mother. Otherwise, she really wants to beat it to death! At the same time, she thought angrily in her heart: You damn vampire, my mother's blood has already been absorbed dried! Where does she blood for you to suck too? It was regret that she could only drive it away. Then she looked at her mother's face and suddenly felt there was something wrong, her face was completely pale, and lips turned grey; she did not have any expression on her face and seemed to have stopped breathing. One of her eyes was open but the other closed. Out of a sudden surprise, Weiying felt extremely nervous and worried. She called "Mom" but received no reaction. She was so desperate as to shout "mom" several times. But her mother appeared like a wooden statue without any demonstration of being alive. A sense of unbearable fear overwhelmed Weiying so that she began to shout out and cried hard. She seemed to lose head and banged on the bedhead without knowing any pain. But her mother lay still without any reaction despite her calls and bangs. She ran outside and cried to Granny Shi, her next-door neighbor, "Granny, please have a look at my mother. Is she…?" Without finishing her words, the old woman answered, "Don't cry, Weiying. It is true. You'd better prepare for your mother's funeral." Hearing that, she was sure that her mother had left her and the world forever; she had gone to the heaven full of severe pain and torture both mentally and physically; she had gone away from this world which had made her desperate. She died so poorly!! Weiying cried hard not only because her mother had left forever... No one could escape death as was their destiny, but was there anything more unbearable than to die from both mental and physical torture?

Soon Juele came back and knew something must have knew happened when seeing his old sister crying on the doorstep. He went at once into the room and his mother's bedside. He knew that mother had left when receiving no reaction from her after shouting "mom" and patting the quilt several times. His tears ran down through his face. Meanwhile he realized that they shall prepare for mother's funeral. Walking to Weiying's side with tears in her eyes, he did not know what to say to her. Weiying walked into the room with her head in a daze and began to clean up the room together with Juele. They totally forgot about lunch.

Weiying boiled some hot water and used it to wash her mother's body with a pair of plastic gloves and Juele went out to inform their relatives and friends and make other preparations. Weiying saw her mother's body was full of cocoons and her belly and feet were swollen because of the cancer and its transfer. It had caused the skin to become thin and visibly shiny. The unbearable sight caused Qiu Weiying to shed tears over and over again as she wiped her mother's body clean.

They held the funeral on a piece of hard concrete earth near home. It was not luxurious but just all right. On the day when her mother's body was sent to the crematorium, they ordered a big open car, and Xiaomao's unit and Weiying's factory both sent an open car respectively. A woman dead of an office with the surname of Huang from Weiying's factory was also in the car to the crematorium. If the "Gang of Four" representing the extremely left had not been beaten down and Mr. Bian who did not treat Weiying with prejudice inaugurated as the new director, it was impossible for the factory to send a car.

Shao Guzheng's body was burnt to ashes in a blink of an eye amidst sorrowful music and put into an ash casket for funerary ashes which was buried there. More than a decade later, the casket for funerary ashes was transported to Hunan Cemetery in Changsha, facing the sunset, as great changes took place in China. The setting sun fell with night coming but the next day it would rise and may brighten the whole world. But her mother's heart stopped beating. Since now, she was, and her mother separated from forever.

Tens of days passed since the funeral. Whenever Weiying thought of her mother's look with one eye open and the other closed, she felt it meant that her mother had undergone various pains and tortures in the mortal world and had no attachment to it on one hand and that she was still concerned with her son-in-law's matter as he hadn't been released from the prison.

No matter when Weiying was reminded of this scene, she couldn't help her tears even in front of her colleagues in the factory. A white-haired woman colleague persuaded her, "You are still crying for tens of days after your mother had left. You will damage your own health." With no words to answer, Weiying thought, my mother did not die from cancer only, and how did you know how much pressure she had to bear spiritually? Who could stand such painful torment in body and heart? It's true that no one can escape death, but she died in enormous pain and desperation…!

One month after Shao Guizhen passed away, Liu's mother next door told Weiying who was on her day off, "Your brother-in-law came back yesterday. I told him, 'Your mother has passed away.' But it seemed that he did not know it and stood outside the locked door for a long while." Hearing the news, Weiying felt sad but meanwhile doubtful. She was sad because her brother-in-law had been in prison in Ningxia for 10 years, her mother's heart closed for 10 tears, and the burden of his whole family pressing on mother for 10 years so that she was too depressed and tried to live on. If he had come back a month earlier, mother might have died with an easier mind so that she would close both eyes.

However, was Li Zhimeng's injustice reversed since he was released about a year after the "Gang of Four" was beaten down? So, she rushed to find Wu. When she got to know that his was reversed and that his salary was issued, she was so happy. But she felt more miserable for her mother, If she passes away a month later and sees her son-in-law go home, it will reduce a layer of painful worry.

She did not even enjoy a better life before going away. The formal public trial of the "Gang of Four" didn't Until December 1980. And the resolution that the Cultural Revolution wrongly launched and led by Mao Zedong was used by the "Gang of Four" represented by Lin Biao and Jiang Qing, causing inestimable losses and turmoil to the Party and the state, was made on the 6th Session of the 11th Central Committee of the CPC ... If Shao Guizhen passes away a month later and sees her son-in-law go home, she will reduce a layer of painful worry.

Shortly after Qiu's mother died, Da Mao brought her son Jianjian over and she asked her brother-in-law about something related to him. Qiu Weiying stroked Jianjian's head and asked, "Jianjian, do you know where maternal grandmother went?" He answered squarely, "maternal grandmother has gone to heaven."

Qiu Weiying felt relieved to hear him say that! She had once heard someone say that children who were a few years old could speak very effectively. Qiu Weiying also believed this, children are innocent, they only know how to speak from their own instincts and will not say anything that goes against their heart.

That night, Qiu Weiying had a dream that would give her a little comfort for the rest of her life. In the dream she saw her mother standing by a laurel tree, her figure delicate, her body shining with golden light. Qiu Weiying said to her mother, "Mum, Tan Jian said you had gone to heaven?" Her mother looked down at her and confirmed it. Qiu Weiying went on to say, "Then you must bless me." Her mother replied, "I will bless you even if I cut my own flesh!"

Qiu Weiying immediately said, "Then I don't want you to cut your own flesh!" While Qiu Weiying was speaking, her mother suddenly turned into a bird with a small laurel crown on its head, standing on a fragrant laurel tree. When Qiu Weiying had finished speaking, the bird, clad in golden light, flew off into the sky ....

At that moment, Qiu Weiying woke up, but it was a dream! How she longed for this dream to come true - the pain her mother had suffered in this world was too much! Too much! Can she be compensated in heaven and live a carefree life as a female divinity? Qiu Weiying silently dedicates a prose poem to her mother,

Fly, fly, fly up to the sky become immortal.
She changed into again a jade lady to accompany Change.
living with the Osmanthus trees and the jade rabbit together.
When she looks back at the world,
her tears turn into pearls and are scattered all over the mortal world.
Wait for the end of her daughter's life and meet in heaven.

5.3 Hapless fate

Qiu Weiying obviously felt lonely after her mother passed away. Although her mother was sick in bed while alive and occupied almost all her spare time, that was a kind of affection hard to give up. Her brother and sister used to get together during festivals when mother was alive but now it totally changed, father liked to have family meetings in his spare time while living in Laozhaobi. But now he was unable to and unwilling to gather the children. Therefore, the Qiu's family never gathered since mother passed away. It seemed that mother played the role of a hoop to unite the family together and when she passed away, the family spited apart.

If Weiying did not go to her younger sisters' and brothers' home when not working, they would hardly go to seen her in the factory, which, perhaps, could explain why she felt more depressed than them after mother left. Moreover, unlike them, she did not have her own family to count on; instead, she appeared an isolated boat floating on the sea of life. When it came to weekends or festivals, a sense of being forgotten almost overwhelmed her, and her born optimistic and humorous nature gradually disappeared with merciless inexorable years. However, without mother's urge, she almost lost confidence in love given her twists and turns in romantic relationships. Furthermore, she was a conservative woman who would not like to get in the initiative touch with men. If no one introduced a boyfriend for her or no man took the initiative to pursue her, she would live on singly, also in response to the then government's advocate of "late marriage and late childbirth". She was wearing down her youth in the ruthless years.

One a day off while Weiying was having lunch cooked by herself, a fortune-telling man walked in, "Would you like to have a divination?" Weiying agreed. But the guy started with such words, "Your father has died but your mother is still alive." A neighboring granny looked at Weiying, wanting to interrupt the guy. Weiying asked the guy at once, "What did you say? I did not catch it." The guy thus repeated, "In your life, your father has died but your mother hasn't." "Hey, the fact is opposite. My mother was just gone away, I don't need you to show me luck."

With nothing to do after lunch, Weiying went to the dormitory of Changsha Traditional Chinese Medicine Factory in Shazitang to visit her middle school classmate Zhuang Ruiying---an overseas Chinese back from Indonesia. Zhuang was pleased to see her, "I haven't seen you for long! Fall in love again?" "I haven't been in any romantic relationship ever since my mother got rectum cancer." Zhuang said, "I heard that Lin told the overseas Chinese colleagues working at Liu's department, when you and your mother visited him, aunt told him, 'If you want to continue with my daughter, she will agree.' is that so?"

Weiying suddenly realized, it turned out like this. She recalled, after she lost her temper and tore the photos, Lu Gengwei's eyes were full of tears, but he controlled himself so much that he would not cry out. So, he must have been told something by others and misunderstood her. At that time, he must have felt poignant but embarrassed to ask her something directly, thus playing a trick to stimulate her. However, he never expected that would push her---a strongly self-esteemed girl---to the contrary! She was so regretful, why didn't you ask me directly about the rumor, Lu Gengwei? So, she told Zhuang, "No, my mother and I did not visit him. My mother just told him, 'You are not married, so it is not good for you to monger rumors.'" Zhuang said, "Since aunt got cancer, uncle came to my home several times. He likes to play with Youqian and says he is clever." "The old like staying with children." Weiying replied and realized that her father was longing for family love and joy.

Back from Zhuang's home, Weiying thought that Lin Jingji once told her, "I have a brother working in Tianjin, another working in Hunan Federation of Supply and Marketing Cooperatives in Changsha. She recalled that when going to Juecong's home in Zhaojiaping, she passed through a lane in which a building was labelled "Hunan Federation of Supply and Marketing Cooperatives". Therefore, on one day off, Weiying went to the building and asked the janitor, "Comrade, I came to visit Mr. Lu---an overseas Chinese back from Japan." Getting his address, she found his place easily and rang the doorbell.

Lu Gengwei's old brother opened the door and Weiying introduced herself first, "I'm Lu Gengwei's ex-girlfriend." Lu's brother looked like their father, and though they had never met, he seemed to know such a thing. Without saying anything, he let Weiying come into the sitting room. Seated herself, Weiying began directly, "Lin Jingji told me that he had such a brother. We haven't met each other before because he is unsatisfied with your wife's attitude towards your parents. But he said you worked here. I passed the building and found you after asking the janitor for your address. When I was with

Injured lonely bird

Lu Gengwei, he told me that he would go to America. So, must have go there and got married." Lu's brother replied, "Yes, but not long. A friend introduced him a girlfriend when he came back last year."

Weiying thought for a moment, he got married last year. I was 30 last year, so he married at 32. However, he told me once, "if you and I break up, I'll go to America alone." He's a man of his word! With these words, Weiying felt a little heartbroken over their previous breakup due to a misunderstanding! She was sure that, they break broke up mainly due to mutual misunderstanding. This is a complicated coincidence, it turns out, "lovers will be married", is not necessarily. And some married Couples may not have love, but they already have a child. Maybe A pair of lovers have been having love, but not having a destiny. These thoughts prompted her to treat love more indifferently.

One day when Weiying went to Xiaomao's home at Changsha Transformer Factory, she came across Mo Shuchun, a classmate in middle school who liked chatting with her, while changing buses at the newly built Changsha Railway Station. Mo greeted her, smiling as before, "Are you married?" "Married? I don't even have a boyfriend." Mo said, "How could it be? I don't believe it." Weiying replied, "Since we are old friends, I don't need to conceal such things from you. I have had several boyfriends but could not get married due to various reasons." Hearing this, Mo was frank, "I'm married and have a child. My husband is the one your colleague had intended to introduce for you. Now we live near the railway station. The government redressed a grievance of his family, they reissued his father's salary and gave two new apartments which are well-furnished. My husband often talked about you and said that both of his parents liked you. If you want to resume your relationship with him, I can quit."

Weiying was surprised at her frank and selfless words! "It seemed that your husband was honest and loyal. Now that his family got good compensate, you are more fortunate than I! Are you willing to leave him in such a happy family?" Mo said, "It doesn't matter as long as he's happy. His family have always been missing you. His mother rarely talked to me but smoked all day long." Weiying asked, "Is his father still alive?" "He passed away not long ago." "In the past, though his parents were old, they were on good terms with each other. 'A couple married young can be lifelong companions.' Maybe his family are now living happily, so his mother misses his father more. I have just been at his home once, and there's no reason she would miss me. Even if his family like me as what you said, you are my classmate and you two have had a child. Therefore, it is impossible for you to divorce." When they parted, Mo wrote her address to Weiying, who felt somewhat this isn't the right. She was embarrassed if to visit them though she wanted to.

Several months later, a female cadre of a bureau in Hunan Province introduced Qiu Weiying to a college graduate from the Department of Mechanical Engineering in Guangdong. He was ix to seven years older than Weiying, the man was about 179 cm high, with a pair of big and sunken eyes and a high and pointed nose. Wu Sha said, "Aunt Weiying, the guy looks like an American!" Weiying found it funny and had the same opinion except that his skin was not white, and his eyes and browns are where black. Whenever this guy come met Weiying, she would think of Wu Sha's words and could not help laughing. The man felt happy as seeing Weiying smiling. Though working in Guangdong, he would take time every month to visit Weiying, who thought he was polite and respected her. But the twists and turns in her romance made Weiying lose interest and confidence in love, so she just treated it calmly. The Guangdong guy told her, "Because I was born in a landlord's family, I was affected in marriage and remained single until now. But they did not confiscate much property from our family as my mother buried it underground. I'm completely able to give a woman I love a happy life."

Weiying understood him and believed what he said to be true as when her family's property was confiscated, there were silver dollars and jewelries. Her mother also had the intention to bury them, but her father's opposition and carelessness led to the huge mistake. She thought that his parents had more experience than hers as her father always insisted that he had not done anything in violation of laws.

Once when the guy came to visit Weiying at the factory, he encountered Secretary Bian, to whom Weiying asked later, "He is a machinery engineer. What do you think of him?" Bian answered, "He's OK in appearance and knows technologies and expertise." Weiying said, "But he works in Guangzhou and came here once a month. How could it be after we get married?" "Since someone introduced you two, so why not ask him or her to look at if he can be assigned to Changsha." Later, Weiying went to ask the matchmaker who told her, "If you get married, there will be no problem for him to work in Changsha as he has expertise and ability." But Weiying still hoped that he could work in Changsha before getting married in of deep anxiety. Nevertheless, she did not tell him her idea but dealt with it casually.

After visiting Weiying several times, the Guangdong guy invited her and Wu Sha on her day off to see a film in near the Martyr's Park nearby. That was a summer evening. After seeing the film, they walked into the fresh open air. A mild breeze made them feel quite comfortable. At that time, the night totally came, with stars twinkling eyes to passers and the moon lighting the whole land. They incidentally went into a pavilion near the cinema. Wu Sha was very happy to see long benches around and she sat down at once and then lied there, while Weiying and the Guangdong guy sat on different benches. Weiying thought it would OK to lie on the bench for half an hour as it was just over nine o'clock then and the factory was not far from there. In addition, she usually went to bed at 11 or 12 at night. At this, she also lies on the bench between that of Wu Sha and of the guy; at the same time, she saw him also lying down. Soon she heard Wu Sha's slight breath in such a quiet environment. Staring at stars in the boundless dark sky, she was also sleepy but opened her eyes because of her vigilance. The Guangdong guy was then standing by her side and staring at her. The darkness disabled Weiying from seeing his expression, but she could see his pointed nose clearly. He seemed to be nearer toward her but stopped. Seeing Weiying waking up, he asked softly in mandarin with a Cantonese tone, "Wake up?" "Yes." Weiying sat up, thinking she should go back to dormitory instead of lying. Therefore, she went to wake up Wu Sha who began to rub her eyes. Weiying asked the guy, "Where are you going to sleep?" "I rented a room." Walking out of the park, they said goodbye to each other.

However, she never expected that was the last time they met. Their relationship might not have ended if they had had been more intimate in the park. Easterners and westerners held quite different opinions in this aspect, easterners, on most occasions, would define their romantic relationship by a kiss, while westerners regarded a kiss on the cheek and near the mouth as a common courtesy. It might be explained like this, eastern women were unlikely to devote themselves in love easily but once they did, they would hardly change their mind.

Not long after that, when Weiying was chatting at an acquaintance's house, that acquaintance said to her, "I know a man doing business in Hong Kong. He intends to find an innocent girl in mainland. If I I introduce you to him, he must be very gratified." Weiying asked, "How old is he? Didn't he have a wife in Hong Kong?" "Is it necessary for him to find a wife if he has one? Even if he had, she must have been dead or divorced. Moreover, a lot of single men with a good fortune in Hong Kong haven't got married."

Weiying think that I didn't of qualifications go to the college after my family possessions were confiscated; now my work and marriage were both affected after my brother-in-law was identified as an anti-revolutionary. I could not learn anything from my job by being on duty every day at the gate of the factory. So, my future would be rather bleak if I went on like this and learning how to do business from him might be a good idea. So, she said, "Let's see if the

Injured lonely bird

person is suitable before mentioning marriage! Now the new society, was to have proposed a marriage alliance get married? That's the old society, parents do arrange marriage it's about the same."

10 days later, the acquaintance brought Weiying to meet with the Hong Kong businessman at Xiangjiang hotel. The man, Mr. Zhong, was about 40 years old and 173 cm high. His sophisticated eyes were twinkling behind a pair of glasses. He talked loudly and vividly and walked confidently as if he was in control of everything. Even a 20-year-old boy might not be as energetic as him. He seemed quite delighted when seeing Weiying. After sitting in the hotel room for a while, he brought Weiying and the matchmaker to the dining hall, indicating his approval.

Zhong Yuquan came to Changsha again soon after that. This time he called to Weiying's factory from the hotel, "This time I came here just for you. Could you come to Xiangjiang Hotel when you are free so that we can chat?"

First, Weiying went to the notary office and asked, "Is there any method for me to know whether a man from Hongkong has a wife or not?" The office replied, "It's very simple. Just ask him to get a certificate to prove that he is single, and we'll notarize it for you."

Then, Qiu Weiying went to the room Zhong Yuquan's Hotel. When sitting down in his room, Weiying first asked, "Don't you have a wife and children in Hongkong?" "My wife has died of illness, and I live alone." "Now that you are satisfied with me in every aspect, bring a certificate which proves you are single. Then I can be assured." Zhong Yuquan promised, "You are my only love. I will never fall in love with anyone else except you. And I'm bound to marry you, but I don't have time to get such a certificate because I'm so busy these days." Weiying felt somewhat uncertain at his words, but she did not inquire more since they just knew each other for a short time.

Then she called Juecong to ask him to come to the hotel. Juecong brought one of his friends, Li Haiqing, there too. Zhong's humor often made them laugh and Weiying couldn't help laughing from time to time. Li said, "He's funny!" Whenever Zhong stared at

Weiying with huge interest and praised her, she would be touched to some degree. He brought her several pieces of clothes, which she never cared as she did not attach importance to gifts. After lunch at the hotel, Zhong said, "I'd like to go to Taiyuan, Shanxi for a week to see whether there is some good business to do. Would you come with me as my assistant?" Weiying thought it was not bad to see what kind of business he is in, and therefore agreed.

She went back to dormitory that night and next day, she asked the leaders of the factory for leave, "I'd like to ask one-week leave to accompany a Hong Kong businessman to the north." A woman leader responded happily, "Hey. You are over 30, so it's time for you to find a boyfriend. Since your mother has passed away and your father, brothers and sisters do not care much for you, our factory supports you in going out for a week." With these words, she signed on the leave note agreed.

Weiying called Zhong as soon as getting approval from the factory. Hearing that, Zhong asked the hotel to buy him two train tickets of soft sleeper carriage. After lunch at the hotel, they took a taxi to the station and went on the train heading north to Taiyuan.

Not long after the train left, a middle-aged waitress with a smiling face went into the compartment with a bottle of boiled water and put it on a small step between two berths. Weiying looked to the corridor through a crack, though there seemed a lot of people in other compartments, this one was rather quiet. The waitress closed the door when leaving. Zhong Yuquan immediately poured water made a cup of tea for Weiying and took out dim sums and fruits bought earlier. It became dark after they had some snacks and tea. Weiying gradually felt sleepy and lied on the berth with a quilt. Soon she was totally asleep. Both felt tired that night. The next morning, they went to the dining car to have breakfast and when they went back to their compartment, Weiying took out a book from her bag to read. But Zhong seemed unhappy to see her reading alone, so she had to talk with him from time to time till they arrived. She followed Zhong and left the Beijing-Guangzhou railway to get on the train from Hebei to Shanxi that afternoon. Though she grew up in mainland, she had never been to any other place except on the Beijing-Guangzhou railway. So Zhong, though from Hongkong, became her guide.

Sine there was not much scenery to see on this train and Weiying did not have much to say to Zhong, she just lied on the berth to read her favorite books. But after dinner, the murky light was not bright enough to read books, so she had nothing to do but lie down and fall asleep. At midnight, she was woken up by something heavy on her body. She opened her eyes and saw Zhong lying on her, attempting to have sex with her. A sense of fear immediately overwhelmed her and pushed her to move her body inside and use one hand to push Zhong outwards. Zhong did not force her, anyway. Weiying dare not fall into sound sleep till dawn. In the dim light, she saw Zhong smoking while on his berth and sometimes thinking something with his hands behind his upheld head. She didn't want to consider anything when tired. The night seemed so long. Weiying opened her eyes and coughed a little when dawn came. Seeing this, Zhong put the cigarette in his mouth and opened the window. Some fresh and cold air rushed in, making Weiying feel better but also a bit cold. Winter came earlier in the north than in the south. Glancing at Zhong, she found him holding his chin in the palm of one hand and pinching a cigarette in the other. He was looking out of the window, thinking something…

When the train arrived at Taiyuan train station, Weiying followed Zhong Yuquan to Yingze Hotel in the city proper, where transportation and shopping were quite convenient. While checking in at the service desk, a worker asked Weiying, "One room or two?" "Two. He's my maternal uncle and came here from Hong Kong to do business. I'm here just to serve as his assistant." Weiying answered quickly before Zhong could interrupt. Glancing at her, he couldn't say anything. With a feeling of relaxation, Weiying walked into her room with her luggage. After a short while of rest in the sofa in the room with a double bed, she heard someone knocking at the door. It turned out to be Zhong Yuquan and a 30-odd-year-old man. Zhong said, "This is the translator and tourist guide the hotel recommended for me and he's going to accompany us to walk around." The gentleman with a pair of glasses was smiling at her. She took the thick suit in light coffee color from the back of the door and went to have breakfast with them. Zhong put tableware in front of her and the translator respectively, but the latter said politely, "I had breakfast before working." Therefore, Zhong poured a cup of tea for him. After breakfast, they walked out of the hotel. Weiying suddenly felt fresh and comfortable when seeing the broad and clean road in the open air. They walked around before going back to the hotel to have lunch.

After a rest, Weiying went out again with Zhong who took pictures for her in the afternoon. When taking pictures, Weiying always felt some passers staring at them and discussing something. Back to the hotel, she wondered whether the passers were discussing Zhong, and she were a couple, or their age gap, for she looked younger than her actual age. When she went to her mother's clinic at 28 or 29, a woman apprentice said to her, "You don't look like your age, and so do your tone and manners." Since she didn't like others to watch her in an examining way, she would not like to take more pictures though the park was nearby. So Zhong suggested, "Then shall we buy some daily necessities in a nearby shop and have dinner in a restaurant before heading back to the hotel?"

Later, while taking a shower in her room, Weiying recalled passers-by the kind questioning eyes, she felt quite uncomfortable. It was true that Zhong was10-odd years older than her, so she thought they might have been wondering whether she was his wife or his daughter.

After the shower, she took on a long-sleeved pajama and began to watch TV in bed. Soon someone knocked. Opening the door, she found it was Zhong Yuquan who asked, "Are you sleeping?" "No, I'm watching TV. Why do you come here instead of taking a shower and going to bed?" "I just want to see you." He replied while closing the door behind him. He took off his coat, put it on the clothes hanger, and sat in a sofa beside the bed. Weiying, who did not like measuring men, was now looking at him up and down full of doubt. She found some obvious wrinkles behind his ears, which mismatched the inconspicuous wrinkles on his face. She once heard that there was an operation called face-lift in foreign countries. So, she asked Zhong, "How old are you?" Zhong turned around, "What? You are my wife, and how could you ask such a question?" "I haven't married with you, so I'm not your wife yet." "I'll go to Hongkong to get a certificate and then go back to Changsha and marry you" Zhong smiled. Weiying continued, "Anyhow I have to know your age." "I'll bring you my passport tomorrow." Weiying felt a bit assured, "That's good."

At that moment, with a false smile, Zhong sat on the bedside, took off his shoes and hugged Weiying. He put her under his body and kissed her lips forcefully and unnaturally, his hands touching her body randomly… Weiying, who had never had sex until more than 30, felt dizzy and became totally blank, she did not yet fall in love with Zhong. She was reminded of the past, "Do all men like to have sex before marriage…?" While in confusion, she could not concentrate…Out of a sudden, she felt a fit of stabbing pain…She tried to push him but without enough strength. It was at that moment that she began to realize she had been over 30 years old under the guidance of "Cannot have sex before getting married". However, the most terrible thing happened, and it was too late to remedy. With enormous horror and pain, she did not at all feel any happy brought about by sex, but her tears poured out…Zhong pretended not to see. Weiying's reaction. Finally, he kissed her cheek, walked out of the room and locked the door, satisfied and calm.

Weiying became more and more heartbroken, sobbing not stop on the pillow…She had never thought that she would lose her virginity, to which she attached the greatest importance, to a man she

433

had not fallen in love with in just half an hour. What's more, she was uncertain about whether he had a wife in Hong Kong and was afraid that she would be pregnant. She fell with these disturbing thoughts and sobbed and fell asleep in the sleepy.

Waken up by Zhong's knock and shouts the next morning, Weiying opened the door and saw him standing there with a smirk. He said, "I'll wait for you to have breakfast together on the first floor." Though indignant, she did not lose her temper but replied unhappily, "OK. You go first." She walked into the bathroom and found her eyes red and swollen in the mirror. Afraid that others would feel strange, she repeatedly put the towel with cold water on her face till the eyes looked well. But she did not walk out of the room after putting on her clothes; instead, she sat in the sofa, finding that there was some blood on the white bed sheet. She therefore put the quilt there to cover it. Then the phone rang. She answered it and heard, "Mrs. Zhong asked you to have breakfast quickly." Weiying walked again into the bathroom and looked into the mirror, finding her eyes not as swollen as before. Thus, she went down to the dining hall.

When she sat at the table, Zhong looked at her with an expression different from before silently and then immediately made tea for her. She put something in her mouth reluctantly and stared outside the window. "Would you like to have more?" Zhong asked her in a low voice. "I'm full." Therefore, Zhong gave the bill to a waiter and brought her out of the hotel. He asked, "Shall we go to the shopping mall? What would you like to buy?" "I cannot think of anything to buy. Shall we take a walk in the nearby park?" However, Weiying was not interested in appreciating the scenery at all; it was the fresh air that made her feel a little sober. After walking and sitting a while, she said, "I'd like to go back to the hotel. I feel very tired." Zhong said, "If you don't want to walk any more, we'll go back early and do something else."

As soon as they walked into the hotel, a woman worker called Weiying, "The leader of the hotel wants to talk to you." At this, Zhong was stuck but then strode after Weiying, attempting to accompany her to the room to which the waitress pointed, but the latter stopped him, "Our leader just wanted to talk to her. Please don't come in." Meanwhile, a man worker walked towards and stopped him. So, he had to go back to his room. Stepping into the room, Weiying saw the translator inside who was looking at her with a surprised and sympathetic look, as well as some middle-aged or older men she had never met. All of them looked serious and mild.

One of them put down his cigarette as Weiying walked in and pointed to a chair, "Please sit down. We just want to inquire you about something. Don't be nervous." At this, Weiying predicted that they would ask her for her relationship with Zhong, but she didn't know why because they did not live in one room. However, the man said directly, "We think you are probably cheated." Scared to death at his words, Weiying could not help shedding tears that expressed her poignancy quietly. The men looked at each other in silence. Weiying could not remember what they said later and what she answered. The translator stood up to send her to her room and left with a sympathetic and pitiful look.

Weiying walked into the room and closed the door, finding everything neat and tidy and the sheet changed. She suddenly realized that their inquiry was totally caused by the marks in the room. Thinking of the first sentence she heard just now, she threw herself in the sofa, confused about her relationship with Zhong Yuquan. Now she found that he was dirty in mind and that she did not love him but began to resent him. She lost her virginity to him before they got married! She could hardly understand, why in this world some married women had an extramarital affair. Apart from forming a family, how much does this mean? It was true that "man proposes, God disposes." She originally intended to give herself to her future husband she loved very much, but everything collapsed in a minute. She didn't know what to do next but to follow her destiny.

Meditating a while, she heard someone knock and opened the door. Zhong stood out there and stared at her face for a minute before rushing into the room and sitting in the sofa. He frowned, "What did they do?" "Asking about our relationship." "What did you say?" "They know what happened last night." He lifted his head, "Stupid! How could you tell them such a thing?" Weiying was don't let go, "You think you are very clever? It was impossible for me to tell them if they did not ask. Perhaps the working staff told that to their leaders when they saw the marks." She pointed to the bed and the floor. Zhong suddenly understood and immediately went out. He came back after a long while, "Are you unhappy? Shall we go to visit Datong tomorrow?" Weiying answered, "Is that an interesting place? I heard it in my middle school. There's only a large coal mine." Zhong insisted, "I heard there are 'Yungang Grottoes' with many different-sized Buddhas. Don't you have interest in them?" She agreed and Zhong booked two train tickets to Datong at the hotel.

They got on the train that evening. After resting a while in the compartment, a waitress came in to check tickets before leaving with a relatively broad crack. Weiying was quite glad about that, but Zhong wanted to get up to close the door. She stopped him, "Don't shut it in they may doubt us. Maybe they did that on purpose." Zhong agreed unhappily and lied down again. Weiying thought, if the hotel reported something to the train staff, she would be so grateful to them.

When they got off the train and arrived in Datong Hotel, Zhong Yuquan who was so daring said to the worker at the reception desk, "Please give me a double room". At that time, a man comrade who was talking with the worker asked, "Have you brought your marriage certificate?" Zhong said quickly, "Next time". Weiying say, "Not yet". The comrade seemed a little angry, "Next time? I ask you if you are married now. If not, you cannot live in one room."

He looked mildly at Weiying, who was then glaring at Zhong, thinking it was shameful with such a man who was not honest. At a result, the hotel arranged two rooms for them. Weiying and Zhong went to have breakfast after putting their luggage in their rooms. Then they went to Yungang Grottoes, where Weiying saw of different sizes and colors built in mountain caves statues. She seemed to have forgotten unhappy things in life and saw the statues with great interest. The only regret was that many statues were faded in color because they had been worn down without repair for so long a time. On one hand, she admired the diligence, wisdom and high-level art attainment of ancestors over 1,500 years ago; one the other hand, she was worried that these art works would disappear with time if not attended and restored, which would an irretrievable loss for the present and future generations. While visiting the Caves, she did not see a single worker except some tourists. But she also thought that perhaps it was just because of the remoteness and desolation that the place could hardly get full attention and reservation. After visiting the Caves located in Datong, they went back to the hotel to stay one night and then to Xi'an the ancient city by train.

In Xi'an, Zhong Yuquan ordered two rooms, making Weiying feel relaxed to some degree. She was used to Zhong's care for her. During the process of visiting, she could feel his considerateness though not happiness. She accepted such kind of care as in her whole life; no one cared for her so much except her mother. Perhaps in her consciousness, she already belonged to him though they had not got married. She spent her childhood and adolescence in a relatively favorable environment, but she would not pursue luxurious life, which might be thanks to her mother's teachings and her go through hazards and hardships in rural areas.

Weiying was affected by her mother who was diligent, frugal, and honest. She would not estimate the price she had paid with her virginity; what she would pursue was just cleanness and tranquility of the soul and purity of love. Therefore, she took Zhong's buying her a pink furred hat in Xi'an a kind of care. She thought that Zhong might be afraid of her getting a cold. She was impressed a lot by the decorated archways, the food of the northern city and the straightforwardness and hospitality of the people. Because her leave was due, she prompted Zhong to buy train tickets and went back to Changsha.

When Weiying back to the factory, the comrade who had been doing her work during her leave told her, "You are back! A Guangdong guy come to see you just two days after you left. I told him not to see you again, because you had become the wife of a Hongkong's boss and together gone to travel." Weiying felt depressed at this and asked immediately, "The wife of a Hong Kong's boss? I haven't been married with him." He objected, "You will not be discarded by men if you yourself don't give up." Weiying replied, "Who knows? There are swindlers in men!" She added, "Certainly. There are swindlers in women too."

Her colleague blinked his eyes, "Oh, I received a phone call from Taiyuan Public Security Bureau and transferred it to Ms. Huang head of an office." At this, Weiying wanted to meet Huang to inquire about what happened. Huang said, "I indeed received a call from there, they asked, 'whether our factory knows that you and a Hongkong guy went to Taiyuan together'. I answered, "Yes, and you had asked for leave. Bian secretary and I said that you are a very conventional girl and there would be no problem. Even if there occurs something, it would be the man's responsibility because you are quite pure. How about the Hong Kong man? Did he bully you?" Weiying was very grateful to them for their trust but did not know how to answer her question.

As Weiying remained in silence, Huang looked at her mildly and doubtfully. At that time, she felt painful in heart but was embarrassed to tell what had happened to Huang, who was also a woman but not her mother after all. Weiying realized that if her mother was alive, she could avoid such a thing after consulting her opinion happen.

Since then, she lost her smile, and the beautiful world of her childhood was becoming more and more obscure. She thought that she had not right to choose an unmarried virgin man who was worth her love but to wait for Zhong Yuquan to come back from Hong Kong to marry her. According to the old feudal thought, she felt that she already belonged to him. At that time, many Chinese women were as traditional as her. She hear of, the Japanese were more open as they thought that it was unimportant whether a woman was a virgin before marriage, but it was important that whether she remained loyal to her husband after marriage. Indeed, no one can prevent something from happening before marriage when people lack experience, especially when parents were not there to give instruction. And what could one do if his or her partner was not loyal after marriage? However, it was indeed a blessing if both husband and wife were maintaining pure and lived happily after.

5.4 Resignation and engagement in medicine

Being conservative Weiying was passively waiting for Zhong Yuquan to bring his single certificate from Hong Kong so that they could get married. Within a month, Zhong came to Changsha again and still lodged at Xiangjiang Hotel. This time he came with a certificate and gave it to Weiying upon meeting her. The certificate confirmed that he was not in his forties, but rather, fifties. But there was nothing she could do about it. When she took the certificate to the notary public, the notary officer told her, "Despite that the age and address on it might be true; it cannot prove that he is single. You can't get married merely on such a certificate." They gave her the documents on marring foreign personages.

Weiying was worried. She went to Xiangjiang Hotel and said to Zhong, "Are you lying to me? If you can't get the certificate done next time, I shall never talk to you again." Zhong said confidently, "Really? It's no big trouble for me to find a dozen of other girls!" Upon hearing his words, Weiying started to doubt his sincerity and her heart ached. She said upsell, "You don't sound like a reliable person." Zhong smirked and said, "I was just kidding! How could I ever give you up?" Weiying stared at him and thought the wrinkles behind his ears had grown more obvious. Suddenly, she felt he was a hypocrite. The invalid certificate he brought her made her worry, on the one hand, he was more than twenty years older than her, enough to be her father; on the other, she began to doubt that he had a wife in Hong Kong and lied to her about his marital status. She said, "The certificate does not tell your marital status, so I cannot have my certificate done. Why don't you bring a single certificate here?" Zhong replied, "I was too busy with my business and forgot about it." Weiying was angry, "I've never seen you doing business once!" Zhong replied firmly, "My big company operates in Hong Kong. How can you see my business here? I'll take you to Shanghai this time and show you some real deal." Weiying said warily, "I'm not going out with you alone again before we get married." At this time, Li Qinghai, who was sitting by Juecong, said, "There's no need to be afraid if there are two bodyguards." Weiying immediately replied, "No. If you two want to go so much, go along." Later, Zhong did take Juecong and Qinghai to Shanghai.

A dozen of days later, the three of them returned to Changsha, and Zhong went back to Xiangjiang Hotel. Weiying met Li Qinghai at Juecong's place. As if to defend her legitimate interest, Li told her, "Zhong hooked up with another woman in Shanghai. The woman is surely somebody. The first thing she did was take him to the huge malls for a shopping spree. Juecong and I had a big fight with Zhong, but the woman would not give up on him, even if she knew he has a fiancée." Weiying asked, "Did anything happen between them?" Li replied, "You don't ask! Why would he buy her so many things? How naïve you are!" What he said made her angry and grieved. She doubted if she would shoot them dead and then commit suicide if she had seen the two in bed; but she had not been there nor had a gun. She thought, "My whole life is ruined by him! He already took away my virginity, and now he hooks up with other women." The anger grew so strong, but she did not know what to do.

Weiying is being upset, she went to Zhong's friend home, Liu, whose place he had been once with Zhong. Upon entering the door, she started wailing. Mrs. Liu was a very nice lady. Seeing Weiying in such grief, she put a basin of water by her to tidy up, put a hot towel into her hand and said, "It's his fault. Don't cry; take care of yourself." Then she put a cup of hot tea on the table in front of her and said, "Have some tea and tell us the story." As if already knew the story, Mr. Liu said, "You should have known before you dated him, how could a man of his age have no wife?" Weiying stopped crying and said, "I didn't know he is so old. I used to read in the newspaper that there are many single men of such age in Hong Kong. I myself am already in my thirties. I'm also single for a bunch of reasons!"

Mr. Liu spoke again, this time as if he did not know the whole story, "He had told me about it before you went to Taiyuan. If I had known you back then, I would have told you not to go with him alone. Later when the Taiyuan Public Security Bureau called, I vouched for him, saying that he had never cheated anyone before he met you, and he did treat you as his fiancé. I had no idea you are thirty and still so naïve. There are many women in this society who are much more sophisticated than you are. You should have made him promise before you went to bed. Why are you so silly?"

Judging from his words, Weiying thought he did not know the truth. So, she said, "It's not a trade. No matter how much he gives me, I would never go to bed with him. I did not know what would happen in the north that time. I had no idea…" She did not feel like explaining any further. Mr. Liu continued, "I heard the Shanghai woman was two years younger than you, but much more sophisticated. Zhong had expected her to be a virgin and did whatever she asked. Later he found her to be a liar and wanted to dump her, but she threatened to sue him, scaring him out of Shanghai. Li and your brother also found out that the woman had a boyfriend. But Zhong is not without conscience. He would not leave you if you don't leave him. As for your marriage, that's something I can't speak sure of." The conversation almost came to an end, and Weiying stood up to leave. Mrs. Liu came out of the kitchen and said, "I have already cooked for you. Wait for my son and daughter-in-law to come back from work and have dinner with us!" She was too friendly for Weiying to refuse her, so she stayed for dinner.

Back to her dormitory, Weiying tidied up and went to bed, but could not fall asleep. Things that had happened to her helped her realize that she could not stay this way forever. Even if Zhong stopped messing with other women, her trust for him had already faded. She even thought that she would not marry him even if he could get all the certificates ready, for she not only had no love for him, but also started to despise him. She believed in spiritual love. Without love, she would never sleep with a man out of material concerns.

In the spring of 1965, our family suffered search the house and confiscate family property, taught her a truth about life, that is "money is by no means omnipotent" and swirl in life can easily take it all away. But the love and relationship between man and wife means that they should share joys and sorrows, to create a new life and to nourish their children. If a couple is not in love, their health would be influenced by the gloomy atmosphere, no matter how nutritious the food is; they would not be happy, no matter how decent they dress. Now she was angry with him even before they got married. What would happen if they were to be together for the rest of their lives…?

Sleepiness took over her, and she felt asleep. The next morning, she started thinking as soon as she opened her eyes, "People are already asking nicely, 'Why still come to work now that you are to marry a rich man in Hong Kong?' There's no doubt that the news has a negative impact on me in the factory! Even if Zhong can complete the procedures, there's nothing nice about living with him, not to mention he can't. Nowadays even the TV universities can issue diplomas, why don't I take correspondence courses on traditional Chinese medical skill and learn from Father? Isn't that much more promising than me keeping the gate every day?" She made a quick decision that she should use her spare time to learn traditional medicine on correspondence as well as other knowledge and skills. The decision was made very quickly but had seeded in her heart ever since Mother's death, when Juele, who had not learnt any medicine before, left the farm and took over mother's job and received medical training, indicating that the policies are much easier since the Gang of Four was brought down.

Private businesses are once again legal, so she could have her own clinic if she could get a doctor's license, which was unimaginable during the time of the Gang of Four! Wasn't her family affected before the Revolution, only because Mother quitted the job in hospital to take care of the children, and then was urged into opening a private clinic as the trend? Misfortune fell on them despite that they had license and was legal, for under the policies against Capitalist Roaders, they found it hard to defend themselves. After the search the house and confiscate family property, she became the daughter of "the twenty-one kinds", was deprived of the right of further education and sent to the countryside to be reeducated by the poor and lower-middle peasants. Now that she could see the morning glow in her life, why not take the chance, quit the unimportant job and set about her own career?

So, when came to work, she went to Director Huang and told her the decision. Huang said to her in a worried voice, "Qiu Weiying, don't give up so easily! It's very hard to find a job now! Your mother had already passed away and you are still single. Once the man you're with leaves you, what should you do?" An elder woman in the lathe work team said nicely, "it's said that our factory will be state-owned again. You'll regret one day! You won't have any pension when you quit. What should you do when you're old?" Weiying replied, "Can't a woman rely on one's own effort be create opportunities? I wanted to quit only because I don't think the man is reliable. Even if the factory is state-owned, I'll have to wait some decades before I retire. I don't like this job, so the years can be long and torturous. Don't worry. I won't be starved to death!" Hearing her words, Huang had no better arguments to discourage her, and within two days, Qiu Weiying completed her resign procedures.

Within a few months, several other workers followed her and quitted the job. Once again Qiu became an example, but this time not to "be reeducated by the poor and lower-middle peasants", but to seek for personal development under new policies and situations! Was it being Capitalist Roaders? If the Gang of Four had known things would change like this, probably they wouldn't have persecuted Liu Shaoqi and Deng Xiaoping for their Capitalist ideas.

After quitting, Qiu Weiying deeply realized that her generation was influenced by the Culture Revolution and lost the precious ten years to study. If she did not quicken her steps and catch up with the learning, splendid future would not come to her. She had never thought of depending on a rich or powerful husband, for she thought those men often attracted greedy women, and relying on men is by no means better than being independent. If she could earn her own money, she could spend a happy life with her husband; if the relationship went wrong, she would not have to be so poor as to stay with someone she hated. Back then, Juecong had left the post as doctor in Changsha Paper Factory and moved to his wife's house, and later was hired by Dalian Ground Force Hospital along with his father. Weiying went home alone and started her self-improvement program. She actively signed up for medicine correspondence courses and She studies English on the side. Because for she believed knowledge is power. Outside the class, she would stay at home and devote herself to various kinds of books.

Mr. Qiu stopped seeing Tu Hua after Mrs. Qiu's death, probably it was because of the children's disapproval, or maybe he realized his own fault. He and Juecong worked two years in the hat Dalian Army Hospital, and then moved to Qingdao, for it was where his ex-wife and eldest daughter lived, and he thought it as good a harbor city as Dalian. One day Weiying received a letter from him, saying, "Now that you have no job and are home along, why don't you learn medicine from me? Being a doctor is much better than other occupations." It was exactly her idea, and Mother also used to hope she could learn medicine. Even though she was learning proctology by herself and taking correspondence course, she would have trouble taking the qualification exam if she could not operate in real-world scenarios.

Without any hesitation, she took a train to Shanghai first. There she settles down at a friend's parents' house. The friend was assigned with a job in Hunan after graduation from college, but his brother and sister-in-law lived with his parents. Qiu could not understand why Shanghai women have had so many quilts with them as dowry – Shanghai had a serious shortage of housing. Was Isn't that a waste of space? The family was very nice to her, so she stayed there a few more days before she got on a ship to Qingdao.

Qingdao was a beautiful city by the seashore. The green sea merged with the blue sky, and Mount Lao even added more to that beauty. Upon arrival, Qiu followed the address Father gave her and found his clinic, which was in a large hotel. Mr. Qiu followed his practice before Liberation, when he was in Jiangsu, He rented two large rooms, one as the clinic, one as the room for him and Juecong, as well as his grandson, who was the son of his daughter from his ex-wife. After Weiying came, he rent another room with two single beds for Weiying and Juecong, while he shared the room with his grandson. The reasons why he need Weiying was that he was too busy with more and more patient coming to him, and that the three of them are often too occupied to cook. So Weiying could learn a trade and help with the patients, as well as take care of their meals. For some unknown reason, Weiying's allergic to blood disappeared since she started helping with proctologic operations, but she only served as an assistant during the surgeries and was mainly responsible for changing the medicinal cottons. She spent a few months serenely.

One day at dinner, she asked Father, "Who you with were at lunch today, that you did not even take your afternoon nap?" Mr. Qiu complained, "How I regret going to lunch with the couple! They seemed to want something from me, for my business is good. At first the woman said they had a big family, but she was busy with the housework, so her husband was the only breadwinner. Now her parents-in-law are seriously ill, but they do not have any money. She asked me to lend some money to them. I said, 'I can treat you for free, but can't lend you any money for your parents-in-law, because all my money is in a bank account in Changsha, and I can't go back and draw them out.' So, they said no more, and neither did I. Later the man asked me if his wife could learn medicine from me. If she becomes a doctor one day, she will thank me a lot, and would not have to borrow money from others. I said, 'I already have many apprentices and have no energy spare for anymore.' At last, the man seemed to threaten me, saying 'We have relatives working in the Public Security Bureau'. I thought I have done nothing wrong and am not afraid of the threat. I was annoyed by them, so I dropped my chopsticks and left their house."

Soon after the incident, two men from the Public Security Bureau came one day. Mr. Qiu pointed to his license on the wall and said, "My business is approved by Qingdao Health Bureau. Why don't you allow me to do my business here?" One man said, "We have not approved it yet. This district is in the charge of our bureau. You have to leave if we tell you to." Mr. Qiu murmured, "All it takes has been the approval of health bureau. I've never heard of that the public security bureau has anything to do with it." His words reminded Weiying of the night before their confiscation of family property, when Chang Wanmin from Changsha Public Security Bureau went to her school, followed by the confiscation of family property in the middle of the night. Even though the Gang of Four had been brought down, it would still take some time for the legal system to be completed. Back then it was no use arguing any further.

To her surprise, the other man said to her rudely, "You live in the same room with your brother?" Weiying grasped what he meant and could not believe her ears, how could he mean something so disgusting? Are human less civilized than animals? She replied at once in despise, "Yes. Each of us has a bed. He's some years younger than me. Is there anything wrong? There are many families, sometimes even two generations sharing a same room, not to mention brothers and sisters. What's more, we are living at hotel now and must save money. There's no way we each rent a room." But the man purposely looked at her in a weird way and said bossily, "Not in hotels. We have the authority to stop such behaviors. I'll tell the manager to stop renting you, his rooms." Some patients who were waiting aside for changing medicinal cottons saw the scene and supported Weiying, "She's right. There's no problem for a brother and an old sister to share a room! What's wrong of the family? They are helping us! We have not healed yet and still need them." The man from Public Security Bureau looked at them in a ruthless way. At this time, Qiu thought of the couple father talked about whom she had met before and felt as if they were watching the show with a provocative smile. Mr. Qiu hesitated for a while and said, "Alright, I'll stop my business. But I must at least finish treating the ones I have already received, right?" Some upright patients said bravely, "Of course! Or who shall I go to for help? Do I have to follow them to Changsha? Are you paying for the tickets?" One man from the Public Security Bureau became less aggressive and replied, "We'll give you a few more days. But you can't take any more patients." Mr. Qiu replied mildly, "Alright. My expertise can get me money no matter was." Days later, almost all their patients had healed, apart from a few who had tiny wounds. Mr. Qiu made some ointment, put it into tiny bottles and taught them how to apply it to their wound. At last, Mr. Qiu, Weiying and Juecong went back to Changsha together.

Mr. Qiu settled down at Juecong's house and assisted him in opening a private clinic. He sometimes helped Juecong with the patients, and sometimes went to the patients' places to help them. Before long, Weiying recalled that she had not met Mr. and Mrs. Liu ever since she went to Qingdao. The couple had been very nice to her, so she went to visit them again during free time. Entering the door, Mrs. Liu asked, "Are you going back to Qingdao again?" Weiying briefly told her about the incident in Qingdao and said, "I don't have a doctor's license for the moment, so I want to learn tailoring first. Even if I don't choose it as my career, it'll be of great convenience if I can make clothes for myself. I have already signed up for a tailoring course." Mrs. Liu said, "That's a good idea. Everybody needs clothing. But why don't you join in your father and brother in running the clinic? Isn't it better to be a doctor?" Weiying replied, "My sister-in-law does not like that. She wants to learn medicine too, and my father values his daughter-in-law more than his daughter." Mr. Liu said, "Tailoring is good too. Ask Zhong to buy you a sewing machine." Weiying said, "I haven't met him since I heard about the woman in Shanghai." Liu told her, "Your brother visited us with Li Qinghai the moment he came back. They were willing to join in my business. I have called Zhong and told him you're back. He'll come a few days later." Weiying said, "I'm sure he has a wife in Hong Kong. I have no plan of being with him." Mr. Liu said, "Even if he does, his wife must be an old woman and already a grandma. It's ok if he is good to you. Forget about his divorce…" Weiying immediately said, "He's too dissolute. I would not be with him even if he divorces." Mr. Liu said, "Don't be so naïve! He owes you big and will surely buy you a sewing machine as long as you ask." Mrs. Liu said, "We can ask for you. He wouldn't mind it. You're not with him anyway. You have already quitted your job, and he can help you as a friend. Alas, you surely are naïve!" Weiying said, "I haven't asked him for anything, for I have never thought of trading my body! That's like selling my soul. What's more, the only reason I went out with him was to be his assistant and learn about business.

Injured lonely bird

Zhong Yuquan did come to Changsha several days later. This time he did not settle at a hotel, but instead, stayed at Juecong's. Weiying did not know Juecong's wife very well, so she never asked about it. One day, Juecong asked her to go to his place, where Zhong said to her gladly, "It' alright that you're not a doctor, or you might dump me." Weiying said angrily, "Dump you? I'm not being with you even if I'm not a doctor." Zhong sneered, "There's plenty of fish in the sea!" Weiying said, "Sure! You're the big boss from Hong Kong! Your money makes all kinds of women beat a path to your door," she continued sarcastically, "Are your Boss Zhong ("Zhong" has the same meaning as "true" in Changsha dialect) or Boss False? Why are you messing with women all day and never getting down to real business?" Zhong simpered and made no response as to his work, but merely asked, "When did you see me messing with women?" Weiying said, "you said it yourself.

Why would women come to you if you're not a philanderer yourself?" Zhong was speechless and could. only say, "You're too eloquent; I'm not arguing with you." Several days later, Zhong went back to Hong Kong, while the summer tailoring course at a primary school was about to start. Weiying said to Liu while visiting him, "I have got my syllabus today.

The school starts the day after tomorrow and will last for four weeks. Cutting lessons are on Monday, Wednesday and Friday, while sewing lessons are on Tuesday, Thursday and Friday. We have to buy our own sewing machines." Liu asked, "Have you got one yet?" She replied, "No. I want a decent one, but that can only be bought with FEC." He said, "Zhong has given me some money and told me to take care of you. I'll buy you a nice machine from Friendship Store the day after tomorrow and have it sent to your school." She did not refuse and told him her address. On the first day of school, Liu came with the driver to bring her the brand new "Butterfly" sewing machine. After the course, she passed the exam easily and got her course-completion certificate. Her cutting teacher said, "You can easily find a job with this certificate." But as she took the certificate to the famous clothing stores and factories, they asked her, "How long have you been in this industry?" She did not like to lie or swagger, so she replied honestly, "Never." As a result, she was turned down, for they wanted experienced old hands.

She thought, "It seems hard for me to have a job at once. Maybe I shall be an apprentice first." She first went to a tailor who used to make clothes for the Qius, who said, "I work from door to door, and it's common for me to carry my machine to different families. You look too tender for this arduous job." Weiying said, "I have been to the countryside for several years have gone through enough difficulties." But the tailor, who was from the countryside, said, "That was but a temporary policy! You urban kids don't have the patience and perseverance to stick to the hard work. Didn't you all come back?" Next, she went to another tailor, who had her own tailoring shop. She refused Weiying directly, "I have many relatives in the countryside that wants to be my apprentices, but I have turned them all down. There's no way I can be your master!"

Weiying was frustrated. As a result, she had to live in the low-rent old house of her parents, learning traditional Chinese medicine by herself and taking correspondence course while waiting for the qualification test of proctology, hoping that one day she could become a doctor. Unexpectedly, Zhong had been very helpful. Knowing that Weiying was jobless, he gave a sum of money to Mr. Liu and asked him to take care of Weiying. Once Liu gave Weiying five thousand yuan, which was enough for a couple of years back then. Being frugal in nature, she put the money into her bank account. For the moment, all she could do was to study as hard as possible and wait for her big chance to come.

Before long, Zhong came to Changsha and once again settled at Xiangjiang Hotel. The next day, before visiting Zhong, Weiying had told Juecong to wait for her in Zhong's room. That day, as she walked by the janitor's room in the hotel, the janitor called her to stop. She stopped at his door near, wondering what the old man had to say with her, for they did not really know each other. The man stood up and exhorted, "Zhang Hao from Hunan Foreign Affairs Office asked me to tell you, Do not fall for the Hong Kong guy! He has a wife back home. Zhang has seen him along with his wife here." Weiying smiled bitterly and said, "Thank you!" On her mind she thought, "Oh, it's too late!" But still she felt grateful, for Zhang was secretly caring for her! With these thoughts, she came to Zhong's door in the hotel, when Juecong and Li Qinghai were already inside. Zhong put on a cocky look and said, "Why is my wife so late? I'm going to stand a treat for my clients and we're all waiting for you!" Weiying asked in retort, "Who is your wife? I'm not living with you, nor have we got married. Don't you already have a wife in Hong Kong?!" Zhong was surprised at first and then asked, "Who told you so?!" She said acrimoniously, "A little bird told me that you have taken her here! Do you dare to say that you don't have a wife?" Zhong frowned, lowered his head and said nothing. Zhang Hao's warning made Weiying even more wary for Zhong. Ever since that day, Zhong had been a totally different figure in her mind.

At lunch that day, she met two Han people from Xinjiang. The elder one of them was sitting next to her, who said, "We would be honored if you and your husband would visit Xinjiang…" Qiu felt uncomfortable with the title and declared at once, "He is not my husband. We are not married. What's more, he is twenty years older than me, old enough to be my dad. I don't want a husband that old…" But the man did not grasp the implication and said, "he said you were his wife. Even if you're not married now, you will be one day." Qiu explained promptly, "That is next to never!" But the foolish man insisted, "Don't be shy! All women must get married. If you really think he is too old, you can always find a younger man when you're rich. Even ten years younger will be no problem… Xinjiang is a very nice place. We will give you the warmest reception if you come." Despite the man tried very hard to persuade her, she showed no interest.

A couple of days later, Zhong agreed to go to Xinjiang. Before leaving, he asked her, "Are you coming with me?" Qiu refused without any hesitation, "No way! And don't you brag to anyone saying I'm your wife!" Zhong was speechless and pinched her tenderly on the face. She pushed his arm away and said, "Get lost!" Zhong was displeased and said, "Screw you! I can pick another woman without the slightest effort!" Qiu was not touched, saying, "Go to whomever you like; I don't give a damn." Later, Zhong took Juecong and Li Qinghai to Xinjiang.

Zhong came back to Xiangjiang Hotel ten days later, and said to Qiu excitedly, "Shame you didn't come! They had a big reception party for me; almost ten thousand people were there. We had great food, fancy accommodation and a fantastic journey..." Qiu did not care at all, saying, "Lucky I did not go! One thousand people? Should I have played the fake wife of yours in front of them? How ridiculous!" Her reply made Zhong very embarrassed.

Zhong never came again in the following months, which was fine with Weiying, who had almost forgotten about him. She engaged her whole energy and attention in learning medicine and hoped that she could get a doctor's license one day.

5.5 Another married man

Qiu Weiying was a rational woman strictly bound by morality and furthermore. She was affected negatively by her first contact with Zhong Yuquan. So, her desire for sex is almost at a standstill and although just more than 30. If no man she liked pursued her, she would not have any sex impulse.

One day she wanted to ask Li Haiqing for something and went to his home just a few minutes' walk away. She went to his house wearing a Red Guard uniform she had made and a pair of gray nylon pants. She pushed the door of Li's home a little when finding the door stood ajar. She saw a tall and handsome man at thirty-something years old years old whom she had never seen sitting in a single chair and looking up at her. She thought he must be Li's guest, so she asked politely, "Is Xiao li in?" That man replied mildly, "No, please have a seat. He'll be back soon." Wondering whether his wife was in the kitchen behind the room, Weiying asked again, "Isn't his wife in?" He said "No, they went out together. Please sit down and have a talk while waiting for them", the man smiled. Although she had enough time, she thought it improper to chat with a stranger alone in someone else's home. Therefore, she said, "Then I'll come another day." While leaving the room, she felt that man stood up and walk to the door. She looked back unintentionally at the turning point of the street and found him still standing at the door, he was leaning on the doorframe with one hand on the half-opened door and had still gazing at her.

Two days later, Weiying went to Li Haiqing's home again. On entering his room, she told him, "I came here two days ago but you and your wife were not home. Only a guest of yours was in." "Oh, it turned out to be you! The guest is a Hong Kong friend and I help him do some business. When I came back that day, he said, 'Just now a pretty and good-shaped young woman came here.' He would like me to introduce you to him, but at that time I didn't realize he was talking about you because you seldom came. He'll come here from the hotel soon." Weiying with her heart is pounding asked, "Doesn't he have a wife?" "No, he's single in Hong Kong."

At this moment, the guest walked in. Li called him, "You're here, Yang Wei Is she who you saw last time?" Yang Wei nodded, smiling. Li said, "She is the elder sister of my friend Qiu Juecong." "Oh", Shao answered and began to talk with Weiying like an acquaintance. In less than five minutes, he said directly, "Could you please let me come to your home in the company of Li Haiqing?" Weiying smiled, "OK. He's my brother's friend and you are his friend." He stood up at once, saying to Li, "Let's go, our business wait for me to turn around and do it!" Thus, the three people walked to Weiying's home in a few minutes.

On arriving, Weiying saw the granny next door sitting in the kitchen shared by the two families. She cast a look at Li Haiqing with an expression of familiarity and then at Yang Wei full of doubt. The two of them sat down in a double sofa on the wall left to the door. He looked over the room with a smile, a new high-quality radio (sent to her by Zhong Yuquan by taxi after he came to Changsha from Hong Kong) was put on the rectangular desk under the window facing the sun; an old black wardrobe stood to the left side of the desk; the wardrobe had two drawers in the upper part and two doors in the lower part and a big wooded was put on it; a new sewing machine was located between a single bed and a double one; a square table and two red chairs were beside the sofa. The decoration of the room, though not luxury, was not dull if measured by the then standards in the demeanor. Yang Wei thought just now Li said she had resigned but she seemed live to be okay. Weiying was sitting on the single bed and thought of Lin Jingji while looking at Shao. She thought it was strange that he looked more and more like Lin Jingji They looked alike not only in appearance but also in have an easy manner. Then the three of them chatted a while and the two guests left.

Saying goodbye to them at the door, Weiying was asked by of next-door neighbor the granny, "Is he Li Haiqing? I have known his mother since his childhood, who is now living at the residents' community down the slope."

In the afternoon of the next day, much to Weiying's surprise, Yang walked into her home alone naturally and easily when she was reading theoretical books on Chinese medicine attentively in sofa. She stood up with a little shy and attempted to go to the kitchen to make some tea. But Yang smiled and stopped her, "There's no need. I already had some tea at Xiaoli's home. I just want to talk with you." After that, he said to her like a host, "Your neighbor's walking around will affect us."

He closed the door and Weiying sat down, upset. Yang sat down beside her at once, watching her softly. Her face blushed as she was reminded of her former boyfriend Lin Jingji, and it seemed that Yang was Lu. Yang asked gently, "Do you live alone?" "Yes. My younger brothers and sisters have been married, my mother passed away and father lives in my brother's home temporarily." Then Yang continued asking, "What are you thinking about?" "Nothing, I'm just listening to you." Yang turned around and sat closer to her, "Let me introduce myself, my family is in Guangzhou and my father is an army cadre from the north. I've been in Hong Kong for nearly 10 years and my brother is at home to accompany my parents." Weiying said, "Li Haiqing knows almost everything about me, and he may have told you all. You can go to ask him if you want to know more." Yang laughed, "No. Why are you so serious as long as I like you?" Weiying felt a burst of heat as another wave of love came around. Her heartbeat faster, but she stayed quite calm in appearance, which embarrassed Yang so that he stood up, "I'll leave and come to see you tomorrow." Therefore, Weiying stood up, going to see him off.

However, at opening the door, Yang turned around out of a sudden and looked down at Weiying, full of reluctancy to leave, making her at a loss as what to do. Locking the door again, he held up her face slightly in his hands and pleaded her, "Can I kiss you?" Weiying's heartbeat fastened but just gave him a smile. Holding her head, Yang began to kiss her lips wildly. Weiying's desire for love was ignited again after several years. She lost all alertness as Yang became totally uncontrolled. She believed he was single and might have even regarded him when he hugged her and rolled to the double bed left by her parents. Then she was just so naive and pure. She thought this man would not deceive her because she would not do so. She didn't know that men were more likely to tell lies than women in terms of love because they didn't have to worry about pregnancy. Many men just wanted to enjoy sex for the moment without considering any consequences. Therefore, in this world, when a woman fell in love with another man and especially a man transferred on another woman, they may completely betray their families if they were not rational enough. "Fire of desire" could end the old relationship and trigger a new one. Lying in his hug, Weiying was being surrounded by his passion… She forgot "marriage" entirely at that time and didn't resist his attack both emotionally and physically… She thought that he was Li Haiqing's friend and Li was his brother's friend, so he was trustworthy. Moreover, he was like Lin Jingji very much, making her feel intimate like an old friend. She let him occupy her entirely and freely in soul and body…

In this situation, his dissoluteness and betrayal to his wife also brought enormous damage to Weiying who paid too much without any sense of alertness! He enjoyed sex for a while and Weiying felt a bit hungry, so she went to the kitchen to prepare a simple dinner. Yang said when they began to eat, "Close the door. It's embarrassing if neighbors see the scene." Weiying said after shutting the door, "Do you think they don't know what we do with the door closed? But both you and I are single, so I'm not that afraid." Yang smiled unnaturally at this. After dinner when Weiying was standing up to open the door, Yang followed her, hugging her from the behind and kissing her. Again, he hugged her to the bed. Knowing that he attempted to have sex again, she thought what had been done couldn't be undone… Weiying asked jokingly, "You don't want to have dinner anymore, just want eat me?" Thus, Yang easily lay on her, Weiying's desire for love was ignited by Yang Wei. Two or three hours passed, and it became dark outside. The wind in the autumn evening was blowing off leaves from trees. Yang suddenly sat up, "Oh, I have appointed with someone to negotiate business. It's too late and I must hurry up to the hotel. I'll come to see you tomorrow." Weiying closed the door quietly and he left in a rush.

Yang Wei came to Weiying's home again the next afternoon and closed the door as soon as entering the room. He opened his portfolio

Injured lonely bird

and took out a thick pile of bank notes, saying to Weiying, "The money is for you." Weiying had never seen such a large amount of money put before her ever since she was born. Neither had she ever expected to get money from a man if she got on a romantic relationship with him. Because She believes that, it is tantamount to using body for exchange, betraying own soul. For her, what was the most important was whether the man loved her sincerely and whether they could live happily after getting married. Though she was surprised at the amount of money Yang gave her, she refused to accept, "Why do you give me so much money? I have savings in the bank, and I don't lack money." Blinking his eyes, Yang couldn't understand, "No one will refuse money." Weiying answered, "I don't lack money now, so give me when I spend all my savings. Furthermore, you have to use it while doing business everywhere." She just tactfully rejected him, and in addition, she knew Yang Wei for a relatively short time, so she was unwilling to use his money at once. Yang did not say more and hugged her quickly to the bed again…

After a long while, Weiying wanted to prepare dinner, but Yang said, "Don't cook for me. I've appointed with Li Haiqing to have dinner and talk about business in the hotel." When he put on his clothes and prepared to leave with his portfolio, Weiying called him, "Take the money away." because she felt in her subconsciousness that she had sex with him but not married yet, so the money would be dirty if she took it. But she was embarrassed to tell him the reason directly. Hearing the words, he took it and said to her, "I'll go back to Hong Kong tomorrow. I'll see you again next time I come to Changsha." Remaining silent in shyness, Weiying saw him off the door. Despite the degree of their relationship, she was watching this man walk out of the house like before.

Yang Wei had left for two or three weeks. One day when Weiying was cooking in the kitchen, the next-door neighbor granny also cooked meat there. She asked, "I haven't seen the Hong Kong boss come here for three to four months." "I heard that he has a wife in Hong Kong, so I gave up." "He must have a wife at such an age, if she doesn't pass away or get divorced." "No matter what situation he is in, I will not consider him even if he doesn't have a wife." The granny continued, "That guy is interesting. His words often made me laugh. But he looked good, and the only disadvantage lies in that he is a little old." Then she began to ask, "A handsome young man came here not long ago. Is he the boyfriend Li Haiqing introduced for you?" "You can say so, he comes from Hong Kong to do business in the mainland." "Does he have a wife in Hong Kong?" "Li Haiqing said he's a bachelor." "Then he's suitable for you, much better than the elder one." At this, Weiying felt pleasant.

Yang Wei came to Changsha again than a month later. When he came to Weiying's home, she was not that shy as before, for she thought he fell in love with her at the first sight and she loved him also from the bottom of her heart. Thereby she was confident in the natural development of their romance. That day, Yang Wei had after satisfying romantic sexual desires in bed, Yang Wei looked up at Weiying, saying to her passionately, "I love you so much, Xiaoqiu. Shall I take you with me this time? I want to take you to Hong Kong to do wife diplomacy." "How?" "We can stow away into Macao from Guangzhou by airship and then it will be easy to enter Hong Kong." Weiying is greatly puzzled and full of doubt asked, "Now that you love me, you should marry me the first place and then apply to Hong Kong legally. Why do we have stolen out of a country? I don't like taking risk stealthily." On finishing these words, she heard Yang say in a sad tone, "Then you have just to stay here forever!" Qiu Weiying became stunned and confused as his words. Seeing her expression, Yang touched her face slightly, "I haven't come up with any other alternative. So, we may talk about it later and I'll come back to Hong Kong tomorrow." An ominous sense overwhelmed Weiying. Both got up from bed almost at the same time. She didn't see Yang off but sat in the room in a daze. She only saw him walk down the steps and disappear.

She was in confusion and felt the matter seemed quite serious, how would this romance play end up? She began to become upset and doubt what Yang said today, what did he indicate to the indirectly? Meanwhile she thought that she could hardly get the truth from Li Haiqing and her brother because they were cooperating with Yang in business. What was more, Juecong was pampered since childhood and very selfish so that he would never care about her interests. His wife didn't even notify him of family Qiu's mother's death by saying and she didn't tell his address in Dalian and let the Qiu family look about for him themselves.

But how could she have trusted him so easily and let him get her on her so easily if she hadn't believed that Yang Wei was a business partner for both!

Weiying thought that now that Yang fell in love with her at the first sight, why did he say ambiguous words to indicate something? Lying in bed, she could hardly fall asleep. Later she remembers Yang once told her, "I have an aunt who plays the violin in the orra of Hunan Song and Dance Ensemble. I'll go there today." The Ensemble was not far from Weiying's home, two or three stations away by bus. She had been there twice before her mother got cancer and after Juele was assigned back to work.

At that time, someone of Hunan Acrobatic Troupe introduced her one friend engaged in a job related with music. That guy told her, "If you marry him, Hunan Culture Bureau can assign you to our troupe to learn conjuring tricks or to the Song and Dance Ensemble to be an announcer." Then she thought that such institutions and jobs were much better and would have a brighter prospect than her own. Furthermore, that man was handsome and looked honest and upright. She had intended to get on terms with him but when he came to her home, her mother got cancer and lay in bed, who with some old thoughts and ideology. Later expressed her objection to him who was occupied in art. Thus, they didn't begin. Now Weiying decided to go to the Song and Dance Ensemble again to find Yang Wei's aunt and get to know about Yang's family actual circumstances.

The weather was nice on Sunday afternoon, Weiying knew that it should be a day off at the Ensemble, so she went there by bus. The janitor said, "It seemed that you had come here two years ago." "Now I'd like to find the aunt of a Hong Kong friend, but I forgot her name. But that guy would have registered here when he came, so you probably knew who she is." Then she described his appearance. The janitor said at once, "There are few people from Hong Kong looking for their relatives. As you said he's from there, I know who's relative he is…"

Later Weiying found his aunt's place according to the door number. The door was open, and his aunt was starting a fire in a stove outside, so she talked with her easily. The woman with wore a suitable pair of glasses. She was exactly a violin player from appearance. However, she was talking with Weiying with a doubtful tone. Of course, Weiying must avoid her real purpose to come here, or she would lose the only clue. Without no alternative, she said, "My brother is a business partner of Yang Wei and now he has an important piece of news to inform him but can't contact him. My brother has no time to come here and since I live nearby, he asked me to come for the phone number and address of Yang Wei's wife so that she can tell it to him."

Yang's aunt said, "I don't know his wife's address, but I can tell you his parents' address in Guangzhou." Hearing the two words "his wife", Weiying almost fainted. Meanwhile, she saw her open her eyes wide to watch her expression, so she strived to control her emotion and went on asking calmly, "Does his wife live together with his parents?" She replied unwillingly, "No, she lives in another place with a daughter and a son. You can find her place since she lives near his parents." While making great effort to prevent her pain from being seen, she continued, "Then could you please give me his parents' address in Guangzhou? I'll send a telegram so that they can tell him." Yang's aunt hesitated a little and perhaps she had doubted Weiying's intention, but she still told her the address.

Injured lonely bird

Now Weiying was totally clear that she had met another married man! She was hurt again! And Zhong Yuquan wasn't the only one to cheat on her! With a broken heart, Weiying feel dizzy back home. She closed the door, fell into bed and burst into violent cries. There was no one who could listen to her when she was cheated, which brought about more pain and suffering. At this under heavy blow moment, she thought of her mother again and felt that they had similarities in destiny because their torment in emotion was totally triggered by men! She cried harder, shouting in agony while glaring at the grey sky, "God! Why are there so many bored bad men in this world?" She hated Yang Wei more and more, he concealed the fact that he had a wife just in order to occupy her body to deceive her emotion when she was entirely unprepared. She was a woman who took love seriously.

But she was too pure, do not see through this world there are so many ugly. She it seemed that thought he looked like Lin Jingji, but they had totally different natures. She thought that if mother had been alive to give her suggestion, her pure and upright mother wouldn't in the least let two married men cheat on her! Now nobody knew her pain and would comfort her. When tired of crying, she stared at the gloomy sky in agony.

Several days later, Weiying went to Juecong's home to ask whether he knew the fact that Yang Wei had a wife and children in Guangzhou. Juecong was not in, but his wife was home. It happened that Li Haiqing and his wife were in one room, Yang Wei sat in the sitting room, and there were several other men and women. Therefore, Weiying walked directly into the room where Li was in, questioning him with indignation, "Since you've been to Guangzhou while assisting Yang Wei in doing business, you must know that he had a wife. Why do you conceal that from me?" Li said, "Yang asked me to keep it a secret. He said you would not see him if you knew it. You yourself are to blame as you-self didn't accept his money."

Weiying was quite cross, for Li did not apologize but his wife also helped him quarrel with her. She angrily accused the couple, "I never sell out my body for money, unlike your wife!" (This was because once Yang went to her home late and told her angrily, "Li Haiqing asked me to stay at his home, but when I came, he'd gone to Guangzhou. So, I asked his wife in a pajama, 'Why didn't you tell me beforehand?' But she didn't take my words seriously and…) At Weiying's words, Li's wife ran to Yang and said something in a rage. Juecong's wife looked at what was happening in silence, neither interfering nor helping Weiying who, therefore, thought there was no need to stay here anymore and left. On the way home, she felt that sense of integrity and family love were becoming blurred and gradually disappear from this world…

Since then, Weiying had not got in touch with the couple and Yang Wei Soon Juecong and Li stowed away into Macao by airship. But Juecong sneaked back in less than one year. Later Weiying received a letter of a girl from Macao who complained Juecong abandoned her mercilessly and at the same time blamed herself for being so stupid as to have fallen in love with a married man. Weiying could feel her pain and was sympathetic for her true love, so she wrote back to her, if you feel painful, welcome to the mainland to travel. And there is a spare bed in my room… But she didn't receive her response, so she asked Juecong directly, "…What's the matter?"

Juecong told her, "I didn't have a legal identity in Macao and thereby lived a hard life there. Her father, who is well-known in Macao of gambling field, firmly opposed our romantic relationship. If I had not leaved her, he would have let a scoundrel to kill me!" With these words, Juecong showed a painful expression as a result of memorizing the past. Yang Wei came to see Weiying once, but they didn't have sex anymore and she would not ask him for money.

But she asked him about the relationship between Juecong and the Macau girl as Shao was clear about it. He told her, "That girl is pretty and quite a few playboys are chasing after her and even her cousin who is perfect in almost every aspect likes her. As a smuggler from the mainland, Juecong had nothing, and it was certain that her father would object! But Juecong is so lucky to get such a girl's love. Weiying asked continuously, "I heard from Zhong Yuquan, 'That girl gave birth to a son after Juecong left.' Is that true?" "Probably." (Yang must have known her relationship with Zhong as he was on close terms with Juecong and Li Haiqing.) Weiying thought, a smuggler had to be looked down upon instead of giving full play to his talent. How uninteresting it was! It was unfortunate to be deceived by or to fall in love with a married man, and it was not easy to be a happy woman!

Before that, Weiying went to Yang Wei's parents' home in Guangzhou. She originally thought that Yang's father who was an army cadre from the north would criticize him, but instead, he cursed her, "I hate such stealthy things between men and women", making Weiying had cry loudly told off, "I'm the victim, what responsibilities do I have?" Finally, Yang's younger brother blamed his father for confusing things and being rude to Weiying. He said to her with sympathy, "He does everything like this as if he's still the general. I understand that you are not the one to blame. It's my brothers should responsibility." At this, Weiying became a little bit relaxed.

When she was born, she was like a life-loving bird soaring high in the sky freely and singing her favorite songs. However, after undergoing thunders, lightning and storms throughout the years, she led a hard and painful life. Cheated by a married man again, she was hurt and tortured gravely both mentally and physically…

CHAPTER 6

Wander about the ends of the earth

6.1 She lingered at the cape

Mao Zedong into launching and leading the Cultural Revolution from 1966 to 1976 ten years, was utilize by the Gang of Four, which lead to a decade of turmoil in the entire China, education and art were paralyzed first, and industry and agriculture followed up. If it was not for Lin Biao's accidental death from air crash and the downfall of the Gang of Four, there could have been a war within the armies? If so, China's future will be unimaginable.

Since Deng Xiaoping inspected the south in 1979 and declared Baoan County is the special economic zone of Shenzhen, a small borderland be close by Hong Kong and the South China Sea - Shenzhen, it was becoming a window of China's reform and be open. It is promoted the economic prosperity of China. In the past, a path breaking group of the more than fifty-something cadres lived at houses made of iron sheet when they first came to Shenzhen. But now, the city is proud to recommend itself with skyscrapers, gardens and villas. People with entrepreneurship, despite their age and sex be completely different, but thy all could not wait to have a try in the promising new land. The population of Shenzhen grew from the primitive twenty thousand to the later one million, and now there are more than ten million citizens and more… Shenzhen, an immigrant city consisting of elates from all over China, has stunned the world with its rapid construction speed, and will keep progressing forever…?

It was early summer, 1985 when Zhong Yuquan came to Changsha again. He lived at Xiang River Hotel, and invited the Qiu's family for dinner, where he declared proudly, "I'm going to take you all to Shenzhen and help you set up a hospital there so you can make big money." Mr. Qiu was elated, "Great! Opportunities come around when one goes around. I hear that Shenzhen is close to Hong Kong and is now a very dynamic city. I can count on my expertise to bring me decent benefits there!" Zhong said cheerfully, "You can count on me! Shenzhen was only a poor countryside some years before. Who could have expected that it can transform into such a large and beautiful modern city so quickly, all because of Deng Xiaoping's one decision?" During dinner, Damao said, "I want to go too. There is nanny at home anyway, so it'll be ok without me." Juecong said, "Go ahead you guys, and I shall wait and see." Juele was silent, looking uninterested.

Weiying did not want to make objections that spoil father's good heart. But she was feeling rather confused, and recalled an Indian folk song, "The world is like a desert to me, wandering everywhere…" She felt as if her heart was a desert, too, devoid of any bright scenery. Father was dissatisfied with her silence, "say something! It's for you own good!" She replied, "There's nothing much to do at home any way, except studying medicine theories of my correspondence course; I haven't finished the books yet, but I can bring them with me." Zhong, observing her face, was pleased, "Pack your bags as soon as possible, and we can leave in a few days' time." Mr. Qiu was glad to hear that, "Fine, no problem!" While Qiu Weiying was indifferent with the plan; she was only trying to make the best of the sudden change opportunity according to Father's will.

Two days later, Weiying, Damao and father together at Shenzhen along with Zhong, and settled in a guesthouse in Shangbu District. Zhong rented three rooms there, one for himself; one for Mr. Qiu; one for Weiying and her sisters. There is a canteen in the guesthouse where they had almost all their meals. Sometimes Zhong would disappear for some hours, which Weiying was quite ok with; however, once the staff learnt that Zhong was from Hong Kong and that he brought the family to Shenzhen only for the sake of Weiying, they decided that Zhong was seeing someone else. The head of the guesthouse said to Weiying, "You don't really like him, don't you? As long as he can take care of you, it doesn't matter who he sees." Weiying said, "It doesn't matter even if he sleeps with someone in front of me. I don't care about this old goat. Actually, I get to enjoy myself when he's away." In her mind, sex was way beyond an instinct. Human were born with thoughts, which distinct them from lower animals. True love was about both body and soul. What was more, she never thought of marrying him, but only treated him like a common friend. Because she is not interested treat with his sex life.

After some days at the guesthouse, she learnt something about the situation and policies of Shenzhen, and said to Zhong one day, "To establish a hospital is impossible! We can't even have a private clinic without a local household residence permit!" Zhong smiled craftily and said, "Don't you worry! You have totally free food and accommodation here, take your time! I will take you to all the fun places if you ask me to." Weiying was so agitated that she did not know what to do. She started to know that the prospect of establishing a hospital was bleak. Her father Mr. Qiu was also losing faith. He stayed at his room all day, watching TV and sleeping. In order to forget about the troubles, Weiying usually went window shopping with Damao. The modernized city showed them many wonders from time to time. Zhong probably sensed that the Qiu Weiying's family was feeling low, so he said one day, "I've booked three rooms in a hotel downtown. Let's move tomorrow." These words lightened Mr. Qiu up, for it would be more interesting downtown; despite that Shangbu District had newly built streets and houses, it was in suburbs, with nothing much to do except watching TV. So, the next day Zhong checked out the guesthouse, and the four of them took a taxi to other a hotel.

The first thing to do their everyday was having breakfast at the hotel restaurant. Sometimes they stay there longer proceed with have lunch. For it was in downtown, more people came to visit Zhong. He displayed great hospitality, asking whoever that comes to stay and have meal with him, never worrying about the budget. But Weiying has never seen a deal made, and she secretly doubted if he had any idea of doing business. Maybe he only enjoyed putting on an air of somebody and squandering his money.

One day, a distant relative of Zhong said to her, "You neither plan to marry him nor will you sleep with him. Going on like this will leave you end up being an old unwanted girl!" Weiying said, "Sleep with him? Are you talking about being his secret lover? Does he have a wife in Hong Kong?" He replied, "That I don't have a clue." Weiying said, "But you are his relative! So, he must have one!" Later she thought to herself, "I owe him much for eating and living here, and I can't marry him. This is not sensible! People don't know he's deceived us; they'll only call me a liar." So, she decided to find a way out to shake off his influence and control.

Fortunately, she met a Mr. Yi in the restaurant, who works at Shenzhen office under No. 6 Construction Company of Hunan. She said to him before he left, "Mr. Yi, you can tell that I don't wish to be with him. My sister is leaving for she misses her son, so could you help rent two rooms nearby for my father and me?" Mr. Yi said, "Won't he blame me?" Weiying said, "Why? Wouldn't it be great to save him the money? And I heard he has a wife in Hong Kong, which he does not admit though. I won't marry him even if he divorces, he's too dissolute for me, and I won't take the trouble to watch over him." Mr. Yi said, "I know that you don't love him at all. You won't bother even if you know he sleeps with other women." Weiying said, "Sure. He's not my husband. I am more than indifferent with his affairs; I hope to stay in Shenzhen as much as possible." So, he finally agreed to help her and said, "We have a guest house in Xiangxi Village, all the staff live there. There are still available, and I'll go and ask my superior." Then he left.

The next day he brought her the good news, and the following day Damao took a train back to Changsha. While Weiying and father went to the hostel office of Hunan Sixth Construction Company in Shenzhen. Before leaving, Yi had informed Zhong. So Zhong rented a taxi to send them there and pay for the month rent. So, despite that Weiying escaped from his presence, she was still connected to him economically. Which made her feel uneasy and triggered her to find another way. She tried asking people at the guesthouse about employment in local hospitals, which worked at once, People in that company were all from Changsha, and many knew Dr. Qiu was an have superb medical skills expert in proctology. They recommended him to Shenzhen Liuhua Hospital. The hospital was lacking in good doctors at that time, so they invited Dr Qiu Zhongyuan to be their physician-in-charge of proctology department.

It was burning hot in July, and the entire city was like a huge steaming pot. But in the afternoon to sign their contract, Mr. Qiu and Weiying were feeling warmer than the weather. Mr. Qiu believed that he could rely on his expertise and welcome another success in life. So, he signed the contract, and started working at the proctology department along with Weiying since August 1, 1985. Liuhua Hospital was established soon after Shenzhen became the special economic zone and was then a very good hospital. Before they officially started working, the hospital authority gave them a senior cadre ward with bathroom and toilet attached as accommodation. Their clinic was opposite the stairs on the second floor, next to the department of gynecology and obstetrics located at the right end.

Shenzhen was a young and modernized city, with a majority of its entrepreneurs being young and mid-aged. With the development of modernization there, the population was becoming younger. Despite that Dr. Qiu was an excellent doctor in proctology that cured every patient, he was nothing more than an old doctor in their eyes, and the fame he enjoyed in Changsha had been much greater. The special economic zone had attracted many celebrities and experts, making it especially difficult for one to stand out. But Weiying got an opportunity to practice her medicine theories from correspondence course and combine traditional methods with western ones under father's instruction. She made quick progress and soon could operate independently. A few months later, she was informed by Changsha Health Bureau that a test for traditional medicine doctor license at city and county level was to be held after spring festival, which made her especially excited, for she knew that if she could get a license, her whole life would be guaranteed. Mother used to say to her, "My girl, it's good for you to learn medicine, for you don't have to worry wherever you go, and can live a rather decent life!" So Weiying immediately wrote to the old nurse who used to assist Mr. Qiu, asking her to come and help her father. The nurse was glad, for she felt quite boring after her retirement, and had always hoped to come and see the new economic zone, not to mention that she could even get a salary for that!

After the nurse came, Weiying left for Changsha at once to take the exam. She got 87 in her theory test, which did not agree with her perfectionism. However, the man in charge of the test told her, "The exam is especially difficult this year, and you're the only one who gets more than 80! You've come first! Last year it was your brother. You're truly from a family of great doctors!" The clinical test came after the theory one, for a person who couldn't pass the theory test was very likely to cause medical accidents operate, for which the health bureau would have to take responsibility. Owing to the practice and learning in Shenzhen, Weiying operated successfully without any help and thus passed the test. Soon after the examination, she got her doctor's license.

Huang and Zhang, the two deans of Liuhua hospital were both happy for her success. Huang praised her, "Good job! I don't think your father cares much about your development; you can start your own career from now on." Weiying said, "My father treasure boys more than girls. I'm his favorite girl already; he's even more indifferent with other ones."

Soon the one-year contract was coming to an end. It was unexpected for them that the authority would inform Mr. Qiu, "We won't renew our contract with you." Weiying asked Huang, "Why? He has never caused any accident!" Huang replied, "We had a meeting, and people all think he's too proud to respect others." Weiying got it, Her father had offended the leader in his hospital he founded, so he was by Wang later. But Liuhua was not established by him, and the deans were not offered by him. Disrespecting the leaders and the staff had left him no prospect of staying. So Weiying asked, "Dean Huang, can I sign a contract with Liuhua? I think I can handle the s in proctology department!" Huang seemed glad about her proposal and asked, "Are you sure?" She said, "You can notify on the contract that I shall take full responsibility if any incident happens. In a word, I'm confident in myself that I won't cause any trouble." Huang nodded at once, "Alright, I'll consider your proposal. I'll tell you if everybody agrees."

Around late July 1986, Dear Huang informed Weiying, "We've decided to renew the contract under your name. All you have to do is sign your name under the original one." Weiying was elated upon hearing the news. She immediately went to his office and signed the contract, while thinking, "Finally I can have my own career. And

Father can keep the job!" She told the news to father at once, which however, did not please him. He said sullenly, "Renew the contract under your name? So now I'm your assistant instead? You can stay if you want, but I'm going back to Changsha!" Weiying knew he was an obstinate person. Mother once commented on him, "As stubborn as a mule! No one can ever reverse his decision!" So, in the end, Weiying could only send him onto a train back to Changsha.

Before long, father got a red booklet in Changsha, he was selected as one of the five top famous traditional medicine doctors in Hunan, and he can enjoy special treatment. In additional, he could travel at public expense. What good news it was at that time!

As to Ms. Wang, the nurse, she would not leave Shenzhen, so Weiying kept her as her own assistant. Despite that father had left, Weiying and Wang kept on with the s in proctology department, and even more people came for help than before. One day Huang said to her, "I did not expect that you could do so well without your father!" But that was all due to her hard work. She kept the sentence in The Making of Steel, "This is how a man should spend his life, when he looks back on his past, he would not be regretful of wasting his years" as her motto. So, after she came back from the countryside, she tried her best to make up for her loss in the golden age. She read books of her correspondence course and various fields to broaden horizon, and worked hard on medicine, especially traditional medicine, all of which contributed to her clinical practice. The experience of combine theory with practice her follow father also helped a lot. What's more, Mother had worked hard on medicine when pregnant with her. It was likely that she had received good antenatal training. Her success was a combination of genius and be hard-working and eagerness to learn!

One day there weren't many patients in the hospital, and a young man who had been in Shenzhen for more than ten years conversed with her. He said, "The locals, except the old and weak, all tried to stow away to Hong Kong when Shenzhen was a poor and backward countryside. Even people outside Shenzhen tried to do so. At that time, it was a betrayal to motherland. The frontier army would with wolfhounds chase these people and even shoot them. I wonder how much blood there is in the sea!" Weiying was hot with emotion, and she said, "If it were me, I wouldn't wager my own life. But people at that time had trouble feeding themselves and only wanted a better life; few really wanted to betray. My brother-in-law was kept custody early stage the Cultural Revolution, and by the time he was declared as counter revolutionary. He had already lost all freedom and could not escape." The patient nodded as if in approval.

During that time at work, Qiu Weiying would sometimes saw a young black man passing by when she opened her clinic door. He was polite and all dressed up. It was said that he was the son of the vice president of an African country, and he came to learn acupuncture from Zhang, the dean, for Zhang was famous for his acupuncture in Shenzhen and Hong Kong.

One day when Weiying finished an operation and was talking with Wang on the chair by her clinic, the black man came inside. Without a word, he sat on the patient chair and started talking like an acquaintance. His English was good, but he could speak only a little Chinese. Qiu studied Russian at middle school, and only learnt a bit English while studying western medicine. So, the two of them just talked according to their own wills and did not really understand each other, while Wang sat by, observing interestedly while making tampons. When he left, Wang said, "Though he's black, he has a face with good regular features. And he talks funny." Many Chinese people think "the whiter, the prettier".

Qiu thought the son of this vice president must have received a good education. Everyone, his demeanor and temperament are important than the color of his skin. What is more important for anyone is, does he have inner beauty - does his existence benefit humanity? Wang Tianliang had a handsome face and body shape, but he looked stupid to Qiu, and never really attracted her. The black man was somewhat interesting to her! But it was nothing about chemistry, for she could tell that he was more than ten years younger than her, apparently not likely to make a couple. He came a few times from that day on.

This day while Qiu was counting the money to hand in to hospital, he quietly came by, swiftly took out a ten yuan note, put on a comic smile and left with a "Bye Bye". Qiu did not care much about the abnormal act, for she thought he was only making a job. But Wang was despising his be indiscreet in one's conduct and commented after he left, "Is this what a son of vice president does? This kind of action really makes me look down!"

But only one day later, when Qiu went back to her dormitory after work, she heard someone knocking on her door. She opened it a bit and saw him smiling amiably out there, so she opened the door and let him in. He gently shut the door and took out ten yuan from his pocket, "Here's your money." Qiu only smiled. She figured out that the reason he took her money was to use it as an excuse to come to her again. What a smart and interesting man! She was mild in dealing with him, asked him to sit on the chair by the door, while she sat opposite him on her bed. But he suddenly stood up and sat by her, said with a frank and honest attitude, "Shall we be friends?" She learnt from his eyes what he meant by "friends". Looking at his smart but inexperienced young face, she realized how much elder she was than him. So, she smiled politely and said, "You're only twenty-something, aren't you? But I'm almost forty, too old for you! Do you have any idea?" But he said, "Really? I don't think it shows. But that's alright. My family like Chinese women! My brother's girlfriend is from Beijing." Qiu asked, "Where is your brother now?" He said, "Sha Tou Jiao. We have a trade company that covers businesses in Shenzhen, Hong Kong, Africa, America and Europe."

Many Chinese people don't like black people, thinking they are crude. However, Qiu Weiying had no such opinion of the young black man in front of him, who was born into an upper-class family in his own country and was well educated. And he is a young man who likes to learn and strive for advancement. No matter what country the person is from or what color he or she is, as long as the person is of high moral character and beneficial to society, he or she deserves respect!

So, Qiu said, "If you want a Chinese girlfriend, there are bunch of young girls out that and I can introduce them to you." He was not moved, "I want a Chinese girl like you." Qiu was stubborn too, "I heard the women in your country shall wear veils when they go out. I would fall if I do so!" He was amused and laughed, and the easy and friendly atmosphere also made she laugh. Before long, he suddenly remembered something, looked at his nice gold watch and said politely, "I have something to deal with." Qiu said nothing and stood up at once to open the door for him.

While Qiu was waving goodbye, she saw Huang dean standing at the end of the corridor, concentrated in observing them. She shut the door and thought, "Is he suspecting our relationship? It is lucky that he did not stay long. Otherwise, he will have a misunderstanding about us." Later she thought that love really could happen between different races, but the man was too young for her. She had never seen him again from that day on, and Huang dean never questioned her on that.

One day she met Yang wife of Long, the dentist. Yang was a nurse at hospital and a close friend of Qiu's, so Qiu told the story to her. She laughed and said, "I'm on your back! He has a good family background, and a face so nice that your future person of mixed race will be very cute." Qiu hit her and said, "What are you talking about? He's more than a decade younger than me!" Yang said, "So what? He likes you! There are a lot of couples in this world with men over ten years younger than women." But Qiu had always been conservative and would not be with a man of that age. Yang said, "I've always felt that you will marry a foreign guy and go abroad." Qiu was curious, "Why? I like it here!" Lil Shao said seriously, "I can tell from your look." Qiu dubitated, "You can tell that from my look?

Which country am I going then?" Li Shao insisted, "You just wait until it comes true!" But Qiu Weiying was not moved, "I don't have much interest in being a second-class citizen in another country."

Half a year later, Qiu became even busier with her work. Sometimes she would have Li Fen, daughter of father's colleague come and help her. Li's parents came from Henan and worked at the proctology department in Shenzhen People's Hospital. Just like Weiying, Li Fen also took up the expertise from her parents, but that she had not taken the license exam yet.

Zhong Yuquan managed to find out where Qiu worked and came to her one day, asking her to have lunch with him. Qiu said, "It takes too much time dining outside, and I have to take my nap." Zhong was displeased, "So now big Doctor has no time for me." Qiu rectified, "I'm not being proud. It's just that I have to maintain sober for the afternoon operations, so I have to take a nap." Later in came a patient, so Qiu left to cater to him behind the white drape, leaving Zhong outside with Li Fen.

A month later, Zhong came to ask her for dinner again. Qiu contemplated for a while and thought it'll be okay to go out with him as ordinary friends. It was late in the afternoon and Li Fen was away, so she said, "Ms Wang has gone to her dormitory for laundry. Let's wait for her and go together." Exhilarated, Zhong nodded and said, "No problem!" Overwhelmed with joy, he couldn't help revealing a secret, "You assistant Li Fen used to take her unmarried lady friend to my hotel, and we had dinner together. Later, her friend act alone came to my room, stripped herself and asked me to sleep with her. Shit! She stinks! She's not even half as good as my Weiying!" Qiu was both amused and disgusted. She glared at him and said, "I'm not yours!" And she thought to herself, "How pathetic a woman is if she has so little self-respect as to hook up with men! They only take play with you and look at you as a lowly woman." She was also aware that the lady must have been infected with venereal disease. She used to visit the department of gynecology and obstetrics next door and happened to saw a woman with the illness, she gave off an extremely unpleasant smell that forced Qiu is quick in action to leave the room.

It's true what her parents told her, "One should cherish his/her own body, for it is endowed by his/her parents!" This is especially true for women, for women might get into the situation of pregnancy. She doesn't know when this social prejudice formed, if a man plays more with women, it seems that he is capable; if a woman plays more with men, she becomes base person. Qiu decided that her future partner must be a man with decency, or else she could even be infected with venereal diseases from him; and that a woman should maintain her self-respect and independence!

For her sense of responsibility, she was honored by her patients, and many introduced their friends relatives and colleagues to her when they get cured. One day a lady came to her for examination and treatment without. registered Qiu said, "Please go downstairs and register first." The lady said, "My colleague recommended you to me. She said she had been seriously ill and got cured by a female doctor in Liuhua Hospital. I have registered the surgical department, but there is only a male doctor, so I came to you." Qiu immediately realized that the hospital office is playing tricks, the contract she signed was about all the proctology s in Liuhua. She had no fixed salary and needed to hand in a certain amount of money to the hospital, namely the more patients she has, the more money she makes.

Because she contracted the entire anorectal department of this hospital and the amount, she pays to the hospital every month is fixed. Now she was serving for someone else's wallet. But she could not object, for firstly, she was not a formal employee, but only an invited doctor with contract; secondly, the proctology department was a branch of surgical department. Later she learned from other patients that the incident that day was not a happenchance, which bothered her a bit.

Later one day, an executive of an import company came to her consulting room. He suffers from a serious and complicated disease. Fiacre's disease, but he soon recovered with Qiu Weiying's help, and even became healthier than before, which made him very satisfied. He was a local in Shenzhen. After knowing Qiu was not a formal employee and was planning new action after two last months in the contract, he volunteered to introduce her to People's Hospital, which was the largest and best-equipped hospital at that time in Shenzhen. Qiu was glad to take the offer. Li Fen's parents worked at the proctology department of People' Hospital, and the Lis lived there too.

Li said her parents were too busy, and so she left Qiu to help them. Qiu used to visit them with her father, when Li's parents revealed that they got their job with the help of their acquaintance in health bureau. In order to keep the job, the couple slid a monthly 500 yuan to the person of health bureau in charge, which was no less than the moon salary of an inland doctor. It was an unbelievable news to Qiu that a state official should seek personal benefit with power in hand, but of course, she did not reveal her real thoughts.

On the big day, Qiu Weiying left work early and told nurse Wang to put the patients on appointments. Then she got on a taxi with the manager to People's Hospital. There she met with the dean, a thin, mid-sized Cantonese around his fifties with smart eyes and polite speech. One could tell he was an intelligent and capable man from his look. It was already after work, but he was still sitting in his office, waiting for Qiu and the manager.

After taking seat, Qiu was asked to make a brief statement, and then the dean asked, "When is your contract due?" She replied, "August 1." The dean said, "Good, only two months left. I believe you will be competent for the proctologic s in our hospital. So, let's start our contract from August 1, and we'll end the contract with Doctor Li by then." Qiu knew who he referred to by Li, and she was surprised to hear that. She said at once, "Li is an old friend of my father's, and I'm acquainted with his whole family. If I just snatch the job from them, how can I maintain their friend? People's Hospital is a very large one, and I can't handle all the s…" The dean seemed rather surprised too, "You know him? Right, his family oversees the proctology department right now. But Li is getting old…"

Qiu interrupted, "But he is healthy and vigorous enough for more years of work." The dean said, "You can take charge of the department." But Qiu insisted, "I can't ruin their business. Let's leave this topic later." However, the dean said, "We won't renew the contract with Li even if you don't come." Qiu hesitated, but still could not take the offer. The interview ended, and she left with no result. Later, the manager told Qiu, "The dean said you're quite an intelligent person! He sincerely hoped that you could work in their hospital." Qiu confessed, "If my friend's father were not in charge of the proctology department right now, I would have gladly taken his offer. But in such situation, I'd feel ashamed if I take the job."

However, Qiu was surprised to find get no thanks for one's good intentions for her. For some people should only base on hearsays and get aggressive easily. A few days later, Li Fen came with her nurse friend and started her rebuke against Qiu the minute she set her feet in, "How ungrateful you are! My parents are so nice to you, how can you try to steal their job?" Before she even finished and Qiu was able to contend, Li's friend put on an air of integrity and shouted at Qiu, "What an evil woman you are! I can't believe you have a baby with the Hong Kong merchant before marriage. He might have got married already in Hong Kong!" Qiu was exasperate, "Baby? Is it a boy or a girl? Who told you so?" She replied, "He told me himself!" Qiu denounced her, "If you really think he's in a relationship with me, why did you try to seduce him behind my back? You have trouble finding a man? Listen carefully, he would never go to you even if I forsake him! You think I have no idea how shameless you are? You better examine your own character first! You will get nowhere without self-respect!" Qiu's anger grew as she spoke. Had she been not a doctor that needed to stay polite, she would have slapped on the face of the jealous, impudent liar. People around the passageway hear the noise and knew something was wrong. Li Fen looked at her friend in doubt, having no idea of what they were talking about. Qiu reckoned that Li Fen introduced her young friend to Zhong, for she knew Qiu did not like him. Zhong showed simply not treat sb as a human being. But she entered his room and took off her clothes… Realized that she could not hide her secrete any more, the woman blushed. Her be sanctimonious gone, and she lowered her head and fled downstairs. Qiu said to Li, "You'll see one day that I did not sign the contract only to save your jobs. But the dean said they won't continue to hire you anyway, even if I don't take the position." Li was doubtful, and silently left to chase her friend.

When they left, Ms. Wang worried for her, "This must have a bad influence on you. The people here don't know the truth, and you're still unmarried; they'll take what she said for granted." Being a person of great person of great self-respect, Qiu's tears almost fell.

A week later, Zhong came again high and mighty, as if knowing nothing about his nonsense. Be beside oneself with anger, Qiu showed no concern for his face and scolded him in front of Ms. Wang, "I just fell for your scam once, and I didn't spend the night with you. When and where did I have any baby with you? I can't believe you made up the story for Li Fen's friend! She came and defamed me, and we had a bad argue! It is you that lied, not me! Why do you do to me like this?!" Zhong only said, "That bitch, I'll tell my friends to teach her a lesson." Qiu declared angrily, "Any of your problems with her is your own business! Don't you ever come to me again?" Zhong was displeased at her attitude and left at once. He did never show up.

A month later, Qiu saw a distant relative of Zhong's by her hospital. He told Qiu, "Zhong has divorced his wife." Qiu said indifferently, "It's none of my business! He's rich enough to find an 18-year-old country girl. I' not the least interested in such a promiscuous man!"

It was only a month before her contract was due, and she began to wonder what she should do. If she continues her cooperation with Liuhua, where the surgical department also take proctology s, her contract makes no sense at all; but if she objects to their doing so, it will be a big contradiction. What's more, the authority had already warned her of maintaining the order of hospital after Li Fen and her friend came. She contemplated, and suddenly came up with the idea of leaving the hospital and opening a personal clinic. She was quite confident in her expertise through her practices.

A Hong Kong patient used to come all the way to her and said, "You'll make big money if you own a private clinic in Hong Kong!" but it took a Shenzhen registered permanent residence to set up a clinic, which she did not have. But she learned she could get the residence by purchasing a house. The housing price was reasonable at that time, taking only around 100 thousand yuan to buy an apartment in Jincheng or Youyi mansion; however, she only had no more than 50 thousand yuan, and had heard nothing of, not to mention to consider bank loans. She had a young female patient who got the permanent residence for her relative in Hong Kong bought a house for her. She told Qiu that some Hong Kong people who had purchased houses in Shenzhen did not need the residence, and people can buy for the residence cards target from them with 20 thousand yuan. So Qiu bought a household register target from a real estate businessman, and later rented a room in Youyi mansion. It was in a first-floor suite with two bedrooms and one living room, owner of which was from Hong Kong. In the other suite lived the niece of the owner, who went to school in Shenzhen.

So, when Qiu's contract with Liuhua Hospital ended, she moved to Youyi Mansion on August 1, 1987. It was not far from the Shenzhen Office of Hunan Foreign Trade, where her former patient worked. She ate in their canteen, and met Sun Jie, a young man f who worked at Shenzhen branch under China Bank. He was also from Changsha and got the job after graduation from university.

Sometimes he would come to Qiu's place for a chat in the name of fellow townsman. He was thirteen years younger than Qiu, over 175 centimeters tall and was a handsome guy with white skin and dark hair. He was smart in nature, but too impulsive and unpredictable for Doctor Qiu. The young guy worked and lived alone in Shenzhen, but his mind seemed to be soaring up in the skies. Most of the urban and economic development forces in Shenzhen were from all over the country. In the modernized new city by the sea, people left their footprints on the history of Shenzhen progress with fancy dreams about new life.

6.2 Shenzhen SAR Entrepreneurship

Youyi mansion included eight buildings with more than twenty floors. It was in an alley behind Jianshe Road and Xiangjiang Restaurant. The buildings made up a square, in the middle of which flowers and grass were planted, for people to have a breath of fresh air amongst the tall buildings. At first Qiu Weiying rented the first-floor room to Jianshe Road's side, and once she settled down, she started sending her credentials including doctor's license and ID card to Shenzhen Health bureau to apply for a private clinic. But the official told her she needed to have a location for business first. So, she had to rent a suite with two bedrooms and one living room. It was to Xiangjiang Hotel's side, on the first floor and attached with a private garden. Apart from the garden, the house covered a small size of around 50 square meters. The kitchen and bathroom were both tiny, and only the living room was larger. The owner was from Hong Kong and charged her a monthly rent of 3800 HKD. Taking the property fees and into consideration, Qiu had to spend no less than 4000 HKD a month, which was about ten month's salaries of an inland common laborer. She also had to change HKD from the black market, where additional fees were charged. She thought at that time that she could make her dream come true if she went through all the procedures; actually, it should have been within the policy for her to open a private clinic.

After she handed in all the credentials needed, she went to Leshan Giant Buddha Sichuan while waiting for the outcome. The Leshan Giant Buddha is from the top to the bottom located on the east bank of the Nanmin River in Leshan City, Sichuan Province. Buddha is from the top to the bottom 71 meters high, and it is the world's largest sitting Buddha. She is planning to return to Shenzhen to open her business after a short tour.

However, August and September flew by after her return. Month after month, even after she had equipped her open a private practice place with all the instrument and medicines needed, the Notification did not come. She was like a cat on hot bricks, time kept on going, and she had only expenditure rather than income. At this rate, she would run out all the money of work hard in Liu Hua hospital. She also had her niece Wu Sha with her, intending to teach her medicine and have her as an assistant. But the two of them only ate, slept, watched TV and went shopping, which won't work out! So, she went to the health bureau to ask the officials, but they only told her to wait. Time flew by, and soon was the end of the month when she had to pay for her rent. Even though she had already paid one month's deposit, she would still have to move out when the money is used up, even if the landlord trusted her. Many who had come to Shenzhen for opportunities eventually had to go back for spending all their money on house expensive rent. If she became one of them, then all her efforts would end up in vain! She had no savings left, and transferred her permanent residence to Shenzhen, so going back to Changsha wouldn't help either. She could neither sleep nor eat and felt like crying all day long. The only comfort was she had been healthy all the way, so she did not need to pay for any doctor for she had no health care insurance.

When she used to be in the countryside, as she often soaked her legs in the cold spring water, to fish for water plants to feed the fish.

But after some years in city, she started to recover, probably because of the better environment and her young age.

One day after dinner, she left Wu Sha watching TV at home and went to Shenzhen International Mall nearby for grocery. She soon finished the shopping, and when she exited the mall, she sensed somebody following her. She quickened her steps, and the follower hastened too; she slowed down, and the man followed suit. She approached the iron gate of Youyi Mansion where home was near, and she stopped to avoid letting him know her address. She turned and glared at him but could not make out his face in dim lights. Her intuition told her that he was a jobless ruffian around his twenties. The man saw Qiu stopped and staring at him, uttered shamelessly, "I'll take you somewhere. How much do you charge?" Qiu grasped his intention and became so furious than she wanted to slap his face. She shouted at him, "What do you mean? Go away your stupid bastard!" The man was about to get angry when a couple of people came close, so he slipped away.

Weiying dropped her things at home and then sat in her wooden sofa, couldn't help shedding tears. Wu Sha said at once, "Aunt, don't worry about the money. I'll go back tomorrow. I can't be of any help here but only add to your burden." But Qiu came up with an idea suddenly, "Don't. You've already waited for so long. It doesn't take much for us to eat only a few hundred a month. The problem is the rent! I'll go to Manager Liu to borrow some money tomorrow." Wu Sha knew Manager Liu, he lived nearby, and he was a nice patient of Qiu when she worked at Liuhua. He would drop by every now and then to visit Qiu. Qiu felt he was respectful to her, and he is rich enough to lend her the money.

Sure, he was. When Qiu Weiying arrived at his place and explained her visit, he gave her 5000 HKD at once to his wife's face. It was the life-saving money, which exhilarated Qiu. She thanked the nice couple and left and paid her rent in time. However, another month went by and a man came to charge her as deputy of her landlord. No matter how Qiu explained to him her difficulties, he was not moved. Before leaving, he said, "I believe in your words. It'll be ok if you put off for some days, but you'll have to pay before long. The landlord only asked me to collect his rents, and he won't have any concern of why you can't afford the rent. If you can pay, you live here. If you can't, you'll have to move." Qiu felt bitter inside. She had already come so far at such a high price; how could she give up? So, she had to call Liu again. She said on the phone, "Mr. Liu, my license has not come yet, so I can't return your money and am having problem with this month's rent."

It was an expected surprise that Liu did not say anything embarrassing; instead, he comforted her over the phone, "That's alright. So, you're out of money again? I'll draw 5000 from bank tomorrow and You come to my house to get it. We live close any way." Qiu had a mixed feeling of happiness and sorrow when she got another 5000. She was happy because she could afford another month's rent, but sad because she could not keep on borrowing money like that. What should she do if the license still wouldn't come? When she gave the money to the client, the man was please, "I knew someone like you won't owe others money." Qiu smiled bitterly and said, "If I hadn't run into a patient I met when I was working at Liuhua Hospital and was able to borrow money to pay the rent, I wouldn't be able to stay now and would have to lose all my money and go home!"

While she left the Liu's home and was waiting for a bus by the roadside, she started thinking, "What am I going to do if the license still doesn't come?" She used to talk with Liu and learnt that he had been through much for his family background and his father's blood relation overseas. Maybe that's why he had sympathy over her. But she could not always borrow from him. Maybe she should go to someone for direct help and find another way out. She looked at her delicate watch which she bought at Shatoujiao, it was already supper time. She remembered that a health bureau chief lived on her way home. When she first started applying for her business license, a kind town fellow of her who was the colleague of his brother-in-law used to write a letter to his wife, asking him to help with Qiu. The town fellow gave the letter to Qiu and told her to give it to Mrs. health bureau Chief. He added, "If you come across any difficulty in future, you can always go to her for help." But Qiu did not like to beg help from others. She did give the letter to the health bureau chief's wife, who said nothing, and so she never bothered her again. But at the special moment, she had no choice but to ask her for help. She looked around a store, had some fried rice noodle in a restaurant before the good time for visit came. Then, she went to the health bureau chief's house to try her luck. Maybe Mrs. health bureau Chief could help her out of her difficulty.

She rang the doorbell, and Mrs. health bureau Chief recognized her at once. It was a delicate lady, looking very smart. The couple came from inland. Mrs. Chie was a seemingly good wife. Chinese people believe that "A man's success owes half to his wife". At least, a man who fights with his wife all day is not likely to focus on his career. Mrs. Chief asked Qiu to sit down, and said, "I've just had my supper. Have you eaten anything?" Qiu replied yes, and the lady asked her young distant relative who lived with them to make Qiu a cup of tea. After some small talk, Qiu explained her difficulty to her. She smiled, as if it was no big deal, "A piece of cake! I know Mr. Wu, the dean of Huaqiang Hospital, a very able man. His hospital is newly set up and in urgent need for specialists. I'll write you a recommendation, and you can go to him yourself." Qiu was happy to hear that. She took over the short note written in haste, put it in her backpack, thanked the lady and left.

After breakfast the next day, Qiu Weiying took a bus to Huaqiang Hospital. Upon seeing Wu dean, she reckoned him to be a very able person. He was around his forties, tall, had a square face, a pair of keen eyes and simple but firm speech. After Qiu introduced herself, he said, "We don't have a inpatients department at this moment; the anorectal are dealt by surgical department. It's no problem if you hope to work here, but we can't offer accommodation; you must deal with by yourself. My family also lived in a temporary work shed made of iron sheet. You can have a look there since you've already come. My wife is free today, so you can talk with her. She's a gynecologist in People's Hospital. We used to be classmates in university." Qiu was at leisure and sat in his office reading newspapers and waiting for him.

When Wu finished work, she followed him to the shed. It was a row of dormitory made of iron sheet, located behind the hospital. Wu showed her around, and she saw all the staff members lived there. The sheds were crowded with not any vacancy left. Behind those sheds was Wu's home, which was nothing different from the temporary shed of construction laborers, except that he had a TV, washing machine and some other electric appliances. It was a poorly furnished house. Wu told his wife, "Doctor Yu, we have a guest." Yu was a tall woman, straightforward and smiling. She kindly asked Qiu to stay for together lunch when their children came back from school. It was an invitation too warm to refuse, so Qiu stayed and chatted with them. She said, "I have not expected you to live in such a simple house. After all, you are the dean!" Yu said, "What's so special about a dean? He serves his country and goes wherever his country asks him to. He has just got everything going in Youyi Hospital in Xiangmi Hu, and soon after that he was dispatched here. It was also this hard in Xiangmi Hu." Qiu admired, "Your husband is truly a construction of the hospital in Shenzhen SAR of open up cultivate wasteland bull!" Upon the words, Wu came over and said to his wife, "Don't complain about the easy accommodation; we should be thankful that we have somewhere to live. Doctor Qiu is having trouble in finding a place to live!" Yu asked her, "So what are you going to do?" Qiu replied, "Then I guess I can't come. Even if I use all my salary to pay for my rent, that would be far from enough! Any house on rent nowadays needs at least one or two thousand. I can only urge them to give me my license while figure some other ways out." Yu said, "It isn't easy starting a career away from home, is it? The housing is so expensive here, and many had to go back for can't afford the rent." Qiu said, "That's true. All my savings have gone to the landlord while waiting for my license. I have now borrowed money to pay my rent".

Yu said, "How about finding another one somewhere cheaper?" Qiu said, "If I move, I will have to start from scratch and apply for my business license with a new address. It'll only add to my trouble!"

At that time, the boy and girl of Wu's came in. the children greeted Qiu politely, and they had lunch in the simple shed. After some rest, the children had to go back to school while Wu had to go to work. Qiu chatted with Yu for some time and asked to leave. Yu stood up and said, "Feel free to drop by!" Qiu accepted pleasantly. Yu walked her out and showed her the shortcut to bus station, and the two of them waved goodbye. Qiu's talk with Huaqiang Hospital did not work out, but the nice family of Wu, and their kindness and friendliness impressed Qiu so much that they became good friends ever since.

Meanwhile, people tried to match Qiu up. They told her there were many rich locals who were well-off on the rents. But Qiu knew the local got married early, while she was already in her late thirties. It was exactly what her mother said, "It's more difficult to find a partner when you're old. You can either get a divorced man or a widower, and you'll end up being a stepmother." Qiu was rather afraid of being a stepmother. She was the eldest child of her mother's, and her brothers and sisters would be displeased if she scolded them for their own good. What if she had to educate a child as a stepmother? What's more, she did not wish to be a housewife without her own career. So, after all that she had been through, she decided not to resort to marriage as a solution.

One day Qiu said jokingly to Sun Jie who dropped by, "My license hasn't come yet. How about you marry Wu Sha? You would make a perfect couple." Sun Jie was angry and shouted at her, "Qiu Weiying, how can you say this to me? You know it is you that I came for! You have no respect for me at all!" Qiu had always sensed that he expected a relationship with her, and that was why she made the joke. Seeing him get angry, she said, "You're thirteen years younger than me, how can this work out?" But Sun only yelled, "I don't believe you're that age!" Qiu said, "You don't? I can show you my ID card." As a result, Sun left indignantly. Qiu began to know that there were some men who willed marry ab elder woman, but she still thought more than ten years is a wide discrepancy that will provide no security at all. When she gets fifty, he will be no more than forty. Handsome as he is, bunch of young girls would come beating a path to his door, and it's very likely that he would change! One cold December day, Qiu was worried to cry for she still didn't get her license. Sun Jie, instead of comforting her, scolded, "Cry, cry, cry! You're really annoying!" In a word, Qiu felt it would be better to be with an elder man. In the end, no matter how independent, women are always weaker emotionally and physically. If a man could not offer the support she needed, would she be happy? To her relive, her license finally came at the verge of breaking down. She was exhilarated, almost laughed out loud in the street. She told the news to Sun when he dropped by the latter held her in his arms and danced with her. He smiled while dancing, and said, "attractive middle-aged woman, still look attractive!" Qiu was both amused and annoyed, and said, "Why do you come to such an old woman?"

She told the exciting news to her previous patients in Liuhua, and they were all happy for her. Some of them had once recommended their friends to go to Qiu cure the sickness in Youyi Mansion, but for Qiu did not have a license. And Qiu Weiying, who never likes to be sneaky, did not accept them, despite all was ready. Now all her waiting is not in vain! She purchased a few drugs, absorbent cotton and medical instruments, medical apparatus and instruments necessities and started her business. Her first patient was the friend of Chen Biyun and Chen is a previous patient of her at Liuhua. At first her clinic was unknown, but business could cover her rent. At the end of the month, she gave in the money earned by herself. The man was happy both for Qiu got her license and gave him the money. Later Qiu earned more, and paid back the money lent by Liu immediately, and Liu thought she was an honest and reliable person. It will always make the next borrowing easier if the debtor pays back in time, but Qiu never borrowed again, for she started to become famous in Shenzhen had no longer had any trouble paying for the rent. Had it not been Liu's help and her confidence that she will make big money once she gets the license, she would probably have lost all her property and hope. She had to go back to Changsha, just like most examples showed. Finally, her dream became true, she got the license, and could give her talents to full play in the promising land of Shenzhen.

Later, when she came to the peak of her life, she was glad that she had not jumped into Xiang River when she walked on the bridge in Changsha. If she had, all the beautiful realities could never come to her. So, no matter how hard life is, men shall never resort to death as a solution! Life is a once-and-only opportunity, but success is likely to revisit. Life is full of miracles that may fall upon you at any time. If you can make the right choice at crucial moments, make it through the difficulty with perseverance, embrace life with a positive attitude and not easily bowing to difficulties, the bright future will eventually become a reality one day!

6.3 Happiness depends on oneself to create

Since the Gang of Four was brought down, <See 1. D> unprecedented changes had taken place in China. The so-called political stains of the Qiu Weiying's – the confiscation of family property and Qiu's brother-in-law being anti-revolutionist, who devastatingly pulled her mar career in education, career and marriage, were erased. The fact that her mother died in mental and physical anguish from a series of economic and political persecutions had branded her innocent heart with incurable wounds. But eke out a difficult existence the past was, it was in the past anyway. Now she was approaching forty and still unmarried, but she wouldn't enter a random relationship and set up a family that easily. Fortunately, she was born with a healthy body and a sensible brain, which contributed much to her independence in career and life. Ever since she got her license, she was more confirmed that life would be beautiful if she worked hard. "A bird cannot fly without the sky and a horse cannot run without the land". If a person's hands and feet were bound, can't fly if you want to fly, and can't move if you want to run. But if you are lazy and don't do it, just lying on the grass and sleeping, happiness will not fall from the sky.

The first few months weren't that easy, though, for the house Qiu Weiying rented was in a quiet alley behind International Mall. People seldom went by unless they are acquaintances come to visit. As first only a few of her previous patients from Liuhua knew her clinic; what's more, it was a private clinic, so her fees are lower because the patients couldn't put their bill on public expenses count. Her starting income was merely enough to make ends meet. But "good wine sells well even deep in an outlying lane", after she cured some serious patients, they recommended her to their friends in Hong Kong, who came all the way for her help and paid her in HKD. She had a special way of charging for her exact prediction of her therapy, after the first examination of a patient, she would settle the total charges according to the state of illness, which included operation, dressings, equipment and pills. After that she wouldn't charge one more yuan and would carry on her service until the patient is cured. She could also tell the patient directly after examination about the time needed for therapy. Almost everyone that came to her was satisfied in the end. Some of them, out of appreciation, wrote letters to the local paper recommending her service, and the paper send journalist to her door. Since then, several thanks-letters and reports were published, and local medias and even a magazine in Hong Kong made several reports about her. As time went by, she gradually grew famous in Shenzhen and even Hong Kong. One day, a manager from Beijing told her, "I've gone to a clinic nearby for you, where the doctor claimed to be Qiu Weiying. But I remember people mentioning you as a 'she', and that was a 'he'." One day, a female patient from Hong Kong said, "There is a clinic in Hong Kong which claims to be your branch…" Qiu thought it was funny, for there should be someone willing to abandon their own sex and names and pretend to be her. As she became more famous, her business also grew larger, occupying more and more of her time.

Once Juecong came to visit her, and after checking her income booklet, he said, "You really ask little! Even I charge more than you, do in Changsha." But Weiying thought people came to her, most are not reimbursed by the workplace, on their own expenses for trust. So, she decided to keep the price reasonable. More and more patients came to her door, and for Hong Kong people always came on Sundays, she would even sacrifice her weekend. It was not rare that she was still hungry when others had already finished their supper for a long while. She was not a greedy person, but if she refused to see the patients after work, they would find excuses like, "I don't live in Shenzhen. I'm from Baoan. I've already waited for so long and won't go home if you help me today." So, she really found it difficult to say no to those patients from far away.

One day when she was occupied with extraordinarily many patients, an official for health bureau paid an uninformed inspection to her clinic. She was too busy to attend to him, who only looked at the patients waiting and said, "That's So many patients!" Then he left without even sitting down. Of course, Qiu began to have extra money to save apart from housing expenditures and wages for Xiao Fang, the nanny. In the past, she usually couldn't or wouldn't afford many of the clothes she liked, but later she was able to get whatever clothes she liked without hesitation, even if it might be a imported piece that cost RMB some hundreds.

In 1989, she celebrated her fortieth birthday in Xiangjiang restaurant where she invited all her friends and ordered two round tables. They dined with beautiful music and did social dancing after the meal. She gradually started to know the happiness and status she won by her hard work. A new patient came with a recommendation from others, and he was surprised to see Qiu, "I thought you were an old doctor to be so experienced, but you're much younger!" Qiu pointed to her doctor's license on the wall, "See, I'm not that young. I'm already forty!" She finally tasted the sweetness in her middle age that the harvest after sweat and happiness won by one's own hands are the utmost pleasures in this world!

However, being alone in this big world as a single woman wasn't easy. Most of her patients were grateful when cured, besides those who wrote letters to newspapers, there were others who bought her gifts, invited her to dinner or even to their companies and homes, and she often found it impossible to turn down those kind invitations. There was an old man from Hong Kong, whose son and daughter in law also treated Qiu as intimate friend after he was cured. The old man had brought expensive ice creams he liked several times all the way from Hong Kong in the hot summer day for doctor Qiu. To keep the ice cream from melting, he would put a large piece of ice under the large plastic box and take it through the customs and on the bus. Qiu thought it was too much trouble for him, and said, "Mr. Lin, I can buy ice creams in Shenzhen. It's so hot in these days and this thing is too heavy. Don't take the trouble!" But he said, "You deserve this for all the trouble you take seeing the patients. This is the best ice cream and I've never seen it on sale in Shenzhen."

For her patients, Qiu realized that curing patients is a doctor's bounden duty. If a doctor serves for her patients maintain a good work attitude with a caring heart, they will return the help with the sincerest respect and love. This is especially true from those seriously ill. Qiu was very proud of her own occupation. What she did was also out of a doctor's sense of responsibility. A doctor works on people's health, which requires him/her to consider people rather than money. It can be said that "teachers are the architects of the human spirit; and doctors are engineers of the human body." As a doctor, if one is not skillful enough or not equipped with medical ethics, one had better quit the position so as not to harm the patients. This should be a fundamental requisite for doctors which should not be discarded at any time or anywhere.

But it might also be a problem if the doctors stick to the ethics while the patients don't. Once had a patient with serious hemorrhoids and fistula, altogether Qiu only charged her about 400 yuan, but when he recovered, he came to ask for "nutrition compensation costs", claiming that he bled after the surgery. A Mr. Hong, manager of a company happened to be there, who was rather delighted for he was cured. He was waiting for Dr. Qiu to finish her work to take her to dinner at his company in Wenjindu – his staffs were preparing a big treat there to show their gratitude to Qiu. When the troublesome patient stated his purpose at the parlor, Qiu was surprised and incensed, but still she calmed herself down and said, "All my patients can go home after the surgery without clinical observation, and I don't have that much space for it too. There was a large piece of decayed flesh taken away from your rear, which necessarily explains a bit of bleeding of the blood capillary. It was quite a normal phenomenon, and nobody calls it a medical accident. I did offer to call a taxi for you, which you refused saying you could walk home. And I believed nothing would evolve into a problem, and I won't have to shoulder any responsibility. If you don't trust me, we can go to a hospital nearby and let the doctors their judge if this is my negligence. If it is, I'll make up for you." The man said, "Alright, let's go right now!" So Qiu took off her white gown and was ready to leave. Mr. Hong glanced at the man and said to her, "The doctors there are about to get off work. Hurry up, I'll wait for you here." Qiu agreed and took the patient to a nearby hospital to consult; but it did not work that easy, there happened to be a proctology department, but the doctor there was not willing to state his opinion after Qiu's explanation of her purpose, so she had to return with no result.

Hong asked as soon as she entered the parlor, "What do they say?" Qiu replied, "They won't say anything. 'People of the same trade can never agree.' But he did not deny my opinion, which means he takes my stand." The patient did not dare to get harsh due to Hong's presence, so he only said shamelessly, "I have to get some money today; my mother has come, and I have to treat her." Hong looked at him, smiled in contempt as if saying, "That's it."

Qiu Weiying knew he was an ungrateful scoundrel, and she still opened her drawer and gave him a 100-paper money, "Take this to your mother and that's all. You think you can bully me because I don't have a man in the house? I could have sued you!" That man was too wrong to argue and knew he could get nothing more. So, he lowered his head and took the money away. Hong said indignantly, "How shameless! This kind of people only works on vicious ideas to get money. Their conscience is in waste!" Qiu said, "True. Why don't they spare the energy and put it somewhere decent? Some even commit crimes for money and never consider the consequences." It was already time to leave, so Qiu got changed and took Wu Sha along to Wenjindu and had dinner in Hong's company. There she and Wu Sha was warmly welcomed and entertain hospitably by the staff and soon left the unpleasant incident behind.

But that was not the only annoyance. One Sunday afternoon, a man with wretched appearance came when she was busy. She took for him a general examination and said, "You have anus dermatosis, and it looks something. I've done two operations in the morning and haven't had lunch yet. I'm hungry now and want some rest for food and tea. Please come again tomorrow." The man was displeased, "I'll have some food also and then come back." Qiu said, "No way, I can't work all week without even an afternoon's break. There was a Hong Kong patient here in the morning waited for me to have tea. But I did not go for patients came. When I finish eating, I must take some rest and do some shopping in the noon. It won't be of any good for you if I undertake the surgery in low spirits." At last, the man agreed to come the next afternoon.

By the time appointed, Qiu had handled to all her other patients and charged the man with all the fees needed. Then she spruced her clinic up, unfolded a clean white cloth on the operating table and had the patient lie down. However, when she put on her disposable gloves and was ready for anaesthetize, she found ulceration on his skin and the edges of which were thickened. She observed more closely and realized it was syphilis rather than anus dermatosis that he had. She used to learn from traditional medical books that syphilis is a highly infectiousness venereal disease, mostly caused by unhealthy sex or passed by through contacts. It had almost disappeared after liberation, and Qiu had neither heard of it from her parents nor saw it herself. But based on the theories she knew, she was rather sensitive about it, or even considered it as a taboo!

She told him at once, "You have syphilis!" He was shocked, but immediately said in a stern voice, "Watch what you say!" Qiu said, "I won't give random judgments. I found something special with your symptoms yesterday, but I was too tired and hungry to look closer, and only knew you had skin problems. I did not expect such situation, and I'm sorry! Please get off the operating table now." Finishing her words, she covered two large absorbent cottons on his wounds, and fixed them with medical proof fabric. The man asked, "Are you sure it is syphilis?" Qiu replied, "You can go to a public hospital to confirm that. My equipment here is limited, and so I can't treat such a special. If they tell you, it's not syphilis, I will give you a free therapy." So, the man had nothing to do but to get off the table. While he was tidying his clothes, Qiu threw the disposable equipment in the dust bin, as well as the new blade and the surgical clamp which contacted his skin. Then she left the clinic, changed into her slippers and went to the parlor, which served as waiting room. She opened her drawer, took out all the money he gave. But before she said a word, the man suddenly said, "I'm not going to a public hospital. You help me with my illness." Qiu said, "Sorry, I don't have strong sterilizer here. Your problem is highly infectious, so I can't help you. I usually throw away all the disposable equipment after a surgery, but the surgical knife holder, the scissors and the clamp are reused after cleansing and sterilization, I am worried about other patients being infected." He started getting impatient, "I can double or even triple the money." Qiu said, "It's not about the money. What if others get infected?" The man was miffed, "they say you only charge once and cater all the way until your patient recovers. The magazine Hong Kong Market says you can cure any proctologic disease except cancer. Today you take my money, and you have to cure me." Qiu explained patiently, "Am I not returning you the money? I return the whole fee as well, if you give me back the receipt. What you have is not proctologic disease but venereal disease, and you have to go to a specialized hospital." That man said ferociously, "If you don't help me today, just wait until my acquaintance in the health bureau comes for your trouble." Qiu was rather strong inside, and dirty threatening was what she hated most. She got incensed too, and replied, "I'm not afraid of your bluff. I support myself with my own professional ethics, and I have done nothing wrong! You have acquaintance, so what?" The man tried to intimidate her, "I'll crash your clinic today if you don't help me." Qiu replied unscarred, "I have my doctor and business license. I'm not a liar any way. If you do anything to my clinic, I'll call the police; I have patient in the police office too." Then she was unwilling to talk with him anymore, so she took up the newspaper at hand and started reading. The man glared at her and left with the money.

That night Qiu said to Wu Sha when watching TV, "Hey, if anything happens, single women are always the weak side!" Wu Shan said, "Weiying aunt, I think you may consider Sun Jie. Even though he's about 13 years younger than you, he's a fun person. At least he'll protect you from being bullied. Anyway, he's a young and handsome man!" Qiu replied, "The problem is young and handsome. He'll be no more than 40 when I get 50. If he is to be a successful man, dozens of young girls in their twenties would go for him, and there's no way he doesn't change. I don't feel secure with him!" Even though Qiu and Sun were not in a relationship, he still had some negative influence on her.

One day Qiu Weiying met a neighbor in the corridor, who came from Fujian. She asked casually, "Mr. Wu, haven't seen you for ages! You've mentioned introducing an able general manager of a five-star hotel, who came from abroad. But I haven't seen him yet. You can really tell a good joke!" Mr. Wu explained, "No way! I'm very respectful to you, and I was serious about introducing that manager. How could I make jokes about that? But that was when I believed Sun Jie was your cousin. Once I met him in the corridor, and said to him, 'I'm trying to match your older female cousin up with a foreign man'. He was displeased and said, 'Doctor Qiu is not my older cousin, she's, my girlfriend! Don't even think about it!' So, I did not dare to talk about it anymore." Qiu ridiculed, "I'm his girlfriend? He's thirteen years younger than me! What a joke! Do you think we can make a pair?" Wu answered seriously, "There's no law about men having to be elder than their girlfriends. He's a tall man, and you have a baby face. You'll make a lovely couple when standing together. Are you afraid of being dumped when you get old? Who knows! A lot of men are being dumped by women nowadays." After these words, the elevator came. Wu manage smiled and walked into the open door and waved goodbye to Qiu. Qiu was not known whether to laugh or cry, and never mentioned this to him anymore.

The day an acquaintance from Changsha came with a man, who was from the north and then became a businessman in Hong Kong. He was tall and rather masculine. The woman from Changsha told Qiu, "He's a bachelor, about your age, well educated. If you know any suitable woman, please introduce to him." Later the man came by his own several times. The first time he brought Qiu a silk dress with small flowers against white background, which he bought in Hong Kong. Qiu said, "I can't take your present for no reason! Please take it back for your relative or friend." The man said, "I bought it in your size, and I don't have any acquaintance of this size." Qiu looked, it was her size indeed. So, she thanked him and put the dress in her wardrobe. Out of professional ethics, Qiu never considered dating her patients, but this man was different. They were introduced to each other as friends, and he left a fine impression on her. Now that she was sure he had out of good will for her, she started feeling special too.

The next time he came she was in the clinic and not aware of his entering. She rolled up the white portiere only to find him and Sun Jie were both there. She put on her slippers, not knowing how to greet the two and feeling uneasy. Sun was a smart man and realized it was not a patient, so he showed the man the whites of his eye and then fixed his sight on Qiu. Qiu sat down in the parlor and was silent at his attitude. The man was sensitive and soon felt uncomfortable. He observed Qiu and Sun and left not utter a word.

After that, Sun said angrily, "Fuck him! Don't even think about it!" Then he smiled bitterly, "Qiu Weiying, you're a beauty snake! I don't know how many people fell under your pomegranate skirt and got into your skirt. "Qiu Weiying dumbfounding to call him, "You and I deal in building friendships than anyone long. You couldn't get into my skirt, so how can anyone get in? Not to mention, you're still behind spying on me, you think I do not know. "After hearing her say this, Sunnier couldn't help but lean forward laughed loudly and said, "Qiu Wei Ying, you learn the wrong line of business, you should engage in public security work!"

There was also a time when Qiu said to Sun, "People might have mistaken you for you're so young, thinking that you came for my fame and wealth." Sun immediately rebutted, "Your wealth? You work so hard day and night, and don't even have a rest on Sundays.

How many does it left after you pay for the rent? There are bunch of young local girls from rich families. How rich are you when compared with them? They don't have to work at all and are well-off on the rents. Those young girls like me, but I don't like them! Those young girls moan and groan, are too troublesome for me!" He finished speaking assertively his speech and left furiously. After that, he seldom came.

At that time Qiu did not fully understand him, for she thought men all likes younger women, and that she was unwilling to be with a man that young. In China, it is eye-catching if a woman is much older than her partner, but it's quite normal for a rich man to be with a much younger woman. She clearly recalled one day not long after she knew Sun Jie, when her business license had not come, she was choosing a tape from her closet in the parlor, while Sun was sitting on a chair between the closet and the office table. Suddenly, he stood up, came over to Qiu, held her face and kissed her lips. It was unexpected, so Qiu neither responded nor escaped. But her heart was beating a bit faster. So, the only once intimate contact with Sun hampered her from denying anything beyond friendship between them. But one day Sun said when no one else was around, "I cannot reconcile to the fact that we're only friends and that's all." After all, Qiu was a healthy woman with normal desires, but that she hated to be indulged in sensual pleasures. She was already pushed to the bedside and were it not for they heard Wu Sha opening the gate with her keys, something might have happened between the two. But it would truly be a worldly mistake if people think Sun were together for Qiu's money and that they did not stop as friends. There are no certain rules to many things in this world.

In the latter half of 1988, Sun suggested to Qiu twice, "How about going to Japan for further education together? After that we'll go to America, which is my destination." It was a surprise to Qiu that Sun would want to go abroad and interpose the idea to her, given that he had already had a very good job in China Bank. She replied without any consideration, "To Japan? What to learn there? I heard

Chinese students in Japan must take hard labors to pay for tuition. I'm almost 40 and going to a foreign country where the language is totally new is too much for me. I can go there to travel when I have the time and money. Isn't it good enough for me to be a doctor in Shenzhen? I have no interest in being a second-class citizen in another country!" But Sun Jie had set his mind, and seeing that Qiu would not go with him, he set out for Japan alone after the spring festival in 1989. Qiu thought him capricious and never took it seriously.

Before the spring festival in 1989, Wu Sha and Damao were going back to Changsha, weren't coming back after the festival. But if so, there would be no receptionist when Qiu's in the clinic operating. What's more, doing surgeries alone might bring many inconveniences. So, after the lunar New Year, she hired Xiao Fang, a country girl from Hunan who was about twenty to help with laundry, cooking, cleaning and reception. Xiao Fang had had some education but dropped out in junior high for economic problems. It had been months since she came to Shenzhen, but she was still jobless then and lived with her aunt. At first Qiu asked her, "Is it ok with your parents if you live with me?" Xiao Fang replied, "They are very happy to know that my employer lives alone and is so nice!" Qiu learned that there were already two girls in Xiao Fang's family. In order to have a boy, her mother was pregnant for the third time. For fear that the village authority should force her to give up the baby, her mother hid in her relative's. As a result of violating the one child policy, the local officials demolished the roof of her family house in accordance. However, the third baby was a boy, her parents now Although a little bitter, gave birth to a brother but also willingly.

Qiu said, "What if it wasn't a boy? Are your parents going to keep on trying? That will be even more tragic! Why is it so important to have a boy?" Xiao Fang replied, "Because men are the major labor forces in the countryside. My parents are too stubborn to change, and I can do nothing about it." Qiu said, "You have some thoughts, judging from your talk; if they had cultivated you, you may have entered a university. Gender won't make any difference then. One college graduate can win over ten illiterates! But if one does not work hard, that'll only be a waste of parents' energy and even tragedy to the family, no matter the sex." As a result, Xiao Fang, the "useless" girl, became her family's only economic support since she got the job at Qiu's. She used to say to Qiu, "My father used to work part-time in the city, but now he's back and we don't have any other income. All my wages here were sent home to cover the daily expenses and my little sister's tuition." That's because Xiaodong didn't have any spending when living with Qiu, not even on clothes, for Qiu had given her old winter clothes and undersized garments to Xiao fang; many of her patients, especially Hong Kong patients knew Xiao fang had a poor family, so they all brought their half-new clothes to let her mail to her hometown.

Qiu treated her better than that. Xiao Fang said once, "Dr Qiu, I wouldn't have agreed to be a nanny if the employer were not you. Some patients even think I'm you relative, for you are so nice with me. I feel really happy with you!" Every time Qiu's patients ask her to dinner, she would always bring Xiao Fang along. She would never leave the girl at home and did treat her like her own niece. It amused Qiu when she first brought Xiao Fang out, they went to a five-star hotel to have dinner with Mrs. Ma and her family, who were from Hong Kong. When they arrived, Xiao Fang curiously examined the surroundings and admired, "Wow—It's gorgeous! Gorgeous! …" Qiu laughed and said, "Xiao Fang, don't be such look around. Others might think you're a silly countryside girl!" Later Xiao fang told Qiu, "My aunt says, 'You're happy to have gone to five-star hotels so many times in a year with Doctor Qiu! My family have been in Shenzhen for a decade, and we've never been to those fancy places.' My girlfriend came to Shenzhen with me and she's also a nanny. The child carelessly fell when she was baby-sitting, and her employer was so angry that he almost beat her. She was scared to tears. She is so jealous of me…"

Qiu thought to herself, "Alas, the country people are too poor to send their kids to school. When the children grow up, they can't find any jobs in the city other than nanny. My mother was born in a poor peasant family too, and she was not higher educated either. Even in pregnancy, she had supported herself hard learned medicine and work and she became have made a respected doctor. It's such a pity that the Gang of Four should trample the legislation system and made Mother a sacrifice to the war between socialism and capitalism; and when my brother-in-law was defined as anti-revolutionist, sister and he three children became a tremendous burden on her shoulder, so heavy that she never stood up again. Moreover, father's betrayal to their love was so devastating that she left the unfathomable earth in mental and physical anguish. If all of which had not happened, Mother should have lived a happy life for the expertise she has…" Qiu Weiying continues to recall:

In the afternoon of October 16, 1979, when mom was confirmed dead by the neighbors, one of her eyes was half open. Maybe the closed eye meant she had too much of sufferings and she was no more attachment this world. But while the half opened one was because she still worried about the mentally abnormal Xiaodong, little Wu Sha and the two teenage boys, for Xiaodong's husband had been in prison for almost ten years and was not given justice. But mom could not help any more. Much as she was worried, she had to forsake the earthly affairs. The memories were a sharp ache on Qiu's heart. She suddenly recalled that mom died in poverty and sickness, and she had never burned her any joss money after she came to Shenzhen. According to the tradition, mom might be poor in heaven. The thought kept her awake during nap hour. So, she told Xiao Fang, "Tell the patients to wait if they come."

She went to the old street under burning sun and bought some big joss papers home. She sat down by her table and wrote on them, "To my mother, Shao Guizhen". Then she opened the iron gate and went to the garden, where she burned the papers with a lighter, threw them on the mud and watched them burned into ashes. It was strange that she dreamed of Mother that night. Mother was dressed like an ethnic minority woman with warm new clothes on. Her cheeks were rosy, and she looked strong. She was not wearing shoes in cold weather, but there were golden bracelets and necklace on her hands and feet, which made her seem young and healthy. She was smiling and looking at Qiu tenderly. Qiu was standing by the iron gate; she wanted to walk to Mother, but her feet were glued to the ground. Then she woke up to find it was only a dream. It was somehow incredible to Qiu, why did she have such a dream after she burned the joss papers? Even though she was not superstitious, she was relieved that Mom got the money. The only regret in the dream was that mom stood on the cold mud with no shoes. Did it mean that lack of a warm family left her nowhere to stand? Right, the birds fly in the sky, only in search of a branch to settle down their nests. Human need nests too. Qiu was almost forty. She was afraid than if she was not to marry soon, she would have to end up being a stepmother, which was not the thing she desired.

The next day Qiu Weiying only redress her old patient's wound and had no new surgeries. In the afternoon when she was comparatively free, she took out a letter and read it through. It was a match-making letter, talking about a forty-something lawyer at an Office Building in Shenzhen, who had not married yet. He was more than 170 centimeters tall, college graduate and very talented… His name and office address were included in the letter, and the place happened to be very nearby. So Qiu took some time off to visit. She took an elevator up and found the room. She asked a female employee by the door, "Excuse me, who is Zhou Siwei?" The woman pointed to the other room over the glass wall, and then lowered her head to indulge in her own business again. At that time, the lawyer happened to stand up and shake goodbye with a male customer. Qiu took a good observation and thought he looked not bad. Instead of staying, she immediately walked out of the door with a satisfaction of accomplishing a task.

After she got back, she immediately found a pen and wrote him a letter, saying, "Someone wrote me a letter and recommended you to me." But she did not mention that she had already gone to see him. She continued, "I'm living in a rented house now, which is small but expensive. I'm using it as both residence and clinic. I wonder if you're living in a rented house too." It was a one leaf letter. She put it into the mailbox under his mansion the same night, and only one day after she got a reply. The lawyer was rather frank and told her by nice hand-writing, "My poor salary is just about enough to cover my rent and food, so I don' have the money to buy my own house." According to the standard then, the monthly salary of a factory worker was a few hundreds, while common white collars got one or two thousand. Even though Wang was a lawyer, his salary was not comparable to one month's rent of Qiu's. She finished reading the letter and thought, "If we are to get married, we will definitely have a child. Then, we can't live at my clinic, while the apartment he rents will be too small for the family. If so, there would be boundless troubles for their marriage. So, Qiu hesitated.

She did not know at that time that they could get loans from the bank – they only needed to pay the down payment and repay the rest to the bank by stages. She was also too realistic at that time, forgetting about father's theory of "wise women choose men with potential". She let go of a marriage which could have been a perfect one. It was just like what mother once said, "Juecong never thought too much about marriage and could marry anyone; while you think too much and can hardly find an ideal partner." A dozen of years later, someone told Qiu that the talented lawyer "can now afford more than an apartment. He can buy a couple of houses and cars if he wants!"

But Qiu Weiying was not merely being realistic; she was born with her unique principles and ethical base line. One day Mr. Zhang, a manager who had immigrated to Canada from Hong Kong and often came to Shenzhen for business, came to her clinic in high spirits. The house he bought for his parents-in-law was right t in Youyi Mansion where Qiu lived. He had come several times for injections, so they were acquaintances. He was about eight years older than Qiu and was a charming man. Juecong had seen him in Qiu Weiying's before he went abroad, and said to his sister, "Judging from his appearance, he must be a rich man." Once he came when there was no other patient. Xiao Fang was out doing groceries, and Qiu was sitting by her table, reading the newspaper. He entered, closed the iron carving door and sat by the other side of the table. He put two property ownership certificates on the table and said delightedly, "I've bought two houses in the newly built mansion downtown. Here are my certificates. I don't like dating girls that are too young, they don't have common topics with me. If you will be my girlfriend, I can give you one of the houses. The other will be put on rent and the money is all yours. It's too tiring being a doctor. You even must stay in on Sundays. Just quit your job. All you need to do is accompany me while I'm here on vacation." With these words, he smiled gently at Qiu, which made her too embarrassed to say a word. She did not want to offend him, but she could not take the offer. After a pause, she blushed and said, "Is your wife ok with this?" He said in an assured voice, "She won't intervene as long as I don't divorce her." Qiu was doubtful for that and made no reply. She thought to herself, "Want me to be your secret lover? why should I be a sneaky person? I can make money on my own, there's no need. I shall rely on one's own effort!" After some silence, Zhang said no more, and quietly took the property title certificate away, which Qiu did not even look at. She recalled twenty years ago when she was first Taste to love. She was so ready to go to Beijing but gave it up in the end for hearing Junjun having a girlfriend. Twenty years later, there's still she cannot destroy a family. Zhang had already had a wife and children too. Her life will never build their own happiness in other people's pain!

A few days later Qiu came across Mrs. Zhang near the building. Mrs. Zhang was coming back from shopping with bags in hands. Qiu came up and greeted her, "So you're in town again. Did you come alone? You really look a sweet couple, judging from the intimacy when you walk together." Mrs. Zhang replied, "Sweet? Maybe. Don't think I'm crazy about him. If he cheated on me, I would divorce him without any hesitation." Her frank attitude surprised Qiu. So, if a man should go to other women, there must have been something wrong within the marriage already. Or else, where did her words come from? It at least proved that the trust between the couple had faded. Qiu had always asked herself to follow the crucial ethics of women – the most important of which was to be self-respectful and never set foot in someone else's marriage. If she did not, she would end up being tangled by affairs, just as Sun Jie had said before.

One afternoon in the summer of 1989, Juecong came to Shenzhen before going abroad, and he visits sister by the way. They chatted over dinner, and Juecong told her, "The properties confiscated cannot be returned. But after implementing the redress false wrong grievance case policy, the house and ownership is back, and now house is me in generating use. It has changed beyond recognition. The garden, kitchen, storehouse, toilet and terrace are all torn down." Weiying said, "Hey! The house was forcibly occupying private house by force after the start of the Cultural Revolution, it's not these people's own houses, will they cherish it? They probably felt uneasy living in someone else's home! But we're finally given return of the house. It's a shame that Mom did not live long enough to see this, especially to see Xiaodong's husband back."

After dinner, Juecong and Xiao Fang watched TV in the living room while Weiying took a shower in the bath. She had just turned on the hot water tape when the phone rang. Then she heard Juecong calling, "Sister, it's your boyfriend from Japan!" Weiying said, "I'm already in the shower, can't answer it!" As she was about to finish, the phone rang again. After the bath, she walked out in her slippers, and was told by Juecong, "It was your boyfriend again. He sounded to have something important to tell you." Before long the phone rang the third time. Qiu picked it up – it was Sun Jie! He sounded unhappy over the phone, "Qiu Weiying, I've had enough being alone here! The Japanese eat raw food, which drives me crazy. The seafood is so fishy when uncooked, making me want to vomit! Forget about your permanent residence in Shenzhen. You can make good money here with your profession. When we finish our study here, we can go to America. I've already asked my Japanese friend to attend to the procedures needed for you to come. Someone will come to you in a few days' time. Get prepared." Qiu said, "I'm not going! My business is getting better. I have a nanny here for the housework and I'm going to hire a nurse. Isn't it better for women of my age to stay in my own country and be a doctor? Why shall I go abroad? I've already told you, I'm not going!" Sun Jie almost roared, "What's so attractive about Shenzhen? If you don't come, I'll kill you when I'm back!" Qiu was incensed to hear that. She hung up at once and said to herself, "Now I won't go even if I wanted to! I can't even think about living with someone with such a personality!" She recalled his words before he went to Japan, "It's better than being alone even if quarrel all day long." "I'm better off alone," she thought, "being angry too often leads to shorter life span."

Juecong told Weiying, "I've quarreled with my wife. Now I'm going to East Germany and other countries for a change of mood." Weiying said, "I can't go abroad for the moment. I'm already a Shenzhen resident, and must consider buying my own house, for the rent takes me more than 4000 Hong Kong dollars per month. Juele can take my house in Changsha, for I won't charge you anyway." Juecong said, "Juele lives at the hospital apartment. Father and I live at Laozhaobi. I gave dad 5000 yuan before I left Changsha. He said father had pensions and perks from occasional patients. He does not need my money for the moment and told me to put them in his bank account."

The next day Weiying gave Juecong 8000 yuan to buy a Japanese TV he transport from Changsha to Shenzhen. At that time, Juecong had an electric appliance shop as his avocation. After paying the money, Weiying glanced at the appliances in herself apartment, her old TV, fridge and washing machine were all made in Japan. No wonder Sun Jie said she could make more money in Japan! So many valuable electrical products in the house are all made in Japan, how can Japan not be rich?

But later, China began its own manufacturing including electric appliances, not only satisfying domestic demands, but also started to export and enjoy the preferential tariffs of the third world. China on a way to rich countries...

In November 1989, not long after Juecong traveled abroad, Weiying learnt from TV that the Berlin Wall was pulled down. A deluge of East Germans flooded to the West. It happened to be the time when Juecong arrived at East Germany. At that time, the West was much richer than the East, so Qiu Weiying anticipated that Juecong would go to the west Germany too...

By then, Qiu Weiying doesn't want to go abroad, although a patient who served as the deputy director of the Public Security Bureau used to say, "People like you can support yourselves even in another country." She knew it by heart that she could go anywhere with her knowledge and expertise. But she thought unfamiliarity with new circumstances and language could be of great trouble. Zhang had told her, "Shenzhen is a rich city even if compared with the developed countries in Europe and America. But the stores in those countries close at night and on Sundays, which is very inconvenient. Sometimes I have to drive very far just to get some ingredients." Qiu felt that China was going through tremendous changes, especially after the down of the Gang of Four. There was no need for her to go abroad. She was confident that Shenzhen was very likely to evolve into the world's most suitable place for her if it kept on developing. She even wished to set up a proctology cancer patient hospital and one day which carries specialized research. Then she shall work hard to be somebody to comfort her mother in heaven.

It was early summer in 1989 when the streets in Shenzhen, one of the southwest cities, were still radiating heat. There weren't many trees by the roadside, not to mention big ones. After a nap, Qiu saw no patients coming when the sun was already tossing its slant glow on the garden wall. So, she said to Xiao Fang, "I'm going to the international mall for some shopping and will be back soon. If anyone comes, tell him to wait for a while." As she walked out of the alley where her Friendship Mansion was, she saw the stock exchange to the right of the street crowded with people. Not an aperture was left in the house that kind of assembled the pawnshop before liberation. She went over curiously, and saw some clerks being busy behind the bars on the counter. The house was filled with babel of noises, and people were struggling forward rampantly to buy or sell the bonds. It was a newly open stock exchange. She recalled in summer there was a board by the road advertising "Yuan Ye", the original stock, which said, "A seed in spring and a harvest in fall". But at that time the stock exchange was unfrequented. She wondered why it became so popular suddenly!

It seemed to be a good thing. She was seized by a whim and immediately went home for her ID and depository receipt without shopping. She drew out all her time deposit of 100 thousand yuan and locked them up in her bedroom closet. At that time, two patients came for dressing changing. After she attended to them, she slipped to the stock exchange, wanting to find an appropriate time to go back, get her time money and buy a stock. When she was standing by the door and staring at the crowd, a short haired mid-aged woman stopped by. The woman was holding a wedge of bonds with face value of 10 yuan, sealed by Baoan Associates Investment Company. She asked Qiu, "Do you want to buy a share?" Qiu replied, "Yes, but it's too crowded inside for me to get in. I'll see." The lady said, "You'll, see? Even the men are having problems of getting inside. Do you really want to buy?" Qiu said, "Sure! I've already drawn 100 thousand from bank and put them at home." The woman said, "If you really do, I'll sell my bonds to you. They are about 100 thousand's worth."

Qiu asked, "These are worth 100 thousand?" She replied excitedly at once, "Yes! Now they're about 100 yuan each!" Qiu was doubtful, "Then why don't you keep them yourself?" She replied, "I've already made tens of thousands. Now I need cash. It's time for me to leave off." Qiu started hesitating. The women encouraged her, "The price will definitely go up! These bonds I have are original. I wouldn't have sold them if I were not in an urgent need for money! See? So many people are trying to get inside, but they can't!" Qiu asked, "Is there any procedure needed?" She said, "It's easy if you have cash. You give them the cash, and I give them the bonds. You'll only need to pay a few commission charges." Qiu thought it reasonable and said, "Ok, I'll have them all. I'll go get the cash now. You can go with me; I live just inside the alley." The woman immediately followed her to the way.

But as they entered the alley, they came across Ms. Pan, who was a neighbor of Qiu's. Pan greeted her, "Doctor Qiu, where are you heading?" Qiu replied, "Home, to get the money and buy her bonds." Pan immediately discouraged her, "Don't! I have many Hong Kong friends who work on stocks. They had a meeting in Xindu Hotel, saying, 'The stock market is going up to fast! Generally, it should go up by only 10%, but now it's already over 60%. It must be brought down!' Don't buy in at such a moment; you'll only lose your money. Don't buy!" Qiu took her certainty for granted and reversed her original planned and said goodbye to the woman.

But to her surprise, "Yuan Ye" had grown more than ten folds by the end of the year. Almost all original stocks in Shenzhen grew hundreds of times over a decade. <See App, 1. H>

The Dutch, being business-sensitive in nature, set up the pioneering Amsterdam Stock Exchanges in 1602. But ever since that, no stock market has ever grown as fast as that in Shenzhen! Luck brushed past Qiu for she believed in Pan's make irresponsible remarks, so lead to the lady luck just miss an opportunity with Qiu. She was born in the year of ox, and her happiness could only derive from pragmatism and a down-to-earth attitude just like the cow, one step and one footprint of walk.

6.4 The test of life

Life is like a voyage, sometimes it is sunny and tranquil, while sometimes it is stormy and perilous. A person should keep progressive and head straight to the destination, or else the ship would not advance, but instead waver and even sink. This is especially true of women, for they are not only born physically weaker than men, but also need to bear children; even the ethical principles for them are stricter. But women have their advantages too, that is, they are more sensitive. So, if a woman wants to stand on her own feet, she must give her hard work and intelligence to full play rather than expecting assistance from men. In the material world, women change, but not as much as men, some males would even forsake his family for immediate physical pleasures.

In the early half of 1990, Qiu had a Beijing patient who had of eminent position a time background. She was younger than Qiu more, her husband was supposed to be young too and this guy has strong backing. It was a man with charisma, and he was treats Qiu become instant friends.

One day after supper, the man came to Qiu's house and said, "Have a walk with me since you are free now, and then we go to the hotel and visit my wife." Xiao Fang had gone to her aunts after work and Qiu had nothing better to do alone, so she followed him out and locked her door. He dragged Qiu in as they went by Youyi Supermarket, which was near the International Mall, and said, "Take whatever you like! I'll pay for them all." Qiu thought they were visiting his wife anyway, so she took some articles for the lady. The hotel was not far from the supermarket and where Qiu's This female patient lived. Qiu walked into this female patient's room with her man.

Qiu did not stay long in their room and left the bag of things there. The couple looked to doctor Qiu with confused eyesight. But Qiu knows that the eyesight of the husband and his wife have different meanings. Qiu explained to the lady at once, "Your husband bought them for you." But before long, this female patient doesn't know, her lovely husband tried to betray his wife…

One-night Qiu and Xiao Fang watched TV together. Later Xiao Fang took a shower, took off her shoes and went for her folded bed sleep in the clinic. When Qiu exited the bath and was about to go to sleep, the phone suddenly started ringing, which made her curious, "Who's calling at such a late hour?" None of her patients had ever had any problem with their surgeries, so no one needed to call her at that late a time. She picked up the phone handset, and it was the man. He said, "This time I come alone. I'm thinking about going to your place tonight. What do you think?" Qiu knew what he was denoting, and circumvented his question with, "What a beautiful wife you have!" But he replied directly, "Figure not as good as you are! Hey, I'll bring 100 thousand cash to you tonight!" His frankness surprised Qiu, for 100 thousand for one night was an astronomical figure then in China. Even a president suite did not cost that much! At that time, you could buy a small suite in Shenzhen. Qiu knew he was being serious, and could only say, "I sleep with my nanny. She's from the countryside and has nowhere else to go." In fact, Qiu is slept alone. The man said nothing more and hung up the phone.

The incident reminded Qiu that most women are way more serious about marriage and family then some men. She saw more clearly that men would even betray their wives at any unexpected time. So, a woman should not depend her happiness on a rich and powerful husband, for this kind of men are more attractive to the easy women going for money. It is better for a woman to be independent, at least not to gravitate around a man. If he is right one, be with him forever; if he happens to be the wrong man, you can always leave him and start your own life. For Qiu, even though the man was young, rich and in power, he was not only married but also the husband to her patient. Qiu had a set of strict rules about social and professional ethics, so she wouldn't be seduced that easily.

Not long after that, Qiu saw a sales ad of Shenzhen Construction Bank and Haifu Garden. She went to East Shennan road and saw the location of the future Haifu Garden, which she was very satisfied with it was close to downtown and the Customs, by the main street but still quiet, and had good transportation and shopping convenient. It is making it convenient for patients from Shenzhen and Hong Kong to come and at the same time perfect for her to live. She consulted the information center and she only need to pay the first installment of more than 90,000, and then pay nearly 4,000 installments every month. A set of nearly two hundred and fifty thousand three bedrooms and one living room, a total of sixty issues in five years, herself can pay off the bank loan and interest. The house covered more than 87 square meters, while her rented house was only three quarters of the size. She estimated that the money she spent on rents was about 100 thousand, but that was gone forever, while the house costing 100 thousand to buy a be her property for a lifetime. The installments almost equaled her rent. So, she immediately signed the contract to buy the house on loans, and exchanged numbers with Madame Huang Biyun, the lady in charge of housing loans in Shenzhen Construction Bank.

She did some calculation after and found out that the installments along with the rents before the end of 1991 and Xiao Fang's wages amounted to more than 10 thousand yuan per month expenses, which meant that her income had to be more than that, leaving alone the cost on food and medical equipment. After she drew all her deposit out for the down payment, she has no more economic backup, while she could not rely on her family to support her. This left her with no choice but to find herself a new way. According to the information she learnt about Shenzhen's renting market, the common suite with two or three bedrooms can cost one or two thousand per month, which meant that the house she rented was two or three times more according to the size. The most unbearable thing was that the house she rented was right above the power distribution room of the entire mansion. When night came and every other noise quiet down, the droning of machines stood out so annoyingly. If she had not been a tight sleeper, she would have got insomnia living in such a house. The machines worked 24 hours a day, but the noises were not that prominent in days, so Qiu did not notice that before she rent the house. But such a house did not charge her any less than others. So, Qiu decided to rent a larger and cheaper suite as accommodation as well as workplace.

She thought she'd better spend a hundred or two for an ad on the Shenzhen SAR newspaper rather than a month's rent on the intermediary, less money, the wider range for choice. So, she set her mind and advertised on Shenzhen Special Zone. The same day the newspaper ad was published a man called to ask her to see his house. He told her on the phone, "It's a new house; no one has ever lived here before. It's on the second floor, one living room and three bedrooms, about 100 square meters. 2,500-yuan Monthly rent."

When Weiying Qiu went to see the house, she saw a selling candy and small food stores in front of the street on the ground floor of this house. On the ground floor of this independent building, a store house seemed to be shut behind, it's with an iron gate that could slide up and down. Right to the small shop was a large wall with a small door, inside of which was the stairs. There was another small door to the left, leading to the house on rent. Walk up to the second floor and there was a large living room after the entrance; to the left was the bathroom and right a bedroom. Opposite the front door was another door to a larger room. There was a hollowed space to the left of the living room, right to which was another bedroom, opposite the kitchen. Qiu's previous house was only 2/3 the size, but the rent was more than 1300 yuan higher with an additional 300

HKD property fee. So, she immediately decided to move in and paid the owner two month's rent and subscription. After she paid off her previous landlord, she moved to the new place.

Therefore, she would basically have no problem with her repaying. She took the largest room in front of the front door as the clinic, where she placed a soft spring mattresses bed under the window air conditioner for the patients to rest on after operation. The new house was larger and more pragmatic, but pitifully few new patients came in the first two months, for it was far away from the main street in a cornered alley, making it hard to locate without the instruction of her previous patients. But as time went by and the recommendation of the ones she had treated, her business took off again.

A patient told her, "I've had this complicated arch syrinx for years, but I was too busy, not have time to see a doctor. After my acquaintances recommended you to me, I went to Youyi Mansion for you, but you had already moved. The new tenant told me he had no idea where you had gone. I was quite anxious until I read an article about you on Shenzhen Demeanor with your picture and new address included that's how I find you." Qiu gave her a knowing smile. Shenzhen Demeanor was a special magazine in celebration of the 10th anniversary of Shenzhen Special Economic Zone, which recorded the jubilance of people in Shenzhen and the tremendous changes in the region after Deng Xiaoping's proposal. A few months later, Qiu's business prospered again, guaranteeing her repayment, rent and daily life.

She firmly believed that bright future would come to her on this perfect-located modernized land. She thought she would live on peacefully and happily in Shenzhen if she gave her effort and skills to full play. However, Weiying Qiu does not live in the Land of Peach Blossom. In this big world, the objective development of many things is often not shifted by people's subjective wishes. She has to continue to bear the continuous pressure of life, all kinds of big and small and from all directions …….

One hot damp day in September 1990, Qiu was watching TV in her living room after supper. Xiao Fang entered the bathroom after cleaning up the kitchen, but she soon stampeded out with untied pants. Qiu asked curiously, "What's wrong, Xiao Fang?" Xiao Fang answered in panic, "S… snake in the toilet!" Qiu said, "It's not even the ground floor. How can there be a snake? Are you sure of what you see?" Xiao Fang said, "Yes! I even stepped my feet on it-quite soft thing looked down, oh my god! It was a snake! It really freaked me out! Do you want to go and have a look?" Qiu said, "I don't if you're sure. Go and ask the elder brother in the shop downstairs if he has the courage to come and catch the snake. I'll pay him for that." Soon the boy came up with Xiao Fang with a long old iron tube in hand. He directly went and opened the half-opened bathroom door after his arrival, looked around and said, "No snake spotted!" It was dark at night, so Qiu turned on the light by the door and looked herself. There was no snake. Xiao Fang said, "It was by the toilet; probably it has gone down the sewer." The boy said, "If you see it again, just call me at once. I don't need the money; I only wish to cook it for a nice meal." The Cantonese have always had a taste for eat snakes.

Not long after that, Qiu Weiying 's father took a retired nurse from Hunan People's Hospital to Shenzhen. It was a plump lady with a smiling face. Wang had a husband and children; she was only accompanied the older Dr. Qiu to Shenzhen Qiu Weiying 's home for a leisure. So Weiying let her stay with them in her house and provided her with food. Mr. Qiu was afraid of heat. For not patient needed the spring bed in the clinic for the moment, Weiying let him sleep on that bed. He would turn on the air-conditioner all night, which Weiying never had an opinion.

One hot day after lunch there was no patient, so Mr. Qiu slept on the wooden sofa in the living room. The nurse Wang was taking her nap in the lower bunk of Xiao Fang's double-deck bed, while Xiao Fang was washing the dishes in the kitchen. Weiying tidied her clinic up, changed into her slippers and was about to exit the room, when she suddenly found a two-foot snake under the wooden sofa where Father slept on. It was sprawling outwards, half of its body showing up. Weiying was frightened and couldn't help shouting, "Dad, there's a snake under the sofa!" Mr. Qiu woke from the terrified scream and so did the nurse. Wang immediately got up, stood by her door and opened her sleepy eyes as wide as possible to look over. The snake hid under the sofa again in Weiying's shout. Mr. Qiu was not panicked at all; he grabbed a long wooden fork which was used to hang the laundry and moved the sofa aside. But to their puzzlement, the snake was missing! There were four drawers down the sofa, but none of them thought of opening them. The nurse thumbed up at Mr. Qiu, "What a man! You're not afraid at all." Weiying thought to herself, "But there are times when he breaks down." For Xiao Fang attended to all the chores, the nurse Wang had much free time to help Qiu with making tampons, cutting cotton and gauzes, while Qiu treated her generously.

Once Mr. Qiu finished his breakfast in the parlor and clinic, and a patient came before Xiao Fang cleaned the table. He saw a thick mixture of sugar, milk and egg in the bowl, and said to Weiying, "You're so nice with your father!" He eats a high price import "Dutch mother and child milk" which was several times the price of its China-made counterparts, and Weiying herself never had a sip of the milk. She was so tolerant that she never said a word of complaint about her father, who wanted to live to 100 years old and often asked her to reimburse his expensive tonics, even if Qiu Weiying tightened her budget and left her no money to buy those decent clothes. Despite she had opinions about Father's betrayal to Mom, but she was his flesh and blood. She also had pity for the unfairness in father's life, the authority of his hospital ignored his contribution to the establishment of Changsha Traditional Medicine Institute and put the boot in by the confiscation of family property, slashed his salaries when he fell off the bike and was about to retire. Until the end, it also plotted to fall on his father's problem with Liang Hua, to beat the nature of the matter into a crime.

Had him not been a tough man, he would have felt tired and pathetic! So Weiying thought it reasonable to satisfy his wish in his late years to make him happier. But before long, Mr. Qiu, not willing to give in to old age, thought he could make money by being a doctor again, wanted to go back to Changsha. So Weiying bought two first class train tickets for him and the nurse to return.

The idea of finding a partner for his father had occurred to Weiying after her mother's death, for the saying going, "Couples in young age, companion in the old". She once visited the home of a woman named Bai who used to live close to her family's private house in Laozhaobi. and whom she had known her she was go to in elementary school.

The Qius all called her Aunt Bai. Aunt Bai and her painter husband had no kids and had a special preference to little Weiying. So Qiu often went to visit them. There she watched Bai's husband paint or listened to Bai's Peking Opera accompanied by her husband's two-stringed Chinese fiddle. But to their surprise, Bai's husband was seduced by a woman downstairs, who probably coveted his painting revenues and even got pregnant with his baby. The honest-looking man left Aunt Bai and ended their marriage. Qiu was sincerely sorry for Bai.

After Mother's death, even though Qiu Weiying had some opinions with her father, she still pitied him, for even though he had made enormous contribution to the Institute, his leader, who actually got her post for father's resignation, not only did not have gratitude for him but even took mom's case of injustice as a chance to undermine his life. It was not easy for Father to make through the tragedies. So Qiu had went to Aunt Bai's home, who was only a few years younger than her father, many times in attempt to match her up with her father. However, when she came to Bai's door, the latter said cheerfully even before Qiu started, "I have a boyfriend now. He's an engineer at Changsha General Mining Machinery, whose wife had died of disease and son is in Canada. He has retired and now lives alone. It's very likely that I would marry him and move in." Qiu was happy for her, "You deserve such a well-educated man for you're so elegant. Or else I would suggest you get on with my father." Of course, she felt pitiful inside, for she knew her father would agree to be with such a nice acquaintance, especially one had no interest in power and wealth. Ms. Bai was especially loyal to love (Qiu could tell how deeply she was hurt when she mentioned her husband's betrayal), and her brothers and sisters all liked her. If she were to be a member of the Qiu's, they would have made a perfect family. However, things do not always turn out as expected, and her blueprint faded. She went to Ms. Bai's new home later and had to admit that she and the engineer were very happy together.

Before long, Qiu Zhongyuan came to Shenzhen again. This time he took with him a divorced woman who was about 20 years younger than him. That is a woman with a low level of education, she only cares about herself enjoyment and dressing. Weiying and the nanny had to follow and attended to her all day long, while she always put on a dissatisfied look. She never took care of Mr. Qiu, but only engrossed in food and fun. It seemed to Weiying that the unprogressive woman had not the least interest in mastering a profession, instead only considered taking advantage of a man whom she did not love. Weiying did not like her at all! She said to her father, "You're already in your seventies. Why be with such a woman? It'll be better for you to stay with your children; we can pay the nanny for her to take good care of you." Mr. Qiu said, "A full room of children is no better than a half-way wife." Weiying said, "That depends on what kind of wife it is!" But Mr. Qiu argued, "All I need is myself home. You're all concentrated on your own business, who would take the time off and be with me?" On the face of it, Mr. Qiu was in good state, or else how could a 70-year-old man with Angio cardiopathy cater to a woman who was more than 20 years younger than him so carefully?

After some days Mr. Qiu said to Weiying, "I'm going back to Changsha. give me 20 thousand yuan." Weiying contemplated for a second and realized it was the woman that was instigating behind his back, so she said, "You live with Juecong in Changsha, and he pays for all your food and stuff. Your pension is more than enough for yourself, plus the 5000-yuan Juecong gave you before he left. All I have now is 10 thousand yuan, which I must keep in bank in of emergency. If I fall ill, all my incomes would be cut up and I even had to pay for a doctor. Now I have to pragmatism and a down-to-earth attitude just like the copay my loans, rent, pharmaceutical products of patient and cost of living, which is a large sum of money. You can stay with me life before Jucong comes back, and I will all life security for you till the end. If you insist on going back to Changsha, you can live in our previous house. You can ask Juele to call me in anything happens, and you can come any time when you want. What's the 20 thousand yuan for?" So sooner than she finished, Father widened his tiger-like eyes and shouted, "I know you have the money, that's why I ask. I gave your life and raised you up, so you are obliged to give me the money." Weiying was angry too, "It's true you gave me life and raised me up. I can give however much money you want. But what does that woman contribute to me? I've been nice enough to allow her to eat and live here. Moms had gone through decades of hardship with you and bear so many children. All her life was percolated with sufferings and in the end, she did not enjoy such a happy life. What will you do with the 20 thousand yuan? Give it to the liar? I won't!" The woman heard their talk and grabbed her handbag to leave at once. A patient happened to come now, so Weiying said, "Go inside the clinic." She rolled up the door curtain to let the patient in and took off her slippers by the door while looking back at her father and said, "I'll buy two tickets for you to go back and give you 1000 yuan." Then she followed the patient in the clinic to change his dressings.

As she sanitized his wounds and was about to spray medicine on, her father dashed inside to snatch the golden necklace on her neck. She held his wrist and did not know what to do next. Xiaochen, the young and strong patient, immediately realize what was going on, and jumped off the bed to hold Mr. Qiu tight by his fingers, got the necklace back and gave it to Qiu. The necklace was snapped, and Mr. Qiu exited in fury walked out. Xiaochen lay back to the bed and said indignantly, "It that really your father? How could he be so mean?" Her sorrow being too deep for tears, she said, "He probably suffers from stress disorder from the confiscation of family property. And now he's old and seduced by a vicious woman." After she followed the patient out the clinic, she saw father sitting on the wooden sofa with his eyes widened by fury, looking over them two. The patient felt improper to make any comment, and so he left without a word.

Weiying recalled Mother's word, "No one could stop him once he gets angry…" Her life was derived from his and was raised up by him. How far could she go in the defiance? Xiao Fang was cooking in the kitchen, and there was no one else except her and her father. She looked at his indignant face and was intimidated, so she entered her own room opposite the kitchen, without a word. She closes the door to her room and started reading an English medicine book. A few minutes later, she heard father shouting outside, "I have to get the 20 thousand yuan today! Don't you dare keep them from me!" Weiying said inside her room, "That's all the money I've got. What about my loans and daily expenditure? What if my business comes to fluctuations?" He shouted back at the top of his voice, "I don't give a damn. I'll crash your door if you don't give me the money." Weiying fumed with anger, "It's not my house! The landlord would ask me to compensate for it!" But Mr. Qiu yelled, "That's none of my business!" Weiying did not want to say any more, for Father has turned such a senseless guy. But after a few minutes' quietness, he started to knock on the door with something hard. She wondered how father changed so much, was it because he was too old and enticed by the woman, or was it because his personality had twisted by merciless fate? She was drowned in sorrow and pity-both for father and herself. Even tears were too light for her sorrow. It was then that she realized the correctness of Dean Huang in Liuhua Hospital, "Your father does not care about you at all!"

But mom was so different from him, during in the Great Cultural Revolution, after brother-in-law was labeled as an anti-cultural revolution current counter-revolution, mother eat breakfast steamed mantou (Chinese bread, usually with no filling) and porridge in the hospital, and even two cents of pickles was loath to spend one's money to buy. Even if the entire Chinese people of the earth are tough times ahead, the children who are growing and developing are not being treated badly. Because is no one had like mother, for the sake take good care of the children of Xiaodong's family, usual to treat herself so live frugally a hard life. The thought of it inflict pain on her heart. She looked out of the window at the floating clouds, controlling her emotions so as not to cry out loud…

The noise kept on going and the door soon cracked into a hole. Weiying was incensed, and her sorrow upgraded into anger. She had been pitying father for he used to be a frank person who might have offended his leaders, but father would never hurt other people, and whose efforts and sweats were paid back by enmity. But now, the pity had faded away! She thought of the Japanese actress, Yamaguchi Momoe, who had reached the limit of one's patience enough of her own father and cut off relations with him. Now she was also at the verge of breaking down. She opened the door, only to see that her father was hitting the door with an iron hammer! The ruthless act took away her last restraint in him. She said furiously, "Father, and this is the last time I call you so. I can give you 10 thousand yuan today, only if you sign on a paper to break off relations with me. After this, we go our separate ways!" Mr. Qiu said ferociously, "Come on! You think I would not do so?" He immediately found a piece of paper from the drawer, sat on the sofa, put the paper on the desk and started writing. Seeing what he did, Weiying honored her commitment and took her ID card to the bank to draw her money. The bank was about to close, so she quickened her steps, went directly to the counter, turned in her bankbook and took all her money out. As soon as she entered her house, she gave the wedge of money to Mr. Qiu, who gave her the ruthless piece of paper in exchange. She tucked the paper in the corner of the closet, and then went to bed. She soon fell asleep.

By the time she woke up, the sun has already set. She stayed in bed and recalled father used to write in his diary, "gamble is in like a down mountain fierce tiger; Sex is yes scraping bone steel knife." He never wagered nor took drugs, but lust alone not only hacked away the love between him and his wife, but also chopped the blood bond between him and his own daughter! Xiao Fang came to her bed, looked at her face and said, "Oh, you've woke up! Your father and the woman took their luggage away. I've had the dinner ready and was waiting for you. Oh, my goodness! It scared me to tears when he took a hammer to strike your door! You're so nice with him. How could he do this to you?" Qiu gave her a bitter smile. She was in total solitude; her mother had gone; She has severed her father-daughter relationship with her father; Her sisters and brothers all have their own families. She was like a lonely boat floating at the sea, having no idea where the storm of life would blow her where…

During the National holiday in 1990, Sun Jie's sister and her boyfriend came from Changsha, and brought some cured meat to visit Qiu. Qiu was happy to see the young couple-both of them were smart, healthy and well educated. She had not contacted them before, and had no idea how they found her, but she felt improper to ask. The young lovers were soon graduating from the affiliated university of Hunan Medical Institute with bachelor's degree in English-taught Medicine, which meant they had to be expert in both medicine and English. They would have a much brighter future than Qiu did! But once when they were having dinner together, Sun Jie's sister said in both praise and sympathy, "Hey, it's hard being a single woman, and even harder being a famous single woman!"

Qiu Weiying was not sure if she had heard something about her, and she did not want to ask. Qiu had always liked to be with educated people, for their speech was profounder and fun to hear. But it was a pity that she had to stay home and could not accompany the two while they were in Shenzhen, for ever since she started her private clinic, she almost had lost the joy of resting all day on Sundays. Even if there was no new patient or surgery, she would have to cater to dressing change, which had no set schedule, and new patients usually came on Sundays, especially those from Hong Kong. They came on non-workdays, because these patients are often treated in private clinics no reimbursement for medical expenses and Qiu found it difficult to turn them down.

One day Qiu went to the store downstairs for groceries. She found the iron gate which used to be shut was open, and to her astonishment, there on the cement ground were piles of round loose woven baskets, inside of which were countless snakes of various kind spiraling and sprawling. She was frightened to a loud scream, "Oh my god! No wonder there were snakes in the new house-they climbed all the way up!" The younger brother of the man who used to go up and help them catch the snake was standing behind the counter. He smiled mystifying at her and said, "I've even seen a snake outside on your bedroom wall. But I did not tell you that in order not to scare you." Qiu was even more afraid. She complained, "That's horrible! I often open my windows on hot days. If the snake had come to my bed, I would have fright died!" The boy said, "No way. These are edible snakes, not poisonous." Qiu said, "You're just saying it. Even if they are not poisonous, I might get scared to death if they come to me at midnight. I have to call my landlord and see if he can deal with it." She made the call as soon as she arrived home, and said, "The house behind the iron gate turns out to be full of snakes. Can you rent it to someone else? The snakes have already entered my house, and very likely to others' home too." Her landlord said, "The houses are all separated; no one has reported seeing snakes." Qiu said,

"But I've seen snakes in my house! The boy downstairs has seen one outside my window. If you don't tell the tenant to move, I'll go." But the landlord only said, "I can tell them to keep the snakes inside. You can move if you insist. The rent downstairs is higher than yours, and someone has made inquiry about your house recently." Qiu said, "So I can move at any time? Alright, I'll go as soon as I find a new place. But remember to return my deposit." The landlord agreed.

Doctor Qiu thought of a newly-build large residence by the corner of the street, Hubei Market. Few had moved in, with plenty of vacancy left. She learnt that the building was the property of Hubei Village, so she went to the village committee to ask them to rent her a suite as private clinic and residence. The officials there receipted her warmly and promised that she could choose any suite in the mansion that she liked. It was a building located at the center of the city, covering an area of thousands of square meters. It was four- story building, with the ground floor being shops of vegetables and fruits, the second of dried and sea food and the upper two for living. Between the first and second floor was a large escalator for the convenience of the shopping customers. Qiu gave no consideration for the fourth floor, for it will be too much for her patients to walk over the stairs after surgery, and so she picked a large suite on the third floor, which was in the middle to the roadside, with one parlor and three smaller rooms. She went down to the village committee behind the mansion, and signed a year's contract at once, for she was planning to move into Haifu Garden a year later. She went home and told Xiao Fang, "I've rented a three-room suite in Dongmen Garden. It is in Hubei Village, to the street over there. They will give me the keys by the end of the month, and then we'll move at once." Xiao Fang was glad, "Great! So, we won't have to worry about snakes coming inside anymore." After, Qiu told the news to her landlord too.

In between of spring and summer, Qiu moved into Dongmen Mansion in Hubei Village by the main street, along with Xiao Fang.

For it was a newly built comprehensive mansion, the furnishing was not completed, and the stores downstairs did not officially open. Consequently, her business was dismal at the beginning. Even though she had glued a piece of red paper with her name and a clinic sign on the glass window to the roadside, nobody would look up and pay any notice; most of the people coming by focused only on food shopping. Few had any idea that a clinic was running in the empty mansion. Xiao Fang was quite worried, and said, "Aunt Qiu, why is nobody coming? You won't even be able to cover the rent, not to mention my wage. Maybe I'll have to ask you to find another job for me." Qiu comforted her, "The rent is one thing, your wage is another. I won't skimp a cent of your money." At the end of the month when Qiu went to pay her rent, she said to the village official, "What shall I do? I made even less than the rent!" Someone joked with goodwill, "Dr. Qiu, you can just marry a rich man in our village. Why take the trouble to be a doctor? That's too much work for a woman!" Qiu smiled and said nothing. She knew many locals were more than rich. Their fate had been transformed by Deng Xiaoping's reform and opening policy, the backward villages in the past turned into a land of fortune overnight, and money flushed into their hands from renting land and houses. Many of them invested the money in stock market, which returned them with hundreds of times more. There were plenty of millionaires in Shenzhen, bunch of multimillionaires and not few billionaires. There was no need to mention how they loved and enthused about Deng-his idea of special economic zone endowed them with happiness that their ancestors had never even dreamed about! But Qiu had never wished to tie her fate to a rich man. She had always thought it most rewarding for a woman to earn her own happiness by her own hands. If a woman only dreams about marrying a wealthy husband to eat, sleep and dress up all day, she will make no contribution to mankind and only be a burden on her family and society. What sense does it make? Qiu hoped to devote all her energy to the course of "serving the people", even though she was not a party member and she hope to emit herself light and heat.

After some while the business started to recover, during which time she knew a pair of brothers from the north. Both were tall and had very frank personality. The elder brother, Zhou Yun, was Qiu's patient, and a quite serious one. He possessed both the toughness of the northerners and the politeness of the southerners. He was 28, two years older than his brother, who accompanied him to Qiu every time. They were quite courteous to Qiu, which made her like them a lot. Once she asked the younger one, "Why is it you to come with him every time? Where is your sister-in-law?" He replied, "She's a great researcher, too busy to come. My brother is in the computer business and can't stay home all day with her." Qiu commended, "Oh, so she's a well – educated lady!" Zhou Yun's home was in the north, but his office expanded to Hong Kong. He usually lived in a hotel when he came to Shenzhen for doctor.

One day after supper, Qiu and Xiao Fang went to his room to visit him, because Qiu operated on him. Xiao Fang was glad to go along and listen to them talk. Qiu knocked on the door and entered with Xiao Fang. Zhou Yun was alone in bed, watching TV. He asked, "Have you had dinner yet? If not, I can make a call and have food sent in here." Qiu replied, "Yes, right before we came." She stood at the window and asked, "Where's your brother?" Zhou replied, "He has his own business and can't stay here all the time. He's back to inland." Qiu said, "We'll come here and visit you after dinner if I'm free. We have nothing else to do except watching TV anyway, and we live quite near." Zhou said, "Alright. I'm here watching TV every night and have nowhere else to go." While Qiu and Zhou were talking, Xiao Fang widened her eyes and ears, which amused Qiu. On their way home, she said to Xiao Fang, "Don't be such a silly girl to stare at us when I'm talking with my patients." Xiao Fang laughed out loud and said, "Did I? I have no idea!" A few days later, Xiao Fang said to her, "Ms. Qiu, my aunt has found jobs for both me and my sister. I must go to work tomorrow. What should you do without me?" Xiao Fang's sister used to live with them for a short period before they moved. She also came from the countryside in

Hunan, looking for a job in Shenzhen, about which Qiu had some clues before. She said, "You should have told me earlier! But off you go! My sister in Changsha has retired in advance and has nothing to do at home. I can make a telegraph and send for her. You're so young, and nanny is not a life-time job. You should go ahead for your future and master a skill to find your own ground in this world." Xiao Fang said, "I'll be working in Baoan Zhenhua Shoe Factory. I'll come back and visit you during breaks." Qiu said, "You can come at any time." Happy to hear that, Xiao Fang smiled. That day after supper, Xiao Fang needed to go shop for some daily necessities, so Qiu went to visit Zhou Yun alone.

She arrived at the hotel and knocked at his door with her fingers. Zhou opened the door in pajamas and led Qiu inside. He opened the cupboards under the TV set, took out two cans of drinks and put them by Qiu. Then he turned right, walked to the corner of the room where his bed was. He slipped inside his quilt, leaned to the bed and watched TV, while Qiu sat on a single couch to the right near the TV. She turned to Zhou in the left and said, "Xiao Fang's leaving tomorrow. She's packing her luggage now." Zhou asked, "Who will cook for you while your work?" Qiu said, "I've called my sister in Changsha; she's coming soon." Zhou asked, "Doesn't she have a job?" Qiu replied, "She used to be a driver in her factory. But it broke down and she retired in advance." About two minutes later, she turned her face again and asked Zhou, "How do you feel after the surgery?" Zhou replied, "Good. Only a bit hurt." Qiu said, "The wound is healing, which explains the pain. You can take some pills." Zhou said, "No, that's alright for me. Didn't I just get off the bed and open the door for you?" The French movie Zorro was on show. Zhou murmured, "Alain Delon is handsome indeed." And he kept on watching. It was a hot day, but the air conditioner was set at a low temperature. Qiu felt chilly, for she was wearing a cool silk dress. So, she went to the other bed and took the white pillow back to the couch, held in her arms and went on watching TV. However, the pillow did not help much, and it was still cold on her back. If she had been visiting a female patient, she would have gone to the other bed and tuck herself in the quilt. But there was only she and Zhou, a man, in the room, and that would be too discourteous. She can only attach her back to the backrest of the sofa and hug the pillow tightly to get warmer.

After some while, she looked at her golden watch, it was not yet nine, an early time in Shenzhen where life did not really start until night. So, she decided to finish watching the movie before leaving. She maintained her position until more than nine o'clock when the door suddenly opened and a group of policemen in uniforms flushed inside. Three or four of them stood at the passageway, looking at her in astonishment, she was sitting still with a big pillow in her arms and watching TV. Another man who looked in charge turned his face to Zhou, who was absorbed in the program as if no one else was around. Smart as Zhou was, of course he knew what was happening, and he chose to ignore the scene and go on watching TV. The situation maintained for a couple of minutes, when one of the policemen went to Qiu and said, "Please show me your identification or border pass (People coming to Shenzhen needed a border pass, for it was a special zone)." Qiu happened to have her ID card with her, so she took it out calmly and gave it to him. Zhou added, "She's, my doctor." One of them asked, "Then why don't you live at the hospital?" Zhou said, "There's no vacancy left!" Those people could not find any fault with them and had to leave in a few minutes' time. Soon the program finished, and Qiu said goodbye to Zhou and left. While passing the service center on that floor, she glared at the waitress, thinking, "There are bunch of shameless young men and women in your hotel, but why did you want to do it to us? You've picked the wrong person if you think in such a despicable way!"

Of course, the world is peppered with people of various kinds, and Qiu did come across a male patient with nasty mind. One day after work, this man asked her to come to his hotel. Upon arrival, the man and some other guys in his company immediately sent for two taxis to take her to diner at a five-star hotel. The man was in sea food business in Guangdong; Qiu could tell he was rich. In dinner, Qiu sat between him and his assistant, who whispered by her ear, "It's the best thing in this world to be a beautiful woman! Men would come to flatter you." Qiu smiled and made no reply. The man, not old or ugly, looked at her and said smilingly, "Doctor Qiu, what makes you so happy? I love to see your smile." Qiu was silent, thinking, "Oh, the guys…!" She finished the two-hour dinner with the men before they got back to the hotel. Out of courtesy, Qiu decided to stay in his room for ten minutes before leaving. As they got back at his room, she sat down in a sofa far away from bed, where the man was. Between the bed and the sofa placed a chair-somebody might have sat there and forgot to move it away. The man leaned over a bit, stared at her and said, "Oh, you do look like my wife! Come closer so I can see clearer…" Qiu thought, "Don't think I'll fall be captured by you! (When she bought something on the outside, the small trades people and peddlers often said too her, "One can tell you're not a local in Guangdong from your look.") This goat is flirting at me!" She gave him a dissimulating smile and said calmly, "It's getting late; I have to go home now." But he tried to keep her, "Why the rush? I have a vacant bed here if it's too late. It's also okay if you want to sleep in my bed!" Qiu only smiled to the amorous man and said, "Goodbye." Then she left the hotel. Either for the basic ethics-for he was a married guy-or for her professional ethics, she would never have slept with him! "It is difficult to achieve anything on one's own." Adultery is an act that involves two sides. People shouldn't have blamed everything on women and look down upon them-that is a complete prejudice! Qiu was single and never married, a doctor that had male patients from all walks of life and admired by many of them. If she had not stuck to her principles, she would have ruined herself by affairs. But she never let that happen. However, she has never let rich, powerful and seductive male patients trip her up, or else she would have destroyed her reputation and future. It's safe to say that she was past countless times tested of life and have a clear conscience.

6.5 People have unpredictable vicissitudes in the life

Life is like a kaleidoscope, colorful and changeable. When you hold a kaleidoscope in hand, can you predict what the next pattern will be with 100% certainty? It will be amazing if you can picture 80% of it. Things often evolve beyond people's imagination. The break-out and prevalence of a plague could easy deprive people of their lives; a cruel political persecution could cost people their freedom, dignity and anima. Even countless wars that humans have fought, often because of a small conflict, it has formed the fuse that caused a catastrophic war. It is really, "in nature there are unexpected storms and in life unpredictable vicissitudes".

Not long after Xiao Fang left, Xiaomao arrived at Shenzhen. Looking especially happy, she said, "Sister, you have gotten the house in order, even if it's not large." After some days she said, "It's a pity that so few people come! I heard that you are quite famous in Shenzhen, and I think that you are busy all day long." Weiying replied, "That was when I lived at Youyi Mansion. I did not start well there either, but my business grew over time. Now I move too much for the patients to find me. But I've asked Mr. Yi from Hunan No.6 Construction Company to make a large wooden signboard for me, which will come with a long-haul truck. I'll put it by the side of the street for people to know and locate my clinic." Xiaomao said, "You'll be busy again then." Weiying said, "That's no problem, I can hire a nurse for the dressing changing. I used to have one assistant from time to time when I was at Youyi Mansion."

Soon the signboard and some other things Yi bought for her came along with the truck driver. Qiu was happy and thankful, but they would not take her money. Yi said, "Our truck did not run a special errand for you; we come to Shenzhen on business and happened to be of help." Yi was busy helping the driver to unload their articles, and not even had time to have lunch at Qiu's this place. He took out a letter from Juele from his pocked gave it to Qiu and left with the driver in haste.

Dr. Qiu was shocked after opening the letter, in which Juele said, "Recently I got a telegraph from Zhengzhou, auntie saying Father had died there. I immediately went there and could not contact. Juecong for I don't have his abroad number and can't make you abandon all your patients to come. So, I went alone and helped with his funeral. On the Mid-autumn Festival Father went to bed after he had some dumplings and did not get up early as usual to work out. They felt strange for he slept so late, so aunt sent her son to wake him up – he did not manage to do that, for father had passed away!" Weiying knew that Father had always lived after a traditional rule of "soup after the food"; he liked to have some dumpling soup after eating dumplings. She reckoned that the habit contributed to overburdened digestive system and blocked blood circulation, which added to his original vascular sclerosis cardiomyopathy. Tears could not help falling at the thought.

Xiaomao noticed and widened her eyes worriedly, "Sister, why are you crying over the letter?" Weiying said, "Juele says that Father had died in Aunt's." "Oh! Really?" Xiaomao paused, the eyes then reddened.

Seeing Weiying dazed at the letter, Tears are still flowing, Xiaomao comforted her, "Don't cry! He had never been nice to us girls anyway, and even smashed your door to ask for money. All people's life has to come end." Weiying said, "I can't help! No matter what he did, he had given me life." Xiaomao disagreed, "He never took up his responsibilities! Give birth require being responsible, not responsible don't birth! Even my foster parents were nicer than him." Weiying said, "They wouldn't have been able to raise you up if mom and dad had not paid them money. But, of course, they really loved you!" Even the blood relations can become estranged if separated for a long time. It can be seen poor handling of affection can also become ruthless.

Weiying had heard Mom said once, "Among all the girls, you're the only one that your dad has ever hugged." Father had also argued for himself, "Yes, I do value the boys more than girls. But if I had seven boys instead, I would have cherished the girls more. Li has given birth to three girls and stopped having babies – that will leave no descendants for the family of Qiu! That's why I married your mother. Before liberation, it was legal to have more than one wife, as long as you can afford to keep them alive!" Father's thought was not particular then, for feudal ideas had taken control of the entire country at that time. Holding the letter in hand, Weiying felt both pity and hatred on him. She pitied him for the mental persecution he had been through! Because he had offended his leader of hospital, so the leader of hospital was unstinting in one's efforts wreak vengeance on. He has despite rendered great services to the hospital.

But he shouldn't have transferred his own trauma and annoyed onto his wife and children; He did not only his cater to the family, but he had also hurt them ruthlessly. Which incensed her more was that she heard Father broke up with that woman after taking 10 thousand yuan away to Changsha. The woman must have sowed discord him into getting the money, and then just took the money away and left! Then he went to the suburbs in Zhengzhou alone, with no one there to take care of him. Aunt was not as various conditions sufficed as Weiying, and there was not even a hospital nearby to save him from the myocardial infarction. Was not his life ruined by that evil woman? That was a bad fruit that he planted himself!

But in this world, even if you are a good person and have a good heart, but if you run into someone who is unable to tell right from wrong, you will come to no good result!

One day before lunch, a woman around her fifties came. She had walking hard and flowing out pained expression. The girl accompanying her sat down, while she could only lean on the wooden couch. Qiu could tell her exacerbation of the disease was serious from her face. She gave the woman an old pillow as cushion, and quickly finished her work at hand to go to her and ask about her situation. The woman told Qiu, "I've had a proctologic surgery in a hospital in-patient department. But now it recurs, and it's keeping me from food and sleep. Three of my colleagues were treated by you, and they told me that your patients can go home directly after the surgery, and most of them can go to work as usual; no one has ever had a relapse. So, I come to you for help."

Dr. Qiu knew that most of such this kind circumstances were caused by mis operation of the surgeon, which led to local irritations and dropsy. She assisted the woman on to the operational desk to have an examination. As the woman took off her pants and lay her head on the pillow, Dr. Qiu pincer the blood-soak tampon away and saw clearly that it was postoperative residue on circular mixed hemorrhoids, which was mainly caused by improper ligation spot in the operation stimulate that led to edema. It was this kind circumstances in which rectum fell out of the anus, while filled with thromboses from blocked blood circulation, bringing extraordinary pain to the patient. In usual thrombosis hemorrhoid s mere removal of the thromboses would alleviate the pain greatly, but circular hemorrhoids, theoretically, is potent to anus narrowness if not treated properly, which meant life-long pain in defecation. So Qiu helped her down the operational desk. She did not tell the woman the estimated period of treatment as usual, nor did she charge her the round fee. She had met with such this kind before and knew very well how to deal with it. Most of the patients, if not informed of Qiu by their relations, would go to a public hospital first, where they can put the fees on account. Only when their problem evolved into a serious situation would they come to Qiu on their own charge. Dr. Qiu just took the examination charges, gave her a prescription and said, "You can't have the surgery today. You must take five days of sitz basin with Chinese herbal fumigant to alleviate your inflammation first."

The woman was a bit disappointed, "Why can't I have the operation today? Is it because I'm too ill and you don't want to treat me?" Qiu explained with patience, "Don't worry. I can help you all out if it's not cancer. My method is a combination of traditional and western medicine. I'm only trying to find the best scheme for you." A bit displeased, the woman took the prescription and with the help of the girl, left the examination bed to home.

Five days later, the woman came again with the girl, limping and still in pain. No one else was around, and Qiu was puzzled to see her face, wondering how she did not the pain ease, but rather exacerbated! So, she asked the woman again for routine examination. To her discovery, the inflammation was expanding – even the skin under the sciatic bone turned red! She remembered clearly when she was at You Yi Mansion, she had a young male patient who came to do business from Jiangsu. He also had fell-out rectum and suffered a lot. People recommended Qiu to him, and he canceled his flight to come for help. It was almost the same as exacerbation this woman, and Qiu also prescribed him a five-day sits bath. After that he came with much fade away inflammation much lessen intense pain. She gave him made the surgery next, and he soon recovered. He was grateful after that, and treated Qiu like family, even hoping to make his girlfriend a student of hers.

But the woman patient at hand was so far from normal! The patient got off the inspection set with Qiu's help, staggered out the clinic and leaned on the couch, waiting for Qiu's treatment. Qiu handed her an old pillow, and asked in doubts, "Have you use the sitz bathtub prescription drugs I prescribed you?" Qiu had guessed that she did not follow her instruction. The woman said casually, "That's too much trouble. There's no one in my home to decoct the medicine for me, so I did not." Before Qiu could say anything, she continued, "I have some acquaintances that were treated by you. They all say that you can operate the surgery directly after examination, and after that they went home right away. So, you can do the surgery for me now..." Displeased at the words, Qiu heightened her voice and said, "Why don't you follow my prescription? It's not a game! Who's the doctor here? Who's to listen and do as instruct? Your exacerbation is different from theirs. I can't do the surgery for you considering you be seriously ill. You must first diminish an inflammation I'll give you one more week of sit bathtub. We have the surgery after that." Then she couldn't help muttering, "What a trouble! You have to get the medicine and take the bathtub as soon as possible, or your exacerbation continue of the disease will aggravate, and I won't take responsibility for that." She made another prescription for the woman, and of course, did not charge her examination fee.

A week had past and Qiu did not see the woman again. She felt it strange, but she thought it was because the hospital did not agree for her to come to a private clinic, and so she stayed still in the public hospital for treatment. Qiu only charged her of examination once and never operated on her and was not to take responsibility for her recover. Then she gradually began to forget about the thing.

Sometimes, people think they are sailing safe and sound on a fine boat and are on a smooth voyage. But no, reality does not go as people wish! Despite that Qiu was independent from parents and partner, unpredicted things also happened to her. Life can play tricks on people, forcing them to make a new choice and step on another route. Although Qiu Weiying's spirit of self-reliance spirit is strong, and she can neither rely on her parents nor does she want to rely on her husband. But the fuse did not grow out of soil or fall from heaven; it was preset by people in advance. Once it was lit, blast began...

Within a month since the woman left, Qiu got a notice from Shenzhen health bureau one day, asking the anus rectum branch of all hospitals to send a person in charge or attending physician to attend a proseminar on "medical attitude". Qiu felt it strange to get such a notice, for she had never been to a meeting in health bureau ever since she became a doctor. Why would they invite a doctor from a private clinic? Of course, Qiu was the person in charge and attending physician of her own clinic and had to go to the meeting.

On the day of the conference, Qiu arrived at the boardroom on appointed time. Most others had arrived then, sitting around the square table and leaving the upper seat vacant. Everyone looked to her as she entered, which was bizarre. A tall, mid-aged woman with short hair looked in charge. She was the chief of Chinese medicine office and sat by the corner near the door. She told Qiu to sit on the upper seat, which puzzled Qiu a lot, "Isn't it the seat for the chair? Why am I sitting here?" But it was the first time for Qiu to come to the boardroom of health bureau (she had only come to the bureau once when she was applying for her business license). So, although feeling odd, she felt it improper to ask questions. She sat down, and soon more people came to fill up all the seats.

The Director of Chinese medicine made clear what he had come for from the very started talking, "Now the proseminar begins. Today we'll discuss medical attitude. Doctor Qiu, some patients have reported that your medical attitude is simple and rude. Please reflect on your behavior." Qiu immediately realized that the meeting was designed against her, which puzzled her even more! Her smiling face switched into a serious look, and the atmosphere of the room altered too. A dozen of people were looking at her peacefully, while some others glared at her in jealousy. Qiu was displeased, and thought to herself, "Oh, a proseminar against me! Who have I offended to put this up?" She said confidently, "Why should I reflect on myself? My attitudes are no worse than anyone else's! If I were rude, how could I support my private business in Shenzhen? I have costly rents to pay. People come to me paying their own money, no reimbursement from the unit. Not only have I been nice to my patients, but I also must make sure of the quality of my service, for public hospitals take care of their doctors, while I take responsibility for everything I do! I wonder what reflection I should make." The director said, "You know it by heart, don't you?" Qiu replied firmly, "No, I don't. Please show me." The director was glaring at her all the way, as if she wanted to swallow Qiu. An older male doctor with sparse hair sitting on the left yelled in jealous, "You've dragged the patients in my hospital to your clinic! You've sabotaged our regular work!" Qiu had never met this doctor before, not to mention dealing with him. But she reckoned from the scenario that he was the doctor whose patients often came to her for help after recurs after his treatment. Then, he must be the chief and resident physician of the proctologic department there. He was reported by the local newspaper several times, but not as favored by the media as Qiu. He must not be willing and harbor a deep resentment.

There had not been s of "doctor's bait" at that time. Qiu defended herself bravely, "The patients walk on their own feet, not mine! I must stay in door while working. How could I drag patients from your door? They come to me, and I must help whoever that comes, according to the professional ethics. Yes, many of my patients have gone to other hospitals once or twice, some are not cured even after several treatments. I helped them recover – is that a sin instead of a virtue?" As soon as she finished, he shouted shamelessly, "You are talk big!" Qiu replied, Is I like to boast? If I cannot ensure the quality of my service, will the patients come to me on their own charge? There are the names, workplaces and phone numbers of my patients on the residence permit book. You can pick some of them in Registered Book and ask them about my work." Qiu was basically arguing with the man, when few others interrupted. Qiu's anger grew, while the man entered hysteria… After about an hour, the mid-aged woman had to declare the meeting was over.

Qiu Weiying thought angrily, "What kind of proseminar this is?

It's just an attempt to screw me! I don't know who the hell is behind this, trying to get me to do something? She was so angry that she didn't greet anyone and left the conference room alone with her head held high after the meeting. She had been calm enough to only have stated her reason. If she chose to shout at others and pound the table when wronged, just like her father had done, the problem would not be solved, but on the contrary, upgrade, unless the leader was a sensible one with broad. Also, she had not made as great contribution to Shenzhen's health care as father had done in Changsha!

She felt gloomy even in the next afternoon. Her muddled father had passed away, and then came the conference incident. She felt that troubles were like the tides, swilling and slapping her... A black cloud came over her head, blocking all the light. Does it seem that the wind is going to pick up? She thought it was a plotted meeting, for the leaders in traditional medicine office wanted to take it as a start to crack her! But for they could not find any fault with her, the meeting turned into a chance for her to reveal many of the public doctors' disqualification. She wanted to find out where the hurricane started, and who was trying to involve her enter and then throw her down?

She reminded Sun Jie sister's words, "It's hard being a woman, and even harder being a famous woman!" She suspected the other doctors were jealous of her for she was reported by the media frequently. She is in Shenzhen, already have Shenzhen Special Zone Newspaper, Shenzhen TV Station, Shenzhen Style, Hong Kong market and other magazines reporter interviews and report. On these coals, she has it not less than ten times. Qiu Weiying's father once said, "People of the same trade can never agree." Especially when some are trying to gain benefits and fame." Dr. Qiu Although considers fame and fortune very lightly, put more emphasis on the value of life, but others are not like that!

The thing was not that simple. She had always thought that she could support herself by her own skills, and never flattered any of the leaders. Was it because they thought she earned much and became jealous? Or else she could not think of any reason: Why are several people attacked her at the meeting so viciously? She had never made any medical accident or political mistake. She had no clue about what was happening. However, that was not the end...

A few days later, Qiu went to a store downstairs for groceries, saw a newly published newspaper, Shenzhen Commercial on the counter and brought one home. As she opened the paper, she saw her name suddenly appear before eyes. It is on a short but prominent article on the right corner. She had not this newspaper been interviewed before, not to mention by a newly published paper, she finished reading at once. It was written under the name of her patient, the name of the author she had never heard of. She specified in proctology, where most patients could recover in a few days after the surgery. But she did not recall any patient under the name and could not find it in her residence permit book either! But the author pretended to be her patient, claiming that he went to Qiu for "rumors about her good service", but was cheated in the end… Qiu was indignant after reading, and knew it was a made-up story aiming at ruining her reputation. First, she was not a liar but a legitimate doctor with local permanent residence and doctor's license; secondly, most of her patients came to her because of their friends' recommendation or having read articles about her on newspapers. No one would come on their own charge merely because of hearsays; thirdly, she only charged her patients once after the examination and saw them through all the way until they recover (She also had a rule that she could treat for free in of recurs, but that had never happened to no one.). There was no way that she would charge any one repeatedly. So how anyone could be "cheated"? After reading the article, she wanted to call the author and argue with him. But she recalled in the spring of 1965, the group of bandits search my family's house and confiscate my property parents. Mother's words, "Sometimes people meant to hurt your reputation and refuse to reason." She thought, "Those people want to bring me down; he knew I did nothing wrong and of course won't argue with me. It must have been under the arrangement of that chief of the Chinese medicine office. Let it be as long as most people know I'm an upright person!" So, she did not make the call to argue heatedly with the rumor-maker.

Even though she was really annoyed, she decided to let it go. However, that was not the end of the incident, for somebody behind the scenes wanted to see the end of her. But one day when Xiaomao was out shopping and she had just finished changing the dressing of a patient and ready to enter the parlor, a group of five rushed in the door, one of which held up a video camera to her face. She immediately realized what was happening, for she had been shot by Shenzhen TV before, that was a program in praise of her. Having read the article in Shenzhen Commercial, she knew that the visitor was not kind-hearted, this endless variety of approaches to me, is not trying to beat me to death with a stick for me?

Incensed, she pointed to the camera and said, "I have many patients who believe me sincerely. I'm not afraid of your conspiracies!" As her anger grew, she couldn't help yelling, "I quit, so that you won't be jealous and so mean anymore to me!" She rushed to the white trolley in the parlor where bottles of medicines were placed. She swept on them all, which smashed on the floor one by one. She kept murmuring, "What have I done wrong for helping the patients? Why would you do all these to me?" Bitter tears fell at her grievance. Those people thought the video won't be of help and soon left. Later Xiaomao came back and asked her, "Weiying Sister, what happened? There's a big-character poster by the door with the seal of health bureau. The crowd is reading it…" Qiu stepped out at once and read it with complex feelings. The general idea of the notice was that her clinic was under rectification, and it urged the patients not come for treatment, or they would have to be responsible for the possible consequences. Alright, Qiu was sure that someone wanted to crack her down. All she could do was to see what would happen next.

The next evening when she took her shower finished and was about to go to bed, she got a call from one of her previous woman patients, who said, "Doctor Qiu, I saw the TV of you being angry on TV today. The video lasted only a few seconds. You've always been a nice person; I did not expect that you would be so angry. You must have offended someone in power, who is setting you up. Hey, it's not easy being all alone like you! Just let them do whatever they want, and you shall focus on your business only." Qiu said, "They have already banned my business. They won't reason with me." The woman said, "Really? What a shame! You are the lucky star of us patients!" The high praise made her comforted and proud. However, the more she thought about it, the more unconvinced she was …!

She started her investigation after that. First, she went to the hospital where many of other proctologic doctors worked and talked with Tang Na's sister-in-law. She is also worked there, only not in the anus rectum Branch. After describing the most have make a personal attack on her, Qiu's suspicion was confirmed! Qiu's father said, "It's true that 'People of the same trade cans never agree'. I've done nothing ill against him, but he has taken actions! He almost wanted to swallow me in the meeting. If it had been in the Cultural Revolution, he would beat me up and wearing a high hat to me…"

That Sunday, Qiu went to a state functionary home who worked at the health bureau, hoping to get some information from him. As soon as she stepped in the door, he couldn't help laughing and said, "Oh my eloquence specialist! They wanted to find faults with you on the meeting but were criticized by you instead. They took some hemorrhoids medicine away from your place for examination, trying to find out what's the magic that you have you cure the disease so well. But they found nothing special." Qiu was puzzled, "Oh, how come I did not notice that? Maybe I was too angry to see it! Doctors should rely on the theories and professional skills to cure the patients. The hemorrhoids are a kind of tumor. There's no such medicine in this world that can remove it without the fine skills of doctor. People who took my medicine are bound to be ignorant!" She continued, "Almost all my patients are nice and grateful to me; but I might have offended one of two of them…" She told the official about the male patient who did not even need a taxi after surgery but distorted the fact and asked for compensation, the man with syphilis whom she turned down, and the recent women sike person who did not follow her instruction of taking the sit bath first and was rebuked by her in the end. After listening to her experience, he said, "You seem to have done nothing wrong; it is especially right to turn down the man with syphilis for the sake of the safety of other patients. But you should have reported to the health and Anti-epidemic Station!" Qiu replied, "He is not a local, and only left his name and age on the residence permit book. He left after the quarrel with me. Where shall I find him?" The official said, "You is taken charge of by the traditional medicine office. Except for the director general of health bureau, no one including me have the power to intervene. You'd better go and talk to the chief of office. I heard that they had secretly placed a recorder to keep track of what you said." Qiu Weiying shuddered when she heard him say that! Who was that someone that wanted to devastate her by the weapon of politics? She did not stay anymore, so she left this cadre's house and went home.

That night, Qiu Weiying lay in bed and had a hard time sleeping. In her mind, she thought, "Secretly, they are going to record my speech - isn't it obvious that they want to find fault with what I said of incorrect statement, so that they can set me up politically? She felt the seriousness of this thing! "Life is like playing chess. Sometimes if you don't adopt a down-to-earth approach to success, you will disrupt plan and lose the whole game. She couldn't take it lightly! Because of all the misfortunes that had happened in her family in the past tell her, if not, she was only one move away from being politically opened by them to kill her.

Since the death of Yaobang Hu, the reformist central leader on April 15, 1989, a federation of students from several universities in Beijing, joined by other people from all walks of life, began a petition for a reevaluation of Hu Yaobang -- against corruption and official buy and resell at a profit, and for democracy, freedom of the press, and freedom of expression and started the hold a demonstration.

On April 26th, the People's Daily of the Party Central Committee published an editorial entitled "There must be a clear-cut against turmoil." The editorial provoked strong protests from the students. They were not convinced and worried that the government would "wait until this thing is over to settle accounts" and demanded to revoke the editorial and dialogue with the government. The government did not agree with the students. As a result, the student's petition has evolved into a hunger strike.

On May 14th, Gorbachev visited Beijing. Not many overseas reporters were interviewed in North Beijing in order to interview the Soviet leader Gorbachev, who was the first Chinese visitor after 30 years, so they all rushed to the square to conduct interviews. The students hoped to use Gorbachev's reforms to help promote China's political reform without exiting the square. However, the government still did not agree to the dialogue, but changed the place of welcoming Gorbachev's ritual to an airport. Because of this, the students took up the Tiananmen Square and carried out a more vigorous petition action.

This movement not only touched the enthusiasm of patriotic Chinese at home and abroad, but also attracted the attention of the world. Affected by the university students' motioning Beijing, hundreds of large and small cities in Shanghai, Guangzhou, Xi'an, and other cities and towns have also witnessed rally protests. At the same time, there are also people from all walks of life joining the protests.

On May 19th, general-secretary Zhao Ziyang, the reformist of the CPC Central Committee, went to Tiananmen to visit the hunger-stricken students. He put forward the idea of agreeing to engage in dialogue with the students but did not reach the opportunity in time due to the suppression of conservatives within the party. Therefore, the students have been insisting on a hunger strike in Tiananmen Square, and some even faint because of fasting, regardless of there were lives in great peril.

On May 20th, the then Premier of the State Council Peng Li impose the martial law order (The martial law order was until

Li Peng signed another State Council order on January 11, 1990, officially lifted).

At the beginning, the crowd did not touch the bottom line of "down the Communist Party" and "opposing socialism". The students also organized a picket to maintain order and conscientiously observe discipline.

On May 23, have three people from Hunan to Tiananmen Square to throw eggs at Zedong Mao's portrait. These three were even seize and turn over to the public security organ by students.

Shenzhen is a special economic zone designated by Deng Xiaoping after the reform and opening. It is adjacent to Hong Kong. It is easy to watch TV programs from Hong Kong. It was difficult to watch Hong Kong TV in the Mainland. Every night after enforcing the martial law, many residents of Shenzhen were sitting at home watching TV. The roads and streets that were full of neon lights and the streets were very quiet.

Of course, there were no exceptions. Almost every day after dinner, Weiying sat in the living room with the babysitter to watched Hong Kong TV. She saw it on TV, the students' sit-in and hunger strike at Tiananmen Square. It caused widespread sympathy and support from Hong Kong and overseas democrats. In particular, the blood of Hong Kong residents is boiling, and everyone actively supports Tiananmen student motioning various forms such as contributions donations and charity performances raise money.

The student motion at that time was spontaneously organized by Beijing University students and some citizens, and there was no leader for the organization. In the final stage of the hunger strike, the chief of the hunger strike, Ling Chai, shouted at Tiananmen with a tweeter "Absolute no retreat "At that time, many students felt that soldiers were approaching Tiananmen from other directions, but under her infection, they still adhered to sitting in front of the Tiananmen Heroes Memorial Monument.

On the evening of June 3, when Weiying Qiu was eating supper, she suddenly heard the Beijing martial law force in the radio recorder broadcasting loudly, the citizens were ordered not to go outside on the night they heard the broadcast. At that time, her heart thumped with a sense of foreboding, and she wondered, "Is this night start a fight about the students?".

After the shower, the babysitter Xiao fang has already slept. Qiu Weiying gently turned on the TV with the question mark in her heart and watched the scene of the Beijing students' motion broadcast by Hong Kong TV station with uneasy feelings.

On the screen, under the cover of the night and smoke, there was a spark in the Tiananmen Square and nearby, and the gunshots sounded. There was a young and middle-aged man on the screen, with his men clutching a shirt appeared. He was facing a group of tanks and trying to block their advance.

At the same time, journalists who risked their lives to conduct interviews, intermittently reported, "The martial law forces in Beijing have begun to suppress the students and the citizens who support the students…".

After a burst of guns, the carnage of war scene appeared, people use various ways to carry and transport the injured students to the emergency station and the hospital; the ambulance screamed through the crowds on the road. Along with military vehicles full of soldiers and a burst of gunfire, some people began to shout in the TV screen, "Down the Communist Party." or even "Down with the Fascists" …

According to media reports, the Fuxin men near Tiananmen Square, especially in the area of Muxide, had the largest number of deaths and casualties.

Weiying Qiu was deeply shocked to see this incredible scene! Although she did not see it on the spot, she believed that what was happening on the screen was true. Because the TV screens of Hong Kong are from the reporters from worldwide taken, and it is all provided live coverage of all events.

She knew that these students who were admitted the university in Beijing were highly qualified in the examinations and are generally highly intelligent. They are China's elites and the future of the motherland. Moreover, their parents often had only one child under the single-child policy at the time. She did not know how these parents of only children would face the tragedy that happened that day?

She was filled with tears in eye, and she wished she could fly at once to Beijing and heal the wounded and rescue the dying. But her predicament prevented her from doing this. After careful consideration, she certainly can't walk away. She regretted that she had already had a little reputation in Shenzhen at this time. Because of the many reports from the local media, she even had many patients in Hong Kong and other places, and many of them were seriously sick patients. When the light of the early morning sun dimly shuttles through the black clouds, she went to bed with a depressed grief.

In the following days, several students and citizens protested in various parts of the country, but they ended up being suppressed and arrested. However, the impact of this Tiananmen protest motion that shocked the world did not completely calm down and end....... Deng Xiaoping and his conservatives accused from beginning to end, this protest was a counter-revolutionary riot with premeditated overthrow of the Communist Party. On June 9th, Xiaoping Deng received and praised the martial law forces. The protest motion in Beijing was also basically quiet on the surface.

Initially, the patient told her, "Doctor Qiu, I heard that Ling Chai fled to Shenzhen and was sent to Hong Kong." Qiu Weiying smiled a bit, didn't say a word. However, she was thinking, "Ling Chai is much luckier than those who have died! I can imagine: "White hair people see off black hair people "is the most sorrowful thing in the world! Who knows, how hard and painful life will be for the parents of these only children in the future!?

She later heard that Hong Kong Alliance in Support of Patriotic Democratic Movements and some righteous people of Hong Kong launched the "Siskin Action" <See App, 2 D)> to rescue those people who joined the movement, even after rigorous search after the event. They still risked a great deal, and at least rescued more than one hundred people who joined the democratic motion and sent them from Hong Kong's neighbor Guangdong to Hong Kong or Taiwan or the Western countries.

Undoubtedly, if at that time it was not because of the need to take care of the patients who had undergone surgery, and Weiying Qiu prepare flew from Shenzhen to Beijing Tiananmen Square, get on "heal the wounded and rescue the dying." like that, she would then be taken into custody and be politically accused.

She began to think deeply, In a one-party state, the key to policy and politics is to look at the people who own the power, and how to use the authority in their hands. It can be said that the fate of thousands of ordinary people in almost the entire country is under his control.

After the victory of the War of Resistance against Japan, the "fight against the landlords and the division of land" by the toiling masses, initiated by Mao Zedong and the Communist Party; Then the Kuomintang was defeated and driven out, and a new China under the Communist Party was established; When Hitler was in power, he planned genocide of the Jews; when the Gang of Four was in power, they created a foul atmosphere of utter confusion for the country.

She recalled how her brother-in-law was stated reactionary in the Cultural Revolution. If there is no mother to overcome all the difficulties and raise Xiaodong's three children, would they end not up as vagrants in streets? If the CPC had not brought the Gang of Four down, and there is no support from Hu Yaobang and Zhao Ziyang redress a grievance policy support, would the Qiu's live under the shadow of the confiscation of family property and anti-revolution forever?

More than ten years had gone by after Deng Xiaoping's reform and opening, but there was still someone who resorted to political means to stab her in the back and trying to devastate everything of her! She just could not accept such a destiny and wondered what it was that she did wrong. She was sure that someone was acting behind the scenes and planned everything.

Qiu was informed that the office chief of Chinese Medicine had studied in America for half a year. For few had the experience of studying abroad at that time, she was bestowed the office.

So Qiu went to health department the next day and talked to the chief of the traditional Chinese medicine. She feeling justice was on herself side, "The so-called seminar was totally against me, right? I wonder what I had done wrong to make you do all these to me. I heard that you guys are actually secretly recording phone calls, so you are trying to set me political frame-up, aren't you?

I've always acted with conscious. None of my patients have supported you, right? Am I that fragile, that easy to be brought down?" The chief frowned, and replied frankly, "No, it's not that easy." Qiu said, "Then you should lift the rectification on my clinic." The chief said, "But there are some patients who report your rudeness in work." Qiu replied directly, "No way! People come to me on their own charge, and I never set any high prices. If I were rude, how would they be so grateful after the treatment? How could I support myself in Shenzhen? The only fault of mine is not having cozied up to you. Who is it that thinks I'm rude? Tell her to come and I will argue with her!" The chief said, "She told us on the phone." Qiu said, "How ridiculous you are to treat me so ill only for a call! You're making trouble out of nothing!" Then she went to her bike angrily and left the health bureau. For this matter, it was always a mystery in her mind …!

After the "Gang of Four" was defeated, during the peaceful period of Hu Yaobang and Zhao Ziyang, great changes took place in China! On the surface Individuals could go to the court to accuse a public department, for the latter did not represent the country and the party anymore. Some people in power were not that virtuous; some of them even traded the power in hand with personal benefits. They also needed the regulation of law and supervision of the people, or else they could still take advantage of the power at hand to bully over the people and create corruption, even if the Gang of Four had been brought down.

During that time, Damao came from Zhuhai to Shenzhen. Weiying told her the incident, and said, "I want to sue the health bureau." But Damao discouraged her, "You'll never win a lawsuit against the health bureau! The weak cannot contend with the strong!"

Weiying recalled their confiscation of family property which her parents had told her about several times, they were confiscated in a midnight of spring, 1965. Their properties were "frozen for the moment and should be dealt with after the concludes". But in the end no result was touched upon, and their properties just went away. They were even continue searched over by the rebel factions several times during the Cultural Revolution. So, she gave up her idea.

The incident that took place on Dr. Qiu was because that she did not fawn on those people, for she was too absorbed in improving her expertise and serving her patients, and became too prominent a target of jealousy after she became famous... No one could tell if there were additional reasons that were not expected. In the situation then, Qiu felt that road ahead of her was in darkness. She was not able to go on with her private clinic anymore, not to mention establishing a proctologic cancer study institute! The saying of "in nature there are unexpected storms and in life unpredictable vicissitudes" cannot be any righter!

6.6 Fly far and high

Qiu Weiying was born in Jiangsu, about a month later, and she followed her parents moved to the provincial capital city Changsha of Hunan. The water of Xiangjiang River nourished her. In her golden years from sixteen to twenty-three, she was deprived of her city household register and sent to the countryside to fix the earth. During which she wasted her youth and gained nothing. What's more, she did not find any of modernization build brought by the educated youth to the backward countryside.

Since 1976 when the Gang of Four was brought down, the shadows over China finally lifted. The land of China, which was made a mess by the Gang of Four, finally saw the light through the fog.

But it was a pity that it was until 1979 when her mother died, that the situation started going back on track and policies were gradually implemented. It was only about a month after mother died in mental and physical torture that brother- in-law was given redress a grievance and sent back, leaving it a forever regret of her that her mother never saw her son-in-law's safe return. Qiu thought death was not that dreadful when one enters a certain age, for death was in the fate of everybody.

But if like her mother, it just was the most regrettable and painful thing in this world if one could not enjoy one' serene late years, because A happy old age which could compensate for all the toils of life.

After Mother's death, Qiu Weiying relied on her on efforts and got her doctor's license and earned herself a constantly improving life. She used to think that the bitter days of tears were gone forever, and that she was a luckier woman than her mother... that was why she never thought of going abroad. It was the soil of China which gave her life and supported her that she loved most! However, under the then situation, the words of a patient who was in a crucial post in the local public security bureau said, "People like you can have one's livelihood assured yourselves even in another country." But now her once-unwavering faith began to wobble.

Qiu Weiying's clinic has been suspend business. If this should continue, how could she make ends meet? Not only had she rents to cover, but she also had loans to of housing loan pay. How should she deal with all of these? After she lost heart in going to court, she thought of going to a higher administration – report to Shenzhen municipal government - to accuse the traditional medicine office of Shenzhen health bureau of suspending her clinic out of no legitimate reason and cut up all her economic source, given that she had done nothing wrong. She recalled once, when she was at Youyi Mansion, an official from the municipal government brought an old distant relative of his to her clinic and asked her to find out what kind of disease the old, skinny, grey-haired lady had that almost killed her. Qiu asked the lady to get on the examining table, only to find hard bleeding ulcers her muscle. Qiu put on her rubber gloves and pressed her finger against it – it is a hard lump that can't be pushed – she was almost certain that it is anus cancer, so she asked the lady, "Are you having painful and bleeding, so you are scared to defecate?" She replied, "Yes! How do you know that?" Qiu said, "From what I see." She walked out the clinic door while the lady was still on the examining table. Dr. Qiu changed into her slippers and went to the official and said, "It's anus cancer." The official was shocked. Sitting on his chair, he raised his head to ask, "Are you sure?" Qiu said, "I'm sure." Before leaving, he gave Qiu a card.

A few days later, he called in extol, "It's really amazing of you to have diagnose her with cancer without any medical instrument! She has had an examination in a hospital and confirmed with that disease. How did you know it?" She replied, "It's not that hard. I only followed the medical theories." The memory reminded her that he would very likely trust her and help her. So, she opened her drawer and found his name card. It read "Li Bingxin, director of letters and visits office, Shenzhen municipal government". Oh, so he was in charge of the director dealing with complaints! Confidence filled up her heart.

Qiu came to the municipal government in a morning. There was a garden in front of the gate, to the left of which was the gate chamber and to the right the reception center of letters and visits office. She filled up a guest form at the chamber and went to the reception first. What she saw there was a crowd of people, each with their own complaints but all shared an identical wish that the government could help with the problem that they could not deal with themselves. But according to the rule, everybody had to fill up a form first and then line up in order, waiting for an official to come and talk to them. So Qiu also filled up a form and handed it over to the staff. After that, she went to the gate and gave the guest form to the guard, who kindly showed her the way to Li's office. Looking to the direction, she saw a broad asphalt road leading to a not tall but imposing office building. She thanked the guard and entered the gate. Walking on the road by elaborately pruned bushes and green grassland, she soon arrived at the building and found Li's office on the right side of the second floor.

She knocked on the half-opened door carefully, heard a "Come in, please!" and quietly opened the door and entered. Li was sitting behind her desk, talking to a mid-aged woman. He was happy to see Qiu, "Hi, Doctor Qiu! What wind brought you here?" Qiu answered, "I don't work today. I have a complaint to lodge." So, Li hinted that she could sit in the single sofa. After the mid-aged woman left, Qiu took out the documents she had wrote from her handbag and gave them to Li. After reading the material she wrote, Director Li asked, "How could such thing happen?" Qiu Weiying told the general situation, and Director Li said, "Okay! I'll take time to go to the Health Bureau and deal with this matter for you personally." Hearing this, Qiu Weiying felt that there was a good hope that this matter could be solved. She thanked Li and left his office confidently.

The statue of "serving the people with the down-to-earth attitude of a buffalo" in front of the government building, as well as Li's hospitality left her an impression that he is always ready to help.

While waiting for Li to handle the thing, she got a notification from Zhonghai property management company, saying that the construction of Haifu Garden was completed, and that the proprietary could check and move in. Qiu was happy with it and took her ID card and relevant documents to the Hai Fu Garden with Xiaomao the next day. There were four buildings, each of more than twenty floors, lining up neatly by Shen Nan Dong Road and Beidou Road, close to both the city center and the Customs. There were not many high-rises in Shenzhen then, so it could be called a high-class domicile of the time. Xiaomao checked out the suite on the third floor, which had a parlor, three bedrooms and a kitchen and a terrace. Standing by the large marble washstand in the bathroom with a large piece of mirror fixed, she said, "My sister, it's fantastic to live in such a place alone!" Qiu said, "I've taken the clinic into consideration when I bought the house, so I have noted on the contract that I could hang up a signboard on the roadside. I shall take one of the three rooms as my own, one for the nanny and the nurse, and one for the patients under treatment. The parlor shall serve as a waiting room. I'll see if any rearrangement will be needed when my business grows larger." She looked around the house and decided to place a washing machine on the terrace outside the kitchen, and sun the clothes on the balcony outside her bedroom. To cater to the patients, she chose a low story so that they could both take the lift and the stairs. For safety considerations, she decided to install stainless steel bars and screen on the window. And a curved iron gate should be installed outside the gate. After she went through the handover procedures, she and Xiaomao took the lift the top floor in excitement. Going through a small door, they arrived at the balcony on top. Qiu looked down and had a complete vision of the burgeoning city of modernization, in front of the building was the

The statue of "serving the people with the down-to-earth attitude of a buffalo" in front of the government building, as well as Li's hospitality left her an impression that he is always ready to help.

While waiting for Li to handle the thing, she got a notification from Zhonghai property management company, saying that the construction of Haifu Garden was completed, and that the proprietary could check and move in. Qiu was happy with it and took her ID card and relevant documents to the Hai Fu Garden with Xiaomao the next day. There were four buildings, each of more than twenty floors, lining up neatly by Shen Nan Dong Road and Beidou Road, close to both the city center and the Customs. There were not many high-rises in Shenzhen then, so it could be called a high-class domicile of the time. Xiaomao checked out the suite on the third floor, which had a parlor, three bedrooms and a kitchen and a terrace. Standing by the large marble washstand in the bathroom with a large piece of mirror fixed, she said, "My sister, it's fantastic to live in such a place alone!" Qiu said, "I've taken the clinic into consideration when I bought the house, so I have noted on the contract that I could hang up a signboard on the roadside. I shall take one of the three rooms as my own, one for the nanny and the nurse, and one for the patients under treatment. The parlor shall serve as a waiting room. I'll see if any rearrangement will be needed when my business grows larger." She looked around the house and decided to place a washing machine on the terrace outside the kitchen, and sun the clothes on the balcony outside her bedroom. To cater to the patients, she chose a low story so that they could both take the lift and the stairs. For safety considerations, she decided to install stainless steel bars and screen on the window. And a curved iron gate should be installed outside the gate. After she went through the handover procedures, she and Xiaomao took the lift the top floor in excitement. Going through a small door, they arrived at the balcony on top. Qiu looked down and had a complete vision of the burgeoning city of modernization, in front of the building was the charge of the director dealing with complaints! Confidence filled up her heart.

Qiu came to the municipal government in a morning. There was a garden in front of the gate, to the left of which was the gate chamber and to the right the reception center of letters and visits office. She filled up a guest form at the chamber and went to the reception first. What she saw there was a crowd of people, each with their own complaints but all shared an identical wish that the government could help with the problem that they could not deal with themselves. But according to the rule, everybody had to fill up a form first and then line up in order, waiting for an official to come and talk to them. So Qiu also filled up a form and handed it over to the staff. After that, she went to the gate and gave the guest form to the guard, who kindly showed her the way to Li's office. Looking to the direction, she saw a broad asphalt road leading to a not tall but imposing office building. She thanked the guard and entered the gate. Walking on the road by elaborately pruned bushes and green grassland, she soon arrived at the building and found Li's office on the right side of the second floor.

She knocked on the half-opened door carefully, heard a "Come in, please!" and quietly opened the door and entered. Li was sitting behind her desk, talking to a mid-aged woman. He was happy to see Qiu, "Hi, Doctor Qiu! What wind brought you here?" Qiu answered, "I don't work today. I have a complaint to lodge." So, Li hinted that she could sit in the single sofa. After the mid-aged woman left, Qiu took out the documents she had wrote from her handbag and gave them to Li. After reading the material she wrote, Director Li asked, "How could such thing happen?" Qiu Weiying told the general situation, and Director Li said, "Okay! I'll take time to go to the Health Bureau and deal with this matter for you personally." Hearing this, Qiu Weiying felt that there was a good hope that this matter could be solved. She thanked Li and left his office confidently.

grassland with a pavilion and a garden, decorating the area between the four buildings and the main street. They added much to the beauty of Haifu Garden and at the same time greened and beautified the city. The downtown, customs and International Trade Building were both near, and by the road near the garden were some bus stops. She looked over to Liuhua Hospital and could even see the sceneries of the New Territories of Hong Kong.

She thought if Shenzhen kept on with the pace of development, it would soon catch up with and even exceed Hong Kong! The reform and opening policy of Deng Xiaoping and raised the once backward countryside into a modernized city, making it a window and role model of China's reform. Looking at everything, Qiu could not help praising herself, "The house did not buy the wrong!" <See 1. E>

One day before Qiu moved into the new house, Zhou Yun came to her clinic at Dongmen Mansion for reexamination. For the official notice of suspend business in order to consolidate on her door had been removed, Zhou Yun and his brother were puzzled, "Why is the business so depressed today?" Qiu replied, "I've been suspended by the health bureau." Zhou asked, "What if new patients come to you?" Qiu said, "I've turned them all down and told them to go to the health bureau. I'm not the sneaky kind of person. They told me to stop, so I stop. I've decided to rent the house out for a year." Zhou asked kindly, "Where shall you live then?" Qiu said, "I've bought a suite in Haifu Garden, Shen Nan Dong Road. I'm moving at the end of the month. You can drop by when you have time!" Zhou said, "Sure. I go to Hong Kong frequently on business. If I go by Shenzhen and time permits, I'll go and visit you." So Qiu wrote him her new address.

When the two brothers left after, Xiaomao said, "Sister, I met a lot of people when working as a lorry driver and traveling around the country. Zhou Yun looks like a smart person who can do something great." Qiu Weiying agreed, saying, "Yes. And the two brothers are very respectful to me. I also have some other male friends in Shenzhen, their wives and other family members are all revere me. If a woman has self-respect, she can have pure friendship with men." Xiaomao said, "Hey, it's always nice to be a woman with her own economic source! I shall die happy if I can have a suite like yours in Haifu Garden!" Qiu said, "The planning lies with Man, the outcome with Heaven. I have no idea what my future will turn out to be. But after all, a woman should be independent and work hard. Some people are poor, for they have been neither diligent in school nor in work, wishing that happiness could fall from heaven – how can things be that easy? But you are an excellent driver, that's your professional skill. The larger environment has changed in the reform and opening up; as long as you're diligent enough, you can at least maintain a life. But I've offended the traditional medicine office under the health bureau…"

Xiaomao said, "That's a typical personality member of the Qiu's family. We don't like to be flattering with leaders, so our family suffer." Qiu Weiying went on to say, "Look at Dad, do not buy the dean's account, he also patted tables and chairs. How could she not look for opportunities retaliate against him? Recommend him to be the dean and he is unwilling to serve, saying that he is only engaged in technology. As a result, he gave way to the cleaner as the dean. As soon as she became the dean, she was biting the hand that feeds one and framed him everywhere. Instead, our family was suffered from the hospital our father founded! Wang Huijun's husband was a party member, and she herself came from a worker's family, and if someone would recommend to her is the dean, the authority would agree on the proposal. But now no one values family background that much; it's all about your performance and education."

A few days later, Juecong sent a letter to Weiying, saying, "I heard that you've been suspended from business. How will you make a living? You shall come to Holland! I'll ask my friends to help you with the procedures…" Weiying thought "Sit idle and you will eat away your fortune" as time proceeded, she would run out of all her savings and have problems paying her 4000-yuan monthly mortgage (At that time, this exceeded the salary of an average worker in the mainland for more than half a year). So, she called Li to tell him that she was ready to move into the new house. Li said, "Good for you to have a house of your own! I've sent the documents to the traditional medicine office, but they have not replied yet." A week went by and Qiu still had not heard anything about the progress, so she went to Li herself. Li told her, "I've rode a bicycle to the health bureau and asked them, 'Doctor Qiu had done nothing wrong. Where should she find her daily bread if you forbid her business?' They promised to investigate you. Why isn't a reply yet? I'm curious too!"

Qiu thanked Li and went home. She was confident that under Li's help and some patients' demand (some of her patients told her, 'I did go to the health bureau, urging them to allow you to treat me'), her clinic would soon come to business again.

But the more she pondered over it, the more she became upset, the confiscation of family property in the spring of 1965, and the following disasters to her family in the cultural revolution had left an eternal shadow over her heart, which might be lessened over time and changes of society, but now it was changing in unpredictable patterns on her mind like a kaleidoscope. Her heart was like a cloud, drifting away too far, far away… Her previous decision of not going abroad was crashed by reality. It dawned on her that the health bureau was her immediate superior. If someone deliberately wants to frame her, sooner or later, rack their brains to give her a "trumped-up" charge. Her future would be a total tragedy, and by that time she wouldn't be able to leave even if she wanted to. What was the telephone recording for if they were not determined to destroy her? She decided to go and have a look abroad. If the situation there is better, she should stay; if not, she could return when the health bureau agreed her business to restart. Just take it as a trip to broaden the horizon!

Once she came upon the decision, she decided to relay the entire clinic in Dongmen Mansion to Damao, who had just come to Shenzhen from Zhuhai. Damao has got doctor's license in Changsha, just haven't done it alone, always doing it for others. Weiying had got everything ready for her, if the health bureau agreed. Weiying could send in a nurse who used to help her when she was busy, and then Damao could take over the clinic. So, even if Weiying had always hated curry favor with one's superiors, she thought she had to deal with it for now. So, she bought some gifts and took Damao to a head's home. Honestly, she was a bit suspicious that all the troubles she got into, including the suspension, were due to lack of flattering. For Doctor Li used to tell her father and her, "It was for his help that I was able to work in People's Hospital. For appreciation, I give him 500 yuan every month…"

Li Fen, the daughter of Dr. Li, indiscriminately blamed Qiu Weiying for the failure of the People's Hospital to renew the contract with her family and led one of her nurse girlfriends to the Liuhua Hospital to find Qiu Weiying, and quarrel over this thing. There was no doubt that someone's the monthly 500 yuan was cut off since Li left the hospital. Was it because the lead of health bureau blamed it on Qiu to revenge? Then he would be the most likely one to intervene her business! Only the chief of traditional medicine office knew who the boss behind the scenes was. But she might not know about the bribery. Bribery was a scar inflicted by the reform and economic development. It would remain a large stumbling block of social progress if it were not to be removed and treated. The officials should not only speak up for people's need; they need to remain probity as well – that's the real spirit of serving the people and the country.

Qiu came across a traditional Chinese medicine shop owner at the heads of Health Bureau house. But the lead was not at home; there were only his wife and the drugstore owner. The drugstore owner was sitting on one site of a couch, by which was a large thick plastic bag filled with gifts, leaning on it. The Marlboro and delicate gift boxes on top of the pile were very eye-catching, as if showing off to Qiu, the stuff you brought here are nothing compared with me! Qiu had only bought a few things. She wanted the health bureau to agree on her sister's taking over her clinic, and she thought it would be a bit trouble for Mrs. head's the gifts she bought were to thank her for taking the trouble. However, they seemed to have failed the mission. She was never good at doing such things. After the drugstore owner left, Mrs. Chief talked with Qiu amiably, saying, "It's really a hot summer, and I still have a room without air-conditioner. When it gets too hot, I don't even dare to enter that room." Qiu, who had been merely absorbed in her own profession, barely knew about the social codes. She did not get the implication and made no answer.

As soon as she stepped out the door, she had a feeling that things wouldn't work out. She told Damao, "She has not said a word about my demand. She took the gifts but did not seem to like them. I don't think she'll help us." Damao said, "I've met that drugstore owner before; he's very rich." Qiu said, "That's it! I've always wondered, according to the regulations, people without permanent residence of Shenzhen could not be doctors here. How come so many other places of them are sitting in drugstores, prescribing? They are definitely richer than me, for they are both merchants and they can also allow doctors who do not have a Shenzhen residence to treat patients in pharmacies." Damao said, "Of course!" The incident brought Qiu to a deeper understanding of the social dynamics. She was especially disgusted with the phenomenon, if this should continue, the entire society would be ruined by corrupt elements! She firmly decided that no matter if things work out with the hand-over or not, she will go abroad!

After some days, Juecong asked a friend from Hong Kong to bring Weiying the invitation and warranty for her to apply for going abroad in the public security bureau. Then she rode her bicycle to the city government and told her decision to Li. Upon her entering Li's office, Li spoke even before she talked, "I've told the traditional medicine office the other day that both of your parents are gone. It's hard for a single woman like you to work in Shenzhen. If they don't reopen your clinic, how could you live on? They promised to make a reply as soon as possible." Qiu said, "They've even stealthily tokened my medicine to examine. If what I did wrong, they would have told me long ago. Up until now, I'm still confused that what I doing wrong? It was that makes me guilty! I heard they even secretly recording during the seminar. They have possible determined to me progress political frame-up. Then I have nothing to do about it, I have already applied for going abroad. If I can't stay there, I'll come back in a year."

Li tried to comfort her, "You want to give up your job as a doctor in Shenzhen? That'll be a pity! You'll find a way out of this if you stay." Qiu said, "You know the policies better than I do! Mr. Li, I really appreciate your trust and help. But I've already submitted the application. If I'm allowed to open up my clinic again, and I can live here in peace, I'll come back. I heard many countries permit Chinese clinics, as long as I avoid doing surgeries; they forbid Western ones by foreign doctors though, for western medicine is an exotic profession. All in all, I've decided to go abroad for a change. I really appreciate your work and help; I haven't even brought you anything." Li said, "No gifts! It is explicitly regulated by the municipal government that we are not allowed to take any gifts from the people. Plus, I don't lack anything; the government has given me a large house." Qiu said, "I've heard that you throw all the brand cigarettes people gave you into the dustbin, even if they put money in it." She went on, "I've decided to put my house in Haifu Garden on rent, the revenue of which I can use to pay my loans. I'll rent the house in Dongmen Mansion to someone else and see what the situation will be in a year." Li said, "Fine. People like you shall have no problem supporting yourselves even in a foreign country; while those who are uneducated and unskilled will find it difficult." Qiu said, "I've come across several chances of going abroad, but I had no interest in being a second-class citizen in another country. Now, I'm already in my forties and going abroad – that's life!" In the end Li said, "You're welcome to my place at any time. There are only me and my wife, no old nor children." Qiu agreed. She said goodbye to Li and headed home.

She told her decision to Xiaomao at home, who said, "Then I shall go back to Changsha. It's more costly living in Shenzhen, and there's no need for me to stay longer." Weiying agreed, bought her a train ticket and told her to take the new TV in the parlor home. In the end of the month, Qiu sublated out the house with her fridge, sewing machine and other furniture with the same price under permission of the village committee. Then, she took her clothes, bed and a bicycle and moved in Haifu Garden.

Qiu waited about a month, and yet still no news about permission on touring and visiting passport came. "Time is money", she felt anxious doing nothing but to wait. She called the public security bureau, but the receptionist said, "You'd better come here and consult the person in charge." So, she went to the credentials department to inquire the office lady in charge of her credentials. She has only to hear bad news – the lady said, "Your brother is not your economic guarantor – you propose cannot be passed!" Qiu was depressed at the news. She said, "Economic guarantee is but a formality. Is there anybody who go abroad only to be raised by his relatives? I won't depend on anybody; I can support myself." But the lady looked serious and said, "What if you run out of all your money, and he isn't able to help? You'll have to be a prostitute then!" Qiu was offended by her rudeness. She heightened her voice and said, "How can you be so mean? It's a personal assault! When I first started my career in Shenzhen, I did not even have the money for food. I'd rather borrow than to sell my body! Now I'm an experienced doctor over 40. Is there any chance that I would give up my self-esteem and national dignity to go abroad and be a prostitute? I want to go now because my income is cut off in my own country. How should I live on?" She grew indignant, and people started to crowd around her. Two men in the office came to the lady, one of whom whispered something by her ear. The lady glanced at Qiu and said nothing. Qiu realized that it would not turn out favorable for her if she stayed, so she left in anger leaved the public security bureau.

She fed herself supper and went to bed, depressed. The next morning turned out being sunny, which erased her sorrows. She suddenly remembered a section chief of the credentials department who was her previous patient, who was very nice and kind to her and even sent her gifts. So, she dialed this Mr. Chen. It was Mrs. Chen who answered the phone. Despite that she had never contacted with Qiu, she sounded like a long-time friend over the phone, "Oh, it's doctor Qiu! You'd better come and have dinner with us; it's the only time that you are sure to see him." Qiu said, "That'll be too much trouble for you; I come for help and get a meal." Mrs. Chen said, "That's alright! I've already known you from my husband." Qiu accepted the invitation. She went to the market behind Haifu Garden and bought some fruit, and then she rode her bicycle to the Chens. It did not take her long to find the address given by Mrs. Chen.

Chen was a local. The minute Qiu looked at their house, she knew it was a personal residence of local people. The broad gate reminded her of her parents' house in Laozhaobi, the gate of which was even wider. It was no wonder for the locals to have one or two large residences, even villas since Shenzhen became the special economic zone; the revenues of rents could keep them wealthy for a whole life… Some of them invested the money in stock market, which returned them with hundreds of times of money. Money seemed to be growing by itself, drowning the locals with wealth. Such phenomenon was absurd even in a dream before the drought-down of the Gang of Four. Before Shenzhen became special economic zone in 1979, almost all the young and middle-aged in the border village steeled out of mainland China to Hong Kong, leaving only the old, weak, sick and disabled at home. Which was the fundamental reason why people in Shenzhen bow down and worship to Deng Xiaoping! <See1. E>

She entered Chen's house, which did not look like one of a wealthy owners, but a place of a happy family. Mrs. Chen led her to the tea table, where she made Qiu a cup of nice tea. She took over Qiu's fruit, put them aside and said, "My husband has made a rule of never accepting any gift, so please take them back when you leave." Qiu smiled and said, "It's not gift anyway; just to thank you for having me for dinner." They talked for a while and heard the brake of Chen's motorbike from the yard. Then, Qiu saw Mr. Chen coming in with his brief. He was tall and thin and had some grey hair. He smiled when seeing Qiu in his parlor, and greeted her, "Doctor Qiu! What brought you here?" Qiu was also glad to see him, saying, "I came for your help." By the table in their clean and delicate dining room, she explained her situation and difficulties to him. Chen pitied her, and at the same time thought the office lady had a sharp tongue too mean. He said, "I'll retire soon, but this should not be tough. I'll send the passport and visa to you once it's done." Qiu was rejoiced and left in gratitude after the meal. She was rather confident that Chen would settle all the troubles for her.

After a dozen of days, there was still no sign of accomplishment. She called Chen, who said over the phone, "It's done already, but I've been too busy recently to send them to you. I'll go to you tomorrow." Qiu said, "Thanks a lot! I can pick them up this afternoon; you can save the trouble." Chen said, "Alright. You can go to the person in charge." Qiu put down the phone, grabbed her handbag and ran downstairs, only to find her new bike by the cement wall was gone. She went to the safeguard of the mansion, who said, "How can it not be stolen if you put such a nice bike here? Bicycle storage in the cellar has been built, for you to put the bike." Qiu was displeased. She had to go to the police office and report the, but there was not much hope of getting her bike back. She was self-consolation, "I'm going abroad anyway; just let it go!"

Then she took a bus to the public security bureau. At the credentials department she waited by the window for the office lady to find her passport. The man who whispered to her the last time Qiu came smiled and asked, "So you permitted it in the end?" The office lady pouted her lips and said, "Chen section chief told me to do." Looking unhappy, she came to the window and gave Qiu the passport and visa. Qiu opened her new passport and saw a clear seal on it, and a form to record her travels. It was not that easy to get a passport at that time, so Qiu put them in her bag and left in excitement.

Qiu recalled the lady's words when she got home and thought despite that the lady had been rude to her, Mr. Chen trusted her. And there actually were people as described. She pondered for a while and decided to sell the house for travel checks just in. What's more, she could use the money if she wanted to set up a clinic abroad. Once decided, she put an ad on the newspaper.

It wasn't long before an Asian woman accompanied by a real estate agent and translator came to see her house. The Asian woman was satisfied with everything there and paid her 10 thousand yuan as deposit. Qiu bought the house with 250 thousand yuan, altogether 400 thousand taking the 5-year bank interest into consideration. However, by then its value had already risen to 600 thousand yuan. The stock market was burgeoning at that time, so Qiu invested the 10 thousand yuan and her savings of 5000 yuan on stock, thinking that she could sell them out before she left the country.

It wasn't long before an Asian woman accompanied by a real estate agent and translator came to see her house woman had promised to pay the rest 590 thousand yuan within a month, but she did not contact Qiu as appointed. Qiu had got everything settled by then, except for the house. So, she called the intermediary, who told her on the phone, "The Asian woman wanted a house on higher floor; she has changed her mind. You only need to pay us half the fee she gave you." Qiu said, "What? The deal's doomed, and you ask me for money? What is wrong with you? The 10 thousand yuan is her deposit! You can refer to the receipt; you and I all have one. It says if I change my mind, I shall have to pay her 20 thousand yuan! I have turned down several people who wanted to buy my house. Now if I am to advertise again, and if somebody does want to buy it, I shall spend much time and energy on the necessary procedures. I must leave within a month; it'll be too late to go after selling the house. Who's going to make up for my trouble and loss? I'm not going to Hong Kong; I'll be away for a long time and don't know when to return. I'm not returning the deposit. You can sue me if you want to."

So, Qiu had to give up on the idea of selling the house. She had to put another advertisement on the local newspaper to put her house on rent. A few of days later, a couple who had just come to Shenzhen from Shen Shao came to see her house. The woman worked at the Customs; her husband was a businessman. They had a boy. Qiu asked them to pay more deposit, for she was going to Europe and did not know when to come back, and she was afraid of having problems paying her bank loans after she left. The couple agreed easily, and immediately paid the deposit and signed the contract.

The next day Zhou Yun came to see her house after having dinner at his hotel. Qiu told him she was going abroad, and said, "I'll set up a clinic there with my brother if possible." Zhou did not support to be in favor of that idea. He said, "I don't understand why so many people want to go abroad. Foreign is not suitable for Chinese people development, for us Chinese; I have a friend who went to USA and came back in the end." Qiu said, "My clinic is suspended; I'm cut off of my economic source." Zhou reminded her, "You can borrow some money to get through the hard time! You already have a career here in Shenzhen, and now you have your own house; there should not be more difficulties for you." He saw that Dr. Qiu did not say anything, and then he said to her, "My company has purchased a second house in the center of Hong Kong; we've just finished furnishing it and it's now vacant. If you're leaving soon, you may stay there for a week." Zhou wrote address of the house and his friend's name, saying, "If I'm not there when you go, you can contact my friend." Qiu had to go via Hong Kong, so that would be very helpful. But Qiu has already set her mind; therefore, she gave no consideration to Zhou's kind suggestion...Zhou Yun looked outside and found it late, so he then got up and said goodbye and went downstairs.

Qiu went to the balcony outside her bedroom and looked up, the stars were twinkling around the moon, which tossed its gentle light, decorating her balcony with mystery. She looked at Zhou, who was crossing the street toward his hotel, and sincerely felt that those friendly patients were respectful to the good doctors, and willing to develop pure friendship with them. So, as an engineer of human health, a doctor should follow his or her mission of saving people, to be trusted and loved. Qiu Weiying took a shower and went to bed. She was lie in bed looking out the window. The moonlight was gradually to disappear, and she fell asleep in a muddled.

It was late autumn in her dream, and with west wind blowing off the yellow deciduous leaves on the trees. She took off from a branch in the forest among a sparse group of birds. They flew over mountains and the beach toward northwest, with white sea wave rolling below them. Suddenly a bird with a sharp beak made a weird scream. As she turned her neck to see what was happening, the bird opened its smelly mouth to make a hard peck on her neck. She soon began to bleed, red blood jetted out the wound and flowed all over her back. In the end, many blood dropped through her feet into the ocean. The cold wind blew harder, she was dazed by the fierce cold wind and lost her way forward. She gritted her teeth with fear and trepidation, trying to restrain the pain of the wounds on her body, feebly flapping her bloody wings as she flew alone, almost falling into the merciless sea and being drown. Suddenly, as if empowered by gods, the see rolled up a large wave of sever meters high, pounding toward of the hysterical sharp bird that pecked her…

She woke up now, and though the dream was ominous. There was a saying that "the foreign moon is round just than the one in China". Was it true? Qiu knew that there was only one moon in the world, and the moon has yin and yang Round lack and full moon no matter when and where it is. Going abroad at her age and low English level could lead to many other difficulties there.

However, the shadow of their illegal confiscation of her family's property in the spring of 1965 remained in her heart.

From the mouth of her parents and bitter experiences of family, she can fully conclude: Many persons were when of the cadres, if you accidentally offend him / her, then it is entirely possible to be "In the name of the country, settle personal scores" deal with you.

My family home was encroachment later, left in disrepair and fractured part of the area. Although it has been returned. However, the parents' life savings were copied away. In a word: "The state can't clear-count and can't payback." The matter was left unsettled. Wy mother was perennating with twin sisters and had been serving patients. It's not like the parents' money came from exploitation! What happened to the United Hospital, which my father invested in himself? lose both the person and the money and the "trumped-up" charges for the whole family to suffer! Although there were once wealthy Hong Kong people interested in investment to open a hospital in Shenzhen, they still need myself to work hard on their own.

Even though it was lightened over time and all changes, the conference held by health bureau reminded her of all the bitter past. She came upon the decision in despair and fear, and there was no way she changes her mind in that situation. The prosperity of a country depends much on how its leaders use the power in hand for their people. Of course, policies and regulations play a crucial rule! A horizontal view of the world's history and longitudinal view Changes before and after the establishment of New China and reform and opening, one can find strong proof for that.

This is just like the dream Qiu Weiying had when she traveled from Beijing to her father's hometown: The dragon that had been sleeping at the bottom of the sea for thousands of years had finally emerged after the Ten-Year Cultural Revolution. If once it could get rid of the contamination of the sludge and murky water caused by the Cultural Revolution, it could one day rise to the sky. It will be able to set up a gorgeous rainbow in the sky with its glittering scales for the prosperity and happiness of all mankind! Even if Qiu Weiying is far away, she is still hoping to see it "avoiding evil and raise good", bringing brilliant light to the cause of the progress of justice for all mankind! Can it inherit and carry forward the 5,000 years of excellent traditions and cultural heritage of the Chinese nation?

Qiu Weiying decided to leave, she was forced to leave this the mountains, rivers and waters that have lived for forty-three years this have the largest population in the world hundreds of millions of hard-working people. She wants to spread her wings, soaring to another country, looking for the value of human survival and urge social democracy and freedom, the great power of prosperity and progress.

Editorial:

The good things and bad things.
The good guys and bad guys.
Constituted darkness and light of the world.
I hate the darkness because it makes people disoriented.
I love the light because it gives people illuminates the future.
Let's cry out for justice!
Let's go into fight for truth!
I'm convinced that,
The truth will defeat the evil,
The world henceforth be forever bright!

RANDOM THOUGHTS

I was born in Jiangsu and the same year that new China was founded. I was growing up in Changsha drinking water on the Xiangjiang River in Hunan province. My growth process and life experience have witnessed, Decades of modern history since the founding of the People's Republic of China.

Although the "right to privacy" is protected by law, I still stark-naked exposed the privacy of myself and my family to the public in this book without any reservation. I can say that this requires a certain amount of ideological struggle and courage!

However, literature comes from life. Without authenticity, it can't touch the readers and inspire them to better understand the essence of life.

To this end, I should unfold a true self and family before the readers' eyes by taking an objective standpoint.

I hope readers can be enlightened to consider: What is the true meaning of our life? How we can establish ourselves in society? What kind of life and society system?

I even thought that I have a sense of mission. Because my nature and my experiences have made me hate evil like an enemy and motivated me to want to complete this final journey of my life. My keenly felt pain taught me that if you want a meaningful and worthy life, you should cherish it and unleash its creativity. Let it emit the light and heat of your life for the advancement of human freedom, prosperity, and progress! That's the real meaning of your precious life.

Dear readers: In this novel, the path of life that mother and daughter really went through is rocky! Does it let you know how everything that happened to this family was caused?

"Every man shares responsibility for the fate of his country", the author hopes that readers will be inspired by Fact-seeking and the pursuit of existence truth! Let us work together to create a better future for China and humanity!

Qiu Niao (Autumn Bird)
The Hague Netherlands

APPENDIX

(closely related to the content of the novel)

1. See notes below:

A. The 25,000-li Long March

In October 1934, the Central Red Army led by Wang Ming, an early leader of the Communist Party, failed to break the fifth siege of the Communist Party by the Kuomintang army. The main Red Army in the south of the Central Committee was forced to carry out the "Long March" strategic transfer.

In 1935, at the Zunyi Conference held during the Long March, the leadership of Mao Zedong in the Party and the army was established. It was a turning point in the history of the Communist Party and the Red Army, a turning point of life and death in the history of China.

On the Long March road, the main force of the Red Army set out from different starting points, passing through Fujian, Guangdong, Guangxi, Jiangxi, Hunan, Hubei, Guizhou, Yunnan, Sichuan, Xikang, Gansu, Henan, Qinghai, Shaanxi, and other provinces; traveling more than 20,000 miles, crossing a dozen rivers, snow-covered mountains, grasslands, and dozens of ethnic minority areas; capturing about 100 counties, fighting nearly 600 battles, and breached the encirclement, pursuit, obstruction, and interception of about 100,000 Nationalist troops.

As the Red Army fought continuously, it was short of medicine, food, and ammunition, and was constantly losing men on the march without replenishment. Nearly 100,000 Red Army troops were left with only about 40,000 men.

After the Red Army's triumphant arrival in northern Shaanxi, it established the revolutionary base areas in the Shaanxi-Ganjiang-Ningxia border region where the Communist Party was able to survive and develop. (After the founding of the People's Republic of China, the cadres of the Long March were treated to a particularly high standard.)

Mao Zedong pointed out, "The Long March is a manifesto, the Long March is a propaganda team, and the Long March is a seed sower. The Long March ended with our victory and the enemy's defeat."

B. The Korean War (The Chinese Communist Party called "Anti-American Aid". War started on June 25, 1950, to the armistice on July 27, 1953)

The Korean War was fought between the Democratic People's Republic of Korea and the Republic of Korea because of their mutual incompatibility and desire to unify each other. Inspired by Mao Zedong's expulsion of the Kuomintang from the mainland and the establishment of the People's Republic of China, Kim Il Sung was burning with ambition and determined to start a war to reunify Korea.

At first, the Soviet Union, which had gone through World War II, did not want to publicly offend the United States or fall into war again; China, which had gone through a civil war between the Communist Party and the Kuomintang, had not yet in time offensive occupying Chiang Kai-shek of Taiwan and want to improve the domestic economy.

But Kim Il Sung's eager request for assist dispatch troops to Korea. Therefore, with the covert support of Soviet-assisted weapons,

Appendix

Kim Il-sung crossed the 38th parallel in the north and south and captured Seoul, the capital of South Korea, within three days.

The Security Council of the United Nations adopted Resolution 84, which concluded that "North Korean forces have committed an armed attack against the Republic of Korea".

As a result, a total of 21 member states of the name of the United Nations provided "military and medical assistance". It is for the first international aid to South Korea under the rule of Syngman Rhee.

Before the outbreak of the war, U.S. President Harry Truman announced that he would not defend Taiwan. After the outbreak of the war, Truman announced that the U.S. would send troops to Korea and that the Seventh Fleet had entered the Taiwan Strait in order to interfere with the continuation of the war between the two sides of the Taiwan Strait.

On October 7, U.S. troops landed and crossed the 38th parallel. Kim Il Sung asked for assistance and the Soviet Union secretly supported and pressured China to send troops.

On October 8 Mao Zedong issued an order and on October 19 the Chinese People's Volunteers led by Peng Dehuai crossed the Yalu River to assist North Korea in its attack on South Korea.

For this reason, bloody the Korean War, which represented the ideological confrontation between China and the West, lasted for more than three years and ended with North Korea still returned and maintaining the 38th parallel demarcation. In the end, Kim Il Sung had failed to achieve his goal of unifying Korea.

But in the socialist camp, Mao was yet seen as a hero who "defeated American imperialism", although because of this war, were sacrificed hundreds of thousands of people. Among them, the Chinese People Volunteers sacrificed the most.

C. The "Anti-Rightist" movement

Mao Zedong was shocked by the events of 1956 in Hungary's Petofi Club, which, he thought, was because "…… had killed too few counterrevolutionaries in some Eastern European countries". The 1957 "Anti-Rightist" motion was a nationwide political persecution campaign by Mao Zedong to "draw snakes out of holes" to establish absolute authority, mainly against intellectuals and democratic parties. At that time, Deng Xiaoping, the General Secretary of the Communist Party of China, was the direct leader of this campaign.

Mao Zedong published in the then authoritative People's Daily "Instructions for Organizing Forces to Counter the Rampant Attack of the Rightists", mentioning that "this is a big battle. Without winning this battle, socialism cannot be built, and there is some danger of a Hungarian incident." But the campaign resulted in many unjust cases and dealt a heavy blow to democratic parties, scholars, and intellectuals from all walks of life. According to official figures, 552,973 people were classified as rightists (the actual number is said to have reached more than 1.7 million or 1.8 million people.). These included party, political and military figures, democrats, and university students). Among those persecuted was Zhu Rongji, later China's premier.

Since so many people were branded as rightists in 1957, mainland China has entered an era of full one-party dictatorship. Intellectuals and democratic parties no longer dared to criticize the Communist Party, and the CCP no longer allowed criticism from people inside or outside the party. Only praise and praise were permitted, and anyone who disagreed with or opposed Mao was an anti-party activist or counter revolutionary.

From the late 1970s to the early 1980s, Hu Yaobang and other state leaders rehabilitated many people who had been "wrongly classified as rightists". In the end, only five people could not be redress.

As a result of living under the double pressure of economy and politics for twenty years, and surviving in the cracks of society, they were so humiliated that they could not raise their heads and were persecuted to death or committed suicide. leaving only about 100,000 people alive at the time of redress a grievance them.

D. 21 kinds of people.

Landlord, rich, anti, bad, and right elements, those who have been rehabilitated through labor and those who have completed their sentences and stayed in the field (factory) for employment, the backbone of the reactionary party groups, the small and medium-sized heads of the reactionary Taoist sects and the professional Taoists, the enemy and counterfeit (referred dregs of the old society of the Kuomintang): military (above the rank of company commander), political (above the rank of bailiff), police (above the rank of sergeant), constitutional (gendarmerie), and special (secret agent) elements, those who have been released from prison and those who have been dismissed from reeducation through labor but have not been rehabilitated well. Play the market, The family members of counterrevolutionaries who were killed, imprisoned, controlled or fled from the country and who maintained reactionary positions.

In fact, it also implicates people who have relatives and friends who fall into this category, as well as people with relatives overseas. They were equally distrusted by the Communist Party and suffered the same political distrust and suppression.

E. Joint public-private operation

In 1956, the Communist Party of China (CPC) implemented a policy and campaign of "socialist transformation "for national capitalists and private individual workers, i.e., "public-private partnership". January 10, Beijing was the first city to announce the realization of industry-wide public-private partnership. Subsequently, all the major cities and more than 50 medium-sized cities in China realized the industry-wide public-private partnership one after another.

The state switched to a fixed-interest system for the redemption of private capitalist shares, with a uniform interest rate of five percent per year; in 1964, the government deprived the families of the original landlords of their inheritance rights to the properties by decree; in 1966, when the Cultural Revolution broke out, the Red Guards looted the properties of the original landlords in large numbers, and were also affirmed by government documents; in September 1966, the fixed-interest year expired, and the PPP enterprises were finally transformed into socialist national ownership.

In effect, it is the nationalization of private property. There were also enterprises that survived by moving to Hong Kong immediately after the establishment of the Chinese Communist Party. Or after being forced public-private partnership and moved to Hong Kong were able to continue to develop.

F. Siqing Motion (Four clean)

Excerpt from <Yanhuang Chunqiu> What I know about the "Taoyuan experience",

…That is, the socialist education movement, according to the requirements of commune members, the accounts of cadres are unclear, extravagance and waste, eat too much of, corruption and dividing the collective financial problems, the methods of clearing work, clearing accounts, clearing money and clearing things were adopted. The "Siqing" at that time only cleared the economy and was called "Little Siqing". From the late period of the "Siqing" Motion to 1965, Proposed to engage in the "Big Four Cleanup", Is the "clear political and Qing economy, clear thinking, clear organization".

To sum up, the "four cleansing" are rectify incorrect styles of socialist work or thinking.

Class struggle, anti-repair and anti-repair, re-educate people and reorganize class ranks, and "Big Corps" operations and so on. For ease of understanding, may wish to use a popular word explanation, "Siqing" is to re-educate people, Class struggle, a combat and prevent revisionism of the "breakthrough point." The brutal struggles it adopted in coercion, confession, faith and corporal punishment, etc. It became a precedent for the Cultural Revolution. This struggle is further expanded in society, it can even persecute people on the charge of "trumped-up".

Later, Mao Zedong believed that neither the Four Cleans nor cultural criticism could solve the fundamental problem. Thus, began brewing and launched the "Cultural Revolution" was. In the end, Liu Shaoqi and his wife Wang Guangmei tasted the ill effects of their own creation. He "under an assumed name, "suffer ill-treatment, and die as a result by inhumane in prison.

G. Knowledgeable youth going up the mountains and going to the countryside

Going up the mountain and going to the countryside did not start with the Cultural Revolution, it has been advocated since the 1950s, it began in the 1960s and ended in the late 1970s. For the educated youths at the time, they went to the countryside, is to eliminate the "three big differences". (I.e., the difference between workers and peasants, the difference between urban and rural areas and the difference between physical work and mental work) the motive of going up the mountain and going to the countryside is in order to solve the employment problem of young students.

From 1966 to 1968, due to the Cultural Revolution caused middle school students stay in society. Made China appear successively Junior high, high school, three sessions of graduates, the spectacle of graduation together. December 22, 1968, Mao Zedong in the "People's Daily" issued instructions, "Educated youth to the countryside, accept the re-education of poor farmers lower middle peasants, it is very necessary. "Immediately launched a massive nationwide. The motion of intellectual youths "Going uphill to the countryside".

Mao Zedong scattered these students into the "broad world" of the countryside, it also eliminated the destructive power of the Red Guards. Because "ten years of tumultuous", leaded political

turmoil and economic regression. During in the Great Cultural Revolution, of educated urban youth must go and work in rural areas for re-education (Cancellation city permanent residence, in the rural labor feed themselves).

The motion of going up the mountain and going to the countryside, also made many government officials was assigned to the "May Seventh Cadre School" at the same time accept "re-education".

Entering the late 70s, central government began to allow the recruitment of young intellectuals, Examinations, sickness withdrawal, fill a position, only child, no one around the parents, students of workers, peasants and soldiers all kinds of nominal gradual return to the city. On May 8, 1980, the then General Secretary of the CPC Central Committee Hu Yaobang proposed, No longer do to engage go to the countryside.

October 1, the central government decided in the past to the countryside Intellectual youth can return to their home city. Which lasted 25-years -long process of the intellectual youths from the cities and towns going to the countryside has come to an end.

H. The Great Proletarian Cultural Revolution ("The Ten Years of chaos" 1966-1976)

In 1949, under Mao Zedong's leadership, the Communist Party expelled the Kuomintang, and change the country name to, "The People's Republic of China". Mao Zedong and the Communist Party became the savior of the Anti-Japanese War in the publicity and education of the People's Republic of China.

Since more than 500,000 were knocked down as rightists in 1957, national People only allowed singing the praises. Whoever makes a different opinion, it is anti-Party elements or counter-revolution. But the failure of the Great Leap Forward led to about 30 million or 40 million people died in "The Great

Famine". Therefore, the prestige of Mao Zedong in the party declined rapidly and suffered opposition from different voices within the party. Especially Liu Shaoqi Vice President and Peng Dehuai Marshal, to put to him directly opposing views. On the other hand, Liu Shaoqi listened to the opinion Deng Zihui of the Minister of Agriculture, engaging in "three -self, a parcel" and other means of economic recovery then made his prestige growing. In desperation, Mao takes a back seat.

However, Mao Zedong is an intolerable other people with critical opinions. He is also a passionate and good at using various means to carry out political struggles.

So, between May 16, 1966, and October 6, 1976, personally, initiated and led by Mao Zedong's, there has been a Cultural Revolution for ten consecutive years in mainland China.

He took advantage of the violent activities of the Red Guards, which were set off by young people's lack of social experience and their susceptibility to incitement. He had achieved one's purpose, eliminate the opponent in his party-Liu Shaoqi and the highest-level leader who disagreed with him different view. His public argument is "Knock down inside the party take the capitalist road people in power", in essence is to put all rights, back into their own hands.

Mao Zedong wrote his "My first big-character poster "fierce attacked at Liu Shaoqi. Finally, causes Liu Shaoqi became within the party "Big traitor, Big internal spy, Big worker thief", and Incognito jailed and persecuted died in prison.

In the early period of the Cultural Revolution, the Red Guards Motion was carried out violent activities of the "Destroy the four old" (That is the so-called old ideas, old culture, old customs, old habits.). However, after the 11th Plenary Session of the 8th Central Committee, the wave of irrational Red Guards, it soon hit the entire land of China like a beast of floods. China have countless excellent ancient and modern Chinese and foreign excellent books were burned, many national cultural relics have been destroyed and looted; The subsequent development become beating, smashing objects, search sb's house and confiscate his property. Country's many pillars' intellectuals and democrats and cadres, being criticized and struggle, even persecuted to death.

Mao Zedong is not afraid of the beat dead person, he said, once a nuclear war occurs between China and the United States, Chinese died half, the earth still turn. "…What is the big deal about a nuclear war, the world's 2.7 billion people, a half dead and half left? China has 600 million people, a half dead and 300 million lefts, I am afraid of who to go."

Summer and Autumn of 1967, Jiang Qing, etc. A group of people took the opportunity put forward, "Completely smash the public, prosecution and law", slogans such as "Wen Gong Wu Wei" incite fighting, the red guards and rebels even hit the military area. Machines throughout the country stopped working normally; Students do not study; workers do not produce; farmers do not plant land; The army has also begun to turmoil; Because "ten years of big chaos ", leaded political turmoil and economic regression. During in the Great Cultural Revolution, of educated urban youth must go and work in rural areas for re-education (Cancellation city permanent residence, in the rural temper oneself through physical labor and feed themselves).

In 1971, Mao Zedong personally selected of successors - Lin Biao fled because of an attempted coup against Mao Zedong. He and his wife and son in a plane crash, dropped in Mongolia burned to death.

In January 1976, Premier Zhou Enlai, Marshal Zhu De in July, Chairman Mao Zedong in September, passed away one after another. Many people in mainland China were a bit nervous and felt: it seemed as if the sky was falling.

On October 6, 1976, one month after Mao Zedong passed away, Hua Guofeng holding Mao Zedong's note, "I'm at ease when you do things" and when the national leaders.

Appendix

Keep abreast of the situation, hold important positions in the Central Committee and the Military Commission Ye Jianying, Wang Dongxing and others, unite put the joint will Wang Hongwen, Zhang Chunqiao, Jiang Qing, Yao Wenyuan Gang of Four and Mao Yuanxin, Mao Zedong's nephew, was detained and sentenced to five people.

Jiang Qing bellow when he was tried, "'I'm at ease when you do things' Behind there is another sentence 'Have problem, find Jiang Qing'!" Is this really? Like that, Hua Guofeng succession, it should be regarded as ""Palace coup".

But foreigners who do not know the inside story of China - Mao fans think it is a right-leaning coup.

It cannot be denied: Hua Guofeng and several other top leaders of the Communist Party of China (CPC) made an amazing and courageous move, "take resolute and effective measures to solve a complicated problem". It is without shedding a drop of blood, to arrest and crush the Gang of Four that had plagued the land of China. At the same time, the whole Chinese people clap with joy!

The Cultural Revolution, which had been scourge China for ten years, finally came to an end and it becomes a glorious and important page that changed the course of Chinese history!

The organizational form of the Revolutionary Committee during the Cultural Revolution, it was not until the 1980 that they were all removed.

What followed was Hua Guofeng push to learn from the West and reform and open up, while it was actively interacted with and further increased by Deng Xiaoping.

In June 1955, Mao Zedong in Changsha to see the plainly dressed, loyal-looking Hua Guofeng, he left a good impression on Mao. From then, Hua Guofeng was almost the only leader in the Communist Party who panned out and was not directly subjected to power struggles. In his later years, he kept his mouth shut about politics even more. The ordinary people have a good feeling about

Hua Guofeng compared, with Liu Shaoqi and Lin Biao, he is considered lucky to get a good die a natural death.

I. Reform and open to the outside world

1978, the Third Plenary Session of the Eleventh CPC Central Committee was held, Deng Xiaoping and others proposed "Reform internally and open to the outside world", the theory of "emancipating the mind and seeking truth from facts". He and Zhao Ziyang, Hu Yaobang headed the reformists of the Communist Party of China, actively lead and promote the implementation of various policies, it was supported by Ye Jianying and many elders of the Chinese Communist Party. Its main policies include privatization of state-owned enterprises and state-owned enterprise contracting system, the government no longer controls prices, and abolish some protectionist policies.

Of course, the state still controls the banking industry and the key industries closely related to the national economy, such as the petroleum industry. In coastal areas, it has born Shenzhen, several special economic zones such as Xiamen and Zhuhai, become a window for mainland China's foreign economic exchange.

In early1990, China successively established the Shenzhen Stock Exchange, Shanghai Stock Exchange.

China joined the World Trade Organization in 2001, take China's reform and opening to the next level.

In 2010, China's gross domestic product (GDP) surpassed that of Japan, become the second largest economy in the world.

The "opening to the outside world" in the reform and opening makes many overseas enterprises enter the Chinese market. A considerable number of Chinese companies have also opened overseas markets. Reform and opening gradually developed into having China the main components of characteristic socialism, it is

Appendix

the Communist Party of China and the People's Republic of China an ideology advocated, including politics, economy, ideology, and culture, as well as a social construction and ecological protection, etc. While defending the one-party dictatorship of the Communist Party of China, introduced the Western capitalist market economy.

It can be said that it is a combination of Chinese and Western economic interests, the ideology has also been added invisibly. When the ideologies of these two conflicts, it is bound to affect the economic interests of both.

What will happen to China's economic and political situation and how will it develop when this so-called unshakeable fundamental state policy is changed? The people of China and the world are waiting to see.

2. Reference:

A) **Wikipedia, He Lu ting** (https, //en.wikipedia.org/wiki/He_Luting)

(July 20, 1903-April 27, 1999) Male, born in Shaodong, Hunan. Chinese composer, music theorist, music educator. Honorary Chairman of China Music Association, Shanghai Music Association, Dean of Shanghai Conservatory of Music.

At the 20th annual meeting of the International Music Council in 1982, Selected as an honorary life member of the International Music Council, It is currently the only musician in China that has won this award.

His beloved daughter, He Xiaoqiu, because "where there is injustice, there will be protest" during the Cultural Revolution, sudden in despair by being implicated by his father committed suicide.

B) The story of the He Xiaoqiu (2006-04-01 University of Chicago Scholar Wang Youqin)

On September 16, 1966, He Lu Ting and his wife Jiang Ruizhi the couple was kidnapped to the school by the school's red guards. He Is luting was blindfolded by a black cloth and beaten by a belt, the clothes that were beaten also rotted and mixed with blood. Jiang Ruizhi also forced in the corner and hit covered with wounds.

After this group of people beat, another group of people came up, they were kidnapped separately and tortured all night. Their home was ransacked, things at home were smashed.

The Cultural Revolution, Shanghai Conservatory of Music only about three hundred people, seventeen so-called "abnormal deaths" occurred. These deaths occurred based on such violent abuse.

On March 21, 1968, He Is luting was imprisoned by the Shanghai authorities in a formal prison. He was imprisoned for 5 years and was only released in 1973. During this period, he repeatedly taken to the "struggle of the General Assembly" on, was the "struggle", these include the "struggle" on television. The "struggle meeting" was opened on TV, which was regarded as a special use of high technology in Shanghai. Although few private individuals had TV sets at the time, there is no TV broadcast outside Shanghai.

After He Is luting was arrested, He Luting's daughter He Xiaoqiu was accused of Luting "reverse the verdict." She did not "draw the line" with her father as the Cultural Revolution required, this was when all parents were "struggled "all young people must do. She expressed views do not agree with his father suffered torture and imprisonment. At that time the so-called "reverse the verdict" is the only appealed his conviction, but it can be seen as "counterrevolutionary" behavior. School ready to "struggle" to her, she turned on the gas to commit suicide, died in the kitchen.

Appendix

C) Tian Han, Tian Han - Wikipedia

(March 12, 1898 - December 10, 1968); Male, Changsha, Hunan; Writer; Songwriter of the Chinese national anthem; great dramatist (Changsha now has the "Tianhan Theatre" named after him). Imprisoned and killed during the Cultural Revolution.

D) Zhao Ziyang and "Siskin action" (https,//youtu.be/vfuuHPFnBLA) **Same day review** 29 May 2019.

"**Siskin action**", Zhao Ziyang's second son was wanted on June 4th, for the first time he disclosed "Siskin action ", assert the CCP,

On June 4, 1989, the CCP dispatched 14 Army Group Army part of the troops deployed and the Beijing Garrison Command, Tianjin garrison area, Beijing Armed Police Corps and other military personnel, about 250,000 people.

Another said means, the CPC Central Military Commission from the five military-regions mobilized the strength of at least 30 divisions, at Tiananmen Square. A demonstration force clearing operation was conducted. Resort to the threat of force put Square in order. Tiananmen Square cleared, it uses of machine gun fire, tanks rolling collision, the overall death figures are still a mystery, but it is estimated that there are tens of thousands of students and citizens killed or injured.

Participants of the pro-democracy motion who escaped the bloody crackdown, get rescued by Hong Kong people's "Siskin action".

Former General Secretary of the Communist Party of China Zhao Ziyang due to the Six-Four incident was deposed, former General Secretary of the Communist Party of China Zhao Ziyang's second son Zhao Erjun current media interview. He first disclosed, "Siskin action", the rescue process, talking about the details of the family in exile in France. He also asserted that the father's reputation and the June 4th Motion can't "redress", because it is "contradiction between us and the enemy".

*In 1980, there was a saying in mainland of China that "you want to eat rice, look for Wanli; you want to eat grain, look for Ziyang.". Zhao Ziyang and Huang Wanli are also pioneering in China of reform and opening.

3. The Kuomintang and The Republic of China -

A. Reasons leading to the ultimate defeated of the Kuomintang:

From "The September 18th "Incident on September18,1931, counting lasted until August 1945, the Republic of China government under the leadership of Chiang Kai-shek, after 14 years of fight bloody battle with the Japanese army, the last with the assistance and intervention of the United States and Britain, after arduous bloody war, finally won the great victory of the Patriotic Anti-Japanese War, defeated the Japanese Devils invading army.

Right after the end of the war against Japan, the Communist party People's Liberation Army then officially launched the three major battles against the Nationalist National Army for power and the fruits of victory.

Lead to the final defeat of the Kuomintang was the "Huaihai Battle" (the Kuomintang called it the "Xu Beng Battle").

It started on November 6, 1948, ended on January 10, 1949. In this war, Chiang Kai-shek respectively lost Huang Baitao (defeated and committed suicide) and Qiu Qingquan (because he was defeated and forced his subordinates to shoot him) two loyal and powerful fighters.

Kuo Rugui, the head of the KMT's War Hall whom Chiang Kai-shek especially trusted and who worked beside him, Chiang did not believe that he was a high-ranking Communist party spy!

Appendix

He informed the Communists in advance of the real military intelligence of the Kuomintang. But he disrupted the KMT's strategic deployment with false information. And Chiang Kai-shek and the Minister of National Defense Bai Chongxi's strategic thinking is not unified and has differences. How could Chiang win the fatal "Xu Bang Battle" when many important factors unfavorable were added together?

*Through the "Xi'an Incident", in which senior KMT generals Zhang Xueliang and Yang Hucheng detained Chiang Kai-shek, led to the complete bankruptcy of Chiang's policy of communist suppression. And the CCP was able to escape from the dead. Zhang Xueliang became the savior of the Communist Party!

So, Mao Zedong once said at that time, "The Xi'an Incident rescued us from the prison disaster." And Zhang Xueliang's main starting point at that time: Was to obtain the support of the Soviet International Communist Movement by assisting the Communist Party in order to deal with the Japanese who had killed his father. At the same time, he gave support to the Communists in terms of money weapons and food, and clothing.

*At the same time, the Communist Party launched a nationwide propaganda campaign against the Kuomintang for "unity against Japan" and "anti-civil war". The civil war was a threat to world peace and was strongly opposed at home and abroad. As a result, the Kuomintang government was helpless and resign oneself to death.

However, after the victory in the War of Resistance against Japan, followed three consecutive "KMT and CCP Civil Wars", in successive years, the mobilized masses of people treated the KMT National Army as an enemy of "protect our homes and defend our country" and assisted the Communists to destroy it. The Communist propaganda tactics were incomparable to those of the Kuomintang!

*The eight-year war of resistance from August 1937 to 1945 had already resulted in the ebb and flow of Communist and Kuomintang power.

The Communist army grew from the initial few hundred thousand to over one million two hundred thousand, the militia over two million. Moreover, the Communists took over the Japanese dominated areas occupied by the Kuomintang as a battlefield behind enemy lines. As a result, the liberated areas of the Communist Party expanded and reached nearly 100 million people.

*The Communist Party had a variety of tricks up its sleeve, making good use of the terrain and being tactically flexible; at the same time, it mobilized the people who had been given fields in the midst of fighting the landlords to actively join the army; in the civil war between the Communist Party and the Kuomintang, the militia transported food and military supplies in large numbers of earth carts and worked together against the artillery of the Kuomintang army.

*And the Kuomintang had already consumed a large amount of combat power of its troops in the war against Russia and Japan successively. Especially in the war against Japan, not only were half of the more than 3.8 million soldiers killed and they wounded, but also 201 senior generals were sacrificed.

*The great warlords around the world were mixed up cutting up their own territories and did not support Chiang Kai-shek's centralization; the KMT troops were scattered like scattered sand, and their army's morale was gradually shaken.

*The KMT overestimated its military strength; there were also defections and uprisings within the KMT. Chiang Kai-shek made improper use of men and poor tactical arrangements at critical moments.

*The Communist Party planted many spies within the KMT and around Chiang to collect military intelligence. This caused the leaking of military intelligence and led to the defeat of the war.

*In fact, in addition to the above-mentioned factors, the real cause of the total collapse of the Kuomintang regime is also fatal. The elite Soviet infantry, air force, armored force, artillery, and the navy that have entered China have participated in the war on a large scale. After the victory of the War of Resistance Against Japan, all the weapons left by the Japanese army on the Northeast battlefield, the Soviet Union's support was handed over to the Chinese Communist army for equipment. This eventually led to the Kuomintang's continual defeat.

*On the other hand, although the U.S. presidential envoy Marshall mediated the armistice agreement between the Kuomintang-Communist Party for a time. But after the failure of the Kuomintang-Communist Party relationship, the U.S. adopted a "look on with folded arms" attitude toward the Kuomintang- Communist civil war.

*Although the KMT had the support of the Americans in the past years, it was corrupt and disunited, mutual suspicious and distrustful, and was wanting to preserve the strength of the troops themselves lead.

At the critical moment of fighting the Communists, there was no timely reinforcements for each other; lack of food to replenish, soldiers were starving and cold and lost their fighting strength.

* The Communists had a variety of tricks that the Kuomintang could not defend itself against; the Communist army was good at using terrain and flexible in tactics; Mao Zedong adopted the main strategic policy of "encircling the cities in the countryside" while the Kuomintang's army was mainly concentrated in the cities; during the Communist Party's fight against the landlords, the people who had been allocated fields actively joined the army.

During the Huai-Hai Campaign, Communist Party the mobilized people used large numbers of earth carts to transport food and military supplies to deal with the artillery of the Kuomintang army.

* In September 1948, the Kuomintang implemented the Gold Yuan Coupons of paper. However, it caused the currency to depreciate wildly, inviting the failure of economic reform and causing public panic and discontent.

The Kuomintang suffered various political, war and economic failures on the mainland. They are eventually fled from strength into weakness and flee in panic- stricken.

B. The Republic of China was forced relocate to Taiwan:

Chiang Kai-shek was defeated in the three major battles of the "Kuomintang - Communist Civil War" and was unable to save the situation.

After the Huai-Hai Campaign (the meet for a decisive battle of Xu Beng) was a complete failure, he had to find a way of the Republic of China.

Chiang Kai-shek once consider moving to Hainan Island, but after a full discussion of his aides thought, Taiwan has superior conditions not found in other regions, therefore he decided to move the Republic of China to Taiwan.

*Because Taiwan faced the mainland and across the sea, there was a natural barrier that was easy to defend and difficult to attack; at the time, the Communists lacked an air force and had a weak navy.

*In the fall of 1948, the KMT, led by Chiang Kai-shek, began the work of moving the Republic of China to Taiwan.

*Chiang Kai-shek and Hu Shih, who valued knowledge and cherished talents, began a plan to "rescue scholars" and persuade them to leave mainland China. However, most of the scholars did not listen to both and remained on the mainland.

(Later, those scholars who did not heed their advice, or who did not have in time to escape from the mainland, or who even returned to the mainland after liberation out of patriotic ideas, almost all suffered from the "The more knowledge you have, the more reactionary you are"; "Down with the bourgeois academic authority" disaster of being drowned.

*Chiang Kai-shek, who act as a director of the Palace Museum in 1928. Beginning on December 22, 1948, before leaving the mainland, more than 700,000 national treasures including antique calligraphy and paintings in the Forbidden City, after many setbacks and difficulties and finally shipped to Taiwan.

Otherwise, these treasures among the Cultural Revolution in mainland China, it will be treated as the product of feudalism and destroyed!

According to the information reported, in the fall of 1948, the Kuomintang, led by Chiang Kai-shek, then began the process of moving the Republic of China to Taiwan.

On December 1, 1948, Chiang Kai-shek was shipped from the Shanghai State Treasury, 990,000 taels gold, 3,000 silver dollars coin, 120 million taels pure silver, 70 million US dollars shipped to Taiwan. This later became the capital that the Republic of China could gain a foothold in Taiwan.

According to the University of California School of Medicine Professor Wu Xingyong testimony,

When Chiang Kai-shek was shipped to Taiwan in batches of gold whole total of about 4 million taels, another 3 million taels of gold equivalent value of silver dollars and foreign exchange, adding up to a total value of about 7 million taels of gold.

The money, which later became the capital of the more than 1.2 million soldiers and civilians of the Republic of China who fled the mainland, was able to gain a foothold in Taiwan for survival and development.

In January 1949, Jiang Zhongzheng stepped down as president and had represented him by Li Zongren, the vice president who advocated peaceful negotiations with the Communist Party of China.

April 23, 1949, the ruling place of the Jiang family Nanjing was occupied by Communist forces. On May 17, 1949, Shanghai lost ground one after another.

After a long period of war consumption, the Kuomintang has been exhausted. It is at various disadvantages and unable to save the situation.

On December 10, 1949, Chiang Kai-shek was already exhausted, and he feel desperate despairing of the "Kuomintang-Communist Civil War" into a victory, secretly flew out of Chengdu to Taiwan.

*When the United Nations organized and sent troops to South Korea to participate in the war, Chiang Kai-shek once actively sought to participate. He wanted to take the opportunity to counterattack the mainland; During the Cultural Revolution, all economic operations were stopped in the cities and villages of mainland China. People even divorced, fought in armed battles, grabbed guns, shot and killed people because of their different political views. Lives and souls were destroyed, and Chiang Kai-shek tried to take advantage of the opportunity to counter-attack the mainland; only to have it all stopped with the disapproval of the United States!

So far, under the influence of the mainland united front ideology, going further and further away from Chiang Kai-shek's wish to counter the mainland.

*In the early days after the founding of New China, Mao Zedong once wanted to win the KMT and occupy Taiwan. Because Kim Il Sung insisted on reunifying South Korea, he asked China and Russia to help send troops. Stalin pressured Mao Zedong to send troops and the Korean War broke out. China sacrificed hundreds of thousands of soldiers in Korea and temporarily lost the ability and opportunity to attack Taiwan.

*Under Mao's leadership for decades, the Communist Party inside fought brutally and ruthlessly, fight to the bitter end. But externally defending the Communist Party's power, they are united like a monolithic block.

Whoever holds the party and political power, especially the military power that comes from the barrel of a gun, will "occupation of the mountain as the king" and can "gang up"; whoever can "be extremely conceited" and represent the party.

Whoever opposes him is a "counter-revolutionary" or even an "anti-Party group". In order to maintain the common interests of the "party the whole country "and the stability of the Communist regime, the opponents became "counter-revolutionary" or "counter - revolutionary clique", opponents have become "prisoners".

That is why Mao Zedong was the "king of the mountain" in the Party and the "magic weapon" that made him invincible from 1945, when he officially started the war to overthrow the Republic of China, to 1976.

*Chinese history summarizes Russia and Japan's aggression against China,

On June 27, 1956, Zhou Enlai said when receiving the Japanese delegation to China, "We are very grateful for some Japanese people, during the war of liberation, they served as doctors, nurses, technicians participated in the war of liberation; these have been enhanced we conclude confidence and friendly relations with the Japanese people. Japanese warlords are cruel, but there are many Japanese who assist us."

During the Anti-Japanese War of the Kuomintang, prisoners of war captured after the defeat of Japan, in the set-up liberation war of New China, for the Communist Party, they wrote a glorious chapter.

*In 1989, Deng Xiaoping told Gorbachev, "From the Opium War, the powers invaded, bullied and enslaved China, Japan has caused the most damage to China. In the end, Tsarist Russia benefited the most from China.

Including Soviet Russia for a certain period and certain problems."

So far, although the Soviet Communist Party has collapsed, the more than 1.5 million square kilometers of land that the Soviet Union used to encroach, plus more than 1.6 million square meters of Outer Mongolia, A total of 3.1 million square meters of land in China was lost in the hands of Russia.

(Mao Zedong once made a statement to Stalin that he wanted to take back Outer Mongolia. Stalin, in turn, hinted that Outer Mongolia and Inner Mongolia. Should be unified. So, Mao Zedong gives the matter was left unsettled.)

*Now, Russia is no longer ostensibly a one-party dictatorship. However, the idea of choosing a successor within the party and insisting on one-party dictatorship was already deeply rooted in mainland China.

*Regardless of Soviet Russia's attitude toward the land and people of China, the CCP still outwardly treats it and North Korea as like-minded friends.

*On the other hand, the CCP always regarded the United States, which never wanted an inch of China's land and even aided China, as an enemy of the CCP from the innermost.

Mao Zedong said. "Either the west wind overwhelms the east wind, or the east wind overwhelms the west wind". Mao Zedong meant that there is no middle way. Therefore, he once criticized his old Soviet friend as revisionist.

Today, human society is already fraught with difficulties and dangers in dealing with natural disasters, so who is there to further create human disasters? Meanwhile, who is truly defending human democracy and freedom, progress and development? This must be left to the facts and the truth to speak!

What will eventually happen to China and the world when the ideological confrontation between East and West becomes more and more acute? The inevitable trend of history is, "He who wins the hearts and minds of the people wins the world"!

In the novel, the real-life path that the mother and daughter experienced was bumpy! However, how did all the bitter experiences in this family result? The author hopes that the reader will get inspired by it and go forward hand in hand to create a better future for humanity!